5/08

D0583445

Historical Dictionary of Socialism

Second Edition

Peter Lamb
James C. Docherty

The Scarecrow Press, Inc.
Lanham, Maryland • Toronto • Oxford
2006

SCARECROW PRESS, INC.

Published in the United States of America
by Scarecrow Press, Inc.
A wholly owned subsidiary of
The Rowman & Littlefield Publishing Group, Inc.
4501 Forbes Boulevard, Suite 200, Lanham, Maryland 20706
www.scarecrowpress.com

PO Box 317
Oxford
OX2 9RU, UK

British Library Cataloguing in Publication Information Available

Library of Congress Cataloging-in-Publication Data
Lamb, Peter.
  Historical dictionary of socialism / Peter Lamb, James C. Docherty. — 2nd ed.
    p. cm.
  Previous edition lists James C. Docherty as author.
  Includes bibliographical references.
  ISBN-13: 978-0-8108-5560-1 (hardcover : alk. paper)
  ISBN-10: 0-8108-5560-7 (hardcover : alk. paper)
  1. Socialism—History—19th century—Dictionaries. 2. Socialism—History—
20th century—Dictionaries. I. Docherty, J. C. II. Title.
HX17.D63 2006
335.03—dc22

                                                          2006012818

Contents

Contents

Editor's Foreword

Socialism has been one of the most resilient modern sociopolitical ideologies. At a time when communism has been "defeated," socialism has continued growing and, if anything, gained from communism's losses. But it still faces incessant criticism from capitalism and neoliberalism and is experiencing difficulty in some places. There is considerable concern among the leadership and sometimes friction with the rank and file, and everybody seems to call for reform, although agreement on just what that means in practice is hard to achieve. Yet, part of this "crisis" is only apparent because many of the early goals of socialism have become so much a part of the general consensus that they are hardly recognized as socialist any more. Among these are the need to overcome unemployment, improve the conditions of labor, create more egalitarian societies, ensure some form of welfare, and provide opportunities for all groups in society to express their opinions.

Socialism is in flux again. Indeed, it seems never to have ceased evolving, so it is important to take another look, not only at the present but also the past, which shows just how much has been achieved and also how often the movement has reinvented itself. That is the task of the new edition of the *Historical Dictionary of Socialism*. This is done partly through 440 entries (considerably more than the previous edition), including many of the significant thinkers, activists, and politicians and especially the new socialist and social-democratic parties of Central and Eastern Europe and the Third World. The other sections have also been updated and expanded, especially the chronology, introduction, and bibliography. This is rounded out by a list of acronyms and glossary of terms.

This second edition was written by Peter Lamb, who is presently a research fellow at Keele University, having taught politics there and at other British universities. Dr. Lamb is a specialist on the socialist thought of Harold Laski and has published many articles and the book

Harold Laski: Problems of Democracy, the Sovereign State, and International Society. Here, he has built on a very strong first edition by James C. Docherty. Dr. Docherty worked for the Australian federal public service and was an honorary research associate with the National Centre for Australian Studies at Monash University. He has written various statistical works and more general articles on Australian history, politics, and labor relations. He is the author of *Historical Dictionary of Australia* and *Historical Dictionary of Organized Labor*.

Jon Woronoff
Series Editor

Preface

This *Historical Dictionary of Socialism* has no pretension to be a comprehensive, single-volume history of socialism. To produce such a volume would probably be an impossible task. This dictionary is, rather, a general guide to the subject—a guide that will, hopefully, encourage readers to find out more. It is, furthermore, a work of information rather than advocacy. It traces the evolution and diversification of socialism from the early nineteenth century to the early twenty-first.

In this second edition of the dictionary, we have extended the scope and updated the relevant entries in order to reflect events and developments in the late twentieth century and early twenty-first century. The dictionary also now includes more material on important and influential socialist thinkers and a range of new entries on intellectual and social movements of the left. Many more political parties have entries, including former communist parties that have been transformed into social-democratic ones, as well as the few remaining ruling communist parties. There are many other miscellaneous new entries. The introductory essay has been revised, as have the chronology, glossary, and bibliography.

This dictionary complements another in the Scarecrow series: James C. Docherty, *Historical Dictionary of Organized Labor, Second Edition* (Scarecrow Press, 2004), which deals with the industrial wing of labor, the trade unions; there is some overlap between the two works, but generally we have kept it to a minimum. The present dictionary is mainly concerned with politics rather than industrial relations. It offers information on writers, activists, ideas, political parties, institutions, and movements that sought, and in many cases are still seeking, to change the social and political order. We try to give due weight to the work of individuals, including many who are now forgotten but exerted much influence in their time. In some cases we indicate why or how such individuals came to be socialists. Turning to the contemporary scene, there are entries on each of the political parties that held full membership of the Socialist International in 2005. There are also entries on a range of parties that are significant today but do not hold such membership. Many party leaders who have led national governments or tried to implement socialist policies have entries. We have also tried to convey something of the idea of socialism as a movement, hence the entries on religion, gender, sport, youth, education, and literature. In all there are 440 subject entries. A few of these entries immediately guide the reader to other relevant entries. The others are of varying length and contain many cross-references. The chronology, glossary, and bibliography are designed to supplement the main body of the dictionary.

As mentioned above, our aim in this dictionary has not been to try to include every topic or personality but rather to present a broad historical view of the subject and, at times, redress some of the imbalances of popular perception. In so doing, complicated and often subtle matters have had to be severely summarized or even omitted. As with any historical material, issues that seem obvious from the present point of view often did not appear that way in the past. It is not possible to convey these kinds of complexities in a work of this kind, and really the only cure is for readers to do their own research, preferably among the primary sources listed in the bibliography. Yet even with the best will in the world, the process of condensing information in itself can lead to a false impression of order and progress not present in the original unfolding of events. Where this has occurred, we can only ask the forbearance of expert readers using a work designed largely to be a first resort. As with any work of this kind, we have relied heavily on the efforts of others. That said, errors and misleading statements remain our responsibility, not theirs. As a general rule we have relied on the more recent works to present what seemed to us to be the latest scholarly consensus.

Finally, a note on cross-referencing: terms are bolded or placed under *See also* in the dictionary. In the glossary words are bolded within the entries if there is an entry in the dictionary and followed by an asterisk if they appear elsewhere in the glossary.

Acronyms and Abbreviations

AD	*Acción Democrática* (Democratic Action) [Venezuela]
ADEMA-PASJ	*Alliance pour la Démocratie au Mali-Parti Africain pour la Solidarité et la Justice* (Alliance for Democracy in Mali-African Party of Solidarity and Justice)
ALP	American Labor Party
ALP	Australian Labor Party
ANC	African National Congress
ANN	*Alianza Nueva Nación* (New National Alliance) [Guatemala]
APRA	*Alianza Popular Revolucianaria Americana* (American Revolutionary Popular Alliance) [Peru]
APSO	Asia-Pacific Socialist Organization
ARF	Armenian Revolutionary Federation (*Hai Heghapokhakan Dashnaktsutyun*)
ASC	Asian Socialist Conference
ASF	Americas Social Forum
BLP	Barbados Labour Party
BSD	*Bulgarski Sotsialdemokrati* (Bulgarian Social Democrats)
BSDP	*Bulgarska Sotsial-demokraticheska Partiya* (Bulgarian Social Democratic Party)
BSP	British Socialist Party
BSP	*Bulgarska Sotsialisticheska Partiya* (Bulgarian Socialist Party)
CHF	*Cumhuriyet Halk Firkasi* (Republican People's Party) [Turkey]
CHP	*Cumhuriyet Halk Partisi* (Republican People's Party) [Turkey]
CLPD	Campaign for Labour Party Democracy

COMISCO	Committee of the International Socialist Conference
COSATU	Congress of South African Trade Unions
CPC	Communist Party of China (*Zhōngguó Gòngchò-nadǎng*)
CPD	*Concertación de Partidos por la Democracia* (Concertation of Parties for Democracy) [Chile]
CpDS	*Convergencia para la Democracia Social* (Convergence for Social Democracy) [Equatorial Guinea]
CSD	*Convergencia Social Demócrata* (Social Democratic Convergence) [Guatemala]
CSEEU	Commission of Socialist Educators of the European Union
CSIT	*Confédération Sportive Internationale du Travail* (International Labour Sports Confederation)
CSPEC	Confederation of the Socialist Parties in the European Community
CSSD	*Česká strana sociálně demokratická* (Czech Social Democratic Party)
CSTEC	Commission of Socialist Teachers of the European Community
CWS	Co-operative Wholesale Society [United Kingdom]
DAP	Democratic Action Party (*Parti Tindakan Demokratik*) [Malaysia]
ĐCVN	Đảng Cộng sản Việt Nam (Vietnam Communist Party)
DGB	*Deutscher Gewerkschaftsbund* (German Trade Union Federation)
Die Linke	*Linkspartie* (Left Party) [Germany]
DLECG	*Demokratska Lista za Evropsku Crnu Goru* (Democratic List for a European Montenegro)
DnA	*Det norske Arbeiderparti* (Norwegian Labor Party)
DPS	*Demokratska Partija Socijalista Crna Gore* (Democratic Party of Socialists) [Montenegro]
DS	*Democratici di Sinistra* (Democrats of the Left) [Italy]
DSA	Democratic Socialists of America
EC	European Community
EDEK	*Eniea Demokratiki Enosis Kyprou* (Unified Democratic Union of Cyprus)
EL	Party of the European Left

ESF	European Social Forum
ESM	European Socialist Movement
EU	European Union
FA	*Frente Amplio* (Broad Front) [Uruguay]
FARC	*Fuerzas Armadas Revolucionarias de Colombia* (Revolutionary Armed Forces of Colombia)
FFS	*Front des forces socialistes* (Socialist Forces Front) [Algeria]
FLN	*Front de Libération Nationale* (National Liberation Front) [Algeria]
FPI	*Front Populaire Ivoirien* (Ivorian Popular Front)
FRELIMO	*Frente de Libertaçao de Moçambique* (Mozambique Liberation Front)
FREPASO	*Frente Pais Solidario* (Front for a Country with Solidarity) [Argentina]
FDSN	*Frontul Democrat al Salvării Naţionale* (Democratic National Salvation Front) [Romania]
FSLN	*Frente Sandinista de Liberación Nacional* (Sandinista National Liberation Front) [Nicaragua]
FSN	National Salvation Front (*Frontul Salvării Naţionale*) [Romania]
HaAvoda	*Mifleget ha-'Avodah ha-Yi'sre'elit* (Israel Labor Party)
HC	Hemispheric Council (of Americas Social Forum)
HDW	*Hizb al Dimuqratiyah al Wataniyah* (National Democratic Party) [Egypt]
HF	*Halk Firkasi* (People's Party) [Turkey]
IASL	International Alliance of Socialist Lawyers
ICA	International Co-operative Alliance
ICFTU	International Confederation of Free Trade Unions
ID	*Izquierda Democrática* (Democratic Left) [Ecuador]
IFM-SEI	International Falcon Movement–Socialist Educational International
IFSDP	International Federation of the Socialist and Democratic Press
IFTU	International Federation of Trade Unions
IJLB	International Jewish Labor Bund
ILP	Independent Labour Party [United Kingdom]
ILRS	International League of Religious Socialists

IRS	International of Revolutionary Syndicalists
ISDUE	International Social Democratic Union for Education
ISP	Indian Socialist Party
ISWC	International Socialist Women's Committee
IUSDT	International Union of Social Democratic Teachers
IUSY	International Union of Socialist Youth
IWMA	International Workingmen's Association
IWUSP	International Working Union of Socialist Parties
IWW	Industrial Workers of the World
JD	*Janata Dal* (People's Party) [India]
JD (S)	*Janata Dal* (Secular) or People's Party (Secular) [India]
JLP	Jamaican Labour Party
JP	*Janata* Party [India]
JSP	Japan Socialist Party
KISOS	*Kinima Sosialdimokraton* (Social Democratic Movement) [Cyprus]
KISOS EDEK	*KISOS Eniea Demokratiki Enosis Kyprou* (Social Democratic Movement EDEK) [Cyprus]
KKE	*Kommunistiko Komma Elladas* (Communist Party of Greece)
KONAKOM	*Parti du Congrès National des Mouvements Démocratiques* (Party of the National Congress of Democratic Movements) [Haiti]
KPRF	*Kommunističeskaja Partija Rossiiskoi Federacii* (Communist Party of the Russian Federation)
KPSS	*Kommunističeskaya Partija Sovetskogo Soyuza* (Communist Party of the Soviet Union)
Labour	British Labour Party
Labour	Irish Labour Party
LADSP	League of African Democratic Socialist Parties
LDDP	*Lietuvos Demokratine Darbo Partija* (Lithuanian Democratic Labour Party)
LRC	Labour Representation Committee
LSAP	*Lëtzebuerger Sozialistesch Arbechterpartei* (Luxembourg Socialist Workers' Party)
LSDP	*Lietuvos Socialdemokratų Partija* (Lithuanian Social Democratic Party)

LSDS	*Latvijas Sociāldemokrātiskā Savienība* (Latvian Social Democratic Union)
LSDSP	*Latviešu Socialdemokrātiskā Strādnieku Partija* (Latvian Social Democratic Workers' Party)
LSE	London School of Economics
LSI	Labor and Socialist International
MAHN	*Mongol Ardyn Huv'sgalt Nam* (Mongolian People's Revolutionary Party)
MAN	*Movementu Antia Nobo* (New Antilles Movement)
MAPAM	*Mifleget Poaleim Meuchedet* (United Workers' Party) [Israel]
MAS	*Movimiento al Socialismo* (Movement Toward Socialism) [Bolivia]
MDP	*Magyar Dolgozók Pártija* (Party of Hungarian Workers)
MEP	*Movimento Electoral di Pueblo* (People's Electoral Movement) [Aruba]
MIR	*Movimiento de la Izquierda Revolucionaria—Nueva Mayoría* (Movement of the Revolutionary Left—New Majority) [Bolivia]
MLP	Malta Labour Party (*Partit Laburista*)
MLP	Mauritius Labour Party (*Parti Travailliste—*PTr)
MMM	*Mouvement Militant Mauricien* (Mauritian Militant Movement)
MPLA	*Movimento Popular de Libertação de Angola* (People's Movement for the Liberation of Angola)
MPLA-PT	*Movimento Popular de Libertação de Angola—Partido de Trabalho* (People's Movement for the Liberation of Angola—Workers' Party)
MRS	*Movimiento de Renovación Sandinista* (Sandinista Renovation Movement) [Nicaragua]
MSDN	*Mongolyn Sotsial Demokrat Nam* (Mongolian Social Democratic Party)
MSM	*Mouvement Socialiste Mauricien* (Mauritian Socialist Movement)
MSzDP	*Magyarországi Szociáldemokratia Párt* (Hungarian Social Democratic Party)
MSzMP	*Magyar Szocialista Munkáspárt* (Hungarian Socialist Workers' Party)

MSzP	*Magyar Szocialista Párt* (Hungarian Socialist Party)
MVR	*Movimiento V República* (Movement for the Fifth Republic) [Venezuela]
NATO	North Atlantic Treaty Organization
NCP	Nepali Congress Party
NDP	New Democratic Party [Canada]
NE	*Nuevo Espacio* (New Space) [Uruguay]
NHS	National Health Service (United Kingdom)
NZLP	New Zealand Labour Party
PAICV	*Partido Africano da Independência de Cabo Verde* (African Party of Cape Verde's Independence)
PAIGC	*Partido Africano da Independência da Guiné e Cabo Verde* (African Party of the Independence of Guinea and Cape Verde)
PANPRA	*Parti Nationaliste Progressiviste Révolutionnaire* (Revolutionary-Progressive Nationalist Party) [Haiti]
PAP	*Partido Aprista Peruano* (Peruvian Aprista Party)
PASOK	*Panellinio Socialistiko Kinima* (Pan-Hellenic Socialist Movement) [Greece]
PCC	*Partido Communista Cubano* (Cuban Communist Party)
PCI	*Partito Comunista Italiano* (Italian Communist Party)
PCTVL	*Par Cilvēka Tiesībām Vienotā Latvijā* (For Human Rights in a Unified Latvia)
PD	Partito de Democratici (Party of Democrats) [San Marino]
PDP/PS	*Parti pour la démocratie et le progress/Parti Socialiste* (Party for Democracy and Progress/Socialist Party) [Burkina Faso]
PDS	*Partei des Demokratischen Sozialismus* (Party of Democratic Socialism) [Germany]
PDS	*Partito Democratico della Sinistra* (Democratic Party of the Left) [Italy]
PDSR	*Partidul Democraţiei Sociale din România* (Party of Social Democracy in Romania)
PDT	*Partido Democrático Trabalhista* (Democratic Labor Party) [Brazil]
PES	Party of European Socialists

PFSDH	*Pati Fizyon Sosyal Demokrat Ayisyen/Parti Fusion des Sociaux-Democrates Haitiens* (Union of Haitian Social Democrats)
PIP	*Partido Independentista Puertoriqueño* (Puerto Rico Independence Party)
PLC	*Partido Liberal Colombiano* (Liberal Party of Columbia)
PLN	*Partido de Liberación Nacional* (National Liberation Party) [Costa Rica]
PMSD	*Parti Mauricien Social-Démocrate* (Mauritian Social Democratic Party)
PNDS	*Parti Nigérian pour la Démocratie et le Socialisme* (Party for Democracy and Socialism of Niger)
PNP	People's National Party [Jamaica]
POUM	*Partido Obrero de Unificación Marxista* (Workers' Party of Marxist Unification) [Spain]
PPD	*Partido por la Democracia* (Party for Democracy) [Chile]
PPP	Pakistan People's Party
PPPL	*Phak Paxãxon Pativat Lao* (Lao People's Revolutionary Party)
PPS	*Polska Partia Socjalistyczna* (Polish Socialist Party)
PR	*Partido Radical* (Radical Party) [Chile]
PRD	*Partido de la Revolución Democrática* (Party of the Democratic Revolution) [Mexico]
PRD	*Partido Revolucionario Democrático* (Revolutionary Democratic Party) [Panama]
PRD	*Partido Revolucionario Dominicano* (Dominican Revolutionary Party)
PRF	*Partido Revolucionario Febrerista* (February Revolutionary Party) [Paraguay]
PRI	*Partido Revolucionario Institucional* (Institutional Revolutionary Party) [Mexico]
PRPB	*Parti de la Révolution Populaire du Bénin* (Benin Party of Popular Revolution)
PRSD	*Partido Radical Social-Demócrata* (Social Democratic Radical Party) [Chile]
PS	*Partido Socialista* (Argentinean Socialist Party)
PS	*Partido Socialista* (Portuguese Socialist Party)

PS	*Partido Socialista de Chile* (Socialist Party of Chile)
PS	*Parti socialiste* (French Socialist Party)
PS	*Parti Socialiste Belge* (Belgian Socialist Party)
PS	*Partit Socialdemòcrata* (Social Democratic Party of Andorra)
PSD	*Parti social-démocrate* (Social Democratic Party) [Benin]
PSD	*Partito dei Socialisti e de Democratici* (Party of Socialists and Democrats) [San Marino]
PSD	*Partido Socialista Democrático* (Democratic Socialist Party) [Guatemala]
PSD	*Partidul Social Democrat* (Romanian Social Democratic Party)
PSDI	*Partito Socialista Democratico Italiano* (Italian Social Democratic Party)
PSDMR	*Partidul Social-Democrat al Muncitorilor din România* (Social Democratic Party of Workers of Romania)
PSDR	*Partidul Social Democrat Român* (Social Democratic Party of Romania)
PSDSh	*Partia Socialdemokrate e Shqipërisë* (Albanian Social Democratic Party)
PSI	*Partito Socialista Italiano* (Italian Socialist Party)
PSM	*Parti Socialiste Mauricien* (Mauritian Socialist Party)
PSOE	*Partido Socialista Obrero Español* (Spanish Socialist Workers' Party)
P-Sol	*Partido Socialismo e Liberdade* (Party of Socialism and Freedom) [Brazil]
PSP	Pakistan Socialist Party
PSP	*Partido Socialista Popular* (Popular Socialist Party) [Cuba]
PSP	Progressive Socialist Party (*Hizb al Taqadummi al-Ishtiraki*) [Lebanon]
PSS	*Parti Socialiste du Sénégal* (Socialist Party of Senegal)
PSS	*Partito Socialista Sammarinese* (Sanmarinese Socialist Party)

PSSh	*Partia Socialiste e Shqipërisë* (Socialist Party of Albania)
PSU	*Partido Socialista del Uruguay* (Socialist Party of Uruguay)
PSU	*Partito Socialista Unitario* (Socialist Unity Party) [San Marino]
PT	*Partido dos Trabalhadores* (Workers' Party) [Brazil]
PUR	*Partidul Umanist Român* (Romanian Humanist Party)
PvdA	*Partij van de Arbeid* (Dutch Labor Party)
PW	*Belgische Werkliedenpartij* (Belgian Workers' Party)
PZPR	*Polska Zjednoczona Partia Robotnicza* (Polish United Workers' Party)
RC	*Rifondazione Comunista* (Communist Refoundation Party) [Italy]
RCD	*Rassemblement Constitutionnel Democratique* (Democratic Constituent Assembly) [Tunisia]
RND	*Rassemblement national démocratique* (National Democratic Assembly) [Algeria]
RPG	*Rassemblement poplaire Guinéen* (Guinean People's Assembly)
SALP	South African Labour Party
SAP	*Sveriges Socialdemokratiska Arbetareparti* (Swedish Social Democratic Workers' Party)
SCD	*Convergencia Social Demócrata* (Social Democratic Convergence)
SD	*Socialdemokraterne* (Danish Social Democratic Party)
SD	*Socialni demokrati* (Social Democrats of Slovenia)
SDA	Social Democracy of America
SDAP	*Sociaal-Democratische Arbeiders Partij* (Dutch Social Democratic Workers' Party)
SDAP	*Sozialdemokratische Arbeiterpartei* (Social Democratic Workers' Party) [Germany]
SDE	*Sotsiaaldemokraatlik Erakond* (Estonian Social Democratic Party)
SDF	*Front Social Démocrate* (Social Democratic Front) [Cameroon]
SDF	Social Democratic Federation [United Kingdom]

SDI	*Socialisti Democratici Italiani* (Italian Democratic Socialists)
SDL	*Strana demokratickej l'avice* (Party of the Democratic Left) [Slovakia]
SDLP	Social Democratic Labour Party [Northern Ireland]
SDP	*Socijaldemokratska Partija* (Social Democratic Party of Montenegro)
SDP	*Suomen Sosialidemokraattinen Puolue* (Finnish Social Democratic Party)
SDP (BiH)	*Socijal Demokratska Partija Bosne i Hercegovine* (Social Democratic Party of Bosnia and Herzegovina)
SDPA	Social Democratic Party of America
SDPH	*Socijaldemokratska Partija Hrvatske* (Social Democratic Party of Croatia)
SdPL	*Socjaldemokracja Polska* (Polish Social Democratic Party)
SdRP	*Socjaldemokracja Rzeczypospolitej Polskiej* (Social Democracy of the Republic of Poland)
SDS	*Saiuz na demokratichnite sili* (Union of Democratic Forces) [Bulgaria]
SDSM	*Socijaldemokratski Sojuz na Makedonija* (Social Democratic Union of Macedonia)
SDSS	*Sociálnodemokratická Strana Slovenska* (Social Democratic Party of Slovakia)
SDUSA	Social Democrats USA
SED	*Sozialistische Einheitspartei Deutschlands* (German Socialist Unity Party)
SF	*Samfylkingin* (Icelandic Social Democratic Alliance)
SFIO	*Parti Socialiste* (*Section française de l'Internationale ouvrière*) or Socialist Party (French Section of the Workers' International)
SGEP	Socialist Group in the European Parliament
Shamin-tō	*Shakai Minshu-tō—Shamin-tō* (Japanese Social Democratic Party)
SHP	*Sosyal Demokrat Halçi Parti* (Social Democratic Popular Party) [Turkey]
SI	Socialist International
SILO	Socialist Information and Liaison Office

SKK EDEK	*Socialistiko Komma Kyprou EDEK* (Socialist Party EDEK)
SLD	*Sojucz Lewicy Demokratycznej* (Democratic Left Alliance) [Poland]
SLPA	Socialist Labor Party of America
Smer	*Smer-Tretia Cesta* (Direction-Third Way) [Slovakia]
Smer-SD	*Smer-Sociálna demokracia* (Direction-Social Democrats) [Slovakia]
SMUSE	Socialist Movement for the United States of Europe
SODEP	*Sosyal Demokrat Parti* (Social Democratic Party) [Turkey]
SP	*Sozialdemokratische Partei der Schweiz* (Swiss Social Democratic Party)
SPA	*Sociaal progressief alternatief* (Socialist Party Different) [Belgium]
SPA	Socialist Party of America
SPD	*Sozialdemokratische Partei Deutschlands* (German Social Democratic Party)
SPÖ	*Sozialdemoktratische Partei Österreichs* (Austrian Social Democratic Party)
SPÖ	*Sozialistische Partei Österreichs* (Austrian Socialist Party)
SSP	Scottish Socialist Party
SUCEE	Socialist Union of Central and Eastern Europe
SV	*Sosialistisk Venstreparti* (Socialist Left Party) [Norway]
SWI	Socialist International Women
SWSI	Socialist Workers' Sports International
TUC	Trades Union Congress [United Kingdom]
UBF	*Union pour le Bénin du Futur* (Union for the Benin of the Future)
UCR	*Unión Cívica Radical* (Radical Civic Union) [Argentina]
UNHCR	United Nations High Commissioner for Refugees
UNO	*Unión Nacional Opositora* (United Opposition Union) [Nicaragua]
UP	*Unia Pracy* (Union of Labour) [Poland]
USFP	*Union Socialiste des Forces Populaires* (Socialist Union of Popular Forces) [Morocco]

USPD	*Unabhängige Sozialdemokratische Partei Deutschlands* (Independent Social Democratic Party) [Germany]
WASG	*Wahlalternative Arbeit und Soziale Gerechtigkeit* (Electoral Alternative Work and Social Justice Party) [Germany]
WLZM	World Labor Zionist Movement
WPK	Workers' Party of Korea (*Chosen Nodong-Tang*)
WPUS	Workingmen's Party of the United States
WSF	World Social Forum
WTO	World Trade Organization
Yachad	Social Democratic Israel/*Yachad*
YPSL	Young People's Socialist League [United States]
ZLSD	*Združeno Lista socialnih demokratov* (United List of Social Democrats) [Slovenia]

Chronology

1516 England: Sir Thomas More publishes *Utopia*, the first secular vision of an ideal society; originally written in Latin, it is first translated into English in 1551.

1576 England: First legislation requiring local government to provide the unemployed with work.

1634 Scotland: Seamen at Bo'ness form a friendly society.

1643 Scotland: Seamen at St. Andrews form a friendly society.

1647–49 England: Putney debates within Cromwell's army concerning the Levellers' efforts to secure a wider franchise, the sovereignty of parliament, and religious, civil, and economic rights (1647–48).

1649 England: The Diggers emerge; they are later hailed as forerunners of utopian socialism.

1699 England: Keelmen in Newcastle upon Tyne agree to form a friendly society to provide money for themselves and their families in the event of sickness, old age, or death.

1760 England: Six bakers deny under oath any responsibility for the burning down of a cooperative flour mill owned and operated by shipwrights employed at the government dockyard at Woolwich, London (March).

1765 Scotland: James Watt invents the condenser, the basis of an efficient new type of steam engine that he builds in 1774 and perfects in 1775.

1769 Scotland: Some weavers at Fenwick form a cooperative society, the first such society formed in Britain.

1776 Scotland: Adam Smith, *An Inquiry into the Nature and Causes of the Wealth of Nations.*

1777 England: Some tailors on strike set up a cooperative workshop in Birmingham.

1789 France: The Declaration of the Rights of Man and of the Citizen affirms the equality of men in their rights (26 August).

1791 England: Thomas Paine, *The Rights of Man* (part 1).

1793 England: William Godwin, *The Inquiry Concerning Political Justice.*

1795 England: Some working-class residents of Hull combine to raise money to build and operate a flour mill. With help from the town council, the mill is built in 1797 and operates as a producers' cooperative until 1895. David Davies, *The Case of Labourers in Husbandry Stated and Considered*; it contains information on the budgets of 127 agricultural laborers between 1787 and 1793.

1798 England: Thomas Malthus, *Essay on the Principle of Population*; this work is used to provide justification for pessimistic attitudes toward the possibility of improving the lot of the working class.

1813 United Kingdom: Robert Owen, *New View of Society.*

1817 United Kingdom: David Ricardo, *The Principles of Political Economy and Taxation.*

1821 France: Claude-Henri Saint-Simon, *Du Système industriel (The Industrial System).*

1824 France: Claude-Henri Saint-Simon, *Catéchisme des industriels (Catechism of the Industrialists)*. **United Kingdom**: William Thompson, *An Inquiry into the Principles of the Distribution of Wealth Most Conducive to Human Happiness.*

1829 France: Charles Fourier, *Le Nouveau Monde industriel (The New Industrial World).*

1834 United Kingdom: The *Report of the Poor Law Commission* leads to the first Poor Law Act.

1839 France: Publication in serial form of Louis Blanc's *Organisation du travail* (Organization of Labor), which is the forerunner of many of the ideas of democratic socialism.

1840 France: Pierre-Joseph Proudhon, *What Is Property?*

1842 France: Étienne Cabet, *Voyage en Icarie* (Voyage to Icaria), a work of utopian socialism. **United Kingdom**: Edwin Chadwick's report on the sanitary conditions of the laboring classes.

1843 France: Flora Tristan (1803–44) advocates a proletarian international in her book *L'Union ouvrière* (The Workers' Union).

1844 Prussia: Weavers' insurrection in Silesia. **United Kingdom**: A consumer cooperative store is opened at Toad Lane, Rochdale, along principles that provide the model for successful British cooperative societies (December).

1845 Germany: Friedrich Engels, *The Condition of the Working Classes in England*; it is not translated into English until 1885.

1847 United Kingdom: William Dixon and W. P. Roberts, two of the leaders of the Miners' Association of Great Britain and Ireland, become the first union officials to stand for election to parliament.

1848 France: The government forcibly closes down national workshops that had been set up to provide employment; several thousand killed and thousands of others are arrested during the "June Days." **United Kingdom**: Marx and Engels publish the *Manifesto of the Communist Party*. The first edition is published in German. The first English translation is published in 1850. John Stuart Mill, *Principles of Political Economy*; this influential work offers a more optimistic view of the possibility for improving the condition of the working class. The emergence of Christian socialism.

1849 Columbia: Socialist club is formed.

1850 Chile: Francisco Bilbao (1823–64), a survivor of the 1848 French revolution, founds the Society of Equality to promote cooperatives and friendly societies. **France**: Edmé Jean Leclaire (1801–72) publishes a pamphlet that advocates profit sharing with employees. **United Kingdom**: Publication of the platform of the National Reform League, which foreshadows the development of evolutionary socialism.

1852 United Kingdom: The Industrial and Provident Societies Act gives legal protection to the funds of cooperative societies. Herbert Spencer uses the term "evolution" in *The Development Hypothesis*. A congress of cooperative societies is held in London (26–27 July).

1853 Italy: Interregional conference of friendly societies.

1855 France: Frédéric La Play, in *Les ouvriers européens* (The European Workers), makes the first international study of working-class incomes.

1859 United Kingdom: Charles Darwin, *The Origin of Species by Natural Selection.*

1861 United Kingdom: Henry Mayhew, *London Labour and the London Poor*; the publication of this work of four volumes is completed in 1862.

1863 France: Three followers of Proudhon stand unsuccessfully for election to parliament. **Germany**: German Workingmen's Association is formed. **United Kingdom**: Foundation of the Co-operative Wholesale Society at Manchester.

1864 France: *Manifesto of the Sixty.* **United Kingdom**: The International Workingmen's Association, or the First International, is formed in London (28 September).

1865 France: Pierre-Joseph Proudhon, *De la Capacité Politique des Classes ouvrières* (On the Political Capacity of the Working Classes).

1866 Germany: August Bebel and Wilhelm Liebknecht hold a workers' congress at Chemnitz that results in the founding of the League of Workingmen's Associations.

1867 Germany: First volume of Karl Marx's *Das Kapital* published but the first English translation is not published until 1887. Volume 2 is published in 1885 and Volume 3 in 1894.

1868 International: Michael Bakunin establishes the *Alliance internationale de la démocratie sociale* (International Alliance of Democratic Socialism). **United Kingdom**: Scottish Co-operative Wholesale Society is formed at Glasgow (August); it merges with the Co-operative Wholesale Society in 1973.

1869 United Kingdom: A congress of cooperative societies is held in London and attended by representatives from several European countries.

1870 Switzerland: A short-lived social-democratic party based on German speakers is formed (March).

1871 Denmark: Socialist Party is formed. **France**: Paris Commune (18 March–28 May).

1872 International: After their expulsion from the International Workingmen's Association, anarchists form their own international at Saint-Imier, Switzerland. **United Kingdom**: The membership of friendly societies reaches four million. The secret ballot is introduced.

1873 Spain: Crushing of insurrections is organized by the International Workingmen's Association. **Switzerland**: A political workers' club (*Arbeiterbund*) is formed; it helps to gain the first factory legislation in 1877 but is defunct after 1878.

1874 Austro-Hungarian empire: All-Austrian Social Democratic Party formed at Neudörfl (April). **United States**: A Labor Party is formed in Illinois and a Social Democratic Workmen's Party of North America is formed in New York.

1875 Germany: Social Democratic Party is formed from the merger of the German Workingmen's Association and the Social Democratic Workers' Party of Germany at Gotha; the Gotha Program of the Social Democratic Party is released.

1876 United States: The International Workingmen's Association formally dissolves in Philadelphia. Workingmen's Party of the United States is formed in Philadelphia (July). The party is renamed the Socialist Labor Party in December 1877 in Newark, New Jersey. **Portugal**: Socialist Party is formed.

1877 Belgium: Flemish Socialist Party is formed; it becomes the Party of Belgian Workers in 1879.

1878 Denmark: Formation of the Social Democratic Party (February). **Italy**: Papal encyclical is issued against anarchism and socialism. **Mexico**: Bakunist League is formed.

1879 Argentina: Anarchist group formed. **Germany**: August Bebel, *Women and Socialism*, advocates equal treatment of the sexes; a second edition of this work (1883) attracts international attention. **Spain**: Socialist Party is formed in Madrid (May). **United States**: Henry George, *Progress and Poverty*, has the unintended result of stimulating interest in socialism.

1880 Austro-Hungarian empire: The General Workers' Party of Hungary is formed; it is reorganized as the Social Democratic Party of

Hungary in 1890. **France**: Formation of the *Fédération des Ouvriers Socialistes de France* (Federation of Socialist Workers of France), France's first socialist party (June). **Sweden**: Social Democratic Party is formed.

1881 United Kingdom: Henry Hyndman and others form the Democratic Federation (June), later renamed the Social Democratic Federation.

1882 France: A split in the Federation of Socialist Workers of France produces the Possibilists, a party advocating evolutionary socialism.

1883 United Kingdom: In London, formation of the Democratic Federation, which is renamed the Social Democratic Federation in 1884.

1884 Peru: Anarchists form a universal union open to all employees. **United Kingdom**: Fabian Society is formed in London (January). William Morris and his followers leave the Social Democratic Federation and form the Socialist League. **United States**: Laurence Grönlund, *The Cooperative Commonwealth*.

1885 Belgium: A united Socialist Workers' Party is formed.

1887 Austro-Hungarian empire: Czech Socialist Party is formed at Brno (December). **Chile**: First socialist political party (the Democratic Party) is formed. **Norway**: Labor Party is founded (August). **United Kingdom**: Trades Union Congress forms the Labour Electoral Association.

1888 Switzerland: Socialist Party is formed. **United Kingdom**: William Morris, *The Dream of John Ball*. **United States**: Edward Bellamy, *Looking Backward: 2000–1887*.

1889 Austro-Hungarian empire: The Austrian Social Democratic Party is formed at Hainfeld (30 December 1888–1 January 1889). **France**: Second International Workingmen's Association, also known as the Second International, is formed in Paris (July); it is dissolved in 1914. **Germany**: Old age pension law is introduced (May). **Sweden**: Social Democratic Workers' Party is formed. **United Kingdom**: Publication of the *Fabian Essays*; edited by George Bernard Shaw, it becomes a bestseller. London dock strike attracts widespread support from organized labor in Britain, Australia, and Germany (19 August–14 September).

1890 Armenia: Socialist Party is formed. **Austro-Hungarian empire**: Hungarian Social Democratic Party is formed (December). **France**: Split among Possibilist socialists over cooperation with bourgeoisie. The split produces the *Parti Ouvrier Socialiste Révolutionnaire*. **Germany**: First international congress considers ways of protecting employees held in Berlin (15–28 March). Industrial courts are set up to adjudicate in labor disputes (July). **Hungary**: Social Democratic Party is formed. **Switzerland**: Social insurance is introduced (June). **United Kingdom**: William Morris, *News from Nowhere*.

1891 Australia: Separate labor parties are formed in the colonies of New South Wales, South Australia (January), and Victoria (June). **Bulgaria**: Social Democratic Labor Party is formed. **France**: "Massacre of Fourmies" occurs when troops fire on demonstrating employees and their families. **Germany**: Social Democratic Party adopts the Erfurt Program (21 October); the program, based on Marxism, remains its official policy until 1921. **Netherlands**: Socialist Party is formed. **Rome**: Pope Leo XIII issues encyclical on the condition of the working classes.

1892 Germany: The socialist feminist journal *Die Gleichheit* (Equality) begins publication. **Italy**: Formation of the Italian Socialist Party (August). **Russian empire**: Polish Socialist Party is formed. **United Kingdom**: Socialist Sunday school movement begins.

1893 France: Auguste Vailland, an anarchist, explodes a bomb in the chamber of deputies. **Romania**: Social Democratic Party is formed. **United Kingdom**: Independent Labour Party is formed at Bradford, England, by Keir Hardie. Robert Blatchford's *Merrie England* is published, is reissued in a cheaper format in 1894, and becomes one of the best-selling works of socialism, doing much to popularize socialist ideas.

1894 Argentina: Socialist Party is formed. **Italy**: Anarchist and socialist organizations are outlawed (11 July).

1895 International: International Co-operative Alliance is formed in London by representatives from Belgium, Denmark, France, Netherlands, Hungary, Italy, Russia, Serbia, Australia, India, Argentina, and the United States. **France**: *Confédération Générale du Travail* (General Confederation of Labor) is founded. **United Kingdom**: London School of Economics is founded.

1896 Russian empire: Socialist Party is formed in Lithuania.

1897 Russian empire: Jewish Labor Bund is formed secretly at Vilna, Poland (October).

1898 Japan: Society for the Study of Socialism is formed (November). **New Zealand**: Old age pensions are introduced. **Russian empire**: Social Democratic Labor Party is formed in Minsk (March); most of the delegates are arrested later. **United States**: Social Democracy Party of America is formed.

1899 Australia: World's first Labor Party government is formed in Queensland; it lasts one week (December). **France**: Alexandre Millerand, a leading socialist, becomes minister for commerce and industry in the cabinet of René Waldeck-Rousseau (1899–1902). He uses his position to introduce many important labor reforms. **Germany**: Eduard Bernstein's *The Preconditions of Socialism*, the first theoretical attempt to update Marxism. **Russian empire**: Socialist Party is formed in Georgia. Socialist Party is formed in Finland; it is renamed the Social Democratic Party in 1903.

1900 Belgium: Cooperative movement forms a wholesale society. **Russian empire**: *Poalei Zion* (Workers of Zion) groups are established by Jewish socialists. **United Kingdom**: Labour Representation Committee is formed (27 February); becomes the Labour Party in 1906.

1901 Denmark: International trade union conference in Copenhagen (21 August); the conference sets up the International Secretariat of the National Trade Union Federations, which is officially renamed the International Federation of Trade Unions in 1919. **Japan**: Formation of the Japan Socialist Party (*Nihon Shakai-ō*). **United States**: Socialist Party is formed.

1902 Luxembourg: Socialist Workers' Party is formed. **Russian empire**: Lenin sets out the role of the revolutionary party in *What Is to be Done?*

1903 United Kingdom: Split in the second conference of the Russian Social Democratic Labor Party in London (August) over the membership of the party; Lenin wins a narrow majority (twenty-four to twenty) and the party becomes divided between his followers (Bolsheviks) and the "minority" (Mensheviks).

1904 Australia: First national labor government is formed with Protectionist support and headed by John C. Watson (April to August). **France**: Socialist newspaper *L'Humanité* is founded. **Russian empire**: Socialist Party is formed in Latvia.

1905 Austro-Hungarian empire: One million people take part in mass marches in support of universal suffrage (28 November). **France**: The United Socialist Party is formed at the urging of the Second International (April). **Netherlands**: Amsterdam Conference of the Second International Workingmen's Association passes a resolution condemning socialists who participate in coalition governments. **Norway**: *Storting* (parliament) declares its independence from Sweden (June); Swedish socialists avert a possible war by threatening a general strike. **Russian empire**: "Bloody Sunday" massacre in St. Petersburg (January). **United States**: Industrial Workers of the World is created in Chicago.

1906 France: *Confédération Générale du Travail* (General Confederation of Labor) adopts the radical Charter of Amiens, which advocates the general strike to eliminate capitalism and affirms the independence of trade unions from any political parties. **Germany**: Mannheim Agreement declares the equality of trade unions with the Social Democratic Party in providing leadership for the working-class movement. Werner Sombart, *Why Is There No Socialism in the United States?* **United States**: Upton Sinclair, *The Jungle*.

1907 Belgium: International socialist women's congress is set up as part of the Second International. **Germany**: Socialist Youth International is formed.

1908 France: Georges Sorel, *Réflexions sur la violence* (Reflections on Violence). **United Kingdom**: Old age pensions introduced. H. G. Wells's *New Worlds for Old* is regarded as one of the most influential works of socialist propaganda since Robert Blatchford's *Merrie England* (1893).

1909 South Africa: Labour Party is formed (October). **Spain**: "Tragic Week" (July) occurs when over 175 people are shot in riots led by revolutionary syndicalists in Catalonia over calling up of reservists for the war in Morocco. Attacks on churches and convents. Execution of anarchist leader Francisco Ferrer. **Turkish empire**: First *kibbutz* is established in Palestine. **United Kingdom**: Keir Hardie attacks capitalist exploitation in *India*. The House of Lords upholds the Osbourne Judgment declaring political levies by trade unions illegal (2 December).

1910 International: General Secretariat of Abstaining Socialists is formed. Balkan Communist Federation is formed. **Denmark**: First international socialist women's conference is held in Copenhagen. **Japan**: Government arrests socialist leaders (May), leading to secret executions in January 1911. **Spain**: Anarchists form the *Confederación Nacional del Trabajo*. **Uruguay**: Socialist Party is formed.

1912 Ireland: Labour Party is formed.

1913 International: Twelve countries are represented at an attempt to form a syndicalist international in London. Sickness, unemployment, and maternity benefits are introduced. First international socialist sports organization is formed.

1915 International: International conference of socialist women is held in Berne to protest World War I (March). Antiwar Zimmerwald Conference held (September). **United States**: Young People's Socialist League is established as a national body.

1916 Brazil: Socialist Party is formed. **Finland**: Social Democratic Party wins a parliamentary majority, the first time a labor/socialist party ever wins a majority in a legislature in Western Europe. **Iceland**: Labor Party is formed. **New Zealand**: Labour Party is formed. **Switzerland**: Revolutionary conference is held at Kienthal (April).

1917 Germany: Independent Social Democratic Party is formed (April); it rejoins the Social Democratic Party in 1922. **Russia**: Alexander Kerensky becomes prime minister of a provisional government (24 July); Bolshevik Revolution (November). **Sweden**: Social Democratic Workers' Party becomes a partner in government for the first time.

1918 International: Scandinavian Cooperative Wholesale Society is formed. **Germany**: Social Democratic Party assumes power after the collapse of the monarchy (9 November). **Russia**: Democratically elected Constituent Assembly is dispersed by the Bolsheviks (18 January). **United Kingdom**: Labour Party is reorganized and adopts a socialization objective that later becomes Clause Four of its constitution; Sidney Webb's *Labour and the Social Order* is adopted as the basis of party policy (June).

1919 International: Second International conference at Lucerne, Switzerland, declares that the communist Comintern tended toward dictatorship and rejects a merger between the two internationals (August). International Labour Organization is formed. **Australia**: the Labor Party adopts a socialization objective that is strengthened in 1921 and 1927. **Germany**: Spartacist uprising is crushed (January). Friedrich Ebert of the Social Democratic Party becomes president of the Weimar Republic (11 February). The federal government suppresses the soviet republic in Bavaria (May). **Soviet Union**: Third International (Communist) is formed (March); known as the Comintern, it is disbanded in 1943. **Switzerland**: Berne conference of the Second International affirms that the reorganization of society along socialist lines has to be based on democracy and liberty (February).

1920 International: Workers' Educational International is formed. **France**: Split in the Socialist Party results in the formation of the Communist Party. **Malta**: Labour Party is formed.

1921 International: International Working Union of Socialist Parties is formed at Vienna (February). International Union of Socialist Teetotallers is formed. **Germany**: Social Democratic Party adopts the Görlitz Program, which drops much of the Marxist analysis of the Erfurt Program of 1891. **Switzerland**: International Cooperative Women's Guild is formed. **United Kingdom**: R. H. Tawney, *The Acquisitive Society*.

1922 International: International Union of Religious Socialists is formed in Switzerland. International of Revolutionary Syndicalists is formed in Berlin (December).

1923 International: Labor and Socialist International is formed in Hamburg (May). The International Socialist Women's Committee and the International of the Socialist Youth are formed at the same time.

1924 International: International Cooperative Wholesale Society is formed. **United Kingdom**: First Labour government is formed, led by Ramsay MacDonald (January–October).

1925 Germany: Social Democratic Party adopts the Heidelberg Program, which restores much of the Marxist analysis removed by the Görlitz Program in 1921. **United Kingdom**: Harold Laski, *A Grammar of Politics*.

1926 United Kingdom: General strike (4–12 May).

1927 United States: Two anarchists, Nicola Sacco and Bartolemeo Vanzetti, executed for murder and armed robbery in Massachusetts (August); the two are publicly exonerated for the crime in 1977.

1928 Germany: Social Democrats become the largest party in the *Reichstag* and form a government with Herman Müller as president (May). **Italy**: Antonio Gramsci is imprisoned.

1929 Australia: Labor Party forms a national government under James H. Scullin, the first since 1917. **Italy**: Antonio Gramsci begins work on his posthumously published *Prison Notebooks*. **United Kingdom**: Labour Party, led by Ramsay MacDonald, forms a government with Liberal support.

1930 Germany: Disagreements over economic policy lead to the fall of Herman Müller's Social Democratic government (March). **Vietnam**: Vietnam Communist Party is formed.

1931 International: International Federation of Socialist Physicians is formed. **Australia**: Split in the federal Labor government over economic policy (March). Some of the Labor parliamentarians join the conservatives to form a coalition which wins the national elections in December. **Spain**: First socialist-led government is formed (June). **United Kingdom**: Labour government under Ramsay MacDonald collapses over disagreements over economic policy (24 August); MacDonald and other Labour parliamentarians enter into a coalition with the conservatives and are expelled from the Labour Party. R. H. Tawney, *Equality*.

1932 International: Formation of an international organization of Zionist labor organizations at Danzig. **Canada**: Founding of the Co-operative Commonwealth Federation. **Sweden**: Election of the first majority Social Democratic government. **United States**: Norman Thomas, the presidential candidate of the Socialist Party, receives 884,781 votes.

1933 Chile: Socialist Party is formed. **Germany**: Social Democratic Party is the only party to vote against the Enabling Act (23 March), which gives Hitler dictatorial powers until 1 April 1937. The Social Democratic Party is outlawed on 10 May and its leadership, as well as that of the trade unions, is imprisoned in Dachau concentration camp.

Palestine: Formation of *Mapai* (January), ancestor of the Israel Labor Party.

1934 Austria: Violent suppression of socialists (11–15 February); the Social Democratic Party is dissolved and not reestablished until 1945. **India**: Congress Socialist Party is formed in Bombay (October). **Tunisia**: Democratic Constituent Assembly is formed.

1935 Denmark: Social Democratic Party wins a majority in both houses of parliament, enabling it to introduce a range of progressive social and economic legislation. **New Zealand**: Labour Party is elected to government for the first time.

1936 Mauritius: Formation of a labor party. **Spain**: Beginning of the Civil War (July), which does not end until 1939 and results in the defeat of the socialist republican government by fascism. **United Kingdom**: J. M. Keynes, *General Theory of Employment, Interest, and Money*. His ideas underpin much social-democratic economic policy in the post-1945 period. Left Book Club is established. "Hunger" march by unemployed men from Jarrow, northern England, to London (October–November). **United States**: American Labor Party is formed in New York state. **Venezuela**: Democratic Action is formed.

1937 Luxembourg: Socialist Workers' Party is elected to government. **Senegal**: First francophone African socialist party is formed. **United Kingdom**: George Orwell, *The Road to Wigan Pier*.

1938 International: Leon Trotsky founds the Fourth International. **United Kingdom**: Introduction of paid holidays.

1939 Dominican Republic: Dominican Revolutionary Party is formed.

1940 International: Last executive meeting of the Labor and Socialist International is held in Brussels (March). **Mexico**: A Stalinist agent murders Leon Trotsky.

1942 United Kingdom: Labour Party conference adopts a policy for a comprehensive social security system, a family allowance scheme, and a national health service (December). Publication of the Beveridge Report which recommends the setting up of a comprehensive national system of social insurance and a national health service (December).

1944 United Kingdom: William Beveridge, *Full Employment in a Free Society*. **Italy**: Communist Party reaffirms its commitment to parliamentary democracy.

1945 International: World Federation of Trade Unions is created in Paris (25 September); the former international trade union federation, the International Federation of Trade Unions, ceases to exist after 31 December. **Austria**: Socialist Party is formed to replace the Social Democratic Party (April). **United Kingdom**: Labour Party wins its first national election in its own right with 47.8 percent of votes and 393 members of the House of Commons (5 July).

1946 Germany: Social Democratic Party in the Soviet zone of occupation is forced to merge with the communists (21 April) after the arrest of twenty thousand of its members. **France**: International Union of Socialist Youth is formed in Paris (October). **United Kingdom**: Socialist Information Office is formed (May). Labour government enacts the National Insurance Act and the National Health Service Act. Ceylon is granted its independence.

1947 International: Committee of the Socialist International Conference is formed (March). Socialist Movement for the United States of Europe is formed. International Falcon Secretariat is formed in the Netherlands (October); it is reorganized as the International Falcon Movement–Socialist Educational International in 1970. **France**: Movement for the Socialist United States of Europe is founded (February). **Italy**: Socialist Party splits; the moderates leave and join the Christian Democrats. **Poland**: Cominform is formed (September); it is dissolved in April 1956. **United Kingdom**: Labour government nationalizes the coal industry (1 January; it is privatized in 1992) and gives independence to India and Burma. Labour government nationalizes the electricity supply industry and introduces a nationalized health service.

1948 International: Forcible mergers of social-democratic parties with communist parties in Czechoslovakia, Hungary, Poland, and Romania. **Israel**: United Workers' Party (*Mapam*) is formed.

1949 International: Socialist Union of Central and Eastern Europe is formed in London. World Federation of Trade Unions splits: the noncommunist countries form their own federation, the International Confederation of Free Trade Unions (December); the World Federation of Trade Unions continues as a communist organization.

1951 International: Socialist International is formed at Frankfurt, Germany; it issues a declaration of the fundamental principles of democratic socialism (July). **Costa Rica**: National Liberation Party is formed. **France**: International Union of Socialist Democratic Teachers is formed (July). **United Kingdom**: Labour government nationalizes the railroads (1 January).

1952 Vietnam: Socialist Party is formed in secret (September).

1953 International: First Asian Socialist Conference is held in Burma (January). International Federation of the Socialist and Democratic Press is formed. **Syria**: *Baath* Party (Arab Resurrectionist Socialist Party) is formed from the merger of two parties to promote Arab unity, freedom, and socialism.

1954 International: Socialist Group in the European Parliament is founded.

1955 International: Socialist International Women is formed in London (July). **Australia**: Split in the Labor Party over communism keeps it out of power in the national parliament until December 1972. **Indonesia**: Socialist Party is defeated in national elections; the party is abolished by President Sukarno in 1960.

1956 International: Second (and last) Asian Socialist Conference is held in India (November). **United Kingdom**: C. A. R. Crosland publishes *The Future of Socialism*, which advocates that the Labour Party shift its emphasis from the nationalization of industry to its modernization. Its revisionist ideas are absorbed by the British Labour Party in practice, though not in theory.

1957 International: Bureau of Social Democratic Parties is founded (January); it is officially reorganized as the Confederation of the Socialist Parties of the European Community in April 1974.

1958 Austria: Socialist Party removes Marxism from its program. **Netherlands**: The Labor Party removes Marxist references from its statement of principles. **United Kingdom**: *New Left Review* begins publication.

1959 Germany: Social Democratic Party adopts a non-Marxist program at its conference at Godesberg (November).

1960 United Kingdom: British Labour Party narrowly adopts a policy that rejects the use of nuclear weapons as the basis for national defense.

1961 Canada: New Democratic Party is formed.

1964 United Kingdom: Labour Party wins general elections. **United States**: Herbert Marcuse, *One Dimensional Man*.

1966 Italy: Moderates rejoin the Socialist Party from which they had split in 1947.

1967 Pakistan: Pakistan People's Party is formed.

1968 Czechoslovakia: Alexander Dubček attempts to liberalize the communist administration.

1970 International: Asia-Pacific Socialist Organization is formed. **Chile**: Socialist Party leader Salvador Allende is elected president. **United Kingdom**: In Northern Ireland Socialist Democratic and Labour Party is formed (August).

1971 Bolivia: Movement of the Revolutionary Left is formed.

1972 France: Socialist Party adopts a program that omits overt references to Marxism. **United States**: Social Democrats USA is formed.

1973 Chile: Socialist president Salvador Allende dies during right-wing coup. **Portugal**: Socialist Party of Portugal is formed.

1974 Greece: Pan-Hellenic Socialist Movement is formed. **Morocco**: Socialist Union of Popular Forces is formed (September).

1975 Portugal: Socialist Party forms government for the first time (April).

1977 Ecuador: Democratic Left is formed. **Spain**: Spanish Socialist Party becomes legal (18 February) for the first time since 1939.

1978 Belgium: Socialist Party splits into two parties based on French and Flemish speakers. **Brazil**: Workers' party is formed. **Egypt**: National Democratic Party is formed. **Guatemala**: Democratic Socialist Party is formed.

1979 Nicaragua: The Sandinista Revolution overthrows the right-wing Somoza dynasty. **United Kingdom**: Labour Party is defeated by the Conservatives led by Margaret Thatcher (May).

1980 International: Socialist International establishes the Disarmament Advisory Council in Spain. **Brazil**: Democratic Labor Party is formed.

1981 International: League of African Democratic Socialist Parties is formed in Tunisia. **France**: Election of socialist François Mitterand as president. The socialists also win a majority in the National Assembly (21 June). **United Kingdom**: Dissident Labour Party parliamentarians form the Social Democratic Party (26 March), which merges with the Liberal Party to form the Liberal Democrats in 1987–88.

1982 France: Socialist government introduces a nationalization law that covers manufacturing, electricity production, banking, and insurance (June). **Spain**: First socialist-led government since 1939 is formed (December); socialists lead Spanish government until March 1996. **United States**: Democratic Socialists of America is formed.

1983 Australia: Australian Labor party wins parliamentary elections. **Italy**: First socialist-led government is formed.

1984 New Zealand: New Zealand Labour Party wins parliamentary elections. **Nicaragua**: The Sandinista National Liberation Front holds and wins general elections.

1985 Fiji: Labour Party is formed (July). **Soviet Union**: Mikhail Gorbachev becomes Communist Party general secretary. **Turkey**: Social Democratic Populist Party is formed.

1986 Austria: Franz Vranitsky of the Social Democratic Party is elected president. **Costa Rica**: Oscar Arias Sanchez of National Liberation Party is elected president. **Haiti**: PANPRA (*Parti Nationaliste Progressiviste Révolutionnaire*) is formed. **Japan**: Takako Doi of the Socialist party becomes the first female leader of a Japanese party. **Portugal**: Socialist Party removes all references to Marxism from its program (June). Mário Soares of the Portuguese Socialist Party is elected president. **Sweden**: Social Democratic Prime Minister Olaf Palme is assassinated.

1987 Bolivia: Movement Towards Socialism is formed. **Haiti**: KONAKOM (*Parti du Congrès National des movement Démocratiques*) is formed. **Poland**: The Socialist Party is secretly reformed as communism begins to collapse. **Taiwan**: Labor Party is formed (November).

1988 Chile: Socialist Party of Chile helps form the Party for Democracy as an ally against the Pinochet dictatorship. **Pakistan**: Pakistan People's Party wins parliamentary elections and its leader, Benazir Bhutto, becomes prime minister. **Solomon Islands**: Labour Party is formed (November).

1989 International: Communism begins to collapse in Eastern Europe. Commission of Socialist Teachers of the European Community is formed. **China**: Demonstrations for political reforms are crushed in Tiananmen Square, Beijing. **East Germany**: Illegal formation of a social-democratic party (October). **Latvia**: Social Democratic Workers' Party is formed (December). **Lithuania**: Social Democratic Party is reestablished (August). **New Zealand**: Labour Party splits over privatization and the formation of the New Labour Party by dissidents (April). **Romania**: Social Democratic Party is recreated (December).

1990 International: Collapse of communism continues in Eastern Europe. **Benin**: Social Democratic Party is formed. **Czechoslovakia**: Social Democratic Party is formed in Slovakia (February) and in the Czech lands (March). **Estonia**: Social Democratic Party is formed (September). **Mongolia**: Social Democratic Party is formed (March). **Nicaragua**: The Sandinistas lose power at general elections. **South Africa**: Nelson Mandela is released from prison and the African National Congress is legalized. **Yugoslavia**: Communism begins to collapse and the country begins to break up in a series of civil wars in the 1990s.

1991 Albania: Social Democratic Party is formed; Workers' Party is renamed Socialist Party. **Austria**: Socialist party is renamed Social Democratic Party. **Canada**: New Democratic Party wins elections to government in Ontario and Saskatchewan. **France**: Edith Cresson of the Socialist Party becomes the first woman to be French prime minister. **Italy**: Communist Party transforms itself into the Democratic Party of the Left (February). **Slovakia**: The former Communist Party transforms itself into a social-democratic party, but is not admitted to the Socialist International. **Soviet Union**: Communism collapses and the country breaks up.

1992 International: The Party of European Socialists is founded as the successor to the Confederation of the Socialist Parties in the European Community. **Israel**: *Meretz* party is formed. **Mali**: Alpha Konaré of AMEDA-PASJ wins presidential elections. **Poland**: Union of Labour is formed. **Turkey**: Republican People's Party is revived.

1993 Burkina Faso: The Party for Democracy and Progress is formed. **Chile**: Radical Party renamed Social Democratic Radical Party. **Denmark**: Poul Nyrup Rasmussen of the Social Democratic Party becomes prime minister. **Greece**: PASOK wins parliamentary elections. **Montenegro**: Social Democratic Party is formed. **Pakistan**: Pakistan Peoples' Party wins parliamentary elections. **Russia**: Communist Party of the Russian Federation is founded.

1994 Denmark: Poul Nyrup Rasmussen of Social Democratic Party is returned to power in parliamentary elections. **Mozambique**: FRELIMO holds and wins free parliamentary elections and Joaquim Chissano of FRELIMO is reelected president under the new constitution. **South Africa**: African National Congress wins majority in first postapartheid parliamentary elections. National Assembly elects Nelson Mandela president.

1995 Portugal: Socialist Party regains government (October). **United Kingdom**: Labour Party replaces the socialization objective adopted in 1918 with a commitment to a mixed economy of the public and private sectors (April).

1996 Czech Republic: The Social Democratic Party wins 26 percent of the vote compared to 7 percent in 1992. **Greece**: Pan-Hellenic Socialist Movement wins national elections. **Italy**: The Olive Tree Alliance led by the Democratic Party of the Left, the former Communist Party, wins the national elections (April).

1997 France: Socialist Party wins government after national elections (May and June). **Mongolia**: Natsagiin Bagabandi of the Mongolian People's Revolutionary Party wins presidential elections. **United Kingdom**: Landslide electoral victory of the Labour Party (May). Tony Blair becomes prime minister.

1998 Germany: Elections bring Social Democratic Party to government in coalition with the Green Party. **Italy**: Democratic Party of the Left is renamed Democrats of the Left. **Latvia**: Latvian Socialist Democratic Workers' Party and Latvian Social Democratic Party merge to form the Latvian Social Democratic Union. **United Kingdom**: Scottish Socialist Party is formed. **Venezuela**: Hugo Chávez of Movement of Fifth Republic is elected president.

1999 Latvia: Latvian Social Democratic Union takes the name of one of its members, the Latvian Social Democratic Workers' Party. **Mozambique**: FRELIMO wins parliamentary elections and FRELIMO's Joaquim Chissano retains presidency. **New Zealand**: Labour Party wins government at elections. **South Africa**: African National Congress retains majority at second postapartheid elections. **United States**: "Battle in Seattle" between police and anticapitalist demonstrators outside a conference of the World Trade Organization.

2000 Finland: Tarja Halonen of the Social Democratic Party is elected president (February). **Greece**: Pan-Hellenic Socialist Movement is reelected to government (April). **Mauritius**: Alliance of Mauritian Militant Movement and Mauritian Socialist Movement wins parliamentary elections (September). **Mongolia**: Mongolian People's Revolutionary Party wins landslide victory at parliamentary elections (July). **Venezuela**: Hugo Chávez is reelected president (July).

2001 International: The first World Social Forum is held in Porto Alegre, Brazil. **Aruba**: People's Electoral Movement wins absolute majority in parliamentary elections (September). **Bulgaria**: Georgi Parvanov of the Bulgarian Socialist Party is elected president (November). **Cape Verde**: African Party of Cape Verde's Independence wins presidential (February) and parliamentary (June) elections. **Former Yugoslav Republic of Macedonia**: Social Democratic Union of Macedonia takes part in government of national unity. **Lithuania**: The Lithuanian Social Democratic Party and Lithuanian Democratic Labor Party merge, taking the name of the former (January). **Mongolia**: Natsagiin Bagabandi of the Mongolian People's Revolutionary Party is reelected president (May). **Montenegro**: Social Democratic Party of Montenegro and Democratic Party of Socialists lead bloc that forms minority government after parliamentary elections (April). **Poland**: Democratic Left Alliance and Union of Labor form a coalition government after parliamentary elections. **United Kingdom**: Labour Party is reelected in general elections (June). **Vietnam**: Nong Duc Manh replaces Le Kha Phieu as secretary-general of the Vietnam Communist Party (April).

2002 International: The first European Social Forum is held in Florence, Italy. **Brazil**: Workers' Party leader Luis Ignacio Lula da Silva wins the presidency and leads minority government (October). **Former Yugoslav Republic of Macedonia**: Social Democratic Union of Macedonia leads coalition government after elections (September). **France**: Socialist Party loses power in parliamentary elections (June) and fares poorly in presidential elections (April). **Germany**: Social Democratic Party (SPD) retains power in coalition with the Green Party after elections, but with reduced majority (September). **New Zealand**: Labour Party retains power at elections but without an overall majority (July).

2003 Barbados: The Barbados Labour Party wins its third successive general election victory (May). **Germany**: Large declines in the SPD vote in the state elections of Hessen and Lower Saxony (February). **Israel**: The Social Democratic Party of Israel (*Yachad*) is formed as a successor to *Meretz*. **Mexico**: The Institutional Revolutionary Party gains control of parliament in coalition with the Ecologist Green Party (July).

2004 International: First meeting of the Americas Social Forum in Quito, Ecuador (July); European Left Party is formed. **Former Yugoslav Republic of Macedonia**: Branko Crvenkoski of the Social Democratic Union of Macedonia is elected president (November). **Lithuania**: Lithuanian Social Democratic Party participates in coalition government after elections (October). **Spain**: Socialist Workers' Party is elected to government (March). Jose Zapatero becomes prime minister. **Greece**: Pan-Hellenic Socialist Movement is removed from government in elections (March). **Mongolia**: The Mongolian People's Revolutionary Party takes part in grand coalition after parliamentary elections (September). **Mozambique**: FRELIMO's Armando Guebuza wins presidential elections (December). **South Africa**: African National Congress wins majority in parliamentary elections for third time in succession (April). **Uruguay**: Tabaré Vázquez of the Socialist Party of Uruguay is elected as the country's first ever leftist president (October). **Venezuela**: Hugo Chávez wins referendum on continuation of his presidency (August).

2005 Bulgaria: Bulgarian Socialist Party wins largest share of votes at parliamentary elections and heads coalition government (August). **Bolivia**: Evo Morales of the Movement Towards Socialism is elected as president (December). **Germany**: Social Democratic Party loses regional elections in North Rhine Westphalia after governing there for thirty-nine years (May). Social Democratic Party fails to win general election but enters into grand coalition (September–October). **Greece**: Károlos Papoúlias of the Pan-Hellenic Socialist Movement is elected president (March). **Haiti**: The Union of Haitian Social Democrats is formed. **Italy**: Olive Tree Coalition makes significant gains in regional elections (April). **Portugal**: Portuguese Socialist Party is elected to government (March). **United Kingdom**: The Labour Party wins a third successive general election for the first time in its history (May).

2006 Cape Verde: African Party of Cape Verde's Independence retains power at parliamentary (January) and presidential (February) elections. **Chile**: Michelle Bachelet of the Socialist Party is elected Chile's first female president (January). **Costa Rica**: Oscar Arias Sanchez of the National Liberation Party is elected president again (February). **Finland**: Tarja Halonen of the Social Democratic Party is reelected president. **Israel**: Labour Party participates in a coalition government led by a new center-right party (May) after general elections (March). **Italy**: Union bloc of the left and center-left narrowly wins general elections (April). **Jamaica**: Portia Simpson Miller of the People's National Party becomes prime minister (March).

Introduction

Throughout history many movements have tried to change the world for the better. As a mass movement seeking general social improvement, socialism has been an influential force for social change for almost two centuries. Socialist philosophy and ideology has inspired millions while simultaneously arousing fear and revulsion in its enemies. Many socialist politicians and activists have devoted their lives to the cause. Yet socialism may seem paradoxical. Although it emerged after the French Revolution in the effort to build upon and develop the egalitarian ideas of the Enlightenment, great crimes against humanity have nevertheless been committed in its name. Democratic in theory, it has sometimes been used by opportunists to justify totalitarian dictatorship in practice.

Despite its importance in history since the early nineteenth century, socialism eludes simple definition. Derived from the Latin word *socius* meaning "ally" or "friend"—the same word that provided the root for *society* and *sociology*—the term *socialist* was used in the English *Co-operative Magazine* in November 1827 as a synonym for "communist." In France the term *socialisme* was used in the *Globe* in February 1832 in contrast to *individualisme* or individualism. The word "socialism" has been in use from 1836.

As G. D. H. Cole suggested in the first volume of his monumental *History of Socialist Thought* (1953), the early socialists opposed the individualism that had come to dominate modern thinking and stressed that human relations had an essential social element that needed to be emphasized. Then, as now, there was no single agreed-upon definition of what socialism actually was. Variety has always been an outstanding feature of socialism. In his *Dictionary of Socialism* (1924), Angelo S. Rappoport listed forty definitions of socialism. Within this diversity many common elements could be found. First, there were general criticisms about the social effects of the private ownership and control of

1

capital—poverty, low wages, unemployment, economic and social inequality, and a lack of economic security. Second, there was a general view that the solution to these problems lay in some form of collective control (with the degree of control varying among the proponents of socialism) over the means of production, distribution, and exchange. Third, there was agreement that the outcomes of this collective control should be a society that provided social equality and justice, economic protection, and a generally more satisfying life for most people. Nevertheless, to a large extent *socialism* became a catchall term for the critics of industrial and capitalist society. Therefore, in trying to define socialism, it is tempting to assume that all that can be said is that it has always defied precise definition.

One need not succumb to such temptation. Indeed, in his introduction to *The Concept of Socialism* (1975), Bhikhu Parekh identified the core of a broad socialist ideology as four values or principles that are essential to any socialist's vision of humans and their society: sociality, social responsibility, cooperation, and planning. Although nonsocialists will often accept some of those four values, they will feel the need, often apologetically, to offer special justification. For socialists each of the four are accepted, and it is the holding of values to the contrary, such as competition as opposed to planning, that requires special justification. Parekh's four values enable one to grasp the socialist vision.

In another attempt to identify the socialist core, Michael Freeden identifies five conceptual themes. Noting in his study *Ideologies and Political Theory* (1996) that some variants of socialism will add other conceptual components to the core or stress that such other components can be added to the periphery to add detail or variation, Freeden says that all socialists will subscribe in some way or another to the five themes he has in mind. The first theme concerns the human relationship, which according to socialists, has a constitutive nature—society is something more than a collection of individuals; second, human welfare is considered a desirable objective; third, humans are by nature active and productive; fourth, the belief in human equality; and finally, history is, in the long term, progressive and will eventually bring beneficial change, so long as humans work to achieve such change.

Now, unlike Freeden, Parekh does not explicitly include equality. This is understandable given the abstract nature of the concept of equality, which is almost meaningless unless other values can be seen to shape a particular conception. The four values identified by Parekh do indeed give meaning to the socialist conception of equality. They also rest on the socialist optimism of Freeden's fifth theme and encapsulate the first three themes identified by the latter author. Sociality, social responsibility, cooperation, and planning do, then, concisely define the socialist vision. On the basis of the four values, one may judge whether those who operate under the socialist banner do so with justification.

LEADERS AND FOLLOWERS

The Emergence of Socialist Thought

Distant precedents for any important topic in political or philosophical discourse can always be found. Some scholars, such as Alexander Gray in *The Socialist Tradition: Moses to Lenin* (1946), have attempted to trace the roots of socialism back to Thomas More's *Utopia* and, even more tenuously, to Plato's *Republic*. Interesting as these antecedents are as forerunners of elements of socialist thought, they are not particularly helpful in understanding socialism as a modern movement, simply because precedents can be found for just about any viewpoint over the past two millennia. Evidence of direct lineage between ideas is all too often assumed rather than proven. As Bernard Crick has observed in his short introductory text *Socialism* (1987), socialism really has no precedent in the ancient or medieval world, which is because there was no precedent for the scale of the explosion of capitalist activity and industrialization that occurred first in Western Europe and then spread to the rest of the world after 1800. By the 1820s and 1830s critics of the new economic order had begun to grow in number and confidence, united, albeit in different ways, in their moral objections to capitalism as an economic and political system. They objected to its emphasis on competition as opposed to cooperation, to the benefits it gave to individuals as opposed to the society, and to its social costs—specifically poverty, unemployment, low wages, inequality, and lack of social and economic protection. These concerns were to become lasting attributes of socialist thought and practice.

Utopian socialism (as it would soon become known) was the dominant form of socialism during the first half of the nineteenth century. If society could not be changed, then one option was to set up model communities either within the society or, more popularly, somewhere else. Hence, communities based on the ideas of Robert Owen and Charles

Fourier were set up in the United States. Although in *The Communist Manifesto* of 1848 Karl Marx and Friedrich Engels criticized utopian socialism as impractical and claimed it did not address the fundamental flaws in capitalist society, interest in socialist communities continued into the 1930s. Utopianism, a form of secular millenarianism, remained a feature of socialism and later, communism. Indeed, the vision of a better society that was widely held between 1880 and 1914 was immensely powerful in sustaining support for socialism.

Socialism varied because it developed under very different conditions within Western Europe. France and England were the twin nurseries of socialist ideas before 1850. Socialism was strongly shaped by the particular political traditions of the two societies, as well as by the very different impact of the process of industrialization on each country. France, to a far greater extent than England, continued its tradition of political change by violent revolution, which was shown vividly in the "June Days" of 1848 and the Paris Commune of 1871, both of which provoked the German thinker Marx to write some of his most widely read pieces. In England the tradition of piecemeal reform was ascendant and fed the socialist tradition in the form of Fabianism. Christian socialism was another response to the problems caused by industrial capitalism. Although its influence waned after 1900, its later influence in shaping the views of later British socialists such as R. H. Tawney or Americans like Norman Thomas should not be dismissed. Another critic of individual capitalism was Claude-Henri Saint-Simon, who stressed its inefficiency and its lack of reward for the truly productive members of society. A more moderate stance was taken by Louis Blanc, a leading democratic French socialist, who saw the potential of using government to implement socialist ideas as early as 1840 and anticipated what was later regarded as revisionism. The very different alternative of anarchism—the denial of the need for government—was effectively, but perhaps unwittingly, begun by Pierre-Joseph Proudhon in 1840.

The general repression that occurred in continental Europe after the failure of the revolutions in 1848 not only suppressed socialism for another decade, but also exposed its weaknesses. With the exception of Proudhon, all the principal writers who today are regarded as precursors of socialism before 1860 came from the middle class. Blanc and Proudhon were among the few to have any kind of political experience. Otherwise, socialism before 1860 was largely confined to a mixed, educated group of middle-class critics of capitalism. Their ideas were sometimes confused and contradictory. Their practicality was questionable. The ideas themselves needed to be refined and made coherent. In this process Marx played a critical role, although it was not until the 1880s that his works became readily available. Even then he was likely to be read through interpreters, such as Karl Kautsky. Marx gave the emerging socialist movement not just a compelling theory of society complete with its own vocabulary, but also a powerful version of socialism's historical theme. His works showed socialists where their theories had came from, where their movement was, and where it could be. Yet sophisticated theory and powerful prose could not disguise the fact that before 1860 socialism as a coherent movement was largely made up of leaders, or those who aspired to lead others. Those leaders needed far more followers in order to create the mass movement that would not only provide a means for the delivery of socialist ideas but also give such ideas practical shape and direction. The place to look for those followers was in the group that socialists seek to help the most, the working class.

The Tradition of Working-Class Collectivism

Marx insisted upon the primacy of productive forces, which included human capabilities and labor as well as technology. Nevertheless, many who trace the history of socialism tend to stress the primacy of ideas published by educated reformers while minimizing the efforts of the working class. What is thus often neglected is that long before the advent of socialist writers a tradition of economic collectivism had been developed by segments of the working class—a tradition that would grow into the mass socialist movement. In England and northern Italy, the first trade unions are recorded as arising in the fourteenth century. Although their lives as organizations were often short, they were persistent. Arising among journeymen (men who had learned a trade through an apprenticeship) and among workers employed at centers of large-scale production, such as mines and textile factories, they were, at least in England, able to become a feature of society by the eighteenth century. Indeed, by the late seventeenth century, labor disputes had emerged in England as a form of working-class collectivism. Despite their illegality, hundreds of such disputes are known to have taken place in the United Kingdom in the century that followed. Events like these could not have occurred without some kind of organization, no matter how rudimentary. In their famous *History of Trade Unionism* (1894), Beatrice and Sidney Webb were inclined to dismiss the pre-1850 trade union movement on the grounds that the organizations were not continuous. This is an excessively bureaucratic interpretation of historical development because although the organizations may not have survived—they were, after all, illegal—their members did endure and so provided the foundations for more impressive institutional achievements after 1850.

Friendly (or mutual benefit) societies were another strand of working-class collectivism. These voluntary associations collected money by installments from members, which would then be paid back to the members or their families in case of unemployment, illness, incapacity, old age, or death. Prussian miners are known to have formed thrift societies in the sixteenth century and early friendly societies were formed in Scotland, England, and France in the seventeenth century, a prominent example being that in 1699 of the coal ship loaders of Newcastle-upon-Tyne, northeast England. During the eighteenth century, the number of these mutual benefit societies increased greatly; by 1803 there were almost 10,000 friendly societies in England with a total membership of more than 700,000. Ironically, slowly rising living standards in England enabled collectivist action by certain groups of workers to diversify and succeed. Mutual benefit societies were one of the most common expressions of working-class collectivism in the United Kingdom before 1850. Often providing a blind for trade union activities (as between 1800 and 1824), they were primarily organizations of the relatively better off. They required their members to have some level of surplus that could be put aside to help out in hard times.

Cooperatives were a third strand in the collectivist tradition. They took various forms but consisted of members pooling their resources to begin some kind of enterprise—such as a mill or a shop—for mutual benefit. The first cooperatives began in the United Kingdom in the 1760s. A cooperative flour mill was established by 1760 by shipwrights employed at the government dockyard at Woolwich, London. In Scotland some weavers at Fenwick formed what seems to have been the first British consumer cooperative in 1769. The links between these forms of collectivist activity were very close; for instance, in 1777 some tailors on strike set up a cooperative workshop in Birmingham. By 1862 there were 450 cooperative societies in England with a total membership of 90,000.

The collectivist strands so far discussed—trade unions, friendly societies, and cooperatives—at first took in only a small minority of the British working class, but they provided a base for expansion once industrialization became more widely established after 1830. Although the membership growth of these collectivist institutions was painfully slow and uncertain before the 1860s, it was vital to socialism's effort to become a mass movement.

The working-class collectivist impulse, whose origins have been sketched here, represented one level of response to the challenges, dangers, and opportunities of a dynamic capitalist economy. It was a practical response to some of the obvious pitfalls of that system, namely, its failure to provide security for all citizens and its unequal distribution of income and wealth. At the same time, this tradition of collectivism among the working class had its limitations. Those who did join tended to be the better-off members of the working class and those who were committed to social advancement. Second, they needed socialist leaders as much as those leaders needed the mass movement. Leaders and ideas would help widen their vision and attain their objectives. After 1860 there was productive cross-fertilization between socialist ideas and working-class institutions. As G. D. H. Cole suggested in *A Short History of the British Working-Class Movement* (1948), the trade unions, cooperative societies, political parties, and socialist organizations became one and indivisible in making up the modern working-class movement in the United Kingdom. They arose out of a common need, depended on one and the same class—a class whose ideas and aspiration needed to be expressed. In different ways, leaders and followers came together.

In the century following the revolution in France of 1789, the conditions in which the French working-class movement grew were quite different to those of the British. The political dominance of the absolute monarchy, the abject poverty of the peasants who had little conception of themselves as belonging to a class, and the underdevelopment of industry meant that the French movement was small, weak, and relatively organized in the late eighteenth century. Discontent, which had simmered under the political surface, erupted when the philosophical influences of the Enlightenment combined with economically motivated disgruntlement as the king demanded more taxes to keep bankrupt France afloat. The republicanism and nationalism that followed the revolution soon dissipated as middle-class dominance took the place of monarchical and aristocratic dominance. The French workers and peasants subsequently endured dictatorial emperors, interspersed with monarchies and a brief new attempt to restore republican rule.

These conditions meant that the French working-class movement, which faced suppression of organized activity and had few legal means at its disposal, was revolutionary rather than reformist in nature, especially when radical interpretations of the ideas of early socialist thinkers such as Claude-Henri Saint-Simon and Louis Blanc began to percolate in society and influence the thoughts of working-class activists, culminating in the failed revolution of 1848. The dictatorship that followed ended with military defeat in the war against Prussia and the brief experiment of working-class participation in the Paris Commune, which ended in bloody repression by the state. In 1884, however, in awareness that toleration of working-class organizations may forestall revolutionary activity, the French government legalized trade unions, but attempted to keep them out of the control of potential revolutionaries. Nevertheless, sections of organized labor did take on a revolutionary approach, adopting syndicalism and its strategy of attempting to instigate general strikes.

In Germany the organization of the labor movement was hampered by political repression for much of the nineteenth century. The first trade union in Germany—the National Printers' Association (*Nationaler Buchdrucker-Verein*)—was not formed until 1848. Even after that, repression for much of the nineteenth century meant that the organized labor movement remained quite small and weak. Radical publications similarly suffered under authoritarian rule in Germany, as Karl Marx witnessed. His work for the liberal newspaper *Rheinische Zeitung* on issues including the poverty and exploitation of the wine growers of Mosselle and his eventual editorship in late 1842 attracted the attention of the Prussian authorities, who suppressed the journal in March the following year. The young Marx set up his own newspaper—the *Neue Rheinische Zeitung*—in Cologne in early 1848. This paper took a radical democratic line against the Prussian authorities, who subsequently suppressed it after less than a year in print. The working-class movement in Germany did, however, slowly develop such that the German Social Democratic Party (*Sozialdemokratische Partei Deutschlands*—SPD) became a significant force. The SPD was hindered when Otto von Bismarck introduced the antisocialist law of 1878. Bismarck's law was repealed in 1890 and thereafter the SPD grew into the leading socialist party in Europe. The trade union wing of the German labor movement also began to develop in the 1890s. By the end of the nineteenth century socialism had become a genuine mass movement in the United Kingdom, France, Germany, and many other countries throughout the world.

Building a Socialist Movement, 1864–1914

In accounting for the emergence of socialism as a mass movement, it is tempting to present it as a rational, orderly progression and to ignore its schisms and mistakes and romanticism. The growth of socialism — the two Internationals and the formation of mass political parties — is familiar territory in European historical writing. Certainly the formation of the International Workingmen's Association — the First International — in London in 1864 was a milestone in socialist history. Marx played a vital role in its early years, activities, and ultimate demise in Philadelphia in 1876. The First International was the first effective international socialist organization. However, a division had already opened up within socialism between those wanting to achieve socialist objectives by reform and those wanting to achieve those objectives by revolution. Essentially this was a division between British and continental socialists. In the United Kingdom those wanting political change could seek it through support for the Liberal Party, whereas on the continent of Western Europe, apart from France, the scope for real political participation was either very limited or nonexistent. Despite a confused start, the Second International Workingmen's Association was formed in Paris in 1889 and managed to provide a forum for all shades of socialist opinion (apart from the anarchists after 1896).

Marxism was particularly appealing in Western Europe after 1880 and became the theoretical underpinning for social-democratic parties throughout continental Europe. The most important program in this respect was the Erfurt Program of the German Social Democratic Party of 1891. British socialism, however, which was carried into the British Empire by emigration, remained largely impervious to formal theory (the Independent Labour Party being a significant exception) and stressed practical ends. The United Kingdom was important too because of the strength of the liberal tradition. Liberalism, or its left wing as represented by John Stuart Mill, went on to play an important role in shaping British socialism. In the *Fabian Essays in Socialism*, first published in 1889 by Bernard Shaw, Sidney Webb, and their colleagues, Webb argued a little too optimistically that Mill's *Principles of Political Economy* of 1848 marked the boundary of the old individualist economics and that each of the several editions that Mill published became more socialistic. Although the influential Harold Laski stressed in *The Rise of European Liberalism* (1936 [1997]) the limitations of liberalism, which served to legitimate capitalism, his socialist thought of the 1930s and 1940s reconciled elements of liberalism and Marxism.

The raw growth figures for working-class and socialist institutions in the late nineteenth and early twentieth centuries are impressive. Between 1870 and 1913 the number of trade union members worldwide rose from 790,000 to 14 million. The individual memberships of socialist or social-democratic parties rose from virtually nothing (for example, there were only about 24,400 members in Germany in 1875) to about 1.7 million in 1914. Worldwide, socialist or social-democratic parties attracted 9.9 million votes in elections on the eve of World War I. The consumer cooperative movement also grew strongly; in the United Kingdom, its total membership rose from 268,000 to 3 million between 1870 and 1914.

From this angle, socialism could be presented as a rational movement, as an attempt to capture the benefits of the Industrial Revolution and use them for the common good. Political parties and their theories, especially when backed by a philosopher of the stature of Marx, have attracted the bulk of attention from scholars of socialism. Yet there was another side to these activities that must not be overlooked, since it was also of great significance in building socialism as a mass movement: dreams and aspirations. Socialism emerged at a time when faith in organized religion had begun to wane and many people began to search for a replacement that would satisfy deeper psychological needs. In Germany and elsewhere on continental Europe the socialist movement was much more than a political party: it was a way of life. There were socialist schools, literature, poems, and music—even socialist cemeteries. Many individuals became socialists in the late nineteenth and early twentieth centuries by a process frequently described as "conversion."

Another way to approach the developments within socialism in this period is to consider socialist themes in utopian literature. Socialism was an affair of the heart as well as the mind. A bibliography of this literature (*British and American Utopian Literature, 1516–1985*) prepared by Lyman T. Sargent in 1988 defined utopian literature as works that provided detailed descriptions of nonexistent societies. Such works can include *utopias* (nonexistent societies that are better than the contemporary society of the reader), *dystopias* (nonexistent societies that are worse than the contemporary society of the reader), and utopian satires, which offer criticisms of contemporary societies or of those proposed by others. Socialist themes in utopian literature include general descriptions of socialist societies, anarchism, Christian socialism, communes and, since 1919, communism. Utopian literature has been used by the opponents of socialism as well as by its proponents. Sargent's bibliography lists 217 works of utopian literature published between 1813 and 1985 that contained socialist themes of some kind: of these 130 were prosocialist or sympathetic and 87 were antisocialist or satirical.

It is interesting to note that the chronological distribution of prosocialist utopian literature is an accurate reflection of the growth of socialism generally. Between 1880 and 1889 twelve prosocialist works were published; this was as many as had been published in English in the whole period from 1813 to 1879. Between 1890 and 1899 thirty prosocialist utopian works were published and thirty more from 1900 to 1909. Thereafter the number of these works gradually dropped off. In other words, of the 130 prosocialist utopian works that were published in English between 1813 and 1985, no less than 72, or 55 percent, were published between 1880 and 1909.

Today these works, which go largely unread, are an embarrassment. Yet they reached large audiences in their day. Who that audience was exactly will never be known for certain, but enough is known of British working-class reading habits in the 1900s to suggest that much of the market must have been among other social classes, most likely the lower middle class, particularly those in white-collar jobs.

The best-known American popularizers of socialism or social reform were Henry George—an ironic inclusion given his opposition to socialism—whose *Progress and Poverty* (1879) fired interest in social reform and sold 60,000 copies in the United Kingdom in the early 1880s, and Edward Bellamy, whose *Looking Backward* (1888) was another bestseller. Yet the greatest sales were achieved by a man whose very name is usually passed over in most secondary works of socialism: Robert Peel Glanville Blatchford. His *Merrie England* (1894) sold two million copies in English and in translation in other languages and is credited with doing more to popularize socialism than any other work published in the late nineteenth century.

Merrie England is part of the anti-industrial literature that was a common theme of British socialists such as William Morris. Despite (or perhaps because of it) being the cradle of the Industrial Revolution, England continued to produce literature antagonistic to industrialization. Blatchford denounced the factory system and saw rural life as the basis for socialism. Morris's *News from Nowhere* (1890) also saw the socialist future in pastoral terms. A study of British Labour Party parliamentarians in 1906 found that the writers and works that most influenced them (apart from the Bible) were Charles Dickens, John Ruskin, and Thomas Carlyle—writers who were often concerned with the negative aspects of industrialization and the positive side of the countryside. Even in the 1930s the British Labour Party leader George Lansbury opposed, in *My England* (1934), the replanning of the United Kingdom's coal mining and industrial regions. He urged their transformation into parks as part of his re-creation of rural, "merry" England, complete with village greens and maypoles. This undercurrent of yearning for a simpler, preindustrial life (that conveniently ignored the harsh realities of that world) should not be underestimated as a theme of socialist aspirations. The very different attitudes toward modernization among socialists provide one indication of the tendency of socialism to fragment.

The Schisms of Socialism

Any movement that sets out to change the world is subject to splits and divisions. In the case of socialism before 1914 these splits sometimes, but not always, assumed institutional form. The grounds for disagreements were many, but the greatest one was between the reformers—those who wanted to implement socialist ideas by peaceful, constitutional means—and the revolutionaries, those who wanted to implement these ideas by revolution. Scholars of socialism therefore need to think of the schisms that have occurred in socialism since 1880 in terms of attitude toward political power and be aware of the varieties of socialism that thus emerged.

THE MAIN VARIETIES OF SOCIALISM SINCE 1880

Syndicalism serves as an example of diversity and subtlety in the range of views and disagreements within the socialist movement. A radical movement in the pre-1914 years in France, syndicalism later broke up, with some of its supporters joining the communists, some joining the socialists, and, in Italy, some becoming fascists. Furthermore, attitudes toward revolution differed markedly among socialists within the Marxist tradition. Rosa Luxemburg envisaged capitalism ending violently as the result of its own defects, but saw this violence coming from spontaneous uprisings by the working class. She did not support V. I. Lenin and Leon Trotsky's concept of a coup by a well-organized group that would then impose its version of socialism by dictatorship and, if necessary, violence.

The Bolshevik seizure of power in Russia in 1917 fundamentally altered the balance between reformists and revolutionaries within socialism and colored subsequent socialist historiography. With the resources of a major country at their disposal—and it needs to be remembered that despite its backwardness Russia was the world's tenth industrial power in 1910—the revolutionary socialists were able to denigrate the reformers by propaganda and weaken their opponents by forming communist parties throughout the world from 1920. The communist parties provided an institutional focus for left-wing groups, which had previously been accommodated within single parties. The extent of the damage to social-democratic parties varied between countries. It was severe in France, far less so in the United Kingdom, but everywhere their support was undercut for much of the interwar period, which promoted the rise of fascism. The social-democratic parties formed their own international body, the Labor and Socialist International (SI), which claimed 6.6 million members at its height in 1928. But it wilted after the Depression and was able to achieve little.

A very different, nonsocialist alternative to liberalism in twentieth-century Europe was fascism. It, too, had roots deep in European thought and represented a reaction to the social and economic changes brought by industrialization and urbanization. It tapped different sources of discontent, specifically among the lower middle class and the rural dwellers, groups conspicuously underrepresented in the membership of the social-democratic parties of Europe. Trapped between communism and fascism, democratic socialism and social democracy were effectively sidelined throughout most of Western Europe until 1945.

The end of World War II saw a strong revival in support for social democracy. In the elections held between 1945 and 1947 social-democratic parties received between 41 and 50 percent of the vote in

Austria, Norway, Sweden, the United Kingdom, Australia, and New Zealand. In other countries, social democrats participated in government through coalitions. Their main achievements were in laying the foundation for the welfare state, a process begun in the 1930s by social-democratic parties in Sweden and New Zealand. The main problem faced by most of these parties was communist competition and the onset of the Cold War after 1948. In that year the social-democratic parties of Hungary, Romania, Poland, and Czechoslovakia were forcibly merged with the communist parties in those countries; this happened in the Soviet zone of Germany (later East Germany) in 1946.

Social-democratic parties, notably those with radical-sounding programs, such as those of Germany and Austria, were forced to distance themselves from the communists by adopting substantially modified programs in 1958 and 1959. In affirming their support for democracy, what had been the democratic socialist tradition merged with the left wing of what had been the tradition of liberalism. The timing of this process differed greatly between countries according to their political environments. The French Socialist Party issued a radical, but non-Marxist program in 1972. Marxist references were removed from the Spanish Socialist Workers' Party in 1972 and from the Portuguese Socialist Party in 1986.

These changes worked together to dilute what many accepted as the meaning of socialism. Nevertheless, the broad tradition of social democracy continued despite criticism from left-wing groups that it was no longer socialist in any meaningful sense. The British social-democratic intellectual Anthony Crosland argued in *The Future of Socialism* (1956) that to work from within and reform the capitalist system was both possible and necessary in the contemporary world. Arguing that the theories of the prewar socialists were outdated, Crosland said that the ideas of Laski, for example, now sounded like an echo from another world. Greater diversity within socialism reemerged, however, when the term "socialist" was increasingly appropriated by radicals such as the ex-communists who made up the nucleus of what became the New Left while the social-democratic parties continued to operate in Western Europe, Australia, and New Zealand.

The difficulty of identifying who is socialist and who is not is reflected in the membership changes of the SI. Formed in 1951 in the depths of the Cold War, the SI began with twenty-eight full member parties, of which twenty were in Europe. By 1969 there had been only one net addition to this membership, but by 1996 its full membership had grown to sixty-nine, of which twenty-two were in Western Europe, nine were in southern and eastern Europe, twenty were in the Caribbean and Latin America, and six were in Africa. These additions to the SI included parties in Latin America with revolutionary pasts and former communist parties of Central and Eastern Europe. In 1992 the Italian Democratic Party of the Left, the former Italian Communist Party, was admitted to full membership. Another interesting addition was the Bulgarian Social Democratic Party; originally formed in 1892, it was suppressed in 1948 but not formally banned. It was revived in March 1991. The admission of parties such as the Bulgarian Social Democratic Party was significant not just for broadening the membership base of the SI, but also for reestablishing a broken historical tradition.

Membership of the SI grew in the late 1990s and the early years of the twenty-first century. Many more of the former communist, but now social-democratic, parties were allowed to join. Revolutionary movements that had liberated poor countries from dictatorship such as the Sandinistas in Nicaragua, the MPLA in Angola, and Frelimo in Mozambique (the latter two of which had in the interim founded one-party Leninist states) were also admitted. The new members included, moreover, parties that were originally formed in the nineteenth century as progressive liberal parties such as the Liberal Party of Colombia and the Argentinean Radical Civic Union, which transformed themselves into social-democratic parties. Altogether there were 106 parties holding full membership in May 2005.

SOCIALISM AND SOCIETY

Socialism and the State

Socialists of all shades of opinion in the nineteenth century could agree on the necessity of changing the economic and social order, but disagreed on how it should be done and, less obviously, about what sort of society they wanted in the end. The first great divide occurred between those socialists who wished to retain the centralized power of the nation-state and those who wanted to decentralize political power and even get rid of national boundaries. The latter point of view was one generally shared by the followers of anarchism and its effective founder, Proudhon, who wanted to replace the nation-state with federations of autonomous communes.

As a defeated movement associated with terrorism and condemned by no less a person than Karl Marx, anarchism may be regarded as the extremist fringe of socialism. Some anarchists are not socialist at all. Yet anarchism was regarded as an integral part of socialism until the late 1870s, and it had a large following in France, Italy, Spain, and Latin America into the 1930s. Terrorist acts were carried out in its name, but (except in the Russian empire) such acts were not organized and were the work of isolated individuals. The anarchist violence that occurred in Latin countries took place in a general climate of violence and oppression. Nevertheless, the emphasis of anarchism on individual freedom and its hostility to authoritarianism in any form makes it worthy of note. Although devoid of the revolutionary connotations of anarchism, other strands of socialism such as guild socialism have also envisaged a reduction in the power of central governments.

Of course this decentralized socialist tradition ultimately failed, and the centralized socialist tradition in various forms succeeded. Socialists before 1914 generally wanted to win the political power of the nation-state and to use it for good ends as they saw them. Anarchism was an embarrassment, for it prevented socialists from attaining the respect and respectability they needed to win elections and be trusted with power. Yet the questions remained: What would socialists do if they gained political power? What sort of society did they wish to make?

With very little likelihood of political power before 1914, socialist thought tended to be concerned with dreams, ideals, and aspirations. As mentioned earlier, the 1890s and 1900s were the heyday of utopian socialist literature. The mechanics of actually winning political power, let alone exercising it, were largely ignored by many socialists. The participation of Alexandre Millerand in the French government between 1899 and 1902 may have offended the ideological purists of European socialism, but his example also showed that a socialist in a position of power could achieve significant reforms. A survey of twenty-nine leading European socialists in 1899 found that twelve supported the participation of socialists in governments and seventeen were against; most of these seventeen respondents lived in countries where socialists had little real chance of gaining political power. Revisionism also caused offense, but not as much as is generally claimed.

The issue of what do with political power assumed greater importance after 1914, when European socialists began to gain some experience of government for the first time, usually as members of coalition governments or as minority governments. In the 1930s electoral victories by social-democratic parties in Sweden (1932), New Zealand (1935), and Denmark (1935) laid the foundations for the welfare state in these countries, initiatives that were taken up more widely after World War II. Indeed the welfare state could be regarded as the main achievement of post-1945 socialist governments. Intended to alleviate, if not solve, problems long a part of capitalism, namely unemployment and economic insecurity, the welfare state has been subjected to increasing criticism since the 1970s for increasing taxation and reducing economic performance, but it was the first concerted attempt to humanely resolve problems that had previously been regarded as insoluble or outside the province of government. Similarly, the goal of nationalization, a common policy of socialist governments, was to end exploitation of employees and to improve the distribution of wealth rather than pursue efficient management for its own sake.

Socialism and Society: A Balance Sheet

Since the early nineteenth century socialism has set out to change the world, to make it more just, more equal, and more fair. The extent to which it succeeded in that objective is indicated by the programs of the various socialist/social-democratic parties of the 1890s. At the time they were drafted, they were on the cutting edge of political radicalism with their demands for free, equal, and direct suffrage, equal rights for women, freedom of association, the private nature of religion, graduated taxation of income and wealth, the replacement of standing armies by militia, an eight-hour working day, prohibition of child labor and night work, and regulation of women's labor. In fact, so much of what they advocated has come to pass that it is easy to take these programs for granted.

This is not to suggest that socialism alone was responsible for the implementation of these measures. Graduated taxation, for example, was introduced by nonsocialist as well as by socialist governments as an effective means for raising revenue, especially to meet the demands of two world wars. Similarly, nonsocialist governments have also developed the welfare state. It could be argued that many of these reforms would have happened anyway, with or without socialist pressure. But one must remember that it was socialism that first placed these items on the political agenda and actively campaigned for their implementation when they were hardly fashionable. The Erfurt Program (1891), furthermore, advocated that international disputes be settled by arbitration, not war, a highly advanced opinion for its time, and one whose failure haunted much of the twentieth century.

Neither must it be thought that socialism has always embodied the best qualities humanity has to offer. It was relatively easy for socialism before 1914 to seem like a golden age of idealism with its justifiable criticism of the gross inequalities of power and wealth of its day, the unremitting toil and low quality of life endured by the working class and the moral bankruptcy of capitalist competition. There was a presumption that ugly phenomena such as anti-Semitism, ethnic violence, and racism, invented and manipulated by capitalism to divide the working class and divert it from its struggle with its capitalist masters, would disappear with capitalism. The tragic experiment of Soviet communism revealed that even if such phenomena disappeared, there was no guarantee that a postcapitalist society would not bring other forms of discrimination, coercion, and brutality. Of course, many Marxists and other socialists would interject that although capitalism had been temporarily removed, critics should not mistake the Soviet Union for the true socialism that might, given time and the development of suitable conditions, be developed.

With their accession to political power in varying degrees after 1914, socialist and social-democratic parties were forced to come to terms with the realities of political life—the decisions and compromises that are part and parcel of politics. Understandably, the marriage of ideals and heightened expectations with the constraint of limited resources was often a difficult one. Long-held principles or commitments such as nationalization were difficult to implement, as in Austria in the late 1940s and early 1950s, or electorally unpopular, as in Australia in 1949 when the Australian Labor Party, then the federal government, wanted to nationalize the banks; the move was one reason why the government was defeated in the election that year. Governments attract critics even among those they try to please, and social-democratic governments have been no exception.

Left-wing critics, including those of the New Left, have often criticized socialist/social-democratic parties and governments for not doing enough to fundamentally reform the capitalist system, with the result that their policies tend to reinforce and perpetuate the system. They have also been criticized for being too conservative in foreign policy such as, for example, their acceptance of the deployment of nuclear weapons in Europe. In addition, the welfare state has been criticized on the grounds of forcing too much of the cost of retirement onto those least able to afford it and by creating poverty traps. Since the 1950s socialist/social-democratic governments have gradually lost faith in many of their former socialist priorities. In order to get themselves elected, these parties need to appeal to a broad spectrum of the electorate. Reliance on the "working class" is not enough, as about a third of them typically vote for non–social-democratic parties. Problems of economic management have come to the foreground since the mid-1970s. In both Australia and New Zealand, governing labor parties in the 1980s pursued policies, particularly with regard to privatization and reductions in government expenditure, that were more associated with conservative governments.

Assessment and Prospects

From unpromising beginnings in the early nineteenth century among a motley group of European thinkers to its alliance with organized labor from the 1860s, socialism has had a remarkable history. It fed on the discontent of its times and directed that discontent into constructive channels. Under the influence of Karl Marx, it asked new kinds of questions about the workings of society. It created a literature that showed how society might be in the future and in the process inspired millions. Seen in a wider context, socialism was a positive response to the challenge and disorientation of industrialization and urbanization. Like all movements, it had its backward-looking aspects but, by and large, socialism stood for worthwhile changes. Socialism stressed the better side of human nature—cooperation, equality, and fraternity—its essential humanity. Its main difficulty was that the world it wanted to change before 1914 could not always be changed peaceably. The transition from autocratic, oppressive regimes to ones that pursue equality and liberty is a difficult undertaking. Indeed, the autocracy that was the Russian Empire was replaced by the relatively efficient communist autocracy after 1917, leading Trotsky, as Josef Stalin's greatest critic on the left, to entitle his critical study of the Soviet Union *The Revolution Betrayed* (1936 [1972]). Countries without a tradition of democracy find it extremely difficult to acquire one.

Traditionally, the study of the history of the last two centuries has been concerned with the cutting blade of change with topics such as the rise of nation states, capitalism, the Industrial Revolution, urbanization, and international migration being staple areas for study. Socialism fits easily into this positive view of historical change, but it is just as important to realize that the pace of economic and social change can be highly uneven and that many parts of society can be left behind.

Fascism, the nemesis of socialism in the interwar years in continental Europe, could also be represented as a response to these same forces, particularly industrialization and urbanization—but a negative one. It was the reverse of socialism. Instead of universal brotherhood, it preached racism; instead of equality and democracy, it exalted obedience to authority; and instead of cooperation, it praised war and violence as a means of cleansing society of those members who did not fit in. Whereas socialism envisaged women as full members of society entitled to all the opportunities of men, fascism regarded them as permanently second-class. Like some of the late nineteenth-century socialists, fascism looked back wistfully to the preindustrial age. Fascism inherently distrusted reason and the rational. It was the revenge of the small rural communities and their petty prejudices against the big cities. It is hardly surprising that socialism and socialists were its foremost enemies.

The reemergence of socialism since 1945 in Western Europe was extraordinary, given the years of fascist persecution, but socialism itself was warped by the politics of the Cold War. In the West socialist/social-democratic parties were usually able to participate in government; in the East they were forced to become part of ruling communist parties. The revival of social democracy in Eastern Europe since 1989 and the apparent conversion of communist parties into social-democratic parties is both fascinating and inspiring. It has amounted to nothing less than a resurgence of the whole democratic tradition of socialism and a triumph of the human spirit, but also has brought about an awareness of the problems of implementing even mild socialist policies in a world dominated by capitalist economic power and capitalist hegemony.

Not everyone within the socialist movement has been happy about the changes which have occurred to democratic socialism since 1945. The earlier generations of socialists seem to have had something the later ones lacked—a faith to fight for. Material improvement has cooled the passion for change; the working class became materialistic—as if it had ever been anything else—and got some share of the prosperity of the post-1945 years.

The increasing role of the middle class in socialist institutions has also been a cause for concern. Yet there was nothing new about its participation. It may have offended vulgar Marxist ideology—the idea of members of a class working against the economic interests of that class—but otherwise it is hard to see how socialism could have emerged as a movement without the active support of its educated middle-class members. It needs to be remembered that leaders like Clement Attlee, Willy Brandt, Eduard Bernstein, Jean Jaurès, and Léon Blum had a choice. They could have opted for safe, well-paid careers. Instead, they committed themselves to a cause which was difficult, poorly paid, potentially dangerous, and whose prospects for success must have seemed remote. In so doing, they, and their movement, helped to make the world a better place.

The landslide election victory of the British Labour Party under Tony Blair on 1 May 1997 has been widely interpreted as a watershed in modern democratic socialism, not just for the United Kingdom but for other countries too. It grew out of a campaign in which the traditional touchstones of socialist policies such as nationalization and income redistribution based on taxation and spending—even the very word socialism itself—were conspicuously avoided. It may be that long-standing chapters in socialism have indeed been closed, or it might simply mean that new ways have to be found to promote the policies democratic socialists have always supported. Just at the time when socialism seemed to be losing its radical edge in much of the world, many on the left began to engage in direct action, perhaps most famously in 1999 at the "battle in Seattle," outside the meeting of the World Trade Organization. Certainly the underlying problems socialism was formed to redress—issues such as inequality, unemployment, and poverty—have not disappeared and until they do, socialism, in some form, is bound to endure. In the early twenty-first century we have witnessed a new diversity of such forms, from the Blair-inspired new social democracies of Europe to the wide range of grassroots activists represented at the annual World Social Forum. Although many would not now subscribe to the ideas of Marx, socialists of various persuasions would still agree that the workers of the world have the world to win.

The Dictionary

– A –

ADLER, VICTOR (1852–1918). Founder of the **Austrian Social Democratic Party** [*Sozialdemoktratische Partei Österreichs* (SPÖ)], Victor Adler was born of a well-to-do **Jewish** family in Prague and qualified as a medical practitioner in Vienna in 1881. He developed an interest in politics and became a socialist following a journey through Germany, Switzerland, and England in 1883 when he met **Friedrich Engels** and **August Bebel**. In 1886 he founded a socialist weekly newspaper, *Die Gleichheit* (Equality), which was banned in 1889. He founded a replacement newspaper, *Arbeiter Zeitung* (Workers' Newspaper), which established itself as the main vehicle of socialism in the Austro-Hungarian Empire. In 1888 he was the main force behind the founding of the SPÖ, which was formally launched in 1889. Adler intended the party to provide a place for all the ethnic groups of the empire, but in 1911 the Czechs formed their own social-democratic party. He was elected to the *Landtag* (parliament) in 1905 and led the struggle for universal **suffrage**, which was granted in 1907. Adler opposed World War I and sought its peaceful ending. After the breakup of the Austro-Hungarian Empire, he argued that the remnant of Austria should become part of Germany.

AFRICAN NATIONAL CONGRESS (ANC). Having for many decades been at the forefront of a social and political movement, the ANC was legalized in 1990 when its leader, Nelson Mandela, was released from 26 years of imprisonment. Four years later it won the national elections with more than 60 percent of the vote, thus becoming the dominant actor and also transforming itself into a political party. After decades as a banned radical organization, the ANC governed with mild social-democratic policies, although the South African

Communist Party and the Congress of South African Trade Unions (COSATU) remained staunch allies. The ANC was formed in 1923 as a moderate organization to campaign against racial discrimination. In 1944 the Congress was transformed into a far more radical force as the leaders of the new **youth** wing, Mandela and Oliver Tambo, began to assert their influence. The apartheid system was set up in 1948, thus firmly institutionalizing oppression of nonwhites, and in 1960 the ANC was banned. Leading figures including Mandela set up an active military wing, leading to the arrest of Mandela. The ANC continued to operate, with Tambo working to gain support abroad, thus promoting an international campaign against apartheid that eventually helped bring the system down.

Since Mandela's release and the 1994 elections, the ANC has dominated the postapartheid era in South Africa. The National Assembly elected Mandela as president from 1994 to 1999. The ANC joined the **Socialist International** in 1999. Although the ANC retained its links with the **Communists**, the Mandela government needed foreign investment and recognized that **capitalism** could not simply be abolished in South Africa. Most on the left of the movement accepted this. Taking a social-democratic approach, the ANC government reformed public finance, widened the scope of **welfare** programs, introduced a constitutional defense of human rights, and encouraged economic revival. Nevertheless, HIV and AIDS remain major problems in South Africa. In 1999 the ANC retained power by gaining 66.4 percent of the vote in the general election, thus winning another majority in the National Assembly but governing in coalition with the mainly Zulu Inkatha Freedom Party. At the general elections of 14 April 2004, the ANC retained power once again, maintaining a huge majority with 279 seats and increasing their share of the vote to 69.7 percent. In August 2005 the previously loyal **trade union** ally COSATU organized a coalition of groups that opposed the ANC's policies of **privatization** and its consequences in terms of **unemployment** and poverty.

AFRICAN PARTY OF CAPE VERDE'S INDEPENDENCE [*PARTIDO AFRICANO DA INDEPENDÊNCIA DE CABO VERDE* (PAICV)]. Formed by **nationalists** in Portuguese Cape Verde and Portuguese Guinea in 1956, the PAICV was originally named the

African Party of the Independence of Guinea and Cape Verde [*Partido Africano da Independência da Guiné e Cabo Verde*—(PAIGC)]. The PAIGC waged a guerilla **war** and in 1974 Portuguese Guinea gained independence as Guinea-Bissau. The following year Cape Verde gained independence. In 1980 the party split when a coup in Guinea-Bissau, where there was growing resentment at Cape Verdians' privileged positions, resulted in the arrest of the president, who was Cape Verdian. The Cape Verdian wing of the party condemned the coup and renamed itself the PAICV, becoming the sole legitimate party in Cape Verde. The PAICV's Pedro Pires was prime minister of Cape Verde from 1975 until the National Assembly abolished the monopoly of power in 1990. At the parliamentary elections in January 1991, the PAICV was defeated by the Movement for Democracy. In February that year an independent candidate won the presidential elections. The PAICV remained in opposition after gaining just 21 of 72 seats in the legislative elections of December 1995 and did not run for the presidency in February 1996. The PAICV gained full membership in the **Socialist International** in 1996 and thereafter reemerged as a credible political force. In February 2001 Pires won the presidential elections for the PAICV in the runoff round by only 17 votes. The PAICV was also successful at the legislative elections of June 2001, taking 40 of the 72 seats with 49.9 percent of the vote. The PAICV formed a government under Prime Minister José Maria Neves. In the legislative elections of January 2006 the PAICV increased its share of the seats to 41 with 52 percent of the vote. Pires was reelected president in February that year with 51 percent of the vote.

AFRICAN SOCIALISM. A general term for an eclectic mixture of traditional collectivist African political and economic practices, social democracy, and **communism** that began in the early 1950s as newly independent African nations adjusted to the postcolonial era. The best-known example of African socialism was carried out in Tanzania, under the presidency of **Julius Nyerere**. In 1967, in a well-meaning but economically disastrous experiment, all large businesses were **nationalized**, and villages were developed as economic units based on cooperative ownership of production, distribution, and exchange. *See also* ARAB SOCIALISM; LEAGUE OF AFRICAN DEMOCRATIC SOCIALIST PARTIES.

AFRICAN SOCIALIST INTERNATIONAL. *See* LEAGUE OF AFRICAN DEMOCRATIC SOCIALIST PARTIES.

AGRICULTURE. With its focus on industrial and urban life, socialism was inclined to neglect agriculture. Although the problems of agriculture, namely the exploitation of the peasantry, debt, and land ownership, were acknowledged early by **Karl Marx**, there was an often unspoken assumption in socialist thought before 1920 that agriculture, particularly its social organization, represented the past, whereas industries and cities represented the future. In fact, agriculture remained a fundamental feature of European life in the first third of the twentieth century. It has been estimated that 70 percent of all Europeans were rural dwellers in 1900 and that this proportion had only fallen to 47 percent by 1940. Similarly, the progress of urbanization was often uneven between countries. England and Wales were highly unusual by having a majority of their residents as urban dwellers as early as 1851. This development did not occur in Germany and Australia until 1891, in Argentina until 1914, in the United States until 1920, and in France until 1931.

The early programs of the social-democratic/socialist parties — with the notable exception of the Belgian Workers' Party (*Belgische Werkliedenpartij*—PW), which later became the **Belgian Socialist Party**—paid little regard to agriculture. The preamble to the **Erfurt Program** of 1891 included peasant proprietors in its claims of the general impoverishment and degradation of labor under **capitalism**, but made no specific demands for assisting agriculture other than calling for agricultural laborers and domestic servants to be given the same legal rights as industrial laborers, a strange omission given that 37.5 percent of Germany's labor force worked in agriculture in 1895. In contrast, the PW's program of 1893 called for the **nationalization** of forests, the reconstitution of or development of common lands, and the progressive assumption by the state or communes of the ownership of agricultural lands. Section C of its economic program was entirely devoted to agriculture.

During the 1890s the need for socialism to appeal to the agricultural sector was recognized as a serious problem by **Karl Kautsky**, George von Vollar (1850–1922), the leader of the **German Social Democratic Party** in Bavaria, **Jean Jaurés** in France, and **Émile Vandervelde** in Belgium, but as a movement, socialism found it hard to win support from most agricultural areas. Where rural discontent was widespread, as in Italy, Spain, and much of Eastern Europe, it often took a violent form that favored **anarchism** rather than parliamentary democracy, which most socialists before 1920 supported. Rural dwellers tended to be less educated and so less amenable to socialist propaganda. Many lived in small communities (even in Germany, 40 percent of the population lived in communities of less than 2,000 people in 1910), which made it hard to market doctrines based on general notions of society rather than community. The result was that European socialism as a movement generally failed to recruit its fair share of supporters from rural areas and remained a movement of the cities. This was reflected in the composition of the **membership of socialist and social-democratic parties** as well as in their vote in elections by region.

AIMS AND TASKS OF DEMOCRATIC SOCIALISM. See FRANK-FURT DECLARATION.

ALBANIAN SOCIAL DEMOCRATIC PARTY [*PARTIA SO-CIALDEMOKRATE E SHQIPËRISË* (PSDSh)]. Formed in 1991, following the demise of Albanian **communism**, the PSDSh stressed its commitments to human rights and particularly the rights of **women**. It formed the group that would later be known as the Social Democrat Women's Committee. It also has close links with some of the independent **trade unions** that were formed in the postcommunist era. The PSDSh first contested a parliamentary election in 1992, winning seven of 140 seats. It provided two ministers in the coalition government led by the Democratic Party, which had become the great rival of the **Socialist Party of Albania** (*Partia Socialiste e Shqipërisë*—PSSh). The PSDSh soon left this coalition and began to develop closer relations with the PSSh. The PSDSh gained full membership in the **Socialist International** in 1996, but did not win any seats that year in the parliamentary elections that were widely considered marred by fraud. The PSDSh obtained eight of the 155 seats in the parliamentary elections of 1997, and entered the coalition government led by the PSSh. In the general elections of June and July 2001 the PSDSh was reduced to four seats, and was a parliamentary ally of the PSSh government. In the parliamentary elections in July 2005, the results of which were withheld until September because of allegations of irregularities, the governing coalition lost power. The PSDSh won seven seats.

ALLENDE GOSSENS, SALVADOR (1908–73). Having become the world's first democratically elected **Marxist** head of state, Salvador Allende died during a right-wing coup against his administration. Born in Valparaíso, northern Chile, Allende studied medicine and was a student leader in his hometown university; he graduated in 1932 and took a post in his country's public **health** service. In 1933 he helped form the **Socialist Party of Chile**. He was elected to Chile's Chamber of Deputies in 1937, and the following year he became health minister in a Popular Front government. In 1943 he became general secretary of his party, a post he still held in 1970. As the result of the elections in 1970 he became president, as head of the Popular Unity alliance, gaining 36 percent of the vote.

As president, Allende established diplomatic relations with Cuba, introduced reforms such as the **nationalization** of banking and the copper industry, and began to redistribute **wealth** to workers and peasants. The economic policies were, however, inflationary, and the freezing of advances by the World Bank did not help the economy. The economic policies and problems led to discontent among the Chilean **middle classes**. Allende's government faced opposition from other forces in the state, including the military. In the legislative elections of March 1973, the alliance increased its electoral percentage to 44 percent, meaning that the two-thirds majority required for constitutional impeachment could not be achieved. In September 1973 a United States–backed military coup forced the Popular Unity alliance from power. The coup involved an attack on the presidential palace on 11 September, where soldiers found the dead body of Allende. It is widely assumed that he took his own life. General Augusto Pinochet took power, forming a right-wing dictatorship in which opposition was suppressed, and many labor leaders and left-wing politicians were imprisoned or exterminated. Pinochet's regime, in which he ruled with the assistance of a military junta, lasted until he stepped down in 1989.

ALLIANCE FOR DEMOCRACY IN MALI–AFRICAN PARTY OF SOLIDARITY AND JUSTICE [*ALLIANCE POUR LA DÉMOCRATIE AU MALI–PARTI AFRICAIN POUR LA SOLIDARITÉ ET LA JUSTICE* (ADEMA-PASJ)]. Formed in 1990 as

ADEMA, this party adopted its full name one year later. At independence from France in 1960 Modibo Kéïta formed a one-party socialist state in Mali. In 1968, faced with economic problems, dissent from within the country, and hostility from the West, the military removed Kéïta's party from power and set up a dictatorship under former Lieutenant Moussa Traoré that ruled until 1991. Toward the end of Traoré's rule civil unrest had turned into violent confrontation between **youths** and soldiers resulting in much bloodshed. Lieutenant Colonel Amadou Touré intervened to overthrow the dictatorship and prepare for the return to civilian rule. ADEMA-PASJ was immediately successful as a center-left social-democratic party. Alpha Konaré of AMEDA-PASJ won the first presidential elections of April 1992. He retained the presidency in the May 1997 elections with 84.3 percent of the vote. ADEMA-PASJ also obtained 130 of 147 seats in the National Assembly in July and August that year. The government experienced problems of violence and corruption and resorted to detaining a number of opposition figures.

In 1999 ADEMA-PASJ gained full membership in the **Socialist International**. In 2000 the party's Ibrahim Boubacar resigned as prime minister. His successor as ADEMA-PASJ prime minister, Mandé Sidibé, allowed several moderate opposition figures into government. In May 2002 the ADEMA-PASJ's Soumaïla Cissé lost the presidency to the independent Touré who retained popularity for overthrowing Traoré. Cissé took 35.7 percent of the vote in the runoff against Touré, who won 64.4 percent. In the elections to the National Assembly in July 2002 ADEMA-PASJ took 45 of 160 seats in a broader alliance with small parties that achieved 51 seats in total.

AMERICAN LABOR PARTY (ALP). The ALP was a progressive political party formed in New York State by representatives of the Congress of Industrial Organizations and over 200 **trade unions** in 1936. The ALP drew much of its support from **working-class Jews** in New York City and provided valuable electoral support for Franklin D. Roosevelt. In 1944 many of the party's supporters withdrew because of **communist** infiltration. The party attracted 509,000 votes in the 1948 presidential election when it opposed Harry Truman and backed the Progressive Party candidate Henry A. Wallace. The party had little effect after 1948 and was disbanded in 1956. *See also* SOCIALIST PARTY OF AMERICA.

AMERICAN REVOLUTIONARY POPULAR ALLIANCE [*AL-IANZA POPULA REVOLUCIANARIO AMERICANA* (APRA)]. *See* PERUVIAN APRISTA PARTY.

AMERICAS SOCIAL FORUM (ASF). The ASF was conceived as a smaller version of the **World Social Forum** (WSF). It is thus a sister forum of the **European Social Forum** (ESF). The WSF was set up as a meeting place for groups and organizations that sought to promote democracy, international justice, and human rights and to oppose neoliberalism and capitalist **globalization**. The ASF has adopted the WSF Charter of Principles, which are broadly **new left** in character, and which express and promote traditionally socialist ideas and themes. Hence, like the WSF, the ASF considers that capitalist globalization consolidates and furthers the global dominance of the large multinational corporations, supported by powerful governments.

The ASF spans North, Central, and South America. It is organized by the Hemispheric Council (HC), which is based in Quito, Ecuador. The HC is under the responsibility of organizations of the WSF International Council. The first meeting of the ASF was held in Quito in July 2004.

ANARCHISM. The term *anarchism* was derived from an ancient Greek word meaning "without government." As such, anarchism was synonymous with chaos and lawlessness. As a political philosophy that regards the absence of government as a positive thing, it owed much to **Pierre-Joseph Proudhon**, who saw the state as a negative element in society that should be abolished. In 1840 he published *Qu'est-ce la propriété?* (What is Property?), an inquiry into the purpose of governments, his best-known work although it was not translated into English until 1890. Proudhon was one of the few socialist theorists to come from the **working class**, which he considered morally superior to the **bourgeoisie**. His ideas were taken up by others and developed into anarchism, which in turn influenced the rise of **syndicalism**.

Michael Alexandrovich Bakunin, an extremist Russian political thinker, propagandist, and activist, absorbed Proudhon's ideas and was one of the leading anarchists of the nineteenth century. Anarchism, as envisaged by Bakunin, sought the overthrow of the state by a general strike and its replacement by democratically run cooperative groups covering the whole economy. He stressed the liberty of the individual and was opposed to **religion** except as a matter of individual conscience. The growth of anarchism could also be seen as an expression of nineteenth-century romanticism, particularly in its emphasis on the importance of the individual and the need for violence against institutions and individuals it judged to be fundamentally evil. Anarchism attracted support from certain intellectuals and from people who lived in rural areas where the local political and economic institutions were repressive and ignored demands for reform. It drew much support from Spain and Italy, where it formed a strand of political thinking with syndicalism. Anarchists held international conferences in Europe in 1873, 1874, 1876, and 1877. In 1881 **Peter Kropotkin** and other anarchist leaders organized the International Alliance of Workers (*Alliance Internationale Ouvrière*) with branches in France, Italy, and the United States.

Anarchists were the bitterest opponents of **Karl Marx** during the 1860s and 1870s. He moved the **International Workingmen's Association** to New York in 1872 so as to prevent it from falling into their hands. Nevertheless, up to the 1880s anarchism was widely accepted as part of socialism. Where it deviated from the other socialists was in its advocacy and practice of violence, or the "propaganda by deed" by some of its individuals. Anarchists assassinated the czar of Russia (1881), the French president (1894), the empress of Austria (1898), the king of Italy (1900), and the American president (1901). In May 1886 a bomb blast at a meeting called by anarchists in Haymarket Square in Chicago over the killing of four strikers led to the deaths of a policeman and seven others. Outside of the Russian empire, these acts of violence were generally the work of individuals, not groups.

Socialists came to realize that, whatever their differences, they had to distance themselves as much as possible from the anarchists, who were excluded from conferences of the **Second International Workingmen's Association** from 1896. In Spain the anarchists formed their own organization, the National Confederation of Workers (*Confederación Nacional del Trabajo*), and anarchists remained important until their destruction during the **Spanish Civil War** (1936–1939). Immigration spread anarchist ideas to Latin America; in 1919 the anarchists attempted to form a federation covering the whole of Latin America. As a movement, anarchism remained a feature of socialism in Europe until it was literally killed off by fascism in the 1920s in Italy, in the 1930s in Germany, and during the Spanish Civil War at the instigation of the **communists**. *See also* ANARCHO-SYNDICALISM; COMMUNES; FEDERALISM; WOODCOCK, GEORGE; SACCO-VANZETTI CASE.

ANARCHO-SYNDICALISM. Anarcho-syndicalism was a synthesis of **anarchism** and **syndicalism** that emerged in the late nineteenth century in France, Russia, Spain, and Latin America. Sympathetic **trade unions** provided anarchism with an organizational base to promote its idea of the use of industrial action to bring about radical social and economic change. In Sweden, an anarcho-syndicalist federation was formed in 1910 after the general strike of 1909 failed; it had 4,500 members in 1914, but 30,000 by 1920. Anarcho-syndicalists set up the **International of Revolutionary Syndicalists** in 1922.

ANTICAPITALISM. The contemporary anticapitalist movement emerged at the end of the twentieth century. There is no agreed name for the movement, which is sometimes known by participants as the **global justice movement**, and by opponents as the antiglobalization movement. Opposition to **capitalism** was nothing new. Socialists have always either opposed or sought to curb the excesses of capitalism. **Marxists** and other radical socialists call for the abolition of capitalism, while social democrats call for greater equality without necessarily overcoming capitalism. Contemporary anticapitalism responds to the changed capitalist, global environment that had developed in the final quarter of the twentieth century. Keynesianism had given way to the international spread and consolidation of free-market policies, deregulation of the economy, and demands for the structural economic adjustment of countries in preparation for overseas investment by the powerful multinational companies. The anticapitalist movement is characterized by a broad alliance of left-leaning organizations that oppose neoliberalism and capitalist **globalization**.

A defining moment in the emergence of anticapitalism came at the end of November 1999, when the World Trade Organization (WTO) held a conference in Seattle, Washington. The function of the WTO is to seek to promote international trade, resolve trade conflicts, and reduce tariffs and other trade barriers. Member states must open up their domestic markets to the others, and in return gain preferential access to those other markets. This involves structural adjustment programs that prepare domestic economies to provide favorable conditions for overseas companies. A large demonstration against the ministerial meeting at Seattle comprised **trade unionists** and activists from a range of nongovernment organizations and coalitions against capitalist globalization. Although mostly peaceful, the "battle in Seattle" also involved some violent protest, resulting in the use by police of plastic bullets and tear gas and in hundreds of arrests.

Following Seattle, there were protests at many international summits of politicians of the powerful states, for example at the WTO summit in Hong Kong in December 2005. Furthermore, opposition to neoliberalism came to be galvanized largely in the **World Social Forum** and associated regional social forums including the **Americas Social Forum** and **European Social Forum**. The social forums, which emphasize peaceful measures, bring together the socialists and others in the broader left who comprise the anticapitalist movement.

ANTISOCIALIST LAW. The Antisocialist Law (*Sozialistengesetz*) was a repressive measure of Otto von Bismarck that was passed to halt the growth of socialism in Germany in 1878. It used as a pretext two unsuccessful assassination attempts on Kaiser Wilhelm I by radical individuals acting on their own initiative. The legislation, which had to be renewed every three years, was aimed at organizations that sought to overthrow the established political or social order or upset the harmony of the social classes. The law was directed primarily against the **German Social Democratic Party** (*Sozialdemokratische Partei Deutschlands*—SPD) and was used to harass its activities. The law was allowed to lapse in 1890 with the fall of Bismarck. While it was in force, 900 people were expelled from their homes and 1,500 were imprisoned. It should be noted that the lifting of the Antisocialist Law did not mean that the SPD was able to operate in a free legal environment because there was continued, though less intense, harassment from the Prussian law of associations (*Vereinsgesetz*) that operated until 1919.

ARAB SOCIALISM. *Arab socialism* is a general term for a fusion of ideas taken from Islam and socialism, particularly **Fabianism**. It arose in the mid-1950s and was largely supported by Western-influenced **middle-class** groups, mainly public servants, army officers, and teachers. Arab socialism advocated the Islamic **religion**, land redistribution, freedom of association, social welfare programs, Arab solidarity, and state economic planning but with the continuance of a private sector. *See also* AFRICAN SOCIALISM; *BAATH*.

ARGENTINEAN SOCIALIST PARTY [*PARTIDO SOCIALISTA* (PS)]. Socialist organization in Argentina began in the 1870s when immigrants formed sections of the **International Workingmen's Association**. Like the parent body, these sections were destroyed by conflicts between socialists and anarchists. German immigrants set up a socialist club in 1882, but it had no appeal to non-German residents. From 1890 socialism began to emerge in a more durable form. In May 1890 the congress of Argentina refused to consider a petition organized by socialists and signed by 7,000 residents calling for an eight-hour day and other labor and social reforms. The advance of socialism in Argentina was slowed by the lack of industrialization, the colonial nature of the economy, and ethnic divisions caused by immigration from Europe. In the early 1890s, for example, French and Italian speakers formed separate socialist bodies. Finally in 1894 some **middle-class** professionals and skilled tradesmen formed the International Socialist Workers' Party (*Partido Socialista Obrero International*) that sent representatives to the **Second International**.

The PS was formed in 1896. Unlike the social-democratic/socialist parties of continental Europe, it adhered to a very moderate program with no **Marxist** analysis of the **capitalist** economy. Confining itself to objectives such as the eight-hour day, free collective bargaining, limited labor for **women** and children, and a graduated income **tax**, the PS could not compete with **anarchism**, which was the strongest external influence on the Argentinean labor movement. The PS also struggled to gain progressive middle-class support, as the **Radical Civic Union** (*Unión Cívica Radical*—UCR) was by the early twentieth century the major force for reform of Argentina's fraudulent electoral system.

Despite a very restricted **suffrage** before 1912, the PS leader Alfredo L. Palacios was elected to congress in 1904. He used his position to introduce laws regulating the working hours of women and children. Even so, the PS faced strong competition for the allegiance of the **working class**, as the anarchists organized large-scale strikes for better conditions and wages. Attempts to form a united socialist organization with the anarchists in 1890 and 1901 failed. **Jean Jaurès** and the Italian socialist Enrico Ferri (1856–1929) both visited Argentina in the 1900s but were unable to increase support for socialism. Failing to build a base of support among the emigrants, many of whom avoided becoming naturalized (and hence eligible to vote) because of the obligation of military service, support for the PS was largely confined to Buenos Aires and it failed. Thus by 1914 it only had about 5,000 members in a country where the **friendly societies** could claim 255,500 members and the **trade unions** claimed 23,000 members.

Nationalism and radicalism further weakened the PS. In 1913 a group of nationalists led by the poet Manuel Ugarte (1878–1932) split from the PS. In 1917 the left wing broke away and became a **communist** party. In 1925 the PS joined the **Labor and Socialist International (LSI)**, but in 1927 another nationalist group left to form an independent socialist party. The LSI failed to reunite the parties. In 1930 the PS sided with the Liberal Party against a military coup supported by the independent socialists, who subsequently lost support. After electoral defeat in 1936 the PS suffered another split, this time by those who wanted a unified front with the communists. In 1938 to 1939 the PS was reorganized but its appeal remained confined to Buenos Aires. In the 1940 election it returned 17 out of 158 deputies in the lower house. The PS became a full member of the **Socialist International** in 1951.

During the rule of Juan Perón (1946–55), the PS and other independent organizations suffered sustained persecution. In 1953 the headquarters of the PS was attacked and the printing presses of the party's newspaper, *La Vanguardia* (The Vanguard), which had been published since 1894, were destroyed. The PS was not able to operate again until Perón was overthrown in 1955. The PS's program of the early 1960s opposed **imperialism**, but it remained a moderate party, opposing cooperation with the communists. It supported democracy, disarmament, and land reform. The PS had some members in the cabinet until democratic government ceased in 1966.

Under repressive military rule, **political parties** were banned in Argentina from March 1976 to December 1979; although those that did not support "totalitarian ideologies" were permitted thereafter, the general ban was not lifted formally until July 1982. Under these conditions, the left, including the PS, fragmented. A confused kaleidoscope of left-of-center parties emerged, none of which attracted mass support. Three new parties were formed by former PS supporters: the Democratic Socialist Party (*Partido Socialista Democrático*) around 1982, the Popular Socialist Party (*Partido Socialista Popular*) around 1984, and the Authentic Socialist Party (*Partido Socialista Auténtico*); of these only the Popular Socialist Party enjoyed membership in the Socialist International. In April 1994 these parties created Socialist Unity (*Unidad Socialista*), which eventually became the Socialist Party once again. Late in 1994 it joined the left-wing Front for a Country with Solidarity (*Frente Pais Solidario*— FREPASO), whose presidential candidate attracted 29.2 percent of the vote in May 1995, a surprising result that made the coalition permanent. In the elections to half of the seats in the Chamber of Deputies in October 1997, FREPASO and the UCR won 61 of the 127 seats with 45.6 percent of the vote.

By the time of the elections to half of the seats of the Chamber of Deputies in October 1999, FREPASO was operating as part of the Alliance for Work, Justice and Education along with the UCR. After the elections the Alliance held 122 seats of the Chamber's 257 seats. In the elections of October 2001 for the 127 seats not contested in 1999 the Alliance obtained 35 with 23.1 percent of the vote. As a result of the election the Alliance held 88 seats, 17 of which were won by FREPASO candidates. FREPASO did not make a significant impact in the presidential elections of 2003, which were held in a period of economic crisis.

ARMENIAN REVOLUTIONARY FEDERATION–ARMENIAN SOCIALIST PARTY (ARF) (*HAI HEGHAPOKHAKAN DASH-NAKTSUTYUN*). Formed in 1890 the ARF sought self-determination for Armenians, social justice, and democracy. In 1907 the ARF joined the **Second International** and in 1918 led the movement that established an Armenian republic and became the ruling party. Two years later under Soviet **communism** the ARF was banned and its leaders exiled. When the Soviet Union began to collapse in 1990 the ARF was reestablished. Armenia gained independence in 1991 and the ARF became the leading opposition party. The ARF was critical of the Armenian government's slow progress in drawing up a constitution and implementing democratic reforms. Under allegations of supporting **terrorism** and planning a coup the ARF was banned and its leaders jailed by the Armenian authorities from December 1994 until February 1998. Notwithstanding the ban, the ARF continued to operate, becoming an observer member of the **Socialist International** (SI) in 1996. In 1998 the ARF supported the winning candidate in the Armenian presidential elections and subsequently received two ministerial posts in the new cabinet. In parliamentary elections of 1999 the ARF won nine seats with 7.7 percent of the vote and also saw its membership in the SI upgraded to consultative status. In the parliamentary elections of May 2003 the ARF took 11 of 131 seats with 11.4 percent of the vote. Observers found that the elections fell below international standards. In October that year the ARF gained full membership in the SI.

ASIAN SOCIALIST CONFERENCE (ASC). The idea of an international conference of Asian socialist parties was first raised at the Asian Relations Conference in Delhi, India, in March 1947, in an effort to redress what was seen as the Western European emphasis of international socialism. Much of the initiative for the first ASC in Rangoon, Burma, in January 1953 came from Burma. The definition of "Asia" adopted by the organizers of the ASC was deliberately broad and included the Middle East (Lebanon, Syria, Iraq, Egypt, and Israel); observers from Tunisia, the Gold Coast, Kenya, Uganda, Nigeria, Morocco, and Algeria; as well as representatives from fraternal international bodies (the **Socialist International [SI]**, the **International Union of Socialist Youth**, and the League of Communists of Yugoslavia). **Clement Attlee** represented the SI. The Asian delegates came from socialist parties in Japan, Malaysia, Indonesia, Pakistan, and India. The themes of the first ASC were opposition to **capitalism**, **communism**, and **imperialism** and support for democracy. The ASC also agreed to set up a permanent administration based on the Consultative Committee of the SI for further conferences.

The second ASC was held in Bombay, India, in November 1956. Representing about 500,000 members of socialist parties, it was dominated by the Suez crisis. The membership of the second ASC was generally the same as at the first except that there were representatives from Cambodia, Sri Lanka, and Vietnam. Also represented for the first time were the **Italian Socialist Party**, the Co-operative Commonwealth Federation, the Popular Socialist Party of Chile, and a Greek socialist party. The ASC condemned French and British intervention in Suez and supported the efforts of Hungary and Poland to regain their freedom. It demanded the withdrawal of Soviet forces from Hungary. Other resolutions called for the recognition of the People's Republic of China by the United Nations, the reunification of Korea, and the unification of Vietnam.

No further meetings of the ASC were held after 1956 and it ceased to function in 1961. The edifice of unity among Asian socialists that had been erected in the early 1950s did not last. The reasons for the disintegration included crackdowns on socialists by the governments of independent Asian nations of Burma and Indonesia and elsewhere as well as competition from communism. In Asia, most democratic socialist parties were newcomers that were founded after the communist parties, whereas in Europe, North America, and Australasia these parties predated communist parties. Asian socialists also had to contend with the absence of a large, educated **middle class** before the 1960s and with political traditions that were biased toward strong leadership, not democracy. In 1970 the ASC was replaced by the **Asia-Pacific Socialist Organization**.

ASIA-PACIFIC SOCIALIST ORGANIZATION (APSO). Formed in 1970 in Wellington, New Zealand, the APSO replaced the **Asian Socialist Conference**, which operated between 1953 and 1961. Originally called the Asia-Pacific Socialist Bureau, the APSO was a committee of the **Socialist International** and in 1988 represented the **Australian Labor Party**, the **Japan Socialist Party**, the **New Zealand Labour Party**, and from Malaysia the **Democratic Action Party**. The APSO has been inactive since 1988.

ATTLEE, CLEMENT RICHARD (1883–1967). British Labour prime minister Clement Attlee was born into a prosperous **middle-class** family in London; his father was a solicitor. He studied modern history at Oxford between 1901 and 1903 and later qualified as a lawyer. In 1905 he visited a boy's club in the **working-class** London suburb of Stepney that was supported by his school. This experience, together with reading works by John Ruskin, **William Morris**, and **Sidney and Beatrice Webb**, turned him into a socialist by 1907 and he became a committed social worker among the working class of east London. He joined the **Independent Labour Party** and belonged for the next 14 years. The death of his father in 1908 gave him a basic but assured income that enabled him to give up law and devote his life to politics. In 1912 he was appointed to a lectureship at the London School of Economics. He joined the army in 1914, rose to the rank of major, and was badly wounded at Gallipoli, Turkey. In 1922 he was elected to the House of Commons. He served in both of the Labour cabinets of **Ramsay MacDonald** in 1924 and 1930–1931. He also served on the Simon Commission on India between 1927 and 1930. He was able to avoid the rancor of the breakup of MacDonald's government, retained his seat in the 1931 election, and was elected deputy leader of the parliamentary **British Labour Party**. He was elected party leader in 1935 after the resignation of **George Lansbury** and in 1942 became deputy prime minister in Winston Churchill's wartime coalition government.

In 1945 Attlee became prime minister of Britain's first majority Labour government. Between July 1945 and July 1947 his government was responsible for the implementation of the **Beveridge Report**, which became the basis for the modern British **welfare state**. He used his specialized knowledge of India to speed up independence for India and Burma in 1947. In foreign policy he wanted to retain an independent role for Britain. To this end he secretly authorized a costly **nuclear weapons** program. The public standing of his administration was adversely affected by the financial crisis of August 1947. Attlee lacked an understanding of economics and his view of socialism tended to stress social administration and **Christian** teachings. He was defeated in the 1951 elections and made an earl in 1955 when he left the House of Commons. *See also* BEVIN, ERNEST.

AURIOL, VINCENT (1884–1966). A moderate French socialist politician, Vincent Auriol was born in Revel, Haute Garonne, and studied law at the university of Toulouse. He worked as a journalist and was elected to the Chamber of Deputies in 1914. He was the secretary general of the parliamentary socialists from 1919 to 1935. Between 1936 and 1937 he served as minister of finance, justice, and coordination in the government of **Léon Blum**. He was arrested for his opposition to Marshall Philippe Pétain's government in 1940 and imprisoned, but escaped to Britain where he joined General Charles De

Gaulle's government in exile. He became minister for state and served as the first president of the Fourth French Republic from 1947 to 1954. His term as president was a difficult one even for so able a mediator as Auriol because of France's severe economic difficulties, chronic political in-fighting and divisions over the war in Indochina (Vietnam). Auriol declined renomination for the presidency in 1954 and in 1960 withdrew from politics. *See also* FRENCH SOCIALIST PARTY.

AUSTRALIAN LABOR PARTY (ALP). The ALP emerged from separate parties organized by the **trade unions** and other groups in the then separate Australian colonies between 1891 and 1893. It was strongest in New South Wales, where it was called the Labour Electoral League. The first branch was formed in April 1891 at Balmain, an inner Sydney suburb. The background to the formation of the ALP was the defeat of the trade unions in the great strike of 1890. Trade unions have continued to provide the basis of the ALP ever since. It represented the culmination of efforts to elect working-class representatives to parliament, which began in the late 1870s. It drew much of its inspiration from the British Liberal Party, the main political outlet for the organized English **working class** in the nineteenth century. Some of its founding members had been members of that party. One of the parties in Tasmania that formed the ALP in 1893 was called the Progressive Liberal League. At the time of federation of the Australian colonies in 1901, the ALP had been set up in all the states and was contesting federal elections. Its use of a platform of policies and disciplined voting by its elected members began a new era in Australian politics. In time the non-Labor parties also adopted platforms of policies and more disciplined voting by their elected members.

Though usually represented by its opponents as a "left-wing" party, the ALP was from its beginnings a moderate social-democratic party, although it did contain some radical groups. Compared to the **British Labour Party** (Labour), the ALP has been a relatively moderate, even right-wing, party. There have been two major splits in the ALP. The first was in 1916 to 1917 over military conscription and the second occurred in 1955 over attitudes toward **communism**.

In 1921 the ALP adopted a **socialization objective**, but this has been progressively diluted since 1957. Public opinion polls show that support for the ALP among blue-collar/manual workers was at least double what was among white-collar/nonmanual workers between 1943 and 1966. Since the 1972 election, support for the ALP has grown among white-collar workers and has been fairly stable among blue-collar workers. In 1993, 57 percent of blue-collar workers supported the ALP compared to 39 percent of white-collar workers.

Despite commanding the most votes of any single Australian political party, the ALP in the postwar period has always had the smallest membership of any of the three major Australian parties. In 1954 the ALP had about 75,000 members, but after the 1955 split, this fell to about 45,000; between 1982 and 1995 ALP membership fell from 55,000 to 35,000. The small membership sometimes made the ALP vulnerable to branch stacking (the enrollment of bogus members to influence voting or decisions). The ALP has been a full member of the **Socialist International** since 1966; this was the first time it joined any international socialist organization.

The ALP was the national government in 1908–09, 1910–13, 1914–15, 1929–32, 1941–49, 1972–74, and 1983–96. In the Australian states, the ALP governed New South Wales in 1910–16, 1920–22, 1925–27, 1930–32, 1941–65, 1976–88, and 1995 to date; in Victoria in 1913, 1924, 1927–28, 1929–32, 1943, 1945–47, 1952–55, 1982–92, and 1999 to date; in Queensland in 1915–29, 1932–57, 1989–96, and 1998 to date; in South Australia in 1905–09 (with the Liberals), 1910–12, 1915–17, 1924–27, 1930–33, 1967–68, 1970–79, 1982–93, and 2002 (minority and coaliton) to date; in Western Australia in 1904–05, 1911–16, 1921–30, 1933–47, 1953–59, 1971–74, 1983–93, and 2001 to date; in Tasmania in 1909, 1914–16, 1923–28, 1934–69, 1972–82, 1989–92 (with the support of the Greens), and 1998 to date. Notable ALP prime ministers have been **William M. Hughes** (1915–16), **James H. Scullin** (1929–32), **John J. Curtin** (1941–45), **Ben Chifley** (1945–49), **Gough Whitlam** (1972–74), **Robert ("Bob") Hawke** (1983–91), and **Paul Keating** (1991–96).

From 1983 to 1996 under Hawke and Keating, the ALP embarked on reforms similar to those later adopted by the Labour governments of **Tony Blair** in the United Kingdom. These reforms included a decrease in state regulation; collective but nonstate forms of provision; tax reform; social policy focusing on employment; and attempts to equip citizens with skills, **education**, and other assets that would mean less reliance on distribution of resources. The ALP thus experimented with measures that would later be considered part of the "third way."

At the national elections on 2 March 1996, the ALP lost control of the government; it attracted 38.8 percent of the vote for the House of Representatives and 36.2 percent for the Senate. The conservative Liberal Party took power and its leader John Howard became prime minister. Under the leadership of Kim Beazley the Labor Party challenged Howard unsuccessfully in the elections of October 1998 and November 2001, gaining 40.1 percent of the vote for the House and 37.3 percent for the Senate in 1998, and 37.8 percent of the vote for the House and 34.3 percent for the Senate in November 2001. Beazley resigned and was replaced by Simon Crean, who resigned in 2003. Mark Latham became leader but was unsuccessful in challenging Howard's conservative coalition at the elections of 9 October 2004, at which Labor won 47.3 percent of the vote for the House (60 seats) and 35 percent for the Senate. In January 2005 Latham quit politics because of ill health and Beazley was elected unopposed to the leadership. *See also* FISHER, ANDREW; WATSON, JOHN.

AUSTRIAN SOCIAL DEMOCRATIC PARTY [*SOZIALDEMOK-TRATISCHE PARTEI ÖSTERREICHS* (SPÖ)]. The first attempt to organize a socialist party in what is now Austria dated from 1867 when a social-democratic party was formed; it organized a mass demonstration in Vienna and presented a petition to the government in favor of the right to hold public assemblies and to form **trade unions**. In 1874 the All-Austrian Social Democratic Party was formed at Neudörfl. But the party did not succeed because of divisions caused by the **anarchists** and police repression. In 1888, following the pattern set by the **German Social Democratic Party** (*Sozialdemokratische Partei Deutschlands*—SPD), the SPÖ was organized and formally established at Hainfeld in 1889 by **Victor Adler**; it claimed 15,550 members by 1890 and 90,000 by 1905 about 40 percent of whom lived in Vienna. There were close links with the trade union movement; indeed, the unions were not clearly differentiated from the SPÖ until 1909. The SPÖ campaigned hard for universal **suffrage** and organized disciplined mass marches through Vienna in 1905.

Before 1918, the SPÖ was dominated by internal divisions between orthodox **Marxists** and reformists and by the ethnic divisions in the Austro-Hungarian empire, of which Austria was a central part. Although largely a German movement, the SPÖ prided itself on its **internationalism** and **education**. The SPÖ under Adler had tried to encompass ethnic diversity within its organization, but this proved impossible after 1911 when the Czechs formed their own social-democratic party. Despite this setback, the SPÖ trebled its membership from 110,000 in 1913 to 336,000 in 1920 and in the 1919 election gained 36 percent of the vote and 69 out of the 159 seats in parliament.

Although the Austrian section of the SPÖ supported participation in World War I, it did so out of fear of the Russian empire, but from July 1915 onward began to support peace initiatives. This shift incurred a crackdown by the monarchical government and led to the assassination of the prime minister Count Stürgkh in October 1916 by Friedrich Adler (1879–1960), the son of Victor Adler. In November 1918 the monarchical government collapsed in chaos and **Karl Renner** emerged as chancellor. After the elections of February 1919 the SPÖ was the largest single party and made an alliance with the **Christian Socialists** to form a government that succeeded in introducing a democratic constitution. This government continued until June 1920 when there was a decline in electoral support for the SPÖ. Although the SPÖ did not hold national government again until 1945, it achieved significant successes in municipal government, notably in Vienna, where it expanded public housing and improved educational, **health**, cultural, and recreational facilities.

After the creation of the Austrian republic in 1918, the SPÖ faced other problems. There was increased antagonism between the SPÖ and the Catholic Church, a conflict that was not resolved until after 1945. The economy of the new republic was damaged by the breakup of the unity that the former Austro-Hungarian empire had provided, and tensions between the rural and urban economy worsened. The SPÖ continued to develop as an organization—for example, in 1925 it established a sports association—but the violence of the 1920s forced it to establish a paramilitary force for self-defense. In its program adopted at Linz in 1926 there was a reference to the possibility of a **working-class** dictatorship to forestall a conservative counter-revolution.

As in other European countries, the SPÖ was unable to overcome the deep social divisions. Although SPÖ membership had reached

718,100 by 1929, making it only second in size to the German SPD in continental Europe, the makeup of that membership was not representative of Austrian society. Of the total membership, 58 percent lived in Vienna (many of the Vienna members were **Jews** who were murdered by the German Nazis between 1938 and 1945), 51 percent were industrial workers, and 16 percent were housewives. Ominously, the SPÖ had almost no members from the agricultural sector of the economy, which accounted for 32 percent of the Austrian labor force in 1934. The division between a countryside increasingly drawn to fascism and large cities drawn toward socialism proved fatal to the SPÖ. Civil war resulted in the right-wing dictatorship of Chancellor Engelbert Dollfuss. After the assassination of Dollfuss in an abortive coup by the German Nazis in 1934, the SPÖ was dissolved in an attempt to consolidate the power of the conservative, authoritarian state. In 1938 Austria was "reunited" with Germany, a move ironically favored by the founder of the SPÖ, Adler, in 1918. But unification was hardly on the terms he wanted. As in Germany, the social democrats and trade union leaders were rounded up by the Nazis along with their Catholic and **communist** counterparts in working-class organizations and sent to concentration camps.

Like the trade unionists, the socialists revived quickly at the end of World War II. The SPÖ was reestablished as the Austrian Socialist Party (*Sozialistische Partei Österreichs*—SPÖ) in April 1945. The SPÖ formed an alliance with the Austrian People's Party, which lasted until 1966. During this time, it served as a partner in coalition governments. In 1958 the SPÖ revised its program to remove its references to **Marxism**. After the defeat of the SPÖ in the 1966 election, **Bruno Kreisky** was elected party chairman in 1967. He reformed the SPÖ and thereby made it possible for it to win outright at the 1971 national election, govern in its own right from 1971 to 1983, and become the dominant partner in coalition governments thereafter. The SPÖ has been a full member of the **Socialist International** since 1951. In 1978 the SPÖ softened its policy on **nationalization** as essential for economic planning; it has accepted the principles of **privatization** since September 1987. In January 1987 it renewed its electoral alliance with the Austrian People's Party and in 1991 reverted to its original title. Franz Vranitsky became chancellor of Austria in June 1986 and chairman of the SPÖ in 1988. In the 1994 election, the SPÖ attracted only 35.2 percent of the vote, its poorest result in the post-1945 period. Vranitsky resigned from his positions as SPÖ chairman and chancellor in 1997. Viktor Klima took over both posts.

After the elections of 1999, at which it won 65 of the 183 seats with 33.2 percent of the vote, the SPÖ was kept out of government when the Austrian People's Party formed a government with the far-right Freedom Party in 2000. In the elections of 24 November 2002, held after the right-wing governing coalition collapsed in an internal power struggle, the SPÖ increased its share of the seats to 69 with 36.9 percent of the vote. Nevertheless, it was kept out of government as the Austrian People's Party once again formed a right-wing coalition with the Freedom Party. In the presidential elections of 25 April 2004 the SPÖ's Heinz Fischer won 52.5 percent of the vote and was thus elected to the largely ceremonial presidency. In the European elections of June 2004, the SPÖ obtained seven of Austria's 18 seats in the European Parliament, compared with seven of 21 in June 1999. The SPÖ members worked in the **Party of European Socialists**, with which the SPÖ was affiliated.

– B –

BAATH. An ostensibly socialist political party, whose name means "renaissance" in Arabic, the *Baath* began as an international movement in Syria in 1940 to press not just for socialism, but also for the unity and freedom of the Arab world. The present party dates from 1953 when the Arab Renaissance Party, which had been formed in 1947, merged with the Syrian Socialist Party, which had been formed in 1950. It was the guiding force behind the union of Syria and Egypt between 1958 and 1961 and has been the ruling party in Syria since 1963 and the dominant political group in Iraq since 1968. In 1994 there were an estimated 250,000 members of the *Baath* in Syria. The Syrian *Baath* is more moderate than the Iraqi, which degenerated into a brutal dictatorship under the presidency of Saddam Hussein. The political **ideology** of the *Baath* stresses a pan-Arabic view (despite the political isolation of Iraq since the Gulf War in 1990–91), **nationalization**, opposition to **imperialism**, and the redistribution of **agricultural** land. The *Baath* has never been a member of the **Socialist International**. In 2003 Saddam's regime collapsed as a result of a United States–led invasion. *See also* ARAB SOCIALISM.

BAKUNIN, MICHAEL ALEXANDROVICH (1814–76). Born on the estate of Premukhino in the Russian province of Tver into a wealthy family, Michael Bakunin was the effective founder of **anarchism** as a movement. After being discharged from the army, he became familiar with the socialist doctrines of **Charles Fourier**, **Claude-Henri Saint-Simon**, and **Pierre-Joseph Proudhon** but not a convert. He moved to Berlin in 1840 and then in 1841 to Dresden where he became a convert to revolutionary change. His subsequent life was one of participating in insurrection and secret societies. In 1849 he was jailed for his part in uprisings in Paris, Prague, and Dresden; he was handed over to the Russians and eventually escaped from exile in Siberia in 1861. Bakunin came to represent the violent, destructive face of anarchism. He joined the **International Workingmen's Association** in 1868, but was expelled for leading the opposition to **Karl Marx**. He responded by establishing a rival body, the **Saint-Imier International**. More than anyone else Bakunin saw the potential of Latin countries in Europe and the Americas as fertile ground for anarchism. He took part in anarchist insurrections in Lyon (1870) and Bologna (1874).

Bakunin was primarily a libertarian who wanted to destroy the state by revolution. He argued in his *God and State* that God and the church were part of the oppressive apparatus of the state; this work was translated into English in 1883. A man of action rather than a man of letters, he envisaged a future socialist society as one characterized by equality and workers' control over the means of production. Unlike **Proudhon** and his successor **Kropotkin**, he maintained that the basis for the distribution of rewards in socialist society should be the labor that individuals contributed, not their needs. *See also* RELIGION.

BARBADOS LABOUR PARTY (BLP). The BLP was founded in 1938 as the Barbados Progressive League and was based on the **British Labour Party**. Its main founder was Grantley Adams (1898–1971), who held office after independence from Britain between 1951 and 1961. The government headed by his son, "Tom" Adams (1931–85), held power from 1976 to 1986. The BLP has been a full member of the **Socialist International** since 1987 and had a membership of 10,000 in 1988. In the general elections of 1994 the BLP won a decisive victory. The BLP leader Owen S. Arthur, who campaigned for a program of economic modernization and job creation, became prime minister. Arthur led the BLP to victory once again at the elections of January 1999, his program stressing economic modernization and this time the severance of links from Britain. Hence, it is expected that the Barbadian constitution will be amended to form a republic in the near future. Arthur and the BLP won the elections of 21 May 2003, gaining 23 of the seats of the House of Assembly with 55.8 percent of the vote. The Democratic Labour Party took the other seven seats with 44.1 percent.

BAUER, GUSTAV ADOLF (1870–1944). A German social-democratic leader, Gustav Bauer was born in Darkehmen, East Prussia, and made his mark in the socialist movement in the **trade unions**. In 1895 he organized the *Verband der Büroangestellten* (Association of Office Employees), which he led until 1908. In 1903 he was made leader of the secretariat for the Berlin trade unions and in 1908 was made vice chairman of the *Generalkommission der Gewerkschaften* (National Federation of Trade Unions), a post he held until 1918. He was elected to the *Reichstag* (parliament) in 1912 and was made secretary for labor in the last imperial government led by Prince Max of Baden in October 1918. He continued in this role under the Weimar Republic government of **Philipp Scheidemann** between February and June 1919. After Scheidemann resigned as chancellor on 20 June 1919, over his refusal to accept the terms of the Versailles Treaty, Bauer took his place and carried out the politically poisoned task of ratifying the treaty. He resigned as chancellor following the Kapp putsch in Berlin in March 1920. He later served as treasurer in the governments of Karl J. Wirth (1921–22) and of **Hermann Müller**. *See also* EBERT, FRIEDRICH; GERMAN SOCIAL DEMOCRATIC PARTY.

BEBEL, FERDINAND AUGUST (1840–1913). One of the principal leaders of German socialism, August Bebel was born near Cologne and became a master joiner and later a manufacturer. In August 1866 he and **Wilhelm Liebknecht** held a workers' congress at Chemnitz that resulted in the founding of the League of Workingmen's Associations of which Bebel was elected president in 1867. At Eisenach in 1869 the league was reconstituted as the Social Democratic Workers' Party (*Sozialdemokratische Arbeiterpartei*—SDAP). The "Eisenachers," as the party was sometimes called, became part of the **International Workingmen's Association**. In 1872 he served a prison term for treason. For Bebel, socialism as defined by **Marxism** was to be achieved by peaceful evolution, a stand for which he was criticized by **Karl Marx** and **Friedrich Engels**. He played an important role in the fusion of the SDAP and the General Association of German Workers at Gotha in 1875. He helped found the **Second International** in 1889 and played a role in the adoption of the **Erfurt Program** by the **German Social Democratic Party** (*Sozialdemokratische Partei Deutschlands*—SPD) in 1891. As editor of *Vorwärts* (Forward), he condemned militarism and **imperialism**. He was also a forthright advocate of equal rights for **women** and argued their case in his book *Women and Socialism* (1879), which was later published as *Woman: In the Past, Present and Future* (1882). He was leader of the SPD for most of the time he spent as a member of the *Reichstag*, that is, from 1871 to 1881 and from 1883 to 1913.

BELGIAN SOCIALIST PARTY [*PARTI SOCIALISTE BELGE* (PS)]. Because of Belgium's early industrialization and proximity to France, socialism there developed early, but was dogged by linguistic and **religious** divisions, specifically between the Flemish in the north and the Walloons in the south. Baron Jean Hippolyte de Colins (1783–1859) advocated a form of **utopian socialism** in the 1850s, and spinners and weavers in the cotton industry organized the first Belgian unions in 1857. In the 1860s and early 1870s César de Paepe (1842–90) represented the Belgian section of the **International Workingmen's Association**. Between 1871 and 1873 there were strikes for the 10-hour working day, but the government suppressed them; the depressed conditions of the period also crushed the emerging **cooperative movement**. In 1875 and 1876 trade union federations were formed in Brussels, Ghent, and Antwerp. The Antwerp federation convened a conference to establish a workers' party, but this initiative floundered on ethnic and religious divisions. The upshot was that two socialist parties were formed: a Flemish party at Ghent and another at Brussels. In 1879 these two **political parties** agreed to work together to agitate for universal **suffrage**, but the Walloon regions refused to join. In 1880 Édouard Anseele (1856–1938) refounded the cooperative movement in Ghent, which became one of the pillars of Belgian socialism along with the **trade unions** and the

friendly societies, or *mutualités*. Because of the restrictive suffrage, the Belgian **working class** was effectively excluded from the formal political system before the 1890s, hence suffrage reform was given top priority by working-class organizations.

The BSP was founded in April 1885 as the Workers' Party (*Belgische Werkliedenpartij*—PW) in Brussels by representatives from the trade unions, cooperatives, and friendly societies. In 1893 the PW called a general strike that was supported by at least 200,000 employees. The strike succeeded in bringing about some suffrage reforms (the vote was given to men 25 years of age and older, but plural voting was introduced) although it should be noted that the support of Catholic working-class organizations for suffrage reform was also an important reason for its success.

Because of the religious and ethnic divisions in Belgium, the PW received its greatest support among the non-Catholic working class. Universal male suffrage (only fully obtained in 1919) was one of the main objectives of this party, which saw the vote as essential to achieving social reform. Otherwise, the PW stressed the practical side of political activity rather than theoretical debates. Like the **British Labour Party**, the PW worked with the Liberal Party before 1914. At the 1895 election, the PW attracted 13 percent of the vote; thereafter its share of the national vote increased steadily to 23 percent in 1900, 30 percent in 1914, and 37 percent in 1919. From 1910 their constructive participation in coalition governments in a junior role won the PW further support. The PW was a member of the **Labor and Socialist International**. By 1931 the PW claimed a total membership of 601,000, but this included affiliates in cooperatives, trade unions, and friendly societies. Despite its success, the PW was not able to win over enough working-class Catholics to govern in its own right. It gained its first taste of political power between 1938 and 1939 when **Paul-Henri Spaak** was prime minister of a coalition government.

After World War II, the trade unions were given equal status with the PW, which took its present title (*Parti Socialiste Belge*—PS). The first postwar Belgian government was a coalition led by Achille Van Acker (1898–1975) who was PS prime minister from February 1945 to February 1946. This was followed by a coalition government headed by Prime Minister **Camille Huysmans** of the PS. The PS has been a participant in most coalition governments in Belgium since

1945. In the late 1940s the PS, trade unions, cooperatives, and friendly societies set up a federation to coordinate their activities. They called a general strike in 1950 to block the return of Leopold III to the Belgian throne. Even so, the PS has never been able to overcome the deep divisions in Belgian society and gain a broad base of support. For example, at the 1974 election, the PS drew 47 percent of its support from Flanders and 44 percent from Wallonia but only 9 percent from Brussels; these regional divisions were also closely reflected in the distribution of the membership of the BSP. In 1978 the PS split along linguistic/ethnic lines: the francophone *Parti Socialiste Belge* (Belgian Socialist Party) and the Flemish *Belgische Socialistische Partij* (Belgian Socialist Party). At the time of the division, the francophone party had 147,300 members and the Flemish party had 111,900 members. Both parties attracted similar proportions of the vote at national elections. In 1995 the francophone party gained 11.9 percent of the vote compared to 12.6 percent for the Flemish party.

In the national elections of 18 May 2003 the francophone party won 25 of the 150 seats in the Chamber of Representatives with 13 percent of the vote. The Flemish Party, by now operating by the name of the Socialist Party Different (*Sociaal progressief alternatief—* SPA) campaigned in the SPA-Spirit coalition, winning 23 seats with 14.9 percent of the vote. Both parties agreed to renew the coalition in government with the Francophone and Flemish Liberal parties. In the elections to the European Parliament in June 2004 the francophone party took four of Belgium's 24 seats and the Flemish party three, up slightly from the 1999 totals of three and two respectively from 25. All of these Belgian members of the European Parliament worked in the **Party of European Socialists**, with which their parties were affiliated. *See also* DE MAN, HENDRIK; VANDERVELDE, ÉMILE.

BELLAMY, EDWARD (1850–1898). Born in Chicopee Falls, Massachusetts, Edward Bellamy qualified as a lawyer in 1871 and became an influential journalist who popularized **utopian socialism**. His best-known book, *Looking Backward: 2000–1887* (1888), attracted a large readership in North America, Britain, and Australasia; he also wrote a sequel, *Equality* (1897). In *Looking Backward: 2000–1887*, Bellamy examined the industrial society of his day from the perspective of a technologically advanced and enlightened society over a century later in 2000. Primarily a writer of utopian fiction, he envisaged a society in which the state would organize large-scale production and ensure economic equality. His ideal world also eliminated the need for human vices such as greed, lying, malice, and hypocrisy. Bellamy's ideas gave rise to a Nationalist club movement in the 1890s. *See also* GEORGE, HENRY.

BEN-GURION, DAVID (1886–1973). An Israeli labor leader and politician, David Ben-Gurion was born in Plonsk, Poland, then part of the **Jewish** territory of settlement on the western boundary of the Russian empire. He emigrated to Palestine in 1916 and became secretary-general of the Jewish Labor Federation in 1926; he held this position until 1933. In 1933 he became leader of the *Mapai* Party, the ancestor of the modern **Israel Labor Party**, holding that position until 1963. He became the first prime minister of Israel in 1948, held the position until 1953 and again from 1955 to 1963. His administration was marked by his determination to ensure the survival of Israel against its hostile Arab neighbors and by the **agricultural** and industrial development embodied in the *kibbutz* movement. In 1963 he retired from politics but returned for a time in 1965 as the leader of a splinter group (the Rafi Party) from the *Mapai* Party, which wanted a more moderate foreign policy toward Israel's Arab neighbors.

BERGER, VICTOR LOUIS (1860–1929). Born in Austria-Hungary, Victor Berger emigrated to the United States in 1878 and settled in Milwaukee, the home of many German-Americans who provided his political power base. He edited three socialist newspapers between 1892 and 1929. With **Eugene V. Debs**, he helped to create the Social Democratic Party of America in 1898, which became the **Socialist Party of America** (SPA) in 1901. Berger was the first member of the SPA to be elected to the House of Representatives (1911–13), where he supported child labor laws, the eight-hour working day, old age pensions, and federal aid for farmers. In other respects he was a man of his time; he believed that African Americans were inferior to Caucasians and was wary of giving **suffrage** to **women** because he feared their conservatism. Because of his opposition to World War I, he was convicted under the Espionage Act of 1917 to 20 years in jail, but successfully appealed to a higher court. His conviction was overturned by the Supreme Court in 1921, and he was readmitted to the House of Representatives where he served until his death. Berger remained in the SPA after 1920 and condemned **Leninism**.

BERNE INTERNATIONAL. The Berne International was the non-communist socialist international that was formed at Berne, Switzerland, between 3 and 9 February 1919. It grew out of a failed attempt by some social-democratic parties to hold a general international conference in Stockholm in 1917. The original members were the leaders of social-democratic parties in Argentina, Austria, Belgium, Bulgaria, Czechoslovakia, Denmark, Finland, France, Germany, Italy, the Netherlands, Palestine, Sweden, Switzerland, and the United Kingdom. The purpose of the conference was to resurrect the **Second International**. The Russians were invited to attend, but refused because the Berne International did not support world revolution. The Berne International held conferences at Amsterdam (April 1919), Lucerne (August 1919), and Geneva (July–August 1920). **Eduard Bernstein** and **Karl Johann Kautsky** assumed major roles in its deliberations. The conferences were stridently in support of democracy and liberty and condemned dictatorship, whether of the left or the right. At the Geneva conference, the Berne International declared its support for gradual **nationalization** of industry. At the same time, the parliamentary emphasis of the Berne International alienated other noncommunist socialist groups who formed the **International Working Union of Socialist Parties**, or **Vienna International**, in February 1921. However, the Vienna International became disillusioned with the methods of the **communists** and their International, the **Comintern**. In May 1923 the Berne International and the International Working Union of Socialist Parties merged to form the **Labor and Socialist International**. *See also* LENINISM.

BERNSTEIN, EDUARD (1850–1932). Eduard Bernstein was a prominent German socialist theorist and politician who argued that the ideas of **Karl Marx**, formulated in the mid-nineteenth century, should be revised to take account of the changed economic and social conditions of the late nineteenth century. Born in Berlin, the son of a locomotive engine driver, his family was **Jewish** but not **religious**. After leaving school, he worked as a bank clerk. He joined the Social Democratic Workers' Party (*Sozialdemokratische Arbeiterpartei—*

SDAP) in 1872 and was present at the unity congress in 1875, which endorsed the **Gotha Program** and founded the **German Social Democratic Party** (*Sozialdemokratische Partei Deutschlands*—SPD). As a result of Otto von Bismarck's **Antisocialist Law**, he went into exile in Switzerland where he edited *Der Sozialdemokrat* (The Social Democrat), the party's newspaper, between 1881 and 1890. The German government issued a warrant for his arrest, which was not withdrawn until 1901. In 1880 he met Marx, whom he impressed by the soundness of his views, in London; after Marx's death, Bernstein became one of Marx's literary heirs. In 1887 he was expelled from Switzerland at the request of the German government and moved to London where he lived until 1901 as the correspondent of *Vorwärts* (Forward). With **Karl Kautsky**, he was one of the main drafters of the party's **Erfurt Program** in 1891.

In the United Kingdom he was influenced by **Fabianism** and the **Independent Labour Party**. In 1896 he published a series of articles on socialist theory and practice in which he argued that socialism would be achieved from accumulated reforms and improvements. In 1899 he defended these articles in his controversial book *Die Voraussetzungen des Sozialismus und die Aufgaben der Sozialdemokratie* (The Preconditions of Socialism and the Tasks of Social Democracy). Using income and consumption statistics, Bernstein argued that the **working class** was not getting poorer and that the **middle class** was growing, trends that undermined Marx's idea of the primacy of the class struggle. He criticized Marx's theory of surplus value and his idea that there is increasing concentration in the ownership of capital. Bernstein was able to show that there were more shareholders than previously and that although large businesses were driving out smaller ones in some parts of the economy, this was not true for every part of the economy. He wanted the **trade unions** to be equal, not subordinate, partners in working toward socialism through collective bargaining. In his prediction that workers would fall victim to dictatorship after a proletarian revolution, Bernstein foreshadowed the Russian experience after the Bolshevik coup in 1917.

In 1902 he was elected to the *Reichstag* (parliament) as deputy for Breslau, a position he held until 1906 and again from 1912 to 1918. **Revisionism** was debated at the Dresden Conference of the SPD in 1903 and rejected once more. At the start of World War I, Bernstein refused to vote for war credits. In 1916 he joined the left-wing Social Democratic Workers' Group (*Sozialdemokratische Arbeitsgemeinschaft*) and in 1917 joined the Independent Social Democratic Party of Germany (*Unabhängige Sozialdemokratische Partei Deutschlands*), but rejoined the majority SPD in 1918. After the collapse of electoral support for the SPD in the elections of 1920 (when the party's support fell to 22 percent), Bernstein took over from the moderate Georg von Vollar (1850–1922) as *Reichstag* deputy for the third electoral district of Berlin. He was appointed a member of a commission to review the SPD program. The Görlitz Conference in 1921 adopted the commission's recommendation for a program that reduced its **Marxist** content, but much of this was restored at the Heidelberg Conference in 1925. Bernstein retired from politics in 1928. In 1930 he published a study of the role of groups like the **Levellers** in the English Civil War.

BEVERIDGE, WILLIAM HENRY (1879–1963). William Henry Beveridge was one of the principal architects of the British **welfare state**. Born in Bengal, India, he was a brilliant student who graduated from Balliol College, Oxford, in (among other subjects) mathematics. Deeply concerned with social problems, he became acquainted with **Sidney Webb** but rejected socialism. He became the first director of the London School of Economics in 1919, a position he held until 1937. He chaired an interdepartmental committee of inquiry into social insurance and allied services, which reported to the government in December 1942. In it, Beveridge advocated the introduction of a comprehensive **social security** scheme that aroused intense interest. In 1944 Beveridge published *Full Employment in a Free Society*, which presented his arguments in favor of his **Beveridge Report**, which were supported by the economics of J. M. Keynes. Although the predominately conservative government of Winston Churchill made some moves toward the implementation of the Beveridge Report before the end of World War II, it was not until the election of the **British Labour Party** in 1945 that a concerted effort was made to implement its recommendations.

BEVERIDGE REPORT. The Beveridge Report was the unofficial title of the *Report on Social Insurance and Allied Services*, which was prepared under the direction of **Sir William Beveridge** in December

1942. The report, which set out a general **social security** scheme largely based on national insurance, was the basis for the social security laws implemented by the Labour government under **Clement Attlee** between 1945 and 1950. The term *welfare state* was coined in this report.

BEVIN, ERNEST (1881–1951). A British **trade union** leader and **British Labour Party** politician, Ernest Bevin was born into a poor rural environment in Somerset. He never knew his father. He held a number of lowly jobs until he found work as a van driver in 1901. His formal education was very limited. Like other labor leaders of his generation, he was a Methodist. He gained some further education from the Quaker Adult School and joined the Socialist Labour Party in Bristol in 1905, becoming a speaker and an organizer. He left the Baptist church and became a socialist because he felt the church was unconcerned with social issues. In 1908 he became active in the Right to Work movement for the unemployed. During the strike by dockers (longshoremen) at Avonmouth, he organized the dock carters as part of the Dock, Wharf, Riverside, and General Workers' Union so they could not be used as strikebreakers. In 1911 Bevin became a full-time official of the Dockers' Union. An outstanding negotiator, he became one of the union's three national organizers in 1913.

In 1915 to 1916 Bevin was the fraternal delegate of the Trades Union Congress (TUC) to the American Federation of Labor, a trip that gave him an international outlook and stimulated him into supporting the integration of Europe. In 1920 his brilliant advocacy for the dockworkers before the Industrial Court won him national recognition, as did his leadership of the Council of Action's campaign to boycott the supply of military equipment to Poland for use against the Russian revolutionaries. In 1921 Bevin was the pivotal figure in the amalgamation of 14 unions to create a new mass union, the Transport and General Workers' Union, which by the late 1930s had grown to be the largest union in Britain and, for a brief time, the largest in the world.

In 1925 Bevin became a member of the general council of the TUC, a position he held until 1940. During the 1930s Bevin successfully fought communist influence and **pacifism** within the labor movement. In 1940 he was made minister for labor, a position responsible for organizing Britain's labor force during World War II. Bevin's last official position was foreign secretary, from 1945 to just before his death in 1951. He fulfilled this office with distinction. He has been called a patriot in the style of **Robert Blatchford**, identifying the British national interest with that of its **working class**. As foreign secretary, Bevin wanted a Europe united against **communism** and played a major role in the implementation of the Marshall Plan, the creation of the Western Union (March 1948), and the North Atlantic Treaty Organization (April 1949). As a result of his tour of the British Empire in 1937 to 1938, he wanted to build an effective multiracial organization bound together by the Columbo Plan (1950). Bevin's main failure in foreign policy was his inability to negotiate a mutually acceptable solution to **Jews** and Arabs in Palestine in the late 1940s.

BLAIR, ANTHONY CHARLES LYNTON [TONY] (1953–). Born in Edinburgh into a **middle-class** Anglican family, his father a university lecturer in law and an aspiring Conservative politician, Tony Blair was educated at a private school. He spent a year in London working a succession of menial jobs before studying law at St. John's College, Oxford University. He practiced as a barrister specializing in labor law from 1976. After marrying Cherie Booth in 1980, he lived in Hackney, a **working-class** area of London's East End. From this time onward, he became active in the **British Labour Party** (Labour) and in April 1983 he was elected to the House of Commons as the member for Sedgefield, a coal-mining center in the northeast of England. He was shadow treasury spokesman between 1984 and 1987; in this position he opposed Labour's support for the closed shop for **trade unions**. Lacking a traditional Labour background in either the working class or the trade unions, Blair's religious beliefs place him in the tradition of **Christian socialism** which was shared by earlier Labour leaders such as Hugh Gaitskell (1906–63), who led the Labour Party between 1955 and 1963, and **Clement Attlee**. In a television interview in 1995, Blair said he had been attracted to Labour because he shared its values and because of his belief that a strong, decent, and cohesive society was necessary for the betterment of the individual.

Blair visited Australia in 1982, 1990, and 1995 and consulted with **Australian Labor Party** leaders **Bob Hawke** and **Paul Keating** when they were in government. A protégé of Neil Kinnock, who led the Labour Party from 1983 to 1992, Blair became leader of the party in July 1994 after the untimely death of Kinnock's successor, John Smith (1938–94), from a heart attack on 12 May. As leader, Blair successfully modernized the image of the Labour Party and enhanced its standing with the electorate, summed up in his term *New Labour*. He advocated a "third way" between the old left and the new right. He succeeded in abandoning the **socialization objective** in clause IV of the party's constitution (a goal unsuccessfully sought by other Labour leaders since 1959) and in adopting a pro-European foreign policy. He indicated support for reform of the House of Lords, especially the removal of hereditary peers.

On 1 May 1997 Blair led "New Labour" to a massive victory in the national elections. He identified **education, health, unemployment**, and crime as priorities for his government. He also began the reform of the House of Lords. In the elections of 7 June 2001 he once again led the party to victory, with only five fewer seats than in 1997. Blair alienated many traditional Labour members and supporters for policies including the allowance and encouragement of business involvement in the public sector. Many in his party opposed him for sending the British military to Iraq in the war led by United States President George W. Bush as of 2003. He won a third term as prime minister when his party won the May 2005 general elections.

BLANC, JEAN-JOSEPH-CHARLES-LOUIS (1811–82). Author and politician, Louis Blanc was one of the most significant figures in the development of socialism. Born in Madrid, where his father had been sent by Napoleon Bonaparte, he founded the *Revue du progrès* in 1839, a journal of advanced social thought. In this journal he serially published his important work *Organisation du travail* (Organization of Labor) in 1840, in which he argued for setting up a system of government-subsidized cooperative workshops to provide employment with a guaranteed minimum wage. The financing for these workshops was to come from **nationalized** railways, mines, banks, and insurance enterprises as well as from general revenue. It was Blanc, not **Karl Marx**, who encapsulated the socialist goal as "from each according to his ability, to each according to his needs." In 1848 he became a member of the French provisional government and was able to use his position to demand that the government provide employment to all who needed it. Because there was much popular support for Blanc's idea of workshops for the **unemployed**, the government set up a travesty of what he advocated with the object of discrediting him. Falsely accused of being part of a revolutionary movement, he was forced to leave France and move to England, where he worked as correspondent until 1871. Blanc assumed that the social classes could cooperate and opposed the **Paris Commune**. On his return to France, he was elected to the national assembly and to the chamber of deputies in 1876. The idea of national cooperative workshops was taken up by **Ferdinand Lassalle**. Blanc's ideas were of lasting importance in wanting to use the state as an instrument to achieve socialism through democratic, parliamentary processes, thus foreshadowing later socialist doctrines such as **Fabianism** and **revisionism**, and workers' self-management or **Guild Socialism**.

BLATCHFORD, ROBERT PEEL GLANVILLE (1851–1943). Journalist and popularizer of socialist ideas, Robert Blatchford was born in Maidstone, England. His father, an itinerant comedian, died when he was two years old. Apprenticed as a brush maker at the age of 14 he ran away when he was 20 and joined the army, where he stayed until 1878. He enjoyed his time in the army and became convinced of the innate goodness of ordinary people. He first began writing for the press in 1883. He moved to Manchester, where the experience of the slums and reading works by **Henry George** and **William Morris** turned him into a socialist, a choice that cost him his well-paid job with the *Sunday Chronicle*. In 1891 he and Edward Francis Fay (deceased 1896) founded a socialist newspaper, *The Clarion*, which he edited until 1935. In 1893 he published *Merrie England*, a book that was originally a collection of articles in *The Clarion*; in 1894 *Merrie England* was reissued as a penny edition and it sold over 2 million copies in Britain, the United States, and in various translations. It was the best-selling work on socialism of its time. Unlike many other writers on socialism such as **George Bernard Shaw**, Blatchford had a gift for communicating with less educated readers. Like William Morris, Blatchford disliked factories and the industrial towns and loved the countryside and its towns. Although he went on to write other works, notably a novel in the tradition of **utopian socialism** called *The Sorcery Shop* (1907), his support for both the Boer War and World War I lost him most of his socialist supporters. After the death of his wife in 1921 he became a spiritualist.

BLUM, LÉON (1872–1950). Born in Paris into a prosperous Alsatian **Jewish** family and raised in a traditional Jewish environment, Léon Blum qualified as a lawyer in 1894 and joined the *Groupe d'Unité Socialiste* in 1899 and the *Parti Socialiste Français* in 1902. He participated in the campaign to exonerate Alfred Dreyfus, a Jewish army officer falsely accused of selling secrets to the Germans. He worked with **Jean Jaurès** and helped found the socialist newspaper *L'Humanité* in 1904. After the murder of Jaurès in 1914 he felt compelled to enter politics. In 1919 he was elected to the chamber of deputies and became a leading member of the **French Socialist Party**. After the **communists** took control of the party in 1921, he left and formed his own moderate party. He became premier of a **Popular Front** government in June 1936 and **nationalized** the Bank of France and the armaments industry. He resigned in June 1937 after being denied special powers by the upper house to deal with the economic crisis. He again served as premier from March to April 1938. In 1942 Blum was put on trial by the Vichy government, but his courageous defense led to the suspension of proceedings. He was handed over to the Nazis and sent to Buchenwald concentration camp, where he was liberated by American troops. He was then premier from December 1946 to January 1947. Blum was a **Zionist** sympathizer from 1918, and strongly supported the creation of Israel in 1948.

BOURGEOISIE. *See* MIDDLE CLASS.

BRANDT, WILLY (1913–92). Born Karl Herbert Frahm in Lübeck, Willy Brandt joined the **German Social Democratic Party** (*Sozialdemokratische Partei Deutschlands* — SPD) and after the Nazis came to power in 1933 was forced to flee to Norway, where he worked as a journalist. He returned to Germany briefly in 1936 to establish an anti-Nazi underground and was a journalist during the **Spanish Civil War**. He joined the Norwegian army in 1940, was captured then released, and went to Sweden. He returned to Germany in 1945 and was elected to the *Bundestag* in 1949. He became chairman of the SPD in Berlin in 1958 and became leader of the party in 1964, a position he held until 1987. He was one of the prime architects of the **Godesberg Program**. He served as chancellor from October 1969 to May 1974, but was forced to stand down after a close aide was arrested as a communist spy from East Germany. In 1976 he became president of the **Socialist International** and used his office to expand its membership into the Third World. His last major public achievement was chairing an international commission that produced the Brandt Report (1979). The report argued that the economic and social problems of nations located mainly in the southern hemisphere threatened world peace and these countries needed more assistance from the industrialized nations located mainly in the northern hemisphere.

BRAUNTHAL, JULIUS (1891–1972). A **Jewish** socialist scholar, publications editor, and administrator, Julius Braunthal was born in Vienna and worked as a bookbinder between 1905 and 1912. He fought with distinction in the Austro-Hungarian army, rose to the rank of lieutenant, and received a silver medal for bravery. Between 1918 and 1920 he served as assistant to the secretary of state for the newly formed Austrian republic. Between 1920 and 1934 he edited various Austrian socialist newspapers. As a result of the Nazi takeover of Austria in 1938, he went into exile and spent the last part of his life in Britain. He was assistant secretary of the **Labor and Socialist International** between 1938 and 1939, edited *International Socialist Forum* from 1941 to 1948, and was secretary of the **Committee of the International Socialist Conference** (1949–51) and its successor, the **Socialist International**, from 1951 to 1956. He was a **Zionist** and today is best remembered for his three-volume *History of the International*, which was originally published in German between 1961 and 1971.

BRITISH LABOUR PARTY (LABOUR). Formed on 27 February 1900, as the Labour Representation Committee (LRC), and renamed the Labour Party in 1906, Labour has been one of the leading **political parties** in the world to be based on organized labor. Labor officials first began contesting British parliamentary elections in 1847, but were unsuccessful until 1874, when Alexander Macdonald (1821–81) and Thomas Burt (1837–1922), two coal miners' leaders, were elected to the House of Commons. In 1867 **suffrage** was widened to include relatively well-off urban **working-class** men. It was broadened again in 1884, but a full adult male suffrage was not introduced until 1918.

Full **women**'s suffrage was not introduced until 1928. Because of its ability to work with the Liberal Party for labor objectives, the Trades Union Congress (TUC), the peak national labor organization, was slow to see the need for organized labor to support its own political party, despite initiatives such as the **Labour Representation League** and the Labour Electoral Committee (1886).

James Keir Hardie founded the Scottish Parliamentary Party in 1888 and the **Independent Labour Party** in 1893, but these were not arms of the **trade unions**. In 1892 Keir Hardie succeeded in having a resolution for separate labor representation carried at the TUC, but no action followed. It was the Taff Vale Case—a legal judgment by the House of Lords in 1901 which made trade unions liable to prosecution for large damages caused by picketing—that galvanized organized labor into supporting a new party; in 1906 the LRC was renamed the Labour Party. The LRC was originally proposed by Thomas R. Steels of the Amalgamated Society of Railway Servants and the ILP. Its founding members were the ILP, the **Social Democratic Federation**, and various trade unions.

The LRC was reorganized in 1903 and increased its subscription rate to pay salaries to its parliamentary representatives, who were henceforth not to identify themselves with any other political party. In August 1903 **Ramsay MacDonald** made a secret deal between the LRC and the Liberal Party, which ended electoral competition between them in constituencies in England; the deal remained in force until 1918, when electoral reforms abolished two-member constituencies. In 1909 the Labour Party was greatly strengthened when the Miners' Federation decided to affiliate; previously, the federation had tended to support the Liberal Party.

Before 1914 the Labour Party was administratively and electorally weak. It therefore preferred to keep the Liberal Party in power, the alternative being the Conservative Party. World War I and the stresses it caused to the social and economic fabric of Britain weakened the Liberal Party and worked to the benefit of the Labour Party. In December 1916 David Lloyd George formed a government and offered some junior ministries to the Labour Party. Growing differences from late 1917 between Lloyd George and Arthur Henderson, the secretary of the Labour Party from 1912 to 1934 and a former Liberal supporter, led Henderson to begin far-ranging reforms of the party to convert it into the major opposition party and supplant the Liberal Party. Under Henderson's leadership, Labour adopted an independent foreign policy and turned to **Sidney Webb** for assistance in preparing policies. In 1918 the party adopted a **socialization objective** as part of its constitution. In June 1918 Webb prepared *Labour and the Social Order*, which was the basis of Labour policy until 1950; it advocated a minimum wage, the democratic control of industry, heavy **taxation** to pay for social services, and expansion of **educational** and cultural facilities. The Labour Party was reorganized to create its own local organizations based on individual members. Previously membership had been open only to trade unions. Between 1928 (when the first figures became available) and 1938, the individual membership of the party doubled from 215,000 to 429,000.

In 1922 Labour won 142 seats in the House of Commons (it contested 414) and became the official opposition party. After the 1923 elections it increased its representation to 191, compared to only 158 for the reunited Liberal Party, thereby enabling Labour to form a minority government under MacDonald with Liberal support. During its brief time in office in 1924, the government's main achievement was a law that provided for government assistance to local government councils to build houses for the less well-off. Otherwise it achieved little; in particular, it lacked the economic expertise to relieve **unemployment**.

At the 1929 election, Labour won 288 seats, making it the largest political party but still short of a clear majority; hence, it formed another minority government. As the Depression set in, the government was unable to agree over unemployment policy. American bankers were only prepared to grant loans if widespread retrenchments were made. In August 1931 MacDonald formed a new government with Liberal and Conservative support, a decision that led to widespread and intense bitterness among Labour supporters, aggravated by Labour's crushing defeat in the elections of October 1931, which saw only 52 Labour members returned.

In 1935 **Clement Attlee** replaced **George Lansbury** as leader of the parliamentary Labour Party, thereby becoming the first leader to come from outside the working class. In the elections of that year Labour won 166 seats and began its slow recovery as a major party. Academic supporters, such as **G. D. H. Cole** and the **XYZ Group**, played an important role in feeding it ideas and producing detailed reformist programs. The Labour Party also abandoned the tendency toward **pacifism** that had been evident under Lansbury's leadership; from 1937 it supported rearmament.

Before 1918 the party's general level of interest in international matters was low, and it was not until 1908 that it joined the secretariat of the **Second International**. The party was an affiliate of the **Labor and Socialist International** throughout its history and during World War II nurtured the bodies in exile that eventually gave rise to the **Socialist International** in 1951.

In May 1940 Winston Churchill formed a war cabinet to fight World War II; it included Attlee as Lord Privy Seal and **Ernest Bevin** as minister for labor and national service. The close working relationship between these two men from very different social backgrounds was the basis for the first majority Labour government after the war. In 1945 Labour achieved this majority with 396 seats in the House of Commons. Of those elected 41 percent had working-class origins compared to 72 percent of Labour parliamentarians between 1918 and 1935.

The Attlee government implemented wide-ranging reforms. It embarked on an extensive campaign of **nationalization** that included the Bank of England, the coal industry, electricity, gas, and transport. It also introduced a national **health** service. It acted quickly to give independence to British India (1947), thereby creating the modern Asian nations of India, Pakistan, Burma, and Ceylon (now Sri Lanka). The government's freedom of action was curtailed by a financial crisis in the late 1940s. The Attlee government was returned to power in the 1950 election, but with a much reduced majority (315 seats), and it lost power in 1951. Its main achievement was the nationalization of the iron and steel industry.

Thereafter Labour entered a long period of electoral decline and internal dissension. Bevin died in 1951 and was replaced by the left-wing Frank Cousins as secretary of the powerful Transport and General Workers' Union in 1955. This deprived Attlee, who remained party leader until 1955, of his most powerful ally. At the same time, the left-wing of the party grew in strength and found an unofficial factional leader in Aneurin Bevan (1897–1960). The left objected to the rearmament of Germany (1954), the decision to produce a hydrogen bomb (1955), and any attempt to remove the socialization objective from the party's constitution (1959). On the issue of **nuclear**

weapons the left succeeded in having the party adopt a policy of unilateral disarmament (1960). Hugh Gaitskell (1906–63), who was party leader from 1955 until his death, led a party in which the views of the parliamentary leadership were often ignored by the trade union voting blocs that dominated the Labour Party. Gaitskell was replaced by **Harold Wilson**, who was then identified with the party's left wing but moved to the right thereafter. Wilson's speech to the 1963 party conference emphasized science, technology, and higher education rather than traditional socialist goals such as nationalization and government regulation of the economy. Labour won national government again at the elections of 1964.

Thereafter the Labour Party's electoral record in national British politics was mixed: Labour lost power in 1970, regained it in 1974, and lost it again in 1979 as it struggled to deal with the country's economic difficulties, notably its adverse balance of payments, high inflation, and low productivity. After its defeat in the 1979 elections, Labour suffered six years of severe internal conflict between parliamentarians and left-wing activists (sometimes known as Bennites), who rallied behind Tony Benn and the **Campaign for Labour Party Democracy**. The shift to the left of the political spectrum alienated some senior Labour parliamentary members—notably Roy Jenkins, David Owen, William Rodgers, and Shirley Williams—who eventually set up the Social Democratic Party in 1981.

At the 1980 party conference, the parliamentary Labour members were blamed for the electoral defeat of 1979. **James Callaghan** resigned as leader and was replaced by the left-winger Michael Foot in November 1980. Under Foot, Labour supported massive government spending, Britain's withdrawal from the European Economic Community, and unilateral disarmament. In April 1981 Benn challenged Denis Healey for the deputy leadership, a move that resulted in six months of struggle, which added to Labour's disunity. Benn lost by less than 1 percent of the vote, largely because Neil Kinnock and his supporters abstained from voting.

The adoption of a left-wing platform in the 1983 elections brought about Labour's worst election result (27.6 percent of the vote) since it became the main party of opposition in 1922. Foot resigned as leader and was replaced by Kinnock, who was at that point another left-winger. By this time, Labour's support according to opinion polls had dropped to 24 percent. Kinnock began the massive task of reforming the organization and policies of the party. The leaders of **Militant Tendency** were finally expelled in 1985 and 1986. In 1986 the traditional party symbol, the red **flag**, was replaced by a red rose. After its defeat in the June 1987 elections, the party's policies were drastically revised to bring them into line with community aspirations. Despite these reforms, the party was again defeated at the national polls in 1992. Kinnock stepped down as leader and was replaced by John Smith (1938–94), who died of a heart attack and was able to do little beyond reducing the power of the trade unions in electing the party leader.

The lack of electoral support for Labour between 1979 and 1992 reflected profound economic and social changes in Britain and in other Western economies. The decline of manufacturing, the growth of part-time employment, and the increased entry of women into the labor force undercut Labour's traditional power base, the trade unions. Between 1979 and 1992 the number of union members of the Labour Party fell from its peak of 6.5 million to 4.6 million, its lowest level since 1948. By 1995 the proportion of British employees who were union members was 32 percent, compared to 51 percent in 1979.

Public opinion polls conducted since 1945 indicate that electoral support for Labour among blue-collar workers was more than double what it was among white-collar workers. Between 1945 and 1974 support for Labour varied between 57 and 62 percent among blue-collar workers compared to between 21 and 28 percent among white-collar workers. Between 1974 and 1992 support for Labour fell among both groups but the fall was greater among blue-collar workers. In 1992 47 percent of private sector blue-collar workers supported Labour compared to only 19 percent of private sector white-collar workers.

After Smith's death on 12 May 1994, **Tony Blair** became party leader. Under him, Labour was moved further into the center of the political spectrum, tending to give community, inclusion, and merit greater emphasis than collectivism, equality, and redistribution. One especially notable feature of Blair's leadership was his successful reduction in the power of the trade unions over the Labour Party; for example, in April 1996 the practice of union sponsorship of individual Labour parliamentarians was abolished. In 1995 Blair relaunched the Labour Party as "New Labour" and dropped its socialization objective. Drawing on the example of the consensus politics of the Australian Labor Party in government in the 1980s and the presidential campaigns of Bill Clinton in 1992 and 1996, Blair led "New Labour" to a landslide election victory on 1 May 1997, gaining 418 of the 659 seats with 43.2 percent of the vote. Among the policies announced in the wake of this victory were support for Britain signing the European Social Chapter to bring it into line with European employment standards, a minimum wage, and increased expenditure on health and education.

At the general elections of 7 June 2001 Labour once again enjoyed a massive victory, winning 413 seats with 42 percent of the vote, albeit in the lowest turnout (59.2 percent) at a British general election since World War II. In the elections to the European Parliament in June 2004 Labour obtained 19 of Britain's 78 seats, which was an even worse result than that of 1999, when it won 29 seats. The Labour members of the European Parliament worked in the **Party of European Socialists**, with which their party was affiliated. In May 2005 Labour achieved a third successive victory in a British general election for the first time in its history. However, its share of the parliamentary seats was reduced to 356, won with 35.2 percent of the vote *See also* BEVERIDGE REPORT; BRITISH SOCIALIST PARTY; CROSLAND, CHARLES ANTHONY RAVEN; CO-OPERATIVE PARTY; LASKI, HAROLD JOSEPH; TAWNEY, RICHARD HENRY.

BRITISH SOCIALIST PARTY (BSP). The BSP was a small radical party that operated between 1911 and 1920. It was formed in opposition to the **British Labour Party** from former members of the **Social Democratic Federation. H. M. Hyndman** was its chairman, but it also included followers of **Robert Blatchford** as well as dissidents from the **Independent Labour Party**. The BSP claimed 15,000 members by 1912, but was unable to sustain itself and in 1914 applied for affiliation with the British Labour Party, which at first refused, but accepted the BSP in 1916. The BSP was weakened by **syndicalism**, which repudiated political activity altogether. In 1920 the BSP joined with other left-wing groups to form the British **Communist** Party, thereby breaking its links with the Labour Party. *See also* MANN, TOM.

BULGARIAN SOCIAL DEMOCRATS [*BULGARSKI SOT-SIALDEMOKRATI* (BSD)]. The Bulgarian Social Democratic Party (*Bulgarska Sotsialdemokraticheska Partiya*—BSDP) was founded in August 1891 as the Bulgarian Social Democratic Labor Party; by 1900 it had 1,761 members. It split in 1903 between the Broad and the Narrow Socialists. The Broad Socialists were comparable to the supporters of **Revisionism** in other parts of Western Europe. They favored a party with a wide social base and cooperation with bourgeois parties to advance economic and political democracy. The Narrow Socialists preferred to concentrate on class struggle as the primary objective and to prepare the **working class** for the future socialist revolution. They later became the Bulgarian Communist Party, and eventually the **Bulgarian Socialist Party** (*Bulgarski Sotsialisticheska Partiya*—BSP).

With the imposition of **communist** rule the BSDP was suppressed in 1948, but not formally outlawed. It was revived in March 1991 after the coup of November 1989, which removed the Todor Zhivkov (1911–98) regime. The BSDP claimed 50,000 members and was admitted as a full member of the **Socialist International**. For the 1991 and 1997 parliamentary elections the BSDP joined the Union of Democratic Forces (*Saiuz na demokratichnite sili*—SDS), which subsequently gained power. A splinter group from the party took the name of BSDP later in 1997 after a legal challenge. This group joined the SDS coalition. Meanwhile, the main body of what had been the BSDP became the BSD. The economic problems that Bulgaria had suffered since the collapse of communism continued. In 2001 the BSD joined with several left-of-center parties to form the Coalition for Bulgaria, led by the BSP. This coalition won 48 of the 240 seats with 17.1 percent of the vote. After the elections of 17 June 2001 the SDS lost control of government, when the party of the former King Simeon II won 120 of the 240 seats in the National Assembly, the former king becoming prime minister. At the parliamentary elections of June 2005 the BSD remained in the Coalition for Bulgaria, which took 82 of 240 seats with the largest percentage of votes—34.17 percent.

BULGARIAN SOCIALIST PARTY [*BULGARSKA SOTSIALIS-TICHESKA PARTIYA* (BSP)]. Formed from the Narrow Socialists, which split from Bulgarian Social Democratic Party (*Bulgarska Sot-sialdemokraticheska Partiya*—BSDP) in 1903, the Bulgarian Communist Party was strong enough in 1919 to provoke fears of revolution in that country. In 1947 the Communist Party took power, following the Soviet occupation and the replacement of the Bulgarian monarchy with a People's Republic. During the collapse of East European **communism** in 1989 to 1990 Todor Zhivkov (1911–98), who had led the Communists since 1954, resigned. The People's Republic was abolished and the Communist Party reformed as the BSP.

The BSP participated in elections in 1990 and dominated the coalition formed with the Agrarians, the Union of Democratic Forces (*Saiuz na demokratichnite sili*—SDS), and others in December that year. Economic problems that would cause problems for Bulgaria throughout the 1980s began to be felt. After mass unrest and a general strike, the BSP vote was reduced in the elections of 1991 to 34 percent, slightly lower than the 34.4 percent gained by the rival SDS coalition, which included the BSDP. In the general election of 1994 the BSP returned to power, their Zhan Videnov becoming prime minister the following year. He resigned in 1996 and the SDS won the elections of 1997. After the National Assembly elections of June 2001, the BSP-led Coalition for Bulgaria took 48 of the 240 seats with 17.1 percent of the vote. The Coalition also included the **Bulgarian Social Democrats** (*Bulgarski Sotsialdemokrati*—BSD), as the former BSDP was now known.

The winner of the elections in 2001 was former King Simeon II, who became prime minister after his party won 120 seats. In November 2001 the BSP candidate Georgi Parvanov was elected president of Bulgaria. The BSP gained full membership in the **Socialist International** in 2003. In the parliamentary elections of June 2005 the BSP operated in the left Coalition for Bulgaria, which obtained 82 of 240 seats with the largest percentage of votes—34.17 percent—under the leadership of Sergei Stanishev, and thus insisted that it must lead a coalition government. The BSP began negotiations with potential coalition partners and in July that year President Parvanov mandated Stanishev to form a government. In August 2005 Stanishev signed a deal that set up a coalition government including the BSP and the main center-right party of Simeon II.

BUND. *See* INTERNATIONAL JEWISH LABOR BUND.

– C –

CALLAGHAN, (LEONARD) JAMES (1912–2005). A leader of the **British Labour Party** (Labour) and prime minister, James Callaghan was born in Portsmouth, England, and was raised by his widowed mother, a strict Baptist in a poor household. He joined the Inland Revenue Service and became secretary of the Inland Revenue Staff Federation. He served in the Royal Navy during World War II. Having been recommended by **Harold Laski** as a potential Labour parliamentary candidate, he was elected to the House of Commons as member for Cardiff South in 1945 and remained a member of the Commons until 1987. When first elected, he was identified with the left of the party, but had moderated his views by the end of the 1940s. He rose through the ranks of the parliamentary party and made an unsuccessful, but credible, attempt at standing for leader of the party in 1963. He was chancellor of the exchequer between 1964 and 1967, home secretary from 1967 to 1970, foreign secretary from 1974 to 1976, and prime minister (of a minority government) and leader of the Labour Party from 1976 to 1980. He was created Baron Callaghan of Cardiff in 1987. His record in power was adversely affected by the economic difficulties of the British economy from the mid-1960s to the late 1970s.

CAMPAIGN FOR LABOUR PARTY DEMOCRACY (CLPD). The CLPD was a group formed in the **British Labour Party** in 1973 to press for members to be given a greater say in decision making within the party. At the 1980 annual conference of the party, the CLPD succeeded in having two of its policies adopted: the compulsory reselection of members of parliament by the party and a broader **suffrage** for the election of the leader of the party.

CAPITALISM. A general term for an economic and social system characterized by the domination of private ownership of the means of production, distribution, and exchange. *Capital*, meaning the accumulated wealth of an individual, company, or community, was used in English by 1611. Meaning the original funds of a trader, company, or corporation and so providing the basis for further operations, the term was used in 1709 in legislation relating to the Bank of England. "Capitalists," meaning moneyed men, was used by Arthur Young in

1792. The first general description of the dynamics of modern capitalism was made by Adam Smith in *An Inquiry into the Nature and Causes of the Wealth of Nations* in 1776. The features Smith described were given far greater force by the **Industrial Revolution**, particularly from the 1830s. Although the benefits of capitalism were evident from its augmentation of national **wealth** and income, it faced increasing criticism after 1820 from critics for causing a skewed distribution of income, depressions in the trade cycle, mass **unemployment**, and, more generally, for moral and ethical reasons. Socialist critics were united in their objections to capitalism as an economic system that promoted competition rather than cooperation. All were influenced by the widespread misery caused by economic depressions in the 1830s and 1840s, which led to movements such as **Chartism**.

That said, socialists were far less united about what to put in its place. **Utopian socialism** sought solutions in the building of separate communities. Radical socialists led by **Karl Marx** for much of the nineteenth century rejected such options and saw the solution in violent revolution by the oppressed workers (proletariat). By the end of the nineteenth century it was evident to acute observers such as **Eduard Bernstein** that the ability of capitalism to adapt had been underestimated by Marx and that the working classes were becoming better off, not worse off. The Depression of the early 1930s led to a major reappraisal by the economist John Maynard Keynes in his *General Theory of Employment, Interest, and Money* in 1936. The Depression provoked widespread disenchantment with capitalism as a system and boosted support for **communism** in Western democracies. From the end of World War II to about 1980, socialist governments in Western countries have accepted the capitalist system, but have sought to ameliorate its drawbacks by intervention, the promotion of full employment, and enhanced **social security** programs. Since 1980 socialist/social-democratic governments have also been more inclined to accept **privatization** as the way to improve economic efficiency and reduce government outlays, as well as to resort to selling off public assets to raise revenue.

CARPENTER, EDWARD (1844–1929). Along with **Robert Blatchford**, Edward Carpenter was one of the ethical socialists who were prominent on the left in late nineteenth-century England. Carpenter was born into a wealthy family and was a student, then fellow, at Cambridge. His socialism was characterized by opposition less to **capitalism** as an exploitative system than to capitalist ethics, whereby humanity was sacrificed to greed, selfishness, and the concern with material gain. This led him to detest modern civilization. He is best known for his long poetic work *Towards Democracy*, in which he expressed his unhappiness with modern life and conceived of an alternative society in which humanity would be liberated. The new society would be one of simple, natural relationships, rather than the corrupt, competitive society of his time. The first edition was published in 1883. In later editions new sections were added and in 1902 a fourth part was published. The complete edition was published in 1905. Carpenter expressed similar concerns in *England's Ideal* (1887), where he appealed to working men and working **women** to cease ducking and forelock tugging, assert the dignity of human labor, and demand the righteous distribution of the fruits of labor.

CHARTISM. Named after the People's Charter, the statement of its demands, Chartism was a radical political movement in England in the 1830s and 1840s. The objectives of the movement were the **suffrage** for all adult males, annual parliaments, vote by secret ballot, public payment of members of parliament, population equality of electoral districts, and the abolition of property qualifications for members of parliament. Although most of these aims were achieved in England by 1914, the most radical demand, for annual parliaments, was not; had it been agreed to, it would have drastically altered the British constitution.

Chartism drew its strength from the depressed economic conditions of the time and the **unemployment** in many industrialized areas. The People's Charter was presented to parliament as a petition in 1839, 1842, and 1848 and was rejected each time. England's rulers saw Chartism as a revolutionary movement and treated it with hostility. The movement was marked by violence (24 were killed at Newport) and internal divisions. With the gradual economic recovery in the late 1840s, Chartism died, but its ideas entered the agenda of **working-class** politics in other English-speaking countries through emigration. It has been suggested that the benign attitude of British governments after 1850 toward the emergence of **trade unions** compared to Chartism was to encourage working-class activism to take an orderly, moderate form.

CHÁVEZ FRIÁZ, HUGO (1954–). President of Venezuela since 1999, Hugo Chávez was born in Sabeneta, in the Venezuelan state of Barinas. He graduated from a military academy and became a major in a Venezuelan parachutist regiment. Having founded the Revolutionary Bolivarian Movement, named after the South American independence leader, Simon Bolivar, he led a coup in 1992 against President Carlos Andres Perez, whose economic austerity measures were causing considerable anger in the country. The coup failed and Chávez was imprisoned. He was released two years later under an amnesty. Representing the poor who never benefited from the country's huge oil deposits, he has dominated the left in Venezuela since the late 1990s, and attracted opposition from the business and political elite of Venezuela. He revived his party, renaming it the **Movement of the Fifth Republic** and achieved a landslide victory in the presidential elections of 1998. In July 2000 he once again won the presidential elections, with 59.5 percent of the vote. In 2002 Chávez was removed in a coup, only to resume the presidency within 48 hours. International observers rejected opposition allegations of fraud.

During Chávez's period in office the economy has been characterized by a huge expansion of the **cooperative movement**, with many new cooperatives being registered. Another initiative has been comanagement, whereby in each case the state holds 51 percent of shares and a workers' cooperative holds the other 49 percent. Politically, however, Chávez has taken an authoritarian stance, introducing a new constitution that strengthened the position of the president and refusing to negotiate with the opposition.

In August 2004 Chávez was successful in a referendum that asked whether he should continue for the remaining approximately two and a half years of his term in office. The referendum, which he won by 59.25 percent to 40.74 percent, was called on the basis of a recall clause in the constitution he had introduced. Chávez had, by then, formed close relations with Cuba and attracted enmity from the George W. Bush administration in the United States.

CHIFLEY, JOSEPH BENEDICT (1885–1951). The **Australian Labor Party** prime minister from 1945 to 1949, Ben Chifley was born in Bathurst, New South Wales. He became a locomotive railroad driver in 1914 and was elected to the national parliament in 1928.

From March to December he was minister for defense in the **James Scullin** government. He lost his seat in the landslide to the conservatives in the elections of December 1931 and did not regain it until 1940. He served as treasurer in the wartime administration of **John Curtin** and took over as prime minister on Curtin's death in 1945. His administration improved social services, established a domestic government-run airline (1946), bought the international airline Qantas for the government, initiated the first large-scale immigration scheme for non-British European immigrants (1947), and began the Snowy Mountains Hydro-Electric Scheme. He lost office in the 1949 election because he was blamed for the effects of the **communist**-led 1949 coal strike that occurred during the winter. His government's plan to **nationalize** the banks and his continued wartime rationing of petrol also contributed to his defeat.

CHRISTIANITY. Although Christianity and socialism are often presented as antagonistic historical traditions, this is an oversimplification of what has been a long and complicated relationship. Christianity contributed much of the ethical basis of what became socialism. Christianity was the source of notions of **egalitarianism** and millenarianism. Egalitarianism was an idea with roots traceable to classical Greece and Rome. Christianity stressed the equality of souls after death, but not during life. The myth of the golden age was revived by millenarian groups from the eleventh to the sixteenth centuries. Common themes among these groups were the need for communities of the faithful and the idea that the second coming of Christ would provide salvation and relief from political oppression. Despite the often violent suppression of these groups by the governments of the day, their ideas lived on in the poorer sections of European society.

During the last half of the nineteenth century socialism as a movement benefited from the decline in support for Christianity. Many found in socialism something like an alternative **religion**. This was especially evident in Germany, where the Catholic church provided an unwitting model for the social organization of the **Germany Social Democratic Party** and its efforts to build an alternative society. Others remained Christians but attempted to fuse socialism and Christianity in the form of **Christian socialism**. In the United Kingdom, many of the socialists of the late nineteenth century came from nonconformist religions. Most of the conflict between socialism and

Christianity has been more between socialism and Catholicism, particularly in France, Italy, and Spain where the Catholic church was closely associated with the established order. An **International League of Religious Socialists** was formed in 1922 in Switzerland to improve dialogue between socialists and Catholics. *See also* SAINT-SIMON, CLAUDE-HENRY.

CHRISTIAN SOCIALISM. From about the 1830s concern about social justice and harmony in the United Kingdom, continental Europe, and the United States gave rise to **middle-class Christian** groups that wanted to apply their faith to help solve social problems. They perceived necessary links between the ideals of **Christianity** and the goals of socialism. They supported **trade unions**, **cooperatives**, adult **suffrage**, **education**, and progressive social reform generally, arguing that the state had a moral obligation to provide for the welfare of citizens. For example, the principles of the American Society of Christian Socialists adopted in Boston in April 1889, declared that God was "the source and guide of all human progress," criticized the economic system for its individualistic basis, and demanded a "reconstituted social order, which, adopting some method of production and distribution that starts from organized society as a body, and seeks to benefit society equitably in every one of its members, shall be based on the Christian principle that 'We are members one of another.'" Although Christian socialism failed to attract a mass following, it continued to form a strand of socialist thought throughout the twentieth century. In the early twenty-first century the British prime minister **Tony Blair** was a prominent Christian socialist. *See also* ELY, RICHARD THEODORE; INTERNATIONAL LEAGUE OF RELIGIOUS SOCIALISTS; RELIGION.

CLARKE, HELEN (1950–). As leader of the **New Zealand Labour Party** (NZLP), Helen Clarke became prime minister in 1999. Born into a wealthy farming family, 23 years later she gained her PhD from the University of Auckland, where she subsequently became a lecturer of political science. Clarke made history in 1981, when, becoming MP for Mt. Albert, she became the first female member of the NZLP to be elected to the New Zealand Parliament. By the late 1980s she had become a senior figure within the party, holding ministerial posts for conservation and housing between 1987 and 1989 and serving as deputy prime minister from 1989 until the following year, when the NZLP lost the general elections. In 1993 she became leader of her party.

Clarke led her party into the 1996 general elections, which were the first to be held under a new electoral system, which combined elements of the old first-past-the-post system with a proportional element (this is the alternative member system). Although the NZLP became the second largest party in parliament, with 37 of 120 seats, the party was excluded from the coalition that resulted from the new proportional element of the system. The right-wing New Zealand First became the pivotal party in the unstable coalition. Nevertheless, by 1999 New Zealand First had lost its appeal and fared disastrously at the general elections that year, when the NZLP returned to power under Clarke, in coalition with the new, left-wing Alliance Party. However, being two seats short of a majority, Clarke relied upon the Greens for support. In 2002 Clarke called elections in which her party retained power but, once again, without an overall majority. After a period of economic stability she became the first NZLP leader to win a third successive term as prime minister when, in September 2005, her party won 50 of 121 seats in the parliamentary elections and formed a minority coalition government with support from two noncoalition parties.

COHEN, GERALD ALLAN (1941–). As a socialist philosopher G. A. Cohen argues for social and economic equality. Born in Montreal, he held office in the Quebec Division of the National Federation of Labour Youth (the **Communist** Party **youth** movement). The Soviet leader Nikita Khrushchev (1894–1971) made revelations of the Joseph Stalin (1879–1953) era in 1956 that divided Cohen's party. In 1957 the Marxist Cohen entered McGill University, Montreal, without party allegiance. After graduating he studied at Oxford. In 1963 he became a lecturer of philosophy at University College London. In 1978 he published *Karl Marx's Theory of History: A Defence*.

An Oxford professor by the mid-1990s, Cohen began to change his socialist position. Traditional **Marxism** had deemed socialism inevitable, as **capitalism** would self-destruct when a revolutionary proletariat realized that productive forces could provide abundance and exploitation was unnecessary. Cohen had taken for granted that from any morally decent point of view socialism would be seen to be superior to capitalism. Like many traditional Marxists, he had neglected the need to explain why socialism was desirable. In 1995, in *Self-ownership, Freedom and Equality*, Cohen argued that Marxists who said they were unconcerned with injustice were deceiving themselves. Historical circumstance would change what justice demanded, but principles of justice were timeless. Furthermore, he considered two traditional Marxist claims regarding inevitability to be false. First, no single class now held all four characteristics that would make revolution inevitable: (1) being the producers on whom society depends; (2) being exploited; (3) being (with their families) the majority of society; and (4) being in dire need. Second, industrial progress could not bring about fluent abundance. The environment was severely degraded, and Western consumption measured in terms of fossil fuel energy and natural resources would eventually, on average, have to fall. So, Cohen believed, it was more important than ever for socialists to set out their cases in normative political philosophy. In 2000 he published *If You're an Egalitarian, How Come You're So Rich?*

COLE, GEORGE DOUGLAS HOWARD (G. D. H.) (1889–1959). A scholar, socialist author, theorist, and historian, G. D. H. Cole was born in Cambridge, England. He was educated at Balliol College, Oxford, and became a socialist by 1906. In 1908 he joined the Fabian Society in Oxford and worked with both the **Independent Labour Party** and the **Social Democratic Federation** in Newcastle upon Tyne in 1913–14. He became critical of the social reformist strand of the **British Labour Party**, for which he would later campaign, and the bureaucratic tendencies in the views of **Sidney and Beatrice Webb**. He left the **Fabian** Society in 1915 and did not rejoin until 1928. He identified with the **trade unions** and believed in organizing change "from below."

In 1913 Cole published *The World of Labour*, a pioneering study of the growth of world trade unionism. For the next five years he was the driving force of **guild socialism**. In 1917 he published *Self-Government in Industry* and in 1920 his most detailed guild socialist work *Guild Socialism Restated*. In 1925 he became a reader in economics and a fellow of University College, Oxford. Cole believed too much in democratic processes to be attracted to **communism**. Nevertheless, in the 1930s his thought comprised an idiosyncratic combination of social-democratic and **Marxist** tenets. He played an important role in providing ideas for the British Labour Party through the Fabian Society and by encouraging debate among pro-Labour intellectuals. In 1940 Cole assisted Sir **William Beveridge** with an inquiry into labor and war production. Cole was a prolific writer. Among his many works of enduring value are *British Working Class Movements: Select Documents, 1789–1875* (with A. W. Filson, 1951) and his multivolume *History of Socialist Thought* (1954–60).

COLONIALISM. *See* IMPERIALISM.

COMINFORM. Short for Communist Information Bureau, the Cominform was the successor to the **Comintern**. Created in Poland in September 1947, its original members were the **communist** parties of the Soviet Union, Poland, Bulgaria, Czechoslovakia, Hungary, Romania, Yugoslavia, France, and Italy. Its stated purpose was to disseminate propaganda and promote international communist solidarity, but it was, like the Comintern, created to carry out the foreign policy of Joseph Stalin (1879–1953). The Cominform was largely unsuccessful; Yugoslavia was expelled for its dissidence in 1948 and the French and Italian communist parties were unable to prevent the implementation of the Marshall Plan. Nevertheless, the Cominform was important as a means of assisting communist parties to undermine social-democratic parties. It was dissolved in April 1956.

COMINTERN. Short for the Communist International, also known as the Third International, the Comintern was formed in Moscow in 1919 as a means of assuming **communist** leadership of international socialism. During the 1920s and 1930s, the Comintern coordinated communist parties so as to meet the needs and interests of the Soviet Union. Joseph Stalin (1879–1953) formally dissolved the Comintern in 1943. *See also* COMINFORM; POPULAR FRONT.

COMMISSION OF SOCIALIST EDUCATORS OF THE EUROPEAN UNION (CSEEU). The Commission of Socialist Teachers of the European Community (CSTEC) was formed in 1989 to represent organizations that were part of the International Union of Socialist Democratic Teachers (now the **International Social Democratic Union for Education**) within the European Community (EC). The

EC became known as the European Union in 1993. Hence, the CSTEC became the CSEEU. In 2005 the CSEEU had member organizations or individual members in 16 countries.

COMMITTEE OF THE INTERNATIONAL SOCIALIST CONFERENCE (COMISCO). The COMISCO was formed in London in March 1948 in the aftermath of the **communist** assumption of power in Czechoslovakia the previous month and the absorption of social and social-democratic parties by communist parties throughout Central and Eastern Europe. It was intended to be a more representative body than its predecessor, the **Socialist Information and Liaison Office**. The COMISCO organized the **Socialist Union of Central and Eastern Europe** to preserve the tradition of social democracy in those countries. At its second conference in Vienna later in 1948, the COMISCO expelled the **Italian Socialist Party** led by Pietro Nenni because of its dependence on the communist party. This conference also agreed to revive the idea of a democratic socialist international, which had been moribund since the demise of the **Labor and Socialist International** at Brussels in March 1940. At the Paris conference of the COMISCO in 1949, **Julius Braunthal** was elected secretary and administrative steps were taken to prepare a declaration of the fundamental principles and aims of democratic socialism. At the Frankfurt conference in July 1951, this declaration (**Frankfurt Declaration**) was adopted and the COMISCO became the **Socialist International**.

COMMUNES. Communes—communities of like-minded individuals—occupy a generally marginal, but symbolically important place in the history of socialism. Before the nineteenth century, communes were generally associated with the dissident traditions of **Christianity** such as the Anabaptist commune of Münster, Germany, between 1534 and 1536, the Pilgrim Fathers in Massachusetts in 1620, and the **Diggers** in England in 1649. Such movements were often linked with millenarianism too. Communes served two main purposes: they were an escape from mainstream society, which the believers judged to be oppressive, and they sought to demonstrate by their example that it was possible to build an alternative society.

Within socialism, communes tended to be most popular in periods of economic hardship, notably the 1840s, 1890s, and 1930s. **Robert**

Owen created a socialist commune in Indiana in 1825; significantly, he bought the land from a dissident Christian sect, the Rappites. In 1829 **Charles Fourier** made the first significant advocacy of communes as a means of bringing about an alternative society to **capitalism** based on cooperation. Thereafter, communes were a persistent theme in socialism, even if they were more discussed than practiced because of their cost.

Most socialist communes that were begun on an entirely new basis were short-lived affairs. For example, the Australian English-born socialist William Lane (1861–1917) led a group of supporters to found a socialist commune in Paraguay in 1893 to get away from the severe economic depression that gripped Australia. Lane was an autocrat and his rule led to discontent and to a split that saw him and some of his supporters leave the original commune and found another one, also in Paraguay. The communes fell apart from 1905.

Where communes were based on wide support, such as the **Paris Commune** or the communes of the **anarchists** in Andalusia during the **Spanish Civil War**, their ends came through repressive violence from national governments. Like the communes of Christian dissidents in the sixteenth and seventeenth centuries, it was their apparent success, not their failures, which made them such a threat to conservative institutions. The great success story of socialist communes has been the *kibbutz* in Israel.

Of the 130 works of utopian fiction published in English between 1813 and 1985 that were sympathetic to socialism, 15 had communes as their principal theme. Of these works, three were published in the 1840s, three in the 1890s, and three in the 1970s. *See also* UTOPIAN SOCIALISM.

COMMUNISM. *Communism* is a general term for the revolutionary tradition of socialism based on interpretations of the writings of **Karl Marx** by **Friedrich Engels** and **V. I. Lenin**. Other strands of communist thought were articulated by **Leon Trotsky** and Mao Zedong. Under **Leninism**, communism rejected the **revisionist** approach of gradually moving toward socialism and opted for a coup followed by dictatorship in the name of the proletariat, an approach ultimately justified by a controversial reference to future socialist society in Marx's critique of the **Gotha Program**. Before 1914, revolutionary socialists—apart from anarchists—were a minority within what was then a unified movement; in addition, there were fundamental differences of opinion among revolutionary socialists. For example, theorists such as **Rosa Luxemburg** opposed Lenin's idea of a small, professional party.

World War I upset the balance of opinion within the socialist movement. The extraordinarily high cost of the **war** in life and goods led to soaring inflation, disenchantment with the war, and political instability. The success of the Bolshevik coup in November 1917, the most dramatic outcome of these trends, transformed the revolutionary part of socialism into a movement in its own right. Although the Soviet government inherited a backward society by the standards of Western Europe and North America, it needs to be remembered that the former Russian empire had been the world's tenth industrial power in 1910 and commanded huge resources of population, **agriculture**, and minerals such as gold. It also inherited a centralized, autocratic political tradition unaccustomed to democratic processes. With these advantages, the communist government began a propaganda war against opposing political creeds, especially their main competitor, reformist socialist **political parties**, through the **Comintern**, the founding of national communist parties, and a campaign to infiltrate **trade unions**.

This aggression and the rejection of parliamentary democracy by the communists shattered the former unity of international socialism. The sticking point for social-democratic parties was the tendency toward dictatorship evident in communism which was condemned by intellectuals as diverse as **Karl Kautsky** and Luxemburg in 1918 and foreshadowed by **Eduard Bernstein** as early as 1899, drawing on the precedent of the French Revolution of 1789. The Western European social-democratic parties tried to revive the **Second International** in 1919, but rejected a merger with the Comintern. A compromise international body, the **International Working Union of Socialist Parties**, was formed in 1921, but it too failed to thrive and merged with the remnants of the former Socialist International to form the **Labor and Socialist International**.

During 1919 the **German Social Democratic Party** (*Sozialdemokratische Partei Deutschlands*—SPD) used military force against communist uprisings in Berlin in January—the Spartacist uprising under **Karl Liebknecht** and Rosa Luxemburg—and crushed the soviet republic in Bavaria that operated from 4 April to 1 May.

Joseph Stalin (1879–1953), Lenin's successor, abandoned the overt policy of fomenting international communist revolution and concentrated on using the state to industrialize the Soviet Union. Agriculture was forcibly collectivized at a cost of millions of lives, a policy originally planned by Lenin. Communist parties were made instruments of Soviet foreign policy and the campaign of denigrating social-democratic parties was continued, epitomized by the term *social fascists*. It has been argued that by weakening these parties, particularly the SPD in Germany, the communists assisted Adolf Hitler's rise to power in 1933. During the **Spanish Civil War** the Soviet Union provided military hardware to the republican government (for the price of its gold reserves) and personnel through the **International Brigades**, but also used its presence to destroy **anarchism** as an effective competitor to communism. The seriousness of the threat posed by fascism led to the temporary alliance of the **Popular Front**. Although Stalin's Non-Aggression Pact with Hitler in August 1939 cost communism much of its idealistic appeal in Western democracies, much goodwill was regained by communist leadership of the partisan movement in Eastern Europe during World War II.

After World War II, Stalin extended his communist dictatorship over the parts of Eastern Europe that had been conquered by the Red Army. The social-democratic parties of East Germany, Czechoslovakia, Hungary, Poland, and Romania were forced to merge with their communist parties between 1946 and 1948; the Bulgarian Social Democratic Party (*Bulgarska Sotsial-demokraticheska Partiya*) was suppressed in 1948 but not formally outlawed. It was this background that fostered the reemergence of noncommunist international socialist bodies culminating in the formation of the **Socialist International** in 1951. The military threat posed by the Soviet Union and the ideological threat of communism in the 1950s forced the continental Western European social-democratic parties to distance themselves from their Marxist heritage, notably in Austria (1958) and in Germany with the **Godesberg Program** in 1958, and to proclaim their adherence to democratic values. In France and Italy, the communist parties competed strongly with the socialist parties for the **working-class** vote. In Italy the Communist Party overshadowed the **Italian Socialist Party** until the 1960s. In France, the Communist Party remained strong until the late 1970s.

The apparent unity of communism after World War II was fractured by the expulsion of Yugoslavia in 1948 from the **Cominform**, but disenchantment with its violence and autocracy among communist party members in Western democracies only began to set in after 1956 with the suppression of the Hungarian uprising at a cost of 50,000 lives, an event that laid the foundations for the **new left**. The military suppression of the reformist Czechoslovak communist government in 1968 by the Soviet Union drained most of the remaining moral capital out of communism in Western democracies and gave rise to the debates over Eurocommunism—reconciling communism with civil rights and the right of political opposition—in the 1970s.

With the collapse of communist regimes in the Soviet Union and in countries dependent on it from 1989, relations between communism and democratic socialism took a new turn. First, there was a revival of social-democratic parties in Eastern Europe. Although they tended to fare poorly in subsequent elections, they became an established part of the political landscape. Second, there was profound questioning within Western eurocommunist parties about their future role. Some, notably the French party, opted to remain more or less as they were, but the Italian Communist Party (*Partito Comunista Italiano*—PCI) transformed itself into the **Democratic Party of the Left** (*Partito Democratico della Sinistra*—PDS) in February 1991. Several members of the PCI who did not want the party to turn to social democracy formed the Communist Refoundation Party (*Rifondazione Comunista*—RC), which sometimes cooperated with the PDS. In 2004 the RC was a significant force with 86,000 members and 11 parliamentary seats won in 2001 with 5 percent of the vote.

In the early twenty-first century the **Communist Party of China** continued to rule in China, albeit over a reformed economy. Elsewhere, communist one-party regimes were led by the **Cuban Communist Party**, **Vietnam Communist Party**, **Lao People's Revolutionary Party**, and the maverick, Stalinist **Workers' Party of Korea**. In Russia the **Communist Party of the Russian Federation** remained a significant, albeit weakened, opposition party, with a strong base of support. In parts of India communist parties continued to attract considerable support, with the Communist Party of India (Marxist ["Marxist" distinguishes this party from other Indian communist parties]) governing in a left-wing coalition in West Bengal. The South African Communist Party remained a key ally of the governing **African National Congress**. *See also* BULGARIAN SOCIAL DEMOCRATS; PARTY OF THE EUROPEAN LEFT; MARXISM.

COMMUNIST INTERNATIONAL. *See* COMINTERN.

COMMUNIST PARTY OF CHINA (CPC) (*ZHŌNGGUÓ GÒNGCHĂNDĂNG*). In 1921 Li Dazho and Chen Duxiu founded the CPC in Shanghai. The following year it began to take direction from the **Comintern**, under instruction from which it briefly cooperated with the **nationalist** Kuomintang, which governed southern China while the remainder of the country was disputed among warlords. By 1927 membership of the CPC had grown to around 50,000, leading the Kuomintang to consider it a threat and attempt to suppress it. However, although thus effectively restricted to the countryside, the CPC began to recruit members from the peasantry, with the result that membership reached around 300,000 by 1931. In response to attacks from the Kuomintang, the CPC established its own powerful Red Army, recruited from the peasantry and, more widely, from Chinese **youth**. This army embarked on the famous "long march" north in 1934 from Jianxi to Yan'an, under the leadership of Mao Zedong and his second-in-command Zhou Enlai. A personality cult began to grow around the authoritarian Mao. Having endured attacks from the Kuomintang along the march, the Red Army arrived at Yan'an battle-hardened and ready to build **communism** in China.

From this point the CPC established itself as a major political force, under the leadership of Mao and Zhou, which would take power in 1949 to form the People's Republic of China. By this time the CPC had around 3 million members. As a single party state, the Republic was dominated by the CPC, a situation that remains unchanged today (2006). In 1950 communist China intervened in the war in neighboring Korea, contributing to the situation that cemented the power of the communist **Workers' Party of Korea** in North Korea. In the 1950s Mao's CPC sought to make China a powerful industrial country and also began the collectivization of **agriculture**. Failures led to famine and the CPC faced further difficulties as relations with the Soviet Union deteriorated, leading to the Sino-Soviet split by the beginning of the 1960s.

Membership of the CPC increased still further to around 17 million in the 1960s and an estimated 57 million in the late 1980s, even though the CPC underwent a series of purges in the 1950s and 1960s, including those during the Hundred Flowers Campaign, the Great Leap Forward (a rapid but disastrous attempt to industrialize and to carry through agricultural reforms), and the Cultural Revolution. During these purges Mao imposed his will upon and cemented his control of the party. Only Mao's absolute authority held communist China together during these ill-considered episodes. Meanwhile communist China became a nuclear power, setting off around 20 nuclear explosions in 1975 and accumulating around 300 **nuclear weapons**.

Zhou and then Mao each died in 1976 and a power struggle within the CPC ensued. After Zhou's death Deng Xiaoping, who had remained an important figure in the CPC even though he had been purged during the Cultural Revolution, expected to take on the role as second-in-command. However, it was Mao's chosen comrade Hua Guofeng who assumed Zhou's post of acting prime minister, then deputy chairman, of the CPC. Upon Mao's death Hua took control, arresting the far-left Gang of Four, led by Mao's widow Jiang Qing. In addition to his post as prime minister, Hua took Mao's position of Chairman of the CPC. In 1980, after much political fighting within the CPC in which Hua and even Mao were discredited, Deng reestablished the long-defunct secretariat, with Hu Yaobang as general secretary. This weakened Hua's position at the top of the CPC and, indeed China. Hu replaced Hua as chairman in 1981. Deng brought the Gang of Four to trial, each member receiving life imprisonment. Deng's group finally defeated that of Hua at the Twelfth Congress of the CPC in 1982. The chairman's office was abolished and the general secretary's office became the most important party office. This office was still occupied by Hu. Deng sat at the top of the party and Chinese politics until his death in 1997, even though he held none of the formal offices that traditionally gave politicians supreme power in communist countries. He did, however, hold the chair of the Central Military Commission that has become a key post in Chinese communism.

Deng began to open up the Chinese economy to Western **capitalism** and, successfully, sought better relations with Washington and Tokyo. Political reform within China did not accompany these economic and diplomatic maneuvers. Deng rejected calls for the introduction of democracy. In 1989 protests by students for democratization within communism were met with a massacre by the military in Tiananmen Square. General Secretary Zhou Ziyang had refused to impose martial law during the Tiananmen Square crisis, and was replaced later in 1989 by Jiang Zemin. Jiang also became the Chinese president in 1993.

In the 1990s and early twenty-first century the CPC continued to introduce capitalist economic reforms and foreign investment while disallowing any political, democratic reforms. The Chinese economy grew rapidly but the CPC continued to stamp out dissent and to ignore demands for human rights to be respected. Inequality between city-dwellers and peasants grew, and corruption became a major problem. By 2000 CPC membership had reached 63 million. The Sixteenth Congress of the CPC in 2002 marked the beginning of the first orderly transition of power since the revolution of 1949, as Hu Jintao succeeded Jiang as general secretary. Hu Jintao was also elected president by the National People's Congress in 2003. He promised to tackle corruption. When Jiang stepped down from the chair of the Central Military Commission in 2004, the orderly transfer of power was complete.

COMMUNIST PARTY OF THE RUSSIAN FEDERATION [*KOM-MUNISTIČESKAJA PARTIJA ROSSIISKOI FEDERACII* (KPRF)]. The KPRF was founded in 1993, and is widely recognized as the successor to the Communist Party of the Soviet Union (*Kommunističeskaya Partija Sovetskogo Soyuza*—KPSS) and its Russian branch. The KPSS was itself formed in postrevolutionary Russia in 1921 as the successor to the Bolsheviks, which **V. I. Lenin** had brought into being. The party became the KPSS in 1925, when **communism** in the Soviet Union had consolidated under Joseph Stalin (1879–1953). The Soviet Union was a one-party **Marxist-Leninist** state. Stalin turned the Soviet Union into a dictatorship. Stalin eliminated most of the senior party members including **Leon Trotsky** who, in exile, denounced the Soviet Union as a degenerated workers' state. The KPSS was the dominant force in the **Comintern**. After the death of Stalin in 1953 Nikita Khrushchev (1894–1971) became leader and denounced Stalin's brutality and corruption of socialism. He, however, supported the use of force to crush the rebellion in Hungary in 1956. Khrushchev continued to attempt limited political reforms but was ousted by hardliners led by Leonid Breznhev (1906–82). Breznhev took over the leadership in the 1964, becoming general secretary in 1966, and ruled until his death in 1982. This was followed by brief spells under the leadership of the general secretaries Yuri Andropov (1914–84) and Konstantin Chernenko (1911–85).

Mikhail Gorbachev became general secretary in 1985. He attempted, with his ideas of *glasnost* (openness) and *perestroika* (restructuring), to slowly transform the Soviet Union into a socialist democracy. Also, the different countries within Russia were given greater autonomy in 1990, when the Communist Party of the Russian Soviet Federal Socialist Republic was created as the Russian branch of the KPSS. Gorbachev had initiated political reforms that escalated out of his control. Following the collapse of communism in Eastern Europe, the Soviet Union itself collapsed in 1991, after hardliners in the KPSS had staged an unsuccessful coup to unseat Gorbachev.

The KPSS was banned in 1991 by the new Russian president Boris Yeltsin. Under Yeltsin Russia descended into economic and political chaos, meaning that when the ban was lifted soon afterward, the new KPRF attracted considerable support, becoming a major political force in the parliamentary elections to the *Duma* of 1993. In those elections the KPRF emerged as the largest party with 157 seats out of 450, but was kept out of power by other parties. Although it had been reduced to 113 seats in the elections of 1999, it was still the largest party. Nevertheless, it was still kept out of power by centrists and supporters of a continuation of **capitalist** economic reform. Moreover, it was unsuccessful in attempting to secure the presidency, the KPRF leader Gennady Zyuganav losing to Vladimir Putin in 1999. The KPRF campaigned for a combination of socialism, with a regulated market, and Russian **nationalism**. It suffered, however, from an aging support base, finding it difficult to attract younger supporters. In elections to the *Duma* in December 2003 the KPRF was reduced to 51 seats with 12.6 percent of the vote, but remained the second largest party behind United Russia, which gained 22 seats with 37.6 percent of the vote. In March 2004 Nikolai Kharitonov of the KPRF unsuccessfully challenged Putin for the presidency. Kharitonov only won 13.7 percent of the vote.

CONFEDERATION OF THE SOCIALIST PARTIES IN THE EUROPEAN COMMUNITY (CSPEC). The CSPEC was set up in Luxembourg in June 1973 as a successor to the Bureau of Social Democratic Parties originally formed in January 1957. As an associated organization with the **Socialist International**, CSPEC aimed to strengthen the European socialist movement, to exchange information between socialist/social-democratic **political parties**, and to guarantee close relations with the **Socialist Group in the European Parliament**. In 1990 the CSPEC represented 16 parties in 13 countries. The CSPEC was succeeded in 1992 by the **Party of European Socialists** (PES).

CONGRESS SOCIALIST PARTY. *See JANATA DAL* (SECULAR).

CONVERGENCE FOR SOCIAL DEMOCRACY [*CONVERGENCIA PARA LA DEMOCRACIA SOCIAL* (CpDS)]. Since gaining independence from Spain in 1968 Equatorial Guinea has been ruled by two presidents from the Nguema family, this being an inhospitable climate for socialism. Obiang Nguema restored constitutional rule in 1982, after a period of military rule since a coup in 1979 led by Obiang to overthrow his father, Macías Nguema. The reforms of 1982 introduced a House of Representatives, but Nguema continued to approve and lead a Council of Ministers. An opposition alliance emerged which included the CpDS but boycotted the 1993 multiparty elections. In November and December 1994 the CpDS became the first opposition party to hold a congress in Equatorial Guinea. In the parliamentary elections of March 1999 the CpDS won only one of 80 seats but rejected the results, alleging irregularities. Later in 1999 the CpDS gained full membership in the **Socialist International**. The CpDS was one of only two opposition **political parties** that did not boycott the parliamentary elections of April 2004, but won only two of 100 seats under continuing repressive conditions for opponents of the ruling party.

CO-OPERATIVE COMMONWEALTH FEDERATION. This Federation was a political movement founded in western Canada in 1932 by farmers, socialist groups, and the Brotherhood of Railway Employees. It advocated the **nationalization** of banks, essential services, and natural resources, programs to stabilize the prices of **agricultural** produce, **social security**, producers' and consumers' cooperatives, programs to create jobs, graduated **taxation**, and government economic planning generally. Representatives of the federation first gained government in Saskatchewan in 1944. During the 1950s it attracted about 15 percent of the vote in national elections. It was a member of the **Socialist International** and in 1961 became one of the founders of the **New Democratic Party**.

COOPERATIVE MOVEMENT. *Cooperative movement* is a general term for groups of voluntary associations whose members work together for their mutual economic advantage through the production or distribution of goods and services. With **trade unions** and **political parties**, the cooperative movement was one of the main strands in the history of democratic socialism and the most practical expression of the collectivist impulse that gathered force during the nineteenth century. Cooperatives began in Britain at least as early as the 1760s. In 1760 a cooperative flour mill was owned and operated by shipwrights employed at the government dockyard at Woolwich, London. The mill was burned down; arson by six bakers was suspected but not proved. In 1769 some weavers at Fenwick in Scotland formed a cooperative society, the first such society formed in Britain. Although there was some revival of interest in cooperatives during the inflationary 1790s, it was not until the late 1820s that there was a more sustained renewal of interest under the stimulus of **Robert Owen**. Although Owen's ideas were impractical as far as cooperatives were concerned, his legacy was important for holding five national conferences between 1831 and 1833, thereby providing a precedent for later developments. Elsewhere in Europe cooperative societies were formed in France and Italy beginning in the 1830s. Although not officially political, national conferences of these societies that were held later in the century contributed to the growth of a wider outlook and added to the cohesion of **working-class** movements in Western Europe.

In the United Kingdom, the cooperative movement was revived permanently at Rochdale, England, when 28 flannel weavers met after a failed strike in 1843 and decided to form a cooperative store based on cash-only sales, charging the going commercial rate for goods, supplying good quality goods at the correct weight, and distributing a dividend to members based on the profits. It is less well known that the principles included the concept of vertical integration—seeking to control the production of goods as well as their selling—and forming links with national and international bodies of a similar kind. The Rochdale store was opened in December 1844. After trading for a year, it had 80 members, a figure that grew to 12,000 by 1894. The principles of the Rochdale store provided a model for cooperatives everywhere.

The British cooperative movement grew from 15,000 members in 1851 to 340,550 by 1872 and to 1.8 million by 1900, within 1,817 locally controlled societies. A very important development occurred in Manchester in 1863 when the **Co-operative Wholesale Society** (CWS) was formed. The success of the CWS gave the whole movement a financial strength it might have otherwise lacked. The cooperative movement was important not just for improving the living standards of members by the payment of the dividend, but also as a source of unadulterated food at a time when adulteration of food by retailers was rife. Cooperatives were strongest in manufacturing and mining areas where they were able to supply large, stable working-class communities. They assisted union members and their families during strikes and played an occasional part in twentieth-century British labor politics. One reason for the success of the British cooperative movement was that it pioneered both retailing and wholesaling and anticipated trends often well before private enterprises. Cooperatives were far less successful in countries where wholesaling and retailing were well organized.

The cooperative movement often figured in debates about what form a future socialist society should take. Producer cooperatives were favored by **Ferdinand Lassalle** and received support in the **Gotha Program** of the **German Social Democratic Party** in 1875. One of the best points **Eduard Bernstein** made about the need to update the ideas of **Karl Marx** in the 1890s was that Marx did not take into account the remarkable growth of the cooperative movement. In 1902 **Karl Kautsky** envisaged that the socialist society of the future would have consumer and producers' cooperatives as well as **nationalized** industries.

In 1895 the **International Co-operative Alliance** was formed in London by representatives from Britain, Belgium, Denmark, France, Netherlands, Hungary, Italy, Russia, Serbia, Australia, India, Argentina, and the United States. Consumer cooperatives also became a feature of retailing in Britain, Belgium, Israel, and Scandinavia but not the United States. By 1919 they claimed 4.1 million members in Britain. In Italy and Germany the cooperative movement was suppressed by the fascists and its considerable assets were seized. Where permitted, the cooperative movement grew steadily after 1945, particularly **agricultural** cooperatives in Asia and Africa. British consumer cooperatives have declined since the 1960s. In Western economies, **producer cooperatives** have not been particularly successful. In the 1970s, however, a radical cooperative movement gained support for its idea of widespread workers' control of the workplace, known as *autogestion*. In Venezuela there was a huge expansion of the cooperative sector after **Hugo Chávez** won the presidential elections of 1998 and 2000. *See also* CO-OPERATIVE PARTY.

CO-OPERATIVE PARTY. The Co-operative Party was formed by the British **cooperative movement** at its congress at Swansea, England, in May 1917. Previously the movement had relied on a joint parliamentary committee (originally formed in 1880 with the Liberal Party) to represent its interests. Although a minority in the co-operative movement had long advocated direct political representation, it was the discriminatory economic policies of the British government against the movement during World War I that tilted the balance of opinion in its favor. Specifically, the movement was denied representation on wheat, sugar, and coal commissions, even though it was then the United Kingdom's largest sugar wholesaler and retailer. It was also threatened with being included in excess profits **tax** legislation. The vote in favor of the formation of the Co-operative Party was carried by 1,979 to 201. In 1918 10 Co-operative Party candidates stood for election, of which one was elected to the House of Commons.

Relations between the Co-operative Party and the **British Labour Party** were harmonious. Although a general understanding between the two parties was reached in 1926 to 1927, no formal agreement was signed until 1938. From 1946 candidates for the Co-operative Party campaigned as "Labour and Co-operative." Despite its unusual nature, the arrangement between the two parties has worked well. The Co-operative Party has declared that it is Labour's sister party. In 1945 23 members of the Co-operative Party were elected to the House of Commons, the party's highest level of representation until 1 May 1997, when 24 members were elected in the landslide to the British Labour Party. By 2005 the Co-operative Party was represented by eight members of the Scottish Parliament, five in the Welsh Assembly, and over 700 councillors in local government. At the general election of May 2005, 29 Labour and Co-operative members were elected to parliament.

CO-OPERATIVE WHOLESALE SOCIETY (CWS). The CWS was formed in Manchester, England, in 1863 to provide a national wholesaling service to the **cooperative movement**. It was not just the first body of its kind in the cooperative movement but also one of the first national wholesalers in the world. Representing 18,000 members in 1864, it had grown to 1.2 million by 1900 and to nearly 4.6 million by 1930. The CWS also undertook a range of educational and other activities designed to promote and extend cooperation. The CWS provided a model for other countries such as Belgium (1900) and the countries of Scandinavia (1918). An International Co-operative Wholesale Society was formed in 1924.

In 1994, despite substantial declines elsewhere in the British cooperative movement since the 1960s, the CWS still represented 8.2 million members and has been commercially successful. For the year ending January 1994 it had a turnover of 7.1 billion pounds and represented 8.2 million members. The CWS merged with Cooperative Retail Services in 2000 and was renamed the Cooperative Group in 2001.

CRAXI, BETTINO (1934–2000). An Italian socialist politician, Bettino Craxi was born in Milan and was active in the socialist **youth** movement and journalism in the 1950s. Using Milan as his power base, he was a protégé of Pietro Nenni (1891–1980) and became a member of the central committee of the **Italian Socialist Party** (*Partito Socialista Italiano*—PSI) in 1957. From there he went on to be a member of the national executive of the PSI in 1965 and deputy president from 1970 to 1976. In 1976 he became general secretary of the PSI, a post he held until 1993. In 1977 he became a vice president of the **Socialist International**. In 1983 he formed a coalition government—the first to be headed by a prime minister from the PSI—that lasted until 1987. In the 1990s Craxi became the focus of attention for his part in the widespread corruption that was revealed in Italian politics. In July 1994 he was convicted of fraud and sentenced to eight and a half years in jail. But as he had moved to Tunisia and claimed he was too ill to return to Italy, the sentence was made in absentia. He died in exile.

CROSLAND, CHARLES ANTHONY RAVEN (1918–77). A British labor theorist, author, and politician, Anthony Crosland was born in

St. Leonard-on-Sea, Sussex. During World War II he served as a parachutist. In 1956 he published *The Future of Socialism*, advocating that the **British Labour Party** should shift its emphasis from the **nationalization** of industry to its modernization. He argued that Keynesian economics solved the main problems of the management of **capitalist** economies, particularly **unemployment**, and that the prime concern of socialism should be to ensure the equitable distribution of the benefits of economic growth. His views were criticized for ignoring the importance of efficient government administration, long a concern of **Fabianism**. Crosland led an unsuccessful campaign in 1959 to 1960 to remove the **socialization objective** from the constitution of the British Labour Party. He served in the cabinets of Labour governments in 1964–66, 1966–76, 1974, and 1974–77. His **revisionist** ideas were absorbed by his party in practice, though not in theory.

CUBAN COMMUNIST PARTY [*PARTIDO COMMUNISTA CUBANO* (PCC)]. The roots of the PCC stretch back to the establishment in 1925 of the Popular Socialist Party (*Partido Socialista Popular*—PSP), which had links with Cuban **trade unions**. For many years the PSP cooperated with Fulgencio Batista's dictatorship in return for toleration of the party's existence. Fidel Castro, operating outside of and indeed in opposition to the communist PSP, led an unsuccessful attempt to overthrow the renewed Batista regime by force on 26 July 1953. Castro was arrested and many of his followers killed. In the suppression that followed not only did Castro's July 26 Movement suffer, but also the communist PSP, which, on the basis of **Leninism**, condemned Castro's spontaneous and, according to the PSP, opportunist action.

Castro was freed in a general amnesty in 1955 and went into exile. He returned under heavy fire the following year with his July 26 Movement. The few survivors of the landing consolidated their resources in the Cuban mountains, where they built support and launched raids on the Batista regime. During 1957 and 1958 a significant section of the PSP lent their support to Castro. After he and his second-in-command, Ernesto [Che] Guevara, had led the revolutionary overthrow of the dictatorship in 1959, Castro, having few political organizational resources, utilized the PSP, even though he had yet to embrace **communism** at this stage. He became prime minister broadly as a radical democrat who also appealed to anti–United States **nationalism**.

At the time of the revolution Cuba was predominantly agrarian, with **agriculture** and the **capitalist** economy more generally heavily dependent on sugar and foreign investment. Finding that private entrepreneurs were unwilling to cooperate with his policies for social justice if this affected their profits, he turned to communism gradually. His conversion led to a deterioration of relations between Cuba and the United States, especially when Castro applied a **nationalization** program to a wide range of enterprises, including American ones. On increasingly bad terms with the United States, Castro improved relations with the Soviet Union. After the unsuccessful, United States–supported invasion of ex-Cubans at the Bay of Pigs in 1961, Castro established links with Moscow and tentatively embraced **Marxism**-Leninism. That year the July 26 Movement merged with the PSP to form the Integrated Revolutionary Organization. The following year Castro barred leading members of the PSP from taking important roles in this organization, which he dissolved in 1963. Castro created in its place the United Party of the Socialist Revolution, ensuring that PSP members did not become dominant. This new party only survived until 1965, when the PCC emerged from it, becoming the sole party in Cuba, with Castro as party leader. Over the next decade communism became firmly entrenched in Cuba, with crucial economic relations with, and assistance from, the Soviet Union.

In 1976 the PCC approved a new communist constitution and Castro was elected president. Since then, the PCC has remained the sole party in Cuba. When the Soviet Union collapsed in 1991 Cuba lost valuable aid and subsequently imposed rationing. Washington tightened its long-established trade embargo on Cuba in 1993. During the 1990s the CCP established closer economic ties with China, which continued to be governed by the **Communist Party of China**. When the left-wing **Hugo Chávez** was elected president of oil-producing Venezuela in 1998 and 2000, Castro developed closer relations with that country.

CURTIN, JOHN JOSEPH (1885–1945). Australian prime minister from 1941 to 1945, John Joseph Curtin was born in Creswick, Victoria. He worked as a printer and a clerk before joining the Victorian

Socialist Party in about 1906. In 1916 he was briefly jailed for his opposition to conscription. In 1917 he moved to Western Australia and became editor of the *Westralian Worker*. He was elected to the federal parliament in 1928 for the **Australian Labor Party** and defeated in 1931 but regained the seat in 1934. He became leader of the federal parliamentary party in 1935. On 7 October 1941, Curtin became prime minister after the failure of the previous conservative government to maintain its majority in the House of Representatives. As wartime prime minister, Curtin recalled the Australian forces committed to the Middle East back to Australia (1941) and appealed to the United States for help (1942). His administration introduced reforms that extended the **welfare state** in Australia, for example, **unemployment** and sickness benefits in 1944. The strain of World War II contributed to Curtin's death at the age of 60.

CZECH SOCIAL DEMOCRATIC PARTY [*ČESKÁ STRANA SOCIÁLNĚ DEMOKRATICKÁ* (CSSD)]. The CSSD was founded in 1878 and functioned as an autonomous part of the **Austrian Social Democratic Party** from 1889 to 1911. A social-democratic party was formed in Bohemia in 1896, and a separate National Socialist Party was formed in 1897. Despite its name, this party was a genuine socialist party with no connections with fascism. At the 1907 national elections, the social democrats attracted 40 percent of the vote. The membership of the CSSD rose from 40,000 in 1900 to 150,000 in 1913. During World War I, national independence became the leading issue for Czech socialists. Thomas Masaryk (1850–1937), a **liberal** and professor of philosophy at Prague University, joined by three socialist groups, achieved a merger of Bohemians and Slovaks to form the Czech Republic in 1918. The CSSD participated in the coalition government for the first time in 1919. At the 1920 elections, the CSSD received 25.7 percent of the vote and the National Socialists, 8.1 percent. The formation of the Czech Communist Party caused a split in the CSSD. In March 1939 the Czech Republic was dissolved with the Nazi occupation.

The CSSD was revived in the Czech lands only in 1945. At the elections in 1946 the CSSD attracted 13 percent of the vote, compared to 13 percent for the National Socialists and 40 percent for the **communists**, who were held in high esteem for leading the resistance to Nazi rule. In 1948 the CSSD was forced to merge with the Communist Party and henceforth existed only as a party in exile.

In November 1989 preparations were made to revive the CSSD and it was officially reestablished in March 1990. Of its 11,000 members at that time, about 20 percent had been members before 1948. By September 1992 the membership of the CSSD had risen to 14,000, and it had become a full member of the **Socialist International**. Yet the CSSD attracted only 3.8 percent of the vote in the June 1990 elections. On 1 January 1993 Czechoslovakia was peacefully divided into the Czech and Slovak Republics despite broad popular opposition to the move. In February 1993 the CSSD adopted as its official title *Česká strana sociálně demokratická*. Between June 1992 and June 1996 the CSSD increased its share of the vote in national elections from 6.5 to 26.4 percent. In the elections to the national Assembly on 14–15 June 2002, the CSSD won 70 seats with 30.2 percent of the vote. This made it the biggest party in the assembly, and its leader Vladimír Špidla became prime minister of a centrist coalition government. Also on the left, the Communist Party of Bohemia and Monrovia performed well, winning 41 seats with 18.5 percent of the vote. The CSSD was unsuccessful in the presidential elections the following year. In elections to the European Parliament in June 2004, the CSSD took two of the Czech Republic's 24 seats, the two members working in the **Party of European Socialists**, with which the CSSD was affiliated. In July 2004 Špidla resigned as both leader and prime minister. He was replaced by Stanislav Gross, who resigned as prime minister in April 2005 after allegations of financial wrongdoings. Deputy CSSD leader Jiri Paroubek took over as prime minister of the coalition government. *See also* DIRECTION-SOCIAL DEMOCRATS.

– D –

DANISH SOCIAL DEMOCRATIC PARTY [*SOCIALDEMO-KRATERNE* (SD)]. Socialism in Denmark had an unpromising beginning. In 1872 the Danish section of the **International Workingmen's Association** tried to hold a meeting in support of striking bricklayers, but it was dispersed by the police. In 1876 some socialists and **trade union** members created a joint political and economic labor organization, but it was not until February 1878 that the SD was formed. In 1884 the SD scored its first electoral success when two of its representatives were elected to the lower house of the Danish parliament (*Folketing*) and gained 4 percent of the total vote. Party membership rose from 14,000 in 1890 to 30,000 in 1901 and to 49,000 in 1913. The SD increased its share of the national vote from 19 to 30 percent between 1901 and 1913. In 1916 the leader of the SD, **Thorvald Stauning**, accepted an invitation to join the cabinet of the Radical Party. For most of the period from 1916 to 1920 he served as minister for labor. After the 1924 elections, the SD formed its first government, which lasted until 1926. In 1928 it declared a membership of 148,500 to the **Labor and Socialist International**.

In 1929 the SD regained power in coalition with the Radical Party. In 1935 the SD and the Radical Party won a majority in the upper house (*Landsting*) for the first time, which enabled the DSDP government to introduce a wide range of progressive laws. The SD was fiercely democratic and anticommunist. In 1936 it issued a declaration against **communism** and refused any cooperation with the Communist Party including the creation of a **popular front** to fascism.

After the Nazi takeover of Denmark in April 1940, the five largest **political parties** put their differences to one side and agreed to unite to secure the "independence and integrity" of Denmark. Following the 1943 elections, the SD received 46 percent of the vote making it the largest party. After the Danish parliament refused to hand over saboteurs to the Nazis in 1943, the Germans declared martial law and arrested thousands. Active resistance to Nazi rule continued for the rest of World War II. After the war, the SD formed a coalition government that lasted from May to October 1945 and governed in its own right from 1946 to 1950 and from 1953 to 1968; it claimed 123,000 members in 1975. The SD led minority governments from 1971 to 1973, 1975 to 1982, and in January 1993 Poul Nyrup Rasmussen became prime minister. In September 1994 the SD received 34.6 percent of the national vote. In the parliamentary elections of 1998 the SD increased its share of the vote to 35.9 percent, with which it won 63 seats. The small Socialist People's Party took 13 seats with 7.6 percent of the vote.

In the elections on 20 November 2001, the SD suffered a decline in support, winning only 52 seats with 29.1 percent of the vote. The election was the first since 1920 at which another party (the Liberal Party with 56) won the highest number of seats. The Socialist People's Party also fared slightly less well than in 1988, obtaining 12 seats with 6.4 percent of the vote. Following the election a right-wing coalition was formed. In the elections to the European Parliament in June 2004, the SD won five, two more than in the elections of 1999, of Denmark's 14 seats. The SD members worked in the **Party of European Socialists**, with which their party was affiliated. On 8 February 2005 an early general election was held. As a result the SD was reduced to 47 votes with 25.8 percent of the vote. The Socialist People's Party was reduced to 11 seats with 6 percent of the vote and another right-wing coalition government was formed. In April 2005 the SD elected Helle Thorning-Schmidt as leader of the party. *See also* KRAG, JENS OTTO; HANSEN, HANS CHRISTIAN SVANE; HEDTOFT-HANSEN, HANS CHRISTIAN.

DEBS, EUGENE VICTOR (1855–1926). Born in Indiana, Eugene Debs joined the railroad at 15, became a locomotive fireman at 17, and served as secretary of the Terre Haute local of the Brotherhood of Locomotive Firemen for three years. He progressed quickly through the **trade union** ranks and served one term in the Indiana legislature as a Democrat in 1885. Despite his success in leading a craft union, Debs was a supporter of industrial unionism and wanted a single union for the railroad industry. In 1892 he resigned his union posts and organized the American Railways Union, which aimed to recruit all railroad employees. A strike by the union against the Great Northern Railroad in 1894 succeeded, but was followed by the massive defeat of a strike against the Pullman Palace Car Company later in 1894; the union was formally wound up in 1897. Debs was charged with conspiring to interfere with the passage of federal mail and served a six-month jail sentence, which transformed him into a socialist. While in jail he read works by **Edward Bellamy**, **Victor L. Berger**, **Robert Blatchford**, **Laurence Grönlund**, **Karl Kautsky**, and **Karl Marx**.

In June 1897 he formed Social Democracy of America in Chicago, a political party that wanted the **nationalization** of monopolies, public works for the **unemployed**, and an eight-hour working day. With Berger he formed the **Social Democratic Party of America** in 1898, which, following mergers with other parties, became the **Socialist Party of America** in 1901. Debs took part in the formation of the **Industrial Workers of the World** in 1905 but disagreed with its policies and left in 1908. He was a presidential candidate for the Socialist Party in 1900, 1904, 1908, 1912, and 1920. In 1912 he attracted 900,369 votes or 6 percent of all votes cast. Opposed to America's participation in World War I, Debs was convicted under the Espionage Act; pardoned by President Warren G. Harding in 1921, he served three years of a 10-year sentence.

DECOLONIZATION. *See* IMPERIALISM.

DELEON, DANIEL (1852–1914). Left-wing American socialist Daniel DeLeon was believed to have been born on the island of Curaçao in the Caribbean to Dutch-Jewish parents. He was educated in Europe and emigrated to the United States sometime between 1872 and 1874. He taught at a secondary school in New York and went on to graduate from the law school at Columbia University. Later he lectured in international law at the university. After being denied a professorship, he resigned in 1889. He entered radical politics by assisting the mayoralty campaign of **Henry George** in 1886 and became a socialist through reading *Looking Backward* (1888) by **Edward Bellamy**. He was also influenced by Darwinism and **August Bebel**; DeLeon made the first American translation of Bebel's *Woman and Socialism*. Dissatisfied with his experience in both the Knights of Labor and Bellamy's Nationalist clubs, DeLeon joined the **Socialist Labor Party of America** in 1891 and became more extreme in his views. He became editor of its journal, *The People*, and used it to promote the idea of class struggle. The depression of the 1890s encouraged him to believe that **capitalism** could not survive. In 1905 DeLeon helped to found the **Industrial Workers of the World**, but he helped to split it too.

DE MAN, HENDRIK (1885–1953). As a politician and political thinker, Hendrick de Man was a prominent Belgian socialist intellectual. Born in Antwerp he had, before World War I, been an organizer of the Belgian Socialist Youth. In the 1920s he became a controversial figure within the Belgian Workers' Party (later **Belgian Socialist Party**), arguing with senior figures within the party, including the leader **Émile Vandervelde**. According to de Man, the party, along with many other socialists, did not understand that the proletariat acting alone could never establish socialism in European parliamentary regimes. Anticipating ideas that would become prominent in social-democratic circles many years later, he argued that socialists needed to realize that the proletariat must seek allies from other sections of society, including small businessmen and peasants. This in turn meant that there should not be a comprehensive **socialization objective**. Socialization should be limited to banks, other credit institutions, and industries that were already under monopoly control. Supporters of the rival Catholic Party could, he hoped, thus be attracted. In 1926 he published *The Psychology of Socialism*, in which he attacked **Marxist** social determinism and workerism.

The critique of workerism, or manualism, was accompanied in de Man's thought by a belief that intellectuals could play a leading role in changing society from above. As one of the intellectuals in the 1930s he formulated his "Plan of Labor." Based on the ideas he had been proposing during the previous decade, the Plan would become hugely influential upon the development of social democracy. Although the Plan was adopted by his party in 1933, and aroused great interest in other social-democratic parties in Europe, it failed to win the support of the Belgian Catholic Party and its **trade union** section. The socialists were restricted to participation in coalition governments. Moreover, many Belgian socialists who feared that class collaboration would undermine their party's **working-class** influence opposed de Man's ideas and plan.

In 1938, upon the death of Vandervelde, de Man became president of his party. In 1940 he became discredited when he collaborated briefly with the Nazi occupiers, acting as the king's advisor. He later tried to exonerate himself, arguing that he had believed that the Nazis had won World War II, and that his role was to remain in Belgium to try to protect his fellow socialists from the occupying forces. Few took notice of his argument. He had been a collaborator who sought to come to terms with the occupiers. His reputation was permanently tarnished and after the war he was unable to return to Belgium. He died in Switzerland.

DEMOCRATIC ACTION [*ACCIÓN DEMOCRÁTICA* (AD)].
Formed in Venezuela in 1936 by **trade unions**, AD took its present title in 1941, when unions were legalized. Its founder, Rómulo Betancourt (1908–81), led a coup that brought in a constitution (1945–47) but he was ousted in a countercoup in 1948. Following the end of a period of dictatorship in 1958, Betancourt was president between 1959 and 1964 and reformed land ownership and nationalized oil and mineral reserves. In 1966 Democratic Action gained observer status in the **Socialist International**, became a consultative member by 1981, and became a full member in the mid-1980s. In 1986 AD claimed a membership of 1.5 million. Despite serious economic problems since 1987—which caused its popularity to drop—the social-democratic AD continued to be Venezuela's largest single political party.

In the early twenty-first century Democratic Action was eclipsed on the left by the radical president **Hugo Chávez** and his **Movement for the Fifth Republic**. In elections to the National Assembly in July 2000 AD won only 29 of the 165 seats. In December 2005 AD withdrew from elections to the National Assembly, arguing that conditions favored the MVR and its allies.

DEMOCRATIC ACTION PARTY (DAP) (*PARTI TINDAKAN DEMOKRATIK*). The DAP was established in 1966 as the Malaysian section of the People's Action Party of Singapore, which was formed in 1954. After protesting the unfairness of the August 1986 election, in which the DAP won 20.8 percent of the vote but only 13.6 percent of the 177 seats in the house of representatives, the party's leadership was subjected to a government crackdown. Sixteen members were arrested and five received two-year jail sentences. The DAP was made a full member of the **Socialist International** in 1987, when it had about 20,000 members. On 21 March 2004 in the elections to the House of Representatives, which now had 219 seats, the DAP obtained 12 seats with 9.5 percent of the vote.

DEMOCRATIC CONSTITUENT ASSEMBLY [*RASSEMBLE-MENT CONSTITUTIONNEL DEMOCRATIQUE* (RCD)]. The RCD was formed in Tunisia in 1934 and took its current name in 1988. Its founder, Habib Ben Ali Bourguiba (1903–2000), was arrested after a general strike in 1938. He was exiled and the party, which sought independence from France, was dissolved. The RCD was reestablished by Salah Ben Yousseff in 1945 to resume the fight for independence, which it gained in 1956. As founding father of independent Tunisia, Bourguiba became president in 1957 and held the post until 1987, when he was deposed in a bloodless coup. The RCD was a member of the **League of African Democratic Socialist Parties** in 1987, when it claimed a membership of 800,000. It has been the ruling party of Tunisia since then and a full member of the **Socialist International** since 1993.

Bourguiba's successor as president, Zine El Abidine Ben Ali, also of the RCD, continued with the modernization of Tunisia, introducing democratic reforms. However, like his predecessor, he experienced the long-running struggle with Islamic fundamentalists. There was sporadic violence and a suspension of political rights. In the elections of October 1999, at which there was a turnout of 91.4 percent, Ben Ali was reelected president with 99.4 percent of the vote. In parliamentary elections that year the ruling RCD took 148 of the 182 available seats in the National Assembly with 91.6 percent of the vote. In a 2002 referendum that infuriated the opposition, a referendum abolished the three-term limit to the presidency. Ben Ali subsequently won a fourth term in 2004. The opposition refused to participate in the elections in protest at the constitutional extension of the presidency.

DEMOCRATIC LABOR PARTY [*PARTIDO DEMOCRÁTICO TRABALHISTA* (PDT)]. A Brazilian Socialist Party was formed in 1916. In 1921, following its decision to join the **Comintern**, a minority broke away and formed a rival party in 1925. In 1928 the **trade unions** formed the Labor Party of Brazil (*Partido Trabalhista Brasilero*), based on the **British Labour Party**; the party claimed 800,000 members by 1930 of whom about 270,000 were trade union members. The party was suppressed by the dictatorship of Getúlio Vargas in the 1930s. Its ability to function in the post-1945 period was limited by government repression, with **political parties** being banned in 1965. The PDT was formed in Brazil in June 1980 by Leonel da Moura Brizola (1922–2004), who had been leader of the Labor Party of Brazil before 1965 and returned in September 1979 after 15 years in exile. The PDT joined the **Socialist International** as a consultative member in 1986 and became a full member in 1989.

Nevertheless, the party has been eclipsed by the **Workers' Party**. In the elections of 1998 the PDT won only 25 seats, with 4.6 percent of the vote, in the lower house of the legislature—the Chamber of Deputies—and no seats in the Senate. The Workers' Party fared better in those elections. In the legislative elections of 2002, the PDT obtained 21 seats in the lower house and five in the Senate. The Workers' Party won greater representation in both houses and secured the presidency that year.

DEMOCRATIC LEFT [*IZQUIERDA DEMOCRÁTICA* (ID)]. The ID was established in Ecuador in November 1977. In 1978 it won 11 percent of the presidential vote in the national elections. It has been a member of the **Socialist International** since 1987. Its membership in 1985 was claimed to be 250,000. In parliamentary elections of May 1998 the ID took 17 of the 123 seats. In the late 1990s the ID, along with the other established parties, suffered a lack of support and populists including Lucio Gutiérrez staged a coup in an atmosphere of economic crisis and austerity. Gutiérrez was imprisoned but in October 2002 won the presidential elections, gaining the support of much of the left and of poor indigenous communities with a call for social justice and an end to corruption. In parliamentary elections also held in October 2002, the ID won 13 of the 100 seats.

DEMOCRATIC LEFT ALLIANCE [*SOJUCZ LEWICY DEMOKRATYCZNEJ* (SLD)]. Successor to the Social Democracy of the Republic of Poland (*Socjaldemokracja Rzeczypospolitej Polskiej*—SdRP), the SLD is Poland's preeminent social-democratic party. The SdRP was itself formerly the Polish United Workers' Party (*Polska Zjednoczona Partia Robotnicza*—PZPR), which was the **communist** party that assumed power in 1947 and governed until 1989. The Polish Communist party was founded in 1918, but was dissolved by Joseph Stalin (1879–1953) in 1938 and then became revived during World War II in the early 1940s. Seeking the support of the peasant majority in Poland, the Communist Party changed its name to the Polish Workers' Party in 1942, and merged with the **Polish Socialist Party** in 1948 to form the PZPR. The PZPR transformed itself into the SdRP in January 1990.

After the collapse of Eastern European communism, the SdRP sought to make its presence known on the political scene by contesting the presidential elections of 1990. The SdRP candidate Wlodzimierz Cimoszewicz obtained 9.2 percent of the vote. In 1991 the SLD was formed as an electoral coalition under the leadership of the SdRP, winning second place with 11.99 percent of the vote in elections to the *Sejm* (parliament) that year. Support began to grow and the SLD was successful at the elections to the *Sejm* in 1993 with 37.17 percent of seats. The SLD formed a coalition government with the Polish People's Party, whose leader became prime minister until he was replaced by the SLD's Jozef Olesky and then Cimoszewicz, both in 1995. That year Aleksander Kwaśniewski of the SLD won a narrow victory over Lech Wałęsca, whose *Solidarność* movement had helped bring down communism. In 1996 the SdRP, still at the head of the SLD, gained full membership in the **Socialist International**.

In 1997, the SLD lost the parliamentary elections to a new coalition centred on *Solidarność*. The SLD needed to consolidate its political activities and was transformed from an electoral coalition led by the SdRP into a political party. In 2000 Kwaśneiewski won a further term as president with 53.9 percent of the vote. In 2001 the SLD, in electoral coalition with the smaller **Socialist International** sister party the **Union of Labour** (*Unia Pracy*—UP), won the parliamentary elections with 216 seats, gained with 41 percent of the vote. The SLD-UP coalition also won an absolute majority—75 seats—in the 100-member upper house that can amend or reject laws passed by the *Sejm*. The SLD and UP formed a coalition government, briefly including the Polish People's Party, until 2003, with the SLD leader Leszek Miller as prime minister. Miller's government took Poland into the European Union in 2004, but in so doing generated much opposition in Poland and within the SLD due to the austerity plan that aimed to balance the Polish budget. In March 2004 seven leaders of the SLD formed a new party—Polish Social Democratic Party (*Socjaldemokracja Polska*—SdPL). Due to the split and lack of support for his government, Miller stepped down on 2 May, one day after Poland entered the European Union. Marek Belka of the SLD replaced him. In elections to the European Parliament in June 2004 the SLD-UP coalition took five of Poland's 54 seats and the new SdPL won three of the seats. These five SLD-UP and three SdPL members worked in the **Party of European Socialists**, with which their parties were affiliated.

Economic problems, along with corruption and involvement in the **war** in Iraq, led the popularity of the SLD government to decrease further. The SLD also lost the support of the UP to the SdPL. In the parliamentary elections of September 2005 the SLD suffered a landslide defeat, winning only 55 seats with 11.3 percent of the vote. They failed to take any seats in the upper house. The SdPL did not win any seats in either house. In the presidential elections of October 2005, the constitution did not allow Kwaśneiewski to stand for a further term. Cimoszewicz initially stood but withdrew following the SLD's poor showing in the parliamentary elections.

DEMOCRATIC PARTY OF THE LEFT [*PARTITO DEMOCRA-TICO DELLA SINISTRA* (PDS)]. *See* DEMOCRATS OF THE LEFT.

DEMOCRATIC SOCIALISTS OF AMERICA (DSA). The DSA was formed in 1982 by the merger of the Democratic Socialist Organizing Committee (formed in 1973) and the New American Movement (formed in 1971) in Detroit. It claimed a membership of 7,000 in 1987 and is a full member of the **Socialist International** (SI). More radical than **Social Democrats USA**—the other SI member from the United States—the DSA seeks an extension to political democracy and democratic empowerment in the economy. The DSA National Director Frank Llewellyn criticized the campaign of John Kerry and the Democratic Party in the 2004 elections for failing to advance a progressive agenda. He insisted that the Democrats did not lose because they were too far left, but because they had not advanced a progressive agenda and campaign for social justice.

DEMOCRATS OF THE LEFT [*DEMOCRATICI DI SINISTRA* (DS)]. Formerly the Democratic Party of the Left (*Partito Democratico della Sinistra*—PDS), the DS is contemporary Italy's most prominent socialist party. The PDS was itself formerly the Italian Communist Party (*Partito Comunista Italiano*—PCI) from 1921 to 1991. The PCI became a moderate **communist** party. In 1968 it denounced the Soviet invasion of Czechoslovakia and took a leading role in Eurocommunism. As a Eurocommunist party, the PCI was the largest and most successful of its kind in any Western country. Moves to form the PDS were made just after the fall of the Berlin Wall in late

1989, and the Party's congress in February 1991 gave its approval to the change. The PDS was admitted to full membership in the **Socialist International** in September 1992. The transition to a noncommunist party at first cost the PDS heavily in electoral support and membership. Between 1987 and 1992 the PDS's share of the national vote fell from 26.6 to 16.1 percent and its membership fell from 1.5 million to 1 million over the same period, but since 1992 its fortunes have improved to the point where the PDS has assumed the leadership of the Italian left, particularly after the demise of the **Italian Socialist Party** in November 1994. The PDS was increasingly accepted by the electorate as a genuinely social-democratic party. In the 1994 national elections the PDS became the largest party of the left, with 115 seats. Another party formed out of the PCI was the Communist Refoundation (*Rifondazione Comunista*—RC). The RC became the second largest left-wing party with 40 seats. However, the winner in the 1994 elections was the media tycoon Silvio Berlusconi's *Forza Italia*, which in a fractious coalition with two other right-wing parties, the Northern League and the formerly neofascist *Alleanza Nazionale*, won a majority of seats. Berlusconi became prime minister for eight months. Upon the collapse of the coalition a crisis government of professionals took charge to try to achieve some stability in Italy.

To contest the national elections on 21 April 1996, the PDS formed the Olive Tree (*L'Ulivo*) coalition with four other parties, including the RC and the Greens, and won 284 of the 630 seats in the Chamber of Deputies—it won 21.1 percent of the vote for the one quarter of seats elected by proportional representation—and 157 of the 315 elective seats in the Senate to form a center-left coalition government under the leadership of Romano Prodi, an academic who, although center-left, had experience as a former minister in Christian Democrat-dominated coalitions. The coalition was weakened by the RC's opposition to a proposed budget and reforms, which had resulted in Prodi's resignation in 1998. Massimo D'Alema of the PDS took over the leadership of the coalition. In 1998 the PDS was renamed as the DS and participated in the Olive Tree coalition, which lost power in the May 2001 elections to Berlusconi's House of Freedom coalition, which obtained a majority in both legislative chambers. The Olive Tree coalition took 252 of the 630 seats in the Chamber of Deputies, of which the DS won 172 and won 125 seats in the Senate. In the elections to the European Parliament of June 2004 the DS, campaigning within the Olive Tree coalition, obtained 12 of Italy's 78 seats, down from 16 of 87 in 1999. The 12 DS members worked in the **Party of European Socialists**, with which their party was affiliated. Also in 2004 Prodi's term as president of the European Commission ended, and he returned to Italian politics to help reform the Olive Tree Coalition, in which the DS was joined by the RC and other parties. In the regional elections of April 2005 the Olive Tree Coalition made significant gains from the House of Freedom.

For the 2006 elections, the Olive Tree was transformed into a smaller but more strictly organized alliance of the DS and two center parties. In this form, the Olive Tree participated in the broader Union (*L'Unione*) coalition, which included the RC and many other left and center parties. Led by Prodi, the Union secured 348 of 630 seats in the Chamber of Deputies with 49.8 percent of the vote. Within this total, the Olive Tree alliance took 220 seats with 31.3 percent. Operating as a single party within the Union for elections to the Senate, the DS won 62 of 315 seats with 17.5 percent of the vote, contributing to the Union's 158 seats. Prodi formed a Union government.

DIGGERS. The Diggers were a radical group that emerged during the English Civil War in 1649. Named after the channels they dug to drain unenclosed common wetlands for cultivation, they also called themselves the True Levellers. They established some settlements in Surrey with the object of distributing the produce from common land to the poor. Unlike the **Levellers**, of whom they were an offshoot, the Diggers opposed private property in principle. They opposed the use of violence in achieving their objectives. Whereas the Levellers saw natural law as the foundation of individual and property rights, the Diggers saw natural law as supporting communal rights. Their settlements in Surrey were destroyed by official harassment and violence. The Diggers have been hailed as forerunners of **utopian socialism**. *See also* COMMUNES.

DIRECTION-SOCIAL DEMOCRATS [*SMER-SOCIÁLNA DEMO-KRACIA (Smer-SD)*]. In 2004 *Smer-SD* absorbed the main social-democratic parties that emerged in Slovakia after the fall of **communism** in 1989—the Party of the Democratic Left (*Strana demokratickej l'avice*—SDL) and Social Democratic Party of Slovakia

(*Sociálnodemokratická Strana Slovenska*—SDSS)—as well as several smaller ones and the original Direction-Third Way (*Smer-Tretia Cesta—Smer*). The SDSS was originally part of the **Czech Social Democratic Party** before it was forced to merge with the Czech Communist Party in 1948. The SDSS was reformed in February 1990, but did poorly in the 1990 elections when it received only 1.9 percent of the vote. Even when led by **Alexander Dubček**, it won only 4.86 percent of the vote in 1992. Thereafter the SDSS was still further marginalized, taking less than 0.5 percent of the vote in 1994, the year it became a full member of the **Socialist International** (SI). The main reason for the poor performance of the SDSS was strong competition from the reformed communist party, the SDL.

The SDL began as the Communist Party of Czechoslovakia, which was formed in 1921. With the end of communist rule in 1989, the Communist Party in Slovakia reformed itself as a democratic party along the lines of members of the SI in 1991. In 1992 the SDL obtained 10 of 51 seats with 14.44 percent of the vote in the Slovak elections and in 1993 claimed a membership of 50,000. It did not contest the 1994 elections but won 23 seats with 14.66 percent of the vote in the parliamentary elections of 1998 and entered a coalition government. In the parliamentary elections of 2002, however, the SDL obtained only 1.36 percent of the vote and did not win any seats. Unlike its rival the SDSS, the SDL did not become a member of the SI.

Smer was formed in 1999. Its leader Robert Fico, once of the SDL, modeled the party on New Labour, as **Tony Blair** had styled the **British Labour Party**. In the parliamentary elections of September 2002 *Smer* won 25 of the 150 seats with 13.46 percent of the vote. In October 2003 *Smer* entered into an agreement on close cooperation with the SDSS. In the elections to the European Parliament of June 2004 *Smer* took three of Slovakia's 14 seats. The three *Smer* members worked in the **Party of European Socialists**, with which their party was affiliated. In December 2004 *Smer* merged with the SDL and SDSS to form *Smer-SD*, which replaced the SDSS in the SI.

DOMINICAN REVOLUTIONARY PARTY [*PARTIDO REVOLU-CIONARIO DOMINICANO* (PRD)]. The PRD was formed as the *Partido Revolucionario Dominicano* in Cuba in 1939 by opponents, led by Juan Bosch (1909–2001), of the Trujillo dictatorship in the

Dominican Republic. After General Rafael Trujillo's assassination in 1961, the PRD won power in the 1962 presidential election with Juan Bosch as president, but he was overthrown by the military in 1963. The United States restored civilian rule in 1965 by military force. The PRD, which led the opposition to military rule, remained in political opposition until May 1978, when Silvestre Antonio Guzmán Fernández won the governmental elections; it was the first peaceful transfer of political power in the history of the republic. The PRD became a full member of the **Socialist International** in 1987, when it claimed a membership of 750,000. One year earlier, in 1986, the PRD had lost the presidency, which it did not regain until 2000, when Rafael Hipólito Mejía Dominguez was elected. In parliamentary elections on 16 May 2002 the PRD won 73 of the 149 seats. On that day it took 29 of 31 Senate seats contested. In May 2004 the PRD lost the presidential elections to the Dominican Liberation Party.

DUBČEK, ALEXANDER (1921–92). A Slovak **communist** and politician, Alexander Dubček was born in Uhrovec and fought in the resistance to the Nazi occupation during World War II. He became first secretary of the Communist Party of Slovakia in 1963. In January 1968, helped by Slovak **nationalists** and reformers, he replaced Antonin Novotný as first secretary of the Czechoslovakian Communist Party. From April 1968 his attempts to liberalize the communist regime—summarized in the slogan "communism with a human face"—included measures such an independent judiciary, human rights, and economic decentralization. His reformist government was crushed by a Soviet invasion and Dubček was removed from office. Dubček's last political role was to lead the Social Democratic Party of Slovakia (*Sociáldemokratická Strana Slovenska*). *See also* DIRECTION-SOCIAL DEMOCRATS.

DUTCH LABOR PARTY [*PARTIJ VAN DE ARBEID* (PvdA)]. The roots of the PvdA can be traced back to Dutch Social Democratic Workers' Party (*Sociaal-Democratische Arbeiders Partij*—SDAP). Like the Belgian Workers' Party (later **Belgian Socialist Party**), the SDAP developed in a society deeply divided by **religion**. **Trade unions** began to emerge after 1866 and became more active during the 1870s. A Social Democratic League had been formed in 1881. Originally committed to securing a classless society by constitutional means, it was hampered by the limitations of the political system and tended toward **anarchism**; it dissolved itself in 1900. Drawing on the **German Social Democratic Party** for financial and policy support, the SDAP was formed in 1894 and developed along similar lines. The SDAP was essentially a moderate party and by 1895 claimed 700 members. In 1909 many of its left-wing members were expelled. Between 1900 and 1913 its membership rose from 3,000 to 26,000, reaching 48,000 in 1920. Its share of the vote in national elections grew slowly. Between 1888 and 1901, the vote for the SDAP increased from 1 to 10 percent. By 1919 it attracted 19 percent of the national vote following the institution of universal male **suffrage** in 1918. In 1920 the SDAP adopted a **socialization objective** for both industry and **agriculture**.

Although invited to participate in a Liberal Party cabinet as early as 1913, the SDAP declined and did not participate in a coalition government until 1939. Rejection by Dutch Catholics limited the ability of SDAP to become a majority political party. In a declaration issued in 1935 the party maintained the need for the class struggle and the ultimate desirability of the classless society, but proposed practical measures for economic stimulation.

Willem Schermerhorn (1894–1977), a leader of the Dutch Anti-Fascist League in the 1930s and a Resistance leader from 1943, was prime minister of a provisional coalition government from June 1945 to July 1946. He was also one of the prime movers in the transformation of the SDAP into the PvdA in 1946 through its merger with the Radical Democrats, the Christian Democrats, and other **political parties**. As in Austria, the spirit of cooperation among parties was heightened by harsh wartime imprisonment. To the disappointment of the PvdA, the **communists** emerged after World War II with enhanced status because of their leading role in the Resistance. The communists won 11 percent of the vote in 1946 and 6 percent in 1952. Religious parties also reestablished themselves. The PvdA continued to poll between 23 and 30 percent of the vote between 1946 and 1972, but was unable to bridge the religious divisions of Dutch society. Surveys of voting preferences in 1968 found that 55 percent of those who were not church members voted for the PvdA (compared to 72 percent in 1956), 36 percent of those who were members of the Dutch Reform church voted for the PvdA (compared to 41 percent in 1956), and only 7 percent of those who were Roman Catholics voted for the PvdA (compared to 5 percent in 1956). In 1959 the PvdA removed all references to **Marxism** in its statement of principles. In 1970 the PvdA claimed a membership of 98,700 and 73,000 in 1992.

The PvdA has been a participant in coalition governments from 1965 to 1966 and from 1981 to 1982; in 1989 the PvdA entered into a coalition government with the Christian Democratic Appeal Party. At the 1994 national elections, the PvdA received 24 percent of the vote. The party's Wim Kok became prime minister at the head of a three-party coalition in August 1994 and the first PvdA leader to exclude the Christian Democrats from the government. At the elections of 1998 Wim Kok retained the post of prime minister and in 2000 his government introduced radical social legislation including the legalization of euthanasia and gay marriage. Kok's government resigned in April 2002 over inaction in preventing the massacre at Srebrenica in the Balkan wars during 1995. In the subsequent elections of July 2002 the PvdA lost power after winning 23 of the 150 seats in the assembly. A center-right coalition was formed, but this collapsed later the same year. In the elections of 22 January 2003 the PvdA improved its position, winning 42 seats with 27.3 percent of the vote. Also on the left, the small Socialist party won nine seats, as it had done the previous year. Nevertheless, the Christian Democrats emerged with the most seats and formed another center-right coalition in May 2003. In elections to the European Parliament in June 2004 the PvdA obtained seven of the 27 seats held by the Netherlands, thus improving on six from 31 in 1999. The PvdA members worked in the **Party of European Socialists**, with which their party was affiliated.

– E –

EBERT, FRIEDRICH (1871–1925). A German socialist politician, Friedrich Ebert was born in Heidelberg. Unlike his father, who was a master tailor, he became a saddler and traveled around Germany to find work. His participation in **trade unions** led to him becoming a socialist by 1889, but his socialism was of a very moderate kind, akin to the **liberalism** of most of the British labor movement, which saw socialism as a means of improving the living standards of the **working class**. In 1905 he became secretary-general of the **German So-**

cial Democratic Party (*Sozialdemokratische Partei Deutschlands—* SPD) and greatly improved its administration, something not possible in the political repression that had characterized most of the party's history up to that time. In 1913 he took over from **August Bebel** as SPD chairman after his election to the Reichstag (parliament) in 1912. In August 1914 he persuaded the SPD to vote for the war appropriations, a policy that committed the party to an unlimited war. By 1917 antiwar feeling had divided the party and in March an independent group was formed that split from the "majority" party.

After the German army's offensive on the Western Front failed in August 1918, Germany's political fabric began to unravel. In October 1918 Ebert was a pivotal player in organizing a coalition government of socialist and nonsocialist parties under Prince Max of Baden. Ebert was strongly opposed to the revolutionary impetus that had developed, but was unable to stop it. On 9 November 1918 Prince Max asked him to take his place as chancellor. Ebert accepted, but the next day **Philipp Scheidemann** proclaimed a republic in Berlin and the two socialist parties (the majority and the breakaway left-wing independents) formed a provisional government and made Ebert its chancellor. The government announced a program of **nationalization** of industries that had become monopolies and the introduction of a democratic constitution. After elections in January 1919 a coalition of the SPD, the Catholic Center Party, and the Democratic Party gained a majority and elected Ebert as the first president of the Weimar Republic (11 February), a post he held until his death.

Ebert, determined not to follow the unhappy example of **Alexander Kerensky**, a moderate socialist who lacked the means to be effective, crushed the uprising led by the socialist radicals **Karl Liebknecht** and **Rosa Luxemburg** in January 1919. To do this, Ebert and his government needed the active support of the political right, including groups such as the *Freikorps* (volunteers of ex-army officers). The price of this support was that the military-industrial complex and conservative power structure that had ruled Germany before 1918 was left largely intact. In the elections of June 1920 the Social Democrats lost much of their electoral support although they continued to be partners in coalition governments.

The next internal crisis was the Kapp putsch in March 1923, which attempted to restore the monarchy. This was followed by other failed right-wing coups in October and by Adolf Hitler's in November in

Bavaria. Externally, Germany faced great economic difficulties. Following the declaration that Germany had defaulted on its obligations to supply coal, the French army occupied the industrial region of the Ruhr. Ebert was wrongly blamed by the German right wing for the country's woes despite the evacuation of the Ruhr and the resolution of the reparation payments issue. The pressures hastened his death in February 1925. *See also* BAUER, GUSTAV ADOLF.

ECONOMISM. Economism was a movement within Russian socialism in the early 1900s that was comparable with revisionism. S. N. Prokopovitch, a follower of **Eduard Bernstein**, argued that the political and economic struggle for socialism should be divided: the political struggle should be the province of the liberal **middle class** and the economic struggle should be left to the **working class**. He was concerned that if the working class entered the political arena, they would alienate the progressive middle class, which would then support the czarist regime. **V. I. Lenin** attacked this argument in *What is to Be Done?* (1902). He argued that the working class needed its own political organization and that the political and economic struggle could not be divided. *See also* LENINISM.

EDUCATION. Education, along with shorter working hours, higher wages, and the extension of **suffrage**, was an objective of social reformers before the rise of socialism as a movement. For example, Thomas Paine listed the education of children as the third point in his suggested eight points of social reform in *The Rights of Man* (1791). **Robert Owen** placed great emphasis on education as an avenue for social and moral improvement in his factory at New Lanark, Scotland, but he also showed that it was not compatible with child labor, particularly the extraordinarily long hours children were expected to work. From the late 1840s education was a part of the socialist agenda. The *Communist Manifesto* (1848) linked free education for all children in public schools and the abolition of child labor among its demands for social reform.

In 1866 and again in 1868 the congresses of the **International Workingmen's Association** resolved to press for legislation for the eight-hour working day and public education for all children. From the 1870s education assumed greater priority as a socialist objective. The lives of British **working-class** socialists from the last third of the nineteenth century testify to their determination to acquire literacy and education despite long hours and harsh living conditions. Nonconformist **religions** such as the Quakers provided important avenues for working-class leaders to acquire an education. For instance, **Tom Mann** and **Ernest Bevin** both gained some of their education from the Quakers. **Peter Kropotkin** and other **anarchists** recognized the importance of education in preparing children for adulthood but were critical of the rote learning of their day and supported technical education, especially mathematics and science.

In Sweden the labor movement established its own schools to provide education for the working class and training for labor leaders. Out of 600 pupils who attended these schools between 1906 and 1920, about 10 percent had parliamentary careers with the **Swedish Social Democratic Workers' Party** (*Sveriges Socialdemokratiska Arbetareparti*—SAP) or in the socialist media. Others were active in the **trade unions** or the **cooperative movement**.

Socialists realized the value of education, not just as a means of social and moral improvement in its own right, but also as a way of easing the way for the spread of socialism. The motto of the Democratic Federation (formed in 1880), the forerunner of the **Social Democratic Federation** (SDF), was "Educate. Agitate. Organize." In 1884 the SDF advocated not only free compulsory education for all but also the provision of one wholesome meal a day for each school child. In 1893 **Henry M. Hyndman**, William Thorne (a socialist and leader of the gas workers' union), and S. D. Shallard formed a deputation to the minister of education to present their case for the free school meals. Education was also a priority for the **Independent Labour Party** (ILP); there were 57 socialists on English school boards by 1897, most of them members of the ILP. By the 1890s free and compulsory education at all levels was a standard feature of the programs of socialist/social-democratic parties in Europe and Australia. The program of the **Socialist Labor Party of America** demanded free, compulsory education for all children less than 14 years of age.

The socialists' support for higher education for the working class also helped to give rise to the Workers' Educational Association in England in 1904; an International Workers' Educational Association was formed in 1920. In the 1920s the British socialist theorists **Harold Laski** and **G. D. H. Cole** both emphasized the importance of education. Laski stressed that one social goal should be to lay genuinely adequate opportunities open to all. Every child must have the opportunity to fully develop his or her faculties. It was important that the talents of those who have special capacity to benefit social **welfare** should not be wasted. Cole said that it was not only more education that was needed for the majority to flourish, but also education of a better sort that would not perpetuate class differentiation. Ignorance was the main enemy and widening the mental horizon of all would mean that there would be far more pressure for improved social conditions and opportunities.

When the SAP began its long tenure of government in Sweden in 1932 it implemented **policies** the rationale of which bore affinities to those urged by Laski in the previous decade. The influential Swedish sociologists Alva and Gunnar Myrdal stressed that money spent by the state on the education of children would reap rewards. Such spending would be an investment in human capital. Society as a whole would thus benefit. Comprehensive education became a central element of the Swedish social-democratic project. Also in the 1930s the first government of the **New Zealand Labour Party** (NZLP) introduced education policies based on equal opportunities and social justice.

The argument for comprehensive education was not confined to socialists. Indeed, in an essay first published in 1943 the British socialist thinker **R. H. Tawney** noted that observers from not only Scandinavia but also the distinctively nonsocialist France disapproved of what he called the "caste system" in the United Kingdom, which was characterized by exclusiveness. Comprehensive education was, though, considered by socialists as a part of their broader project to end social inequality and promote social justice, a project that considered equal access to education as a human right. In this project the **British Labour Party** was one of a number of social-democratic parties that called for reform of educational processes in the postwar era. In its **Godesberg program** of 1959 the **German Social Democratic Party** (*Sozialdemokratische Partei Deutschlands*—SPD), for example, argued that education should develop the full capacities of each individual. Socialists also began to collaborate internationally in the **International Falcon Movement–Socialist Educational International**. Socialist teachers, furthermore, began to organize in the International Union of Social Democratic Teachers, which subsequently became the **International Social Democratic Union for Education**.

In a well-known lecture of 1966, reprinted in his book *Socialism Now* in 1974, the British Labour Party politician and theorist **C. A. R. Crosland** made an influential socialist case for comprehensive education, arguing that education and society interact with each other at every point. He argued that separation is unjust, labeling children for life when in fact measured intelligence is not fixed and innate, but develops according to nurture, stimulus, and response which vary among children of different environments and backgrounds. This meant that the odds in terms of life chances were loaded against working-class children. This was also a waste of valuable resources that could be used for the good of society.

In the late 1970s socialists in the advanced industrial countries came under pressure to adapt to the global recession. By the early 1980s public indebtedness was becoming a serious problem. Demands upon public expenditure were growing while tax-generating growth declined. A large share of the growth of expenditure was on welfare services including education. The NZLP and **Australian Labor Party** responded with programs of deregulation and **privatization**, policies that many regarded as a betrayal of the ideals of the parties. Schools in New Zealand were to be run on a competitive basis along the lines of market economics, with parental choice. In Australia there was a similar market-inspired emphasis, where attempts were made to enable children and adults to gain skills and education without relying wholly upon the distribution of resources. Nevertheless, these measures were made in an attempt at efficiency rather than cost cutting in the short-term, and spending on education was left largely intact in each of these countries.

These responses would influence social-democratic parties in Europe and elsewhere in the 1990s, encouraged by the "third way" politics of the **British Labour Party**. **Tony Blair** brought Labour back to power in 1997 after languishing in opposition, promising to focus on and increase spending for education. Blair introduced performance targets and national strategies for literacy and numeracy. After winning the general election of 2001 Blair, inspired by the earlier reforms by the ALP and NZLP, began to introduce more in the way of parental choice and competition between schools. Also, in response to budgetary problems, he argued for greater expenditure by the private sector in education and a reduction of local authority control. After winning the general election of 2005 Blair faced increasing dissent within his party regarding his education reforms, which many considered to be endangering the public good and disadvantaging working-class children. *See also* SOCIALIST SUNDAY SCHOOLS; YOUTH.

EGALITARIANISM. Egalitarianism—the doctrine asserting that all people should enjoy significant equality—has been central to the theory and practice of socialism. Early notions of egalitarianism arose during the English Civil War among the **Levellers** who in turn were linked with radical elements of millenarianism that had been present in **Christianity** in Western Europe at least since the eleventh century. The **Diggers** were more radically egalitarian. Egalitarianism was given sharper focus by the American Declaration of Independence (1776) and the French Declaration of the Rights of Man and of the Citizen (1789) and was absorbed and adapted by socialist writers from the 1840s.

ELY, RICHARD THEODORE (1854–1943). Economist and academic, Richard Ely was a leader of **Christian socialism** in the United States. His books included *French and German Socialism* (1886), *The Labor Movement in America* (1886), *The Social Aspects of Christianity* (1889), and *Socialism: An Examination of Its Nature, Its Strengths and Its Weaknesses with Suggestions for Social Reform* (1894). He was professor of political economy and director of the school of economics, political science, and history at the University of Wisconsin.

ENGELS, FRIEDRICH (1820–95). With **Karl Marx**, Engels is one of the central figures in the history of socialism. The son of a wealthy textile manufacturer, he was born in Barmen, Germany, but was a rebel at heart. Through business trips to England from 1842 he became acquainted with **Chartism** and the followers of **Robert Owen**. In 1845 he published his best-known work, *The Condition of the Working Class in England* in German; it was not published in English until 1885.

In 1842 Engels met Marx, who became his lifelong friend, collaborator, and financial supporter. In 1848 Engels was expelled from Germany for participating in the revolts of that year. From 1850 until his death he lived in England; he was an employee and then partner in his father's business between 1849 and 1869. With Marx, he wrote the *Communist Manifesto* (1848) and *The German Ideology.* He edited the second and third volumes of Marx's *Das Kapital.* He also helped found the **International Workingmen's Association** in 1864. Engels was important in socialist history for the way he sustained Marx and publicized his works. Despite his **wealth,** Engels was a founder of the revolutionary tradition of socialism that evolved into **Leninism** and **communism.** *See also* MARXISM.

ERFURT PROGRAM. The Erfurt Program was the official policy of the **German Social Democratic Party** adopted at the party's conference at Erfurt in October 1891. Drafted by **Karl Kautsky** and **Eduard Bernstein,** the preamble to the Erfurt Program set out a Marxist view of economic and social development that depicted the crushing of small businesses by large ones, the growing impoverishment and exploitation of the urban proletariat and peasant proprietors, and increasing levels of **unemployment.** It identified the private ownership of the means of production as the source of this social misery, and it advocated as the solution a political struggle to capture power in order to achieve a social revolution that would abolish class distinctions and create a society in which there was equality of rights and duties for both sexes. This struggle was recognized as international in character.

The program demanded universal, equal, and direct **suffrage** by secret ballot; the people's right to initiate or veto legislation; a militia rather than a standing army; freedom to express opinions, hold meetings, and form associations; abolition of laws which treated **women** as inferior to men; a declaration of **religion** as a private matter; compulsory, public, secular, and free **education;** free legal administration and assistance; free medical assistance and burials; and a graduated income and property **tax.** For the protection of labor, the program demanded: the eight-hour day; the prohibition of child labor (under 14 years of age) and night work for most employees; an unbroken period of at least 36 hours rest per week; prohibition of payment in kind instead of wages; government inspection of factories; the legal equality of agricultural laborers and domestic servants with industrial employees; confirmation of the rights of association; and giving employees a share in the administration of their insurance scheme. It remained the party's official policy statement until 1921, when the Görlitz Program replaced and omitted much of the **Marxism**, which was largely replaced in 1925 by the Heidelberg Program.

ERLANDER, TAGE (1901–85). A Swedish social-democratic leader, Tage Erlander was born in Ransater and graduated from the University of Lund in 1928. He entered local government politics in 1930 for the **Swedish Social Democratic Workers' Party** and was elected to the *Riksdag* (parliament) in 1932. In 1938 he became minister for social welfare in the government of **Per Albin Hansson**. After Hansson's unexpected death in 1946, Erlander became prime minister and was one of the architects of the **welfare state** in Sweden. He supported Sweden's political neutrality and the United Nations. He was prime minister in a series of coalition governments from 1946 to 1968. He retired from politics in 1969.

ESTONIAN SOCIAL DEMOCRATIC PARTY [*SOTSIAALDEMO-KRAATLIK ERAKOND* (SDE)]. Estonia was part of the Russian empire between 1721 and 1918, gaining independence along with the other Baltic states, Latvia and Lithuania. The Estonian Socialist Worker's Party (*Eesti Sotsialistlik Tööliste Partei*) was created in 1925 from the merger of the Social Democratic Workers' Party (which had been formed in 1917 from the Russian Social Democratic Party) and the Independent Socialist Party (previously the Party of the Social Revolutionaries). At the election of 1923, the two parties that formed the Estonian Socialist Workers' Party together received 18.7 percent of the vote. They participated in a coalition government between December 1924 and June 1926, and the new party provided the prime minister for a government between November 1928 and May 1929. In 1928 this party had 4,500 members and was a member of the **Labor and Socialist International**.

After receiving 24 percent of the vote in the 1931 elections, the socialists entered into a coalition government that remained in office until January 1932. Adolf Hitler's victory in Germany in 1933 encouraged fascist sentiment in Estonia and the other Baltic states. The government was replaced and a state of emergency was declared. The socialists were forced underground and Estonia was incorporated into the Soviet Union.

The first freely conducted elections since the early 1930s were conducted in Estonia in March 1990, and the country's independence was formally recognized by the Russian government in September 1991. The SDE was formed in September 1990 and became a member of the **Socialist International** that year. In 1996 the SDE merged with the Estonian Rural Centre Party to form the People's Party Moderates (*Rahvaerakond Mõõdukad*). From 1999 to 2002 the Moderates participated in a three-party, center-right coalition, which broke down due to disagreements between the parties. In elections to the National Assembly in March 2003 the Moderates won six seats with 7 percent of the vote. In February 2004 the Moderates held a congress, at which it was agreed to rename itself as the Estonian Social Democratic . Party, with a manifesto entitled "For Equal Society." The party campaigned for a **welfare state** and stressed the importance of cooperation with **trade unions** and other European social-democratic parties. In June 2004, the Party won three of Estonia's six seats in the European Parliament, the three members working in the **Party of European Socialists**, with which the SDE was affiliated. *See also* LATVIAN SOCIAL DEMOCRATIC WORKERS' PARTY; LITHUANIAN SOCIAL DEMOCRATIC PARTY.

EUROPEAN SOCIAL FORUM (ESF). The ESF is a continental initiative based on its parent **World Social Forum** (WSF). After the success of the first WSF, which in 2001 had brought together in Brazil **anticapitalist** organizations and groups from around the globe, the ESF aimed to serve a similar function in Europe. Like the WSF, it is broadly **new left** rather than specifically socialist. Socialist themes and groups are, though, prominent. The ESF invites people and groups opposed to war, **racism**, and corporate power, and seeks to promote global justice, workers' rights, and a sustainable society.

The first ESF was held in Florence in 2002, and the second in Paris the following year. The third gathering, in London in 2004, which attracted around 20,000 people, hosted over 250 speakers and involved over 500 meetings. The themes of forums are broadly those of the WSF, reflecting the adoption of the WSF Charter of Principles, which expresses support for peaceful opposition to neoliberalism and capitalist **globalization**.

EUROPEAN SOCIALIST MOVEMENT (ESM). The ESM was created in February 1947 as the **Socialist Movement for the United States of Europe**; it was reorganized as the ESM in 1961; its title can also be translated as the European Left Movement. The purpose of the ESM was to promote a politically united Europe based on socialism. In 1995 the ESM had sections in five countries: Belgium, France, Germany, Italy, and the United Kingdom. The movement was, however, marginalized by other continental socialist parties and alliances. *See also* INTERNATIONALISM.

– F –

FABIANISM. Fabianism was named after the ancient Roman Republican general Quintus Fabius Maximus (deceased 203 B.C.) who was famous for his delaying tactics in dealing with a superior adversary, Hannibal. Fabianism was essentially a **middle-class** organization that sought to convert Britain to socialism by gradually infiltrating the decision-making process, particularly the governing bureaucracy. It sought to win over educated opinion to socialism through well-reasoned publications. Beginning as a quasi-religious group in London in January 1884, its membership came to include some of the most important personalities in British socialism, notably **Beatrice and Sidney Webb**, **George Bernard Shaw**, **G. D. H. Cole**, **Harold Laski**, and **H. G. Wells**. The Fabian Society never had a large membership—it only had 173 members by 1890 and 730 in 1904—but it gained adherents in other English-speaking countries, for example, the Fabian society that was begun in Australia in 1895 and influenced **revisionism**. In 1900 the Society helped found the **British Labour Party** (Labour), with which it has always been affiliated. In 1931 there was a split in the society when the New Fabian Research Bureau was established, although this body reunited with the Fabian Society in 1939. In 1943 the Fabian Society claimed a membership of 3,600 in the United Kingdom, scarcely a mass movement, but it included many influential people in its ranks.

Assessments of the direct impact of Fabianism, apart from special members such as Sidney Webb, are difficult because Fabianism aimed for gradual change over long periods of time, changes that could occur for reasons other than Fabianism. Fabian societies continue to produce pamphlets on a range of issues of public importance and remain committed to generating ideas, good government, informed discussion, and the dissemination of socialism. Following the general elections of 1997, at which Labour returned to power, there were around 200 Fabian MPs in the House of Commons.

FEBRUARY REVOLUTIONARY PARTY [*PARTIDO REVOLU-CIONARIO FEBRERISTA* (PRF)]. The PRF was formed in Paraguay in 1936. It led a coup on 17 February 1936, which established Colonel Rafael Franco as leader of the government. He was overthrown by a countercoup in August 1937, and the PRF was banned until mid-1946. It participated in government in 1947 but was expelled for plotting a coup. Franco led a liberal-**communist** rebellion against the right-wing Colorado Party government. In 1954 a coup brought the Colorado Party's General Alfredo Stroessner Mattiauda to power. Stroessner's one-party regime, in which elections were meaningless, ruled until 1998. In 1959 the PRF purged its left wing and allied itself with the Liberal Party. It was legalized but boycotted elections after 1968, claiming they were fraudulently conducted. The PRF has been a full member of the **Socialist International** since the 1970s but has not enjoyed success. It did not win any seats in Paraguay's parliamentary elections of 2003.

FEDERALISM. Federalism was an important concept in the political thought of **Pierre-Joseph Proudhon**. As outlined by him in 1863, it meant the administrative reorganization of society based on **communes** or associations of individuals. The nation state was to be replaced by confederations of smaller administrative units. The goal of federalism was to place the control of administration as close to the people as possible. *See also* ANARCHISM: NATIONALISM.

FINNISH SOCIAL DEMOCRATIC PARTY [*SUOMEN SOSIALI-DEMOKRAATTINEN PUOLUE* (SDP)]. Socialist ideas began to be promoted in Finland in 1895, and a labor party was created by a national **trade union** convention in 1899. In 1903 this party, drawing on the example of the **Austrian Social Democratic Party**, renamed itself the SDP, adopted a socialist program that included the preamble from the **Erfurt Program**, and joined the **Second International**. As part of the Russian empire until 1917, Finnish socialists were preoccupied with national independence. After the 1905 uprising in Russia, the vote was granted to all Finns aged at least 24 years, a reform the SDP was able to use to gain representation in the unicameral parliament. It proposed progressive labor and socialist legislation but the czar overruled these initiatives. Finnish opposition to Russia resulted in direct rule from Moscow in 1909 and 1910. Finnish opposition to participation in World War I brought further repression. Even so, the SDP gained 43 percent of the national vote in 1913, the highest level achieved by a European labor/social-democratic party at that time. World War I brought a loosening of Russian control, and in the 1916 election, the SDP won 103 of 200 seats, the first time that a labor/socialist party had ever won a majority in a legislature in Western Europe. The March 1917 revolution in Russia did not bring the independence requested by the Finnish government, and the severe economic hardships brought by World War I encouraged political extremism.

With the German defeat in 1918, Finland was left alone to organize its own affairs. The government declared Finland to be a republic in June 1919. In 1926 the SDP formed a minority government under **Väinö Alfred Tanner** who was also leader of the **cooperative movement**. Although it lacked a majority, Tanner's government was able to institute old age pensions, **health** insurance, and a reduction in duties on food. It was brought down by the other parties in December 1926. The SDP was a member of the **Labor and Socialist International** in 1928 and claimed a membership of 37,700.

The SDP attracted 34 percent of the vote in 1930 but remained in opposition until 1937, when it joined the Agrarian Party in a coalition government that lasted until 1943. Karl August Fagerholm (1901–84), an SDP member and minister for social affairs, was forced to resign from the cabinet of this government for refusing to deport **Jews** who fled to Finland from Nazi persecution in Germany.

Relations with the Soviet Union polarized Finnish politics from 1939 with adverse effects on the support of the SDP, which became increasingly opposed to Finnish participation in Germany's war with the Russians. The SDP was a partner in governments to varying degrees from 1946 to 1958. The government of Fagerholm (July 1948 to March 1950) was overshadowed by Soviet relations and by internal struggles with its **communist** sympathizers.

Pressure from the Soviet Union, whose rulers saw the SDP as pro-American, ensured that no social democrat served in a coalition cabinet between 1958 and May 1966. Rafael Passio (1903–80), who was SDP chairman from 1963 to 1975, was prime minister from May

1966 to March 1968. His administration was dominated by internal economic difficulties and by the need to placate the Soviet Union over the neutrality of Finland.

By 1975 the SDP had 101,000 members and it has been a major participant in coalition governments from 1966 to 1970, 1972 to 1975, 1977 to 1991, and since 1995. Between 1991 and 1995 the SDP increased its share of the national vote from 22 to 28 percent. Tapio Paavo Lipponen of the SDP became prime minister of Finland in April 1995 at the head of an unusual "rainbow coalition," ranging from the conservative National Coalition Party to the Left Alliance. The rainbow coalition was renewed after the elections of 1999, once again with Lipponen as prime minister.

On 6 February 2000 Tarja Halonen of the SDP won the second round of the presidential elections, having taken first place with 40 percent of the vote in the first round on 16 January. She thus became Finland's first female president. In the parliamentary elections of 16 March 2003 the SDP won 53 of the 200 seats in the parliament (*Eduskunta*) with 24.5 percent of the vote. The SDP formed a coalition government along with the Center Party and Swedish People's Party. In elections to the European Parliament in June 2004 the SDP won three of Finland's 14 seats, having taken three of 16 in 1999. The SDP members worked in the **Party of European Socialists**, with which their party was affiliated. In January 2006, Halonen was reelected as president with 51.8 percent at the second round of voting.

FIRST INTERNATIONAL. *See* INTERNATIONAL WORKING-MEN'S ASSOCIATION.

FISHER, ANDREW (1862–1928). Coal miner and **Australian Labor Party** (ALP) leader, Fisher was born in Crosshouse, Ayrshire, Scotland. He began work as a coal miner at the age of 10 and was elected secretary of the Ayrshire Miners' Union in 1879; he was an admirer of **Keir Hardie**. In 1881 he was blacklisted by the coal mine owners for taking part in a 10-week strike. He emigrated to Queensland, Australia, in 1885 where he again worked as a coal miner, read works on social science and economics, and became an active member of the Amalgamated Miners' Association, which provided him with a base for entry into politics. In 1893 he was elected as a member of the Queensland parliament and served in the brief ministry of Andrew

Dawson (1863–1910) in 1899, the first labor government in the world.

In 1901 Fisher moved from state to federal politics and in 1907 became minister for trade and customs in the labor government of **John Christian Watson**. He was elected leader of the parliamentary ALP in 1904 and served three terms as prime minister and treasurer (1908–09, 1910–13, and 1914–15).

At the April 1910 election, the ALP won a majority in both houses of the federal parliament, which enabled Fisher's administration to introduce many important reforms, including a graduated land **tax** (1910), a federal government-owned bank (the Commonwealth Bank, 1911), and a maternity allowance (1912). His administration also sought (unsuccessfully) through referenda to give the federal government the power to make laws with respect to monopolies (1911), trade and commerce and corporations (1913), trusts, and the **nationalization** of monopolies (1913). Fisher retired from politics in October 1915 in favor of **William Morris Hughes**.

FLAGS. Following its use by the **Paris Commune**, the red flag was the flag of socialism from the 1870s. Children carried red flags to socialist **Sunday schools** in Britain in the years leading up to 1914. This custom was continued by the **communists** after the success of the Bolshevik coup in Russia in 1917. To distinguish themselves from the communists, the Spanish **anarcho-syndicalists** adopted a black and red flag divided diagonally; the red component was maintained as a gesture of international solidarity. Later the **anarchists** used the black flag. The **British Labour Party** used a red flag as its emblem until 1986 when it was replaced by a red rose with a long stem.

FOURIER, FRANÇOIS-MARIE-CHARLES (1772–1837). Charles Fourier was one of the leading theorists of **utopian socialism**. The son of a tradesman, he was born at Besançon, which was also the birthplace of **Claude-Henri Saint-Simon**. He was an unsuccessful commercial clerk and then a clerk at Lyon. In 1812 he inherited his mother's estate, which enabled him to devote himself to full-time writing. Fourier's thought derived from Newtonian physics as well as from criticisms of contemporary **capitalist** society. He wrote *Théorie des quatre mouvements et des destinées générales* in 1808 (translated in 1857 as *The Social Destiny of Man; or, Theory of the Four Movements*) and *Le Nouveau Monde industriel* (The New Industrial World) in 1829. He envisaged a harmonious society based on cooperative communities that he called *phalanstères* (phalanxes). Their purpose was to ensure equitable distribution of economic rewards and to lower wastage. He was one of the earliest proponents of profit sharing. Fourier's ideas were primarily aimed at **agriculture**, not manufacturing, which was only a small part of the French labor force. His ideas attracted support and phalanx-style settlements were set up both in France and the United States. At least 40 phalanxes were established in the United States, one of which, the North American Phalanx at Red Bank, New Jersey, survived in a much modified form until the late 1930s. *See also* COMMUNES.

FOURTH INTERNATIONAL. In 1938 **Leon Trotsky** founded the Fourth International in response to the failure of the **Comintern** to act as a progressive revolutionary organization. The Fourth International remains a small organization that has always suffered from splits. After the most serious split in 1953, when some leading members sought to distance the organization from Trotsky's insistence on the revolutionary role of the **working class**, the International Committee of the Fourth International was founded to lead the International according to Trotsky's ideas. The International Committee continued to lead the Fourth International in the early twenty-first century.

FRANCHISE. *See* SUFFRAGE.

FRANKFURT DECLARATION. The Frankfurt Declaration was the general name for the *Aims and Tasks of Democratic Socialism*, which was a statement of the fundamental principles of democratic socialism issued by the **Socialist International** at its inaugural congress in Frankfurt, Germany, on 3 July 1951. Set in the context of the Cold War, the declaration was intended to place as much distance as possible between social democracy and **communism**. The declaration began by condemning **capitalism** for placing the "rights of ownership before the rights of man," for its economic inequality, and for its support of **imperialism** and fascism.

The main points of the declaration were that although socialism was an international movement, it was a plural one that did not demand uniformity of approach; there could be no socialism without the freedom of democracy; the economic goals of socialism were full employment, the **welfare state**, raising living standards, and a fairer distribution of income and **wealth**; **nationalization** was one way of achieving public ownership of the means of production, distribution, and exchange, but not necessarily the only way, and institutions like the **cooperative movement** could play their part in replacing the private profit motive of capitalism with the public interest of socialism; **trade unions** were affirmed as a necessary part of a democratic society; economic and social planning did not necessarily have to assume a centralized form and might be decentralized; there were other ways, apart from money, of rewarding individuals for their labor; all forms of discrimination, whether legal, political, or economic, must be abolished regarding **women**, races, regions, and any other social groups; any form of colonialism or **imperialism** is rejected; **war** is largely the outcome of struggle for freedom. *See also* GODESBERG PROGRAM; LIBERALISM.

FRASER, PETER (1884–1950). Born in Rosshire, Scotland, Fraser became **New Zealand Labour Party** (NZLP) prime minister from 1940 to 1949. His father was a member of the Liberal Party, which was then the political avenue for British **working-class** activists. Fraser joined the **Independent Labour Party** in London in 1908. He emigrated to New Zealand in 1910 and worked as a longshoreman in Auckland and edited a socialist newspaper, *The Worker*. He opposed conscription during World War I and served a jail term. In 1918 he was elected to the House of Representatives for the NZLP. He became deputy leader of the NZLP in 1934. After the party's victory in the national election of 1935, he was made minister of **education**, health, and marine, a position he held until April 1940 when he was elected prime minister after the death of **Michael Savage**. As prime minister, he devoted himself to the mobilization of New Zealand to the Allied **war** effort. After World War II, he continued to build the **welfare state** in New Zealand. He ceased to be prime minister in December 1949 because of ill health.

FRENCH SOCIALIST PARTY [*PARTI SOCIALISTE* (PS)]. Although France was one of the cradles of European socialist thought and one of the main centers of left-wing activity generally, the level of electoral support for socialism and its actual successes have been historically low compared to the United Kingdom and Germany. The reasons for this contrast lie in the peculiarities of France's political and economic development. Industrialization and urbanization, the two preconditions of socialism, were much less in evidence in France than they were in either the United Kingdom or Germany. **Agriculture** and small communities retained their importance until the middle of the twentieth century. As late as 1946, 36 percent of the French labor force worked in agriculture and 47 percent of the people lived in rural communities. Industrialization in France was characterized by small-scale industries and industrial growth before 1920 was inhibited by the large amount of capital invested in other countries, particularly the Russian empire.

There has also been a significant anticlerical strand within French society. After the French Revolution of 1789 there was a general separation between Catholicism and **liberalism**, with the Catholic Church becoming identified with the forces of privilege and conservatism. Thus those who wanted to change society were, by that fact, defined as anti-Catholic. Similarly, sincere Catholics could not be part of the left wing. This made it extremely difficult for socialist parties to win over practicing Catholics. In 1956, 28 percent of the members of the French **working class** were practicing Catholics and the socialist vote in areas with high active Catholic populations was low before the 1970s. French radical politics also had a greater tendency toward factionalism than was apparent in the United Kingdom and Germany. This factionalism was widely seen as a weakness by socialists outside France, especially by the well-organized Germans.

In April 1905, at the urging of the **Second International**, two of the leading socialist parties in France—the **Possibilists** and the followers of **Jules Guesde**—were united under **Jean Jaurès** to form the *Parti Socialiste* (*Section française de l'Internationale ouvrière*— SFIO) or Socialist Party (French Section of the Workers' International), although these two very different parties continued to maintain separate organizations. Electoral support for the Socialist Party rose from 10 percent in 1906 to 17 percent in 1914 and to 21 percent in 1919. During World War I, three socialist deputies, Guesde, Marcel Sembat, and Albert Thomas (who became the first director of the International Labour Organization in 1919), served in the government between 1914 and 1917 so as to preserve national unity.

But in 1920 the SFIO was badly damaged when it split into rival **communist** and socialist parties. Between 1920 and 1921 the membership of the SFIO fell from 179,800 to 50,400. The strength of the Communist Party was such that it split the left-wing working-class vote and prevented the SFIO from winning government in its own right. Despite being a reformist socialist party, it was forced to sound more radical than it really was or the communists would have denounced it.

In the early 1930s mutual concern about the threat of fascism drew socialists and communists closer together. In February 1934 the two parties held antifascist demonstrations and in July 1934 they signed a pact creating the **Popular Front**. In the national elections in May 1936 the Popular Front won and formed a government under **Léon Blum**. At the election, the SFIO attracted 21 percent of the vote and the Communists 15 percent. The Blum government was responsible for introducing the modern framework for collective bargaining in France (1936) and attempted to make progressive reforms in France's overseas colonies. The Popular Front government lasted until April 1938. After the German conquest of France in June 1940, the SFIO was outlawed. Blum and other leaders were tried. Others were executed or sent to concentration camps. Socialists and communists worked together in organizing resistance to German rule from June 1941.

After 1947 the SFIO faced a resurgent Communist Party (*Parti communiste français*) that had substantial support among the working-class electorate and controlled the largest national **trade union** federation, the *Confédération Générale du Travail*. In the 1945 elections, the communists attracted more votes (26 percent) than the socialists (25 percent) and maintained this share of the vote until 1956.

Between 1946 and 1973, the SFIO entered a period of long-term decline and disunity. Between 1946 and 1962 its share of the national vote fell from 21 to 13 percent. Over the same period the number of party members fell from 355,000 to 91,000. In 1970 membership reached its lowest point since 1945 — 71,000. This drop also affected the social composition of the membership. In 1951 44 percent of the 116,000 members were employed in blue-collar occupations, but by 1979 only 23 percent of its members worked in blue-collar jobs.

Relations between the socialists and the communists deteriorated after World War II under the impact of the Cold War. In 1945 the

SFIO declined the communists' offer of a political merger (August) and their proposal to form a government (October). The Socialists participated in tripartite governments between April 1944 and May 1947. In 1947 the communists were expelled from the government, and in December the socialist unions left the communist-led national federation and established their own federation (*Force Ouvrière*). In July 1951 the Socialists left the government. In August 1954 the Socialist deputies divided over the European Defense Community. In September 1958 the SFIO split over a new constitution and the participation of **Guy Mollet**, the general secretary of the party, in de Gaulle's government in 1958 to 1959 with dissidents forming the *Parti Socialiste Autonome* (Automomous Socialist Party) which was renamed the *Parti Socialiste Unifié* (United Socialist Party) in 1960. The SFIO continued to decline during the 1960s.

In January 1968 Mollet issued a call for a new socialist party, a call that was taken up in December 1968 when steps began to be taken to form a new party, the *Parti socialiste* (PS), from the merger of the SFIO, the *Convention des Institutions Républicaines* led by **François Mitterrand**, and other left-wing groups. Mitterrand, who became the new party's secretary in 1971, brought together a diversity of socialist and noncommunist groups and worked to make the PS a party of government. In March 1972 the PS issued a new program that was radical in intention but without **Marxist** language. By 1976 the PS had taken the lead from the Communist Party in national elections.

In 1981 the PS won power in its own right for the first time. Mitterrand was elected president on the second ballot in May, and in June 1981 the PS won a large majority in the parliamentary elections that it retained until March 1986. The PS government continued the Gaullist tradition of the president determining general policy with the prime minister and other ministers carrying it out. The government in this period was headed by Pierre Mauroy from May 1981 to July 1984 and by Laurent Fabius from July 1984 to March 1986.

The PS inherited a poorly performing economy in 1981 and sought to stimulate it and reduce unemployment by higher government expenditure. It introduced a **wealth** tax and began a **nationalization** program in 1982. It also reduced the working week, lowered the retirement age, lengthened holiday entitlements, and improved social welfare benefits. These policies ran counter to international economic trends and economic orthodoxy. Inflation continued to be higher than Germany's, and France's general economic performance fell, which was reflected in the deterioration of its balance of payments. In March 1984 there was a reversal of economic policy; government spending was reduced and the government was forced to pay greater attention to international economic pressures. In March 1986 the PS lost its majority in the national assembly elections, although it continued to be the largest single party. A conservative government under Jacques Chirac ruled from 1986 to 1988. Although the PS lost power in its own right in 1986, Mitterrand was able to use his position as president to force compromises on Chirac's policies.

Mitterrand was returned as president in May 1988, and in June 1988 the PS made sufficient gains for it to lead a minority government under Michel Rocard. But the party's support was eroded by continuing high unemployment and the generally mediocre performance of the French economy. Rocard resigned in May 1991 and was replaced by Edith Cresson, who became France's first **woman** prime minister. She was replaced in April 1992 by Pierre Eugène Bérégevoy, a close associate of Mitterrand, after the PS received only 18.3 percent of the vote in regional elections (compared to 29.9 percent in 1986). Bérégevoy remained prime minister until March 1993 when the PS received only 20 percent of the vote in the national elections, and a conservative administration took power. Although Mitterrand was again able to use his position as president to modify conservative policies, his ability to do so was diminished by the unpopularity of the previous socialist administrations. Even so, in the presidential elections of April 1995 the PS candidate, **Lionel Robert Jospin**, who replaced Mitterrand as first secretary of the party in 1981, attracted 23.3 percent of the vote, the highest for any candidate and although he lost to Chirac on the second round of voting by 52.6 to 47.4 percent, his margin of defeat was much less than had been expected.

Persistently high levels of **unemployment** and voter dissatisfaction with the conservative economic policies enabled the Socialist Party under Jospin to win the government in the national elections in May–June 1997, leading a left alliance including the Communists and Greens. When Jospin became prime minister François Hollande took over as first secretary. The government's main achievement was the introduction of a 35-hour working week. However, in April 2002 Jospin came in an extremely disappointing third in the presidential elections, taking only 16.17 percent of the vote in the first round, thus being eliminated from the second round. In June 2002 the Socialists were removed from government in elections to the assembly, winning only 140 seats with 24.1 percent of the vote. This brought to an end five years of cohabitation in French politics. The Communists won 21 seats with 4.8 percent.

In March 2004 the Socialist Party, still led by Hollande, enjoyed a revival at the regional elections. A left coalition led by the Socialist Party and including the Communist Party and Greens won approximately 50 percent of the vote, taking 21 of the 22 regional councils. Furthermore, in elections to the European Parliament in June 2004, the PS obtained 31 of France's 78 seats, an improvement upon the 22 of the country's 87 seats in 1999. The PS members worked in the **Party of European Socialists**, with which their party was affiliated. *See also* AURIOL, VINCENT.

FRIENDLY SOCIETIES. Friendly societies are voluntary associations originally designed to provide members with money in case of **unemployment**, illness, incapacity, or death. Before the twentieth century, they were the main source of **social security** for the **working class**. Prussian miners are known to have formed thrift and friendly societies as early as the sixteenth century. The first friendly societies in France and Britain began in the seventeenth century. In Britain the first friendly (or mutual benefit) societies were formed by sailors who contributed to a common "sea chest." Friendly societies of this kind were formed in Scotland (Bo'ness in 1634 and at St. Andrews in 1643). From the late seventeenth century, other employees began to form friendly societies. They grew out of the trade societies and clubs formed by journeymen, often in taverns and public houses, which catered to the needs of traveling artisans for accommodation and work. They were the ancestors of **trade unions** in many parts of Western Europe and enjoyed steady growth after 1760.

In 1793 genuine friendly societies received legal protection in England provided they could pass inspection by the justices of the peace to prove that they were not really trade unions; in 1801 there were about 7,200 friendly societies with a total membership of 648,000. Because they required regular contributions, friendly societies attracted those in better-paid employment with relatively high job security. By 1815 the membership of friendly societies in England had risen to 925,400. Over the next 60 years the societies enjoyed substantial growth. In 1872 a parliamentary committee found that the membership of friendly societies making official returns was almost 1.9 million. But the true figure was about 4 million members spread among 32,000 societies with a further 4 million having potential access to their benefits. After 1850 some of the better-off trade unions, notably the Amalgamated Society of Engineers, also provided similar kinds of benefits to those provided by friendly societies, but these were exceptions. In Italy, friendly societies developed from the 1830s and they held their first interregional meeting in 1853. *See also* BELGIAN SOCIALIST PARTY; COOPERATIVE MOVEMENT.

FRONT FOR THE LIBERATION OF MOZAMBIQUE [*FRENTE DE LIBERTAÇAO DE MOÇAMBIQUE* (FRELIMO)]. Formed as a resistance movement in 1962 to fight against Portuguese **imperialism** in Mozambique, FRELIMO became the single party after independence in 1974. Independence leader Samora Machel became president in 1975. Adopting **Marxism** and **Leninism**, FRELIMO introduced a **communist** state in Mozambique under the leadership of Machel. FRELIMO faced armed opposition from the guerrillas of RENAMO (*Resistëncia Nacional Moçambicana*) that were established by white Rhodesians and subsequently supported by South Africa as they sought to destabilize Mozambique. FRELIMO faced many years of civil **war** with RENAMO and thus economic hardship. Nevertheless, Machel remained hugely popular until his death in an air crash in 1986.

Machel was succeeded by Joaquim Chissano who was, similarly, a communist. Nevertheless, he began to take a more pragmatic approach to building socialism in Mozambique, eventually denouncing Marxism-Leninism in 1989. The following year FRELIMO adopted a new constitution that introduced multiparty politics, which accommodated RENAMO. Two years later a peace deal was reached. FRELIMO held and won free elections in October 1994, winning 129 of the 250 parliamentary seats. At the same time Chissano was reelected as president with 53.3 percent of the popular vote. The presidential elections were monitored by 2,500 international observers. Soon afterward, FRELIMO achieved full membership in the **Socialist International**. FRELIMO was transformed into a social-democratic party that introduced a managed market economy. In the elections of 1999 FRELIMO was once again successful as Chissano was reelected president with 52.3 percent of the vote and the party improved its share of the parliamentary seats to 133. Renamo declared the elections unfair, leading to rioting the following year. International observers said that the elections had been free and fair, and thus did not accept the RENAMO complaints. In December 2004 Chissano retired from politics and hence did not stand for the presidency that month. The FRELIMO candidate Armando Guebuza won the election. Although RENAMO complained about irregularities, monitors declared the elections largely fair and Mozambique's top judicial body declared Guebuza president in January 2005.

FULL EMPLOYMENT. *See* UNEMPLOYMENT.

– G –

GEORGE, HENRY (1839–97). Although not a socialist, American journalist and single-tax advocate Henry George was an influential figure in late nineteenth-century labor in English-speaking countries. Born in Philadelphia, Pennsylvania, he eventually joined the staff of the *San Francisco Times* in 1866 after a variety of failed business ventures. In his *Progress and Poverty*, published in 1879, he promoted a single capital **tax** on land as the means to eliminate poverty. A popularizer rather than an original thinker, George promoted his ideas through lecture tours to England and Australia. Although his ideas attracted support from the urban **working class**, they failed to be implemented. During his career, George ran for public office a number of times unsuccessfully; for example, in 1884 he ran for mayor of New York City with union backing. George was opposed to socialism. He was also opposed to protectionism, a stand that alienated most of the leaders of organized labor in the 1890s. Ironically, George was important in the history of socialism because he stimulated widespread debate about social reform. For example, **George Bernard Shaw** was partly inspired to become a socialist after attending a lecture George gave in 1882. George's other main works were *Social Problems* (1882) and *The Condition of Labor* (1891). *See also* BELLAMY, EDWARD.

GERHARDSEN, EINAR HENRY (1897–1987). A Norwegian social-democratic leader, Einar Gerhardsen was born in Oslo and began work as a road repairer in 1914. In 1919 he became head of the **trade union** representing road repairers. He became secretary of the Oslo branch of the **Norwegian Labor Party** (*Det norske Arbeiderparti*—DnA) in 1925 and was elected to Oslo town council in 1932. In 1935 he became party secretary. In 1940 he became mayor of Oslo but was forced from office after the Nazi invasion. He joined the Resistance and was arrested by the Gestapo in 1941. He was imprisoned in Sachsenhausen concentration camp until 1944. He was returned to Oslo in 1945 and was released only with the Nazi capitulation in May 1945. As mayor of Oslo, he became leader of the DnA in 1945. He formed a coalition government that lasted from November 1945 to November 1951 and introduced important social welfare programs. He also approved of Norway joining the North Atlantic Treaty Organization in 1949. He held office from January 1955 to August 1963 and from August 1963 to September 1965.

GERMAN SOCIAL DEMOCRATIC PARTY [*SOZIALDEMO-KRATISCHE PARTEI DEUTSCHLANDS* (SPD)]. From its formation in 1875 until 1933 the SPD was the largest and best-organized socialist party in Western Europe. As such, it provided a model for similar parties in Belgium, Austria, and Switzerland. In 1891 it adopted the **Marxist**-influenced **Erfurt Program**, which remained its official program until 1921. Despite its radical posture, the SPD was essentially a moderate organization; in practice, but not in theory, it followed **revisionism**. Denied access to real political power before 1918, it concentrated its efforts on building up supporting social institutions, even to the extent of creating what amounted to an alternative society. For example, by 1893 the SPD published 31 daily newspapers, 41 weekly and semi-weekly newspapers, one scientific review, one family magazine, two humorous publications, and 55 trade journals.

The executive of the SPD worked to maintain the unity of the competing groups within its ranks. Before 1914 the SPD refused to form coalitions with other **political parties** or to vote for any budget of a nonsocialist government. It expected to gain power by constitutional means, but never developed policies designed to attract support from the important **agricultural** sector whose share of the labor force was

37 percent in 1907 and had only fallen to 29 percent in 1933. The radical-sounding theory of the SPD, despite its moderate electorate practice, made it unattractive to land-owning peasants and landless agricultural wage earners. It was also difficult for the SPD to win support in states such as Prussia, where there was no secret voting before 1914.

With the lifting of Otto von Bismarck's repressive **Antisocialist Law** in 1890, the SPD made impressive growth in membership and elections. Between 1905 and 1913 membership rose from 400,000 to 983,000. At the 1912 national election, the SPD attracted 35 percent of the vote, compared to 23 percent in 1893. These results made the SPD the dominant party of its kind in continental Europe, providing a direct model for Austria and Switzerland. It was one of leading parties of its kind in the world; in terms of membership only the **British Labour Party** (which relied on **trade unions** for its institutional base) was higher.

World War I created many tensions for the SPD. It came to support the **war**, although not as strongly as the trade union movement. Despite opposition to war, there was widespread fear of czarist Russia within Germany. In 1917 antiwar elements, many of which had been expelled from the SPD, met at Gotha and formed the Independent Social Democratic Party (*Unabhängige Sozialdemokratische Partei Deutschlands*—USPD). In December 1918 **Rosa Luxemburg** and **Karl Liebknecht** founded the Spartacists, the forerunner of the German Communist Party, which later competed strongly with the SPD for the **working-class** vote.

The German military failures on the Western Front in August 1918 doomed the imperial government, which faced widespread discontent with the war. In October 1918 several members of the SPD joined the cabinet of Prince Max of Baden, but this conciliatory gesture was swept aside by events. On 9 November 1918, **Philipp Scheidemann** proclaimed a provisional republican government to preempt Liebknecht who was said to be about to proclaim a Soviet-style revolutionary government. Despite disruptions, elections were held in February 1920 and the SPD had its first experience of political power when, with the support of other parties, **Friedrich Ebert** was made president and Scheidemann became the first chancellor. The new government faced immense economic and political problems. The war was brought to an end by the acceptance of the Versailles Treaty by Scheidemann's SPD successor, **Gustav Bauer**, and revolts from the left (the Spartacists and the Bavarian soviet republic) and right were suppressed between 1919 and 1923. Germany was accepted back into the family of nations, but at the high price of the continuance of right-wing power structures based on the military and heavy industry, which never accepted the legitimacy of the democratic government.

In July 1919 the largest trade union federation announced its political neutrality, but after the USPD rejoined the SPD in 1922, it gave the party its support from 1924 to 1932. The SPD was returned to power in 1928 under **Hermann Müller**, but his government was powerless once the Depression began. He was forced to resign in March 1930.

At the state level, the record of the SPD as a political force was also mixed. On the evening of 7–8 November 1918 Kurt Eisener (1867–1919), a member of the USPD, deposed the monarchy in Bavaria and proclaimed a republic. The Independent party fared poorly in the ensuing elections in January 1919 and Eisener was assassinated a month later. A moderate SPD government led by Johannes Hoffman held power until March 1920. In 1923 the radical social democrat Erich Zeigner formed a government in Saxony in coalition with the communists, but this government was deposed by the national government of Gustav Stresemann in October 1923. The SPD was a partner in coalition governments in Saxony until 1929. The main political success achieved by the SPD occurred in Prussia, where the party formed the main party of government from 1918 until 30 July 1932, when it was ousted by the national government under Franz von Papen. Its main leader in Prussia in this period was Otto Braun (1872–1955).

The membership of the SPD changed markedly between 1905 to 1906 and 1930. First, the proportion of non-working-class members rose from about 10 percent to 24 percent. Second, in the 1920s the Communist Party seems to have been more successful than the SPD in gaining the allegiance of the lesser-skilled working class. In 1930 the SPD had 1,037,400 members, an impressive result, but one which disguised a profound maldistribution in the social base of its support; of the total membership, 78 percent were manual or blue-collar employees and virtually none came from the agricultural sector of the labor force, which employed 29 percent of Germans in 1933. In 1933 the Nazis forcibly dissolved the SPD and many of its leaders were arrested and sent to Dachau concentration camp. The executive was set up again in Prague in June 1933, then Paris in 1937, and finally London in 1940. By a cruel twist of fate, the large cities of western Germany and the Ruhr, which were the backbone of support for the SPD both before and after 1945, suffered the greatest devastation from Allied bombing during World War II.

The SPD was reconstituted in the Allied zone of occupation in August 1945 under the leadership of **Kurt Schumacher**, composed of those who had survived the horrors of the Nazi period. In the Soviet zone of occupation the SPD was forced to merge with the Communist Party on 21 April 1946; in the previous seven months, 20,000 members of the party had been arrested by the Soviet secret police for "discussions." The merger was the model for the forced mergers of social democrats and **communist** parties in Czechoslovakia, Hungary, Poland, and Romania in 1948.

In West Germany, the SPD had no organic connection with the trade union movement, unlike the British Labour Party. After 1945, the main trade union federation *Deutscher Gewerkschaftsbund* (DGB) was officially politically neutral, but actively supported the SPD in 1953 and 1972. Although the links between the DGB and the SPD are unofficial, they are important in exerting a conservative influence on the SPD.

In 1956 the Communist Party was banned in West Germany, thereby removing an electoral competitor to the SPD. But the left did not go away. For example, the Paulskirche movement opposed the proposed West German membership of the North Atlantic Treaty Organization in 1954 to 1955. The left also waged campaigns within the SPD during the 1960s and 1970s, one of the left-wing parliamentary factions being the *Leverkusen* Circle. The SPD also faced competition from the environmental party, the Greens. In November 1959 the SPD adopted a new platform of policies in its **Godesberg Program**, dropping its Marxist language and seeking to broaden its electoral appeal. The SPD was a participant in government from 1966 to October 1982. Between 1960 and 1990, the SPD governed from four to seven *Länder* (states) at any one time.

From 1983 to 1994 the SPD's share of the national vote fell from 43 to 32 percent. State elections results since 1992 confirmed a general loss of support for the SPD. The idea of an alliance with the

Greens was raised but was not yet supported by a majority of the party. A social-democratic party was revived in former East Germany in October 1989, but after the reunification of Germany in 1989, the SPD faced unexpectedly strong electoral competition in the east from the Party of Democratic Socialism (the former communist party of East Germany). For example, in the state elections during 1994 the SPD won only one of five contests in the states that had constituted East Germany—the state of Brandenburg, where it attracted 54.1 percent of the vote.

In November 1995 a congress of the SPD at Mannheim voted by 321 to 190 votes to replace Rudolf Sharping as party leader with the left-leaning Oskar Lafontaine. Three years later, at the elections to the *Bundestag* in October 1998, the SPD won 298 seats with 40.9 percent of the vote. They formed a coalition government with the Green Party, which took 47 seats with 6.6 percent of the vote. **Gerhard Schröder** of the SPD became chancellor. Schröder placed a high priority on reducing the level of **unemployment**. He also promised to gradually curtail Germany's nuclear energy program, which became an issue with the Green partners who called for swifter action on this matter but were overruled. In March 1999, in protest to a lack of support from his party, Lafontaine resigned as party chairman and also as a minister and member of the *Bundestag*. Schröder became chairman of the SPD. By mid-1990 the SPD was losing support after introducing austerity measures to appeal to the business sector and reverse the fall in economic growth. Many Germans considered that with these measures the party had abandoned the commitment to social justice. This was reflected in poor performances in *Länder* elections later that year.

In 2000 the SDP government took a strong stance against far-right, neo-Nazi extremism, demanding tougher sentences in dealing with violence by the extremists, and banning some neo-Nazi groups that breached the German constitution. After elections to the *Bundestag* in September 2002 the SPD-Green coalition was renewed, albeit with significant losses by the SPD, which was reduced to holding 251 seats, adjusted from the directly won 171 seats, because of winning 38.5 percent of the party list vote. The Greens took an adjusted total of 55 seats with 8.6 percent of the party list vote. In March 2004 Franz Münterfering became party chairman as Schröder resigned to concentrate on his role as chancellor. At the elections to the European

Parliament in June 2004 the SPD won 23 of Germany's 99 seats, down from 33 in 1999. The SPD representatives worked in the **Party of European Socialists**, with which their party was affiliated.

In January 2005 the SPD-Green coalition introduced labor reforms in which unemployment and **welfare** reforms were merged, in an effort to boost the economy and reduce unemployment. Many critics argued that this would mean increased poverty for the unemployed. Lafontaine led several disgruntled members into a new party: the Electoral Alternative Work and Social Justice Party (*Wahlalternative Arbeit und Soziale Gerechtigkeit*), which merged with the Party of Democratic Socialism (*Partei des Demokratischen Sozialismus*) later that year to form the **Left Party**. In a key regional election in May 2005 the SPD lost control of North-Rhine Westphalia (Germany's most populous state), after having governed the state for 39 years. The party's declining popularity led Schröder to call for an early election, which was held in September to October 2005. The SPD obtained 222 seats, including 145 constituency seats, with 34.2 percent of the vote, losing narrowly to the conservative Christian Democratic Union/Christian Social Union. Münterfering resigned from the chair after his preferred candidate for the position of secretary general was beaten by the left-winger Andrea Nahles in a vote by the party board. In November Matthias Platzeck became party chairman and the SPD entered a grand coalition with the conservatives. The SPD lost the chancellorship but Münterfering became vice chancellor and also minister for labor and social affairs. Another seven SPD members took cabinet posts, including those of finance and foreign affairs. *See also* BERNSTEIN, EDUARD; BRANDT, WILLY; KAUTSKY, KARL; GOTHA PROGRAM; LASSALLE, FERDINAND; SCHMIDT, HELMUT HEINDRICH WALDEMAR; ZETLIN, CLARA JOSEPHINE.

GLOBALIZATION. One of the most prominent political issues of the early twenty-first century is globalization, which had become an increasingly debated notion throughout the 1990s. *Globalization* is a contested term, but an influential interpretation of it is that it involves the diminution of geographical restraints upon economic, social, and cultural activities. The hallmarks of globalization, it is argued, are the integration of the world economy, the mobility of capital, the transnational nature of much economic activity, and thus the decline of the power of nation states in the face of global economic forces. Exponents of neoliberalism often consider the process of globalization to be positive, emphasizing the liberated working of the free market and the decreasing ability of states to obstruct the efficient movements of global capital.

Many socialists and others on the broader left are skeptical of the globalization thesis, arguing first that nation-states have always faced severe restraints by international capital and second that states in fact retain significant capacity to make and implement policy and thus govern. Powerful states serve to support **capitalist** interests on the world stage. What is presented as globalization is, skeptics argue, linked with neoliberalism and what opponents sometimes refer to as the Washington Consensus on international economic policy.

Socialists of various persuasions, including Alex Callinicos and Susan George, have criticized the tendency of some to use the term *antiglobalization*. As socialism has always been international in character, it is absurd to use that term in opposition to global capitalism. Indeed, neoliberal or capitalist globalization is sometimes distinguished from globalization as an international movement against poverty and capitalist domination, and for human solidarity and the protection of the natural environment. The Charter of Principles declared by the **World Social Forum** emphasizes that it opposes and seeks alternatives to capitalist globalization dominated by large multinational corporations and their supporting governments. The contemporary **global justice movement** against capitalist globalization indeed styles itself as one of **anticapitalism**, rather than antiglobalization.

GLOBAL JUSTICE MOVEMENT. *See* ANTICAPITALISM.

GODESBERG PROGRAM. The Godesberg Program was the statement of values and policies adopted by the **German Social Democratic Party** at its conference at Godesberg in November 1959. The program broke with the **Marxist** tradition begun with the **Erfurt Program** in 1891 by identifying two fundamental values of democratic socialism: allowing every individual to develop freely and, as a responsible member of the community, to take part in the political, economic, and cultural life of mankind; and fighting for democracy and freedom of speech and against all forms of dictatorship. It claimed that the roots of democratic socialism in Europe were rooted in **Christian** ethics, humanism, and classical philosophy. A similar retreat from Marxism took place in the Austrian Socialist Party (formerly and since 1991 **Austrian Social Democratic Party**) in 1958 and in the **Swedish Social Democratic Workers' Party** in 1960.

The Godesberg Program supported the reunification of Germany, affirmed the need for national defense, condemned the manufacture or use of **nuclear weapons** by the German Republic, and supported international cooperation to preserve peace. On the economy, the program warned of the dangers of monopolies and the need to defend consumers and free collective bargaining by **trade unions** and employers' organizations. The program upheld the right to **social security** and the equality of **women** in all respects. It declared that socialism was "no substitute for religion" and upheld the autonomy of the churches. On **education**, the program stressed the importance of developing the full capacities of the individual. *See also* BRANDT, WILLY.

GONZÁLEZ, FELIPE (1942–). A Spanish socialist politician, Felipe González (Márquez) was born in Seville and graduated from the Catholic University of Louvain, Belgium, in law. He joined the Spanish socialist **youth** in 1962 and became a full member of the **Spanish Socialist Workers' Party** (*Partido Socialista Obrero Español—* PSOE) in 1964. In 1966 he began a law practice to assist employees with work-related accident cases. He entered the national executive of the PSOE in 1969 and became first secretary of the party in 1974. During 1979 González defeated the doctrinaire **Marxists** within the PSOE and worked to make the party more like a social-democratic party. In December 1982 he became Spain's first socialist prime minister since the **Spanish Civil War** and held the post until his defeat in March 1996. As the leader of a number of coalition administrations, his term was notable for the expansion of the **welfare state**, the reduction of the importance of state enterprises in the economy, and Spain's entry into the North Atlantic Treaty Organization despite long-standing opposition within the PSOE. In 1982 he became vice president of the **Socialist International**.

GOTHA PROGRAM. The Gotha Program was a joint statement of **ideology** and **policies** by two German parties in 1875. These parties were the General Association of German Workers (*Allgemeiner Deutscher Arbeiterverein*), founded by **Ferdinand Lassalle** in 1863 (and often referred to as the Lassalleans), and the Social Democratic Workers' Party (*Sozialdemokratische Arbeiterpartei*—SDAP), formed in 1869 by **Wilhelm Liebknecht** and **August Bebel** on the core of the League of Workingmen's Associations they founded in 1866. Under the statement these two parties agreed to merge to form the German Socialist Workers' Party (*Sozialistische Arbeiterpartei Deutschlands*). The latter was renamed the **German Social Democratic Party** (*Sozialdemocratische Partei Deutschlands*—SPD) in 1890.

After the suppression of the **Paris Commune** in 1871, Otto von Bismarck had turned against any form of socialism, thereby making it imperative for the two rival parties to combine forces. Parliamentary members of the two groups operated as a *fraktion*, and moves for the merger were begun by the Lassalleans in October 1874. The merger was achieved at the "Unity Conference" held at the town of Gotha the following year. The Gotha Program was designed to accommodate the Lassalleans and the **Marxist** SDAP. It reflected the political realities of the time and made the compromises necessary to ensure that the merger worked. At the same time, it reflected positions that were agreed to on both sides; for example, both sides wanted to achieve a "free state and socialist society" by legal means. It was not, as **Karl Marx** claimed, an agreement to get unity at any price. At the time of the merger, the Lassalleans had 15,322 members and the SDAP had 9,121.

The specific objectives of the Gotha program were the abolition of the wage system; the elimination of all forms of exploitation, including social and political inequality; the establishment of a system of producers' cooperatives with state assistance covering industry and **agriculture** that would form the basis of the socialist organization of labor in the future; free, compulsory elementary **education**; a "normal" (the duration was unspecified) working day; the restriction of female labor and the prohibition of child labor; the state supervision of factories, workshops, and domestic service; the regulation of prison labor; and an effective employers' liability law. Concessions had to be made to the Lassalleans because they were originally the numerically greater group. Because of the **Anti-Socialist Law**, it was not possible to hold congresses in Germany to revise the Gotha Program. Thus it remained the official policy of the SPD until 1891 when the Erfurt Program replaced it.

Despite its success, the Gotha Program is better known as the target for Marx's criticisms of its Lassallean ideas, especially what Marx considered the vagueness of terms such as "equality" and "proceeds of labor" in the proposals for distribution, and the assertion that the "free" nation-state was the framework through which the **working class** could achieve its freedom. Originally written as margin notes in May 1875 on a draft version of the program (which was largely adopted in that form), his remarks were not published at the time because the unity negotiations were too far advanced. Both Marx and **Friedrich Engels** thought that the Gotha Program made too many concessions to the Lassalleans. Engels published Marx's criticism in 1891; it was usually referred to later as the *Critique of the Gotha Programme*. The importance of this work for Marxist theory was that it contained Marx's prediction that in the transformation from a capitalist to a communist society, there would be a period of political transition in which the state would be the "revolutionary dictatorship of the proletariat," an idea later reinterpreted and amplified by **V. I. Lenin**.

GRAMSCI, ANTONIO (1891–1937). Widely considered to be the most innovative **Marxist** thinker of the twentieth century, Gramsci has influenced socialist thinking both within and beyond the Marxist tradition. Born in Sardinia, Italy, he grew up in poverty and ill **health**. His family endured hardship to ensure he gained a proper secondary education. In 1911 he won a scholarship to the University of Turin. Two years later he became active in the **Italian Socialist Party** (*Partito Socialista Italiano* — PSI). He was involved in the Turin factory council movement of 1919 to 1920, publishing articles and editiorials in the newspaper *l'Ordine Nuovo* (The New Order) that he edited.

As a Marxist, Gramsci held that people expressed themselves in their labor, transforming nature to meet changing needs. In council **communism**, people would associate with one another in the industrial organization. They would directly control their labor and material existence. Workers' democracy would involve a worldwide network of factory and farm councils that would elect members of ward and regional councils. This was not achieved. The industrialists of Turin broke the Council movement.

In 1921 the PSI split and Gramsci joined the new Italian Communist Party (*Partito Comunista Italiano*—PCI). He was elected at once to the central committee of the party and sent to Moscow to serve as the Italian representative on the executive of the **Comintern**. In 1924 he returned and was elected to serve the PCI in parliament and become secretary general of the party. By this time **Benito Mussolini** had seized and begun to consolidate fascist power in Italy. Gramsci, who was considered dangerous, was arrested. In 1928 he was imprisoned, after the public prosecutor famously stated that his brain should be prevented from functioning for 20 years. Although he died in prison within 20 years, his brain had continued to function. In his notebooks he worked on a range of topics, often combined to throw the prison censors off track. The notebooks were published later as Gramsci's *Prison Notebooks*.

A prominent theme of the *Notebooks* was the survival of **capitalism** and the failure of the **working class** to gain its consciousness in the twentieth century. The explanation, according to Gramsci, revolved around the concept of hegemony. As a Marxist he maintained that the economic base ultimately determines, or sets the limiting conditions for, politics, ideology. and the state. He stressed, however, that to understand hegemony it was necessary to study the political and ideological superstructure. The modern state may resort to its coercive resources to suppress challenges to capitalism, but usually relied upon ideological hegemony. The system of values, morals, beliefs, and attitudes that maintained support for the existing order was thus sustained through culture, **education**, churches, the family, and other resources. Consent was generated for the class-divided and dominated society by masking the tensions therein.

Gramsci argued that socialists must make strategy with this situation in mind. There would need to be a war of position and a war of maneuver. The war of maneuver, or in other words, a rapid push against the state, was appropriate in some, but not all, circumstances. In modern society what would usually be required to overcome the class dominance of capitalism would be the war of position. This would be a protracted series of campaigns guided by the intellectuals of the revolutionary party, involving alliances with other progressive forces. This may involve campaigns in parliament, industry, and other parts of civil society. The hegemony of the dominant class would be gradually weakened and an alternative hegemony developed.

Gramsci suffered from ill health throughout his imprisonment. When his release date arrived, his sentence shortened by remissions, he was too ill to move. He died in the prison clinic a few days later. His sister-in-law, Tatiana Schucht, smuggled his notebooks from his prison cell.

GRÖNLUND, LAURENCE (1846–99). Born and educated in Denmark, Laurence Grönlund emigrated to the United States in 1867 where he became a lawyer and a writer in the tradition of **utopian socialism**. A popularizer of European socialism rather than an original thinker, his works had wide appeal and included *Dialogue on the Coming Revolution* (1880), *Our Destiny* (1891), *The New Economy* (1898), and *The Cooperative Commonwealth* (1884), his best-known work. He was a member of the executive of the **Socialist Labor Party of America** in 1888.

GUESDE, JULES (1845–1922). Jules Guesde was the pseudonym of Mathiew Basile, one of the leading figures in French socialism and one of its best organizers in the 1870s and 1880s. Born in Paris into a **middle-class** family that was not well-off, he nonetheless received a good education and became a journalist. In the 1860s he was associated with the **anarchists** of the **International Workingmen's Association**. He was jailed for writing in support of the **Paris Commune** and spent the next five years in Switzerland and Italy. In November 1877 he founded *L'Égalité* (Equality), one of the earliest socialist journals in France, with the help of **Wilhelm Liebknecht**. In 1878 he was jailed again for defying a government ban on holding an international labor conference. In 1879 he emerged as the dominant personality at the national **trade union** conference in Marseilles, which agreed to set itself up as a socialist political party, the *Fédération des Ouvriers Socialistes de France* (Federation of Socialist Workers of France). Guesde drew up a program for the party and visited **Karl Marx** in London who approved it. Guesde wanted the party to be centralized, based on the example of the **German Social Democratic Party**, with the trade unions occupying a subordinate role in the struggle for a socialist society.

These ideas did not square well with the realities of either the trade unions or French socialism. Although trade unions in France had only been legalized in 1884, they still predated the socialists as organizations and were unwilling to be controlled by them, preferring their independence even though they usually agreed with socialist doctrines. French socialism itself gloried in its individuality in the nineteenth century with factions forming around dominant individuals like Guesde himself. Guesde was influential in the trade unions despite his opposition to **syndicalism** at conferences of the **Second International**. His ideas were those of an orthodox **Marxist** of the 1880s. He was not against using parliamentary means to achieve reforms, but believed that **capitalism** could only be overthrown by revolution. In 1882 the **Possibilists** broke away and he reformed his party as the *Parti Ouvrier Français* (French Workers' Party), which formed a federation with the followers of the insurrectionist Auguste Blanqui (1805–81) in about 1899 called the *Parti Socialiste de France* (Socialist Party of France). In 1905 this group became part of the united **French Socialist Party**. Guesde was elected to the French Chamber of Deputies in 1893. Ironically, for an opponent of the participation of **Alexandre Millerand** in government and **revisionism**, he joined the French coalition government as minister without portfolio at the outbreak of World War I in 1914, a position he held until 1915.

GUILD SOCIALISM. Guild socialism was an important variety of British socialism that flourished between 1912 and the early 1920s. Whereas other forms of socialism viewed the state as something to be captured and used to implement socialism, or, following **anarchism**, abolished altogether, guild socialism advocated a third course, namely, the decentralizing of the political power of the state through the creation of democratically run guilds or **communes** in each industry. The origins of guild socialism were mixed. In part it was influenced by French **syndicalism** and the **Industrial Workers of the World**, but it owed more to British thinkers such as John Ruskin, Thomas Carlyle, and **William Morris**, who condemned the **Industrial Revolution** and its works on aesthetic grounds and looked back romantically to the Middle Ages when independent craftsmen, organized in guilds, were alleged to be able to take pride in the products of their labor. Guild socialism began with the guilds' restoration movement in 1906 and entered into British socialist debate in 1912 following articles by A. R. Orage and S. G. Hobson. When **G. D. H. Cole** lent his support from 1913 onward, guild socialism began to be molded into an effective force. Although Cole failed to persuade the

Fabian Society to adopt guild socialism, he quickly became its ablest and most persuasive publicist.

Like the American Knights of Labor, guild socialism wanted to abolish the wage system. It sought to create a system of self-government in all parts of the economy by means of national guilds working in cooperation with the state. The National Guilds' League was formed in 1915. In 1920 the reference to the state was omitted from the League's platform. Guild socialism saw **trade unions** rather than parliament as the basis for building the guild state. Although never a mass membership movement — the League only had about 500 members mainly in and around London in 1917 — it nevertheless exerted considerable influence in the United Kingdom and elsewhere, largely through Cole's writings. Defunct as a movement by 1931, guild socialism was important for drawing attention to the need for democratic participation in the management of the productive side of the economy. It exerted influence on Swedish socialist thought through **Ernst Wigforss**. Many of the ideas of guild socialism were revived by advocates of industrial democracy in the 1970s. *See also* PELL-OUTIER, FERNAND LÉONCE EMILE.

GUINEAN PEOPLE'S ASSEMBLY [*RASSEMBLEMENT POP-LAIRE GUINÉEN* (RPG)]. The RPG emerged in the 1980s as an unofficial political organization whose activities were suppressed by the military government of Lansana Conté, which took power in a coup of 1984. Before the emergence of the RPG, Guinea's previous experience of socialism had been Sékou Touré's disastrous experiment. Touré took power immediately after Guinea gained independence from France in 1958. He sought ties with the Soviet Union but, seeking to unite **trade unionists**, peasants, and progressive members of the **middle class**, rather than appeal solely to the **working class**, refused to follow the orthodox **communist** model that many in his *Parti Démocratique de Guinée* recommended. The experiment declined into dictatorship as, in response partly to invasions from opponents abroad and partly to imagined enemies, Touré suppressed and eliminated many of his opponents. Furthermore, the **nationalization** policies and state control that were central to the experiment were executed and administered incompetently.

Following the death of Touré in 1984 and the commencement of Conté's regime, Guinea remained a country that suffered from poverty and authoritarian rule. Nevertheless, after appeals from Conté for political exiles to return, the RPG leader Alpha Condé returned to Guinea in May 1991 after a long period of exile. After popular disturbances led Conté to introduce civilian rule in 1992, a range of parties including the RPG were legalized. In the presidential elections won by Conté in 1993 Condé's share of the vote was recorded at 19.6 percent, a figure widely considered to be artificially low. In 1994 the RPG alleged harassment of its supporters by the security forces and in 1995 pulled out of the legislative elections, alleging fraud. The final results gave the RPG nine of 114 seats. In 1998 Condé was arrested on charges of plotting to overthrow Conté's regime. The opposition parties withdrew from the presidential elections that year. In September 2000 Condé was sentenced to five years imprisonment but after a campaign by Amnesty International he was released in 2001 and resumed his parliamentary duties. In June 2002 the RPG boycotted the parliamentary elections at which Conté's ruling party retained power. In December 2003 the RPG boycotted the presidential elections at which Conté was reelected. Also in 2003 the RPG gained full membership in the **Socialist International**.

GUTERRES, ANTÓNIO (1949–). Guterres became leader of the **Portuguese Socialist Party** (*Partido Socialista*—PS) in 1991. Born into a lower-**middle-class** family in the rural Fundão region, he was educated at Lisbon University and qualified as an electrical engineer. He began his parliamentary career in the provisional government of **Mário Soares** in 1974 as a minister without portfolio. Guterres was unusual for being a practicing Catholic in a party noted for its secularism. Originally on the left of the party, he became a moderate during the 1980s and supported free-market economics, **privatization**, and economic integration with the rest of Europe. After the PS's victory in the national elections of October 1995, when it won 44 percent of the vote, he was asked to form a government. As leader of the PS he won the general elections of October 1999. Also in 1999 the Congress of the **Socialist International** (SI) elected him as president. Following defeats in local government elections in December 2001, he resigned as prime minister. In 2003 he was reelected president of the SI, but he resigned when in May 2005 he was appointed head of the office of the United Nations High Commissioner for Refugees (UNHCR).

– H –

HANSEN, HANS CHRISTIAN SVANE (1906–60). A Danish social-democratic politician, Hans Christian Svane Hansen was born in Arhus. He became secretary of the **youth** organization of the **Danish Social Democratic Party** in 1929 and its chairman in 1933. He was elected to parliament in 1936 and was party secretary during the German occupation in World War II when he also published a Resistance newspaper. He was minister for finance from 1945 to 1950 (a post he used to facilitate Denmark's economic recovery), minister of foreign affairs from 1953 to 1955, and prime minister from 1955 until his death.

HANSSON, PER ALBIN (1885–1946). A Swedish social-democratic leader, Per Albin Hansson was born in Scania province and joined the staff of the newspaper of the **Swedish Social Democratic Workers' Party** in the 1900s. He was elected to parliament in 1918. He served in the cabinet to Karl Hjalmar Branting (1860–1925) as minister for war and national defense, but resigned in 1926 because of his anti-militarist views. He became leader of the party in 1936 and prime minister in September 1936, a post he held until his untimely death. His administration was notable for the strict maintenance of Sweden's neutrality during World War II and the development of the **welfare state**.

HARDIE, JAMES KEIR (1856–1915). Born in a poor rural environment near Holytown, Scotland, James Keir Hardie began his working life at the age of seven. He worked in coal mines in Lanarkshire from the age of 10 until he was 22. During the late 1870s he actively agitated for better pay and conditions for coal miners, activities that cost him and his two brothers their jobs. Keir Hardie obtained some income by working as a journalist for the *Glasgow Weekly Mail*, but did much unpaid work as an organizer for the coal miners. He became corresponding secretary for the Hamilton miners in 1879, led an unsuccessful strike by Lanarkshire miners in 1880, and helped to form a **trade union** of coal miners for all of Scotland. By the mid-1880s, if not earlier, Keir Hardie became a committed socialist who recognized the importance of labor representation in parliament. He advocated the **nationalization** of the coal mines as early as 1887. In 1888 he failed to get elected to a vacant seat and formed the Scottish Labour Party, which merged into the **Independent Labour Party** (ILP) in 1893. Keir Hardie's activities as a labor publicist through his newspapers, *The Miner* (1887–89) and the *Labour Leader* (1889), made him well-known and assisted his election to the House of Commons in 1892 as member for West Ham South (to 1895) for the ILP. He scandalized parliament by making his entrance in a deerstalker hat and being preceded by a cornet player. In 1893 Keir Hardie became chairman of the ILP and held the position until 1900. He was again elected to the House of Commons as member for Merthyr Tydfil, a seat he held until his death. In 1906 he was the first leader of the **British Labour Party**.

Keir Hardie also played an active role in international organized labor from 1888. He visited the United States in 1895. After his visit in 1909 he published *India*, which exposed the destruction of native crafts by large-scale **capitalism** and the oppression of the peasants by moneylenders. Like other British labor leaders of his time, such as **George Lansbury**, he was a total abstainer; many radical reformers saw alcohol as a means of oppressing the **working class**. He was chairman of the British section of the International Socialist bureau in 1914. He was greatly grieved by the inability of international labor to prevent World War I. *See also* TEMPERANCE.

HARRINGTON, MICHAEL (1928–89). An American socialist organizer and author, Michael Harrington was born in St. Louis into a **middle-class** Catholic family. He received a Jesuit education, but became a socialist after studying law at the University of Yale. From there, he went on to complete a master's degree in English at the University of Chicago. His social work with the poor in the 1950s provided the material for his study of poverty, *The Other America* (1962), which helped to bring into being the antipoverty programs of the John F. Kennedy and Lyndon B. Johnson administrations. By 1953 he had ceased to be a Catholic and had become leader of the **Young People's Socialist League**. He disagreed with **Norman Thomas** over the Korean War. Harrington, a strong anticommunist, became chairman of the **Socialist Party of America** (SPA) in 1968. Although he opposed the Vietnam War, he did not support the unconditional withdrawal of American troops, a stance that cost him support among the **new left**. In October 1972 he resigned as cochairman of the SPA and went on to form the Democratic Socialist Organizing Committee the following year. In 1972 he became a professor of political science at Queen's College. In 1982 the committee merged with the New American Movement to form the **Democratic Socialists of America**.

HAWKE, ROBERT JAMES LEE [BOB] (1929–). Australian Labor Party (ALP) prime minister from March 1983 to November 1991, Bob Hawke was born in Bordertown, South Australia. He was educated at the universities of Western Australia and Oxford, which he attended as a Rhodes scholar. In 1958 he joined the Australian Council of Trade Unions as a research officer and industrial advocate and was elected its president in 1970. He held the position until 1980, when he was elected to the national parliament. In February 1983 he became leader of the federal parliamentary ALP and, with the ALP's victory at the March 1983 election, became prime minister. Among other things, his government encouraged greater communication between **trade unions** and employers. The deterioration of the economy after 1987, particularly the continuing adverse balance of trade and sharply rising foreign debt, were major problems for his government. The recession, which afflicted the economy from September 1990 and throughout 1991, eroded Hawke's popularity in opinion polls and made it possible for his former treasurer, **Paul Keating**, to successfully challenge him for the position of prime minister in December 1991; he resigned from federal parliament in February 1992.

HEALTH CARE. The provision of health care is a key concern for all socialists from the radical left to mainstream social democrats. It is seen as crucial to the broader **egalitarian** tenet of socialism. Moreover, the organized, collectivist provision is justified by the socialist tenets of sociality, social responsibility, cooperation, and planning. The organized provision of health care is not an exclusively socialist concern. The first organized system was established in Otto von Bismarck's Germany in the nineteenth century. This was done largely to dampen support for socialism. In the twentieth century social liberal thinkers and governments have advocated and offered such provision as part of the **welfare state**, and even many conservatives accepted that some degree of publicly provided health care was necessary for a harmonious and orderly society. Other conservatives have, along with libertarians, stressed that health care is the responsibility of individuals rather than the state. The size of the gap between social **liberalism** and socialism regarding health care will depend partly upon the strength of egalitarianism of the socialist in question, and partly upon the weight attributed to sociality, cooperation, and social responsibility.

The demand by socialists for health care for those in need is often accompanied by a call for private health provision to be abolished. This call is made on the grounds that private medicine infringes the rights of the poor. The only relevant ground for health care, according to abolitionists of private provision, is the state of a person's health. Private provision means that it is likely that the poor will receive inferior medical treatment, as the more wealthy can afford to jump the queue or purchase drugs that are not widely, or cheaply available. This means that grounds other than the state of a person's health are allowed to influence the provision of health care, which many socialists consider to be an injustice. Moreover, the restriction of medicine and care on the basis of the price that can be secured on the market is considered to restrict the freedom to enjoy good health.

Efforts to provide some kind of public provision have often taken the form of subsidized private insurance funds or compulsory levies to support national insurance schemes. However, closer to the socialist ideal is the national health service (sometimes referred to as socialized medicine). This involves state ownership of the health care institutions and also the employment of personnel in those institutions. Aneurin Bevan, minister for health in the **British Labour Party** (Labour) government, introduced the first example of such a service in the United Kingdom in 1948. An earlier report by **William Beveridge** was highly influential upon the decision to build the British National Health Service (NHS). Social democrats within the Labour Party saw this and the welfare and **nationalization** program as a way to sufficiently tame capitalism. More radical socialists saw this as a stage in the campaign to abolish **capitalism**.

Rather than lead to the abolition of capitalism, the British NHS existed within a capitalist system. The NHS survived the final two decades of the twentieth century, during which time many nationalized industries passed into private hands. Elsewhere in Europe, national health services had by then been introduced in Sweden, Italy, and Spain. However, as health care became increasingly expensive, national budgets came under strain.

The problem was rooted in the global recession that began to bite in the late 1970s. There was, moreover, an increase in the numbers of elderly people in the Western democracies. The shortage of growth-inspired **tax** revenues to pay for health care meant that socialist parties came under pressure to rethink their strategies. The need for welfare cutbacks led to renewed debate on the role of the state. Many **Marxists** argued that the problems the recession posed for social democrats reflected the deeper problem of trying to reform the capitalist state, rather than abolish it. Social democrats had to experiment with efficiency reforms without making health care expenditure the target of government spending cuts. Indeed, even when the **New Zealand Labour Party** in the 1980s and the **Australian Labor Party** in the 1980s and 1990s began to introduce market-based reforms, health care spending remained largely intact. When Labour was elected to government in the United Kingdom in 1997 **Tony Blair** introduced public-private partnerships in health policy to enhance efficiency and allow a channeling of resources, rather than to introduce cuts to health care spending. The importance of health care to supporters of socialist parties was in evidence as the **Swedish Social Democratic Workers' Party** (*Sveriges Socialdemokratiska Arbetareparti*—SAP) increased its share of the vote at the parliamentary elections of 2002, after committing itself to high levels of spending on health care. The SAP leader Göran Persson was rewarded with a third term as prime minister, forming a minority government. In the United Kingdom Labour continued to experiment with private sector involvement, such as the Private Finance Initiative, after its victories in the general elections of 2001 and 2005.

HEDTOFT-HANSEN, HANS CHRISTIAN (1903–55). Danish social-democratic leader and politician Hans Christian Hedtoft-Hansen was born in Arhus and became a printer. He served as president of the **youth** organization of the **Danish Social Democratic Party**, beginning in 1928. He used this position to become secretary of the party by 1935, when he was elected to parliament (*Folketing*). He remained in parliament until 1940 when he resigned after the German occupation and joined the Resistance. After the **war**, he served as minister for labor and social affairs in a coalition government in 1945. Hans Hedtoft (as he was known from this time onward) was the prime minister of a minority social-democratic government from 1947 to 1950 and served a second term as prime minister from 1953 to his death. His period in power was notable for his support for a strong defense policy and Danish membership in the North Atlantic Treaty Organization. His defense views were shaped not just by the German occupation of Denmark but also by the **communist** coup in Czechoslovakia in February 1948. *See also* KRAG, JENS OTTO.

HILLQUIT, MORRIS (1869–1933). American socialist Morris Hillquit was born Moses Hillkowitz in Riga, Latvia, then part of the Russian empire. He adopted the name Hillquit in 1897. His parents were assimilated **Jews**. He emigrated to the United States in 1885, worked in the garment industry in New York City, helped to organize Jewish garment workers, and joined the **Socialist Labor Party of America** (SLPA). He qualified as a lawyer in 1893 and used his legal talents to defend employees in accident and civil liberty cases. During the 1890s he became a **Marxist** and a supporter of **Daniel DeLeon**. He led a large dissident group within the SLPA in 1899, which divided the party in two. In 1901 his group joined with the Social Democratic Party of America of **Eugene V. Debs** to form the **Socialist Party of America** (SPA). Hillquit's socialism was close to that of **Karl Kautsky**, and it also made him an opponent to **syndicalism**. From 1907 until his death he contested public office in New York unsuccessfully, but attracted significant support nonetheless. He wrote *The History of Socialism in the United States* (1903). Later attacked by communists, he denounced **Leninism**. From 1920 he continued, by default, to be the leading figure in the SPA and supported **Norman Thomas**.

HUGHES, WILLIAM MORRIS (1862–1952). Australian Labor Party (ALP) prime minister, William Morris Hughes was born in London to Welsh-born parents. He became a schoolteacher and spent some years teaching in Wales. He emigrated to Australia in 1884, where he eventually settled in Sydney. In 1894 he entered New South Wales politics as a Labor member and in 1901 entered federal politics. He was also one of the founders of the national union for longshoremen—the Waterside Workers' Federation. In *The Case for Labor* (1910) Hughes argued that socialism required a long evolutionary period to occur and could not be achieved quickly. He succeeded **Andrew Fisher** as prime minister in 1915 and devoted most of his administration to organizing Australia's **war** effort; this included leading two exceptionally bitter campaigns in support of conscription in 1916 and 1917, which split the ALP. In 1916 he switched sides and joined the conservatives to form the Nationalist Party. At war's end in 1918, he used the size of Australia's contribution to gain a separate place for Australia at the Versailles peace conference. His efforts resulted in Australia acquiring control of the former German territories in New Guinea. Always a polemical figure, Hughes continued as prime minister until 1923.

HUNGARIAN SOCIAL DEMOCRATIC PARTY [*MAGYAROR-SZÁGI SZOCIÁLDEMOKRATIA PÁRT* (MSzDP)]. The first signs of **working-class** and socialist activity in what is now Hungary were evident from 1868, when the first **trade union** was formed. In 1869 employers sponsored a workers' educational association that was soon converted into a socialist organization. In 1870 these two groups got together to produce the first Hungarian socialist newspaper with a German-language edition and agreed to accept the **Marxist** program of the German Social Democratic Workers' Party (*Sozialdemokratische Arbeiterpartei*—SDAP) adopted at Eisenach in 1869. Universal **suffrage** and freedom of association and assembly were the early fundamental objectives of Hungarian socialists and remained so until 1918. Hungarian socialism operated under political repression. The trade unions, for example, operated as **friendly societies** under a law of 1872.

In 1880 a new socialist party was formed, the *Magyarországi Általánon Munkáspárt* (General Workers' Party of Hungary), and adopted a program demanding political rights, free and compulsory **education**, the end of child labor for those children under 14, the separation of church and state, a 10-hour working day, the abolition of night work, regulation of women's labor, and improved occupational **health** and safety conditions. The economic backwardness of Hungary made it difficult for the party to attract a mass following. The party joined the **Second International** in 1889 and, with assistance from the **Austrian Social Democratic Party**, it was reorganized as the MSzDP in December 1890. In 1905 the MSzDP organized mass meetings in Budapest to agitate for universal **suffrage**, but to no avail. Although party membership grew from 43,000 to 53,000 between 1910 and 1912, it achieved little. The failures of the MSzDP were attributable not just to the repressive political environment in which it had to operate but also to its inability to harness rural unrest (there were widespread rural disturbances in 1896–97) and to its adherence to the idea of a unitary Magyar state, which alienated Slavs and Romanians.

In the political turmoil at the end of World War I, there was a political revolution in Hungary in October 1918 and the MSzDP was able to participate in a coalition government for the first time between 1918 and 1919. Béla Kun (1886–1936), who had been sent from Russia to foment a communist uprising in Hungary, agreed to a merger with the MSzDP. A government that he dominated took power and tried to nationalize all property. Faced with Allied attacks designed to destroy the left-wing government, Kun resigned on 1 August 1919 and a social-democratic government took over, but it only lasted a few days after the Romanian army entered Budapest. This was followed by a right-wing coup organized by Admiral Miklós Horthy, who instituted a reign of terror against communists and moderate socialists alike. A period of effectively fascist rule followed; in 1939 only five of the 323 seats in the lower house of the Hungarian parliament were occupied by members of the MSzDP. Despite its troubles, the MSzDP was a member of the **Labor and Socialist International** in 1928, to which it reported a collective membership of 138,500.

In 1948 the MSzDP was forced to merge with the Communist Party to form the Party of Hungarian Workers (*Magyar Dolgozók Pártija*), which was later renamed the Hungarian Socialist Workers' Party (*Magyar Szocialista Munkáspárt*). In 1988, during the demise of one-party communist rule in Eastern Europe, the MSzDP reformed as a small opposition party under the leadership of Andras Revesz. In 1990 the MSzDP gained membership in the **Socialist International** (SI). Revesz soon helped split the party, forming an Independent Social Democratic Party. In 1994 Laszlo Kapolyi became leader of the official MSzDP. Although the MSzDP included both Marxists and social democrats, the latter prevailed. However, the party has not enjoyed electoral success, failing to reach the 5 percent threshold at parliamentary elections. Its rival **Hungarian Socialist Party** has been the dominant social-democratic party since the collapse of **communism**. The MSzDP's status in the SI was changed to full membership in 2003.

HUNGARIAN SOCIALIST PARTY [*MAGYAR SZOCIALISTA PÁRT* (MSzP)]. As the result of a merger of the **Hungarian Social Democratic Party** (MSzDP) and the Hungarian Communist Party, the Party of Hungarian Workers (*Magyar Dolgozók Pártija*—MDP) was formed in 1948, following three years of Soviet occupation after the removal of a Nazi-sympathetic government. The MDP declared a **communist** people's republic the following year. The MDP was, from the outset, under such tight Soviet control that, when the moderate Imre Nagy took over as prime minister in 1953, a power struggle commenced within the MDP, leading to the Nagy's replacement in 1955 by the Stalinist wing. A political crisis ensued, at which point the Soviet Union intervened, replacing the Stalinist Matyas Rakoski with the slightly less hardline Erno Gero as party leader. Mass demonstrations in 1956 calling for Nagy to resume the leadership led to conflict between demonstrators and police. The unrest was met by Soviet military intervention. Nagy was reinstated as prime minister and the party leadership passed to Janos Kadar. Nagy announced the restoration of a multiparty system and, under pressure from demonstrators, stated his intention to withdraw from the Warsaw Pact (the international military organization of communist states). The Soviet Union intervened with troops and tanks, killing thousands of demonstrators, many of whom put up armed resistance. Nagy was executed.

Although Kadar thus controlled Hungary, he relaxed central economic control, allowing some private initiatives, especially on the part of the peasants. Unlike the other Comecon countries, Hungary became self-sufficient in food production. Nevertheless, by the 1970s the rising price of oil led the state to borrow heavily, creating debt from which the country never recovered. Dissatisfaction led the leaders of the Hungarian Socialist Workers' Party (*Magyar Szocialista Munkáspárt*—MSzMP), as the MDP had by now been renamed, to contemplate change, leading the party to become a pioneer in the transition of the European communist parties. Kadar was replaced as leader in 1988 and, with the beginning of the demise of one-party communist rule in Eastern Europe the following year, the MSzMP split. A section of the membership formed the Social Democratic Movement, which was soon renamed the *Magyar Szocialista Párt*— MSzP. A larger section remained in the orthodox MSzMP, which became the Hungarian Workers Party, which has not enjoyed electoral success, and joined the **Party of the European Left** in 2004.

The MSzP, rather than the MSzDP, became the dominant democratic socialist party in Hungary. However, the MSzP lost the 1990 elections to a bourgeois bloc. In opposition during 1992 the MSzP was granted observer status by the **Socialist International** (SI) and membership of the party in the 1990s was at various levels between 30,000 and 40,000. In the May 1994 national elections, under the leadership of Gyula Horn, the MSzP received 33 percent of the vote, compared to 11 percent in 1990. As a result of the election the MSzP increased its share of the seats from 33 to 209, giving it an overall majority in parliament. Nevertheless, largely to convince the West that the return of an ex-communist party to power was nothing to fear, the MSzP formed a coalition with the center-right Alliance of Free Democrats. The coalition introduced an austerity program to attempt to deal with the Hungarian economic problems that had not gone away. The MSzP achieved success in gaining full membership in the SI in 1996. Domestically, however, notwithstanding warnings from the left of the party not to alienate the mass of the populace, the unpopularity of a supposedly socialist government introducing such measures led to defeat at the hands of the right-wing Young Democrats-Bourgeois Party at the parliamentary elections of 1998.

In the parliamentary elections of 2002 the MSzP returned to power, once again in a center-left coalition with the Alliance of Free Democrats, under the leadership of Peter Medgyessy of the MSzP. At these elections the MSzP won 178 seats with 42.1 percent of the vote. In elections to the European Parliament in June 2004 the MSzP obtained nine of Hungary's 24 seats, the nine members working in the **Party of European Socialists**, to which the MSzP was affiliated.

HUYSMANS, CAMILLE (1871–1968). A leading Belgian socialist, author, and politician, Camille Huysmans was born at Bilsen and completed his higher education at Liège where he studied German philosophy. He went on to hold academic positions at the Liberal College of Ypres and then at the New University of Brussels. He was attracted to socialism as a young man and wrote articles for its press. He gained his first political post in 1905 when he was elected to the city council of Brussels; in the same year he became the secretary of the international bureau of the **Second International**. Although the international bureau had been established in 1900, it was Huysman's linguistic and political skills that transformed it into an effective vehicle for the dissemination and coordination of socialism. He held the post until 1922. In 1910 he was elected to the Belgian parliament. After World War I he became the chief organizer of the Belgian Workers' Party (later **Belgian Socialist Party**) in Antwerp and served as minister for science and arts in 1925, president of the chamber of deputies in 1936, and as a prime minister of a coalition government from August 1946 to March 1947.

HYNDMAN, HENRY MAYERS (1842–1921). Henry Mayers Hyndman was an important figure in left-wing British socialism in the late nineteenth century. Born into a wealthy family in London and educated at Trinity College at Cambridge University, he became a socialist after reading *Das Kapital* by **Karl Marx** in French while sailing to the United States in 1880. In the United States he read *Progress and Poverty* by **Henry George**. On his return to the United Kingdom, he contacted Marx. Friedrich Engels disliked Hyndman, as Marx did when Hyndman refused to acknowledge the intellectual debt he owed to him in his pamphlet of 1883, *Socialism Made Plain*, which he wrote on behalf of the newly formed Democratic Federation (based on radical clubs in London), which demanded the **nationalization** of capital and land. In 1884 the federation was renamed the **Social Democratic Federation**, which briefly included the membership of **William Morris**. Hyndman had a poor opinion of **trade unions** and the value of strikes. He had a dictatorial style of leadership and his socialism took the form of a doctrinaire **Marxism**, which alienated potential supporters. He also wanted to revive **Chartism**. In 1886 he was arrested and tried and acquitted for inciting riots among the **unemployed** in London, along with John Burns and H. H. Champion. Hyndman and his first wife, Matilda Ware, took an active interest in **education**. Hyndman helped form the **British Socialist Party** in 1911. His wing left this party when other members opposed his support for Britain's role in World War I. In 1916 he formed the National Socialist Party. As well as writing pro-Marxist books such as *The Historical Basis of Socialism* (1883), Hyndman used his personal **wealth** to further the socialist cause.

– I –

ICELANDIC SOCIAL DEMOCRATIC ALLIANCE [*SAM-FYLKINGIN* (SF)].

The Icelandic Social Democratic Party (*Alþýðuflokkurin*) was formed in 1916 as a labor party based on the **trade unions**. It became independent of the unions in 1940, but its effectiveness was weakened by the defection of its left wing to a **communist** group. The *Alþýðuflokkurin* participated in coalition governments in 1958 to 1959, 1959 to 1971, 1978 to 1979 and 1991 to 1995. It has been a member of the **Socialist International** since about 1987, when it had a membership of about 5,000. In the parliamentary elections of 1995 the *Alþýðuflokkurin* saw its share of the national vote fall to 11.4 percent. A right-wing coalition of the Conservative Independence Party and Progressive Party won that election, and also those of 1999 and 2003. In 1999 discontented members of the *Alþýðuflokkurin* and of other parties formed the more radical Left-Green Alliance, combining traditional social-democratic concerns for equality and social justice with environmentalism and a goal of neutrality in foreign policy. In the elections of 1999, the *Alþýðuflokkurin* joined in an electoral coalition with the People's Alliance and the Women's List. This coalition won a disappointing 17 seats, with 27 percent of the vote. The Left-Green Alliance took six seats with 9 percent of the vote. In 2000 the *Alþýðuflokkurin*-led coalition was made formal, creating the SF, which, notwithstanding divisions resulting from a wide range of views, won 20 seats in the parliamentary elections of 2003 with 31 percent of the vote. The Left-Green Alliance took five seats with 8.8 percent of the vote.

IDEOLOGIES. Socialism is, along with **liberalism** and conservatism, one of the main ideologies whereby political outlooks and commitments are categorized. Ideologies are belief systems, each of which leads to an understanding of the world based on a combination of ideas regarding concepts such as equality, freedom, justice, and obligation. The ideology one holds leads to a view of how the problems of the world may be resolved. Political movements, groups, and parties comprise people who understand the world in similar terms and share ideas of how that world may be bettered, even though there is usually disagreement among members of groups on the details of such understandings and ideas. Ideologies are notoriously difficult to define, as there is often disagreement among holders of a particular ideology. Nevertheless, all socialists are committed to some degree of social equality, cooperation, responsibility to one's fellow humans, and the belief that people can only be understood as members of society, rather than as atomistic individuals. Socialism itself can be divided into variants, such as **Marxism, Fabianism, Leninism, utopian socialism, Christian socialism, guild socialism,** and others, which are sometimes considered ideologies in themselves.

Ideologies overlap one another. Hence, for example, the liberal philosopher **John Stuart Mill** declared tentatively on occasions that he might be considered as a kind of socialist. Some ideologies such as **anarchism** and feminism overlap two or more other ideologies. While anarchism is often, for example, considered to be part of the socialist family, some thinkers adhere to certain anarchist tenets while opposing those that many anarchists share with socialists. Hence, some ultralibertarian thinkers who are committed to the free market are sometimes described as anarcho-capitalists. Within the broader feminist ideology is **socialist feminism**. *See also* AFRICAN SOCIALISM; ANARCHO-SYNDICALISM; ARAB SOCIALISM; CHARTISM; COMMUNISM; ECONOMISM; FEDERALISM; IMPERIALISM; INTERNATIONALISM; MUTUALISM; NATIONALISM; PACIFISM; REVISIONISM; STATE SOCIALISM; SYNDICALISM; ZIONISM.

IMPERIALISM. From the late nineteenth century the empires of the Western European countries began to receive increasing attention from the socialist movement. In 1904 the Amsterdam conference of the **Second International** established a colonial bureau, but there were important divisions of opinion among its leaders regarding socialist policy about imperialism. Imperialism was condemned outright by the British **Independent Labour Party** (ILP) and the **Social Democratic Federation** because of the passions aroused by the Boer War (1899–1902) but others disagreed. **Eduard Bernstein** supported Germany's imperialism on the grounds that it assisted the German economy and brought benefits to the native populations. Dutch socialist leaders opposed the exploitation of imperialism, but also believed it brought benefits to indigenous peoples. In his *India* (1909), **Keir Hardie** exposed the destruction of native crafts by capitalist competition and the oppression of the peasantry by moneylenders.

The Belgian Workers' Party (later **Belgian Socialist Party**) opposed the outrageous abuses of human rights in King Leopold II's colony of the Congo Free State (modern Zaire and, since 1997, Democratic Republic of the Congo), but found it hard to form an alternative response. Some wanted the Congo to be placed under international supervision, an unrealistic option given the fierce competition for African lands among the European powers. Others opposed imperialism in principle, but declined to offer an alternative policy. Many opposed the proposal of **Émile Vandervelde** to transfer the Congo to the control of the Belgian parliament (which was done in 1908) on the grounds that it made Belgium a participant in imperialism. In Britain, one of the leaders of the campaign against Leopold's brutal rule in the Congo was Edmund Dere Morel (1873–1924), who was then a supporter of the Liberal Party but joined the ILP in 1914.

In 1940 the **British Labour Party** included an end to imperialism and the rapid progression of colonies to self-government in its aims for peace—programs it implemented after its election victory in 1945. From that time onward, democratic socialist and social-democratic parties played a leading role in dismantling the empires of the European powers. The main exceptions were the **Dutch Labor Party**, which was ambivalent about independence for Indonesia (the former Dutch East Indies in 1949), and France, where the socialist ministers of the government of **Guy Mollet** (1956–57) affirmed that country's harsh rule in Algeria and the decision to send troops to the Suez Canal after its **nationalization** by Colonel Gamel Abdel Nasser in 1956. Mollet, however, was also responsible for granting some autonomy to France's colonies south of the Sahara. *See also* WAR.

INDEPENDENT LABOUR PARTY (ILP). The ILP was a British socialist political party formed at Bradford, England, by **Keir Hardie** in January 1893. Its purpose was to assist the election of labor candidates who were independent of the Liberal Party in local and national elections, the Liberal Party at the time being the only political election vehicle for candidates representing the **working class** in Britain. The ILP sought the eight-hour working day, social services for the widowed and sick, work for the **unemployed**, and the abolition of overtime. It drew most of its support from the Midlands, Lancashire, Yorkshire, and Scotland. Party organization was loose with a large number of branches that enjoyed a high degree of autonomy. The ILP was an affiliate of the **Second International**. Its socialism was **pacifist** and international. It opposed the Boer War, World War I, and World War II.

In February 1900 the ILP, along with the **Fabian** Society, the **Social Democratic Federation**, and representatives of 41 **trade unions** formed the Labour Representation Committee, which became the **British Labour Party** in 1906. Before 1914 the ILP was the main source of leaders, ideas, and individual members of the Labour Party. It also provided an extensive regional presence that the Labour Party then lacked. In 1914 the ILP had 672 branches, compared to 150 local Labour parties and affiliated trade union councils. **Ramsay Mac-Donald** was its leading figure before 1920. After the 1906 elections 29 members of the Labour Party were elected to the House of Commons of whom seven were ILP candidates and 11 were ILP members. The membership of the ILP grew during World War I from 16,000 to 35,000. In Glasgow, Scotland, it played an important role in the shop stewards' (trade union delegates) movement and organizing strikes from 1916 to 1918.

In 1922 the ILP adopted a revised constitution that declared that it sought a "Socialist Commonwealth" in which "Land and Capital are communally owned, and the process of production, distribution, and exchange are social functions." It affirmed its belief in political and economic democracy and that the interests of workers were the same regardless of race, color, or creed. From this time onward the ILP faced increasing competition for left-wing support from the Labour Party, which adopted a **socialization objective** in its 1918 constitution, and from the Communist Party. The ILP entered a period of instability. Membership fluctuated, rising from between 25,000 to 30,000 in 1922, to between 55,000 and 60,000 in 1926, and then falling to 16,800 in 1932. Lacking a broad base in the **trade unions**, the ILP could never hope to become a mass political party. Yet it remained strong in Glasgow, where its leading figures were David Kirkwood and James Maxton.

Growing differences between the ILP and the Labour Party led to the disaffiliation of the ILP in 1932. The process of separation actually began in 1917 when the Labour Party amended its constitution to exclude affiliated organizations with less than 50,000 members from making a direct nomination to the party's executive, a move which was directly aimed at the ILP. By 1935 the membership of the ILP had fallen to 4,392. Some who left in the 1930s joined the

Communist Party and others joined the fascists. In 1937 the ILP conference condemned the idea of the **Popular Front**. Moves to reaffiliate with the Labour Party were pushed aside by World War II. In 1945 three ILP members were elected to the House of Commons. One, James Maxton, the party's leader, died in 1946 and the remaining two joined the Labour Party. There were no ILP members elected to parliament after 1950 and no candidates were nominated after 1959. The ILP continued into the 1960s. It opposed conventional as well as **nuclear weapons**, but its membership had fallen to about 300 compared to about 3,000 in 1948. The ILP continued to operate as a small organization under its original name until 1975, when it was transformed into a pressure group named Independent Labour Publications (hence still ILP).

INDUSTRIAL REVOLUTION. The *Industrial Revolution* was a term coined in the early 1900s to describe a massive shift in the economy that was marked by technical innovations (in particular the invention of the steam engine), improvements in transportation, and the large-scale production of goods. Although industrial revolutions have been claimed for earlier periods and countries, the origin of the Industrial Revolution is traditionally associated with late eighteenth-century England. Once developed, its features were emulated by other countries to varying degrees from the 1830s. The Industrial Revolution both reflected and fortified **capitalism** even though **communist** governments, particularly those of the former Soviet Union and China, used its techniques to speed up economic development in the twentieth century. The Industrial Revolution hastened the development of socialism by creating the changes necessary for it to become a mass movement. It led to a rapid increase in the number of urban wage-and-salary earners employed by large enterprises, thereby providing the basis for large-scale **trade unions** from the 1880s. The increase in the social distance between employers and employees accentuated class divisions and provided favorable conditions for the spread of socialist doctrines. **Karl Marx** saw the industrial revolution in terms of the development of productive forces necessary for a change from capitalist to socialist relations of production.

INDUSTRIAL WORKERS OF THE WORLD (IWW). The IWW was the American expression of **syndicalism**, which was influential in international organized labor from the early 1900s until about 1920. Although the works of European theorists such as **Karl Marx** and **Georges Sorel** were known, the IWW, which came to be widely known as the "Wobblies," owed its origins to the violent labor environment of the mining industry in the western United States. The prime mover in the formation of the IWW was the radical Western Federation of Miners, a body that originated in the Butte Miners' Union established in 1878. After defeats in disputes in 1903 to 1904, particularly at Cripple Creek, Colorado, the Western Federation of Miners called a convention in Chicago to create a single organization for the **working class** in 1904, which led to the creation of the IWW in 1905. The convention adopted a radical platform, declaring that employers and workers had nothing in common and agreeing to build an organization that admitted all employees regardless of sex, race, or nationality, an idea dormant in American organized labor since the demise of the Knights of Labor in the late 1880s.

By 1906 the IWW claimed 14,000 members but was able to mobilize far greater support among poorly paid and exploited workers. It campaigned for free speech in the late 1900s, which provoked vigilante violence, and conducted America's first sit-down strike at the General Electric plant at Schenectady, New York, in 1906. The IWW proved adept at mobilizing working-class discontent but not at creating lasting organizations. With the entry of the United States into World War I in 1917, the IWW, which opposed the **war**, came under direct attack from the federal government, which raided IWW offices and arrested the bulk of the leadership. At its height, between 1919 and 1924, the membership of the IWW ranged between 58,000 and 100,000, some of whom joined the American **Communist** Party. The IWW was not a significant force after 1924. Although primarily an American organization, the IWW was an important force in Canada and was a focus for left-wing activity in Argentina, Australia, Mexico, New Zealand, and South Africa. *See also* DELEON, DANIEL.

INHERITANCE. As a mechanism for the perpetuation of inequalities of **wealth** and income, socialism regarded the principle of inheritance of property with suspicion, if not hostility. **Karl Marx** and **Friedrich Engels** in the *Communist Manifesto* (1848) called for the complete abolition of inheritance rights. At that time inheritance would not benefit most of the **working class** because they had no property to pass on to their descendants or relatives. The **Erfurt Program** (1891) of the **German Social Democratic Party** moderated this position; it demanded instead that inheritances should be subjected to graduated tax according to the size of the inheritance and the degree of the relationship between the deceased and the beneficiary. The Brunn Program (1901) of the **Austrian Social Democratic Party** regarded a graduated tax on inheritance along with income and property as a substitute for all indirect forms of **taxation**. In the post-1945 period, nonsocialist as well as socialist governments have imposed inheritance taxes to pay for greatly increased government expenditure on defense and the **welfare state**.

INSTITUTIONAL REVOLUTIONARY PARTY [*PARTIDO REV-OLUCIONARIO INSTITUCIONAL* (PRI)]. The PRI, then called the National Revolutionary Party (*Partido Nacional Revolucionario*) was formed in 1929 to unite the revolutionary factions that survived the factional rivalries, violence, and assassinations that followed the Mexican revolution, which began in 1910. It ruled Mexico until 2000, working under several names in its early years. The party was eventually renamed the PRI by President Manuel Ávila Camacho in January 1946, shortly before the presidency (1946–52) of Miguel Alemán Valdés (1902–83) began. Although the PRI officially governed according to the revolutionary constitution of 1917, which expressed socialist ideas of land redistribution and workers' rights, it gradually became more concerned with keeping power, through patronage and manipulation of election results. It dominated the presidency and both houses of parliament. In the 1970s and 1980s the PRI suppressed many among the Mexican left.

Under the presidency of Carlos Salinas from 1988 to 1994, the PRI introduced economic reforms including **privatization** and membership in the North American Free Trade Agreement (NAFTA). Many on the left in Mexico and elsewhere considered that the most significant result would be that Mexico would become a source of cheap labor for the United States and Canada. Once economic reform had begun, the PRI found that its powers of patronage were waning. Moreover, **trade unions** were able to act independently of the PRI. In addition to the economic reforms, the PRI began to end electoral irregularities. In the parliamentary elections of 1997 the PRI lost control of the Chamber of Deputies. In the presidential elections of July

2000 the PRI candidate Francisco Labastida, who won 36 percent of the vote, lost to the candidate of a center-right coalition, Vicente Fox. The PRI reformed itself as a social-democratic party, opposing some of Fox's free market–oriented economic measures. In July 2003 the PRI enjoyed success at the parliamentary elections, winning 224 of the 500 seats. With its ally the Ecologist Green Party, which took 17 seats with 4 percent of the vote, the PRI gained control of the Chamber of Deputies. The PRI also became the biggest party in the Senate in July 2003, with 58 of the 128 seats. The PRI gained full membership in the **Socialist International** in October 2003. *See also* PARTY OF THE DEMOCRATIC REVOLUTION.

INSTITUTIONS. *See* COOPERATIVE MOVEMENT; FRIENDLY SOCIETIES; POLITICAL PARTIES; TRADE UNIONS.

INTERNATIONAL ALLIANCE OF SOCIALIST LAWYERS (IASL). The IASL was formed under the auspices of the **Labor and Socialist International** at its Brussels congress in 1928 to advise it on legal matters and to assist it with socialists who were victims of persecution. The IASL was built on existing organizations in Germany and Austria. In 1931 the IASL had 1,500 members in 15 countries.

INTERNATIONAL BRIGADES. The International Brigades were left-wing volunteers who fought on the republican side during the **Spanish Civil War** (1936–39) against General Francisco Franco. The **war** was generally regarded as a fight against fascism among socialists of all persuasions. The Brigades were organized mainly by the **Comintern** and operated between October 1936 and October 1938; many, although not all of its participants, were **communists**. American volunteers were organized in the Abraham Lincoln Brigades, of which about 60 percent were communists. The main places where the Brigades fought were Córdoba, Brunete, Guadalajara, and Zaragoza. In all, about 59,000 men fought in the International Brigades; of these, nearly 10,000 were killed and 8,000 badly wounded. Most of the volunteers came from France (28,000), Belgium (14,000), Italy (4,500 of whom 3,000 were living in exile), United States (2,800), and the United Kingdom (2,440), but most other parts of Europe were represented, as well as volunteers from

Canada and Australasia. Although **George Orwell** was the best-remembered British fighter on the republican side, he was not in the Brigades. In January 1996 the Spanish parliament agreed to grant citizenship to the 400 worldwide survivors of the International Brigades, thereby fulfilling a promise made by the dying republican government in 1938. *See also* ANARCHISM.

INTERNATIONAL CONFEDERATION OF FREE TRADE UNIONS (ICFTU). The ICFTU has been the largest international body representing organized labor in noncommunist countries since its formation in 1949. After the **International Federation of Trade Unions** was replaced by the **World Federation of Trade Unions** in 1945, there was growing concern over infiltration of the new body by **communist** organizations controlled by the Soviet Union. This concern was strongest in the United States, the United Kingdom, and the Netherlands, which set up the ICFTU in 1949. At its founding, the ICFTU had 51 countries as members, which represented 48 million union members of whom 43 percent were in Western Europe and 31 percent in North America. Despite its strong support for independent **trade unions**, many of the ICFTU's members in Latin America, Africa, and Asia violated this principle. By the 1960s the ICFTU had broadened its perspective to include progressive social goals. In 1969 the politically conservative American Federation of Labor-Congress of Industrial Organizations withdrew from the ICFTU and did not rejoin until 1981.

In 1984 the ICFTU began to conduct annual surveys of violations of trade union rights in the world. After 1989 some labor federations from former East European communist countries were admitted to membership in the ICFTU. By 1996 organized labor in Eastern Europe accounted for 9 percent of the 125 million members in the ICFTU. When in 2000 Russian labor federations were admitted as affiliates, the total membership rose by 30 million, thus making the membership from Eastern Europe grow to 24 percent. As well as country members, International Trade Secretariats, bodies representing employees in particular industries, have also been associated with the ICFTU, although they retain their autonomy. In December 2004, at its eighteenth World Congress, the ICFTU elected its first female president, Sharon Burrow of the Australian Council of Trade Unions. By the end of the conference more than 25 percent of the positions on the ICFTU's executive were held by **women**. In 2005 the ICFTU claimed to represent 145 million workers in 234 affiliated organizations and from 154 countries and territories.

INTERNATIONAL CO-OPERATIVE ALLIANCE (ICA). The ICA was set up in London in August 1895 with a mixed membership of individuals and organizations in the **cooperative movement**. It originated in the Co-operative Union, a centralized body designed to assist, represent, and promote the interests of the various British consumer cooperatives, which was set up in 1870. An international conference of cooperatives held in London was attended by representatives from Belgium, France, Germany, Italy, and the Netherlands as well as the United Kingdom. In 1895 the Co-operative Union agreed to become the British section of the ICA. After 1901 only organizations were allowed to remain members. Individuals were excluded. The aims of the ICA were to promote the principles and methods of consumer and producer cooperation, to provide a forum for friendly relations between cooperatives internationally, and to further economic and social progress for all people in every country through cooperation. An International Cooperative Women's Guild was formed in Basle, Switzerland, in 1921.

The early growth of the ICA was impressive; by 1921 it claimed a global (mainly European) membership of 25 million. But growth was hampered by totalitarian suppression of free cooperatives in Italy (1924), Germany (1933), and the Soviet Union. By 1940 the ICA claimed 40 million members. With the admission of other forms of cooperative societies after 1940 and the push to build membership outside Europe after 1945, the membership of the ICA reached 214 million by 1964. Since that time, the ICA has again expanded impressively; in 2003 the ICA had 230 affiliated member organizations in over 100 countries representing more than 760 million people. *See also* CO-OPERATIVE WHOLESALE SOCIETY.

THE "INTERNATIONALE." As the anthem of international socialism, the "Internationale" is intended to rally **working-class** unity and action. The lyrics were written by Eugène Pottier (1816–87) in 1887, a former member of the **International Workingmen's Association** and a participant in the **Paris Commune**. The music was composed by Pierre de Geyter (1848–1932) in 1888. The "Internationale" was adopted by the **Second International** and was made the national anthem of the Soviet Union in 1921, retaining this status until 1944. As a result, the "Internationale" became more associated with the revolutionary tradition of socialism rather than with the reformist tradition.

INTERNATIONAL FALCON MOVEMENT–SOCIALIST EDUCATIONAL INTERNATIONAL (IFM-SEI). The IFM-SEI was formed in Amsterdam in October 1947 to coordinate and promote the educational and political efforts of democratic socialist member organizations. It was intended to replace the Socialist Education International, which operated between 1924 and 1940. **Youth** is a particular target of the IFM-SEI in its promotion of **education**. The present title of the organization was adopted in 1970. In 2005 the IFM-SEI had 55 members from more than 40 countries, and was a fraternal organization of the **Socialist International**.

INTERNATIONAL FEDERATION OF THE SOCIALIST AND DEMOCRATIC PRESS (IFSDP). Established in 1953 and based in Milan, Italy, the IFSDP aims to promote cooperation between the publishers and editors of socialist newspapers. The IFSDP is an associated organization of the **Socialist International**.

INTERNATIONAL FEDERATION OF TRADE UNIONS (IFTU). The IFTU was the first continuous general international organization of **trade unions**. Officially called the International Secretariat of the National Trade Unions Federations until 1919, the IFTU was formed in Copenhagen on 21 August 1901 by labor representatives from Belgium, France, Germany, Denmark, the United Kingdom, Sweden, Norway, and Finland. The original impetus for the formation of the IFTU came from J. Jensen, the leader of the Danish trade unions, who had attended a conference held by the General Federation of Trade Unions in London in 1900. Its largest affiliates between 1901 and 1913 were the United Kingdom and Germany. The American Federation of Labor joined the IFTU in 1911, but left officially in 1919; it did not reaffiliate until 1937. Before 1913 the IFTU devoted itself to collecting money to help unions and strikers and to exchanging information. World War I split the IFTU along national lines, and it was not reestablished until 1919.

After 1919 the IFTU participated in European politics, a policy that led the American Federation of Labor to withdraw. The IFTU invited the Russian trade unions to its conferences, but these moves were met with hostility from the communist government, which regarded the IFTU as a competitor for the leadership of organized labor. The Russians established Profitern, the labor arm of the **Comintern**, as a rival to the IFTU. The IFTU continued to aid trade unions in affiliated countries and carried out fact-finding missions of workers' conditions in Austria and Belgium (1920) and the Saar and Upper Silesia (1921).

Throughout its life, the IFTU was essentially a moderate, European-based organization and the voice of organized labor in the International Labour Organization. In 1927 the IFTU established an International Committee of Trade Union Women, which lasted until 1937. It considered issues such as equal pay for equal work, domestic service, working from home, and the peace campaign conducted by **women**.

In the 1930s the IFTU tried to widen its membership; India joined in 1934, Mexico in 1936, New Zealand in 1938, and China in 1939. The Australian Council of Trade Unions was invited to join in 1936, but did not accept. At conferences in 1931 and 1932 the IFTU adopted the 40-hour working week and a comprehensive social program as objectives.

Despite its best efforts, the IFTU was weakened by the suppression of organized labor by fascism and was undermined by **communism** and lack of support from the American Federation of Labor for most of its life. The IFTU gave way to the World Federation of Trade Unions and ceased to exist on December 31, 1945. *See also* INTERNATIONAL CONFEDERATION OF FREE TRADE UNIONS.

INTERNATIONALISM. Internationalism—the doctrine of support for cooperation and friendliness between nations and between ordinary people from all nations—has always been a theme of socialism. Given their emphasis on cooperation as a fundamental principle of how society should operate ideally in a nation, it was logical for socialists to apply that idea across nations. **Karl Marx** and **Friedrich Engels** called in the *Communist Manifesto* for working men of all countries to unite. A sustained movement toward internationalism within socialism began in the 1860s in the **cooperative movement**.

The **International Workingmen's Association** was formed in 1864 and a congress of English cooperatives in 1869 was attended by representatives from several European countries. Thereafter the internationalist impetus sagged until the late 1880s as socialist parties sought to establish themselves within countries. Its revival was shown by the establishment of the **Second International** in 1889, the formation of the **International Co-operative Alliance** in 1895, and the **International Federation of Trade Unions** in 1901. The 1900s were the high point of socialist internationalism. Socialist international bodies were formed among **youth** and **women** in 1907 and an international socialist sports organization was formed in 1913. The outbreak of World War I, and the orgy of **nationalism** that accompanied it, together with the success of the Bolshevik coup in Russia in 1917, destroyed the unity of internationalism within socialism; from 1919 international socialism was split into democratic and communist camps. The democratic elements were represented by the **Labor and Socialist International** and the communists by the **Comintern**. Competition from fascism weakened effective democratic socialist internationalism by the 1930s. Practical socialist internationalism has been most successful in Scandinavia and German-speaking countries.

Outside of its immediate ranks, democratic socialism made its interest in internationalism clear by supporting the economic integration of Europe in the **German Social Democratic Party** in the 1920s and in the **British Labour Party** in the 1930s. Since 1945 support for internationalism among democratic socialist parties in Western Europe has continued, but it has been tempered by the need to face the realities of government, the domestic focus of social-democratic governments' policies, and the diversion of attention and resources caused by competition from **communism**. Since the 1970s democratic socialist support for internationalism has been expressed largely through the **Socialist International** and its concern for redressing the huge economic balance between the industrial developed countries and the Third World and issues such as disarmament. *See also* EUROPEAN SOCIALIST MOVEMENT; KRAG, JENS OTTO; NATIONALISM; SOCIALIST MOVEMENT FOR THE UNITED STATES OF EUROPE; SPAAK, PAUL-HENRI.

INTERNATIONAL JEWISH LABOR BUND (IJLB). The IJLB was set up in the United States by Polish-Jewish refugees in 1941.

"Bund" referred to a Jewish labor organization formed secretly in Vilna, Poland, in October 1897 that included **Jews** in Lithuania, Poland, and Russia. Its original title was *Algemyner Yidisher Arbeter Bund in Lite, Poyin un Rusland*, and it claimed 20,000 members by 1904 and 40,000 by 1917. The IJLB held its first international conference in Brussels in 1947 when it adopted its present title. Based in New York, the IJLB is dedicated to the elimination of anti-Semitism and achieving equality and self-determination for Jews, that is, the right of Jews to their own culture within their countries of residence by neither assimilation nor **Zionism**. The IJLB has been an associate member of the **Socialist International** since the founding of the International in 1951. In 1997 the IJLB celebrated the centennial of the Bund.

INTERNATIONAL LABOUR SPORTS CONFEDERATION [*CONFÉDÉRATION SPORTIVE INTERNATIONALE DU TRA-VAIL* (CSIT)]. The CSIT, as it is universally known, was established in Brussels, Belgium, in 1946 as a continuation of the **Socialist Workers' Sports International**. Its aims were to promote equality and solidarity in sport, physical education, and intellectual and moral **education** for all people. It has been an associated organization of the **Socialist International** from 1951. In January 2005 it claimed 35 member organizations in 26 countries, and between 12 and14 million individual members.

INTERNATIONAL LEAGUE OF RELIGIOUS SOCIALISTS (ILRS). Founded in 1922 as the *Union internationale des socialistes religieux* (International Union of Religious Socialists) at Bad Eptingen, Switzerland, and reorganized in 1938, the ILRS was intended to unite **Christian socialists** in a worldwide brotherhood and promote socialism. It is now open to all **religions** and opposes religious fundamentalism and the religious right. The ILRS campaigns for tolerance of religious diversity and social and economic equality throughout the world. In 2004 the ILRS membership consisted of religious socialist organizations in Australia, Austria, Bulgaria, Costa Rica, the Dominican Republic, Finland, Germany, Hungary, Italy, Latvia, Lithuania, the Netherlands, Norway, the Philippines, South Africa, Spain (Basque country), Sri Lanka, Sweden, Switzerland, the United Kingdom, and the United States. Individuals can only join indirectly, through the affiliated organizations. In 2004 the ILRS claimed to represent over 200,000 socialists of different faiths in the world's socialist, social-democratic, and labor parties. The ILRS is an associated organization of the **Socialist International**. *See also* CHRISTIANITY; JEWS.

INTERNATIONAL OF REVOLUTIONARY SYNDICALISTS (IRS). The IRS was an **anarcho-syndicalist** body that was established as an independent body to the Profintern—an arm of the **Comintern** designed to infiltrate **trade unions** in July 1921—in Berlin in December 1922. The congress resolved to adopt its formal title, the **International Workingmen's Association**, as a gesture of continuity with the first international socialist organization, but it is not generally known by this name. Its delegates represented about a million members. In 1923 the Spanish *Confedración del Trabajo* (Confederation of Labor) joined the IRS and raised its membership to more than 2 million. Other organizations that joined the IRS were located in Bulgaria, Poland, and Japan. In 1928 the anarcho-syndicalist unions in Argentina, Brazil, Bolivia, Costa Rica, Guatemala, Mexico, Paraguay, and Uruguay formed their own international, which became the American division of the IRS and raised its membership to about 3 million. The strength of the IRS was destroyed by fascism, first in Italy in 1924, and then in the 1930s in Germany, Spain, and Portugal. Its headquarters was moved to Stockholm where it survived, at least on paper, into the 1960s. *See also* SYNDICALISM.

INTERNATIONAL SOCIAL DEMOCRATIC UNION FOR EDUCATION (ISDUE). Formed as the International Union of Social Democratic Teachers (IUSDT) at Versailles, France, in July 1951, the International Social Democratic Union for Education provides a worldwide forum for socialist educators. The ISDUE is a union of socialist and social-democratic organizations for **education**. It stresses the importance of lifelong learning and of education for human rights, social justice, international understanding, and citizenship. Affiliated with the **Socialist International**, the USDT had members in autonomous organizations in 23 countries in 2005. *See also* COMMISSION OF SOCIALIST EDUCATORS OF THE EUROPEAN UNION.

INTERNATIONAL SOCIALIST WOMEN'S COMMITTEE (ISWC). The ISWC developed out of an international women's conference, which was held in Hamburg in connection with the first congress of the **Labor and Socialist International** (LSI) in 1923. Its origins can be traced to the International Women's Congress, which was created in 1907 as part of the **Second International**; the first international women's conference had been held in Copenhagen in 1910. The 1931 congress of the ISWC, which was held in Vienna in connection with that of the Labor and Socialist International, discussed women's **suffrage**, their right to work, the organization of **women**, women in **agriculture** and domestic service, and the status of housewives. In 1928 there were 973,900 women members of the LSI. *See also* INTERNATIONAL WOMEN'S DAY.

INTERNATIONAL UNION OF SOCIALIST TEETOTALERS. *See* TEMPERANCE.

INTERNATIONAL UNION OF SOCIALIST YOUTH (IUSY). The IUSY was originally founded in 1907, but after being suspended during World Wars I and II was reestablished in Paris in October 1946 as a successor to the International of Socialist Youth, which operated between May 1923 and 1939. The aims of the IUSY were to promote the cause of democratic socialism among young people, to fight against **racism**, fascism, and **imperialism**, and to fight for the right of all people for free and independent social development. The IUSY is a fraternal organization of the **Socialist International** and has relations with international bodies concerned with **youth**. In 2005 the IUSY had 143 affiliated member organizations in 100 countries.

INTERNATIONAL WOMEN'S DAY. The first practical steps to institute an international day to draw attention to the needs of **women** were taken in Germany by **Clara Zetkin** and Louise Zietz just before the congress of the **Second International** in Stuttgart in 1910 based on the example of May Day. However, the initiative failed. Women's Day was not held in Western Europe until 18 March 1911, the fortieth anniversary of the **Paris Commune**. In the United States, in accordance with a declaration by the **Socialist Party of America**, a National Woman's Day was begun on Sunday 28 February 1909. The last Sunday in February was also adopted by socialists in the Russian empire. It was on International Women's Day, on 23 February 1917 according to the Gregorian calendar, but 8 March 1917 according to the Julian calendar, that Russian women in Petrograd effectively launched the "February" Revolution. Zetkin persuaded **V. I. Lenin** to declare International Woman's Day a holiday in **communist** countries from 1922. In 1967 feminist students in Chicago revived the idea of an international Women's Day. The date for International Women's Day became 8 March. In 2005, as in previous years, International Women's Day was celebrated in many countries throughout the world. *See also* INTERNATIONAL SOCIALIST WOMEN'S COMMITTEE.

INTERNATIONAL WORKINGMEN'S ASSOCIATION (IWMA). Also known as the First International, the IWMA was the first attempt to found an international body to protect and advance the interests of the **working class**. Although the idea was suggested by **Flora Tristan** in 1843, the IWMA was formed in London in September 1864 against a background of a depressed economy (the late 1850s saw a slump in the building trades in London and Paris, and the American Civil War hurt employment in the British textile industry) and importantly the presence of some French labor leaders who were in the United Kingdom at the time to support the Polish revolt against Russian rule in 1863. Once the IWMA was established, **Karl Marx** and **Friedrich Engels** took the leading role in its affairs. The IWMA was mainly composed of the leaders of English organized labor and political émigrés from continental Europe. A split developed between these two groups, particularly after 1867 when the better-off English urban working class was given the vote; they tended to support reformist solutions for labor's problems, whereas continental European members could not envisage their governments ever granting the necessary concessions; they tended to support revolution.

These tensions eventually proved fatal to the IWMA. It broke up at its Hague conference in 1872, and Marx moved it to New York to avoid it coming under **anarchist** control. It was formally wound up in Philadelphia in 1876. Although primarily a radical political organization, the IWMA assisted the campaign in northeast England in 1871 to 1872 for the nine-hour day and frustrated the employers' attempt to recruit strikebreakers from continental Europe. In return, the

IWMA was allowed to raise money in Britain to assist strikers in other parts of Europe. A short-lived offshoot body of the IWMA, the Democratic Association of Victoria, operated in Australia in 1872. The maximum total membership of the IWMA was about 350,000. *See also* SECOND INTERNATIONAL.

INTERNATIONAL WORKING UNION OF SOCIALIST PARTIES (IWUSP). Also known as the Vienna Union, this body, which was dubbed the Two-and-a-Half International by **V. I. Lenin**, was formed in 1921 by the socialist parties of Austria, France, and Switzerland, the German Independent Socialist Party, and the British Independent Socialist Party, all of which did not want to join either the **Second International** or the **Comintern**. A unity conference between these three bodies in Berlin in 1922 broke down. In May 1923, at a second congress in Hamburg, the IWUSP joined the remnants of the former Second International to form the **Labor and Socialist International**.

IRISH LABOUR PARTY (LABOUR). Like the **British Labour Party**, Labour was created by the **trade union** movement. Formed in 1912, it has been a minor party for most of its history. The reasons for the weakness of the party lay in the rural nature of Irish society, the overriding importance of **nationalism** in Irish politics, and the separation of Ulster from the Irish Republic, which denied the party access to the only large concentration of urban **working-class** people in the country. Concerned with issues such as social justice, poverty, and **unemployment** but faced with a conservative Catholic electorate, the party's appeal was limited; between 1923 and 1957, the party only gained 10 percent of the vote on one occasion, 1948. Conflict with the Catholic hierarchy arose in 1939 when the church declared that the reference to the setting up of a workers' republic in the party's constitution of 1936 was contrary to Catholic teaching; the reference had to be removed.

The party suffered because of conflicts within the trade union movement, particularly the split between the British-based unions and Irish unions. In 1943 founder member James Larkin (1876–1947), a radical socialist and general secretary of the Workers' Union of Ireland, succeeded in being elected to parliament as Labour member. This caused the Irish Transport and General Workers' Union leadership to disaffiliate from Labour, to accuse the Party of being in-filtrated by **communists**, and to establish a separate labor party, the National Labour Party, which existed until 1948. Two years later Labour was reunited. In the 1960s the party grew and enjoyed in-creased support. Several times in the 1970s and 1980s it joined the Fine Gael party as a partner in coalition government. It withdrew in 1987 over Fine Gael's proposal of cuts in the **health care** budget.

In 1990 the Labour candidate Mary Robinson was elected president. She was the first Irish **woman** to hold that office, serving until 1997. In the early 1990s the party merged with two small Irish socialist parties. After making significant gains in the November 1992 elections, which increased the number of seats they held from 15 to 33, Labour entered into a coalition government with the Fianna Fáil party in January 1993. Disagreements in November the following year led Labour to leave the coalition. The following month the party entered into a coalition gov-ernment with the Fine Gael and Democratic Left parties, an arrange-ment which ended in June 1997. The party lost support in the 1997 par-liamentary elections, with its share of the seats reduced to 21. Its candidate also failed to win the presidency. Long-standing leader Dick Spring resigned that year. In 1999 Labour and the Democratic Left merged under the name of the former. In the parliamentary elections of 2002 Labour once again won 21 seats. That year Ruairi Quinn stepped down as party leader and was replaced by Pat Rabbitte. *See also* SO-CIAL AND DEMOCRATIC LABOUR PARTY.

"IRON LAW OF OLIGARCHY." A phrase coined by the German po-litical theorist Robert Michels (1876–1936) to describe what he re-garded as the inevitable tendency for large **political parties** to be-come bureaucratic and less democratic, with decision making dominated by a small number of leaders. The organization may be democratic in theory, but in reality it is an oligarchy. Michels was ac-tive in the **German Social Democratic Party** (*Sozialdemokratische Partei Deutschland*—SPD) before 1907 and used it as the model for the élite theory he published as *Political Parties* in German in 1911 and in English in 1915. He eventually became a fascist, admiring **Benito Mussolini**. Michels's views have been criticized for ignoring the effects of the repressive **Antisocialist Law** on the SPD and the growth of the lower levels of the party's organization after 1907. *See also* LEADERSHIP/RANK AND FILE TENSIONS.

ISRAEL LABOR PARTY [*MIFLEGET HA-'AVODAH HA-YI'S-RE'ELIT (HAAVODA)*]. Founded in January 1968 *HaAvoda* is the direct descendent of the oldest Israeli **political parties**. It was formed by the merger of the *Mapai* (which had been founded by **David Ben-Gurion** and others in January 1933), the *Rafi* (a breakaway party from the *Mapai* also founded by Ben-Gurion in 1965), and another party, the *Achdet Avoda*. The *HaAvoda* led coalition governments from 1948 to 1977 and participated in governments of national unity of varying political complexions from 1984 to 1996. Shimon Peres—a member of the *Mapai* since 1959, general secretary of the *Rafi* from 1965 to 1968, and chairman of *HaAvoda* from 1977 to 1992—served as prime minister from 1984 to 1986. He was replaced as chairman in February 1992 by Yitzhak Rabin (1922–95), who led *HaAvoda* to victory in the elections of June 1992 and formed a coalition government in July.

HaAvoda is a **Zionist** and a socialist party. Its socialism has been evident in its support for the **welfare state**, **trade unions**, the separation of state and **religion**, and, most controversially, equal treatment for minorities, including Israel's Arabs, especially in the Israeli-occupied Palestinian West Bank and (until August 2005) Gaza Strip. Its foreign policy has been one of seeking a negotiated settlement with Israel's Arab neighbors, a policy that led to hostility from Jewish settlers in the face of rising **terrorism** from Arab extremists: one of these Jewish settlers assassinated Rabin on 11 November 1995. Peres again became prime minister but was defeated in the election of 29 May 1996, the first election in which the prime minister was chosen by the direct vote of the electors.

In 1999 Ehud Barak of *HaAvoda* was elected prime minister, following the collapse of a right-wing coalition. Barak promised to end the Israeli-Arab conflict within a year. Although he succeeded in ending Israel's occupation of Lebanon, violence between Israelis and Palestinians began to increase. In February 2001 Barak lost the presidential elections to the right-wing candidate Ariel Sharon, whose tougher approach to the problems appealed to many Israelis. Nevertheless, Sharon included *HaAvoda* ministers in his coalition government. In October 2002 the Labor ministers resigned over the policy of funding Jewish settlements in the West Bank. Sharon, who was unable to govern without *HaAvoda* support, called an early election for January 2003. Sharon formed a right-wing coalition without

HaAvoda, which won 19 of the 120 seats. Amidst continuing violence, *HaAvoda* joined Sharon's coalition in January 2005. The *HaAvoda* leader Peres explained that this was to ensure that the plan to disengage from the Gaza Strip and parts of the West Bank would go ahead. In November 2005 *HaAvoda* narrowly elected Amir Peretz as leader, thus unseating Peres. Peretz opposed free-market reforms and spending cuts because of their impact upon the poor. Believing that his party should return to traditional social democracy, he pulled *HaAvoda* out of the governing coalition. Later that month Peres resigned from the party. In the parliamentary elections of March 2006, *HaAvoda* took 19 seats, and in May, it entered a coalition government led by the new center-right *Kadima* (Forward) Party. *HaAvoda* has always been a full member of the **Socialist International**.

ITALIAN DEMOCRATIC SOCIALISTS [*SOCIALISTI DEMOCRATICI ITALIANI* (SDI)]. Founded as the Italian Socialist Party (*Partito Socialista Italiano*—PSI) in Genoa in August 1892, the party now known as the SDI has had an unhappy history of major splits because of the polarized character of Italian society and politics and because Italy lagged behind other Western European countries in achieving genuinely democratic government; for example, universal male **suffrage** was not granted until 1912 and the right could not be exercised until the 1913 national elections. As well, Italy was torn by widespread rural discontent from the late 1890s. The PSI faced strong competition from **anarchism** and **syndicalism** before 1914 and from **communism** after 1920. These pressures, plus the lack of political experience of the leadership of the PSI in government, promoted an air of unreality and impracticality within the PSI. The growth in electoral support for the PSI was comparatively slow; in 1895 it secured 7 percent of the vote. In 1900 this had doubled to 13 percent, but in 1913 this support had only grown to 18 percent. Reformists ("minimalists") and revolutionaries ("maximalists") fought for control of the PSI in 1912 and 1917. **Benito Mussolini** was one of the leaders of the left wing of the PSI before 1914.

Party membership fluctuated wildly. In 1914 the PSI had 58,000 members, but only 24,000 by August 1918 and then 216,000 by 1920, a reflection of the upsurge in rural and industrial unrest at the time. In 1919 the PSI officially left the Second International and agreed to join the **Comintern**. Despite intervention by **Clara Zetlin**, the PSI refused to expel the reformists as demanded and by 1921 negotiations had broken down. The political immaturity of the PSI was shown in November 1919 when 156 socialist deputies were elected (131 from the north), an impressive result that was drained of significance because many did not bother to attend parliament, confidently expecting an imminent revolution. But the threat of revolution alienated the **middle class** and fed the ranks of the fascists.

In January 1921 the left wing of the PSI, including **Antonio Gramsci**, split and formed the Italian Communist Party (*Partito Communista Italiano*—PCI). From this time onward all the left-wing parties faced physical assault from Mussolini's supporters (the "blackshirts"). The formation of the PCI split the left and cost the PSI about a third of its membership. In October 1922 a Reformist Socialist Party was formed with Giacomo Matteotti as secretary; Matteotti's murder by the fascists on 10 June 1924 is generally regarded as the formal beginning of Mussolini's dictatorship. In November 1925 a member of the Reformist Party tried to assassinate Mussolini, who used the incident to outlaw the party. In November 1926 the PSI was formally outlawed, but by then its membership had slumped to 15,000.

The PSI was reconstituted in Paris and was recognized by the **Labor and Socialist International** (LSI). In 1930 the PSI was reunited in exile when the maximalists and the reformists came together. Otherwise the PSI took no effective part in the resistance to Mussolini. In contrast, the PCI maintained an active resistance movement and 3,000 of its members were imprisoned. In August 1934 the PSI and PCI reached an accord to consult and cooperate with each other on matters of mutual concern. This Unity of Action agreement, which, with a break between 1939 and 1942, ran until the mid-1950s, worked to the advantage of the communists, who were the best-organized force in the Italian left. Under the leadership of Palmiro Togliatti (1893–1964), the PCI shrewdly adopted a policy of working for "progressive democracy" in April 1944. Togliatti realized that no Italian revolution was possible without Soviet intervention and that the party would have to work with the Catholic church and the liberals to further its ends. Despite its impotence and general lack of coherence as a party, the PSI attracted 20.7 percent of the vote in the national elections of 1946, compared to 18.9 percent for the Communists. In January 1947 the reformists in the PSI led by

Giuseppe Saragat split over cooperation with the PCI and formed the Italian Workers' Socialist Party (IWSP), which in 1952 joined with other parties to become the Italian Democratic Socialist Party (*Partito Socialista Democratico Italiano*—PSDI). In 1949 the PSI was excluded from the **Committee of the International Socialist Conference** because of its dependence upon the PCI. In 1966 the PSDI rejoined the PSI but broke away again in 1969.

After the Soviets crushed the Hungarian uprising in 1956, the dominance of the PCI within the Italian left began to decline and the PSI began to develop slowly into a truly independent party; for example, it accepted Italian membership in the North Atlantic Treaty Organization (NATO). In 1962 the Christian Democrat Amintore Fanfani formed a government with PSI support, even though its support at the 1963 elections was only 13.8 percent, compared to 25.3 percent for the Communists. In 1976 **Bettino Craxi** became leader of the PSI. A social-democratic, non-Marxist program was adopted in 1978 and the traditional PSI symbols of the rising sun and the hammer and sickle were replaced by the red carnation. At the same time the Communists continued to provide significant competition to the PSI by becoming more moderate. This process continued until in February 1991 the PCI transformed itself into a noncommunist party, the Italian **Democratic Party of the Left** (*Partito Democratico della Sinistra*—PDS).

Between 1946 and 1973 the membership of the PSI fell from 850,000 to 463,000. Over the same period the proportion of members who lived in the north fell from 50 to 43 percent, and the proportion which lived in the south rose from 30 to 38 percent. What is even more striking about the PSI in the post-1945 period has been its poor electoral showing. Even when their votes were combined, the Italian socialist parties, until the emergence of the PDS, attracted at most only about a fifth of the vote; in 1987, for example, they received 17 percent of the vote—the PSI receiving 14 percent and the ISDP receiving 3 percent. Nevertheless, Craxi led a socialist government—the first in Italy's history—from 1983 to 1987. From 1989 to 1994 the PSI was a participant in national coalition governments. In June 1990 the PSI renamed itself the *Partito Unità Socialista* (Socialist Unity Party), but reverted to its former name in 1992. Although the PSI won 13.6 percent of the national vote in 1992, Craxi's conviction for fraud (and charges against 30 other party leaders) in July 1994 destroyed its image. At its congress in Rome on 13 November 1994 the

PSI resolved to dissolve itself; a new party, the Italian Socialists (*Socialisti Italiani*), was formed in the hope of rebuilding public support, but to no avail.

In 1998 the PSI remerged with PSDI, which since the split in 1967 had only attracted 5 percent or less of the vote in national elections. The united party took its present title: the SDI. As such it retained its place as a full member of the SI. Under the leadership of Enrico Bosselli the SDI stressed that socialism is inseparable from democracy and freedom. In the parliamentary elections of May 2001 the SDI participated in the Sunflower (*Il Girasole*) alliance with the federation of Greens. This alliance itself joined the broader Olive Tree coalition, in which the **Democrats of the Left** was the prominent force. The Olive Tree coalition obtained 252 of the 630 seats in the Chamber of Deputies, of which the Sunflower alliance won 16 seats. Although the SDI won less than the threshold of 4 percent of the total vote, it gained parliamentary representation as a result of an agreement that it contest safe seats and thus win substantially. Party leader Enrico Bosselli was one of nine SDI representatives in the Chamber of Deputies. In the elections to the European Parliament of June 2004 the SDI, campaigning within the Olive Tree coalition, won two of Italy's 78 seats. The two SDI members worked in the **Party of European Socialists**, with which their party was affiliated. In the general elections of April 2006, the SDI operated in the new Rose in the Fist (*Rosa nel Pugno*) alliance, which, as part of the Union (*L'Unione*) coalition, took 18 seats in the Chamber of Deputies with 2.6 percent of the vote.

ITALIAN SOCIALIST PARTY. *See* ITALIAN DEMOCRATIC SOCIALISTS.

IVORIAN POPULAR FRONT [*FRONT POPULAIRE IVOIRIEN* (FPI)]. The FPI was formed in 1990 when opposition parties were legalized in Côte D'Ivoire. Since independence in 1960 Côte D'Ivoire had been ruled as a single-party state by Félix Houphouët-Boigny and his Democratic Party. Houphouët allowed foreign interests to export resources and profits. World recession and thus lower prices meant increased poverty, leading to unrest that, along with international pressure, led Houphouët to introduce the democratic reforms of 1990. Laurent Gbagbo of the FPI, a **trade union** activist, challenged Houphouët unsuccessfully at the presidential elections that year, winning 18 percent of the vote. Houphouët died in 1993 and his successor at the head of the Democratic Party won the presidency in 1995 unopposed due to a boycott by the FPI and other opposition parties in protest at parentage conditions stipulated for candidacy. The Democratic Party also won the elections to the National Assembly that year, at which the FPI took 12 of 225 seats.

In 1996 the FPI gained full membership of the **Socialist International**. In the remainder of the 1990s the economy worsened leading to popular unrest, increasing repression, and, in 1999, a military coup, in which Robert Guéï assumed power. Under international pressure Guéï allowed presidential and legislative elections to take place in 2000. The FPI's Gbagbo won the presidency with 59.4 percent of the vote against Guéï's 32.7 percent. Guéï disputed the result and clung to power until violent unrest led him to accept defeat. In elections to the Assembly that year the FPI took 96 of the 225 against 94 for the Democratic Party. Gbagbo formed a coalition government but elements in the army began a civil **war** in which, for all practical purposes, the country was divided into a northern and a southern section. In March 2003 a power-sharing government was formed in an attempt to end the war, but in March 2004 the Democratic Party withdrew its ministers. In April 2005 the government and rebels agreed on an immediate and final end to hostilities, but little came of this.

– J –

***JANATA DAL* (SECULAR) [JD (S)].** The JD (S), or People's Party (Secular), has its roots in the Indian Socialist Party (ISP), which was formed in Bombay as the Congress Socialist Party at a conference in October 1934 at which **Jayaprakash Narayan** played a leading role. The party wanted independence for India, full adult **suffrage**, land distribution to the peasants, the elimination of civil and **religious** divisions, and support for **cooperatives**. Although very similar in **ideology** to the Indian **Communist** Party (which had formed in 1924), the two parties were enemies throughout the 1930s. The party was banned by the British between 1942 and 1946. In 1948 it left the Indian National Congress (which had been formed in 1885) and adopted a new constitution, making membership available to anyone who supported democratic socialism; it also changed its title to the

ISP. It sought economic and social reforms that would bring about *sarvodaya*, or uplift of all. In 1952 its membership was claimed to be 295,550, of whom 117,820 were individual members; a study of its Bombay membership suggested that most were **middle class** and only 29 percent were industrial workers.

The party was a full member of the **Socialist International** between 1951 and 1953, but was only a consultative member from 1955 to 1969. In 1952 it joined with the Kijan Mazdoor Praja Party to form the *Praja* Socialist Party All-India. After internal dissent, this party split in 1955 over collaboration with the Indian National Congress and its appeal declined further after the congress adopted a **socialization objective** in 1957. It also suffered from the more moderate stance adopted by the Indian Communist Party. A new Socialist Party was formed in 1972, when the *Praja* Socialist Party merged with former members who had formed the Samyukta Socialist Party. In May 1977 this Socialist Party joined a coalition with four other parties to create the *Janata* (People) Party (JP) and thereafter ceased to have an independent existence.

The JP campaigned on the principles of democracy, equality, and secularism, and won the national elections of 1977. Under the leadership of Morarji Desai, the JP formed a government. The JP included the populist *Jana Sangh* members, who had a history of paramilitary style discipline. These members left to form the *Bharatiya* (Indian) *Janata* Party, which originally claimed to be socialist but soon became a right-wing Hindu party that criticized special measures that helped the majority Muslims. The JP also enjoyed success in regional elections in the 1980s and 1990s. In 1988 the party changed its name to *Janata Dal* (JD). After the national elections of 1996 JD led a minority coalition government, with its leader H. D. Deve Gowda as prime minister. In 1999 the JD split into the *Janata Dal* (Secular) (JD [S]) and *Janata Dal* (United). The JD (S) was headed by H. D. Deve Gowda, and claimed to be committed to the cause of farmers, urban poor, and the common man. In national parliamentary elections of April and May 2004 the JD (S) did not join any of the three major coalitions and only obtained 1.6 percent of the vote, thus winning only four of the 545 seats. The Left Front Coalition, dominated by two Communist Parties, obtained 7.6 percent, winning 59 seats. In 2005 the JD (S), having observer party status, was the only Indian party affiliated with the **Socialist International**.

JAPANESE SOCIAL DEMOCRATIC PARTY [*SHAKAI MIN-SHU-TŌ* (*Shamin-tō*)]. The JSDP was known for many years as the Japan Socialist Party—JSP (*Nihon Shakai-tō*). Like **trade unions**, socialism was imported into Japan in the late nineteenth century. The first trade unions were formed among metal manufacturing employees in 1897, although labor disputes were reported from at least 1870. **Sen Katayama**, who had been active in the formation of trade unions, began publishing a column about socialism in his journal *Rodo Sekai* (Labor World) in 1897. In 1898 Katayama and others formed a society to study socialism and converted itself into the *Sakaiminshuto* (Social Democratic Party) in 1900. **Christians**, particularly Unitarians, played a leading role in the early years of Japanese socialism, four of the six founders of the *Sakaiminshuto* being Christians. The program of the party included the **nationalization** of the means of production, universal **suffrage**, civil equality, disarmament, and legalization of trade unions.

The government banned the *Sakaiminshuto* and it was reformed as the JSP in 1901. During the Russo-Japanese War (1904–05) the socialists became more active. Katayama was sent to the Amsterdam conference of the **Second International** in 1904 where he and the Russian delegate Georgi Plekhanov (1857–1918) shook hands to express the solidarity between the working classes of their two countries. The gesture led to further repression of socialists in Japan. The JSP became divided between those who wanted to reform the constitution and those who wanted change by revolution. In 1910 the JSP was not only banned but its leadership was tried in secret: 12 were executed and 12 were sentenced to lifetime imprisonment. Before 1914 socialism in Japan was largely confined to intellectuals. It revived after 1918 mainly as a result of wartime inflation and the subsequent drop in **working-class** living standards. Universal male suffrage was granted in 1925.

The JSP was reestablished in November 1946 and adopted a reformist program that sought to make Japanese society more **egalitarian** through constitutional means. After the 1947 election the JSP became the largest party and formed a coalition government with Katayama Tetsu as prime minister. The JSP/*Shamin-tō* has been a full member of the **Socialist International** (SI) since 1951. However, the JSP suffered from internal conflict between reformists and revolutionaries. In 1959 the right wing of the JSP broke away and established the Japan Social Democratic Party (later renamed the Democratic Socialist Party) in January 1960. This new party became a member of the SI in 1961. It drew much of its support from the labor federation *Domei*. In 1986 it attracted 6.4 percent of the vote in the national elections and claimed a membership of 40,000. At the same elections, the JSP received 17.2 percent of the vote and claimed a membership of 55,000. Both parties sought a more self-reliant defense policy for Japan.

In 1986 Takako Doi became chairperson of the JSP, thus becoming the first **woman** to lead a Japanese political party. She resigned in July 1991, her party having lost the national elections in April that year. Also in 1991, the JSP was renamed, taking its present title *Shamin-tō*. In December 1994 the rival Democratic Socialist Party joined with some other parties (but not the JSP) to form the *Shinshinto* or New Frontier Party; this political grouping won 156 of the 500 seats in the House of Deputies in October 1996 to become the largest opposition party.

Meanwhile, in June 1994 the *Shamin-tō* leader **Tomiichi Murayama** became prime minister of a coalition government and held the post until January 1996. During a period of coalition government with its long-time enemy, the conservative Liberal Democratic Party, *Shamin-tō* was forced to abandon or moderate many of its long-held policies, particularly its **pacifism** and general opposition to American foreign policy. In contrast to European social-democratic parties, *Shamin-tō* has not taken a leading role in promoting domestic reforms with respect to matters like social welfare, consumer protection, or the environment, preferring to leave them to the Liberal Democratic Party. This period of coalition government—and its attendant policy compromises—alienated many of its traditional supporters, and led to an extraordinary convention in September 1995. The convention agreed to reform *Shamin-tō* as the Democratic League and, to adopt policies designed to win more support among the middle ground of Japanese politics.

Nevertheless, the Party continued to operate as *Shamin-tō*. In the national elections for the House of Deputies in October 1996 *Shamin-tō* won only 15 of the 480 seats, compared to 30 before the elections. As well as alienating its own supporters by its policies in coalition, *Shamin-tō* also suffered from a new rival party, the Democratic Party of Japan, which had been formed in September 1996. In practice, the

Democratic Party of Japan provided the main opposition to the Liberal Democratic Party in the elections to the House of Deputies in 2000 and again in November 2003. Indeed, in November 2003 *Shamin-tō* took only six seats with 5.2 percent of the vote, a worse performance than the Communist Party of Japan, which won nine seats with 7.7 percent of the vote. The ruling party called a general election for September 2005, at which the *Shamin-tō* increased its share of seats to seven, while the Communists retained their nine.

JAPAN SOCIALIST PARTY (JSP). *See* JAPANESE SOCIAL DEMOCRATIC PARTY.

JAURÈS, JEAN-JOSEPH-MARIE-AUGUSTE (1859–1914). Born in Castres in southwestern France to a **middle-class** family with a background in the professions and business, Jean-Joseph Marie-Auguste Jaurès developed into an outstanding intellectual. He lectured in philosophy at the University of Toulouse from 1883 to 1885 and from 1887 to 1893. He was familiar with **Karl Marx** and his work, but was never a **Marxist**. He was elected to the French Chamber of Deputies from 1885 to 1887, 1893 to 1898, and from 1902 until his death. From 1892 when he was selected in a by-election, Jaurès began the transition from **liberalism** to socialism. He began voting with the socialist deputies but remained outside any faction. He was a **pacifist** who believed that socialism could be best achieved by gradual means. He took a leading role in the campaign to overturn the conviction of Alfred Dreyfus, a Jewish military officer who had been falsely accused of selling military secrets to Germany. Jaurès was a fine orator, with a striking appearance, who conveyed sincerity and integrity. As a scholar, he is best remembered for his large-scale history of socialism beginning with the French Revolution and closing in 1900. In 1904 he founded the socialist journal *L'Humanité*, later better known as the organ of the French **Communist** Party. At the Amsterdam conference of the **Second International** in 1904 he criticized the **German Social Democratic Party** for attempts to impose its tactics on other countries, although he accepted their call for unity and was the main force behind the unification of what became the **French Socialist Party**. Jaurès had planned to stop World War I by a general strike but tragically was murdered by a demented monarchist.

JEWS. Jews have played an outstanding role in the history of socialism as both revolutionaries and reformists. Among the many socialist thinkers and leaders who were Jews (although often not practicing Jews), were **Karl Marx, Ferdinand Lassalle, Eduard Bernstein, Rosa Luxemburg, Leon Trotsky, Victor Adler, Léon Blum, David Ben-Gurion, Julius Braunthal, Harold Laski**, and **Bruno Kreisky**. Outside the Russian empire, most of the leading Jewish socialists had **middle-class** origins. Because of its inclusive nature and its general emphasis on equality, cooperation, and justice, socialism attracted many Jews, especially in view of the endemic anti-Semitism in most of northern and eastern Europe, which grew worse in many areas from about 1850 with the growth of **nationalism**. Jews occupied a peculiar position in European society as permanent outsiders and as an unforeseen challenge to many socialist assumptions. The ideas of the French Revolution of 1789 recognized the rights of Jews as individuals but not as a people; to do otherwise would have violated the foundations of the nation-state as understood in the nineteenth century. Among Jews themselves there were enormous differences of economic circumstances and adherence to their **religion** and culture. Many in Eastern Europe were poor, oppressed, and subject to officially sanctioned violence in pogroms. Others, most famously the Rothschilds, were the bankers and financiers of Europe, individuals identified in anti-Semitic propaganda with exploitation.

As a movement, socialism before about 1920 regarded the problems faced by the Jews as the product of manipulation by **capitalism**. Anti-Semitism was seen as a temporary aberration and a device intended to divide the **working class** and divert it from the struggle with its capitalist oppressors. Therefore replacing capitalism by socialism would automatically mean the end of anti-Semitism. Although this was true to some extent in Eastern Europe at least, the deeply rooted nature of anti-Semitism was little understood by socialists who based their analysis of society on economic relationships and social class. Both **Mensheviks** and Bolsheviks wanted to denationalize Russia's Jews. In 1900 about half of the world's Jews then lived in the Russian empire and of these about 90 percent were forced to live in the pale of settlement, a zone created by legislation between 1795 and 1835 covering a swath of territory in the western part of the empire. Jews were particularly important in the membership of the

Austrian Social Democratic Party. About 40 percent of the party's membership in 1910 lived in Vienna, which then contained nearly 175,000 Jews or about 9 percent of its total population.

Revolutionary Jewish socialists like Luxemburg rejected their Jewish culture and embraced socialist internationalism. They wanted Jews to assimilate into their societies and give up their distinctiveness. **Zionism**—the creation of a separate Jewish nation in Palestine—was not the favored choice of all Jews. The Jewish Labor **Bund** denounced Zionism and held (in 1903) that the solution to the Jews' problems was a proletarian revolution, but it recognized that a separate organization was needed to protect Jews. Bernstein was approached in 1902 by Chaim Weizmann to lend his support to Zionism. Bernstein declined and indeed criticized the movement, although he was impressed by the pioneering efforts of Jewish settlers in Palestine in the 1920s. In 1930 Ben-Gurion approached Bernstein to try to persuade the British government to drop its threat to halt Jewish immigration to Palestine. *See also KIBBUTZ*; INTERNATIONAL JEWISH LABOR BUND; ISRAEL LABOR PARTY; SOCIAL DEMOCRATIC ISRAEL; WORLD LABOR ZIONIST MOVEMENT.

JOSPIN, LIONEL ROBERT (1937–). **French Socialist Party** prime minister from 1997 to 2002, Lionel Robert Jospin was born in Meudon, Hauts-de-Seine, a district of Paris. He was educated at the École Nationale d'Administration and was secretary of the Ministry of Foreign Affairs from 1965 to 1970. He then became professor of economics at Paris-Sceaux University from 1971 to 1980. In 1981 he was elected to the Chamber of Deputies, the lower house of the French parliament. Having joined the French Socialist Party in 1971, he succeeded **François Mitterand** as first secretary of the party in 1981. Jospin held this post until 1987. He then became minister for education from 1988 to 1992. Although defeated in the 1992 elections, he was reelected in 1994. In the presidential elections of April 1995 he received 23.3 percent of the vote during the first round—the highest figure for any single candidate—and although he was defeated by the conservative Jacques Chirac in the second round of voting in June 1995, the margin of his defeat (52.6 to 47.4 percent) was far less than had been predicted.

In the national elections in 1997, Jospin led the party to victory winning 43.1 percent of the vote in the first found (25 May) and 38.5 percent in the second round (1 June). With the support of the **Communist** Party (which took 10 percent of the vote in the first round and 3.6 percent in the second round), Jospin formed a government. His administration was elected on a platform to create 700,000 jobs for young people, reduce the working week from 39 to 35 hours, restrict **privatization**, introduce a broader **taxation** system, and impose conditions on French support for a single currency for Europe. Although he fulfilled the promise to reduce the working week to 35 hours, Jospin suffered a humiliating defeat at the 2002 presidential elections. He finished third in the first round behind Chirac and the far-right candidate Jean Marie Le Pen (Chirac won at the second round). Jospin subsequently resigned as prime minister.

– K –

KATAYAMA, SEN (1860–1933). Katayama was the best-known Japanese socialist before 1930 and an important activist in international socialism. He was born in the village of Hadeki in central Okayama. An able and hard-working student, he moved to Tokyo in 1881. After enduring much poverty, he became an apprentice printer. He followed a friend to the United States in 1884 and supported himself by menial jobs in San Francisco. He converted to **Christianity** while attending English classes in a Chinese mission. He continued his education at institutions in Tennessee, Iowa, and Massachusetts. He was influenced by the writings of **Richard T. Ely**, particularly *The Social Aspects of Christianity* (1889), and became familiar with **Ferdinand Lassalle** from reading an article in the *Atlantic Monthly*.

Katayama returned to Japan in 1896 and took a leading role in labor agitation and the formation of **trade unions**. He helped to form a society for the study of socialism (*Shakai Shugi Kenyā-kai*) in November 1898. He set up the first socialist newspaper in Japan (the *Naigai Shimpō*) in 1902 but the venture failed. Katayama wanted socialism to be a mass movement, but this was difficult to achieve in Japan because of its late industrialization and the strength of the government. Katayama returned to the United States in 1903 and in 1904 attended the Amsterdam conference of the **Second International**, where he was honored as the only Asian delegate. He was elected first vice president and was taken by the hand by the Russian delegate, Georgi V. Plekhanov, as a gesture of peace and to show the socialists' support for peace, even though Russia and Japan were then at **war**. He returned to the United States and lived in Texas until 1907, thereby avoiding the infighting and the repression of socialists in Japan. He returned to Japan, married a second time, and was arrested and jailed for five months in 1912 after a successful streetcar strike in Tokyo. He left Japan for the United States again in 1914 with a reputation greater internationally than in Japan.

At the invitation of S. T. Rutgers, a leader of the left wing of the Dutch Social Democratic Workers' Party, Katayama left San Francisco and moved to New York in 1916. While in New York he wrote the book that he became best remembered for, *The Labor Movement in Japan* (1918), in which he exaggerated his own role and denigrated that of his opponents. With his move to New York, Katayama became part of the extreme left of socialism. He immediately realized the importance of the Bolshevik coup in 1917. He went underground to avoid the Palmer Raids of 1920 against **communists** and from then on played an active role in the **Comintern**. He engaged in revolutionary agitation in Mexico from March to November 1921 before leaving for Russia, where **Leon Trotsky** welcomed him. In 1922 he assisted with the formation of the Japanese Communist Party. Katayama not only survived in the Comintern, an unusual accomplishment, he prospered. He was given a lavish state funeral in Moscow. *See also* JAPANESE SOCIAL DEMOCRATIC PARTY.

KAUTSKY, KARL JOHANN (1854–1938). Socialist theorist and author, Karl Johann Kautsky was a leading figure in German socialism before 1920. Born in Prague, he was educated at Vienna University. He often visited **Karl Marx** in 1881 and was **Friedrich Engels's** secretary between 1881 and 1883. He lived mainly in London until 1890. He founded a journal of theoretical **Marxism**, *Die Neue Zeit* (The New Time), at Stuttgart in 1883 and remained its editor until 1917. But he was forced into exile in Switzerland and then London, and he was not able to bring *Die Neue Zeit* back to Germany until 1890. Among the works he wrote were a study of More's *Utopia* (1888) and *Karl Marx' ökonomische Lehren* (The Economic Doctrines of Karl Marx) in 1887, which was widely read as a textbook and translated into a number of languages. In this and other works, Kautsky has since been criticized for presenting Marx as a more dogmatic and systematic thinker than he really was. As the leading theorist of the **German Social Democratic Party** (*Sozialdemokratische Partei Deutschlands*—SPD), he drafted the Marxist analysis in the preamble to the **Erfurt Program** in 1891. He worked closely with **Eduard Bernstein** until they split over **revisionism** in 1899. Between 1905 and 1910 he edited three volumes of Marx's notes on the history of the theory of surplus value.

In 1902 Kautsky wrote *Die soziale Revolution* (The Social Revolution) in which he attempted to sketch the likely features and priorities of the proletarian state after the revolution. He envisaged the socialist conquest of power in terms of a peaceful progression that used propaganda and the gained power in **trade unions**, parliament, and other institutions in line with the inevitable atrophy of **capitalism** caused by its internal contradictions as exposed by Marx. There was no suggestion in his thought of the Leninist notion of seizing political power by violence.

He imagined the socialist state as centralized, independent of established religion, defended by a citizen's militia, having a graduated system of **taxation**, without rights of **inheritance**, and having a mixture of **nationalized** industries and consumer and producers' **cooperatives**. Kautsky was a leading personality in the **Second International** and was widely regarded as an arbiter of Marxist theory. He hated violence and saw **war** as a product of capitalism. He remained in the SPD until 1917 when the party was becoming too conciliatory and its discipline too constraining. Like Bernstein, he briefly joined the breakaway Independent Social Democratic Party (*Unabhängige Sozialdemokratische Partei Deutschlands*). He opposed World War I and from 1917 he and Bernstein worked together again. Like Bernstein, Kautsky stressed the importance of democracy and ethics in achieving socialism. He opposed the Bolshevik Revolution and criticized **Leninism** and the dictatorship of the proletariat in his *Die Diktatur des Proletariats* (1918), which prompted a ferocious reply from **V. I. Lenin** and a rejoinder by **Leon Trotsky** in *Terrorism and Communism* (1920). Kautsky returned to the SPD in 1922, four years after Bernstein had done so. Kautsky left Germany for Austria in 1924, but was forced to flee to Amsterdam in 1938 after Adolf Hitler's takeover. His last book concerned socialism and war.

KEATING, PAUL JOHN (1944–). Australian Labor Party (ALP) prime minister Paul Keating was born and educated in Sydney, New South Wales. He began his working life as a research officer with the Federated Municipal and Shire Council Employees' Union. He joined the ALP at 15 in 1959 and became president of the New South Wales Youth Council of the ALP in 1966. His political education included an association with the former ALP premier **John T. Lang** as well as serving as president of the New South Wales branch of the ALP between 1979 and 1983. In 1969 he was elected to the federal parliament for the outer Sydney suburban seat of Blaxland. He served as minister for northern Australia in the government of **E. G. Whitlam** for six weeks before it was dismissed in November 1975. While in opposition, he was shadow minister for minerals and energy (1976–80) and resources and energy (1980–83) until becoming spokesman for treasury matters on 14 January 1983.

After the victory of the ALP in the federal election of 11 March 1983, Keating became treasurer of **Bob Hawke**'s government and, with Hawke, its principal policy maker. He oversaw the progressive deregulation of the financial system, the floating of the Australian dollar, and reforms to the **taxation** system. His close association with the Australian Council of Trade Unions, the national body of **trade unions**, was essential in maintaining an accord on prices and incomes that had been reached with the council in February 1983. Personal and policy differences between Keating and Hawke led to his resignation as treasurer on 3 June 1991 after losing a challenge for the office of prime minister by 66 to 44 votes. A second challenge, on 19 December 1991, was narrowly won by Keating. He became prime minister on 20 December 1991. Keating continued as prime minister until his landslide defeat in the elections on 2 March 1996 and resigned from the federal parliament shortly afterward.

KERENSKY, ALEXANDER FEODOROVICH (1881–1970). Russian democratic socialist and politician, Alexander Feodorovich Kerensky was born in Simbirsk (later Ulyanovsk). His father was the headmaster of the high school where **V. I. Lenin** was educated. Kerensky qualified as a lawyer at St. Petersburg University and joined the Russian Socialist Revolutionary Party in 1905. He suffered arrest, imprisonment, and exile in 1905 and 1906. On his return to St. Petersburg, he worked as an advocate for political dissidents. He was elected to the *Duma* (parliament) in 1912. After the revolution in March 1917 he became minister for justice in the provisional government. His main initiatives in that position were abolishing ethnic and religious discrimination—a czarist policy that particularly affected **Jews**—and the death penalty.

Kerensky believed that socialism was not possible without democracy, but without a mass constituency to support him, Russian politics remained dominated by extremists of the right and the left and his initiatives were never implemented. Further, his continued support for the Allies in World War I doomed his efforts to find a moderate, socialist middle path that emphasized the rule of law. Kerensky became prime minister of the provisional government on 24 July 1917. His government was effectively ended by the Bolshevik coup on 7 November 1917. He left Russia in May 1918 and spent the rest of his life in exile in France (from 1919 to 1940), Australia (1940 to 1946), and then the United States. He published *The Kerensky Memoirs* in 1966 and worked for a time at the Hoover Institution at Stanford University. *See also* MENSHEVIKS.

KIBBUTZ. Derived from a Hebrew word meaning "gathering," *kibbutzim* were developed as a form of cooperative farming in Palestine by Russian **Jewish** immigrants from 1909. The *kibbutz* was based on the collective ownership of the means of production, its organization, and allocation of labor. By 1991 there were 270 *kibbutzim* with 129,300 members compared to 254 with nearly 120,000 members in 1979. However, in the 1980s and 1990s, there was a relative decline and some of the more egalitarian aspects were toned down. The *kibbutz* was a practical application of the socialist aspects of **Zionism**. Most *kibbutzim* are affiliated with the national **trade union** federation, the *Histadrut*, and are a major source of support for the **Israel Labor Party**. *See also* COMMUNES.

KIENTHAL CONFERENCE. Called by the International Socialist Commission established by the **Zimmerwald Conference**, this conference was held at Kienthal, Switzerland, in April 1916. Attended by 44 delegates and comparable in composition to those who attended the Zimmerwald Conference, the Kienthal Conference was far more left-wing and revolutionary in feeling. It denounced the failure of the international socialist bureau of the **Second International** to act to stop World War I and asserted that socialism, achieved through the victory of the proletariat, was the only way to ensure an enduring peace.

KRAG, JENS OTTO (1914–78). Danish social-democratic politician Jens Otto Krag was born in Randers. Like **Hans Hedtoft-Hansen**, he made his progress in the **Danish Social Democratic Party** through its **youth** organization, which he joined in 1930. In 1940 he completed a master's degree in political science at the University of Copenhagen and took a position with the economic council set up by the **trade unions** of Denmark. In 1947 he was elected to parliament and was made minister of commerce and shipping in the Hedtoft government, a post he held until 1950 when he went to Washington, D.C., as a counselor on economic matters with the Danish embassy. He was elected to parliament again in 1952 and served as minister of economics and labor from 1953 to 1957 and as foreign minister from 1958 to 1962. He served two terms as prime minister, the first from 1962 to 1968 and the second from 1971 to 1972. Like Hedtoft, he opposed neutrality for Denmark and supported an active national defense policy. Related to this was his strong support for European economic cooperation. He served as head of the European Economic Community delegation to Washington in 1974. For his work on European unity, he was the recipient of the Charlemagne Prize in 1966 and the Robert Schuman prize in 1973.

KREISKY, BRUNO (1911–90). A leading Austrian socialist, Bruno Kreisky was born in Vienna into a wealthy Jewish family. He joined the **Austrian Social Democratic Party** in the 1920s and worked for it until its banning in 1934. He was imprisoned (1935–36) and on his release completed his legal studies. He was arrested again after Adolf Hitler's absorption of Austria and went into exile in Switzerland, where he worked for a consumer cooperative. On his return to Austria in 1946 he joined the diplomatic service and was made state secretary for foreign affairs. He played an important role in the 1955 agreement that guaranteed Austria's independence and neutrality. Kreisky was elected to parliament in 1956 and became leader of the Austrian Socialist Party (formerly and since 1991 the Austrian Social Democratic Party) in 1967. He led it to victory in the 1970 elections and became chancellor, a position he held until 1983. He used his diplomatic skills to negotiate a special relations agreement with the European Economic Community in 1972 and to work for a peaceful resolution of the Arab-Israeli conflict.

KROPOTKIN, PETER ALEXEYEVICH (1842–1921). Born in Moscow into an aristocratic family, Peter Alexeyevich Kropotkin became the leading theorist of **anarchism** after the death of **Michael Bakunin** in 1876. As a geographer in Siberia, contact with political exiles made him familiar with the writings of **Pierre-Joseph Proudhon**. Like Proudhon, he advocated devolution of political power to **communes**, that is, voluntary, local administrative units that, in union with other communes, could form cooperative networks that would replace centralized governments. Unlike Bakunin, Kropotkin emphasized need, not work, as the criterion for the distribution of goods and services. He opposed any form of wage system and wanted the means of exchange to be based on the labor time of the individual worker. His books include *The Conquest of Bread* (1892), *Fields, Factories and Workshops* (1899), and *Mutual Aid* (1902). Kropotkin served terms of imprisonment in Russia and France and lived in England from 1885. He returned to Russia after the March 1917 revolution, but opposed Bolshevik policies.

– L –

LABOR AND SOCIALIST INTERNATIONAL (LSI). The LSI was formed in 1923 in Hamburg, Germany, by 620 delegates from 30 countries representing socialist and labor parties drawn from the remnants of the **Second International** and the **International Working Union of Socialist Parties**. It regarded the class struggle as a means of achieving socialism. Competition from the **Comintern** and the rise of fascism greatly reduced the effectiveness of the LSI, even though it claimed 6.2 million members in Europe and North America at its last conference in 1931. The LSI had close links with the **International Federation of Trade Unions**. Its main achievement was to provide assistance for refugees from fascism. The LSI was made defunct by World War II and was replaced by the **Socialist International**, a noncommunist body, in 1951.

LABOR UNIONS. *See* TRADE UNIONS.

LABOUR PARTY. *See* BRITISH LABOUR PARTY.

LABOUR REPRESENTATION LEAGUE. This league was formed by organized labor in Britain in 1869 to promote the election of **working-class** candidates to parliament. Despite enjoying some electoral successes in 1874, political concessions to labor and a lack of resources doomed the League. It was defunct by 1889, but its activities were continued by the parliamentary committee of the Trades Union Congress. *See also* BRITISH LABOUR PARTY.

LAIDLER, HARRY WELLINGTON (1884–1970). American socialist author and publicist Harry Wellington Laidler was born into a **middle-class** family in Brooklyn, New York City. Educated at Wesleyan University, Connecticut, he joined the **Socialist Party of America** in 1903. With **Upton Sinclair**, Jack London, and Clarence Darrow, he founded the Intercollegiate Socialist Society in 1905. Laidler was the society's executive head from 1910 to 1921. In 1923 the society was reorganized as the League for Industrial Democracy to promote socialism, employee participation in decision making in the workplace, social planning, public control or ownership of essential services, **trade unions**, and **cooperatives**. Laidler served as the League's executive director until 1957. The author of many books and pamphlets on socialism and social issues, he was best known for his *Social-Economic Movements* (1944), which he revised and updated as *History of Socialism* (1968), the most comprehensive single volume on the subject in English to that time.

LANG, JOHN THOMAS (1876–1975). John Thomas Lang was twice **Australian Labor Party** (ALP) premier of the state of New South Wales (1925–27 and 1930–32) and one of its most controversial. Born in Sydney, he was elected to the New South Wales parliament in 1913 for the Sydney suburban electorate of Granville. He was a member of the New South Wales parliament until 1946. He opposed conscription during World War I and in 1923 became leader of the ALP in New South Wales. His first term as premier in 1925 to 1927 was notable for two pioneering initiatives in building the **welfare state**: child endowment and widows' pensions. His second term as premier (1930–32) was dominated by the Depression. Lang's populist economic policies, which included a reduction in the interest rate on Australia's large overseas borrowings, were opposed by the federal ALP government of **James Henry Scullin** and even more so by its successor, the conservative United Australia Party government. Lang's attempt to resist federal law over the collection of money claimed by it for interest charges led to his dismissal by the state governor, Sir Philip Woolcott Game (1876–1961), but privately the two men remained friends for many years. Lang's government was defeated at the June 1932 New South Wales election. Lang lost his leadership of the New South Wales ALP in 1939 and in 1943 was expelled from the ALP for opposing **John Curtin**'s federal ALP government over conscription. He was readmitted to ALP membership in 1971, having outlived his enemies.

LANGE, DAVID RUSSELL (1942–2005). New Zealand Labour Party (NZLP) prime minister David Lange was born in Thames and qualified as a lawyer in 1965. He moved to Auckland in 1974 to practice law, became active in local politics, and was elected to parliament in 1977. He became leader of the parliamentary NZLP in 1983 and, on its electoral victory, prime minister in 1984. His administration was notable for its economic deregulation and free-market policies that were associated with his finance minister Roger Owen Douglas. His administration received international attention over its refusal to allow American warships that were carrying **nuclear weapons** into New Zealand ports. The United States government's refusal to either confirm or deny that its warships were carrying nuclear weapons led to a stalemate and the effective withdrawal of New Zealand from the defense treaty with Australia and the United States (ANZUS). After Labour's win in the 1987 elections, Lange and Douglas fell out over economic policy; Lange felt that the economic policies of Douglas were too extreme. After continued conflict, Lange resigned as prime minister in 1989.

LANSBURY, GEORGE (1859–1940). British socialist and leader of the **British Labour Party** George Lansbury was born near Halesworth, Suffolk, England, but later moved to London. In 1884 he and his family emigrated to Queensland, Australia, to improve their circumstances but returned to England after a year, blaming misleading emigration propaganda. Lansbury became a partner in his father-in-law's saw milling and veneering business in Whitechapel, London. Lansbury's socialism came from a number of sources, but primarily from his devout **Christianity**. Unlike most other British socialists who were usually Nonconformists, he was an Anglican. Like many of them, he was a total abstainer.

At first associated with the Liberal Party, Lansbury was at various times in the 1880s a member of the **Social Democratic Federation**, the **Independent Labour Party**, and the **Fabian** Society. He first stood for parliament in 1895. Like **Keir Hardie**, he cared passionately about **unemployment** and helped to found a colony for the unemployed in Suffolk. He was one of the members of the royal commission on the poor laws (1905–09) and, with **Sidney Webb**, one of the signatories of its minority report. In 1910 he was elected to parliament for the British Labour Party, but resigned to fight as an independent for votes for **women**. He was reelected in 1922 as Labour member for the seat of Bow and Bromley in London's East End. He held the seat until 1935. He was one of the founders of the British Labour Party's first daily newspaper, the *Daily Herald*, in 1912.

After the disastrous 1931 election, Lansbury was the only member of Ramsay MacDonald's cabinet to retain his seat and was elected leader of the much-reduced parliamentary British Labour Party in 1932. As well as being a socialist, Lansbury was also a complete pacifist. He wanted the United Kingdom to unilaterally disarm as a model for other nations. At the party's conference in 1935 **Ernest Bevin** trenchantly attacked him for his failure to support the party's executive decision calling on the government to enforce sanctions against Italy for its invasion of Ethiopia, which, like Italy, was also a member of the League of Nations. Unable to reconcile his **pacifism** with this course of action, he resigned as leader and was replaced by **Clement Attlee**. Lansbury later visited the heads of government of Western Europe to try to win them to the cause of peace and pacifism. *See also* TEMPERANCE.

LAO PEOPLE'S REVOLUTIONARY PARTY [*PHAK PAXÃXON PATIVAT LAO* (PPPL)]. The origins of the PPPL lie in the Indochinese Communist Party, formed in 1930 by Ho Chi Minh. This party would become the **Vietnam Communist Party**. In 1936 the Lao section of that Party was formed. In 1955 the Lao People's Party emerged from this Lao section, but operated secretly, operating through the *Pathet Lao* (Land of Laos) **communist** revolutionary movement. One year earlier a civil **war** had broken out between the ruling monarchy and the *Pathet Lao*. In the early 1970s Laos suffered an intensive U.S. bombing campaign to halt supplies that were transported through the country to reach the Vietnamese communists. In 1975 the *Pathet Lao* seized power from the monarchy. The Party, now renamed the PPPL, took control, setting up a one-party communist state. The small industrial sector was **nationalized** and **agriculture** collectivized. In 1986 some market economic reforms took place and in 1989 political reforms included the first national elections in communist Laos. However, only PPPL-approved candidates were allowed to compete. In 2002 parliamentary elections were held, and all but one of the candidates was from the PPPL. The other candidate was elected. The PPPL remained the only legal party. The president of Laos, Khamtai Siphandon, won his third term after being elected by the National Assembly in 2001.

LASKI, HAROLD JOSEPH (1893–1950). Principally a political theorist, Harold Laski was also a senior figure in the **British Labour Party**. Born in Manchester, England, and educated at Oxford, he began his academic career at McGill University, Montreal, in 1914 before moving to Harvard in 1916. He soon became recognized as a socialist pluralist theorist, arguing that functional associations should largely control their own affairs, and that a state should integrate functional groups, promoting a common purpose. For Laski, moreover, state sovereignty was a fiction that served to uphold vested interests while giving the impression of social unity. At Harvard he supported the Boston police strike to the annoyance of the president of the university.

In 1921 Laski took a lectureship at the London School of Economic (LSE). He also joined the Labour Party and **Fabian** Society. Having already published widely, he presented a collection of his pluralist essays in *The Foundations of Sovereignty and Other Essays*. In 1925 he was appointed to the chair in government at the LSE. That year he published *A Grammar of Politics*, in which his pluralist position was modified. He still advocated widespread political participation through functional organizations, but saw a more extensive role for the state, guided by input from the functional spheres. He continued to describe sovereignty as disguised power, arguing that consent should involve scrutiny of, and influence upon, the actions of the state.

Laski developed a broadly **Marxist** position as he reflected upon the rise and spread of fascism, the British general strike of 1926, and the collapse of the Labour government in 1931. Adolf Hitler's seizure of power in Germany confirmed his change to Marxism. His critique of sovereignty now stressed that the state was an instrument of the dominant class. In 1938 Laski published a fourth edition of *A Grammar of Politics*, which included an introductory chapter explaining his change to the more radical position. His books in the 1930s and 1940s included *Democracy in Crisis* (1933), *The State in Theory and Practice* (1935), *The Rise of European Liberalism* (1936), and *Reflections on the Revolution of Our Time* (1943). In 1936 he was elected to the Labour Party's National Executive Committee, a post he held until 1949. In 1945 Laski was elected as chairman of the committee. During Labour's successful electoral campaign that year he was wrongly accused in the press of calling for a violent revolution. He sued the newspapers involved, arguing that he was warning of the danger of such revolution if the vested interests did not allow constitutional change toward socialism, but lost the case in 1947. He continued to publish at a prolific rate and spoke at a number of rallies in the year of Labour's reelection in 1950. Soon afterward he developed bronchitis and died of a collapsed and infected lung.

LASSALLE, FERDINAND (1825–64). Lassalle was the leading figure in German socialism from 1848 until his death. Born at Breslau, then part of Silesian Prussia, he was the son of a well-off **Jewish** silk merchant. His original surname was Lassal, which he changed to Lassalle probably to make it sound more French (and thereby link it with revolution) and more aristocratic. A highly intelligent, flamboyant, and romantic man, he had experienced discrimination by the Prussian **education** system, which was biased toward Protestantism. He studied philosophy at the Universities of Breslau and Berlin. Lassalle became well acquainted with **Karl Marx** and his works, but was not prepared to be dominated by him. Unlike Marx, he remained a follower of G. W. F. Hegel. He saw the state as the expression of the people, not as a construct of social class. He also supported the ideas of **Louis Blanc**. He argued that the German **working class** had to organize itself to demand and attain male **suffrage**, capture political power, and use the power of the state to advance their interests. Lassalle saw himself as a champion of the working class but he also wanted social advancement. In December 1862 he was asked to organize a congress of the working class, which he used to set up the General Union of German Workers in May 1863, the first and numerically largest German socialist party until 1875. Fittingly, Lassalle died in a duel. *See also* GERMAN SOCIAL DEMOCRATIC PARTY; GOTHA PROGRAM.

LATVIAN SOCIAL DEMOCRATIC WORKERS' PARTY [*LATVIEŠU SOCIALDEMOKRĀTISKĀ STRĀDNIEKU PARTIJA* (LSDSP)]. The LSDSP was formed in 1904. At that time Latvia had been part of the Russian empire since 1772 (and did not attain independence until 1918 along with the other Baltic states, Estonia and Lithuania). Under these conditions the LSDSP could achieve little apart from surviving. At the 1922 elections it received 250,000 votes, that is, 31.5 percent of the total, and won 33 of the 100 seats in the Diet or parliament. Four members of the LSDSP participated in a coalition government between December 1926 and December 1927. The LSDSP was a member of the **Labor and Socialist International**, but from the late 1920s the party's fortunes declined. Its vote in national elections fell from 231,000 in 1928 to 192,000 in 1931, when it claimed a membership of 9,000. Adolf Hitler's accession to power in 1933 encouraged fascism within Latvia. In May 1934 the Farmers' Party Government staged a coup d'état and proclaimed martial law. The leaders of the LSDSP were arrested or forced into exile. In 1940 Latvia was incorporated into the Soviet Union.

Latvia formally declared its independence from Russian rule in August 1991 and was recognized by the Russian government in September 1991. The LSDSP was reestablished in December 1989 but attracted less than 1 percent of the vote in the 1993 national elections, compelling it to form coalitions with other **political parties**. The LSDSP became a full member of the **Socialist International** in 1994.

The LSDSP began to cooperate with the Latvian Social Democratic Party, which, under the leadership of Juris Bojars, had emerged from the Latvian Communist Party that split up after independence. Like the LSDSP, this party won just under 1 percent of the vote in 1993. In the national elections of 1995 the two parties together obtained 4.6 percent of the vote, which was below the threshold required to take seats. The two parties together enjoyed success at the local elections of 1997. Cooperation was increased, thus strengthening the position of both parties.

In May 1998 the LSDSP and its former communist partner merged to form the Latvian Social Democratic Union (*Latvijas Sociāldemokrātiskā Savienība*—LSDS). Bojars was appointed party leader. A joint list was formed for the 1998 parliamentary elections. The parties kept a significant measure of independence. The LSDS won 14 seats—eight of which were for the LSDSP—with 12.9 percent of the vote. In 1999 the merger was completed with the adoption of the LSDSP title, with Bojars as leader.

In early 2002 a number of members of the party followed several leading figures who left the LSDSP to form a breakaway faction because of the close links that the party had formed with the left-wing coalition For Human Rights in a Unified Latvia (*Par Cilvēka Tiesībām Vienotā Latvijā*—PCTVL), which comprised the ethnic Russian Socialist Party and communists. At the elections of October 2002 the LSDSP took 4 percent of the vote but because of the 5 percent threshold this did not secure any seats in the 100-member parliament. The PCTVL won 25 seats with 19.1 percent of the vote. After those elections a right-wing coalition was formed. The LSDSP did not win any of Latvia's nine seats in the European Parliament in the elections of 2004. The PCTVL obtained one seat, although by that time some members, including the Socialist Party, had departed from the coalition. *See also* ESTONIAN SOCIAL DEMOCRATIC PARTY; LITHUANIAN SOCIAL DEMOCRATIC PARTY.

LEADERSHIP/RANK AND FILE TENSIONS. Mass democratic movements that seek social and economic change are especially prone to tensions between their leaders and their rank and file. When tensions are publicly displayed, they may create an impression of continual disunity. If serious, these tensions can lead to breakaway parties, but more often they are simply symptomatic of the democratic process of debate and exchange. The sources of tension may be excessive control by the leadership—what Robert Michels called the **"iron law of oligarchy"**—or dissatisfaction with particular policies of the leadership by a significant section of the rank and file. These kinds of tensions increased in the post-1945 years when social-democratic parties gained political power, often for the first time.

Unresolved leadership/rank and file tensions can lead to party splits and the formation of new parties. Opposition to World War I led to a split in the **German Social Democratic Party** (*Sozialdemokratische Partei Deutschlands*—SPD) in 1917 and the formation of a separate party that was not reunited with the parent party until 1922. In 1955 the **Australian Labor Party** (ALP) suffered a major split over the attitude of the leadership to **communism**; the split, and the anticommunist anti-Labor party that grew out of it (the Democratic Labor Party), formed by breakaway members (or "groupers"), resulted in the ALP remaining out of power in the national parliament until December 1972. In April 1989 a split occurred in the **New Zealand Labour Party** over **privatization**; those who opposed privatization formed an independent party, the New Labour Party, which attracted 5.2 percent of the vote in the national election in 1990 compared to 35.1 percent for the parent party.

In the 1950s and 1960s tensions between the leadership and the rank and file of the SPD over **nuclear weapons** were expressed through extraparliamentary movements. In the **British Labour Party** there were marked differences between the views of rank and file, which were dominated by blocs of **trade union** delegates, and Hugh Gaitskell (1906–63), the leader of the party from 1955 to 1963, over his support for the campaign to remove the **socialization objective** from the constitution and his opposition to unilateral disarmament. In 1977 the congress of the **Dutch Labor Party** voted against its leaders and supported a republican form of government. Between 1980 and 1983, the British Labour Party was racked with tensions between militant left-wing activists and its parliamentary members. Another example of leadership/rank and file tensions occurred within the **Norwegian Labor Party** in November 1994, when many of its supporters voted against a referendum on Norway joining the European Union, even though a party conference had decided in favor by majority of two to one.

The British Labour Party, under **Tony Blair**, who led the party to victory in the parliamentary elections of 1997, 2001, and 2005, suffered from dissatisfaction among many rank and file members over the abandonment of the socialization objective, the increased involvement of the private sector in public services, and support for the U.S.-led **war** in Iraq. In Germany members of the SPD dissatisfied with Gerhard **Schröder**'s reforms of the **welfare state** left to form a new party that allied itself with the **Left Party** in 2005. *See also* MEMBERSHIP OF SOCIAL-DEMOCRATIC/SOCIALIST POLITICAL PARTIES.

LEAGUE OF AFRICAN DEMOCRATIC SOCIALIST PARTIES (LADSP). Based in Tunis, Tunisia, the LADSP was established in 1981 as the Socialist InterAfrican. The LADSP provided an international forum for socialist parties in Africa. Its statement of aims proclaimed that democratic socialism is the only way to develop African countries and deliver their people from all forms of exploitation and oppression. Its founders were Léopold Sédar Senghor, the former president of Senegal, and Habib Bourguiba, the president of Tunisia. In 1988 the LADSP had 11 member parties in Djibouti, Gambia, Mauritius, Morocco, Senegal, Somalia, Sudan, and Tunisia and was still an active organization in 1995. *See also* AFRICAN SOCIALISM.

LEFT BOOK CLUB. The Left Book Club was influential in spreading informed debate about socialism and social reform in the United Kingdom in the late 1930s. It was an initiative of the publisher Victor Gollancz (1893–1967), the socialist writer and future Labour member of parliament John Strachey (1901–63), and the political theorist **Harold Laski**. Launched in 1936, it was designed to resist fascism and promote socialism by providing the public with informed works of nonfiction. Its membership rose from 10,000 at its formation to nearly 60,000 by 1939, but fell rapidly after the Hitler-Stalin Pact. Among its most notable works were **George Orwell**'s *The Road to Wigan Pier* (1937) and Ellen Wilkinson's *The Town That Was Murdered* (1939). The club was wound up in 1948.

LEFT PARTY [*DIE LINKSPARTIE (Die Linke)*]. In July 2005 the German Party of Democratic Socialism (*Partei des Demokratischen Sozialismus*—PDS) was renamed as *Die Linke*. It simultaneously merged with the recently formed Electoral Alternative Work and Social Justice Party (*Wahlalternative Arbeit und Soziale Gerechtigkeit*—WASG). The PDS had emerged in 1989 to 1990 from the old East German communist Socialist Unity Party (*Sozialistische Einheitspartei Deutschlands*—SED).

The SED was formed in 1946 by a merger of the Communist Party and the section of the **German Social Democratic Party**

(*Sozialdemokratische Partei Deutschlands*—SPD) that found itself in the Soviet-controlled eastern part of Germany after World War II. In 1949 Germany was divided and the SED ruled the eastern German Democratic Republic from 1949 until the collapse of East European **communism** in 1989.

The PDS then reoriented itself as a democratic socialist party, to the left of the SPD. Although the rank and file membership demanded that the old leadership be replaced, the PDS continued to appeal to the reformist communists. It also stressed its **pacifist** and antifascist principles. Although it has operated throughout Germany since reunification in 1990, its support was concentrated in the eastern *Länder* (states). In those *Länder* the PDS's socialism has appealed to many who continued to look to the state to provide **welfare** and social justice and who were dissatisfied with the relative poverty of the east in comparison with the west.

Although in elections to the united *Bundestag* in 1992 the PDS won only 2.4 percent of the party list vote, it attracted 11.1 in the eastern *Länder*, and 0.3 percent in the west, thus gaining representation due to special quotas for new eastern-based parties, despite failing to reach the 5 percent threshold. In 1994 the PDS won 4.4 of the list vote throughout Germany, this time securing its share of the party list vote because it won the four direct mandates from territorial districts. This gave the PDS 30 seats. In 1998 the PDS secured 5.2 percent of the party list vote and 35 seats. However in September 2002 the PDS attracted only 4 percent of the party list vote and two seats by direct mandate, thus taking only two seats in the *Bundestag*. Nevertheless the PDS continued to enjoy some success in local government, sometimes participating in local coalition government with the SPD. In the elections to the European Parliament in June 2004 the PDS won seven of Germany's 99 seats, one more than in 1999. In 2004, the PDS, under chairman Lothar Bisky, became a founder member of the **Party of the European Left**.

The WASG was formed in January 2005, gathering together a splinter group from the SPD led by Oskar Lafontaine with various others on the left dissatisfied with the SPD. In July 2005 the ninth PDS Congress agreed to a change of name from PDS to *Die Linke*. Earlier that month members of the WASG agreed by a large majority to a merger of campaign efforts with *Die Linke*, thus creating the new organization campaigning under the Left title. In the general elections of September 2005 *Die Linke* took 54 seats in the *Bundestag*, including three constituency seats, with 8.7 percent of the vote.

LENIN, VLADIMIR ILYICH (V. I.) (1870–1924). "Lenin" was, from late 1901, the pseudonym of Vladimir Ilyich Ulyanov, the preeminent Russian revolutionary who was born in Simbirsk (later renamed Ulyanovsk in his honor) into an educated **middle-class** household. In 1887 his elder brother was hanged for taking part in a conspiracy to kill the czar, an event that made Lenin a determined revolutionary for the rest of his life. He first became acquainted with the works of **Karl Marx** in 1890. A brilliant student, Lenin studied law at the Universities of Kazan and St. Petersburg and practiced law between 1891 and 1894 but was a full-time revolutionary thereafter. He was exiled to Siberia in comfortable circumstances between 1896 and 1899 and was then forced to spend most of the next 17 years in exile in Western Europe. In 1903 he won a narrow victory at the second conference of the Russian Social Democratic Labor Party in London over the composition of the membership of the party. Lenin wanted party membership to be restricted to full-time, committed individuals whereas his opponents, the **Mensheviks**, were prepared to include sympathizers. A prolific and polemical writer, Lenin founded **Leninism** and, with **Leon Trotsky**, organized the coup in November 1917 that established the Soviet Union. His time in power was notable not only for the establishment of Soviet **communism** but also for the repression of opponents, the formation of an efficient totalitarian regime, the suppression of **religion**, and plans to collectivize **agriculture** that were implemented by his successor, Joseph Stalin (1879–1953). *See also* COMMUNIST PARTY OF THE RUSSIAN CONFEDERATION.

LENINISM. Also known as Marxism-Leninism, Leninism was the leading **ideology** of revolutionary socialism in the twentieth century. **V. I. Lenin** blended **Marxism** with his personal experiences of czarist Russia and the extraordinary opportunities offered by the disastrous participation of the Russian empire in World War I. The main features of Leninism, as set out in his *What Is to Be Done?* (1902) and other works, were the need for a professional, dedicated party of revolutionaries who were to be the vanguard of the proletariat and were to guide it both before and after the revolution; "the dictatorship of the proletariat" based on a particular reading of Marx's criticisms of the **Gotha Program**; hostility toward social democrats, liberals, and parliamentary democracy generally; hostility to **religion**; and a view of **imperialism** that saw it as the last stage of **capitalism**. Leninism provided the basis for communist parties after 1920.

Leninism differed radically from most other forms of socialism current before 1915. Specifically, most socialists, even those who accepted the idea of the eventual downfall of capitalism by revolution, such as **Karl Kautsky**, believed that the revolution would occur spontaneously and that there was no need to hasten it, much less to replace a capitalist government by dictatorship and to deny democratic processes. A second vital difference concerned religion. Leninism was opposed to religion in principle as a means of deluding and oppressing the masses. Before 1920 mainstream European socialism could be generally described as nonreligious. There was certainly hostility to established religions where they were part of oppressive government machinery, owned excessive amounts of property, or had a monopoly in areas such as **education**. But the dominant view, as expressed in the **Erfurt Program**, saw religion as a private matter. *See also* LUXEMBURG, ROSA.

LEVELLERS. The Levellers were a group of reformers who emerged in the army of Oliver Cromwell during the English Civil War between 1647 and 1650. Despite their name, which was suggestive of severe **egalitarianism**, the Levellers were not as radical as their conservative opponents painted them. Claiming traditional birthrights derived from the Magna Carta (1215), the Levellers sought recognition of political, civil, religious, and economic rights. They asserted the sovereignty of parliament over any form of monarchy and the election of members of parliament by a broadly based **suffrage**. The extent of the suffrage was never precisely defined by the Leveller spokesmen, but it was not a universal suffrage. They presented their case during debates at Putney between 1647 and 1649. The Levellers were later suppressed by Cromwell. Because of their support for individualism and property, they have been since described as radical liberals rather than radical democrats. *See also* DIGGERS; LIBERALISM.

LIBERALISM. Liberalism may be broadly defined as a range of beliefs that have at their center an emphasis on the importance of the individual and the freedom of the individual. As a political tradition, such as existed in the nineteenth-century United Kingdom, liberalism was often seen as the enemy of socialism, particularly its insistence on the sanctity of individual property and the minimum degree of interference by governments in economic and social affairs. In contrast, socialist theories rejected the **capitalist** system and advocated (with the notable exception of **anarchism**) collectivist solutions to economic and social problems with government expected to play a leading role. Notwithstanding these divisions, liberalism made important contributions to the practice if not the theory of socialism. Liberals and socialists could agree, for instance, on their opposition to autocracies. Modern liberalism, in contrast with the classical liberalism that opposed state intervention, showed in Britain at least that it was possible to make significant improvements to the social order and to alleviate the worst features of the capitalist system through incremental change. There was disagreement about the pace of that change, but liberalism showed it could be done through constitutional means. It was a measure of the success of British liberalism that most **trade union** leaders before the 1880s were liberal supporters. Most importantly, liberalism contributed the idea that the lives and liberty of individuals were precious and had to be taken into account in the process of political change.

The experience of repressive regimes, both communist and noncommunist, demonstrated repeatedly how easily such concerns could be lost. After 1945 the Cold War forced Western social-democratic and labor parties to move further to the right to remove themselves from the charge of association with **communism**. The formal expunging of **Marxism** by the **German Social Democratic Party** in its **Godesberg Program** of 1959 was symbolic of this broader development. As a result, many elements from liberalism and the democratic socialist tradition merged. The ideological overlap of liberalism and socialism may be illustrated by two Latin American parties—the **Liberal Party of Columbia** and the Argentinean **Radical Civic Union**—that were formed in the liberal tradition during the nineteenth century but have since adopted social democracy and achieved full membership in the **Socialist International**. *See also* BERNSTEIN, EDUARD; FABIANISM; FRANKFURT DECLARATION; LEVELLERS; MACPHERSON, CRAWFORD BROUGH; MILL, JOHN STUART.

LIBERAL PARTY OF COLOMBIA [*PARTIDO LIBERAL COLOMBIANO* (PLC)]. Formed in 1849, as its name suggests the PLC was originally a party in the tradition of **liberalism**. In recent decades it has become a social-democratic party. In the early 1930s the PLC president Alfonso López Pumarejo introduced constitutional and economic reforms that came to be known as the "revolution on the march." This helped increase the party's support among the **working class**. Party loyalties to either the PLC or the Conservative Party have been intense and passed down through the generations of many Colombian families. This even resulted in undeclared civil **war** between the parties from 1947 to 1958. The parties agreed to form a National Front in 1958 to restore peace and stability. The Front's attempt to stabilize Colombia was interrupted in the 1960s when the PLC faced strong challenges in congressional elections by the populist Popular National Alliance, which also challenged the PLC's victory in the presidential elections of 1970 and subsequently began a guerilla campaign. The Alliance collaborated with the left-wing Revolutionary Armed Forces of Colombia (*Fuerzaz Armadas Revolucionarias de Colombia*—FARC), which had been formed in 1966.

The cooperation between the PLC and Conservatives was revived, although now informally, from 1974 until 1986, in an attempt to deal with the various left-wing guerilla groups and the major drug cartels. In 1986 the PLC won the elections to the presidency and both houses of Congress convincingly, and continued the attempt to control the guerillas and convince the FARC's political wing to turn to conventional politics. However, increased violence by the guerillas and drug cartels continued to undermine Colombia. In 1990 the PLC retained control of both houses of Congress and in May 1990 César Gaviria Trujillo of the PLC won the presidency, but again formed a government of National Unity with the Conservatives in an attempt to deal with the FARC and the drug cartels. After the elections of 1994 the PLC continued to control Congress but lost the presidency to the Conservatives. In March 1998 the PLC retained a narrow majority in Congress with 84 of 161 seats in the House of Representatives and 53 of 102 in the Senate, but again lost the presidential elections.

Declaring that it belonged to the democratic left, the PLC gained full membership in the **Socialist International** in 1999. The PLC announced its opposition to neoliberalism and its support for human rights and equality between men and **women**. In the elections of

March 2002 the PLC remained the largest party but with a substantially reduced share of the seats in the House of Representatives and Senate, with 54 of 166 seats and 28 of 102 respectively. The PLC, Conservatives, and independents together formed the government. In March 2002 the PLC failed to win the presidency, as an independent candidate was elected.

LIEBKNECHT, KARL (1871–1919). Karl Liebknecht, the son of **Wilhelm Liebknecht**, was born in Leipzig. He qualified as a lawyer and used his legal training to defend socialists. In 1907 he founded the Socialist Youth International, the first body of its kind, and became its leader. With **Rosa Luxemburg**, he was identified with the far left wing of the **German Social Democratic Party**. He opposed Germany's policies during World War I and organized the Spartacist League in 1915 in response. He was jailed for the rest of the **war**. In 1919 he converted the League into the Communist Party of Germany and led a **communist** uprising in Berlin in January 1919. He was captured and shot dead by right-wing former army officers (the *Freikorps*).

LIEBKNECHT, WILHELM (1826–1900). With **August Bebel**, Wilhelm Liebknecht was one of the founders of the League of Workingmen's Associations, which was reconstituted as the Social Democratic Workers' Party (*Sozial Demokratische Arbeiterpartei*) in 1869 and became part of the **International Workingmen's Association**. Liebknecht was born in Giessen, Hesse. He took part in the 1848 to 1849 revolution in Germany and then lived in exile in London where he became acquainted with **Karl Marx** and **Friedrich Engels**. On his return to Germany, he joined the General Union of German Workers, which had been founded by **Ferdinand Lassalle** in 1863. Disagreement with Lassalle's policies led Liebknecht and Bebel to found their own party, which merged with Lassalle's followers to form the **German Social Democratic Party** in 1875. Liebknecht took an active part in both the **International Workingmen's Association** and the **Second International**. His son **Karl Liebknecht** was a prominent left-wing German socialist.

LITERATURE. The literature most relevant to the history of socialism falls into two main categories: utopian or visionary works concerned with imaginary societies and works critical of existing society that stimulated social reform. The most famous of these works, although not a socialist work, or even the first work of its kind, was Thomas More's *Utopia* (1516), which presented a distant, secular, ideal society that was implicitly critical of the society of his day. In the nineteenth century utopian literature provided a vehicle for the promotion of socialist visions. Between 1813 and 1985 at least 217 works of utopian literature that contained socialist themes of some kind were published in English. Of these 130 were prosocialist or sympathetic and 87 were antisocialist or satirical. Between 1880 and 1889 12 prosocialist works were published, compared to 14 that had been published in English in the whole period from 1813 to 1879. Between 1890 and 1899 30 prosocialist utopian works were published and 30 more from 1900 to 1909. Thereafter these works were gradually fewer. In other words, of the 130 prosocialist utopian works that were published in English between 1813 and 1985, no less than 72 or 55 percent appeared between 1880 and 1909. Among the best-known works of utopian literature were **William Morris**'s *News from Nowhere* (1892), **Robert Blatchford**'s *The Sorcery Shop* (1907), and two works by **H. G. Wells**, *A Modern Utopia* (1905), and *New Worlds for Old* (1908). After 1917 the number of works of utopian literature inspired by socialist visions dropped off sharply and the literary medium became increasingly used by antisocialists and anticommunists to present antiutopias of society under **communism** or socialism.

Among novelists who were socialists and used the literary medium to promote socialism, the author with the most enduring reputation was **Upton Sinclair**, especially in his work of 1906, *The Jungle*, which had the unintended effect of initiating federal food legislation. Another work written around that time, first published in 1914, is Robert Tressell's *The Ragged Trousered Philanthropists*, which has become a classic of socialist literature. Another notable work was Walter Greenwood's *Love on the Dole*, first published in 1933. Like that of Tressell, Greenwood's novel is a critical commentary upon English **working-class** conditions and the problems of promoting socialism in such conditions.

LITHUANIAN SOCIAL DEMOCRATIC PARTY [*LIETUVOS SO-CIALDEMOKRATŲ PARTIJA* (LSDP)]. The LSDP was formed in 1896. Lithuania became part of the Russian empire in 1795 and remained so until it achieved independence along with the other Baltic states, Estonia and Latvia, in 1918. The formation of the LSDP reflected an upsurge in **nationalism** in Lithuania, which had begun in 1883. The LSDP became a member of the **Labor and Socialist International** and claimed 2,000 members in 1925. At the elections in 1926 the LSDP received 170,000 votes and won 15 out of 78 seats in the Diet, or parliament, thereby making it the second largest party in the country. It participated in a coalition government until December 1926, when it was violently overthrown by a right-wing coup. The leadership of the LSDP was either arrested or forced into exile. In June 1940 Lithuania was occupied by the Soviet Union. Lithuania declared its independence in March 1990, which prompted Soviet military intervention. Lithuania's independence was formally recognized by the Russian government in September 1991. The LSDP was reestablished in August 1989, and has been a full member of the **Socialist International** since the early 1990s.

In the parliamentary elections of 1992 the LSDP won eight seats. The former Communist Party, which had been reformed as Lithuanian Democratic Labour Party (*Lietuvos Demokratine Darbo Partija*—LDDP), secured a majority (73) of the seats and formed a government. The LDDP's Algirdas Brazauskas was also elected as independent Lithuania's first president. In the parliamentary elections of 1996 the LSDP won 10 seats and the LDDP 12, thus losing power to a conservative coalition. In the parliamentary elections of October 2000, the LSDP and LDDP participated with two other parties in Brazauskas's Social Democratic electoral coalition (*A. Brazausko socialdemokratinė Koalicija*), which obtained 51 seats with 31.1 percent of the vote. Although this was the biggest share of the vote, they were not able to compose a majority government. A center-right coalition took power. In January 2001 the LSDP and LDDP merged. The LSDP was the senior partner and thus the party continued under the LSDP name, while the former LDDP leader was elected chairman of the party, which campaigned for freedom, social justice, and solidarity. The center-right coalition collapsed in 2001 when the social liberals left the coalition. Without new elections the LSDP agreed to form a ruling coalition with the New Union (social liberals). Brazauskas became prime minister on behalf of the LSDP.

In elections to the European Parliament in June 2004 the LSDP won two of Lithuania's 13 seats. The LSDP members worked in the

Party of European Socialists, with which their party was affiliated. Before the parliamentary elections of October 2004 the LSDP, along with the social liberal New Union, formed an electoral coalition entitled Working for Lithuania (*Už darą Lietuvai*), which took 31 of 141 seats, including 20 for the LSDP. It formed a governing coalition with a new populist party entitled the Labour Party, which with 39 seats became the biggest party in parliament. Brazauskas retained the post of prime minister. *See also* ESTONIAN SOCIAL DEMO-CRATIC PARTY; LATVIAN SOCIAL DEMOCRATIC WORKERS' PARTY.

LONGUET, CHARLES FÉLIX CÉSAR (1833–1903). A French socialist, Charles Longuet was born in Caen. He was initially a follower of **Pierre-Joseph Proudhon**, but became a **Marxist** after his marriage to **Karl Marx**'s eldest daughter, Jenny, in 1872. He was a member of the **International Workingmen's Association** and was a leader of the **Paris Commune**. After 1889 he moderated his views and attracted a following. His followers, Longuetites, were **pacifists** during World War I. They supported the Bolshevik revolution, but not the dictatorship of the proletariat, and helped to set up the **International Working Union of Socialist Parties** in 1921.

LONGUETITES. *See* LONGUET, CHARLES FÉLIX CÉSAR.

LULA DA SILVA, LUIS IGNACIO (1945–). Born in the state of Pernambuco, North East Brazil, Luis Lula da Silva became the country's first left-wing president for 40 years when elected in 2002. As a child Lula da Silva had lived in extreme poverty, working as a peanut seller and a shoeshine boy. He trained as a metal worker and at the end of the 1960s became an enthusiastic **trade union** activist for the metalworkers. He made his name in Brazilian trade unionism, which had traditionally been very moderate. As a radical he became president of the Metalworkers' Union in 1975. In the late 1970s he was a major figure in the radical movement that would form the **Workers' Party** (*Partido dos Trabalhadores*—PT) in 1978.

"Lula," as he is almost universally known, remained a prominent activist in this new, grassroots-based party, standing as presidential candidate in the elections of 1989. He lost those elections by only 5 percent to the right-wing, neoliberal candidate Fernando Collor de

Mello. Lula's party continued to consolidate its strength in Brazil, and one year before the presidential elections of 1994, he led his rivals in the polls by approximately 20 percent. Nevertheless, in those elections he lost to the former radical Henrique Cardosa, who had now shifted to the neoliberal right. The PT did, however, continue to enjoy considerable success in local government, although the radical and social-democratic wings sometimes collided, leading importantly to the end of the Party's four-year administration of São Paulo. Nevertheless, Lula argued that experience in local government had allowed the PT to mature, gaining consciousness of its responsibilities without becoming less radical.

After failing to succeed in the next presidential elections, losing once again to Cardosa, Lula did win the presidency in October 2002, gaining 61.3 percent of the votes in the second round of the elections. Although the social-democratic wing of his party had gained the ascendancy, he had been able to hold the various forces together. Although the PT did not have majorities in the two houses of the Brazilian Congress, he was able to gain the support of other parties on the left and center-left and even one small party further to the right. He achieved this by not only maintaining his party's commitment to give priority to the poor and encourage grassroots participation, but by also promising to work with the International Monetary Fund.

Lula raised his profile on the international stage. In April 2004 Brazil gained the support of the World Trade Organization with the argument that cotton subsidies to U.S. farmers artificially and illegally depressed world prices. In August that year he led the G20 group of poor nations in campaigning against subsidies to farmers in countries with great **wealth**. However, his government suffered from an inability to implement some of its platform and charges of corruption against collaborators of Lula but not Lula himself.

LUXEMBOURG SOCIALIST WORKERS' PARTY [*LËTZE-BUERGER SOZIALISTESCH ARBECHTERPARTEI* (LSAP)].
The LSAP was founded in 1902 as the Luxembourg Social Democratic Party and adopted its present title after World War II. It suffered a reverse in 1921 when its left wing split off and formed a **communist** party. In 1928 it declared a membership of 1,200 to the **Labor and Socialist International**. In 1937 the LSAP was elected to government and laid the foundations for a **welfare state**. It was a partic-

ipant in government from 1945 to 1947, 1951 to 1959, 1964 to 1968, 1974 to 1979, and 1984 to 1999, usually in coalition with the conservative Christian Social Party. Its right wing having split in 1968, the LSAP was reorganized in 1974. In 1987 it claimed a membership of 5,000. The LSAP has been a full member of the **Socialist International** since 1951. In the elections of June 2004 the LSAP won 13 seats and once again joined a coalition government with the Christian Social Party, which took 19 seats. In elections to the European Parliament in June 2004 the LSAP obtained one of Luxembourg's six seats, one fewer than in the elections of 1999. The LSAP member worked in the **Party of European Socialists**, with which the LSAP was affiliated.

LUXEMBURG, ROSA (1870–1919). Rosa Luxemburg was a leading left-wing German socialist. She was born in Zamość in Russian Poland into a **middle-class Jewish** family. On her mother's side she was descended from a long line of rabbis, but she knew no Hebrew and only a little Yiddish. She probably became a socialist to protest the enforced Russification of Poland in Warsaw in 1887. In 1889 she was forced to flee to Switzerland, where she completed a doctorate on Poland's development as a **capitalist** society. She moved to Berlin in 1898 and took an active role in the **Second International** and opposed **revisionism**. She was on the far left of the **German Social Democratic Party**. Luxemburg saw the collapse of **capitalism** as inevitable on the grounds that in order to expand it needed precapitalist economies that it absorbed and then killed off. Eventually there would be no more precapitalist economies and the system would break down. The revolution in her view needed the spontaneity of working class. She entirely disagreed with the idea of **V. I. Lenin** that the revolution required a small, disciplined, and dedicated party.

In 1918 Luxemburg wrote a pamphlet on the Russian Revolution that was published in 1922. In it she attacked the Bolsheviks for the suppression of the peasantry, national groups, and their denial of democratic freedoms. She was a critic of separatist movements such as **Zionism** and the **International Jewish Labor Bund**, but wanted protection for Russian Jews from pogroms and the abolition of the pale of Jewish settlement in the Russian empire. She doubted the ability of small nations to defy large ones. Luxemburg opposed World War I and was jailed several times. With **Karl Liebknecht**, she was captured by right-wing former army officers after their **communist** uprising in Berlin in January 1919 failed. She was bashed with rifle butts and then thrown still alive into the Landwehr canal to drown.

– M –

MACDONALD, JAMES RAMSAY (1866–1937). Ramsay MacDonald was the first prime minister to come from the **British Labour Party** (Labour). Born to poor parents in Lossiemouth, Scotland, he briefly belonged to the **Social Democratic Federation** before joining the **Independent Labour Party** in 1894 (after he had been rejected by the Liberal Party as their candidate for the seat of Dover). He was secretary of the British Labour Party from 1900 to 1911 and chairman of the parliamentary Labour Party from 1911 to 1914 and again from 1922 to 1931. He was first elected to the House of Commons as the member for Leicester in 1906. He was also a key strategist and theorist for Labour, publishing three books before 1914: *Socialism and Society*, *Socialism and Government*, and *The Socialist Movement*. These works added nothing new to socialist theory; they presented an orderly evolutionary view of socialism and its compatibility with **liberalism** in order to create a party that would appeal to all social classes. Expanding state control was seen as the means to implement socialist policies; class struggle was rejected. He opposed both British participation in World War I—a decision that caused his resignation from the leadership of the parliamentary Labour Party—and British intervention in Russia after the Bolshevik revolution.

Between January and November 1924 MacDonald was prime minister of a minority government that depended upon the support of the Liberal Party. In 1929 he again became prime minister in an administration that was overwhelmed by the Depression. Faced with a cabinet hopelessly divided over domestic economic policy, particularly **unemployment**, MacDonald decided to enter into a coalition with the Conservatives to form a "National" government in August 1931; this bitterly denounced decision adversely colored MacDonald's reputation down to the late 1970s. MacDonald's career was the basis for a novel by Howard Spring, *Fame Is the Spur* (1940), which deals with a politician who begins by dedicating his life to the **working-**

class struggle but is corrupted by the trappings of political power. It was made into a film in 1947.

MACPHERSON, CRAWFORD BROUGH (1911–87). C. B. Macpherson was a socialist political philosopher who sought to retrieve what was valuable in both **liberalism** and **Marxism**. Born in Toronto, he studied at the University of Toronto, being influenced greatly by his lecturer Otto B. van der Sprenkel, who had been an enthusiastic student of **Harold Laski**. In the early 1930s Macpherson went on to study for a master's degree at the London School of Economics, under Laski's supervision. From there Macpherson returned to Toronto. Later conceding that he remained under Laski's spell into the 1940s, Macpherson became an important political philosopher and teacher in his own right, and was active in professional activity regarding political science in Canada. He also participated in the Canadian Campaign for Nuclear Disarmament.

While he considered that the nineteenth-century liberals **John Stuart Mill** and T. H. Green had written much of great value concerning human development, Macpherson was sharply critical of liberal market society. He argued that the political philosophy of such thinkers as Thomas Hobbes and the early liberal John Locke had reflected the development of the market economy in the seventeenth century. The culture that had arisen in market society and had come to dominate twentieth-century capitalist society could be summarized as, in his words, "possessive individualism." This culture was based on the theory that the unlimited right of accumulation is a necessary incentive for productivity in a situation of scarcity in society. This, according to possessive individualism, is the best means of satisfying unlimited desire.

Macpherson argued that the contemporary liberal democratic state and society could not accommodate significant human development. Like Laski, Macpherson embraced the liberal-democratic tenets of individualism, liberty, and human flourishing, but stressed that the historical association between liberalism and capitalism had resulted in the frustration of those tenets. Although liberal democracy was justified partly upon the claim that it maximized human powers, in fact market society enabled some human beings to benefit from a transfer of powers from others. He thus distinguished between developmental power and extractive power.

Technological progress had created the conditions for humans to develop their powers both individually and collectively. Such development was, as Macpherson understood it, what freedom really meant. If the impediments to human development were removed, democracy need not be merely protective, defending individuals from one another and the state, but also participatory, in which people could take control of their lives in an atmosphere of cooperation. In 1976 he declared that his life's work had been to reconcile elements of liberalism and Marxism. He died in Toronto.

MALON, BENOÎT (1841–93). French socialist theorist, Benoît Malon was born at Précieux, Loire. He worked as a laborer, a dyer, and a shepherd. He was self-educated and joined the **International Workingmen's Association**. As a parliamentary representative for Seine department, he opposed peace with Germany in 1870 and participated in the **Paris Commune**. In 1885 he founded the influential journal *Revue socialiste*. Malon's socialism was an eclectic blend of the ideas of various French activists and thinkers, including François-Noel Babeuf, Antoine Nicolas Condorcet, Auguste Comte, and **Claude-Henri Saint-Simon**, that stressed morality and humanitarianism. He and his followers promoted a gradualist approach to the achievement of economic and social reforms through legislative change and they were an important influence on **Jean Jaurès** and **Alexandre Millerand**. *See also* REVISIONISM.

MALTA LABOUR PARTY (MLP) (*PARTIT LABURISTA*). The original Maltese Labour Party was formed in 1920. The following year it attracted 22 percent of the vote and was thus represented in the legislative assembly in 1922 for the first and only time until the end of World War II, as its support quickly declined. The party formed a government in October 1947 under the leadership of Paul Boffa. In October 1949 Boffa left the party, which was reorganized and renamed the MLP that year under the leadership of Dominic Mintoff. The MLP, which became strongly anti-imperialist, lost the parliamentary elections of 1950. Boffa formed a moderate Malta Workers' Party which, after briefly participating in a coalition government, ceased to exist in 1953.

The MLP gained full membership in the **Socialist International** in 1955 and was elected to power that year under Mintoff (who was leader until 1984). Mintoff resigned as prime minister in 1958 after his once anticolonial party failed to gain agreement in the country for integration with the United Kingdom. Malta gained full independence in 1964. The MLP did not regain power until it won the parliamentary elections of 1971, when Mintoff became prime minister once again. He introduced extensive **nationalization** and expanded the **welfare state**. Mintoff resigned in 1984 but the MLP remained in government until 1987, with Carmelo Mifsud Bonnici as prime minister. In 1987 the MLP claimed a membership of 30,000.

The MLP came to see itself as a bridge between Europe and the Arab world. In 1996 it attracted 50.7 percent of the vote in the national elections, and regained power with Alfred Sant as prime minister. The MLP shelved the application made by the previous Nationalist government to join the European Union (EU). In 1998 the MLP lost power to the Nationalist Party at the national elections. The MLP failed to regain power in the elections of 12 April 2003, winning 30 of 65 seats, with 47.5 percent of the vote. The Nationalists took Malta into the EU in 2004. At the elections to the European Parliament in June 2004 MLP candidates took three of Malta's five seats. They worked in the **Party of European Socialists**, with which the MLP was affiliated.

MANIFESTO OF THE SIXTY. The Manifesto of the Sixty was issued by some of the followers of **Pierre-Joseph Proudhon** in 1864. It asserted that although the French Revolution of 1789 had won political equality, **capitalism**, reinforced by the parliamentary system, denied the **working class** economic equality. The manifesto argued that the working class needed to be represented by other working-class men who alone would truly represent their own interests. In 1863 this group unsuccessfully sponsored three working-class candidates for election to parliament. Proudhon reacted to the manifesto by writing *De la capacité politique des classes ouvrières* (On the Political Capacity of the Working Classes).

MANN, TOM (1856–1941). Tom Mann was one of the leaders of organized labor in England and a radical political activist who operated internationally. He was born near Coventry; his mother died when he was two years old. He received only three years of formal schooling. His working life began at the age of nine. He was employed as a pit worker at the age of 10 and was apprenticed as a toolmaker in 1872. Mann benefited directly from the successful campaign by the Tyneside Nine Hours League and used the shorter working day for further study. He also concluded that **trade unions** alone could not achieve such victories. In 1881 he joined the Amalgamated Society of Engineers and read *Progress and Poverty* by **Henry George** but rejected its central idea of the single **tax**. Mann was a friend of **Friedrich Engels** and of **Karl Marx**'s daughter Eleanor. These friendships strengthened Mann's political radicalism, as was shown by his leading role in the campaign for an eight-hour working day in the late 1880s.

In 1885 Mann joined the **Social Democratic Federation** and in February 1894 he became secretary of the **Independent Labour Party**, a post he held until January 1897. In 1895 he stood unsuccessfully for election to the House of Commons and in 1896 helped to organize the London conference of the **Second International**. In 1889 he became the first president of the London Dockers' Union, a position he held until 1893. He was one of the main founders of the International Federation of Ship, Dock, and River Workers in 1896, which became the International Transport Workers' Federation and the Workers' Union in 1898. Mann visited the United States twice, in 1886 and 1913. Between 1901 and 1910 he lived in New Zealand and then Australia (and briefly South Africa), where he was active in organized labor and in the Socialist Party of Victoria. He returned to the United Kingdom a committed supporter of **syndicalism**. In 1916 he joined the **British Socialist Party** and was a founding member of the British Communist Party in 1920.

MARCUSE, HERBERT (1898–1979). A central figure in the Frankfurt School for **Marxist** social research in the 1930s, Herbert Marcuse became a key figure of the **new left** in the 1960s. Born in Berlin, he joined the **German Social Democratic Party** in 1917 but left two years later, in response to his party's role in suppressing the socialist revolution in Germany. In the 1920s he studied philosophy at Berlin and Freiburg. In 1933 he joined the Frankfurt School. As the Nazi dictatorship made the position of the left precarious the School left Germany and in 1934 settled in the United States. Marcuse remained in America for the rest of his life, becoming a professor at the University of California and a guru during the student protests of the 1960s.

In 1953 Marcuse published *Eros and Civilization*. In response to Sigmund Freud, he argued that repression of human instincts would not be necessary in a society where technology could provide abundance. If classes were abolished tension and conflict would disappear. Human instinct, which need not be channeled into work, could be liberated. Humanity and the power of reason could thus develop. However, Marcuse was not optimistic that this would come about. He did not believe that the solution could be found in Soviet **communism**. In *Soviet Marxism* in 1958 he argued that although there were important ideological differences between communism and advanced **capitalism**, regarding property relations for instance, in both systems individual autonomy had been replaced by centralized regimentation. The masses were coordinated through communications, entertainment, industry, and **education**. As the Soviet Union attempted to catch up with the West industrially, its original aims had been lost, technological rationality becoming the dominant concern.

In *One Dimensional Man* in 1964 Marcuse presented a radical alternative to both liberal capitalism and orthodox Soviet Marxism. He argued that in the twentieth century technology satisfied all the reasonable desires of people in the modern capitalist societies. Largely through advertising, mass culture, and the media the **bourgeoisie** manipulated the interests of the proletariat. This constituted indoctrination and a new form of social control. False needs integrated individuals into the existing system of production and consumption. Ideas, aspirations, and objections that transcended or criticized established patterns were either repelled or reduced to the terms of this pattern. The critical power of reason was suppressed and humans were not free to flourish. Capitalist society had thus become totalitarian. Although he considered that social forces and tendencies could break this containment, he stressed that not enough people recognized social control, as class distinctions were masked and people held false consciousness. The proletariat, which had been assimilated and thus contained within bourgeois society, was no longer a revolutionary force. Society had become one dimensional, involving consensus and agreement between classes.

In *An Essay on Liberation*, published in 1969, Marcuse sought a way out of the problem he had discussed in *One Dimensional Man*. He identified "the great refusal" of some people to accept the norms of society. People were discovering new instincts, with some hippies adopting a whole new way of living. The counterculture, radical protests, movements, and new lifestyles gave him hope. The solidarity required for socialism may indeed thus be developed. Nevertheless, in an interview in 1973, when the 1960s protests had dissipated, he suggested that his arguments in *One Dimensional Man* were being corroborated. The protest movement would need to rethink its strategies and tactics.

MARKET SOCIALISM. Advocates of market socialism, such as David Miller, John Roemer, and David Schweickart, argue that even if the ownership of capital is socialized, market mechanisms can be the means to provide most goods and services. In the 1930s Oscar Lange offered an early theory of market socialism in his essay "On the Economic Theory of Socialism." There would be a division of function between a central planning board and the management of socialized enterprises. Management would respond to consumer demand but in a situation of scarcity the board would manipulate prices. Late twentieth-century market socialists offered theories that were quite different from that of Lange. They considered it futile to seek a nonmarket economy in modern industrial society, in which there would inevitably be conditions of scarcity. Not only had central planning eventually failed wherever it had been established, certain problems had made such failure almost inevitable when economies grew more complex, even if great strides had been made in the developmental stages. These problems concerned, first, information in a complex economy; second, incentives to make innovative decisions, take risks, make harsh but necessary decisions, and work harder than necessary; and third, authoritarian tendencies that central planning fostered.

Nevertheless, market socialists stressed that the market need not be associated with **capitalism**. Moreover, market socialism could be both preferable and more economically viable than capitalism. Enterprises would be self-governing—some theorists advocating **cooperatives**. There would be investment agencies from which the enterprises could draw capital, but this capital would find its way back to common ownership either through **taxation** or interest. The capital should not be a source of income. Productivity and growth would, though, bring financial rewards. Either the workers in an enterprise would gain financially, providing some incentive, or in another model of market socialism each citizen would have a stock portfolio and gain when the enterprises controlling stocks generate dividends. In the latter case the stocks would be received at birth, may be exchanged but not sold, and returned to society at death. Some socialists argue that the competition and inequality that would ensue in any of the variants would mean that market socialism is not really socialism at all.

MARX, KARL HEINRICH (1818–83). Karl Marx is the towering figure in the history of socialism. No other socialist thinker has had comparable influence, although his followers have hotly disputed the nature of his legacy since the 1890s. Born in Trier, Germany, Marx was descended from a family that had produced many rabbis, but he was baptized as a Protestant. In 1837 he began studying philosophy and was eventually awarded a doctorate on the Democritean and Epicurean theory of nature in ancient Greek philosophy from the University of Berlin in 1841. In 1842 he became editor of the radical newspaper *Rheinische Zeitung* (Rhine Newspaper) and wrote some articles on poverty that were published in January 1843. Two months later the newspaper was shut down by the authorities. After refusing a post with the Prussian civil service, Marx moved to Paris where he met **Pierre-Joseph Proudhon**, **Michael Bakunin**, and **Friedrich Engels**. In 1844 he wrote the work in which he set out his theory of alienation. Never published in his lifetime, that work would later be known as the *Economic and Philosophical Manuscripts*. In 1844 he also began his lifelong collaboration with Engels.

In January 1845 Marx and his family were expelled from France for his radical writings. They moved to Belgium where he and Engels founded the Communist Correspondence Committee, which was mostly made up of German émigrés; at its first congress in London, the committee renamed itself the Communist League. It was the League that commissioned Marx and Engels to write the *Manifesto of the Communist Party* (Communist Manifesto), which appeared in February 1848. After his radical activities in Germany in 1848 Marx was expelled in 1849 and moved to Paris and then London, where he remained for the rest of his life, often living in great poverty despite regular financial help from Engels and occasional help from others. In London Marx studied, conducted research into economics and history in the British Museum (now the British Library), and engaged in radical politics. He was the European correspondent for the *New York Tribune* between 1851 and 1862 and wrote articles on the Crimean War and the American Civil War. In 1852 he formally dissolved the Communist League. In September 1864 he was invited to attend the inaugural meeting of the **International Workingmen's Association** and soon became its leading figure. In 1871 he was accused in France of being the instigator of the **Paris Commune**, a claim he denied in a letter to *The Times* of London. In 1875 his application for British citizenship was rejected.

Apart from the *Manifesto of the Communist Party*, Marx's most influential writings included *The Class Struggles in France, 1848–1850* (1850), *The Eighteenth Brumaire of Louis Bonaparte* (1852), *Grundrisse der Kritik der politischen Ökonomie* (Outline of a Critique of Political Economy, 1857), *The Civil War in France* (1871), and *Das Kapital* (Capital) which was published as three volumes in 1867, 1885, and 1895. The roots of Marx's socialism were in the millenarianism of the Old Testament, the tradition of **egalitarianism** spawned by the French Revolution, the **middle-class** rationalism of the Enlightenment, German philosophical idealism (specifically as espoused by Hegel and the dialectic), political economy (the original title of the modern discipline of economics), and the growth of the **working-class** movements such as **Chartism** and **trade unions**.

The main elements of Marx's thought may, for convenience, be approached under five headings: class struggle, historical materialism, alienation, the labor theory of value, and **communism**. Marx saw society as made up of classes that were defined in terms of the means of production—particularly the extent to which certain classes monopolized the ownership of the means of production—and used that power to exploit other classes, which gave rise to incessant struggle between the classes. Historical materialism was an interpretation of history that saw it as largely a predictable, dialectical process reflecting changes in the nature of the means of production, which themselves reflected the development of productive forces (such as technology and developing human capabilities) in society. Alienation, a feature more of Marx's earlier writings than his later ones (which tended to stress the economic exploitation of class relations), referred to the estrangement of most workers under capitalism from the control of the process of work and the products of their labor.

The labor theory of value was an idea Marx took from the English economist Ricardo. It held that labor was the source of all wealth. Marx used the theory to argue that the excess of "surplus" produced by the worker under capitalism was confiscated by the owners of the means of production. In practice, this meant that the worker was not fairly paid for the value of his or her labor. Rather, under the wage system, workers were paid enough to reproduce their labor power. Communism would be the state of society in which the means of production had been taken over by the proletariat. It presupposed that capitalism had collapsed through its own internal contradictions or through violent revolution. Private property would be abolished as would the social division of labor based on social class and its economic exploitation. Communism would enable a wealthier, better-educated society in which each individual would be able to achieve his or her full potential and want would be eliminated. This summary gives only a cursory impression of the breadth and complexity of Marx's thought and the way in which his ideas were interrelated.

Because much of Marx's works remained incomplete at his death, others, such as **Karl Kautsky** and Georgi V. Plekhanov (1857–1918), attempted to present his thought in a more coherent way than appeared in Marx's manuscripts, many of which did not become available until long after his death. Marx left behind a vast, complex, and ambiguous legacy that gave rise to Marxism. He had little direct influence in his lifetime, but the rise of communism gave his ideas, or at least his ideas as interpreted by **V. I. Lenin**, a world prominence that they probably would not otherwise have enjoyed.

The term *dialectical materialism* was not actually used by Marx himself, but was coined by the Russian Marxist theorist and codifier of **Marxism**, Plekhanov, in the 1890s. Dialectical materialism was an idea based on a radical revision of the work of the German philosopher G. W. F. Hegel. The dialectical part refers to argument or discussion and the materialism part refers to a theory of existence that holds that everything that exists is material in that it occupies some amount of space at some time. In dialectical materialism conflict between opposites (*thesis* and *antithesis*) leads to a new outcome (*synthesis*). Marx had applied the idea of materialism to understand historical and social developments, but his followers later applied dialectical materialism to other fields of knowledge.

Marx's ideas were important for continental socialism, but much less so for English-speaking countries. The ambiguity of his legacy is important to appreciate because there is evidence that toward the end of his life Marx considered that the economic and social revolution he envisaged could be achieved by peaceful means in the more industrially advanced and politically progressive parts of Western Europe. Brilliant as his ideas were, they were not without problems of their own. For instance, after the 1840s Marx never renewed his knowledge of British manufacturing firsthand. He therefore failed to appreciate its development and the diversification of occupations and skills. He saw the development of craft unionism and the growth of a labor aristocracy as a backward step, not as a reflection of changed industrial conditions. As a result, Marxism was frozen in the memory of the misery of industrial Britain in the 1840s; ironically, this helped Marxism to seem more relevant for less developed economies. A second important difficulty concerned his view of the working class. Marx emphasized what its members had in common and was inclined to ignore those things that divided them, such as **religion**, ethnicity, and skill levels. Marx was a remarkable analyst and system maker on the world scale. But as in the case of all such thinkers, it is important to distinguish him from his interpreters. *See also* LENINISM.

MARXISM. The general term *Marxists* means literally "followers of **Karl Marx**," but has nevertheless encompassed a great range of meanings. European socialist parties, particularly the **German Social Democratic Party**, drew on the theories of Marx as interpreted by **Friedrich Engels**, but these parties were reformist, not revolutionary, in practice. **V. I. Lenin** extracted the revolutionary aspects from Marx and created Marxism-**Leninism**, which became the basis for a dictatorship in the name of socialism. In contrast to the doctrinaire oppression of Marxism-Leninism and other antidemocratic variants of **communism** such as Maoism, the **New Left** sought to create a humane version of Marxism. This diversity in Marxism arose not just because of different political environments—notably in societies that had democratic traditions and those that did not—but also because of the ambiguities in Marx's writings that provided support for a variety of interpretations.

For most social-democratic parties since 1945 there was an electoral imperative to distance themselves from Marxism, which was equated with communism, totalitarianism, and repression. Accordingly, references to Marxism in the statement of principles of the social-democratic parties were removed in Austria in 1958, Germany and the Netherlands in 1959, France in 1972, Italy in 1978, Spain in the early 1980s, and Portugal in 1986. *See also* KAUTSKY, KARL JOHANN.

MAURITIAN MILITANT MOVEMENT [*MOUVEMENT MILITANT MAURICIEN* (MMM)]. Formed in 1969 at a time of labor unrest, the MMM, led by Paul Berenger, developed a considerable base of support. In the parliamentary elections of 1976 the MMM gained the most seats, but the **Mauritius Labour Party**—MLP (*Parti Travailliste*—PTr) formed a coalition government with the Mauritian Social Democratic Party (*Parti Mauricien Social-Démocrate*). In 1982 the MMM formed a coalition government with the Mauritian Socialist Party (*Parti Socialiste Mauricien*—PSM). This, however, lasted only one year, as some members of the MMM left to form the Militant Socialist Movement (*Mouvement Socialist Militant*), which was soon renamed the Mauritian Socialist Movement (*Mouvement Socialiste Mauricien*—MSM) when it combined with the PSM. In 1991 the MMM joined an alliance with the MSM and a smaller party and won the parliamentary elections. In the parliamentary elections of 1995 the MMM won 25 of the 62 seats and formed a winning alliance with the MLP. In 1997, when its leader Berenger was dismissed, the MMM withdrew from the coalition. In the parliamentary elections of September 2000, the MMM and the MSM reunited in an alliance to win the elections, gaining 54 of 62 seats with 51.7 percent of the vote (adjusted to 58 of 70 when the seats for best losers were constitutionally allocated). The MSM's Sir Anerood Jugnauth became prime minister until 2003 when, as agreed before the election, Berenger took over as prime minister. The MMM gained full membership in the **Socialist International** in 2003.

In the parliamentary elections of July 2005 the MMM/MSM coalition lost power to the MLP-led Social Alliance (*Alliance Sociale*). The losing coalition obtained 22 of 62 seats (adjusted to 24 of 70). Berenger thus resigned as prime minister.

MAURITIUS LABOUR PARTY (MLP) [*PARTI TRAVAILLISTE* (PTr)]. The MLP (or PTr as it sometimes known) was formed in

February 1936 by Dr. Maurice Curé, a medical practitioner, and was based on the Hindu community. Its first goal was the extension of the **suffrage** to the **working class**. In the 1950s the MLP became less left-wing and abandoned its policy advocating the **nationalization** of the sugar industry. Mauritius gained independence from the United Kingdom in 1968. The MLP became a full member of the **Socialist International** in 1969.

The MLP enjoyed electoral victories in 1948, 1959, and 1963 and in coalition with the Mauritian Social Democratic Party (*Parti Mauricien Social-Démocrate*—PMSD) in 1967, but suffered from internal dissension after 1976. This contributed to its loss of power in 1982 to the **Mauritian Militant Movement** (*Mouvement Militant Mauricien*—MMM)/Mauritian Socialist Party (*Parti Socialiste Mauricien*—PSM) alliance. The MLP participated, along with the PMSD and the newly formed Mauritian Socialist Movement (*Mouvement Socialiste Mauricien*—MSM), in a coalition government briefly from August 1983 to February 1984. The MLP suffered splits in 1986 and 1987 but again participated in a coalition government from 1987 to 1991. After the elections of December 1995, at which it won 35 of the 62 seats, the MLP entered government in alliance with the MMM. In 1997 the MLP Prime Minister Navinchandra Ramgoolam dismissed the MMM coalition members, meaning that the MLP was left to govern with just a few minor parties in alliance. In September 2000 the MLP contested the parliamentary elections in a coalition with the Mauritian Party of Xavier-Luc Duval (*Parti Mauricien Xavier-Luc Duval*). This coalition obtained only six of 62 seats with 36.5 percent of the vote (adjusted to eight of 70 when the seats for best losers were constitutionally allocated), and the MLP lost power to a coalition of the MMM and the MSM.

In the parliamentary elections of July 2005 the MLP returned to power at the head of the Social Alliance (*Alliance Sociale*), which, consisting of several parties including the PMSD, defeated the MMM/MSM coalition. This Alliance won 38 of 62 seats with 48.8 percent of the vote (adjusted to 42 of 70). Ramgoolam became prime minister and formed a new government, promising to tackle inflation and **unemployment**.

MEMBERSHIP OF SOCIAL-DEMOCRATIC/SOCIALIST PO-LITICAL PARTIES. Information about the membership of social-democratic/socialist parties first became available from the 1890s and became more generally available from the early 1900s. Excluding cases of political repression, the membership statistics show a substantial growth from this time to 1913 and on to 1920; one notable exception was the **Socialist Party of America**, whose membership declined sharply after 1912. The growth pattern of the individual membership of social-democratic/socialist parties has usually paralleled that of the **trade unions**. For some parties, notably the **British Labour Party** (Labour) and the Belgian Workers' Party (later **Belgian Socialist Party**), individual membership figures were included with those of trade unions and cooperatives before 1930. In many of the countries for which the data are available, membership reached a peak during the 1950s or 1960s and then tended to level off or decline.

Although much scarcer, it is information on the composition of the membership of the social-democratic/socialist parties that is of even greater interest, for it shows clearly where the strengths and weaknesses of political socialism lay. Data on the pre-1940 period are available for the parties of Norway (1887 to 1971), the Netherlands (1909), Bulgaria (1909), Austria (1929), and Germany (1930). Making allowances for the differences in dates and countries and the different occupational classifications used, a distinct pattern becomes apparent in regard to the social groups that were attracted to these parties. In the main, the principal groups represented in these parties were urban industrial workers and tradesmen, males, and the better-educated. The most notably absent group was **agriculture**. Although the growth in **middle-class** representation in these parties has been cause for comment (and even concern) since 1960, it is evident from these earlier data that the educated and the middle class have always had an important presence in such parties. For example, a sample of 140 members of the leadership of the **Norwegian Labor Party** (*Det norske Arbeiderparti*—DnA) from 1887 to 1903 shows that 34 percent were from the liberal professions or were employees in the higher levels of the private sector. Since the 1960s there has been a general decline in the proportion of manual or blue-collar employees in the membership of such parties. Because this decline has often been faster than in the whole labor force, the figures have been used as evidence for **working class** disenchantment with social-democratic/socialist parties. For instance, in the **French Socialist Party** the proportion of manual/blue-collar members fell from 44 to

19 percent between 1951 and 1973. Yet over the same period, the proportion of manual/blue-collar members in the **Austrian Social Democratic Party** (*Sozialdemoktratische Partei Österreichs*—SPÖ) only fell from 40 to 37 percent.

The members of these parties have also displayed remarkable endurance under the most difficult conditions. For instance, it has been estimated that when the **German Social Democratic Party** (*Sozialdemokratische Partei Deutschlands*—SPD) was reestablished in 1946, about 75 percent of its 701,448 members had been members before its suppression in 1933. When the **Czech Social Democratic Party** (*Česká strana sociálně demokratická*—CSSD) was reformed in 1990, about 20 percent of its 11,000 members had been members before 1948, which was before the imposition of one-party **communist** rule.

In the late twentieth-century party membership of European political parties declined in general. Many socialist/social-democratic parties experienced this problem. In Austria the SPÖ suffered a decline from more than 700,000 in 1980 to 400,000 in 1999. Membership of the **Swedish Social Democratic Workers' Party** fell from around 214,000 in 1974 to approximately 162,500 in 1998. The **Danish Social Democratic Party** experienced a decline from more than 101,000 in 1980 to 59,500 in 1998, while in the same period membership of the **Finnish Social Democratic Party** fell from around 100,000 to just over 64,000. In Norway the DnA saw its membership decline from around 153,500 in 1980 to just over 64,400 in 1997. In Germany membership of the SPD fell from nearly 987,000 in 1980 to around 755,000 in 1999. The **Dutch Labor Party** suffered a decline from nearly 113,000 in 1980 to 61,000 in 2000. In Britain membership of Labour fell from just over 348,000 in 1980 to around 293,000 in 1989. However, when **Tony Blair** took over the leadership, membership rose, reaching 385,000 in 1998 before declining again in the early twenty-first century.

Membership of many political parties in the recently democratized countries of Europe grew in the late twentieth century. This included a number of socialist/social-democratic parties. In the Czech Republic membership of the CSSD rose from 13,000 in 1993 to 18,000 in 1999. The **Spanish Socialist Workers' Party** enjoyed a rise from around 97,000 in 1981 to 410,000 in 2000. Membership of the **Pan-Hellenic Socialist Movement** in Greece grew from 75,000 to 200,000 in 1998. The **Portuguese Socialist Party** had around 64,000

members in 1980 and 100,000 in 2000. *See also* LEADERSHIP/
RANK AND FILE TENSIONS.

MENSHEVIKS. *Menshevik* is a Russian term meaning "a member of the
minority." It was originally applied to members of the Russian Social
Democratic Labor Party who supported **economism** and a gradual approach to the introduction of socialism. They were a distinct faction in
the party after a split at the party's second conference in London in
1903, when they then constituted a minority as opposed to the Bolsheviks, who were then the majority. Unlike **V. I. Lenin**, the Mensheviks
were prepared to admit individuals as members who were not full-time,
professional activists. They had the support of **August Bebel** and **Karl
Kautsky**. The leaders of the Mensheviks were L. Martov, G. V.
Plekhanov, P. D. Axelrod, and **Leon Trotsky**. Most of the Mensheviks
were expelled by the Bolsheviks in their reorganization of the party in
1912. They opposed Lenin's idea of the dictatorship of the proletariat.
After the March 1917 revolution in Russia the Mensheviks enjoyed
considerable support in the soldiers' and workers' councils and tried to
achieve unity among the socialist groups. The Mensheviks supported
Alexander Feodorovich Kerensky, who led a provisional government.
After the Bolsheviks, with Trotsky now on board, seized power in November 1917, the Mensheviks became the effective opposition. But
they were progressively removed from positions of influence and were
declared illegal in 1921. *See also* LENINISM.

MIDDLE CLASS. Often referred to as the bourgeoisie, the middle class
occupies a paradoxical place in the history of socialism. The term
class as a label for social rank entered the major European languages
during the last half of the eighteenth century and in English by 1767.
The plural term *middle classes* appeared in print in England in 1797
and in the singular form in 1812, but it did not become dominant until after 1840. Identified by **Karl Marx** with the owners of property,
the middle class was identified as the natural enemy of the proletariat,
or **working class**. It must be appreciated that in the 1840s these terms
had vastly different meanings than they do today. The middle class
was proportionately much smaller than at present and the working
class much larger; for instance, in 1911 only 18.7 percent of the employed labor force in Britain worked in white-collar occupations.
There were also far greater disparities in income and **wealth**.

The problem for the growth of socialism was that **education** and organizational expertise in the nineteenth century were largely in the hands of the middle class. It therefore needed much assistance from the middle class to grow. It was no accident that the ideas and writings that contributed so much to the development of socialism in the nineteenth century came almost exclusively from sympathetic members of the middle class and even the wealthy. A sample of the leadership of the **Norwegian Labor Party** between 1887 and 1903 found that 34 percent came from liberal professions or highly placed white-collar members of the private sector. When traditional working class parties and other institutions develop substantial middle class membership this is sometimes called embourgoisement. An example of an influential middle grouping is the H. J. Vogel circle in the **German Social Democratic Party**, which allied itself with the working-class party workers known as the *kanalarbeiten* from the 1960s. Another German example is the *Sozialdemokratische Wählerinitiative* (social-democratic voter initiative) intellectual forum. Members of the middle class who voice social and political concerns and influence policy makers are sometimes dubbed "chattering classes," or in Australia "new class." *See also* MEMBERSHIP OF SOCIAL-DEMOCRATIC/SOCIALIST POLITICAL PARTIES.

MILITANT TENDENCY. Militant Tendency is a cover name for the **Revolutionary Socialist League**, a well-organized, disciplined left-wing group that used the tactic of entrism and infiltrated the **British Labour Party** (Labour) in the early 1970s and 1980s. Claiming to follow Trotskyist **ideology**, it became the dominant group in the council of the city of Liverpool. Two Labour members of parliament were among its adherents. Although declared a party within a party (and therefore illegal under the Labour constitution), it was not banned until 1983 and 200 of its leaders and supporters were expelled in 1985 and 1986. At the time of its banning, the Militant Tendency had 8,000 members. *See also* CAMPAIGN FOR LABOUR PARTY DEMOCRACY; SCOTTISH SOCIALIST PARTY.

MILL, JOHN STUART (1806–73). Although widely recognized as a founder of modern **liberalism**, the English philosopher Mill made a contribution to the development of social democracy. This contribution came chiefly in his influential book *Principles of Political Econ-*

omy (1848), which went through seven editions during his lifetime. In that book Mill made a clear distinction between production and distribution. He was sympathetic to what would later become known as the **utopian socialism** of writers such as **Robert Owen** and **Charles Fourier**, especially from the third edition of 1852 onward. Nevertheless he was also critical, arguing that the existing economic system could be improved.

Although he considered that production was constrained by economic laws and other impediments, Mill believed that the imbalances these barriers created could be redressed by intervention in the distribution process, thereby opening the possibility for society to expropriate and redistribute the **wealth** created by production. He saw the existing distribution of wealth as being set by the "laws and customs of society," not by iron-clad economic laws. He introduced a more optimistic view into economics than that engendered by Thomas Malthus and David Ricardo. Both conservatives and radicals criticized Mill for overestimating the extent to which society was prepared to redistribute wealth. Later in life, in his posthumously published *Chapters on Socialism*, Mill came to adopt mildly socialist views, arguing, however, that socialism must be developed gradually and be based on small-scale, self-acting units such as towns or villages. Revolutionary, centralized socialism would lead to tyranny. He believed that social behavior could be changed and that the **working class** could avoid the population trap of Malthus and, by means of **education**, have fewer children of their own will.

MILLERAND, ALEXANDRE (1859–1943). Born in Paris, Alexandre Millerand was a leading exponent and practitioner of evolutionary socialism. A lawyer, he was elected to the French Chamber of Deputies in 1885, where he led an independent group of socialists. His acceptance of the position of minister for commerce and industry in the government of René Waldeck-Rousseau in 1899 caused uproar among French socialists and in the **Second International**, which condemned socialists accepting positions in bourgeois governments in 1905. Unfortunately this controversy overshadowed Millerand's considerable achievements as a government minister. He used his position to introduce the first effective French legislation to restrict working hours—the previous legislation was not enforced—from 11 hours in 1899 to 10.5 in 1901 and to 10 hours from 1903; to actively encourage government labor inspectors to investigate complaints by **trade unions**; to set up a system of labor councils made up of employer and employee representatives (*Conseils du Travail*); to enforce the payment of accident insurance premiums by employers, not employees; and to improve conditions for the employees of successful government contractors for public works and supplies.

A **nationalist** and a republican as well as a socialist, Millerand wanted to develop the public ownership of large-scale production and to improve the distribution of **wealth**. He saw socialism as an inevitable trend in social development and believed that socialists should play an active role in government, including working with bourgeois governments if necessary. His efforts to have this position adopted as general policy by socialists failed in the wake of their revulsion against politics generally following the Dreyfus Affair in 1897. Millerand and the trade unions disagreed over his efforts to give them the legal status of persons so they could be parties to contracts; the trade unions feared they might be destroyed by litigation, especially following the Taff Vale Case in the United Kingdom in 1901, which made them liable for potentially huge damages if they engaged in picketing. They were also determined to preserve their independence from all forms of political control and so clashed with Millerand's plans for a labor court based on the New Zealand law of 1894. Millerand published a collection of his speeches as a book, *Le Socialisme Réformiste français* (French Reformist Socialism), in 1903. He was formally expelled from the ranks of the socialists in 1905. He served as minister for works in 1909 to 1910, of war in 1912 to 1913, and as president of the French Republic (1920 to 1924), by which time he had become part of the political right wing. *See also* REVISIONISM.

MITTERRAND, FRANÇOIS MAURICE MARIE (1916–96). The leading moderate French socialist of the post-1945 period, **François** Mitterrand was born in Jarnac, Charente, eastern France; his father was a railroad station master who later inherited a vinegar distillery. From his father Mitterrand imbibed a sense of economic injustice, particularly over the uneven distribution of **wealth** in society. Otherwise, Mitterrand was a political paradox. Although firmly linked with democratic socialism from 1946, he had flirted with fascist organizations in the mid-1930s. He was drafted into the army in 1938 and was wounded and captured by the Germans during their invasion of France in 1940. He escaped and worked on the administration of veterans' affairs with the Vichy government in 1942. In 1943 he formed a resistance group. After qualifying as a lawyer he was elected to the chamber of deputies in 1946. He held ministerial positions in nine Fourth Republic governments and emerged as a leader of the non-**Marxist** socialists. He was minister of justice in the government of **Guy Mollet** between 1955 and 1957.

Mitterrand first stood as a socialist presidential candidate in December 1965 and received 44.8 percent of the vote in the second ballot. He became president of the *Convention des Institutions Républicaines* in 1970, a non-Marxist socialist group that merged with the old *Parti Socialiste* (*Section française de l'international ouvrière*) in June 1971 to create the new **French Socialist Party** (*Parti socialiste*—PS). Mitterrand became the first secretary of the PS and succeeded in molding a united left-wing party from varied groups that was able both to work in coalition with the **communists** and also to supplant them as the dominant party of the French left. In May 1981 he was elected president, and the PS won power in its own right for the first time in the chamber of deputies. His administration embarked on the **nationalization** of industry and banks and an expansionist economic program, but these policies had to be moderated in the face of economic difficulties, particularly **unemployment**, unfavorable balances of trade, and inflation. In foreign policy, Mitterrand maintained independence while remaining part of the Western bloc and suspicious of the Soviet Union. He used his position between March 1986 and June 1988 to weaken his political opponents when he was forced to share power with the Gaullist coalition led by Jacques Chirac. Mitterrand ceased to be president of France in May 1995.

MOLLET, GUY ALCIDE (1905–75). Born in Flers, Normandy, to **working-class** parents (his father was a weaver), Guy Mollet became a schoolteacher and joined the Socialist Party in 1923. During World War II he served in the French Resistance and rose to the rank of captain. In 1946 he was elected as deputy of and in 1946 he became secretary-general of the Socialist Party, a position he held until 1969. He was a minister in five French governments from 1946 to 1958 and was prime minister from 1956 to 1957. For a socialist, Mollet's record in government was contradictory in that he played a part in the decision-making process that saw an increased military effort by France against Arab **nationalists** in Algeria and France's participation with the United Kingdom and Israel in the invasion of Egypt in 1956, but he also granted some autonomy to France's colonies south of the Sahara. *See also* AURIOL, VINCENT; FRENCH SOCIALIST PARTY.

MONGOLIAN PEOPLE'S REVOLUTIONARY PARTY [*MON-GOL ARDYN HUV'SGALT NAM* (MAHN)]. Emerging from the struggle against the Chinese occupation of Mongolia from 1919 to 1921, the MAHN formed a people's republic after victory. The First Party Congress was in 1921 and the MAHN adopted **Leninism**, ruling thereafter as a **communist** party until 1990. In response to street demonstrations that year the MAHN democratized Mongolia, allowing opposition parties to compete in elections. The MAHN won the elections of 1990. In 1992 the MAHN introduced a new constitution, which respected human rights and established a regulated free-market economy. The MAHN won 71 of the 76 seats in the new legislature that year. In 1996 the MAHN lost the parliamentary election to the Democratic Unity Coalition. In 1997 the MAHN formally adopted a democratic socialist **ideology**. Also in 1997, Natsagiin Bagabandi of the MAHN won the presidential elections. In 1999 the MAHN became an observer member of the **Socialist International** (SI), and in July 2000 won a landside victory in the parliamentary elections, taking 72 of the 76 seats. Bagabandi was reelected president in May 2001, with 57.9 percent of the vote. In October 2003 the MAHN gained full membership in the SI. After the parliamentary elections of June 2004 there was deadlock. After months of negotiations a grand coalition was formed in September that year between the MAHN and the Motherland Democratic Coalition that consisted of the Democratic Party, the Democratic New Socialist Party, and the Republican Civil Will Party. *See also* MONGOLIAN SOCIAL DEMOCRATIC PARTY.

MONGOLIAN SOCIAL DEMOCRATIC PARTY [*MONGOLYN SOTSIAL DEMOKRAT NAM* (MSDN)]. The MSDN was formed in March 1990 and existed for one decade. In September 1992 it was accepted as a consultative member of the **Socialist International** (SI), which sent a fact-finding mission to Mongolia in 1993. It achieved full membership in the SI in 1996. The membership of the MSDN, variously estimated in 1992 to 1993 at between 10,000 and 20,000, was described as drawn from the educated sections of Mongolian society. About a quarter were **women**. Although nominally social-democratic, the MSDN received support and advice from U.S. Republicans throughout the 1990s. In 1996 the MSDN joined several parties in the Democratic Unity Coalition that won the parliamentary elections that year, defeating the **Mongolian People's Revolutionary Party** (*Mongol Ardyn Huv'sgalt Nam*—MAHN). The Coalition introduced neoliberal reforms. Mongolians demonstrated their dissatisfaction in 2000 by electing the MAHN back to power. The MSDN merged with five other parties after the elections to form the Democratic Party.

MORALES AIMA, EVO JUAN (1959–). Born in Orinoca in the eastern Bolivian Oruro department, Evo Morales belongs to the Aymara, who make up over half of Bolivia's populace. As a child he migrated with his family to Chapare in eastern Bolivia. He became the leader of Bolivia's coca growers, the *cocaleros*, and was elected to the Bolivian parliament in 1997. Early in 2002 he was removed from his seat after allegations of involvement in **terrorism**. This action against Morales was subsequently declared unconstitutional. In the presidential elections in June that year he came in second with 20.9 percent of the vote. In the parliamentary elections of 2002 his party, the Movement Towards Socialism (*Movimiento al Socialismo*—MAS), won 27 of the 130 seats in Bolivia's lower house with 11.9 percent of the vote and 8 of 27 seats in the Senate.

In 2003 Morales played a part in demands for the **nationalization** of Bolivian gas and oil. These protests brought about the resignation of Bolivia's President Gonzalo Sanchez, who was replaced by the caretaker President Eduardo Rodriguez. Morales continued to support the coca growers while opposing the production of cocaine from coca. In the presidential elections of December 2005 he promised to give Bolivia's impoverished indigenous people greater political control of their country. He was successful at the first round by securing 53.7 percent of the vote, thus becoming Bolivia's first indigenous president. In the parliamentary elections also held in December 2005 the MAS won 72 seats in the Chamber of Deputies and 12 in the Senate.

MORRIS, WILLIAM (1834–96). Artist, designer, poet, writer, and unwilling political leader William Morris was one of the leaders of English socialism in the late nineteenth century. Born into a wealthy family in Walthamstow near London, he was much influenced by the ideas of John Ruskin (1819–1900) and was entranced by an idealistic vision of a preindustrial world that provided a high level of job satisfaction in craftsmanship and cooperative living. He loathed violence and wanted to restore to work the idea (as he saw it) of craftsmanship and the satisfaction of skill, as opposed to the tedium and low skill inherent in factory work for most employees. Disillusioned with its doctrinaire leadership, he and his followers left the **Social Democratic Federation** in 1884 and formed the Socialist League, which was gradually taken over by **anarchists**; Morris, who now took a broadly **Marxist** position, left the league in 1890. Ironically, his popular utopian novel, *News from Nowhere*, foretold a society without government institutions. He saw art and **education** as means of improving society. *See also* UTOPIAN SOCIALISM.

MOVEMENT OF THE FIFTH REPUBLIC [*MOVIMIENTO V REPÚBLIC* (MVR)]. Formed in the mid-1990s by **Hugo Chávez**, the MVR came to dominate left-wing politics in Venezuela. As the leader of the Movement Chávez was elected to the presidency in 1998, reelected in 2000, and won a referendum on the continuation of his presidency in 2004. In elections to the Venezuelan National Assembly on 30 July 2000 the MVR won 76 of the 165 seats. The **Democratic Action** (*Acción Democrática*—AD) party, which as a social-democratic party had been a major force in Venezuelan politics for several decades, obtained 29 seats. Also on the left, the Movement Towards Socialism (*Movimiento al Socialismo*) won 21 seats. Led by the charismatic Chavez, the MVR took 114 of the 167 seats at the elections to the National Assembly in December 2005. Allies of the MVR secured the other seats. Opposition parties including the AD had withdrawn, complaining that conditions favored the MVR. The turnout was only approximately 25 percent of registered voters.

MOVEMENT OF THE REVOLUTIONARY LEFT–NEW MAJORITY [*MOVIMIENTO DE LA IZQUIERDA REVOLUCIONARIA–NUEVA MAYORÍA* (MIR)]. The MIR was formed in

Bolivia in September 1971 from a number of political groups, notably the Christian Democratic Party, which opposed the coup against the left-wing president General Juan José Torres González. The MIR is usually referred to without stating "Nueva Mayoría." It began life as a noncommunist **Marxist** party that included left-wing Catholics. MIR participation in government was interrupted in the early 1980s by coups and in 1985 several factions split from the party. The MIR has been a consultative member of the **Socialist International** since about 1987 and a full member since about 1992.

In 1989 Jaime Paz Zamora of the MIR was elected president and in a country characterized by coalitions of diverse parties, the MIR entered a coalition government with the right-wing party of General Hugo Banzer Suárez, who had led the repressive military government from 1971 to 1978. In 1993 the MIR lost power and in the presidential elections of 1997 Zamora won only 16.7 percent of the vote. After the elections of June 2002, in which it took 26 of 130 seats in the Chamber of Deputies with 19.8 percent of the vote and five of 27 seats in the Senate, the MIR entered a coalition with the once left-wing but more recently neoliberal Nationalist Revolutionary Movement. Along with a smaller party they formed a Government of National Responsibility. Among the MIR's opponents was the left-wing Movement Towards Socialism (*Movimiento al Socialismo*—MAS), led by **Evo Morales**. As the MAS became the major party on the Bolivian left the MIR's significance waned. The MIR did not contest the presidential or congressional elections of December 2005.

MÜLLER, HERMANN (1876–1931). German social-democratic politician Hermann Müller was born in Mannheim into a **middle-class** family. He first came to prominence in the **German Social Democratic Party** when he was made editor of one of its many newspapers, the *Görlitze Zeitung*, in 1889. A moderate, he was elected to the party's executive in 1906 and in 1914 took part in a mission intended to ward off the imminent **war** with France. In 1916 he was elected to the *Reichstag* (parliament) and after the fall of the imperial government he was made foreign minister of the government of **Gustav Adolf Bauer**. In this capacity, he had the thankless task of signing the Versailles Treaty for Germany. He replaced Bauer as chancellor in March 1920 and held the post until June 1920. He also became party leader in 1920, but could achieve little until the

1928 elections, which gave the party the opportunity to become the largest group in a coalition government.

Müller served as chancellor from June 1928 to March 1930. His administration was responsible for the reduction of reparation payments and the introduction of a program to rebuild the German navy. Otherwise, Müller's term was engulfed by the Depression, which severely affected Germany, sending its **unemployment** rate up to 44 percent by 1932, compared to 22 percent for the United Kingdom and 25 percent for the United States. Müller's government floundered on the issue of maintaining unemployment benefits—against those who wanted them reduced—in a crisis that was paralleled by the crisis of the **Ramsay MacDonald** government. Müller also played a role in international socialism and served on the executive of the **Labor and Social International** from 1925 to 1931.

MURAYAMA, TOMIICHI (1924–). Japanese socialist politician Tomiichi Murayama was born in Oita, southern Japan, the fifth of 11 children. His father was a poor fisherman. He was educated at Meiji University and gained his first political experience in local government in 1955. He became an official of the seamen's **trade union** and was elected to parliament for the Democratic Socialist Party in 1972. In June 1994, now leader of the **Japanese Social Democratic Party**, he became prime minister of a coalition government after corruption scandals in the Liberal Democratic Party government, the first time a socialist had occupied the post since 1947. As such he was able to do little to implement the policies of his party, namely opposition to the self-defense forces, use of the national anthem and the **flag**, the American alliance, and economic deregulation. He tried to issue an unequivocal apology for the atrocities committed by Japan's military forces during World War II, but was forced to water down the statement. He resigned as prime minister on 5 January 1996. His term in office was notable for the debt crisis among Japan's banks, the Kobe earthquake, and his personal frugality and incorruptibility.

MUSSOLINI, BENITO (1883–1944). Although best known as the founder of Italian fascism, Benito Mussolini spent his early political career as a socialist. Born in Dovia, his father supported **Michael Bakunin** and the need for the violent overthrow of the political system. In 1908 he was jailed for 10 days for participating in rural agitation. He edited three socialist newspapers, including *Avanti* (Forward), the official socialist publication, between 1908 and 1914. In 1911 he led the opposition to Italy's attack on Libya and was jailed for five months for urging resistance to the government. Mussolini was expelled from the **Italian Socialist Party** in November 1914 for agitating for Italy to join the Allied side in World War I; the party's official policy was opposed to the **war**.

MUTUALISM. Mutualism was an important concept in French socialist thought in the nineteenth century. The idea of mutualism seems to have originated with the eighteenth-century French philosopher Antoine Nicolas Condorcet, who used the term *mutualité* to describe a mutual association for the **working class** to provide protection from downturns in the trade cycle. **Charles Fourier** used the term *mutualisme* in the 1820s. "Mutualists" was also the name of a secret society among Lyon textile workers in the 1830s. Fourier's followers had been active in Lyon. The term *mutualist* was later applied to the followers of the **anarchist** theorist **Pierre-Joseph Proudhon**. Their thought emphasized producer cooperatives as a means to regenerate society and opposition to political revolution.

– N –

NARAYAN, JAYAPRAKASH (1902–79). An Indian socialist and author, also known as Jai Prakash Narain, Jayaprakash Narayan was born in Sitab Diyara in Bihar into a **middle-class** family. He attended Patna University before abandoning his studies to join the noncooperation movement directed at British rule in India. An outstanding student, he was awarded a scholarship in 1922 to study in the United States. He supported himself with menial jobs and studied at the Universities of Iowa, Chicago, Wisconsin, California, and Ohio until 1929, becoming acquainted with **Marxism** and socialism while at Wisconsin. After his return to India he was made professor of sociology at Benares Hindu University, but left after being offered the position of head of the labor research department of the Indian National Congress. In 1931 he helped found the Bihar Socialist Party. In 1932 he was made acting general secretary of the Indian National Congress and was jailed for his participation in Mohandas (Mahatma) Gandhi's civil disobedience campaign against the British. Released in 1933, he was prime mover in the formation of the Congress Socialist Party. In 1936 he published *Why Socialism?* He was jailed again in 1939, escaped in November 1942, was recaptured in October 1943, and was not released until April 1946.

Narayan envisaged socialism as being based on the **nationalization** of major industries and improving the lot of the Indian peasants through land ownership. He supported large-scale industrialization under government control as a means of reducing **unemployment**. He was one of the leaders of the Indian delegation to the first **Asian Socialist Conference** in 1953 and also attended its second gathering in 1956. In April 1954 he left party politics because of his support for the *Bhoodan* (land-gift) movement. He went on to write *A Plea for the Reconstruction of Indian Policy* (1959) and *Swaraj and the People* (1961). Although Narayan never held any public office, he remained an influential figure. His last national role was as leader of the fight against corruption under Indira Gandhi for which he was again jailed. *See also JANATA DAL* (SECULAR).

NASH, WALTER (1882–1968). New Zealand labor politician Walter Nash was born in Kidderminster, England, where he studied law and worked as a merchant. He emigrated to New Zealand in 1909 and was an early member of the **New Zealand Labour Party** (NZLP). He became a member of the national executive of the NZLP in 1919 and its secretary in 1922, a position he held until 1932. In 1929 he was elected to the House of Representatives and served as minister for finance and customs in the ministry of **Michael Joseph Savage**. As minister for **social security** in 1938, he played an important role in creating the basis of the **welfare state** in New Zealand. He served as prime minister from 1957 to 1960, but his government was defeated by his attempt to extend social welfare by increased **taxation**.

NATIONAL DEMOCRATIC PARTY [*HIZB AL DIMUQRATIYAH AL WATANIYAH* (HDW)]. The HDW was formed in July 1978 and has been the ruling party of Egypt since 1979. Muhammad Hosni Mubarak of the HDW has been president of Egypt since the assassination of President Anwar Sadat in 1981, being reelected by referendum as the sole candidate approved by the Egyptian People's Assembly in 1987, 1993, and 1999. In 1999 he gained 93.97 percent support with a turnout of 79 percent. Although nominally a socialist, Mubarak has introduced neoliberal reforms under pressure of the world economy. The HDW was a member of the **League of African Democratic Socialist Parties** and has been a full member of the **Socialist International** since 1992. In elections to the National Assembly in October and November 2000 the HDW gained 388 of the 444 seats (including 35 members who stood officially as "independents"). In May 2005 the Assembly agreed to Mubarak's request to change the constitution to allow multiple candidates to contest presidential elections. In the election, held in September 2005 with a low turnout of 23 percent, Mubarak attracted 88.6 percent of the vote, defeating nine candidates. In elections to the National Assembly in November and December 2005 the HDW took 311 seats.

NATIONAL LIBERATION PARTY [*PARTIDO DE LIBERACIÓN NACIONAL* (PLN)]. The PLN was formed in Costa Rica in October 1951 based on the membership of the *Partido Demócrata Social* (Social Democratic Party), which had been set up in 1948. Jóse Figueres of the PLN was elected president in 1953 and held the post until 1958. The PLN was the source of presidents between 1962 and 1966 and 1970 to 1978. In 1982 the former general secretary of the PLN, Alberto Monge Álvarez, was elected president. In 1984 the PLN claimed a membership of 367,000, and since about 1987 it has been a full member of the **Socialist International**.

In 1986 Oscar Arias Sanchez of the PLN was elected president until 1990, when the opposition took power. In 1994 Jose Maria Figueres Olsen of the PLN was elected president. The opposition took the presidency in 1998 and again in 2002, when the NPL candidate Rolando Araya Monge lost in the runoff, gaining 42 percent of the vote. In the parliamentary elections of 2002 the PLN won 17 of 57 seats with 27.1 percent of the vote. Arias Sanchez was elected president once again in February 2006 with 40.9 percent of the vote. In the parliamentary elections that month, the PLN increased its share of the vote to 36.4 percent, with which it secured 25 seats.

NATIONALISM. Nationalism fits uneasily into the history of socialism because socialists tend to see social divisions as based on class rather than nation or ethnicity. The **internationalist** socialist ideal expressed by organizations such as the **International Workingmen's**

Association and the **Second International** was often at odds with nationalist ideas that brought about conflicts. Socialists often regarded nationalism, like **war**, as a product of class conflict within **capitalism** and a means to divide and divert the attention of the **working class** from fundamental social and economic change. A resolution to this effect was passed by the Second International at its congress at Brussels in 1891 when it was asked by an American Jewish organization for a policy response to anti-Semitism.

Nationalism was a particular problem for the **Austrian Social Democratic Party** because of the many ethnic groups that made up the pre-1918 Austro-Hungarian Empire. In 1897 the party adopted a federal structure designed to accommodate representation from Germans, Czechs, Poles, Slovenes, Ruthenians, and Italians; each group was given autonomy under a single executive. This compromise did not satisfy the Czechs, who wanted their own party. They tried to get the Second International to approve this action in 1907 and 1910, but it would not, and the Czechs formed their own party in 1911.

Within the **German Social Democratic Party** (*Sozialdemokratische Partei Deutschlands*—SPD) national pressures were also evident from many Poles who lived within the pre-1918 boundaries of Germany. A Polish Socialist Party was formed in 1892, but its formation was opposed by the SPD, which believed that the Poles' best protection was to stay within a unified German framework.

In 1903 the Bulgarian Social Democratic Party (later **Bulgarian Social Democrats**) split into a "Broad" Party comparable with the **revisionists** of Western Europe, which recognized nationalism, and a "Narrow" Party, which concentrated on the class struggle. In the United Kingdom before 1914, there was little interest in foreign policy in the **British Labour Party** beyond criticizing military expenditure as socially wasteful. Its concerns were those of its own working class. The complexities of the relationship between nationalism and socialism were also shown by the case of the **Jews**. In Asia nationalism and socialism reinforced each other in the post-1945 period in their opposition to **imperialism**. The same applied to Africa and parts of the Caribbean.

NATIONALIZATION. Nationalization refers to the acquisition by the government of private property with or without compensation. The term was first used in the United Kingdom to refer to the acquisition of large estates in the 1870s. By the end of the nineteenth century the idea of nationalization was widely adopted by social-democratic/socialist parties as a means of ending exploitation of employees and improving the distribution of **wealth**. Attitudes to nationalization differed greatly within socialism. In *Das Kapital*, **Karl Marx** used the term *socialization* to describe the general trend toward monopoly and concentration of ownership of the means of production, distribution, and exchange. The term was later taken by parts of organized labor to press demands for giving employees a direct say in the operation of a nationalized industry, enterprise, or service. The preamble to the **Erfurt Program** of the **German Social Democratic Party** (*Sozialdemokratische Partei Deutschlands*—SPD) discussed nationalization but did not include it among its specific demands for reform. The party, following **Karl Kautsky**, wanted to capture political power first and then introduce nationalization. Without political power, it was believed that nationalization would simply strengthen the reactionary German government that was in power up to November 1918.

At its London conference in 1896 the **Second International** discussed a report of its economic and industrial commission that advocated the universal "socialization" of the means of production, transport, distribution, and exchange and their control by a democratic organization in the interests of the whole society. Yet another strand of socialist opinion was held by the **Fabians**, who were inclined to support nationalization because it would improve economic efficiency. In contrast, the **Independent Labour Party** favored nationalization because it would help the poor and unskilled among the **working class**. **Robert Blatchford** advocated collective ownership not just because it would lead to the more equitable distribution of goods and services but also to higher production.

Another aspect to nationalization concerned what form it would take. Although nationalization is generally associated with control by the central government following the early example of the Soviet Union, there was a widespread view throughout socialism that control of nationalized industries and services should include local governments as well as the **cooperative movement**. On 31 July 1920 an international socialist conference at Geneva, Switzerland, supported gradual nationalization with compensation for owners to be paid from **taxation**. Its administration would be shared by national and local governments and the cooperative movement. Pressure to give employees a say in running nationalized industries and services came from organized labor and was especially strong in coal mining. In January 1917 the annual conference of the **British Labour Party** (Labour) passed resolutions in favor of the nationalization of the railroads and coal mining. In 1919 this issue aroused considerable debate in Germany. It was opposed by the majority of the SPD, which feared that it would mean exploitation of the public through higher prices if agreed to. In the United Kingdom a royal commission into the coal industry under Sir John Sankey (1866–1948) supported the principle of public ownership and the miners being given a voice in the operations of the industry; the representatives of the coal owners prepared dissenting reports. These general developments led Labour in Britain and the **Australian Labor Party** (ALP) each to adopt a **socialization objective**.

With the participation of socialist/social-democratic parties in government, the issue of nationalization had to be faced in practical terms. In 1936 the government of **Leon Blum** in France succeeded in nationalizing the munitions industry, but this could have been justified more on the grounds of national interest than on support for socialist principles.

With the victory of these parties in elections in a number of countries immediately after World War II, nationalization moved from policy to implementation. The Austrian Socialist Party (formerly and since 1991, **Austrian Social Democratic Party**) nationalized some industries in the early 1950s, but was prevented from nationalizing German assets in the Soviet-controlled zone until the end of the occupation in 1955. After its victory in the 1945 British general elections the Labour Party implemented a broad range of nationalization measures, including a national health service, the Bank of England, the coal industry, gas and electricity production and distribution, and public transport.

Nationalization has been a contentious policy. For instance, the proposed nationalization of the banking industry by the ALP aroused fears of job losses among the banks' employees, who campaigned against it and helped to bring down the Labor government in 1949. Nationalized industries have also been accused of being less efficiently run, employing too many people, and being captive to **trade unions**. Finally, it should be noted that nationalization is not an idea peculiar to socialism and has been used to strengthen national sovereignty, for example, by Iran over its oil industry in 1951and most famously by Egypt over the Suez Canal in 1956. In Spain and Portugal, large state-owned enterprises were a feature of the fascist dictatorships of General Francisco Franco and Oliveira Salazar with the result that there was no commitment to nationalization by their respective socialist parties.

Since 1980 **privatization**—the selling of publicly owned assets, that is, the reverse of nationalization—has been used by social-democratic governments (with the notable exception of France) as well as by conservative governments in the attempt to improve economic efficiency. In June 1982 the French Socialist government introduced a law that nationalized major firms in chemicals, electronics, metals, steel, electricity, space, and armaments, plus 36 banks and insurance companies. This program, which was the last general application of nationalization by a socialist/social-democratic government in a large democracy, originated from the need to maintain the support of the French Communist Party, but was later used to rationalize and restructure these concerns. The ALP, the **Portuguese Socialist Party**, and the **Spanish Socialist Workers' Party** all have reduced the role of state-owned enterprises in the economy while in government.

NEPALI CONGRESS PARTY (NC). Formed in exile (Calcutta) in 1950, through the merger of the Nepali National Congress (established in 1947) and Nepali Democratic Congress (established in 1948), the NC sought to overthrow the Rana dynasty that had ruled feudal Nepal since 1846. The Ranas dominated the powerless monarchy. The NC waged an armed struggle, supported by King Tribhuyan who thus went into exile to escape the Rana regime. In 1951 the king returned to persuade the Ranas to end their regime and play a constitutional role in coalition government with the NC. In November of that year, having been nominated by the king, Matrika Prasad Koirala of the NC became prime minister. Koirala was expelled from the NC in 1952 for acting against his party and passing power effectively into the hands of the monarchy. The elections promised by the constitution were not held.

In 1956 the NC adopted democratic socialism as the principle for change. A campaign of civil disobedience led the new king—King Mahendra—to agree to parliamentary elections, at which in 1959 the NC won 74 of the 109 seats. B. P. Koirala became prime minister of an NC government that embarked on a program of social reform until the king and army took power in a coup, dissolved the government and parliament, banned **political parties**, and set up the *panchayat* system of local councils ruled by the monarchy in 1960. The NC went into exile in India and for the next two decades resorted at different times to armed struggle and peaceful means of protest, including civil disobedience, to demand a return to multiparty politics. In 1990 the Nepali Communist Party (**Marxist-Leninist**) was one of several parties that joined the NC-led Movement for Restoration of Democracy.

In 1990 the *panchayat* system fell and was replaced by a multiparty system with a constitutional monarchy. Parliamentary elections were held in May 1991, at which the NC obtained 112 of 205 seats. An NC government was formed under Prime Minister Girija Prasad Koirala. In 1994 Koirala's government fell after a vote of no confidence and a Communist minority government was formed until this was dissolved in 1995 by a combination of anticommunist parties, including the NC. The following year another **communist** party—the Communist Party of Nepal-Maoist—began a campaign of insurrection, aiming to replace the monarchy with a communist republic. In the second half of the 1990s Nepal was governed by a series of weak coalition governments as the NC and other parties made deals. This period ended in May 1999 when the NC won an absolute majority with 110 of 205 seats in parliamentary elections. The NC formed a government under Prime Minister Krishna Prasad Bhattari. In November 1999 the NCP gained full membership in the **Socialist International**. After disputes within the NC Bhattari was replaced the following year by former Prime Minister Girija Prasad Koirala, and then by Bahadur Deuba.

In October 2002 King Gyandra dismissed the government after Deuba asked for the parliamentary elections due in November of that year to be postponed by a year because of mounting Maoist violence. The king appointed a new government dominated by Nepali conservatives and postponed elections indefinitely. In May 2004 the royalist prime minister resigned after street protests and in June Deuba was reappointed as prime minister. In February 2005 the king once again dismissed Deuba and the government in order to rule directly in response to the escalating Maoist violence.

NEW ANTILLES MOVEMENT [*MOVEMENTU ANTIA NOBO* (MAN)]. Formerly a Dutch colony, the Netherlands Antilles became an autonomous political entity within the kingdom of the Netherlands in 1954. Based on the island of Curaçao, the MAN is a social-democratic party that holds full membership in the **Socialist International**. The MAN has usually played a minor role in Antilles politics. An exception was the 1980s, when Dominico Martina of the MAN was prime minister from 1979 to 1984 and from 1986 to 1988. In the legislative elections of January 1998 the MAN won two of 22 seats. In elections held in January 2002 its 5.2 percent of the vote was not enough to hold any seats.

NEW DEMOCRATIC PARTY (NDP). The Canadian NDP was formed in 1961 by the **Co-operative Commonwealth Federation** and the **trade unions**. Now Canada's fourth largest political party, the NDP is broadly social-democratic and a member of the **Socialist International**. The NDP supports economic planning and **social security** and opposes **nuclear weapons**. Between 1968 and 1988 its share of the vote in national elections varied from 15.4 to 20.4 percent. It enjoyed a surge of support in 1991 when it won government in Ontario and Saskatchewan, but its support slumped thereafter. Between 1989 and 1995 it was led by Audrey McLaughlin, the first **woman** to lead a notable political party in North America. In June 1997 it won 21 seats with 11 percent of the vote in the national elections (compared to only 6.9 percent in 1993) under its leader Alexa McDonough. In the elections of November 2000, however, the share of the vote slipped to 8.5 percent, giving the party 13 of the 301 seats in the House of Commons. In 2003 Jack Layton took over the leadership from McDonough, who remained a prominent member of the party. Under Layton the NDP attracted 15.7 percent of the vote in the elections on 28 June 2004, obtaining 19 of the 308 seats. When in November 2005 the minority Liberal government refused to rule out private **health care** the NDP withdrew its support. Later that month the NDP, the Conservatives, and the *Bloc Quebecois* brought the government down by a no-confidence vote over alleged corruption. In January 2006 the NDP took 29 seats with 17.5 percent of the vote at the elections won by the Conservatives without an absolute majority of seats.

NEW LEFT. The New Left was a loose group of political movements originally developed by former members of Western **communist** parties who were disaffected by the violent Soviet suppression of the Hungarian uprising in 1956. They were also influenced by **Karl Marx**'s *Economic and Philosophical Manuscripts of 1844*, of which a complete English translation was finally published in 1963. These works, which focused on alienation and exploitation, were interpreted as stressing the need for social commitment and seemed to show a more humanistic side to Marx's ideas. One of the founders of the New Left in the United Kingdom was the social historian Edward P. Thompson (1924–93), author of *The Making of the English Working Class* (1963). The name New Left was taken from the journal *New Left Review*, which began in 1959 after the merger of the *New Reasoner* (founded by Thompson and John Saville in 1957) and *Universities and Left Review*. In contrast to the New Left, the "old" Left tended to cling to a doctrinaire form of **Marxism** as interpreted by Moscow. Although there were important differences among the New Left, it was commonly held to be independent-minded, socially committed, and anti-American (Americans with economic and political power, rather than Americans in general), particularly with respect to the deployment of **nuclear weapons** in Western Europe, the North Atlantic Treaty Organization (NATO), and America's war in Vietnam.

In the United States, the New Left was influenced by the philosopher **Herbert Marcuse** and was more associated with the 1960s, especially the civil rights movement and opposition to the war in Vietnam. Its leading organization was the Students for a Democratic Society. In France and Germany, the New Left was at the forefront of massive protests in 1968, especially the disruption of universities. The violence of the era often led to repressive measures by those in authority. With the end of the Vietnam War in 1975, the New Left lost much of its momentum and the differences between it and the "old" Left became less obvious. The legacy of the New Left is hard to measure, but it can claim credit for focusing attention on social issues such as poverty, civil rights, the role of **women**, and the dehumanizing effect of much assembly line work, that is, broadening the political agenda to include all aspects of society. Above all it offered a stimulating challenge to the complacent assumptions that underpinned institutions of all kinds.

NEW SPACE [*NUEVO ESPACIO* (NE)]. Formed in 1994, NE gained full membership in the **Socialist International** in 2003. It is a small Uruguayan social-democratic party. In 2002 NE joined the Broad Front, *Frente Amplio* (FA) center-left coalition, of which the **Socialist Party of Uruguay** (PSU), is a member. The FA was successful in the presidential and legislative elections of 2004, at which many Uruguayans rejected the free-market polices that had brought their country to economic crisis. The FA in total obtained 52 of 99 seats with 50.4 percent of the vote in the lower legislative chamber and 17 of the 31 seats in the Senate.

NEW ZEALAND LABOUR PARTY (NZLP). The NZLP was founded in 1916. The first socialist organization in New Zealand was formed in 1902 by followers of **Robert Blatchford**. Dissatisfaction with the Liberal Party led to the formation of a political labor league in 1904 by the **trade unions** based on the Australian model. After 1907 New Zealand labor began to be influenced by the ideas of the **Industrial Workers of the World** from the United States. In 1910 the Labour Party was formed by moderate trade unions and renamed the United Labour Party in 1912. Militant labor formed the New Zealand Socialist Party and the Social Democratic Party (1913). But in 1913 the power of militants collapsed after strikes by longshoremen and miners were crushed.

The NZLP was formed at Wellington in July 1916 at a conference convened by the Social Democratic Party, of which **Peter Fraser** was secretary. After gains at the 1931 elections, the NZLP became the main opposition party. Under the administrations of **Michael Joseph Savage** and Fraser, the NZLP created a comprehensive **welfare state** between 1935 and 1949. Since 1950 the party has had mixed fortunes. The NZLP government of **Walter Nash**, elected in 1957, lost power in 1960 over attempts to extend the welfare state by increased taxation. The NZLP governments of 1972 to 1975 and 1984 to 1990 were bedeviled by economic problems that had at their root the entry of the United Kingdom in the European Economic Community and the greatly increased difficulty of the entry of New Zealand agricultural products to the Western European market. The NZLP has been a full member of the **Socialist International** since 1952. In 1982 the NZLP claimed a membership of 80,000. Left-wing dissatisfaction with the policies of the NZLP under Prime Minister **David Lange**—mainly over its support for **privatization**—led to the formation of the

New Labour Party in April 1989, which won 5.2 percent of the vote in the elections of 1990.

In the national elections of October 1996, under the new leader **Helen Clarke**, the NZLP won 37 out of 120 seats to become the second largest parliamentary party, but it was not included as a partner in the subsequent coalition government. It only attracted 28.2 percent of the vote in 1996 compared to 34.7 percent in 1993. The NZLP returned to government on 27 November 1999 in coalition with the new left-wing Alliance Party. The NZLP took 49 seats and the Alliance 10. Just two seats short of a majority, the coalition relied upon the Greens for support. In the elections on 27 July 2002 the NZLP retained power, gaining 52 seats of 120 seats with 41.26 percent of the vote. This time the Alliance won no seats. The NZLP formed a minority coalition with Jim Anderton's Progressive Coalition, which won two seats, thus having to rely on support from the Greens. In the elections of September 2005 the NZLP's share of seats was reduced to 50 of 121, gained with 41.1 percent of the vote. The Party once again formed a minority coalition government with Anderton's group, which, now known as the Progressive Party, won one seat. The minority government secured the agreement of a center-right party and, surprisingly, the right-wing New Zealand First Party, in critical votes in parliament.

NORWEGIAN LABOR PARTY [*DET NORSKE ARBEIDER-PARTI* (DnA)]. Officially founded at Arendal in August 1887, the DnA was the culmination of a series of developments within Norwegian organized labor, beginning with the formation of a national printers' union in 1882. The first district **trade union** federation was founded in 1883 (in Oslo) and a social-democratic newspaper, *Vert Arbeit* (Our Work), was established in 1884. Influenced by Danish socialists, in January 1885 the Social Democratic Association (*Socialdemokratisk Forening*) was formed in Oslo. Advocating the 10-hour working day and universal **suffrage**, the Association assumed responsibility for the production of *Vert Arbeit* and for the leadership of the DnA. More intellectuals joined the party, which adopted a program closely modeled on the **Erfurt Program** in 1891. The DnA participated in the **Second International** from 1889. There was a close relationship between the DnA and organized labor, particularly after the formation of the Norwegian Confederation of Trade Unions

(*Landsorganisasjoine i Norge*) in 1899 although there was also strong support for **liberalism** among the **working class**. The DnA contested its first election in 1894. In 1903 it established a national **youth** organization. The DnA supported **education** and culture not just to make it fit for government but also to convince the bourgeoisie of its responsibility.

During World War I the DnA moved to the left. It was a participant in the **Zimmerwald Conference** in 1915 and became a member of the **Comintern** in 1919, but its membership ceased when it refused to take direction from Moscow. In 1921 the DnA split between the social democrats and the **communists**, but was reunited as a party in 1927 at the urging of the trade unions. In January 1928 the DnA was able to form a government, but its support fell quickly because of its proposals to redistribute **wealth**. In the aftermath of the Depression the DnA used support for popular measures like **unemployment** relief and assistance for farmers to divide the conservative parties and gain the support of the Agrarian Party to form a minority government in 1936 under Johan Nygaardsvold (1879–1952), a trade union leader who had worked on railroads in the United States. The DnA introduced a public works program, an old-age pension scheme, and extended unemployment insurance and factory legislation. In 1939 it adopted a program that advocated a planned economy and the gradual "socialization" of large-scale industry, banks, trade, and transportation. As a result of the Nazi invasion, the leadership of Norway's **political parties** fled to London and formed a government in exile in June 1940.

In May 1945 the government in exile led by Nygaardsvold returned, and the DnA won a majority in the October 1945 elections for the first time under the leadership of **Einar Henry Gerhardsen**, who had been released from a Nazi concentration camp. The DnA has been a member of the **Socialist International** since 1951. In 1956 it was responsible for the introduction of a national health program and in 1963 raised annual holidays from three to four weeks and reduced working hours. The DnA supported Norway's membership in the European Community in 1972, but the proposal was defeated in a national referendum and the government resigned. Between 1957 and 1989 support for the DnA among working-class voters fell from 76 pecent to 47 percent. In 1976 the DnA claimed a total membership of 143,900, but this figure included organizations as well as individuals.

There has also been significant support for other noncommunist socialist parties. The DnA led minority governments for most of the post-1945 period: 1955 to 1963, 1963 to 1965, 1971 to 1972, 1973 to 1981, 1986 to 1989, 1993 to 1997, and 2000 to 2001.

At the national elections in September 1993, the DnA won 37 percent of the vote compared to 34.3 percent in 1989; over the same period support for the rival Socialist Left Party (*Sosialistisk Venstreparti*—SV) declined from 10.1 to 7.9 percent. In 1994 a conference of the DnA decided in favor of membership in the European Union, but there was considerable rank and file opposition, which contributed to rejection of the idea by the electorate in a national referendum. At the national elections of 1997 the DnA fell from government, as a center-right minority coalition took power until 2000, when an environmental dispute led to its collapse. The DnA leader Jens Stoltenberg took over in a minority government. At the national elections of 2001 the DnA lost once again, taking 43 of 165 seats with 24.3 percent of the vote. This was the DnA's worst electoral result in nearly a century, and a center-right coalition took power. The SV won 23 seats with 12.4 percent of the vote.

At the national elections of September 2005 Stoltenberg led the DnA to victory in partnership with the SV and the Center Party. Together the three parties obtained just over half (87) of the 169 seats. The DnA won 61 seats with 32.7 percent of the vote, while the SV took 15 seats with 8.8 percent. Stoltenberg pledged to spend more money on education, **health care**, and **welfare**.

NUCLEAR WEAPONS. Nuclear weapons and socialists have had a complex relationship since 1945. In 1946 the **British Labour Party** government secretly embarked on a campaign to develop such weapons. In the 1980s the **French Socialist Party** government began a neutron bomb program and continued the policy of the previous conservative governments to build nuclear submarines. With the outstanding exception of France, socialist opinion in most European countries turned against nuclear weapons as a deterrent to **war** during the 1950s. In 1960 the annual conference of the British Labour Party narrowly adopted a policy that rejected the use of nuclear weapons as the basis of national defense.

Hostility to nuclear weapons grew among European socialists, particularly among the left wing of the British Labour Party and the

German Social Democratic Party. A particular area of contention arose in the early 1980s over the deployment of Pershing and Cruise missiles by the United States in Western Europe. Grassroots socialist opposition to nuclear weapons also drew support from the environment movement and the Green **political parties**. *See also* PACIFISM; SCANDILUX.

NYERERE, JULIUS KAMBARAGE (1922–99). As independence leader, prime minister of independent Tanganyika, president of Tanzania (which Tanganyika became), and also political theorist, Julius Nyerere was a senior and widely respected figure of **African socialism**. He was born in Butiama, Tanganyika. His father was the chief of the Zanaki tribe.

Nyerere was educated in mission schools before he went on to university in Makarere and Edinburgh. As president in the 1960s he took Tanzania out of the British Commonwealth, without violence, in response to the **British Labour Party** prime minister's failure to take action over the Rhodesian Unilateral Declaration of Independence. As president he also condemned **racism** of all types and considered freedom to be the central goal. For Africans this would involve freedom from minority, racist rule; economic freedom from external domination; freedom from poverty, oppression, and injustice at the hands of other Africans; and freedom from mental subjugation to ideas other than their own. Along with Nyerere's **egalitarianism**, this concern for freedom characterized the socialism he sought for Africa, which must, he stressed, build on African tradition. Africans, he once famously said, needed to be neither converted to socialism nor taught democracy.

Indeed his Arusha Declaration (named after the town in which it was announced) of 1967—*Ujamaa na Kujitegemea*—meant in English "Socialism and Self-reliance." Socialism or *ujamaa* also meant brotherhood or, bearing in mind Nyerere's great respect for the role of **women** in society, familyhood. Socialism, in his view, required the large-scale **nationalization** of a country's economic assets, with great emphasis on the importance of **agriculture**, which would become a central feature of African socialism. He also encouraged the highly centralized single-party system that became another feature of African socialism. One-party rule was, he believed, central for unity and stability. Nyerere's idealistic and theoretically just policies never bore fruit. As he would later concede, those policies were poorly applied in practice, resulting in economic disaster for Tanzania. Nyerere retired voluntarily from the presidency in 1985 and died 14 years later at the age of 77.

– O –

ORWELL, GEORGE (1903–50). George Orwell was the pseudonym of Eric Blair—one of the leading writers on socialism in the 1930s and 1940s. Born in India, he was educated at Eton. Between 1922 and 1928 he served in Burma as a policeman with the Indian Imperial Police. He fought in the militia of the Workers' Party of Marxist Unification (*Partido Obrero de Unificación Marxista*—POUM) on the side of the republicans during the **Spanish Civil War** and was badly wounded. He was commissioned by the **Left Book Club** to investigate social conditions in the industrial areas of England. His book *The Road to Wigan Pier* (1937) was the result of his investigation and was one of the most powerful modern cases for socialism. He also gave his views of Spanish left-wing politics in his *Homage to Catalonia* (1938). Orwell's writings on socialism were distinguished by his honesty, his appreciation of practical difficulties, and his fears of how socialism was being used to justify dictatorship and oppression. These concerns were made plain in his well-known works of **literature** attacking the Soviet Union, *Animal Farm* (1946) and *1984* (1949). Orwell never lost sight of the need to reconcile socialist **ideology** with human dignity and freedom. He made this clear in *The Lion and the Unicorn: Socialism and the English Genius* (1941).

OWEN, ROBERT (1771–1858). A major figure in **utopian socialism**, Robert Owen was born in Newtown, Montgomeryshire, Wales. He left school at nine and completed an apprenticeship as a draper. He then worked in London and Manchester (1787–88). He entered the cotton-spinning industry in 1791 with a business partner. Bought out, he started a cotton-spinning factory on his own, which prospered. In 1799 he and a partner bought the New Lanark mills near Glasgow, Scotland, from David Dale. Owen continued and greatly extended the tradition of philanthropy and **educational** reform that had been begun by Dale. New Lanark became an industrial showcase that attracted many visitors from Britain and other parts of Europe. In 1813 Owen published his best-known work, *A New View of Society*, which argued that a person's character was formed by his or her environment, explained the reforms of New Lanark, and advocated a national **educational** system, public works for the **unemployed**, and reform of the Poor Laws. In 1818 Owen presented a memorial to the Congress of Aix-la-Chapelle in which he urged that the governments of Europe should appoint a committee to visit his factory at New Lanark and use its lessons to place legal limits on the normal working hours in manufacturing in their countries; his initiative was ignored.

Although opposed to **religion**, his main ideas, particularly those relating to communities, had their origins in **Christian** thought and practice. By the mid-1820s Owen had developed a theory of utopian socialism based on communities, social equality, and cooperation. To this end, in 1825 he bought the community of New Harmony, Indiana, from a German religious sect, the Rappites, a move that cost him most of his fortune. Owen was too autocratic and too paternal to become a direct leader of organized labor, but his many initiatives provided a focus for its activities, particularly the formation of the Grand National Consolidated Trades Union in 1834 and the cooperative congresses held between 1831 and 1835. Owenism as an ideology became influential among **working-class** leaders. Owen was also important among the social critics of his time in his acceptance of industrialization and the possibilities it offered for general material improvement. Four of Owen's sons settled in the United States. The eldest, Robert Dale Owen, was elected to the state legislature of Indiana in 1835 and to the U.S. House of Representatives in 1843. In 1958 a Robert Owen Association was formed in Japan to study and promote his ideas. *See also* COMMUNES.

– P –

PACIFISM. Pacifism—the belief that **war** could and should be abolished—has been an important theme in the history of socialism. By its very nature, socialism stresses cooperation in human relations, which war, by its very nature, denies. This is not to imply that support for pacifism has been universal among socialists. Indeed, the most widely supported socialist position by the end of the nineteenth century was the recognition that the world was a dangerous place and that self-defense against aggression was a responsible policy in keeping with socialist ideals. **Keir Hardie** and Edouard Vaillant both hated violence and tried unsuccessfully to persuade the **Second International** between 1910 and 1914 to declare a general strike to prevent war. **Ramsay MacDonald** shared their antiwar views. The **Independent Labour Party** was a pacifist body, a position that won it few supporters before 1914, apart from Quakers. Pacifist feelings were also strong in the **Danish Social Democratic Party**, which opposed any kind of armed forces other than border guards. **G. D. H. Cole**, like many others, became a pacifist because of the carnage of World War I. In the 1930s **George Lansbury** was the leading pacifist in the **British Labour Party**, but **Ernest Bevin** crushed his influence.

Pacifist sentiments surfaced again in the British Labour Party in the 1950s in the form of opposition to **nuclear weapons**. In September 1960 a resolution in favor of "unilateralism" (that is, the United Kingdom rejecting the use of nuclear weapons as the basis of a defense policy on its own initiative without reference to other countries) was narrowly carried at the party's annual conference (3,282,000 votes in favor to 3,239,000 against). Opposition to nuclear weapons was also a feature of socialist/social-democratic parties in Western Europe and Japan. The British Labour Party effectively abandoned unilateralism after May 1989. *See also* JAURÈS, JEAN; LONGUET, CHARLES FÈLIX CÈSAR.

PAKISTAN PEOPLE'S PARTY (PPP). The PPP was formed in Lahore in November to December 1967. Its founder Zulfikar Ali Bhutto became chairman. The PPP adopted the principle that socialist ideas would lead to economic and social justice. Its goal was an **egalitarian** democracy. It also explicitly declared that Islam was the party faith. This religious emphasis had been absent from the earlier Pakistani party of the left—the Pakistan Socialist Party (PSP)—that was founded as the Punjab Socialist Party in 1932. The PSP was part of the Congress Socialist Party, later the **Indian Socialist Party**, from 1936. It opposed the partition of India and the creation of Pakistan. It wanted a classless socialist society and equal treatment for all regardless of race and **religion**. Thus, being completely at odds with

nationalism and the religious environment of Pakistan, the PSP was unable to gain any support from other **political parties**. In 1956 it had only about 1,250 members when it was represented at the **Asian Socialist Conference**.

Under military rule that began in 1955, political parties were banned in Pakistan between 1958 and 1962. The military still controlled Pakistan when Bhutto, who had been foreign minister in the limited democracy introduced by the military, formed the PPP in 1967. In response to mass unrest in the years that followed, the military declared that elections with universal suffrage would be held. In 1970 the PPP won the elections in West Pakistan. The military intervened against the winner of the elections in East Pakistan. After Indian military intervention, the Pakistani military president resigned and East Pakistan became the new state of Bangladesh. Bhutto became the president of Pakistan. Under Bhutto the PPP introduced social and economic reforms and started the **nuclear weapons** program. Bhutto was removed from power by the military in 1977 and executed in 1979. The military retained power, and continued the nuclear program. Martial law and a ban on political parties continued until 1985. The following year Benazir Bhutto (daughter of Zulfikar Ali) returned from exile.

In 1988, after the death of President General Zia Ul-Haq in an air crash, military rule ended and general elections were held. With Benazir Bhutto as leader the PPP was the biggest party in the assembly. Bhutto became prime minister in a PPP-led coalition. The president dismissed her in 1990, charged with incompetence and corruption. Repression, the introduction of Islamic Shariah law, and neoliberal economic reforms followed. In the general elections of 1993 the PPP returned to power with Bhutto as prime minister, only to be dismissed once again on allegations of corruption in 1996. The following year the PPP lost the general elections. In 1999 the military once again staged a coup and General Pervez Musharraf took power and became president in 2001. After granting himself another five years in office and the power to dismiss an elected parliament Musharraf allowed general elections to be held in October 2002 but retained the presidency. Led by Bhutto, the PPP won 71 of the 342 seats with 25.8 percent of the vote and remained in opposition as a pro-Musharraf coalition entered government. In 2003 the PPP became a full member of the **Socialist International**.

PALME, SVEN OLAF (1927–86). A leading post-1945 Swedish social-democratic politician, Palme was born in Stockholm and educated in Sweden and the United States. He graduated with a law degree in 1951. After serving as personal secretary and speechwriter to
Prime Minister **Tage Erlander**, he was elected to the *Riksdag* (parliament) in 1956 and was minister without portfolio until 1963. He
participated in protests about America's **war** in Vietnam and the Soviet invasion of Czechoslovakia in 1968. In October 1969 he became
prime minister, but lost power in 1976 after Sweden's ailing economy
cut support for the **Swedish Social Democratic Workers' Party**. He
returned to power in October 1982 as prime minister of a minority
government. He was shot dead in Stockholm in February 1986.

**PAN-HELLENIC SOCIALIST MOVEMENT [*PANELLINIO SO-
CIALISTIKO KINIMA* (PASOK)].** PASOK was formed in 1974 by
Andreas Papandreou out of the Pan-Hellenic Liberation Movement, which he had formed in 1967 to oppose military rule. PASOK
claimed a membership of 150,000 in 1987 and has been a full member of the **Socialist International** since about 1990. At the beginning
of 1996 Costas Simitis took over the leadership of PASOK from the
dying Papandreou. In the national elections in September 1996,
PASOK received 46.9 percent of the vote, compared to 41.5 percent
in 1993, and retained control of the government. In December 1995
a left-wing group split from PASOK and formed the Democratic Renewal Group that attracted 4.4 percent of the vote in the 1996 elections. PASOK was victorious once again at the April 2000 elections,
winning 158 seats with 43.8 percent of the vote. Of the other left parties the Communist Party of Greece (*Kommunistiko Komma
Elladas*—KKE) obtained 11 seats with 5.5 percent of the vote and the
Synaspismos Left Coalition won six seats with 3.2 percent.

Simitis resigned from the leadership shortly before the general
elections of 7 March 2004. George Papandreou, son of the party's
founder, became the new leader. George Papandreou's inexperience
proved costly in the elections, which were held amidst economic
problems in the country and perceived corruption involving some
members of PASOK. Having governed for 19 of the previous 22
years, PASOK lost the elections to the conservative New Democratic
Party, PASOK taking 117 of 300 seats with 40.5 percent of the vote.
Of the other left-wing parties the KKE won 12 seats with 5.9 percent

of the vote, and Synaspismos took six seats with 3.3 percent. On 12 March 2005 Károlos Papoúlias of PASOK became president of Greece after securing the votes of 279 of the 300 members of the Greek parliament.

PAPANDREOU, ANDREAS GEORGE (1919–96). Leading Greek socialist Andreas Papandreou was born on the island of Chios. He qualified as a lawyer at the University of Athens in 1939 and completed a doctorate in economics at Harvard in 1943. He became an associate professor at the University of Minnesota in 1947 and went on to hold professorships at the universities of Minnesota (between 1951 and 1955) and California (from 1955 to 1963). He returned in 1964 to Greece, where his father, George, served as prime minister until he was dismissed by the king in 1965. Imprisoned by the military after their coup in 1967, he was released after eight months without trial. Then he left Greece and continued his campaign against its military rulers. He addressed the congress of the **Socialist International** in 1969. He founded a new socialist party, the **Pan-Hellenic Socialist Movement** (*Panellinio Socialistiko Kinima*—PASOK) in 1974. It grew out of the Pan-Hellenic Liberation Movement that he had founded in 1967 to oppose the military rulers.

PASOK won the 1981 election, and Papandreou became the first Greek socialist prime minister. He dominated the government and was able to impose his own interpretation of socialist policies. Despite his long residence in the United States (he relinquished his American citizenship in the 1960s), Papandreou adopted anti-American and anti-Western policies during his first term as prime minister (1981–89). Domestically, he initiated policies designed to redress social inequalities, such as improving the status of **women**, overhauling **education**, and promoting **nationalization**.

His government was defeated in 1989 though a combination of infighting in PASOK and the scandal over the failure of the Bank of Crete. Papandreou was reelected leader of PASOK in 1992 and led it to victory in 1993. His second term as prime minister was notable for its **nationalism** and moderation. Social welfare continued to be improved, but the nationalization program ceased in response to concerns by Greece's European neighbors. Papandreou was hospitalized in late November 1995 and formally resigned as prime minister on 15 January 1996, shortly before his death.

PARIS COMMUNE. The Paris Commune was a left-wing government that functioned between 18 March and 28 May 1871. It originated in the provisional government's acceptance of the harsh peace terms imposed on France by Otto von Bismarck after the defeat of Napoleon III in the Franco-Prussian War of 1870. These terms included not only the surrender of Alsace-Lorraine but also the occupation of Paris by a Prussian army. The Commune was organized in an atmosphere of general discontent. It proceeded from no particular plan and harked back in concept to the Jacobins and the Commune of 1793. The armed forces of the Commune were provided by the National Guard that had been created to defend Paris during its five-month siege. The central committee of the National Guard in Paris held elections for a body of 90 to be called the "Commune of Paris" on 28 March 1871; the 229,000 electors elected moderates as well as radicals, some of whom were linked to the **International Workingmen's Association**. The nonradicals largely withdrew, leaving the followers of Auguste Blanqui in the majority although the followers of **Pierre-Joseph Proudhon** were also important.

The Commune wanted to introduce labor and **educational** reforms, but was forced to spend much of its time fighting. It committed violence, executing the archbishop of Paris and other hostages and burning some buildings, but its violence paled before the savage reconquest of Paris by President Adolphe Thiers's forces, which destroyed much of inner Paris and killed thousands. Estimates of the casualties vary, but it is thought that about 30,000 supporters of the Paris Commune were killed in the fighting and a further 45,000 were arrested, of whom 17,000 were executed and 13,000 were imprisoned or deported to New Caledonia.

The crushing of the Paris Commune had important implications for the history of socialism. First, it greatly weakened France as the European center of socialism and so hastened the demise of the **International Workingmen's Association**. Second, it was the subject of a work by **Karl Marx** called *The Civil War in France*, which **V. I. Lenin** used to support his case for the dictatorship of the proletariat. Third, the Paris Commune supplied martyrs for the socialist cause in France and elsewhere; the Paris Commune was featured on some of the posters after the Bolshevik takeover of Russia in 1917. Fourth, it showed that any attempt to introduce socialism by revolution was bound to provoke a violent conservative response. *See also* COMMUNES; LENINISM.

PARTY FOR DEMOCRACY [*PARTIDO POR LA DEMOCRACIA* (PPD)]. As one of three Chilean parties holding full membership in the **Socialist International**, the PPD is now a significant force in Chilean politics. The PPD was launched in 1988 by the **Socialist Party of Chile** (*Partido Socialista de Chile*—PS) as a temporary measure in the plebiscite against General Augusto Pinochet's dictatorship and to gain the support of Chileans who would not be attracted to a traditional socialist party. However, the PPD became an independent party on the Chilean left, working in partnership with the PS in the early 1990s. In 1996 the PPD gained full membership in the **Socialist International**. On 16 January 2000 the PPD's leftist candidate Ricardo Lagos (1938–) became president. Representing the left and center coalition entitled the Concertation for Democracy (*Concertación de Partidos por la Democracia*—CPD), Lagos polled 51.3 percent of the vote at the second (runoff) round of elections. In the general elections to the Chamber of Deputies on 16 December 2001, the PPD contributed to the CPD's success against the rightwing coalition. Of the CPD's 62 of the 120 seats, the PPD won 20 under the leadership of Victor Barrueto. After the elections to half of the seats in the Senate that day, the CPD held 20 of the total of 38 electable seats (ten other seats were appointed until 2005), of which the PPD occupied three. In the elections of 11 December 2005 the CPD increased its share of the seats in the Chamber of Deputies to 65, gained with 51.8 percent of the vote. The PPD took 21 of those seats with 15.5 percent. The CPD obtained 11 of the 19 contested Senate seats, with one going to the PPD. The CPD maintained its total of 20 Senate seats and the PPD its total of three.

PARTY FOR DEMOCRACY AND PROGRESS/SOCIALIST PARTY [*PARTI POUR LA DÉMOCRATIE ET LE PROGRÈS/ PARTI SOCIALISTE* (PDP/PS)]. The PDP/PS of Burkina Faso was formed in 1993 and became a full member of the **Socialist International** by 1995. It was formed by a breakaway party from the Popular Front that took power in October 1987 after the violent overthrow of Thomas Sankara's military government. Between 1980 and the fall and execution of Sankara, no **political parties** were permitted in Burkina Faso ("country of honest men"), which was known as Upper Volta before 1984. The PDP/PS's opponent Blaise Compoaré took over as president of Burkina Faso in 1987 and won the presidential elections of 1991 and 1998, elections boycotted by the opposition (including the PDP/PS in 1998). The PDP/PS was also unsuccessful in parliamentary elections, which Compoaré's party, in its different forms, dominated. In the parliamentary elections of May 2002 the PDP/PS won 10 of the 111 seats. The PDP/PS was led by Joseph Ki-Zerbo, who had links to the **French Socialist Party**. In November 2005 the PDP/PS's candidate Ali Lankoande obtained only 1.74 percent of the vote in the presidential elections won yet again by Compoaré.

PARTY FOR DEMOCRACY AND SOCIALISM OF NIGER [*PARTI NIGÉRIAN POUR LA DÉMOCRATIE ET LE SOCIALISME* (PNDS)]. In 1974, 14 years after independence from France, Niger fell under military rule that continued until 1989, when a civilian one-party system was introduced. In 1990 opposition parties, including the PNDS, were legalized following strikes and demonstrations. The PNDS joined five other parties in the Alliance of the Forces for Change, which won 50 of 83 seats in the parliamentary elections of February 1993. The PNDS's Mahamadou Issoufou, who had lost out to another Alliance candidate in the presidential elections that year, was appointed prime minister. After a period of political, social, and economic tension the PNDS withdrew from the Alliance in September 1994 and Issoufou resigned as prime minister, in protest at some of the powers of his office being transferred to the presidency.

The coalition broke up and a military-backed party won most seats at the 1995 parliamentary elections. After continuing political instability the military took control again in January 1996 and Issoufou was placed under house arrest. A military leader was also installed as president in August that year in the elections, during which the opposition was suppressed. The PNDS and other opposition parties boycotted the parliamentary elections of November that year. The military again seized power temporarily in April 1999 following the assassination of the president. In the presidential elections of October to November 1999 Issoufou lost in the runoff with 40.1 percent of the vote. In parliamentary elections, also held in October to November that year, the PNDS won 16 of 83 seats. In March 2001 the PNDS led 11 other parties to form an opposition alliance.

The PNDS gained full membership in the **Socialist International** in 2003. In the presidential elections of November to December 2004 Issoufou again lost in the runoff, with 34.5 percent of the vote. In the parliamentary elections of December that year the PNDS and its allies obtained 25 of 113 seats, of which the PNDS took 17 with 13.4 percent of the vote.

PARTY OF EUROPEAN SOCIALISTS (PES). The PES was founded in 1992, as the successor to the **Confederation of the Socialist Parties in the European Community**. The PES brings together the socialist, social-democratic, and labor parties of the European Union. The PES was founded following the Treaty on European Union, one article of which recognized the importance of **political parties** at a European level. The PES seeks to strengthen the socialist and social-democratic movement in Europe. It also tries to develop close working relationships between the national member parties, their parliamentary groups, and the parliamentary group of the PES (the **Socialist Group in the European Parliament** [SGEP]). In 2004 there were 32 member parties from the 25 nations of the new Europe and Norway. There were also eight associate and five observer parties. The PES is an associated organization within the **Socialist International**.

PARTY OF SOCIALISTS AND DEMOCRATS [*PARTITO DEI SOCIALISTI E DEI DEMOCRATICI* (PSD)]. The PSD was formed in San Marino by the merger of the Party of Democrats (*Partito de Democratici*—PD) and the Sanmarinese Socialist Party (*Partito Socialista Sammarinese*—PSS). The roots of the PD can be traced back to the Socialist Unity Party (*Partito Socialista Unitario*—SUP), which existed alongside the PSS. The SUP was established in 1975 from the left wing of the Independent Social Democratic Socialist Party, which was formed in 1957 and had been a consultant member of the **Socialist International** (SI) since 1961. The SUP became a full member of the SI in 1980. The SUP disappeared in 1991 and its leader, Emilio Della Balda, led a new party—the Democratic Movement—that likewise disappeared at the beginning of the twenty-first century. Della Balda became a member of the newly formed PD. Coalition government between diverse parties, which is the norm in

San Marino, continued after the parliamentary elections of June 2001, at which the PSS won 15 of the 60 seats in the Grand and General Council with 24.2 percent of the vote. The PD took 12 seats with 20.8 percent of the vote. The PSS entered government with the Christian Democratic Party and the PD later joined this coalition, which collapsed in June 2002. The PSS and PD formed a new coalition government along with the Popular Democratic Alliance. This coalition collapsed in December 2002. A new coalition was formed which once again comprised the PSS and the Christian Democrats. The merger of the PSS and PD took place in February 2005, and the new PSD became the sole Sanmarinese party with full membership in the SI.

PARTY OF THE DEMOCRATIC REVOLUTION [*PARTIDI DE LA REVOLUCIÓN DEMOCRÁTICA* (PRD)]. The PRD was formed in 1989 as a left-wing alternative to the **Institutional Revolutionary Party** (PRI). In 1996 it gained full membership in the **Socialist International**. During the second half of the 1990s the PRD began to enjoy an increase in support, as many Mexicans protested against the PRI amidst economic crisis. Hence, in regional elections the PRD gained control of some of Mexico's states in which the PRI had traditionally enjoyed strong support. In the presidential elections the PRD did not fare well, coming in third behind the successful center-right candidate Vicente Fox and also the PRI's candidate. In the parliamentary elections of July 2003 the PRD won 95 of the 500 seats in the Chamber of Deputies, with 17.6 percent of the vote.

PARTY OF THE EUROPEAN LEFT (EL). Formed in 2004 by parties, including **communist** parties, more radical than those of the **Party of European Socialists**, the EL attempts to articulate the left at the level of the European Union (EU). The idea for such a party had been aired in 1999, at a conference of the Confederated Group of the United European Left/Nordic Green Left, which had been formed that year by members of the European Parliament from radical left parties. The EL does not, however, exclude parties from countries outside the EU. The aim is a Europe that is anti**war**, rejects capitalist **globalization**, redistributes power, **wealth**, and influence, and deepens democracy in each state. At the time of formation the EL comprised 14 member parties, ranging in size from the French Communist Party—which had 135,000 members and in 2002 won 21 parliamentary seats with 4.8 percent of the vote—to the San Marino Communist Refoundation, which had 100 members and won two parliamentary seats in 2001 with 3.4 percent of the vote. The other parties were the German Party of Democratic Socialism (renamed the **Left Party** in July 2005), the Italian Communist Refoundation Party, the Greek *Synaspismos*: Coalition of Left, of Movements and Ecology (which won six Greek parliamentary seats with 3.3 percent of the vote in 2004), the Austrian Communist Party, the Estonian Social Democratic Labour Party, the Hungarian Workers Party, the Romanian Socialist Alliance Party, the Czech Party of Democratic Socialism, the Party of Labour of Switzerland (which won two parliamentary seats with 0.7 percent of the vote in 2002), and three parties from Spain—the Spanish Communist Party, the United Left, and the Catalonian United Alternative Left. The EL held its first congress in Athens during October 2005. *See also* HUNGARIAN SOCIALIST PARTY.

PELLOUTIER, FERNAND LÉONCE EMILE (1867–1901). A French radical labor leader of **middle-class** origins, Fernand Pelloutier was one of the leading exponents of **syndicalism**, the doctrine that saw the general strike as the most effective way of overthrowing the social order. Born in Paris, he was secretary of the *Fédération des Bourses du Travail* from 1895 until his death. Pelloutier envisaged the socialist society of the future as a federal grouping of producers, with each industry organized on a local basis by **trade unions** that enrolled all occupations within their ranks. He wanted unions to control the supply of labor and the apprenticeship system. To be effective managers, employees needed to be well informed and have access to good libraries. *See also* GUILD SOCIALISM.

PEOPLE'S ELECTORAL MOVEMENT [*MOVIMENTO ELECTORAL DI PUEBLO* (MEP)]. The MEP was set up on the Caribbean island of Aruba in 1971. It took a leading role in the struggle for domestic autonomy from the Netherlands, which was granted in January 1986. However, in June 1990, at the request of Aruba, an agreement was made with the Netherlands to delete references to eventual full independence. The MEP participated in coalition government between 1989 and 1994, with Nelson Orlando Oduber of the MEP as prime minister. Plans for independence were finally shelved in 1994. The MEP has been a full member of the **Socialist International** since 1994. In the parliamentary elections of September 2001 the MEP won 12 of the 21 seats with 52.4 percent of the vote. This was the first absolute majority gained by a party in Aruba. Oduber became prime minister. He retained this post when the MEP was returned to government after obtaining 11 seats with 43 percent of the votes in the elections of September 2005.

PEOPLE'S MOVEMENT FOR THE LIBERATION OF ANGOLA [*MOVIMENTO POPULAR DE LIBERTAÇÃO DE ANGOLA* (MPLA)]. Formed in 1956 during the struggle against Portuguese **imperialism**, the MPLA was forced into exile. It formed a government in exile in the early 1960s while also conducting a guerilla **war** against the Portuguese. The military dictatorship in Portugal ended in 1974, and Angola gained independence the following year. The MPLA became the sole legal party and immediately had to fight a civil war against guerilla groups supported by the United States and South Africa. The MPLA gained the support of Cuban troops. In 1976 the MPLA formed a socialist people's republic of Angola, guided by **Marxist-Leninist ideology**. From 1977 until 1992 the party became known as the MPLA-Workers' Party (MPLA-PT) (*Partido de Trabalko*).

In 1979 the MPLA's founding president, Agostinho Neto died and José Eduardo Dos Santos, who had become foreign minister at independence, became president of Angola. As the civil war lingered on in the 1980s, Dos Santos and the MPLA gradually took a less hard-line Marxist-Leninist approach, introducing some market reforms into the essentially planned economy and legalizing private property. Dos Santos was reelected president in September 1985. In 1990 the party committed itself to democratic socialism and in 1992 won the presidential and parliamentary elections. In the presidential contest Dos Santos obtained 49.5 percent of the vote. Jonas Savimbi as leader of the main opposition guerilla movement—National Union for the Total Liberation of Angola—participated in the election but refused to accept the result. Although a peace treaty was signed in 1994 and a government of national unity including opposition figures set up in 1997, the civil war continued intermittently until 2002 when Savimbi died in fighting and his movement's armed wing disbanded. In 2003 the MPLA gained full membership in the **Socialist Interna-**

tional. Dos Santos retained the Angolan presidency, but said that he would be unlikely to stand again in elections planned for 2006.

PEOPLE'S NATIONAL PARTY (PNP). The PNP was formed in Jamaica in September 1938 by Norman Washington Manley (1893–1969), who based it on the **British Labour Party**. The PNP's socialism was, indeed, influenced by **Fabianism**. A split between Manley and a major **trade union** led to the formation of the Jamaican Labour Party (JLP) in 1943, led by Alexander Bustamente. Each party had strong support from sections of the labor movement. The JLP was populist, appealing to the poor, even though the PNP was the socialist party. Since then, the PNP and JLP have alternated in government and opposition. The PNP was first elected to government in 1955. It has been a full member of the **Socialist International** since 1952.

In the 1950s the PNP and JLP converged at the center, each pursuing industrialization based on foreign investment. This led to economic growth but also a large trade deficit, **unemployment** and inequality. The PNP resigned in 1962 after Jamaicans chose independence at a referendum, and remained out of government for the next 10 years. In 1972 the PNP was elected to government under the leadership of Michael Manley (1924–97). Manley also led the PNP to victory in the general elections of 1976, thus remaining as prime minister until 1980. Under Manley in the 1970s the PNP returned to its earlier strong commitment to democratic socialism. It expanded state control over sections of the economy, made improvements in **health care** and **education**, and increased the income of the poorer Jamaicans. The PNP also pursued closer relations with Cuba and adopted a foreign policy of nonalignment. Although such measures in domestic and foreign policy appealed to many poor and **working class** Jamaicans, they did not appeal to the United States. A balance of payments deficit developed and the PNP had to accept International Monetary Fund conditions in 1977 and 1978. The JLP governed in the 1980s led by Edward Seaga, and pursued warmer relations with the United States and a change to free-market policies. Nevertheless, the economy did not improve and a World Bank structural adjustment loan was followed by spending cuts and a huge debt burden.

The PNP was elected to government again in 1989 and reelected at the next three general elections. The PNP had now shifted toward the

center-left. After the elections of 1992 Percival J. Patterson represented the PNP as prime minister. Patterson also led the PNP in the
electoral victories of 1997 and 2002. In 1997 the PNP won 50 of the
60 seats in the House of Representatives. In 2002 this was reduced to
34 of the 60 seats, obtained with 52 percent of the vote. Patterson resigned in March 2006. Portia Simpson Miller was elected to lead the
PNP later that month. As leader of the ruling party she became prime
minister.

**PERUVIAN APRISTA PARTY [*PARTIDO APRISTA PERUANO*
(PAP)].** In its original form the PAP was called the American Revolutionary Popular Alliance (*Alianza Popular Revolucionaria Americana*—APRA), popularly known as the Aprista Movement. The
APRA was formed in Mexico in 1924 by the Peruvian exile Victor
Raúl Haya de la Torre (1895–1979), who had been driven from Peru
for his student activism against the dictator Augusto Leguía. Haya intended the APRA to be an international movement. However, it faced
problems of **nationalism** and also opposition from the **communist**
parties, including the Peruvian Communist Party that was founded by
the former APRA supporter José Carlos Mariategui (1891–1930).
The communists opposed the APRA's commitment to parliamentary
democracy and Haya's opposition to class struggle. Haya attempted
to build a common front involving the **working class**, intellectuals,
progressive sections of the **middle class**, and, importantly, blacks and
native Americans. This front would, on a continental scale, oppose
the landed aristocracy, foreign capitalists, and north-American **imperialism**. Haya aimed for international public ownership of land and
major industries and also a system of **social security** that would tran-
scend the national boundaries of South America. Haya's ultimate
goal was world solidarity of all the oppressed peoples and classes.

The opposition of nationalists and communists and the task of
overcoming the differing economic and demographic conditions of
the South American continent meant that the APRA did not succeed
in building a mass international following. In 1930, following the
overthrow of Leguía, the APRA transformed itself into an essentially
Peruvian political party that became known as the PAP. In Peru it secured a strong base of support among the working class and native
Americans. In the presidential elections of 1931 Haya was defeated
by General Luis M. Sanchez Cerro, who jailed Haya and violently

suppressed the PAP. Two years later Cerro was assassinated and Haya freed. However, Peru fell under the new dictatorship of General Oscar Benavides, forcing the PAP underground until 1945, when it led a center-left National Democratic Front to victory in the presidential elections that year. José Luis Bustamente of APRA was president until 1948, when the PAP was once again outlawed by the dictatorship of General Manuel A. Odría, with Haya restricted to his refuge in the Columbian embassy until 1954, when he was allowed into exile in Europe. Peru transferred back to civilian rule in 1956 and in 1962 Haya contested the presidential elections but no candidate achieved the level of support required to win. The army vetoed Haya's accession anyway and new elections the following year produced a president acceptable to the military, who ruled until 1968 when the generals saw fit to remove him from power. Peru passed into military rule until 1980.

Although the PAP joined the **Socialist International** it moved to the center ground of Peruvian politics. In 1985 Alan Garcia Perez of the PAP won the presidential elections, which were the first in Peru under universal **suffrage**, with 53 percent of the vote. The PAP also gained a majority that year in both houses of the legislature. However, Garcia's reliance on government spending caused Peru's economic situation to worsen, bringing a decline in living standards and high unemployment. Garcia also attempted to deal with a resurgence of guerilla activity by the **Marxist** *Sendero Luminoso* (Shining Path) movement. Garcia was defeated by Alberto Fujimori at the presidential elections of 1990, at which Garcia's share of the vote was only 19.2 percent. Fujimori performed an *autogolpe* in 1992 suspending the constitution, judiciary, and congress. The following year he introduced a new constitution that placed constraints on the democratic system. In protest at the new constitution the PAP boycotted the presidential elections of 1995, which Fujimori won. The PAP did contest the presidential elections of 2000, which Fujimori won yet again amidst allegations of corruption.

When Fujimori fled to Japan after it emerged that his secret service was linked to the operations of the Columbian drug cartels, the United Nations prepared new elections in 2001. Garcia stood for the PAP in the presidential elections of April and June that year, losing in the runoff with 46.9 percent of the vote, against 53.1 percent for Alejandro Toledo Manrique. In legislative elections in April 2001 the

PAP secured 26 of 120 seats with 19.7 percent of the vote, and remained in opposition to a coalition government.

PLAID CYMRU. Full national status for Wales in the European Union is the aim of *Plaid Cymru* (Party of Wales). Stressing that it does not discriminate against any race, nationality, gender, color, creed, sexuality, age, ability, or social background, its constitution states the party's aim to promote economic prosperity, social justice, and a healthy natural environment on the basis of decentralist socialism. Formed in 1925, *Plaid Cymru* sought to promote a revival of Welsh culture and language. In 1966 Gwynfor Evans (1912–2005) won the Carmarthen by-election to the British parliament. In the 1974 general election the party won two more seats. The party conference of 1981 agreed that community socialism should formally be a main aim. The party continued to win three to four seats at general elections and after the election of 2001 it held four seats. A new role emerged in 1997 when a referendum in Wales led to the formation of the Welsh Assembly in 1999, when the party held 17 seats in the assembly. Also in 1999 the party won one seat in the elections to the European Parliament. In the 2003 elections to the Welsh Assembly, the party's representation was cut to 12 seats. In the general election of May 2005 the party lost one of its seats in the British parliament, thus being reduced to three.

POLICIES. Political parties and groups select goals and consider methods of achieving those goals. They make decisions concerning those goals and methods. Individual decisions or sets of decisions made on the basis of value-systems are policies. **Ideologies** consist of value systems and the effort to formulate policies. Socialists make policies from a value-system in which equality, cooperation, social responsibility, and sociality feature strongly. Their policies are made on a wide range of issues, typically including **education, social security, health care,** and the **welfare state.** They can be at national level or below—for example, in the case of municipal socialism, at local government level. *See also* EGALITARIANISM; IMPERIALISM; INHERITANCE; PACIFISM; RELIGION; UNEMPLOYMENT; WAR; WEALTH; WOMEN.

POLISH SOCIALIST PARTY [*POLSKA PARTIA SOCJALISTY-CZNA* (PPS)]. Socialism in what is now Poland (but before 1918 was divided among the empires of Russia, Austria-Hungary, and Germany) emerged in the 1870s. In 1881 Lugwig Wariński (1856–89) organized a socialist organization, Proletariat, which conducted some strikes before it was suppressed. Wariński was arrested and died in jail. Proletariat was later reestablished and operated as an underground political body; one of its members was **Rosa Luxemburg**, who joined in 1886. In Galicia, then part of the Austro-Hungarian empire, the Poles formed a section of the **Austrian Social Democratic Party**. Other socialist groups were also organized and merged with Proletariat to form the PPS in 1892. The PPS adopted a policy of **nationalism**, which put it at odds with the **German Social Democratic Party** and vocal critics such as Luxemburg.

In 1906 most of the left wing of the PPS broke away and many of them joined the Polish Communist Party in 1919. A second split in the PPS occurred in 1916 when Josef Pilsudski (1867–1935) led many on the right wing out of the party. World War I radically altered Polish politics. Poland declared its independence in November 1918 (the first time it had been an independent nation since 1795) and fought a brief but successful war with the new Bolshevik state in 1920. The PPS was represented in the lower house of parliament (the *Sejm*) from 1919 and even participated in government in the early 1920s, but its support declined. Poland was then a heavily agricultural country and nationalism had far greater appeal than the kind of radical socialism espoused by the PPS. In 1926 Pilsudski, the former socialist, staged a coup d'état and was effectively a dictator until his death. In 1928 the PPS declared a membership of 63,400 to the **Labor and Socialist International**, but this included 8,400 members of an independent socialist party.

The PPS was devastated by World War II. Many died in the resistance to Nazi rule and others were executed by the Soviet government, which did not want the PPS to compete with the Communist Party. Two leading Polish socialists who were executed on the orders of Joseph Stalin (1879–1953) in 1942, despite international protests, were Henry Erlich and Victor Alter.

In 1948 what remained of the PPS was forced to merge with the Polish United Workers' Party, by then the ruling **communist** party. In November 1987 the PPS was secretly reformed, but it failed to attract support. The reason for its lack of support lay partly in the Polish United Workers' Party transforming itself into the Social Democracy of the Republic of Poland in 1990, which apologized for the repression of the past. *See also* DEMOCRATIC LEFT ALLIANCE.

POLITICAL PARTIES. Parties are central to socialist politics. Parties seek election to political office at the central, regional, or local levels of government. Whether free and fair or merely formalities, elections give the successful parties an air of legitimacy. Even parties that have virtually no realistic chance of winning office usually have aspirations to do so at some level, examples being past and present parties of the left in the United States: the **American Labor Party**, **Social Democratic Party of America**, **Socialist Labor Party of America**, **Socialist Party of America**, **Workingmen's Party of the United States**, **Democratic Socialists of America**, and **Social Democrats USA**. Parties are also the organizations through which people are recruited for candidacy. Parties, furthermore, serve to make the various demands of their supporters and members into manageable packages to campaign upon and hopefully implement.

Some political parties are more radical at some times than at others. For example, the **German Social Democratic Party** embraced **Marxism** in the late nineteenth century, but became a mainstream social-democratic party in the early twentieth century. Another example is the Italian Communist Party, which transformed itself into the social-democratic **Democratic Party of the Left** and subsequently **Democrats of the Left** when **communism** suffered a major decline in the late twentieth century. This Italian Party became more prominent than the **Italian Socialist Party** which, having once dominated Italian social democracy, suffered rapid decline and reemerged as the minor **Italian Democratic Socialists**.

During the period of communist decline many former ruling communist parties reorganized themselves as democratic socialist or social-democratic ones, sometimes changing their names. These include the **Bulgarian Socialist Party**, **Democratic Left Alliance**, **Front for the Liberation of Mozambique** (FRELIMO), **Hungarian Socialist Party**, **Mongolian People's Revolutionary Party**, Party of Democratic Socialism (PDS), **People's Movement for the Liberation of Angola** (MPLA), **Social Democratic Party [Benin]**, and **Socialist Party of Albania**.

The PDS changed its name once again, becoming the **Left Party** in 2005. Another prominent example of a renamed party is the

Japanese Social Democratic Party, which had operated as the **Japan Socialist Party** until around 1990. Some major parties of the left either compete or cooperate with other social-democratic parties such as the **Albanian Social Democratic Party**, the **Bulgarian Social Democrats**, and the **Mongolian Social Democratic Party** until it merged with several other parties. The **Mauritius Labour Party** and **Mauritian Militant Movement** operate in frequently changing coalitions and alliances with other Mauritian social-democratic parties.

Sometimes newly formed parties enjoy electoral success quite quickly. Examples are the **Workers' Party** in Brazil and the **Movement of the Fifth Republic** in Venezuela. On some occasions established parties merge to form new social-democratic ones, recent examples being the formation of **Social Democratic Israel** in 2003, the **Direction-Social Democrats** in Slovakia in 2004, the **Party of Socialists and Democrats** in San Marino in 2005, and the **Union of Haitian Social Democrats** in 2005. Sometimes even quite new parties merge to form a new one, as was the case in Slovenia in 1993 with the formation of the United List of Social Democrats (*Združeno Lista socialnih demokratov*—ZLSD), which became the **Social Democrats of Slovenia** in 2005.

The roots of some existing parties can be traced back to old established ones that split; for example, roots of the *Janata Dal* **(Secular)** party can be traced back to the old Indian Socialist Party. Another example is the **Republican People's Party** in Turkey, which was revived in 1992, having roots in an older Turkish party of that name. In some countries one party has dominated socialist politics. An example is the **British Labour Party** in the United Kingdom. Smaller socialist parties in that country faded into obscurity, such as the **British Socialist Party**, **Independent Labour Party**, and **Social Democratic Federation**. However, in Britain's parliamentary elections, the **Social Democratic and Labour Party** competes for seats in Northern Ireland and, with limited success, *Plaid Cymru* and the **Scottish Socialist Party** (SSP) compete in Wales and Scotland. The SSP has yet to win seats in the British Parliament, but has won a number of seats in the Scottish Parliament.

Some parties have strong links with **trade unions**. Such parties include the **Australian Labor Party**, the Labour Party in Britain, the **Belgian Socialist Party**, and **Norwegian Labor Party**. Some parties began life as liberation movements against **imperialism**, dictatorship, or institutionalized discrimination. These include the **African National Congress, Armenian Revolutionary Federation, Sandinista National Liberation Front, African Party of Cape Verdi's Independence**, FRELIMO, **Nepali Congress Party**, and the MPLA. Some parties that became social-democratic, such as the **Liberal Party of Columbia** and **Radical Civic Union** (UCR), started out in the broad tradition of **liberalism**. The UCR was generally more successful than the **Argentinean Socialist Party**.

By the beginning of the twenty-first century five one-party communist states remained, governed by the **Chinese Communist Party, Cuban Communist Party, Korean Workers' Party, Lao People's Revolutionary Party**, and **Vietnam Communist Party**. In Russia following the collapse of the Soviet Union the communist party was reformed as the **Communist Party of the Russian Federation**. Two international parties, comprising parties from a range of countries, are the **Party of European Socialists** and **Party of the European Left**. See also ALLIANCE FOR DEMOCRACY IN MALI/AFRICAN PARTY OF SOLIDARITY AND JUSTICE; AMERICAN REVOLUTIONARY POPULAR ALLIANCE; AUSTRIAN SOCIAL DEMOCRATIC PARTY; BARBADOS LABOUR PARTY; CONVERGENCE FOR SOCIAL DEMOCRACY; CZECH SOCIAL DEMOCRATIC PARTY; DANISH SOCIAL DEMOCRATIC PARTY; DEMOCRATIC ACTION; DEMOCRATIC ACTION PARTY; DEMOCRATIC CONSTITUENT ASSEMBLY; DEMOCRATIC LABOR PARTY; DEMOCRATIC LEFT; DOMINICAN REVOLUTIONARY PARTY; DUTCH LABOR PARTY; ESTONIAN SOCIAL DEMOCRATIC PARTY; FINNISH SOCIAL DEMOCRATIC PARTY; FRENCH SOCIALIST PARTY; GUINEAN PEOPLE'S ASSEMBLY; ICELANDIC SOCIAL DEMOCRATIC PARTY; INSTITUTIONAL REVOLUTIONARY PARTY; IRISH LABOUR PARTY; ISRAEL LABOUR PARTY; IVORIAN POPULAR FRONT; LATVIAN SOCIAL DEMOCRATIC WORKERS' PARTY; LITHUANIAN SOCIAL DEMOCRATIC PARTY; LUXEMBOURG SOCIALIST WORKERS' PARTY; MALTA LABOUR PARTY; MOVEMENT OF THE REVOLUTIONARY LEFT; NATIONAL DEMOCRATIC PARTY; NATIONAL LIBERATION PARTY; NEW ANTILLES MOVEMENT; NEW DEMOCRATIC PARTY; NEW SPACE; NEW ZEALAND

LABOUR PARTY; PAKISTAN PEOPLE'S PARTY; PARTY FOR DEMOCRACY; PARTY FOR DEMOCRACY AND PROGRESS; PARTY FOR DEMOCRACY AND SOCIALISM OF NIGER; PARTY OF THE DEMOCRATIC REVOLUTION; PEOPLE'S ELECTORAL MOVEMENT (ARUBA); PERUVIAN APRISTA PARTY; POLISH SOCIALIST PARTY; PORTUGUESE SOCIAL-IST PARTY; PUERTO RICAN INDEPENDENCE PARTY; REVO-LUTIONARY DEMOCRATIC PARTY; ROMANIAN SOCIAL DEMOCRATIC PARTY; SOCIAL DEMOCRATIC CONVER-GENCE; SOCIAL DEMOCRATIC FRONT [CAMEROON]; SO-CIAL DEMOCRATIC PARTY OF ANDORRA; SOCIAL DEMO-CRATIC PARTY OF BOSNIA AND HERZEGOVINA; SOCIAL DEMOCRATIC PARTY OF CROATIA; SOCIAL DEMOCRATIC PARTY OF MONTENEGRO; SOCIAL DEMOCRATIC PEOPLE'S PARTY; SOCIAL DEMOCRATIC RADICAL PARTY; SOCIAL DEMOCRATIC UNION OF MACEDONIA; SOCIALIST PARTY OF SENEGAL; SOCIALIST PARTY OF URUGUAY; SOCIALIST FORCES FRONT; SOCIALIST PARTY OF CHILE; SOCIALIST UNITY PARTY; SOUTH AFRICAN LABOUR PARTY; SPANISH SOCIALIST WORKERS' PARTY; SWEDISH SOCIAL DEMO-CRATIC WORKERS' PARTY; SWISS SOCIAL DEMOCRATIC PARTY; SOCIAL DEMOCRATIC MOVEMENT EDEK.

POPULAR FRONT. The Popular Front was the name of a temporary alliance between **communists**, social democrats, and other left-wing groups designed to resist fascism. It operated between 1936 and 1939. The idea of the Popular Front was proposed by the **Comintern** in 1935 and was a reversal of its previous policy of denigrating social democrats, who were described as "social fascists." The need for unity among left-wing parties was shown when they were suppressed by fascists in Germany and Austria in 1933 to 1934. Popular Front governments were formed in France under **Léon Blum** (1936–37) and Camille Chautemps (1937–38), in Spain (1936–39), and in Chile (1938–41). Soviet support for the idea of the Popular Front was dropped after the signing of the Non-Aggression Pact between Nazi Germany and the Soviet Union in August 1939.

PORTUGUESE SOCIALIST PARTY [*PARTIDO SOCIALISTA* (PS)]. Although formed in 1876, the PS was mainly notable for its insignificance in Portuguese affairs before the 1970s. The poverty and economic backwardness of Portugal encouraged political extremism and discouraged the development of democratic socialism. **Anarchism** and **syndicalism** were the dominant forces in the **trade unions**, which operated independently of the PS. What little support the PS had was concentrated in the north in and around the town of Oporto. After the monarchy was overthrown in 1910, a constitutional republic was instituted. But Portuguese politics remained highly unstable. In the 1915 election to the lower house on a limited franchise (the illiterate were denied the franchise), the PS received only 5,100 votes, or 1.6 percent of the votes cast. A **communist** party was formed in 1919, but like the PS it attracted limited support. In 1928 both parties were suppressed by a military-based dictatorship led by Oliveira Salazar, who remained in power until his death in 1968.

The PS was reestablished in 1973 by **Màrio Soares** and soon became a full member of the **Socialist International**. After the collapse of the old dictatorship, which had extended beyond the death of Salazar, the PS won 40.7 percent of the valid vote in April 1975, making the PS the largest single party and enabling it to form a government. The PS claimed 96,000 members in 1976. In June 1986 all references to **Marxism** were removed from its declaration of principles. Soares was president of Portugal from 1986 until 1996, when another socialist, Jorge Sampaio, succeeded him. Sampaio was reelected president in 2001 with 55.8 percent of the vote. The PS governed between 1975 and 1978, 1983 and 1985, and 1995 and 2002. It lost the elections of March 2002, after which the confusingly named Social Democratic Party and the Popular Party formed a center-right coalition. In elections to the European Parliament in June 2004 the PS obtained 12 of Portugal's 24 seats, the PS members working in the **Party of European Socialists**, with which their party was affiliated. The PS was returned to power in the parliamentary elections of March 2005, winning an absolute majority of seats—121 of 230 with 45.1 percent of the vote. José Sócrates, who had become leader of the PS the previous year, became prime minister and set to work on Portugal's serious economic problems. *See also* GUTERRES, ANTÓNIO.

POSSIBILISTS. The Possibilists, a breakaway group from the *Fédération des Ouvriers Socialistes de France* (Federation of Socialist

Workers of France), France's first socialist party, formed in June 1880 under **Jules Guesde**. In 1882 the *Fédération* split into two groups: one group followed Guesde and called itself the *Parti Ouvrier Français* (French Workers' Party). The other, under Paul Brousse (1844–1912), called itself *Parti Ouvrier Socialiste Révolutionnaire Français* (French Socialist Revolutionary Workers' Party) and became known as the Possibilists. The Possibilists dropped *Révolutionnaire* from the party title and became the more moderate of the two parties. The split occurred because the Possibilists wanted a decentralized organization whereas the Guesdists favored a centralized **Marxist** party based on the **German Social Democratic Party**. The Possibilists remained committed to the class struggle but wanted to exploit every opportunity possible to advance socialism, such as through local government, social legislation, and alliances with bourgeois radicals. Unlike the party of Guesde, the Possibilists supported the freedom of the **trade unions** to develop in their own way and did not try to direct or dominate them. They were supported by Parisian artisans and the lower levels of the middle class. In March 1888 the Possibilists issued a public invitation for an international conference in Paris in July, which gave rise to the **Second International**.

In 1890 the Possibilists themselves split. Jean Allemane (1843–1935), a survivor of the **Paris Commune** who had been transported to New Caledonia, was the leader of the breakaway group that advocated direct strike action by trade unions and was critical of parliamentary methods. The group adopted the original title of the Possibilists—the *Parti Ouvrier Socialiste Révolutionnaire Français*; in 1896 this party split when an even more radical group broke away and set itself up as the *Alliance Communiste Révolutionnaire* (Revolutionary Communist Alliance). In the meantime, the original Possibilists, the followers of Allemane and the Independent Socialists, formed a federation called the *Parti Socialiste Français* (French Socialist Party) that enabled them to retain their individual organizations. In April 1905, at the behest of the **Second International**, this federation joined with another socialist federation, the *Parti Socialiste de France* (Socialist Party of France) formed by the followers of Guesde and Louis-Auguste Blanqui, to create the *Parti Socialiste Unifié* (United Socialist Party) under **Jean Jaurès**. *See also* FRENCH SOCIALIST PARTY; REVISIONISM.

POST-MARXISM. A **new left** project that has provoked much controversy is post-Marxism, the leading theorists of which are Ernesto Laclau and Chantal Mouffe. Their book *Hegemony and Socialist Strategy: Towards a Radical Democratic Politics*, first published in 1985, argued that a radical, but credible, socialist position would need to jettison almost all of **Marxism**, which perceived a societal division between two opposing classes, thus overlooking the complexity of modern societies. The post-Marxists radically revised **Antonio Gramsci**'s theory of hegemony. Gramsci held that although the strategy must be to seek allies to build and continually secure an alternative hegemony to that of the capitalist class, the proletarian class remains the key agency of social change and the party is its vehicle. Post-Marxism considers that, as it focuses only on the **working-class** movement, this is an essentialist position that should be rejected. Laclau and Mouffe argued that Marxism's privileging the working class had led to authoritarianism. Marxism could not come to terms with forms of differentiation in society. The working class itself was fragmented, there were anticolonial movements not restricted to class, and there were, more recently, the new social movements which campaigned for the recognition of rights in societies characterized by consumer **capitalism** and the **welfare state**. Socialist projects would need to take into account the antiracist, environmentalist, feminist, and gay movements that highlighted other significant forms of oppression in societies.

Laclau and Mouffe argued that a new, hegemonic, liberal-conservative discourse was emerging that sought to articulate the neoliberal defense of the free-market economy with the profoundly antiegalitarian cultural and social traditionalism of conservatism. In response, the Left should expand the chains of equivalents between the various struggles against oppression. Laclau and Mouffe set out to build a theory of hegemony that avoided the problem of class privilege. This involved articulatory practices, the totality of which would constitute a discourse formation. Discourse formation continues as different people and groups begin to feel as though they are oppressed or subordinated. Hegemony would require some form of unifying discourse.

Only hegemony based on an alliance between the Left and the other oppressed groups could counter the neoconservative hegemony. Valuable elements inherent in modern democratic theory could be subject to critique in order to develop them in a pluralist, radical direction. Socialists could thus realize democratic ideals.

Critics of post-Marxism stress that not all social identities are discursively created. The example of working-class material interests is cited. To overlook this is to rule exploitation out of the picture. Also, the logic of equivalence does not allow one to identify which groups might be progressive. Furthermore, democratic discourse is itself shaped by class interest. Finally, there is no reason why privileging the working class in the struggle against capitalism must rule out other groups, many members of which might also be members of the working class, from the struggle.

PRIVATIZATION. *See* NATIONALIZATION.

PRODUCER COOPERATIVES. Cooperative production refers to the collective ownership of enterprises that produce goods or services. Producer cooperatives were widely advocated by a wide range of socialist writers in the nineteenth century as a practical remedy for many of the abuses of **capitalism**. Between 1860 and 1914 producer cooperatives were formed by employees in the United Kingdom to produce coal, flour and bread, footwear, metal goods, and clothing and to provide printing, laundry, and banking and insurance services. Despite these initiatives, producer cooperation was always small-scale and never attained the success of consumer cooperatives. During the twentieth century, the British **Co-operative Wholesale Society** extended its activities into the production of goods and the provision of services, some of which had been pioneered by producer cooperatives. *See also* COOPERATIVE MOVEMENT; GOTHA PROGRAM; MUTUALISM.

PROGRESSIVE SOCIALIST PARTY (PSP) (*HIZB AL-TAQAD-UMMI AL-ISHTIRAKI*). The PSP was founded in Lebanon in 1949 as a Moslem Druse party committed to implementing socialist policies by constitutional means. It was founded by a group led by Kamal Jumblatt (1917–77). After Jumblatt's death his son Walid took over the leadership. The PSP has been a full member of the **Socialist International** since 1980. In the civil **war** of 1975 to 1990 the PLP's militia took part in the fighting. After the civil war Walid Jumblatt supported Syria, which occupied Lebanon. However in the early years of the twenty-first century he called for Syria to leave. For the parliamentary elections of May to June 2005 the PSP, still led by Jumblatt, joined the anti-Syrian Rafik Hariri Martyr List that, winning 72 of 128 seats of which the PSP took 16, gained a majority in parliament.

PROUDHON, PIERRE-JOSEPH (1809–65). Proudhon was the founder of **anarchism** as a political **ideology**. Born near Besançon in the Jura mountains of France, he, almost alone among the main early socialist thinkers, was of the **working class**. His father was a cooper who later tried to be a brewer and tavern keeper. Proudhon completed an apprenticeship as a printer and was largely self-educated. In 1829 he supervised the printing of *Le Nouveau Monde Industriel* (The New Industrial World), one of the main works of **Charles Fourier**, and spent six weeks in his close company. In 1843 he arrived in Lyon to work as a clerk for a water transport company. Lyon was then home to all kinds of socialists. In 1840 he published *Qu'est-ce la propriété?* (What Is Property?), in which he set out the fundamental tenets of anarchist doctrine. He became famous for his declaration that "property is theft," one of the most misused quotations of socialist thought. He did *not* mean that all property was theft; what he condemned was the use of property to exploit the labor of others. Far from condemning all property, he regarded property in the form of the ownership of a house, land, and tools by workers as a right essential for liberty. Even though he later fell out with Proudhon, **Karl Marx** initially admired *Qu'est-ce la propriété?* In 1848 to 1949 Proudhon served as a deputy in the national assembly but was disillusioned by his parliamentary experience. Proudhon was a prolific writer, but not a systematic thinker. His views caused official offense and led to his serving several jail terms.

Apart from his journalism and books, Proudhon's main achievement was his attempt to set up a people's bank in 1849 to foster the exchange of the products of labor between works based on a system of vouchers for labor. Credit was to be provided at a nominal rate. The purpose of the bank was to promote the welfare of independent craftsmen. It attracted 27,000 potential subscribers, but failed to become operational. Before 1890 Proudhon's ideas were very influential in French socialism. His views shaped **syndicalism**, and he counted among his supporters the artist Gustave Courbet (1819–77),

Alexander Herzen (1812–1870), and **Michael Bakunin**. He influenced **Peter Kropotkin** and the Russian novelist Leo Tolstoy (1828–1910). *See also* FEDERALISM; MANIFESTO OF THE SIXTY; MUTUALISM.

PUERTO RICAN INDEPENDENCE PARTY [*PARTIDO INDEPENDENTISTA PUERTORIQUEÑO* (PIP)]. The PIP was founded in 1946. In addition to independence, the PIP campaigned for democracy and social justice. Gílberto Concepción de Gracia was president of the PIP from 1946 until his death in 1968. It was not until 1984 that it gained its first parliamentary representatives. This was because for most of its history, independence was not supported in Puerto Rico; in a referendum in 1967 less than 1 percent of voters supported independence. In about 1987 the PIP became a consultant member of the **Socialist International** (SI), claiming a membership of 6,000. It became a full member of the SI in 1994. In November 2004 the PIP president Rubén Berríos, who was the only PIP senator elected in 1992 and 1996, came in a distant third in the gubernatorial elections.

– R –

RACISM. For most of its history, socialism as a movement paid less attention to racism than it has since World War II. The **Frankfurt Declaration** of 1951 by the **Socialist International** condemned discrimination on the grounds of race. Nevertheless, before 1965 the **Australian Labor Party** officially supported an immigration policy that excluded non-Europeans. The **British Labour Party**, in contrast, adopted a new statement of aims in March 1960 affirming that its "central ideal" was "the brotherhood of man" and accordingly repudiated "discrimination on the grounds of race, color or creed." This statement represented the more usual position taken by socialists. *See also* JEWS.

RADICAL CIVIC UNION [*UNIÓN CÍVICA RADICAL* (UCR)]. Formed as a party in the tradition of progressive **liberalism** in 1890, the Civic Union (*Unión Cívica*) sought to reform the fraudulent presidential electoral system in Argentina. In 1891 the Union split into two parts, one of which agreed to a compromise with the government that the other, the UCR, could not accept. The UCR, popularly known as the Radical Party, continued to press for secret, universal, and obligatory voting. The methods it employed included abstentions and uprisings with the support of some sectors of the armed forces. In 1912 the reforms were introduced. In 1916 Hipólito Yrigolen of the UCR was elected president and moved toward the social-democratic tradition with the introduction of a minimum wage.

Although it retained the word *radical* in its title, the UCR became a moderate, center-left party. The UCR retained the presidency and controlled both houses of the Argentinean Congress until the coup of 1930 that brought military dictatorship until 1938, when constitutional politics was restored. The UCR held the presidency until 1943, when a coup brought another period of military dictatorship that lasted until 1946, when the Peronist movement took power in elections. In 1956 a group that was opposed to dialogue with Juan Perón split from the UCR and formed the Intransigent Radicals. The UCR formed governments from 1958 to 1966. From the 1940s to the early 1980s Argentina alternated between unstable democracy, often under the Peronist movement, and military dictatorship until 1982, when the Argentinean junta collapsed after the war with the United Kingdom. In the new presidential democratic republic Raúl Alfonsín of the UCR was elected president in 1983 and the UCR won 129 of the 254 seats in the Chamber of Deputies that year. However, inability to deal satisfactorily with Argentina's economic problems led the UCR to lose power to the Peronists in the presidential elections in 1989. The UCR also fared poorly in the elections to half of the seats in the Chamber of Deputies that year, taking only 47 of the 127 seats with 29 percent of the vote.

In 1999 Fernando de la Rúa Bruno of the UCR, in an alliance with the left-wing Front for a Country with Solidarity (*Frente País Solidario*—FREPASO), won the presidential elections. Also in 1999 the UCR gained full membership in the **Socialist International**. Argentina's economic problems escalated and a corruption scandal emerged. The public lost confidence in the administration and De la Rúa resigned under public pressure in 2001. A UCR alliance with FREPASO in elections to half of the seats in the Chamber of Deputies in October 2001 gained 35 seats in total with 23.1 percent of the vote, resulting in the alliance holding 88 seats in total, of which the UCR held 71. In the presidential elections of April 2003 the UCR candidate Leopoldo Raúl Guido Moreau won only 2.3 percent of the vote. After elections to half of the seats in the Chamber of Deputies in October 2003 the UCR held 46 of the 256 seats. *See also* ARGENTINEAN SOCIALIST PARTY.

RELIGION. There was often a strong undercurrent of hostility toward organized religion within socialism, particularly where it was allied with conservative or reactionary governments or where it diverted the **working class** from the economic and social struggle for improvement as defined by **Karl Marx**. But there was also, usually, recognition that individuals have a right to a religion. The association of socialism with militant antireligious policies was a feature of **Leninism**. Socialist/social-democratic **political parties** in the 1890s were well aware of the divisive nature of religion as they worked to create and maintain the united working class necessary for political reform. This compromise view was evident in the **Erfurt Program** of the **German Social Democratic Party** (*Sozialdemokratische Partei Deutschlands*—SPD), which demanded that religion be declared a private matter, that all state expenditure on churches and religious bodies cease, and that churches and religious bodies be treated as private associations, that is, a complete separation of church and state. It also demanded that **education** be completely secularized. The Brunn Program (1901) of the **Austrian Social Democratic Party** also demanded that civil marriage be compulsory.

Although many socialists tended to regard socialism as rational (as opposed to religion which was seen as irrational) not all observers agreed. Gustav Le Bon (1841–1931), a pioneer of social psychology and an unsympathetic observer of the rise of socialism, wrote *The Psychology of Socialism* (1899), in which he presented socialism as essentially a religious movement. Some socialists themselves, including **Claude-Henri Saint-Simon**, have argued that there is a strong link between socialism and **Christianity**, and **Christian socialism** has sometimes attracted considerable support. The **Pakistan People's Party** has argued for a combination of socialist and Islamic values, and there is a **World Labor Zionist Movement**. There is also an **International League of Religious Socialists**. In contrast, Leninism was distinctive in socialist thought for its hostility to all forms of religion as a means of oppressing the working class. The socialist republican government of Spain in the 1930s was also exceptional in its antireligious policies.

Public opinion polls conducted since 1950 indicate that there is still a significant divide between support for social-democratic parties by religion in Western Europe, particularly in France, Italy, and the Netherlands. The **Godesberg Program** of the German SPD was careful to proclaim in 1958 that "socialism was no substitute for religion" and it respected religious freedom. The **British Labour Party** officially rejected discrimination on the grounds of religion in its statement of aims in 1960. *See also* DUTCH LABOR PARTY; SPANISH SOCIALIST WORKERS' PARTY; TEMPERANCE.

RENNER, KARL (1870–1950). Austrian social-democratic theorist and politician Karl Renner was born in Unter-Tannowitz, Bohemia, and came from a peasant background, which was unusual for a socialist of the time. A moderate socialist, he qualified as a lawyer at the University of Vienna, joined the **Austrian Social Democratic Party**, and represented the party in the parliament from 1907. After the collapse of the monarchical government in November 1918, he became chancellor heading a coalition government, a post he held until October 1919 and again from October 1919 to June 1920. Because of the severe territorial losses suffered by Austria following the dismemberment of the Austro-Hungarian empire, Renner supported union (*Anschluss*) with Germany, but the Allies rejected this. In his pre-1920 writings Renner gave much attention to the problems of the various nationalities within the former empire. As chancellor he advocated that Austria play a constructive role in international affairs. Identified on the right of the party from 1920 onward, Renner was president of the Austrian parliament from 1930 to 1933. He was jailed for a year by the regime of Engelbert Dollfuss, but released. In 1938 he made a public statement in apparent support of Adolf Hitler's takeover of Austria, but this seems not to have been made voluntarily.

Renner moved out of Vienna during World War II and was associated with the underground resistance to the Nazis. He was chancellor once more after the end of the German occupation in April 1945 as head of a coalition government that declared its independence from Germany and threw out all the Nazi laws. In December 1945 he was elected president by parliament, a position he held until his death. *See also* ADLER, VICTOR.

REPUBLICAN PEOPLE'S PARTY [*CUMHURIYET HALK PARTISI* (CHP)]. The CHP is a Turkish left-wing party that traces its origins to the People's Party (*Halk Firkasi*—HF) created in 1923 by the founder of modern Turkey, Kemal Atatürk. The HF became the Republican People's Party (*Cumhuriyet Halk Firkasi*—CHF) in 1924 and was renamed the CHP (the English title remaining the same as before) in 1935. Turkey became a multiparty democracy in 1950 but the CHP did not govern again until 1961. The CHP lost the elections of 1965 but, led by Bülent Ecevit, was successful at those of 1973. It lost power again at the elections of 1975 but in 1977 formed a coalition government with some smaller parties. This government collapsed in 1979 and the military took power by means of a coup d'état in 1980. The military government banned the CHP and other existing parties.

The CHP was revived in 1992 by 21 members of the Social Democratic Party (*Sosyal Demokat Parti*—SODEP). In February 1995 the Social Democratic Populist Party (*Sosyal Demokrat Halkçi Parti*—SHP) became part of the reformed CHP. The SHP had been formed in Turkey in 1985 by the merger of the Populist Party (*Halkçi Partisi*) that was formed in 1983 and the SODEP, which was formed at about the same time but not allowed to contest the 1983 election. The SHP received 24.8 percent of the vote in the 1987 elections and became the main opposition party. The SHP became a full member of the **Socialist International** (SI) in 1990.

The CHP took the SHP's place in the SI. In the parliamentary elections of November 2002 the CHP obtained 178 of the 550 seats with 19.4 percent of the vote, losing to the Justice and Development Party that won a landslide victory. The Democratic Left Party (*Demokratik Sol Parti*), which had been formed in 1985, was led by the former CHP leader Ecevit, and had governed in coalition and minority governments since 1998, gained only 1.2 percent of the vote—below the 10 percent needed for parliamentary representation.

REVISIONISM. As a general term for a doctrine that emerged within socialism around 1880, *revisionism* advocated constitutional, gradual means (rather than revolution based on class struggle) to achieve socialist objectives. Revisionism, or reformism, was foreshadowed by **Louis Blanc**. In France, revisionism dates from 1882 with the **Possibilists**. In the United Kingdom, the first systematic form of revisionism was **Fabianism**, which influenced the ideas of **Eduard Bernstein**, with whom revisionism in continental Europe is traditionally associated. In Germany, Bernstein's ideas were anticipated by a Munich socialist deputy, Georg von Vollar (1850–1932) who argued in 1891 for the importance of immediate practical reforms and laws to protect labor, regulate business cartels, and reform **taxation**. In France, the foremost revisionist in the 1900s was **Alexandre Millerand**. Because it accepted the fundamental economic relationships of **capitalism**, revisionism was condemned by **Marxists**, at conferences by the **Second International**, and later by **communists**. Yet revisionism recognized the enormous practical difficulty of making far-reaching social and economic changes quickly. In practice, if not in theory, it was adopted by the social-democratic parties in countries with democratic, parliamentary governments.

REVOLUTIONARY DEMOCRATIC PARTY [*PARTIDO REVOLUCIONARIO DEMOCRÁTICO* (PRD)]. The PRD was formed in Panama in1979, following the legalization of **political parties** the previous year, after a decade in which the military regime had banned them. The PRD was formed by the military ruler Omar Torrijos who, two years earlier, had gained enormous popularity for negotiating the treaty that led to the transfer of the Panama Canal from the United States in 2000. The PRD was initially designed to unite the pro-Torrijos forces in Panama. These forces ranged from left to right, but the dominant strain became the social-democratic one. The PRD retained close ties with the military for many years. In the parliamentary elections of 1980 the PRD won 40 percent of the vote and in 1984 27.4 percent. This was still enough to give the PRD 34 of 67 seats. The party supported the successful presidential candidate that year. Along with a range of other parties the PRD participated in coalition governments throughout the 1980s. The PRD also became a consulting member of the **Socialist International** (SI) in 1986. Nevertheless Panama was dominated by General Manuel Antonio Noriega, who had come to effectively control the country in 1983. Like Torrijos, Noriega manipulated the PRD and the presidency. Although the 1989 presidential elections resulted in a large majority voting for anti-Noriega and anti-PRD candidates, his regime annulled the elections and continued to dominate until the United States removed him from power later that year and the electoral result stood.

In the parliamentary elections of May 1994 the PRD took 32 of 72 seats and subsequently led a coalition government. In September 1994 Ernesto Perez Balladares won the presidency for the PRD with 33 percent of the vote. In May 1999 Martin Torrijos, son of the PRD founder, contested the presidential elections for the PRD but lost with 37 percent of the vote. Also in May 1999 the PRD obtained 35 of 72 seats in the parliamentary elections and subsequently formed another coalition government. After the 1999 elections Martin Torrijos became PRD leader and began to reform the party, removing some members who had been established figures since his father's regime. In 2003 the PRD gained full membership in the SI. In May 2004 Torrijos won the presidential elections with 47.5 percent of the vote. In the parliamentary elections held on the same day the PRD won 41 of 78 seats and subsequently once again formed a coalition government.

REVOLUTIONARY SOCIALIST LEAGUE. *See* MILITANT TENDENCY.

ROMANIAN SOCIAL DEMOCRATIC PARTY [*PARTIDUL SOCIAL DEMOCRAT* **(PSD)].** The roots of the PSD can be traced to the formation of the Social Democratic Party of Workers of Romania (*Partidul Social-Democrat al Muncitorilor din România*—PSDMR) in 1893. The first manifestation of socialism in Romania occurred in 1834 when Teodor Diamant (1810–41), a minor aristocrat, established an **agricultural**-industrial community of 60 people at Scăieni, north of Bucharest. It was based directly on the "phalanstery" concept of **Charles Fourier**. The community was closed down by the ruler of Wallacia in 1836. Interest in socialism revived in the late 1870s. It was strongest among university students studying law and medicine and was stimulated by Russian exiles, particularly Constantin Dobrogeanu-Gherea (1855–1920), who was the main source of **Marxist** theory in the country. From its formation the PSDMR sent representatives to all congresses of the **Second International** apart from that at Amsterdam in 1904. The leadership of the PSDMR was dominated by intellectuals. Although the party had 6,000 members by 1897, most were confined to Bucharest. Ideological differences, as well as financial weakness, ensured the party stayed weak.

In February 1900 there was a split between those who wanted to maintain a separate socialist party and those (mainly intellectuals) who wanted to merge all **political parties** that wanted democracy. It was not until after 1905 that socialism and the **trade unions** revived. The Socialist Union was formed by socialists from the PSDMR and trade unions to coordinate their political activity, but apart from strikes and rural unrest, little was achieved. In February 1910 the Union decided to reform the PSDMR first as the Social Democratic party of Romania (*Partidul Social Democrat Român*—PSDR) and then the PSD. At the 1911 election the PSD campaigned on a platform of universal **suffrage**, a graduated income **tax**, and **social security**, but it received only 1,459 votes out of 73,633 cast (2 percent). The progress of socialism was hampered by a restricted franchise, a rigged electoral system, a lack of industrialization, and the overwhelmingly rural (82 percent in 1913) character of Romanian society.

The PSD sent a representative to the **Zimmerwald Conference** in 1915, but was able to do little else. In February 1921 the party split: 18 members of the executive opted to join the **Comintern** and 12 dissented. The dissidents reorganized the PSD, which joined the **International Working Union of Socialist Parties**. In 1921 the Communist Party was outlawed and only one social-democratic candidate, Jacob Pistiner (deceased 1930) was elected as a deputy in 1922; he became Romania's representative to the **Labor and Socialist International**. In 1926 Pistiner lost his parliamentary position because the government passed a law denying representation to political parties that polled less than 2 percent of the vote. In a climate of electoral manipulation and effective government by dictatorship, the PSD could do little in the 1920s and 1930s.

The PSD was forced to merge with the Romanian Communist Party in February 1948. However, it effectively became a party in exile during the period of **communist** rule and was a consultant member of the **Socialist International** (SI) from 1963. On 24 December 1989, the day before the communist period ended with the execution of President Nicolae Ceausescu, the PSD was recreated under the title PSDR and succeeded in gaining legal recognition as the legitimate continuation of the pre-1948 party.

Meanwhile, immediately after the execution of Ceausescu, some former communists formed the National Salvation Front (*Frontul Salvării Naționale*—FSN), which took over the governance of Romania and won the elections to the Chamber of Deputies in May 1990, taking 263 of the 396 seats with 66.31 percent of the vote. Ion

Iliescu of the FSN was elected president of Romania that month with 85 percent of the vote. A struggle for power within the FSN led Iliescu to withdraw his faction and form the Democratic National Salvation Front (*Frontul Democrat al Salvării Naționale*—FDSN) in April 1992. The FDSN contested the September 1992 elections and, after receiving 117 of the 341 seats with 27.72 percent of the vote, participated in a coalition government. In October that year Iliescu was reelected as president with 61.43 percent of the vote at the runoff between the leading two candidates. The FDSN merged with three small parties in July 1993 to form the Party of Social Democracy in Romania (*Partidul Democrației Sociale din România*—PDSR).

In November 1996 Iliescu lost the presidency to the center-right led by Emil Constantinescu. The PDSR lost the elections to the Chamber of Deputies that month to the Romanian Democratic Convention coalition. The PDSR took 91 of 343 seats with 21.52 percent of the vote. The PSDR, which had been readmitted as a consultant member of the SI in 1992, enjoyed a minor revival at those elections. Operating in the Social Democratic Union (*Uniunea Social Democrata*) that won 53 seats with 12.93 percent of the vote, the PSDR obtained 10 seats.

In 2000, the PDSR and PSDR contested the parliamentary and presidential elections together, along with the centrist Humanist Party (*Partidul Umanist Român*—PUR), in the Romanian Social Democratic Pole (*Polul Democrat Social din România*). In November this coalition won the elections to the Chamber of Deputies, taking 155 of 345 seats with 36.61 percent of the vote. The PDSR's Adrian Nastase became prime minister in a minority government supported by centrist parties. In December Iliescu was reelected president, taking 66.83 percent of the vote in the runoff elections with the votes of his center-right opponents, as Romanians acted to prevent a neofascist candidate from taking power. On 16 January 2001 the PDSR and PSDR merged to become the PSD. The PSD gained full membership in the SI in October that year.

In 2004 the constitution did not allow Iliescu to run for another term. Nastase stood as presidential candidate for the PSD but lost by 51.2 percent to 48.8 percent in the second round in mid-December to the centrist candidate Traian Basescu. The parliamentary elections in November 2004 failed to produce an outright winner. The PSD campaigned in an alliance with the PUR entitled the National Union, which obtained 132 of 332 seats in the Chamber of Deputies with 36.8 percent of the vote, and 47 of 147 seats in the Senate with 37.2 percent. Of those seats the PSD won 113 and 36 respectively. However, the PSD lost power as Basescu's centrist alliance won the support of some smaller parties—including the PUR, which swung to the right—and formed a government.

– S –

SACCO-VANZETTI CASE. The Sacco-Vanzetti case concerned the conviction and execution by electrocution of two Italian **anarchists**, Nicola Sacco and Bartolomeo Vanzetti, in Massachusetts in August 1927. They were charged with the murder of a paymaster and the theft of more than $15,000 from a shoe factory in 1921. Sacco and Vanzetti always denied the charges. It was widely suspected they were blamed because they were anarchists rather than because they were genuinely guilty. Their case and their eloquent final statement attracted international support. One of the socialists who expressed such support was **Harold Laski**. The case also inspired literary works such as *Boston* (1928) by **Upton Sinclair**. In 1977 the governor of Massachusetts exonerated Sacco and Vanzetti of any wrongdoing.

SAINT-IMIER INTERNATIONAL. After the victory of the **Marxists** over the **anarchists** at the Hague congress of the **International Workingmen's Association** in 1872, a mainly anarchist congress was held at Saint-Imier, Switzerland, to found a rival international. At its Geneva congress in 1873 this body attracted delegates from Spain, Italy, the Jura mountains, France, the Netherlands, Belgium, and the United Kingdom. At the 1874 congress at Brussels, the Lassalleans were also represented. Subsequent congresses were held at Berne (1876) and Verviers in the Netherlands (1877); this last congress attracted delegates from Mexico, Uruguay, and Argentina.

SAINT-SIMON, CLAUDE-HENRI DE ROUVROY, COMTE DE (1760–1825). Social and religious theorist Claude-Henri Saint-Simon was born in Paris. Despite his aristocratic lineage—his family claimed descent from Charlemagne (who once appeared to Saint-

Simon in a dream)—Saint-Simon was a democrat. He fought in five campaigns during the American War of Independence. He returned to France and stayed there during the revolution. In 1825 he published his proposal for a new **religion**, *Nouveau Christianisme* (New Christianity), in which he advocated a return to **Christianity**'s traditional concern for the poor. He carried his concern for social justice to his works on the efficient reorganization of the economy so as to give the productive and useful members of society a greater share of **wealth**, although he never explained how this was to be done. As a result, his ideas were subject to varying interpretations. After his death his followers formed a religious **commune** but it soon fell apart. Saint-Simon's ideas were studied by individuals as diverse as **John Stuart Mill**, **Karl Marx**, and **Friedrich Engels**. Marx and Engels referred to Saint-Simon in their critique of **utopian socialism**.

SANDINISTA NATIONAL LIBERATION FRONT [*FRENTE SANDINISTA DE LIBERACIÓN NACIONAL* (FSLN)]. Formed in 1961, the FSLN started as a revolutionary organization to wage guerilla **war** on the Somoza dynastic dictatorship that had ruled Nicaragua since 1936. Following independence from Spain in 1821 power in Nicaragua alternated between antagonistic and often warring Liberal and Conservative parties, representing small and large landowners respectively. The peasant majority lived in poverty during Conservative rule from 1857 to 1893. The Liberals then took power, drawing hostility from the United States. U.S. marines were dispatched to back a Conservative uprising in 1908 and bring down the Liberal regime. In 1912 and 1926 the U.S. marines crushed Liberal revolts. A Liberal officer, Augusto César Sandino, began a guerilla campaign against the U.S. occupation. In 1934 Sandino was assassinated and in 1936 Anastasio Somoza seized power.

The formation of the FSLN was a response to the poverty and repression. The earthquake that destroyed much of the capital, Managua, in 1972 worsened conditions of ordinary people. In the revolution of 1979 the FSLN overthrew Anasasio Somoza II. A revolutionary government of national reconstruction was formed on 20 July 1979. A 51-member council of state was later created. The FSLN began to introduce reforms that protected the long-neglected rights of **women** and workers, brought about agrarian reform, and began initiatives in **education** and **health care**. In 1984 the FSLN held and won general elections that were deemed fair by most international observers and analysts. The FSLN leader Daniel Ortega Saavedra became president of Nicaragua.

The United States, which did not accept the results, backed the Contra rebels in a counterrevolutionary war. The war undermined many of the reforms, as did the fragility of the FSLN's credit policies and subsidization of basic necessities with export revenues. The FSLN continued with democratic reform, introducing a constitution in 1987 that combined **liberal** practices and norms with the revolutionary aims for society. In 1990 the FSLN held general elections but lost to the U.S.-backed National Opposition Union (*Unión Nacional Opositora*—UNO) coalition. The FSLN accepted the result, Violeta Chamorro assumed the presidency, and the new administration set about dismantling many of the postrevolutionary reforms and introducing a neoliberal policy of structural adjustment. The FSLN regained significant support in Nicaragua and remained the main opposition party. Nevertheless, a split in 1994 led to the formation of the Sandinista Renovation Movement (*Movimiento de Renovación Sandinista*—MRS). The split damaged the FSLN's electoral prospects.

The FSLN secured full membership in the **Socialist International** in 1996. With Ortega still leader the FSLN failed to retake power in the 1997 elections, losing to an anti-Sandinista Liberal Alliance by 37 seats to 42. The FSLN achieved success in the local elections of 2000, winning at the expense of the unstable Alliance. Ortega was reelected as leader in 1998. Before the presidential election of 2001 he stressed that he would recognize private property rights and seek a good relationship with the United States. Nevertheless, he lost to the businessman Enrique Bolaños who left his Liberal Constitutional Party to form the Alliance for the Republic. Ortega obtained 42.3 percent of the vote. At the parliamentary elections of 2001 the FSLN won 43 of the 90 contested seats (three of 93 were not contested) with 42.1 percent of the vote. In 2002 Ortega was once again reelected leader of the FSLN. In 2005 the FSLN entered into an unlikely alliance with the Liberal opponents of Bolaños. This alliance controlled parliament and entered into a power struggle with the president.

SARAGAT, GIUSEPPE (1898–1988). Italian social-democratic politician Giuseppe Saragat was born in Turin into a **middle-class**

household. After graduating from the University of Turin with a degree in economics and commerce, he worked as a bank clerk. He joined the **Italian Socialist Party** (*Partito Socialista Italiano*—PSI) in Turin and became its secretary. With the imposition of **Benito Mussolini**'s dictatorship, Saragat was forced into exile in Austria and France between 1926 and 1943. After Mussolini's fall, he returned to Italy where he helped fight the Nazi occupation; he was captured by them, but escaped. Between 1945 and 1946 he served as minister without portfolio and as ambassador to France. On his return, he was elected president of the constitutional assembly at a time when a new constitution was being drawn up. Saragat was a pro-Western and anticommunist politician. In 1947 he led a breakaway socialist party from the PSI because of its cooperation with the **communists**. He was secretary of this party, the Italian Workers' Socialist Party, from 1947 until it merged with others in 1952 to form the Italian Democratic Socialist Party (*Partito Socialista Democratico Italiano*), of which he was secretary until 1964 and from 1975 to 1983. He was deputy prime minister of Italy from 1947 to 1949 and from 1954 to 1957. He was minister for foreign affairs from 1963 to 1964 and was president of Italy from 1964 to 1971, the first socialist to hold this post. His political career was notable for his efforts to improve housing, **health**, and **education**.

SAVAGE, MICHAEL JOSEPH (1872–1940). Born in Benalla, Victoria, Australia, Michael Savage was the first prime minister to come from the **New Zealand Labour Party**. After leaving high school in 1886, he worked in various jobs before becoming secretary of the Political Labor Council of Victoria in 1900. He also opened a cooperative store. In 1907 he emigrated to New Zealand and was elected to the House of Representatives in 1919. He became leader of the NZLP in 1933 and prime minister in 1935 after the party's electoral victory. He held office until his death. Savage's government brought in a comprehensive range of social and labor laws that laid the foundations of the **welfare state** in New Zealand until the 1990s. These measures included a 40-hour working week, a minimum wage, compulsory **trade unionism** for many employees, a housing program, increased public works, and, most importantly, the Social Security Act (1938). Savage's government supported the League of Nations and the United Kingdom's increased defense efforts.

SCANDILUX. A forum set up by the social-democratic parties of Scandinavia and the Low Countries in 1980 to coordinate opposition to the deployment of Pershing and Cruise missiles by the United States in Western Europe. Although these **nuclear weapons** were deployed in 1983, Scandilux continued to act as a forum for debate about arms control.

SCHEIDEMANN, PHILIPP (1865–1939). German social-democratic politician Philipp Scheidemann is best remembered as the man who proclaimed a provisional republican government from the balcony of the *Reichstag* (parliament) on 9 November 1918 without any authorization from his party. Born in Kassel, Scheidemann became a journalist and was elected to parliament for the **German Social Democratic Party** in 1903. In October 1918 he was appointed minister without portfolio in the government of Prince Max of Baden. He proclaimed the republic to forestall the radical socialist **Karl Liebknecht**, who was said to be planning to proclaim a Soviet-style government following the example of **V. I. Lenin**. Scheidemann was a member of the provisional government that took over after the collapse of the monarchy and became the first chancellor of the Weimar Republic after the elections in February 1919. He was strongly opposed to **Leninism** and militarism. As chancellor he refused to ratify the Versailles Treaty and resigned his post on 20 June 1919. He was replaced by **Gustav Adolf Bauer**. Scheidemann was to the left of **Friedrich Ebert**, whom he disliked. He returned to his native Kassel where he served as mayor until 1925 and survived an assassination attempt in 1922. After Adolf Hitler came to power, he fled Germany and died in Copenhagen.

SCHMIDT, HELMUT HEINRICH WALDEMAR (1918–). Born in Barmbeck, Germany, Helmut Schmidt was chancellor for the **German Social Democratic Party** (*Sozialdemokratische Partei Deutschlands*—SPD) from 1974 to 1982. Conscripted during World War II, he was captured by the British and joined the SPD while a prisoner of war. After World War II, he qualified as an economist and was elected to the *Bundestag* (parliament) in 1953. He succeeded **Willy Brandt** as chancellor in May 1974 and held the position until his defeat in 1982. Schmidt came to power at a difficult time in the international economy that saw the ending of the post-1945 boom and large increases in petroleum prices. He was politically more conservative than Brandt, and his administration emphasized sound economic management rather than social reform; this was shown by the careful control of government expenditure to dampen inflation and a tacit agreement with **trade unions** in 1976 to provide economic stability and employment growth in return for restraint by unions in making pay claims. In foreign policy he supported the policy of improved relations with the **communist**-run Eastern Europe (*Ostpolitik*) and, with **James Callaghan**, the U.S. proposal for the deployment of the neutron bomb in Europe, a position that cost him support among young and **middle-class** supporters of the SPD. He resigned from parliament in 1987.

SCHRÖDER, GERHARD (1944–). Coming from a poor background from which he began his working life as an apprentice salesman, Gerhard Schröder rose to become Social Democratic chancellor of Germany in 1998. He was born in Mossenberg, Lower Saxony. Having gained the required qualifications in his spare time, he left his apprenticeship to study law at Göttingen University. After joining the **German Social Democratic Party** (*Sozialdemokratische Partei Deutschlands*—SPD) in 1978, he was enthusiastic and ambitious and soon began to play a prominent role. His first major office was head of the party's **youth** organization. Only two years after joining the party he was elected to represent it in the *Bundestag* (the lower house in Germany's federal parliament). In 1990 he was elected minister president, or prime minister of his home *Land* (state) within Germany.

In 1998 the SPD nominated Schröder to challenge the Christian Democrat Helmut Kohl, who had been chancellor since 1982, defeating a succession of Social Democratic rivals for the office. With Schröder as the candidate the SPD performed strongly in the elections and, in coalition with the Green Party, secured a majority in the *Bundestag*. Under Schröder the SPD also held a majority in the *Bundesrat* (upper house comprising representatives from the 16 *Länder*) for a short period. Within one year the latter majority had disappeared. Nevertheless, in April 1999 Schröder took over the chairmanship of his party, after the resignation of Oscar Lafontaine, and was able to consolidate his position in December that year when he was reelected chairman with a higher margin of support than he had achieved in April.

Influenced by **Tony Blair**, Schröder proceeded to move his party further toward the center ground. He adopted the idea of the "third way," in German *neue Mitte*. In 2002 Schröder's coalition was returned to power with a reduced majority. His **welfare state** reforms and the rise in **unemployment** that Germany experienced during his tenure eroded his popularity considerably. Under party pressure in 2004 he was replaced as leader by Franz Müntefering, but remained chancellor of Germany. After losing the key regional election in North-Rhine Westphalia in May 2005 Schröder announced that he would seek to bring forward the date of the next general election, gaining President Horst Koehler's backing in July. The SPD was narrowly beaten by the conservative Christian Democrats in the elections that went ahead in September 2005. Schröder served as caretaker chancellor while the parties entered negotiations which resulted in a grand coalition between the SDP and the Christian Democratic Union/Christian Social Union under the conservative Chancellor Angela Merkel.

SCHUMACHER, KURT (1895–1952). Kurt Schumacher was a central figure in the successful revival of the **German Social Democratic Party** (*Sozialdemokratische Partei Deutschlands*—SPD) after World War II. He was born in Kuhm, Prussia, and his father was a merchant. He obtained a doctorate in political science from Münster University. As a result of military service during World War I, his right arm was amputated. He joined the SPD in 1920 and worked as an editor for socialist publications and a legislator. He was a member of the *Reichstag* from 1930 to 1933. An ardent anti-Nazi, Schumacher was arrested under the infamous Enabling Law and spent most of the period from 1934 to 1945 in Dachau concentration camp; like many other SPD and **trade union** leaders imprisoned there, he suffered greatly. Despite his experiences, he was authorized by other SPD figures to convene a conference at Wennigsen, near Hanover, in August 1945. This conference, which was held in October 1945, reestablished the SPD largely with survivors from the pre-1933 years. In May 1946 Schumacher was elected chairman of the SPD and as leader sought to broaden the appeal of the party to include the **middle class** and Catholics.

SCOTTISH SOCIALIST PARTY (SSP). Formed in 1998, the SSP declares itself to be **anticapitalist**, proindependence, **internationalist**, anti-imperialist, and democratic. Its most widely recognized member is former convener Tommy Sheridan. He was elected as a Glasgow City councilor while serving a jail sentence for his activities against the Community Charge (poll tax), which was introduced by the British Conservative Party in 1990. The Charge was replaced with the Council Tax in 1993. Although it has strong roots in the Trotskyist Scottish Militant Labour, which was itself formed from the **Militant Tendency**, the SSP operates in part as a parliamentary socialist party, which campaigns in British general elections and elections for the Scottish Parliament. Sheridan was elected to the newly formed Scottish Parliament in 1999. In 2003 five more SSP members were elected to the Scottish Parliament. Sheridan stood down as leader in November 2004 and in February 2005 Colin Fox was elected leader with the backing of Sheridan. The SSP is active outside Parliament, for example, supporting **trade unions**, campaigning against **nuclear weapons**, and working on local and international campaigns. It did not win any seats at the general elections of May 2005.

SCULLIN, JAMES HENRY (1876–1953). Australian Labor Party (ALP) prime minister from October 1929 to January 1932, James Scullin was born at Trawalla, Victoria. Largely self-educated, he joined the ALP in 1903 and was a member of the federal parliament from 1910 to 1913. He was a leading anticonscriptionist during the campaigns of 1916 and 1917. He reentered federal parliament in 1922 and became leader of the parliamentary ALP members in 1928 and prime minister after the national election in October 1929. However, the ALP failed to win a majority in the upper house, the Senate, whose members frustrated his government's efforts to ease the very high **unemployment** caused by the Depression. His government faced opposition from the ALP in New South Wales, led by the colorful **John T. Lang**, and from the conservative board of the Commonwealth Bank. His own cabinet was divided about the best **policies** to adopt toward the Depression. His government was defeated in the election of December 1931 by the newly formed United Australia Party. Scullin remained leader of the ALP in the federal parliament until 1935 and was a member of parliament until 1949. The experience of the Scullin government with the banks convinced his minister for defense, **J. B. Chifley**, to try to **nationalize** the banks when he was prime minister in the late 1940s.

SECOND INTERNATIONAL. The more common name for the Second International Workingmen's Association was the Second International, which was a loose association of socialist parties founded in Paris in 1889 and dissolved in 1914 when World War I began. Its founding was a logical extension of the growth of socialist **political parties** as well as international organizations of **trade unions** in Western Europe in particular occupations. The initiatives for the Second International began in 1887; in September, the British Trades Union Congress (TUC) voted for an international conference to press claims for an eight-hour working day, and in October the **German Social Democratic Party** voted to convene an international socialist conference at its congress at St. Gallen, Switzerland. In November 1888 the parliamentary committee of the TUC organized a conference in London that was attended by French and Belgian socialists. On 11 March 1889 Paul Brousse (1844–1912), the leader of the **Possibilists**, issued a public invitation to attend an international conference in July in Paris.

A division quickly occurred between the **Marxists**, following **Friedrich Engels**, and the others, including the Possibilists and most of the United Kingdom union leaders. As a result, two conferences were held at different venues; the Marxists held theirs at a hall in the rue Petrelle; the Possibilists conference was held at a hall in the rue de Lancy, although there was some movement by delegates between the conferences. The Marxists' conference was attended by 391 delegates, mainly from France and Germany but also some from the United States. The Possibilists' conference passed resolutions in favor of the eight-hour day, better working conditions, and standing armies.

After the inaugural Paris congress, the Second International met at Brussels (1891), Zürich (1893), London (1896), Paris (1900), Amsterdam (1904), Stuttgart (1910), and Basel, Switzerland (1912). Vienna was to have been the venue for the congress in August 1914 but with the outbreak of World War I it was changed to Paris and then canceled. A congress was planned for Stockholm in 1917 but had to be abandoned.

The Second International was subject to many disagreements, but it did manage to initiate 1 May as a day for international demonstrations by trade unions in favor of the eight-hour day. May Day, which owed its origins to Labor Day in the United States, was first celebrated in this way in Europe in 1890. The Second International, which did not have a secretariat until 1900, proved unable to agree on many important issues, specifically whether socialism could be achieved through parliamentary means and whether socialist parties should join in parliamentary coalitions with other parties, a practice condemned by the 1905 conference in Amsterdam. The Second International opposed **anarchism**, and after 1896 anarchists were excluded from its membership. The outbreak of a European war in which **nationalism** would override the interests of the **working class** was foreseen by the Second International, which tried to prevent it. Nationalism proved stronger and destroyed the organization. A number of bodies since 1914 have claimed to be the rightful successor to the Second International. *See also* COMINTERN; LABOR AND SOCIALIST INTERNATIONAL.

SECOND INTERNATIONAL WORKINGMEN'S ASSOCIATION. *See* SECOND INTERNATIONAL.

SHAW, GEORGE BERNARD (1856–1950). Born in Dublin, Ireland, George Bernard Shaw went on to achieve international renown as a dramatist and a critic. A concern with social problems led him to attend a **Henry George** lecture and made him interested in socialism. He was familiar with **Marxism** and **anarchism**. In the early 1880s he wrote five failed socialist novels, but was only able to get one published, *An Unsocial Socialist* (1883). In 1884 he joined the Fabian Society in London and made the acquaintance of **Sidney Webb**. He edited an English edition of *The Co-operative Commonwealth* (1884) by **Laurence Grönlund** and *Fabian Essays* (1889), a work that brought **Fabianism** to the attention of educated readers in Britain. Shaw's other works included *The Early History of the Fabian Society* (1892) and *The Intelligent Woman's Guide to Socialism and Capitalism* (1928). Like **Robert Blatchford**, he supported the Boer War. His socialism, like other aspects of his life, was eccentric. Like other socialists he was opposed to unearned income, but unlike many cared little for democracy and favored rule by experts, even if it meant dictatorship.

SHELLEY, PERCY BYSSHE (1792–1822). Although he wrote and indeed died shortly before the word *socialism* was coined, Percy

Bysshe Shelley was concerned with social problems and issues that would concern socialists. Born in Sussex, England, he was educated at Eton and then Oxford, until he was expelled at the age of 19. In many of his poems, including *Queen Mab*, *The Mask of Anarchy*, and *Prometheus Unbound*, he attacked social inequality, exploitation, and the use of **religion** to justify oppression. He was ever concerned with social improvement and believed that the overturning of oppression and exploitation was a historical inevitability. He drowned on a boating voyage.

SINCLAIR, UPTON BEALL (1878–1968). American author and unorthodox socialist Upton Sinclair was born in Baltimore into an unsuccessful branch of a prosperous and prominent family. His father was an inebriate and a liquor salesman. Sinclair worked his way through college and supported himself by journalism and odd jobs. In the early 1900s he lived in poverty with his wife. He joined the **Socialist Party of America** in 1902 and, at the party's instigation, conducted an investigation of the meatpacking industry in Chicago. *The Jungle* (1906), his novel exposing the shocking conditions of the industry, made him briefly well-off and assisted in the passing of the federal Pure Food and Drug Act, an ironic result for a work intended to fire enthusiasm for social reform.

Sinclair used the profits from *The Jungle* to finance an experimental housing cooperative, but the project was destroyed by fire in 1907 and Sinclair lost his money. He resigned from the Socialist Party over its opposition to World War I, but later rejoined. In 1915 he moved to California and in 1934 campaigned as the Democratic candidate for governor on an antipoverty campaign; he was only narrowly defeated. Thereafter he concentrated on his writing, enjoying large sales of his works. Of particular importance in the history of socialism were his critiques of **capitalism** in specific industries: *The Moneychangers* (1908), which dealt with Wall Street; *King Coal* (1917), which was concerned with the miners of Colorado; *Oil* (1927); and *The Flivver King* (1937), which was about the automobile industry. He also wrote an account of the **Sacco-Vanzetti case**, called *Boston* (1928).

SOARES, MÀRIO ALBERTO NOBRE LOPES (1924–). The leading Portuguese socialist of the post-1945 period, Mário Soares was born in Lisbon into an educated, **middle-class** family. He was educated at the Universities of Lisbon and the Sorbonne and graduated in law. His active opposition to the dictatorship of Oliveira Salazar brought him imprisonment on 12 occasions and exile. In 1973 he reestablished the old **Portuguese Socialist Party** and was its general secretary from 1973 to 1986. He returned to Portugal in April 1974 after dictatorial rule was ended and served as prime minister from 1976 to 1978 and from 1983 to 1986. On 16 February 1986 he was elected president of Portugal. He was reelected to the post for a further five years on 13 January 1991. He was vice president of the **Socialist International** from 1976 to 1986 and honorary president from 1986. As minister for foreign affairs in 1974 to 1975, he ended Portuguese **imperialism** by granting independence to Portugal's remaining colonies. In 1977 he was granted the International Prize of Human Rights. In the same year he initiated the negotiations that led Portugal into the European Community.

SOCIAL DEMOCRATIC AND LABOUR PARTY (SDLP). The SDLP was formed in Northern Ireland in August 1970 by Catholic civil rights campaigners. It aimed to end deprivation and achieve a more equal distribution of **wealth**. The first leader was Gerry Fitt (1926–2005), and the deputy John Hume. The SDLP wanted the peaceful unification of Ireland. In 1973 the SDLP helped establish a new Assembly and power-sharing executive for Northern Ireland. The power-sharing executive, established in 1974, included six SDLP members. However, in May the executive and assembly were brought down by a workers' strike. Also in 1974 the SDLP secured full membership in the **Socialist International**. The SDLP participated in a constitutional convention in 1975 but consensus was not reached, as the Unionist majority rejected power sharing. In the two British general elections of 1974 and that of 1979 Fitt was reelected to parliament, having first been elected in 1966. Also in 1979 Hume was elected to the European Parliament and joined the **Socialist Group in the European Parliament** (SGEP). He retained this seat in 1984, 1989, 1994, and 1999, working from 1992 as an SGEP member of the **Party of European Socialists** with which the SDLP was affiliated.

Hume became party leader in 1979 and was elected to the British parliament in 1983. In British parliamentary elections the SDLP won three seats in 1987, four in 1992, three in 1997, and three in 2001, with Hume retaining his seat each time. In the May 1996 elections for a constitutional forum, the SDLP attracted 21.4 percent of the vote. In 1998 the Good Friday Agreement was reached. This devolved power to a Northern Ireland Assembly with its executive in 1999, but was suspended in October 2002, following a breakdown of trust among the participating **political parties**. In 2001 Hume stepped down as party leader. Mark Durkan became leader. Hume retired from the European Parliament before the elections of 2004 and the SDLP failed to retain his seat. In the general elections of May 2005 the SDLP once again took three seats, including Hume's old seat won by Durkan. *See also* IRISH LABOUR PARTY.

SOCIAL DEMOCRATIC CONVERGENCE [*CONVERGENCIA SOCIAL DEMÓCRATA* (CSD)]. The CSD was formed in 2000 during a period of political instability. In 1995 open politics had resumed after decades of civil **war** in Guatemala. Nevertheless, frequent reports of torture and killings by right-wing death squads continued until the ceasefire of 1996. Fernando Enrique De León became the leader of the CSD, which was admitted to the **Socialist International** (SI) as a consultative member in October 2003. Unlike the New National Alliance (*Alianza Nueva Nación*—ANN), which represented three of several other left-wing parties that were formed after the war, the CSD was not ready to contest the congressional elections of 9 November 2003. The ANN won only six of 158 seats, with 4.9 percent of the vote. Neither the CSD nor the ANN contested the first round of the presidential elections held on the same day as those for Congress.

Guatemala had previously been represented in the SI by the Democratic Socialist Party (*Partido Socialista Democrático*—PSD). This title was first used in 1944 by opponents of Jorge Ubico's dictatorship, but the new PSD was formed in 1978, during the civil war. After death squads murdered many of its members in 1979 to 1980, most of the leadership of the PSD went into exile in Costa Rica. At the 1984 national elections, the PSD attracted 3.4 percent of the vote. It became a full member of the SI in 1987. Unable to make a political impact after the civil war, the PSD ceased to operate before the presidential and congressional elections of 2003.

SOCIAL DEMOCRATIC FEDERATION (SDF). Originally formed as the Democratic Federation by **Henry Mayers Hyndman** in 1883, this party was renamed the SDF in 1884. It represented the extreme left of British socialism in the late nineteenth century. Under Hyndman, it adhered to a dry interpretation of the works of **Karl Marx** that emphasized class struggle. Within a year of its founding, it included five distinct groups: **anarchists**, municipal socialists, those led by Hyndman who favored a party based on the **German Social Democratic Party**, **trade unionists**, and a mixed group of individuals who were in the process of forming their own views of socialism. In 1884 **William Morris** and his group departed and formed their own organization, the Socialist League. In 1900 the SDF joined the Labour Representation Committee, the forerunner of the **British Labour Party**, but left in 1901 because it wanted the issue of class **war** to unify the new organization. The SDF was never a mass party; in 1894 its membership was estimated at between 2,000 and 4,000. In 1903 some of its Scottish members departed to form the Socialist Labour Party.

SOCIAL DEMOCRATIC FRONT [*FRONT SOCIAL DÉMO-CRATE* (SDF)]. Formed in March 1990, the SDF has remained in opposition in Cameroon, a country in which civil liberties have always been restricted. French Cameroon gained independence in 1960 and in 1966 several **political parties** formed the National Cameroonian Union, which has dominated Cameroon ever since. This party became the Cameroon People's Democratic Movement and in 1972 created a repressive, conservative one-party state. In 1992 popular discontent led the ruling party to allow multiparty presidential elections. The SDF candidate Ni John Fru Ndi lost to the incumbent president in an election marred by violence on the part of the state. After alleged irregularities in the parliamentary elections of May 1997, which the ruling party won, the SDF, along with the other Cameroonian parties, boycotted the presidential elections in October that year, which too were marred by irregularities. In 1999 the SDF gained full membership in the **Socialist International**. In parliamentary elections of June and September 2002, which were once again marred by irregularities, the SDF obtained 22 of 180 seats. The ruling party, in coalition with a smaller party, won by a huge majority. In October

2004 Ni John Fru Ndi of the SDF once again challenged for the presidency, but was unsuccessful, winning 17.4 percent of the vote.

SOCIAL DEMOCRATIC ISRAEL (*YACHAD*). Formed in 2003, *Yachad* is a social-democratic party that became a full member of the **Socialist International** (SI). *Yachad* was formed through a merger of two previous social-democratic parties—*Meretz*, which was founded in 1992 and *Shahar*, founded in 2002. *Meretz* was formed as an alignment of three parties including the United Workers' Party (*Mifleget Poaleim Meuchedet*—MAPAM). MAPAM had been founded in 1948 by left-wing **Jewish** intellectuals in Israel who were part of the *Kibbutz* movement. MAPAM, which held full membership in the SI, had been the only **Zionist** political party to admit Arabs as members, and had a policy of peace and social and economic equality.

In 1992 *Meretz* entered into a coalition government with the **Israel Labour Party**, after gaining 12 seats in parliamentary (*Knesset*) elections that year. In the *Knesset* elections of January 2003, *Meretz* won six seats. Recognizing that Israel is a multicultural society, *Yachad* was formed as a party of both Jews and Arabs. Believing in human equality *Yachad* campaigned for social justice, human rights, the narrowing of social gaps, and the defense of the **welfare state**, as well as economic growth. It supported the two-state solution to conflict (Israel and Palestine) in line with the Geneva Accords. In the parliamentary elections of March 2006, *Yachad* won 5 seats.

SOCIAL DEMOCRATIC MOVEMENT EDEK [*KINIMA SOSIALDIMOKRATON EDEK* (KISOS EDEK)]. The acronym EDEK in the title of this party stands for *Eniea Demokratiki Enosis Kyprou* (Unified Democratic Union of Cyprus). EDEK was formed in 1969 by Vassos Lyssarides, who became party leader when the party was established the following year. EDEK sought to promote social justice and solidarity, and soon changed its name to Socialist Party EDEK (*Socialistiko Komma Kyprou EDEK*—SKK EDEK). It has always opposed the Turkish occupation of northern Cyprus. Its newspaper circulation suggested a membership of about 6,000 in the mid-1980s. It has been a full member of the **Socialist International** since about 1987. None of the **political parties** in Greek Cyprus has been strong enough to gain the presidency of Cyprus independently, and none has been able to dominate the parliament. Nevertheless,

SKK EDEK has regularly held a presence in parliament. In 1998 it participated in a coalition government, holding two ministerial posts. However, SKK EDEK pulled out at the end of that year. Also at the end of 1998 SKK EDEK took steps to unite forces sympathetic to social democracy, and in February 2000 the Social Democratic Movement (*Kinima Sosialdimokraton*—KISOS) was formed. The KISOS supported the market economy but emphasized the need for greater state intervention to achieve social justice. In the parliamentary elections of May 2001 the KISOS won four of the 56 seats with 6.5 percent of the vote. The largest party in parliament was the Communist Progressive Party of the Working People, but with only 20 seats this party was unable to control parliament. In the presidential elections of February 2003 the KISOS joined with several other parties spanning the left to right spectrum to support the center-right candidate Tassos Papadopoulos, who subsequently became president. The KISOS participated in the new coalition government, holding two ministerial posts. In June 2003 the acronym EDEK was restored, the party title becoming KISOS EDEK.

SOCIAL DEMOCRATIC PARTY (BENIN) [*PARTI SOCIAL-DÉMOCRATE* (PSD)]. The PSD was formed in 1990, the year after the Benin Party of Popular Revolution (*Parti de la Révolution Populaire du Bénin*—PRPB) began to usher in multiparty democratic government. The PRPB had taken power in 1972 in the last of several military seizures of power after independent Benin was formed. Led by General Mathieu Kérékou, the PRPB installed a **Marxist-Leninist** regime that established **communism** in Benin, introducing a new constitution with itself as the single party. The PRPB's successor party, the Union of the Forces of Progress, failed to win any seats at the parliamentary elections of 1991. Kérékou himself retained much support, but nevertheless lost the presidential elections that year. The PSD became a supporter of Kérékou, who was now a civilian, as Benin's politics came to be characterized by alliances and coalitions of the **political parties**. Although in the parliamentary elections of March 1995 the PSD won few seats, its leader Bruno Amoussou was elected speaker of the legislature. In the presidential elections of 1996 Amoussou won 7.8 percent of the vote and was thus eliminated from the second round, which Kérékou won. Kérékou installed a new government in which the PSD held three portfolios. In 1999 an alliance of opposition parties beat the alliance of pro-Kérékou parties by 42 to 41 seats, but reassured voters that it intended to cooperate with the president and seek consensus where possible.

In the presidential elections of March 2001, Amoussou stood for the PSD, obtaining only 8.6 percent of the vote in the first round, and was thus initially eliminated. He encouraged supporters to vote for Kérékou, who headed the Action Front for Renewal and Development in the second round. However, the other candidates withdrew amidst allegations of electoral irregularities. Amoussou stood as a token candidate against Kérékou in the second round. Although Amoussou retained his position as a minister of state, he was now the sole PSD member in the government. Having gained consultative membership in the **Socialist International** in 1999, the PSD was granted full membership in 2003. In the parliamentary elections of March 2003 the PSD participated in the Union for the Benin of the Future (*Union pour le Bénin du Futur*—UBF), which was led by Amoussou. The UBF won 31 seats as part of the broader Presidential Movement (*Mouvance Présidentielle*) that obtained 52 of the 83 seats with 55.8 percent of the vote.

SOCIAL DEMOCRATIC PARTY OF AMERICA (SDPA). The SDPA was formed by **Eugene V. Debs** and **Victor L. Berger** in 1898 from the remains of Social Democracy of America (SDA), a political party set up by Debs in Chicago in June 1897, and those members of the **Socialist Labor Party** who were opposed to **Daniel DeLeon**. The SDA originally included a contingent of **utopian socialists** who wanted to form cooperative colonies. The organization ceased when Debs and Berger withdrew their followers. The SDPA was one of the main groups that formed the **Socialist Party of America** in Chicago in January 1901.

SOCIAL DEMOCRATIC PARTY OF ANDORRA [*PARTIT SO-CIALDEMÒCRATA* (PS)]. **Political parties** were not established in the principality of Andorra until the introduction of a new constitution in 1993. The PS was founded in 2000, after the National Democratic Group (*Agrupament Nacional Democràtic*) split into two factions that became the PS and the Democratic Party. As a result of the parliamentary elections of March 2001, won by the Liberal Party of Andorra, the PS held six of 28 seats. The PS gained full membership in the **Socialist International** in 2003. In the parliamentary elections of April 2005 the PS increased its share of the 28 seats to 11, with 38.1 percent of the vote. The Liberal Party won the election but without an absolute majority.

SOCIAL DEMOCRATIC PARTY OF BOSNIA AND HERZEGOVINA [*SOCIJAL DEMOKRATSKA PARTIJA BOSNE I HERCEGOVINE* (SDP BiH)]. Formed in 1909 by **trade unionists** and intellectuals, the SDP BiH became a member of the **communist** parties of Bosnia and Herzegovina and of Yugoslavia. During World War II the communist-led People's Liberation Movement formed the People's Republic of Bosnia and Herzegovina, which became part of communist Yugoslavia. When communist Yugoslavia collapsed in the early 1990s the SDP BiH reassumed its original title and in 1992 briefly joined the Government for National Unity. The party left the government that year, when nationalist parties within it called for the formation of national armies. The SDP BiH seeks to represent people of all nationalities in multiethnic Bosnia and Herzegovina—a county that, because of rival **nationalisms**, has struggled to build itself as a viable state since the **wars** that tore Yugoslavia apart in the 1990s. The peace accord of 1995 that ended the civil war in Bosnia and Herzegovina divided the country into two administrative parts. One, controlled by Bosnian and Croat armed forces, was the Federation of Bosnia and Herzegovina. The second, controlled by the Bosnian Serb Army, was the Republic Srpska. The SDP BiH participates in elections for the legislatures of both of these parts, as well as the state-level legislature. In the general elections of 1996 the SDP BiH campaigned as a part of a "joint List" that won 5 percent of the vote. In the general elections of 1998 it campaigned alone and won around 10 percent of the vote. In November 1999 the SDP BiH gained full membership in the **Socialist International**. In the legislative elections of November 2000 the SDP BiH became the largest party at the state level with nine members gained with 21.5 percent of the vote. The SDP BiH joined several moderate parties in the Alliance for Change, which won power at state level and at both administrative levels, although the SDP BiH was weakly represented at the Republic Srpska level.

The Alliance suffered from negative campaigning on the part of the nationalist parties, which blamed the Alliance for the country's economic problems. After the legislative elections of 2002 the SDP

BiH was not represented in government at either the state level or the levels of the Federation of Bosnia and Herzegovina and the Republic Srpska. The governments were all composed of representatives from center-right and right-wing nationalist parties. In the state level elections the SDP BiH obtained 10.4 percent of the vote. Four SDP BiH members thus won seats, but one soon left to become an independent. The SDP BiH took 15 of 98 seats in the legislature of the Federation of Bosnia and Herzegovina, with 15.6 percent of the vote. It won three of 83 seats in the legislature of the Republic Srpska, with 3.4 percent of the vote. After the elections a small minority who wanted to make deals with the nationalists left the SDP BiH to form new parties. A special congress confirmed the decision of the main board of the SDP BiH not to make such deals.

SOCIAL DEMOCRATIC PARTY OF CROATIA [*SOCI-JALDEMOKRATSKA PARTIJA HRVATSKE* (SDPH)]. The SDPH was formed in 1990, at a time when **communist** Yugoslavia, of which Croatia was a federal republic, had begun to break up amidst **war** between its republics. The SDPH grew out of the reformist branch of the League of Communists of Croatia. At the parliamentary elections of 1992 the SDPH attracted 5.4 percent of the vote. Another social-democratic party had been formed at about the same time as the SDPH and in 1994 the two parties merged under the SDPH title. In the parliamentary elections of 1995, this strengthened party increased its share of the vote to 8.9 percent of the vote. In 1999 the SDPH gained full membership in the **Socialist International**.

In the 1990s Croatia was barely democratic, governed under the grip of the right-wing, **nationalist** president Franjo Tudjman. After his death in 1999 the powers of the presidency were greatly reduced. In the parliamentary elections of January 2000 Tudjman's Croatian Democratic Union lost power after dominating Croatia for nine years. A coalition of the SDPH and the Croatian Social Liberal Party won 71 of the 152 seats, and were joined in a broader governing coalition by the Croatian Peasant Party, the Istrian Democratic Assembly, the Liberal Party, and the Croatian People's Party. During this government coalition some of the SDPH's partners left government or split up. In the parliamentary elections of November 2003 the SDPH-led coalition lost power to Tudjman's old party, which formed a new governing coalition after the elections. The SDPH coalition obtained 43 seats with 22.6 percent of the vote. The SDPH itself won 34 of those seats.

SOCIAL DEMOCRATIC PARTY OF MONTENEGRO [*SOCI-JALDEMOKRATSKA PARTIJA* (SDP)]. In 1993 two parties—the Social Democratic Reform Party and Socialist Party of Montenegro—merged to form the SDP. The SDP's independent campaign for Montenegro was successful in 2006. Montenegro remained united with Serbia as **communist** Yugoslavia disintegrated in the 1990s. In April 2001 the first parliamentary elections were held in Montenegro since the beginning of the Balkan crisis of the 1990s. There was no clear winner, but the SDP, in a bloc with the Democratic Party of Socialists (*Demokratska Partija Socijalista Crna Gore*—DPS) that had formerly been the League of Communists, won most seats and formed a minority government with the support of a Liberal alliance. The SDP and the Liberals withdrew their support from the government when in 2002 an agreement was made to establish the two remaining Yugoslavian entities as Serbia and Montenegro. Parliament was dissolved and new elections were held in October 2002. The SDP and DPS formed into the proindependence Democratic List for a European Montenegro (*Demokratska Lista za Evropsku Crnu Goru*—DLECG), and won the elections with an absolute majority with 39 of 75 votes, gained with 47.9 percent of the vote. The SDP took seven of those seats, and the DPS 30.

In 2003 Yugoslavia became internationally recognized as Serbia and Montenegro with a 126-member parliament (91 in Serbia and 35 in Montenegro) elected in February 2003 by the members of the former federal parliament and the republican parliaments in proportion to party strength in those parliaments. The SDP gained 5 of these seats but did not enter the government. The DPS, still operating as the DLECG, gained 19 of the seats. It did enter the coalition government, with its Svetozvar Marovic as president of Serbia and Montenegro. In the Montenegrin presidential elections of May 2003 the proindependence candidate Filip Vujanovic, supported by the SDP and DPS, was successful with 63.3 percent of the vote. Later in 2003 the SDP gained full membership in the **Socialist international**.

SOCIAL DEMOCRATIC RADICAL PARTY [*PARTIDO RADICAL SOCIAL-DEMÓCRATA* (PRSD)]. One of three Chilean parties holding full membership in the **Socialist International**, the PRSD is actually a party of the center rather than the left. Formerly the Radical Party (*Partido Radical*—PR), the party adopted its present title in 1993. The PR was originally founded in Chile in 1863. It was the party of government from 1938 to 1952. During the 1950s it was anticommunist, but it moved to the left in the 1960s and joined the government of **Salvador Allende** in the 1970s. Banned after the military coup, the PR went into exile in Mexico where it split into center and left factions. After 1983 the center faction built alliances with other groups to form a united opposition to military rule. The PR worked closely with the Chilean Christian Democratic Party in the late 1980s, after the close of Augusto Pinochet's right-wing dictatorship. The PRSD operates in coalition with a range of left and center parties entitled Concertation of Parties for Democracy (*Concertación de Partidos por la Democracia*—CPD).

The CPD was successful at the 2001 general elections for the Chamber of Deputies, winning 62 of the 120 seats, thus defeating the opposing right-wing coalition. The PRSD became a minor player in the CPD, holding only six of its seats. After the elections to half of the seats in the Senate that day, the CPD held 20 of the total of 38 electable seats (ten other seats were appointed until 2005), of which the PRSD occupied two. In the elections of 11 December 2005 the CPD increased its share of the seats in the Chamber of Deputies to 65, gained with 51.8 percent of the vote. The PRSD took seven of those seats with 3.5 percent. The CPD obtained 11 of the 19 contested Senate seats, with one going to the PRSD. The CPD maintained its total of 20 Senate seats, and the PRSD its total of two.

SOCIAL DEMOCRATIC UNION OF MACEDONIA [*SOCI-JALDEMOKRATSKI SOJUZ NA MAKEDONIJA* (SDSM)]. Following the independence of the Former Yugoslavian Republic of Macedonia from the disintegrating **communist** Yugoslavia in 1991, the SDSM was formed as the successor party to the League of Communists. Kiro Gligorov, who was the first president of the republic from 1990 to 1999, helped found the party. Branko Crvenkovski later became SDSM leader. Following the parliamentary elections of 1992, in which it won 31 of 120 seats, the SDSM participated in a coalition government with the Liberal Party, the Socialist Party, and the Democratic Party of Albanians. Crvenkovski was prime minister from 1991 until 1998, when the coalition disintegrated because of corruption and a breakdown of relations between the parties. The SDSM, as a party with a **working-class** support base, had also lost popularity among it supporters and **trade unions** due to its **privatization** policies. In the parliamentary elections of 1998 the SDSM was reduced to 27 seats.

In 2001 the SDSM participated in a temporary government of national unity in response to ethnic hostilities in the multicultural republic. The parliamentary elections of September 2002 were held in a period of tension between Macedonian and Albanian **nationalists**. The SDSM participated in the Together for Macedonia coalition of four parties, which obtained 60 of the 120 seats. The SDSM won 43 of those seats. Along with the nationalist Albanian Democratic Union for Integration the electoral coalition formed an SDSM-led coalition government. This government set out on an anticorruption purge of public administration and finance. In 2003 the SDSM gained full membership in the **Socialist International**.

In the presidential elections of April 2004 the former party leader Crvenkovski secured the presidency for the SDSM with 60.5 percent of the vote at the second round between the two leading candidates. Some opposition parties alleged that the SDSM had manipulated the electoral process, but international observers were satisfied with the process. Crvenkovski reshuffled the SDSM-led government in June but this collapsed in November due to disagreements over decentralization with the Albanian nationalists represented in the coalition government. The country had suffered from interethnic tension since independence. In November 2004 Vlado Buckovski was elected leader of the SDSM. He became prime minister and formed a new SDSM-led government in December 2004.

SOCIAL DEMOCRATS OF SLOVENIA [*SOCIALNI DEMO-KRATI* (SD)]. The SD was formerly the United List of Social Democrats (*Združeno Lista socialnih demokratov*—ZLSD), which was formed in 1993 by a merger in Slovenia of three parties that had emerged at a time when **communist** Yugoslavia was breaking up— Slovenia having been a federal republic within Yugoslavia. The three parties that formed the ZLSD were the Party of Democratic Reforms, which was formed in 1990 and was an opposition party in parliament, and two parties that had not been represented independently in parliament—the Workers' party of Slovenia, founded in 1991, and the Social Democratic Union, founded in 1990. In the parliamentary elections of 1992 the three parties, along with the Democratic Party of Pensioners in Slovenia, won 14 seats as a center-left coalition by the name of United Left. In 1993 the new ZLSD participated in government with four ministerial positions. The ZLSD became a full member of the **Socialist International** in 1996.

In the parliamentary elections of 2000 the ZLSD won 11 seats and remained a member of the coalition government that also included the Liberal Democratic Party of Slovenia and Slovenia People's Party. The ZLSD has never held the largely ceremonial Slovenian presidency, its candidate winning only 2.23 percent of the vote in the presidential elections of 2002. In the parliamentary elections of October 2004 the ZLSD was reduced to 10 seats, gained with 10.3 percent of the vote. It was excluded from government as a center-right coalition took power. In the elections to the European Parliament in June 2004 the ZLSD won one of Slovenia's seven seats. The ZLSD member worked in the **Party of European Socialists**, with which the ZLSD was affiliated. At its fifth national congress in April 2005 the party became the SD.

SOCIAL DEMOCRATS USA (SDUSA). The SDUSA was formed in 1972 from the **Socialist Party of America**, after the latter party's cochairman, **Michael Harrington**, left to form the Democratic Socialist Organizing Committee. The party has been a member of the **Socialist International** since 1972 and in 1987 claimed a membership of 3,000. The party has, almost since its formation, been criticized by many on the American left for its conservatism. It nevertheless continued to support organized labor, insisting in a resolution in January 2003 that **trade unions** have an important role in making the market system a fairer one.

SOCIAL SECURITY. Social democrats, who seek to reform **capitalism**, stress the importance of social security to alleviate poverty and social injustice. As a key function of the **welfare state**, social security, or social insurance, typically helps provide for such benefits as old-age pensions, regular payments for the **unemployed**, and provision of necessities for families who suffer deprivation. Social security can contribute to a social wage. Like **health care**, social security is not an exclusively socialist concern. Social **liberalism** argues for social security to help individuals fulfill their potential. Indeed, **William Beveridge**, whose plan to abolish want was adopted by the **British Labour Party** in government during the 1940s, was a liberal. Even conservatives often concede that the maintenance of order and harmony requires some degree of social security, however minimal. Other conservatives, along with libertarians, stress the importance of self-reliance, arguing that the **taxation** that is usually required to pay for social security represents an injustice. Socialists are more interested in stressing the sociality of human beings, the importance of co-operation and social responsibility, and the social benefits of planning. Planning for social security is an example of cooperation, whereby social democrats seek to institute social responsibility.

Social-democratic governments faced demands from international business and finance in the late twentieth and early twenty-first centuries to review and reduce social security spending. **Globalization** was said to involve integrated international markets, mobile capital, and thus a decrease in the power of the governments of nation states. Under the leadership of **Tony Blair** and **Gerhard Schröder** respectively, the British Labour Party and the **German Social Democratic Party** represent two prominent examples of parties that tried to juggle those demands with social-democratic principles and the continued backing of their natural supporters.

"SOCIALISM WITHOUT DOCTRINE." This phrase was coined by the French labor investigator Albert Métin (1871–1919) to describe experiments in labor and economic regulation by the nonsocialist governments of Australia and New Zealand, which seemed to be a form of state socialism, but were devoid of any reference to socialist theory. Métin visited Australia and New Zealand in 1899 and published his book *Socialisme sans doctrines* (generally translated as "socialism without doctrine") in Paris in 1901; it introduced these experiments to a French audience that included **Alexandre Millerand**.

SOCIALIST FEMINISM. Drawing on some resources of **Marxism**, socialist feminism is sometimes referred to as Marxist feminism. However, socialist feminism departs from traditional Marxism. Inspired by the **women**'s liberation movement of the 1960s, socialist feminism developed as a tradition of Western political thought in the

1970s. Like Marxism, socialist feminism holds that it is not enough to seek for equality and justice in the existing **capitalist** system. This is because the relationship between the sexes is rooted in the social and economic structure of society. Socialist feminism attempts to show that economic factors and others must be taken into account if we are to get a true picture of sexual inequality in capitalist society. Hence, socialist feminists have been concerned with the relationship between two types of oppression—those of class and those of sex. Influential socialist feminists include Juliet Mitchell, Alison Jaggar, and **Iris Marion Young**.

Socialist feminists argue that theory aiming to emancipate women should portray the world from the standpoint of women. While **liberalism** attempts to take the standpoint of the neutral, observing from outside the reality of what is being observed, socialist feminists argue that there is no neutral standpoint. All standpoints reflect certain social interests and values. While the dominant in society are convinced by the **ideology** from which they view the world, oppressed groups experience directly the system that oppresses them, even though they are sometimes duped by the ruling ideology.

Socialist feminists argue that women's subordination serves capitalist interests. They also hold that women face a special form of exploitation and oppression. Women thus gain a distinctive standpoint from which to understand society, but will not arrive at this standpoint while their perceptions of reality are distorted by male-dominant ideology and the male-dominated structure of everyday life. The standpoint will be discovered in collective struggle. Women's subordination is not a permanent, natural, or inevitable feature of human relationships. This subordination has, rather, developed most fully in the capitalist era. Because subordination is so entrenched within class society, it will not be ended by arguments that raise abstract notions such as justice. Indeed, it will not be ended by argument at all. For Marxist feminists, nothing short of substantial social change, or social revolution, will bring about genuine emancipation for women.

SOCIALIST FORCES FRONT [*FRONT DES FORCES SOCIAL-ISTES* (FFS)]. Formed in 1963, the FFS was immediately overshadowed on the Algerian left by National Liberation Front (*Front de Libération Nationale*—FLN). The FLN had led the **war** of independence against France (1954–62) and, under the leadership of Ahmed

Ben Bella, took over the functions of government in the new Algerian republic. Algeria formally became a single-party socialist state under the FLN. However, real power lay with the military and bureaucracy and in June 1965 the government was overthrown by a military revolutionary council that ruled until a new constitution was introduced in 1976. The military leader Colonel Houari Boumédienne became president unopposed. In 1978 he died and the military took control once again. In February 1989 a new constitution signified the end of the nominally socialist one-party state, and permitted the formation of **political parties** outside the FLN—although there were restrictions and parties needed to be licensed by government. In this environment the FFS was revived. In 1996 it gained full membership in the **Socialist International**.

In the multiparty parliamentary elections of December 1991 to January 1992, the FFS won 25 of 430 seats and the FLN took just 15. However, the strong performance of an Islamic fundamentalist party led to allegations of irregularities and the second round of the elections was canceled by a military-dominated High Council of State, which approved a new head of state who inaugurated a National Transition Council. Parliamentary elections were held again in June 1997 and the Council formed a centrist National Democratic Assembly (*Rassemblement national démocratique*—RND) that obtained 156 of 380 seats. The FFS won just 20. The RND formed a government along with the FLN and a moderate Islamic party. In April 1999 the FFS withdrew its candidate Hocine Aït Ahmed from the presidential elections, alleging massive fraud in favor of the Abdelazïz Bouteflika, who was supported by the FLN and RND. The FFS boycotted both the parliamentary elections of May 2002 and the presidential elections of April 2004.

SOCIALIST GROUP IN THE EUROPEAN PARLIAMENT (SGEP). The SGEP was established in 1954 to provide a forum for socialist politicians who were members of the European Parliament. It is the parliamentary group of the **Party of European Socialists** (PES). It is also an associated organization with the **Socialist International** and the **Confederation of the Socialist Parties in the European Community** and has links with the **International Union of Socialist Youth**. In 1990 the SGEP had 180 members, making it the largest single grouping within the European Parliament. After the

1999 European elections the SGEP held 232 seats, making it the second-largest group, behind the conservative European People's Party–European Democrats. Although the European Union was enlarged in 2004, when 10 new member states were admitted, the SGEP membership dropped to 200 members from 23 of the 25 member states, under the group presidency of Martin Schulz. The SGEP was still the second largest grouping, behind the conservatives.

SOCIALIST INFORMATION AND LIAISON OFFICE (SILO). The SILO was formed at Clacton-on-Sea, England, in May 1946 to restore the links broken by World War II between groups of exiled socialists from continental Europe and, if possible, to develop common policies on problems of mutual interest. It represented 19 socialist or social-democratic parties and was made part of the secretariat of the **British Labour Party**, which had been sponsoring meetings of these groups during World War II. Anti-German feeling carried over into the SILO with opposition to admitting the **German Social Democratic Party** as a full member, a cruel irony given the party's suffering and resistance to the Nazis. At further conferences at Zurich (June 1946) and Antwerp (November 1947), it was agreed to organize the SILO into a more representative body, the **Committee of the International Socialist Conference**, which occurred in March 1948.

SOCIALIST INTERAFRICAN. *See* LEAGUE OF AFRICAN DEMOCRATIC SOCIALIST PARTIES.

SOCIALIST INTERNATIONAL (SI). The SI was formed in Frankfurt, Germany, in July 1951 out of the **Committee of the International Socialist Conference**. Intended to be the successor to the **Labor and Socialist International** as a forum for social-democratic parties, it pledged itself to work for world peace and freedom, resist exploitation and enslavement, eliminate mass **unemployment** and poverty, advocate for the development of the individual personality as the basis for social advancement, and affirm its support for collective security to resist totalitarian governments. Since its inception, the SI has provided a focus for international efforts to fight dictatorships, provided support to socialist/social-democratic parties in exile, upheld liberties and the rule of law, increased aid to Third World countries, and increased expenditures on **health**, housing, **education**, and

social security. The SI has always supported the use of peaceful means to bring about social and economic improvement. By 1966 the SI had representatives from **political parties** in 30 countries representing about 60 million electors. Since the 1960s the SI has worked to promote arms control, disarmament, human rights, the peaceful conflict of international disputes, and understanding and amelioration of the problems of the Third World.

The SI has two permanent committees—the Ethics Committee and the Committee for Finance and Administration. It also sets up committees with regard to matters of contemporary interest. Those committees established for the period 2003 to 2007 included the following, among others: Economy, Social Cohesion and the Environment; Peace, Democracy and Human Rights; Africa, Asia and the Pacific; Latin America and the Caribbean; South Eastern Europe. Based in London, the SI grew significantly in membership in the late twentieth and early twenty-first centuries. The SI had 69 full member parties in 59 countries in 1996. By 2005 this had increased to 104 full member parties in 90 countries. *See also* SOCIALIST INFORMATION AND LIAISON OFFICE.

SOCIALIST INTERNATIONAL WOMEN (SWI). The SWI was founded in London in 1955, as the International Council of Social Democratic Women. It was the successor to the **International Socialist Women's Committee**, which had been formed in 1907 as the International Women's Congress by the **Second International**. The SWI adopted its present title in 1978. Affiliated with the **Socialist International**, the SWI is the international organization of **women**'s organizations of many socialist, social-democratic, and labor parties. The aims of SWI include sharing information and promoting democratic socialism, equality of treatment between the sexes, human rights, economic development, and international peace. In 2005 the SWI comprised 152 organizations from around the world.

SOCIALIST LABOR PARTY OF AMERICA (SLPA). The SLPA was established in 1877 as a successor to the **Workingmen's Party of the United States**. It relied heavily on immigrant socialists, particularly Germans and **Jews**, rather than the native-born. It conducted much of its activity in taverns, which discouraged participation by **women**. The SLPA enjoyed some success in the late 1870s when it was able to benefit from labor discontent and won some electoral support in Illinois. One of its members, **Laurence Grönlund**, wrote *The Cooperative Commonwealth* (1884), which enjoyed an international readership in English countries. Otherwise the SLPA failed to harness immigrant **working-class** discontent in the mid-1880s. Nor did it form lasting links with other labor reformers, specifically the native-born and the Irish Americans. This contributed to the image of socialism in the United States as "foreign." **Daniel DeLeon** became its leader, but faction fighting doomed the SLPA. Its pre-1900 membership was never more than 5,000. Nonetheless, it continued as an organization into the early twenty-first century. *See also* SOCIALIST PARTY OF AMERICA.

SOCIALIST MOVEMENT FOR THE UNITED STATES OF EUROPE (SMUSE). Support for the idea of the economic integration of Europe among socialists, using the United States as a model, was expressed as early as 1925 in the Heidelberg Program of the **German Social Democratic Party** (*Sozialdemokratische Partei Deutschlands*—SPD); it was a response to the economic dislocation caused by World War I. In 1927 **Ernest Bevin** succeeded in carrying a motion in support of this idea by the British Trades Union Congress. By 1939 **Clement Attlee**, the leader of the **British Labour Party**, favored the creation of a politically and economically federated Europe. In 1947 Philip Andre (1902–70) created the SMUSE to cater to small but influential minorities in the British Labour Party and the SPD that supported European integration. The SMUSE largely lost its reason to exist when the Council of Europe was set up in 1949; subsequent other pan-European organizations further removed the need for the SMUSE. *See also* EUROPEAN SOCIALIST MOVEMENT; INTERNATIONALISM.

SOCIALIST PARTY OF ALBANIA [*PARTIA SOCIALISTE E SHQIPËRISË* (PSSh)]. After ruling Albania as a single-party communist state since 1946, the Albanian Workers' Party (the communist party) allowed independent parties to be formed in 1990, following the collapse of Eastern European **communism**. Albania had turned to communism in the 1940s when the Anti-Fascist National Liberation Committee, which was dominated by communists, took power after becoming the strongest political force as an organization that had opposed the Nazi occupation. The communists took power without a serious challenge. Albania became an isolationist communist state when the party leader Enver Hoxha broke diplomatic relations with the Soviet Union. In 1985 Hoxha died and was succeeded as leader by Ramiz Alia, who ruled for the remainder of the communist era. The party retained power after the first multiparty parliamentary elections held in April 1991, having along with its allies won 169 of the 250 seats. However, a government of national salvation was formed. In June 1991 the party changed its name to the PSSh. Formally committed to improving the social and economic position of **women**, the PSSh is connected to the Albanian Socialist Women's Forum, founded in 1992. Another general election was held in 1992, at which the PSSh was reduced to 38 seats.

In the decade following the demise of communism the Albanian multiparty system was marred by violence and fraud. The PSSh leader Fatos Nano was imprisoned for 12 years in 1993 for mass fraud. In the elections of 1996, the PSSh share was reduced still further to 10 seats. Alleging irregularities, the PSSh refused to take those seats. Also in 1996, Nano, having been reelected PSSh leader while in prison, declared that the party had abandoned **Marxism**. He was pardoned and released in 1997. The PSSh won the parliamentary elections that year, with 99 of the 155 seats. Nano became prime minister but resigned in 1998 after political violence intensified in Albania. Nano's supporter and fellow PSSh member Pandeli Majko became the new prime minister. Relations within the PSSh deteriorated and Majko resigned when Nano was once again reelected party leader. Another of Nano's rivals within the PSSh, Ilir Meta, became the new prime minister in 1999. In November 1999 the PSSh gained consultative membership in the **Socialist International** (SI).

At the parliamentary elections in June and July 2001, the PSSh obtained 73 of the 140 seats. Three other parties were allied to the PSSh, including the **Albanian Social Democratic Party**. The combined total of the PSSh and its allies was 87 seats. Meta once again became prime minister. However, rivalries in the PSSh continued, especially between Meta and Nano, and Meta resigned as prime minister in January 2002. Another previous PSSh prime minister, Majko, once again took the office, attempting to achieve a balance in his government ministers between supporters of Nano and Meta. This was unsuccessful and in July 2002 Nano took over as prime minister. He formed a new PSSh government, promising economic reforms and a clampdown on corruption. Meta was included in the government as deputy prime minister, but resigned in 2003. Meta and his allies, who complained that the PSSh was run undemocratically, formed a new organization entitled the Socialist Movement for Integration.

In October 2003 the PSSh gained full membership in the SI. The party lost power to a coalition headed by the Democratic Party in the parliamentary elections in July 2005, the results of which were withheld until September because of allegations of irregularities. The PSSh was defeated, taking 42 seats. Nano resigned as party leader, assuming responsibility for the defeat but continuing to allege malpractice on the part of the victors. Gramoz Ruci became the party leader.

SOCIALIST PARTY OF AMERICA (SPA). The SPA was the principal socialist/social-democratic party in the United States from its founding in 1901 until its breakup in 1972. It was formed by the **Social Democratic Party of America** and former members of the **Socialist Labor Party of America** (SLPA). The bulk of its supporters came from the skilled **working class**, tenant farmers, and German and **Jewish** Americans. At first the SPA enjoyed a surge of support: between 1903 and 1912 its membership rose from nearly 16,000 to 118,000. But the SPA was too diverse to sustain this massive growth. Like early American socialist parties, such as the SLPA, it was extremely reliant on immigrants; of its 79,400 members in 1915 about 40 percent were immigrants. The SPA conspicuously failed to attract native-born Americans of British or Irish stock. Internally, it was weakened by conflict between the "left" and the "right" as well as by competition from the **Industrial Workers of the World**. Apart from racial and regional divisions, the SPA lacked a **trade union** base. The peak national labor body, the American Federation of Labor, opposed alliances with any particular party, opposed socialism on principle, and showed no interest in organizing the unskilled.

Despite some successes in local government elections between 1910 and 1912 (in all about 2,000 socialists held local government posts in 1912), the membership of the SPA fell from 118,000 in 1912 to 82,300 by 1918. The SPA was harassed by the federal government for its **pacifism** during World War I, but the main reason for its decline thereafter was a severe split caused by conflict between the older SPA officials and the **communists** in 1919 to 1920. The membership of the SPA, which had recovered to 108,500 in 1919, was slashed to 26,800 by 1920. The subsequent history of the SPA was one of a small interest group that depended heavily on a few able individuals, specifically **Norman Thomas**, who ran for president between 1928 and 1948, and energetic personalities such as **Harry Laidler**. Although the SPA never attracted the mass following it had before 1913, it continued to be an important source of ideas for the political agenda in the United States. Throughout its history the SPA was the American representative in the **Second International**, the **Labor and Socialist International**, and the **Socialist International**. *See also* AMERICAN LABOR PARTY; HARRINGTON, MICHAEL; SOMBART, WERNER; YOUNG PEOPLE'S SOCIALIST LEAGUE.

SOCIALIST PARTY OF CHILE [*PARTIDO SOCIALISTA DE CHILE* (PS)]. One of three Chilean parties holding full membership in the Socialist International, the PS was founded in 1933 by among others, **Salvador Allende**, who as president of Chile would die during General Augusto Pinochet's right-wing coup in 1973. The support for the PS at its formation came from the **working class** and socialist intellectuals. After Pinochet's coup the PS split into factions and socialists were repressed under the dictatorship. Nevertheless, in 1988 the PS made a contribution to the plebiscite that would end Pinochet's rule. In the campaign the PS set up the **Party for Democracy** (*Partido por la Democracia*—PPD) as a temporary measure to attract support from Chileans who would not wish to be associated with the socialists of the past. The PPD actually became a permanent fixture of Chilean politics in its own right, challenging the PS. The PS did, though, manage to unite some of its factions in 1990. In the 1990s the two parties worked together in a sometimes tense relationship. In 1996 the PS gained full membership in the **Socialist International**.

The PS is a member of the left and center Concertation of Parties for Democracy (*Concertación de Partidos por la Democracia*—CPD). The CPD won the elections to the Chamber of Deputies on 16 December 2001 with 62 of the 120 seats, of which the PS took 11 under the leadership of Gonzalo Martner. After the elections to half of the seats in the Senate that day, the CPD held 20 of the total of 38 contestable seats (ten seats were appointed until 2005), of which the PS occupied five. On 11 December 2005 the CPD won 65 of the seats in the Chamber of Deputies with 51.8 percent of the vote. The PS took 15 of those seats with 10 percent of the vote. The CPD obtained 11 of the 19 contested Senate seats, with the PS taking four. The CPD maintained its total of 20 Senate seats and the PS increased its total to eight. Michelle Bachelet of the PS won the presidential elections at the second round on 15 January 2006 with 53.5 percent of the vote.

SOCIALIST PARTY OF SENEGAL [*PARTI SOCIALISTE DU SÉNÉGAL* (PSS)]. The PSS was formed in 1958 from the *Parti Socialiste Sénégalais*, which was begun in 1929 by Lamine Guèye (1891–1968). In 1937 Guèye was made the director of the Senegal section of the metropolitan **French Socialist Party.** The bulk of what was to be the PSS split from the party in 1948, and went its own way winning elections in 1951 and 1955. The PSS was the governing party of Senegal for 40 years from gaining independence in 1960 until the presidential elections of 2000. It has been a full member of the **Socialist International** since the 1970s and claimed a membership of 1.3 million in 1987. The president of Senegal from 1960 to 1981 was Léopold Sédar Senghor (1906–2001). Abdou Diouf of the PSS succeeded Senghor as president that year, and was reelected in 1988 and 1993. Diouf's administration was undermined by a secessionist civil war waged from the Casamance region. This and the accompanying deterioration of the economy led to his defeat in the presidential elections of 2000. Although Diouf obtained 41.3 percent of the vote at the first round and Abdoulaye Wade of the Democratic Party 31 percent, Wade won on the runoff. The PSS was also defeated in the parliamentary elections of April 2001. A coalition led by Wade's Democratic Party won 89 of the 120 seats. The PSS took only 10, with 17.4 percent of the vote.

SOCIALIST PARTY OF URUGUAY [*PARTIDO SOCIALISTA DEL URUGUAY* (PSU)]. Formed in 1910, the PSU split 10 years later. Some former members sympathized with **communism** and formed the Communist Party of Uruguay. Others, who rejected **Leninism,** including the PSU founder Emilio Frugoni, maintained the PSU. In 1971 the PSU became one of the founders of the progressive Broad Front (*Frente Amplio*—FA) coalition. Among the other parties of the FA were the Communist Party and the Christian Democratic Party. The latter party later left the FA, which became established as the center-left coalition in Uruguayan politics. In 1999 the PSU gained full membership in the **Socialist international** (SI). In the early twenty-first century Uruguay suffered a severe economic crisis under the administration of the right-wing Colorado party and there was mass opposition to **privatization**. In October 2004 the PSU member Tabaré Vázquez contested the presidential elections, promising social justice. He defeated the incumbent free-market Colorado party candidate, winning almost 52 percent of the popular vote, becoming the first-ever Uruguayan president of the left. At legislative elections in 2004 the PSU won 15 percent of the votes secured by the FA, which in total obtained 52 of 99 seats with 50.4 percent of the vote in the lower legislative chamber and 17 of the 31 seats in the Senate. The FA formed a government. *See also* NEW SPACE.

SOCIALIST SUNDAY SCHOOLS. In the early 1830s followers of **Robert Owen** and **Chartism** set up their own secular Sunday schools, using the example of **Christianity**, that operated until the 1850s. The next secular Sunday schools did not appear in the United Kingdom until 1886. In 1892 Mary Gray, a member of the **Social Democratic Federation**, began the socialist Sunday school movement in London; the movement was started in Glasgow, Scotland, in 1896 and spread into northern England. In 1910, when a national union of these schools was formed, there were 100 schools with nearly 5,000 children and 1,000 adults. In the United States German and Finnish immigrants formed the first socialist Sunday schools before 1900, but the main development occurred with the growth of the **Socialist Party of America** (SPA). These schools sought to impart socialist ideas to the young. They never recovered from the split in the SPA in 1919 to 1920. The last of these schools ceased to exist by 1937. *See also* EDUCATION.

SOCIALIST UNION OF CENTRAL AND EASTERN EUROPE (SUCEE). SUCEE was founded under the auspices of the **Committee of the International Socialist Conference** in London in 1949 to keep alive the traditions of social democracy so long as Central and Eastern Europe were under **communist** domination, promote the cooperation of **political parties** in exile, and appeal for moral support from Western democracies. In 1989 the SUCEE consisted of exiled social-democratic parties from Bulgaria, Czechoslovakia, Estonia, Hungary, Latvia, Lithuania, Poland, Romania, the Ukraine, and Yugoslavia. With the overthrow of communist regimes in Central and Eastern Europe in the late 1980s and the emergence of democratically elected governments, the reason for the existence of SUCEE disappeared.

SOCIALIST UNION OF POPULAR FORCES [*UNION SOCIALISTE DES FORCES POPULAIRES* (USFP)]. The USFP was founded in Morocco in September 1974. It was a member of the **League of African Democratic and Socialist Parties** in 1987 and claimed a membership of 100,000. It was a full member of the **Socialist International** by 1994. The government suppressed the USFP in June 1981 for its role in a strike over rising prices. The USFP was closely linked with the main labor federation of Morocco, the *Confédération Démocratique du Travail* (Democratic Confederation of Labor). The previous year it had criticized the fairness of the conduct of the national election. Opposition to the monarchy was suppressed more generally until the mid-1990s. In the parliamentary elections of 1997 the USFP gained most seats—57 of 325—and thus became the first opposition party to lead a government. In the parliamentary elections held in September 2002 the USFP's share of the seats was reduced to 50. Nevertheless the USFP participated in the new government. The USFP's Driss Jettou became prime minister.

SOCIALIST WORKERS' SPORTS INTERNATIONAL (SWSI). An international socialist gathering for sports and games was originally set up in May 1913 in Ghent, Belgium, as the International Socialist Federation. It was reestablished as the SWSI in 1920 to encourage sports as a means of promoting world peace. In order to help the underprivileged it held two large-scale International Workers' Olympiads in Frankfurt in 1925 and Vienna in 1931. The SWSI worked closely with the **Labor and Socialist International**. In 1938 the organizations affiliated with the SWPI had a combined membership of 380,000. The SWSI was revived in 1946 as the **International Labour Sports Confederation**.

SOCIALIZATION OBJECTIVE. The *socialization objective* is the term commonly used to refer to the presence of objectives in the platforms of social-democratic parties that advocate public ownership or control of the economy. Such objectives were in the platforms of the British and Australian labor parties after World War I when inflation had reduced real wages for employees. This caused widespread discontent and substantially increased support for left-wing policies.

The 1906 constitution of the **British Labour Party** (Labour) made no mention of the general **ideological** goals of the party, and was confined to organizational details. In contrast the program of the **Independent Labour Party** in 1907 declared that the aim of the party was "to establish the Socialist State, when land and capital will be held by the community and used for the well-being of the community, and when the exchange of commodities will be organized also by the community, so as to secure the highest possible standard of life for the individual."

In the United Kingdom Labour adopted a socialization objective in 1918 as part of its reorganization. Drafted mainly by **Sidney Webb**, the objective read: "To secure for the workers by hand and brain the full fruits of their industry and the most equitable distribution thereof that may be possible upon the basis of the common ownership of the means of production, distribution and exchange, and the best obtainable system of popular administration and control of each industry or service." This later became clause IV of the constitution. An attempt to abolish clause IV in 1959 to 1960 failed, and the clause remained formal Labour policy until 29 April 1995, when, under the leadership of **Tony Blair**, it was replaced by a wholly new clause. This new clause declared the party to be a democratic socialist party that "believes that by the strength of our common endeavor, we achieve more than we achieve alone so as to create for each of us the means to realize our true potential and for all of us a community in which the power, **wealth** and opportunity are in the hands of the many not the few, where the rights we enjoy reflect the duties we owe, and where we live together, freely, in a spirit of solidarity, tolerance and respect." Other parts of the new clause IV recognized the importance of a dynamic economy based on the private sector with only those enterprises "essential to the common good" being owned by the public sector. Social justice, accountable government, environmental protection, defense, and cooperation with international bodies were vital "to secure peace, freedom, democracy, economic security and environmental protection for all."

In 1940 the **Socialist Party of America** included a detailed socialization objective in its platform aimed at breaking monopolies in coal, oil, lumber, railroads, and aluminum to give consumers greater economic choices, but the platform made it clear that socialization was not to be pursued just for its own sake.

In 1919 the federal conference of the **Australian Labor Party** (ALP) agreed to insert as an objective of the party the "democratic control of all agencies of production, distribution and exchange." At the 1921 federal conference, this objective was broadened to read: "The socialization of industry, production, distribution and exchange." In 1927 the federal conference again revised the socialization objective to include extending the power of the government-owned Commonwealth Bank until "complete control of banking is in the hands of the people." Since 1957 the socialization objective has been progressively diluted on the grounds that it enabled the conservative parties to portray the ALP as an extremist party that could not be trusted with government. By 1991 the objective had been amended to read "the democratic socialization of industry, production, distribution and exchange, to the extent necessary to eliminate exploitation and other anti-social features of these fields."

The Dutch Social Democratic Workers' Party (*Sociaal-Democratische Arbeiders Partij*), which later became the **Dutch Labor Party** (*Partij van de Arbeid*—PvdA), adopted socialization objectives for industry and **agriculture** in 1920. Since 1945 the PvdA has adopted more moderate policies, removing **Marxist** references from its principles in 1959. *See also* NATIONALIZATION.

SOMBART, WERNER (1863–1941). The son of a wealthy liberal politician, Werner Sombart was born in Harz, Germany. He studied in Italy before returning to Germany, where he gained his doctorate from Berlin. He became a socialist and his academic work led him to be recognized as an expert on Marxian economics and **capitalism** (a phrase he coined). In 1906 Sombart wrote the influential essay *Warum gibt es in den Vereinigten Staaten keinen Sozialismus?* (*Why Is There no Socialism in the United States?*). He was interested in offering his reasons why a mass socialist/social-democratic party based on the **working class** had failed to emerge in the United States. He offered several reasons: the favorable attitude of American workers toward the capitalist system; the support of American workers for their system of government and their high level of civic integration through **suffrage**; the strength of the Democratic and Republican Parties, which made the establishment of a third major party very difficult; the affluence of American workers compared to the working class of Europe; the increased chances for upward social mobility in the United States compared to Europe; and the opportunities for an independent life on the land offered by the open frontier of settlement.

Sombart based his judgments on a visit to the United States in 1904 as well as published sources. His views have been criticized on various grounds. For example, his concentration on the "average" worker ignored the large section of the working class who lived well below the average. Nonetheless, Sombart's essay raised a significant question: why had socialism in the United States failed to attract a mass following as it had in Germany? The ways in which suffrage was extended and the relative affluence of the American worker were certainly important differences between the United States and Germany at that time, but they were far from being the only reasons why socialism failed to win mass support in the United States. Consider the counterexample of Australia, which had male suffrage from the mid-nineteenth century and a relatively affluent economy until the 1890s, but which yet still managed to produce the **Australian Labor Party**.

Other reasons that have been advanced by **G. D. H. Cole** and others include an electoral system that favored two parties only; the lack of solidarity in the American working class, particularly the great divide between skilled and unskilled employees and divisions of nationality, race, and region; the hostility of the American Federation of Labor to socialism in any form; the failure of German immigrants (who made up a quarter of all immigrants to the United States between 1871 and 1891) to adapt their socialist ideas to American conditions; the agrarian/small-town ethos of the United States (urbanization did not exceed 50 percent until 1920 in the United States); and the strength of Catholicism, which had been boosted by immigrants from Ireland before 1890 and then by immigration from Italy and Eastern Europe.

There is some dispute regarding Sombart's political leanings in later life. Some have suggested that he was sympathetic to the Nazis. Others have denied this. *See also* SOCIALIST PARTY OF AMERICA.

SOREL, GEORGES (1847–1922). Engineer and political theorist Georges Sorel was born in Cherbourg, France, to **middle-class** parents. In 1892 he retired to devote himself full-time to writing. He became interested in **Marxism** and **anarcho-syndicalism** after 1893. In 1898 he published a theoretical analysis of **syndicalism**. Although a critic of **utopian socialism** and **revisionism**, he respected **Eduard Bernstein**. In 1908 he published the work for which he became best known, *Réflexions sur la violence* (Reflections on Violence), which went though four editions by 1919. He opposed socialist/social-democratic **political parties** on the grounds that they were merely seeking political power and would simply substitute one system of privilege with another. More generally, he opposed the emphasis on rationalism in socialist thought and wanted greater attention paid to the role of custom and tradition in the complexity of real life. The idea of myth was central to his thought. Myths were not necessarily true, but they were indispensable in inspiring, mobilizing, and maintaining groups that sought change. Sorel cited the example of the myth of the Second Coming of Christ in sustaining **Christianity**. He saw the general strike as the myth of the proletariat; it might fail, but failure created martyrs whose memory would reinforce the myth. Combined with his rejection of democracy, the myth of the general strike emphasized the importance of fighting to sustain the struggle against **capitalism**. Essentially Sorel's myths were intuitive and beyond rational argument and discussion. With this emphasis on irrationalism and myths, Sorel's ideas occupied an uncertain ground between socialism and fascism. **Benito Mussolini** admired his work and Sorel briefly admired Mussolini.

SOUTH AFRICAN LABOUR PARTY (SALP). Socialism in South Africa has a tenuous history because of entrenched racial divisions and government violence. For many years the socialism that existed was imported by skilled workers from Europe. Between 1902 and 1914 versions of the **Social Democratic Federation** and the **Independent Labour Party** were set up and a South African Socialist Federation was formed at Johannesburg in 1907. South Africa was represented at the conferences of the **Second International** in 1904 and 1907. But all the South African socialist bodies remained small and well aware of the lack of community support for racially mixed **political parties**. **Ramsay MacDonald** (1902), **Keir Hardie** (1908), and **Tom Mann** (1910) all visited South Africa, but had to be mindful of racial divisions among the European **working class**. Racial segregation was reinforced by the craft exclusiveness of British immigrants and by Australian immigrants who brought with them ideas of racial exclusion based on immigration policy. Working-class Europeans wanted to restrict the supply of low-wage, non-European labor.

The SALP was officially formed in October 1909 in the aftermath of the 1907 strike by Rand miners. Its first leader was a mining engineer, Colonel F. H. P. Cresswell (1866–1932). Like the **trade unions**, the SALP made slow progress. It obtained 5 percent of the vote in the lower house in the 1910 elections and 13 percent in 1920, winning 21 out of 134 seats. The SALP operated in a climate marked by much official violence. Strikes in 1913, 1914, 1918, 1919, and 1922 were suppressed by the government with violence and much bloodshed. The SALP had some success, achieving a majority on the Transvaal provincial council between 1913 and 1917, but otherwise its support was limited. During World War I the left wing split from the SALP and joined the **Communist** Party in 1920. Thereafter the SALP was only a marginal presence in South African political affairs. It won five out of 156 seats at the election in 1953 and none thereafter. *See also* AFRICAN NATIONAL CONGRESS.

SPAAK, PAUL-HENRI (1899–1972). A leading Belgian social-democratic politician after 1945, Paul-Henri Spaak was born near Brussels and qualified as a lawyer, a profession he practiced from 1921 to 1931. He came from a prominent **middle-class** family. One of his grandfathers had been a prime minister for the Liberal Party in the nineteenth century. His mother was a socialist who was elected to parliament in 1921. Spaak was elected to parliament for the Belgian Workers' Party (later **Belgian Socialist Party**) in 1932, edited a left-wing socialist newspaper, served as foreign minister from 1936 to 1938, and was prime minister of a coalition government from 1938 to 1939. Because of his move to the right of the party, Spaak was more acceptable than the more obvious choice of **Émile Vandervelde**. After the German invasion, Spaak left for the United Kingdom and joined the Belgian government in exile. After World War II, he again served as foreign minister from 1945 to 1947 and led a coalition government from 1947 to 1950. His government was responsible for giving **women suffrage** in 1948 and placing the national bank under government control. He also helped to persuade King Leopold to abdicate in 1951 after strong opposition to the king from Belgian socialists.

Spaak's main achievements lay with his role in forging greater European unity. He was instrumental in the preparation and signing of the Brussels Treaty, which provided for mutual aid between the Benelux countries, the United Kingdom, and France. He played a leading role in the formation of the European Economic Community. He was leader of the negotiations for the Treaty of Rome that was signed in 1957 and was secretary-general of the North Atlantic Treaty Organization (NATO) from 1957 to 1961. Spaak left the Belgian Socialist Party in 1966.

SPANISH CIVIL WAR. The Spanish Civil War was an important rallying point for left-wing activists in the 1930s. Widely interpreted as a proxy **war** against fascism generally, it was also a complicated and controversial conflict on many levels. In February 1936 a **Popular Front** government supported by republicans, socialists, **syndicalists**, and **communists** was elected to govern, but excluded the Communists, who did not hold any positions within the government. In July 1936 General Francisco Franco began a military revolt against the republican government in Spanish Morocco. He was generously aided by the fascist government of **Benito Mussolini**. In particular, Adolf Hitler's transfer of Franco's troops by aircraft (commonly regarded as the first of its kind in history) in the early stages of the revolt helped tip the military balance in Franco's favor. The United Kingdom and France declared a policy of nonintervention, which in effect denied assistance to the republican government. Franco deliberately fought the war slowly to draw out his opponents to kill them. The republican government was assisted by the Soviet Union (which was paid ultimately with the government's gold reserves) and by the **International Brigades**.

On the republican side, there was much internal conflict. Its aggressive anticlerical policies (such as the confiscation of all religious property on 28 July 1936) alienated much internal and international support despite its positive programs of land redistribution and **educational** development. There was also much hostility between **anarchists** and other left-wing republican supporters. Anarchists, who had staged some local uprisings previously, were admitted to the republican government in Catalonia in September 1936 and in Madrid in December 1936. The conflict came to a head in May 1937 when the communists in Barcelona, the anarchists' stronghold, attacked the anarchists, whom they accused of sabotage. The attack marked the beginning of the end of anarchism in Spain as a significant force and the loss of moral authority for the republican cause. *See also* ANARCHO-SYNDICALISM.

SPANISH SOCIALIST WORKERS' PARTY [*PARTIDO SOCIALISTA OBRERO ESPAÑOL* (PSOE)]. The PSOE was formed in Madrid in May 1879. In 1886 it began to produce a socialist newspaper, *El Socialista* (The Socialist), but otherwise was able to achieve little on its own. The Spanish economy was overwhelmingly agricultural; up to 1910 two-thirds of the employed labor force worked in **agriculture**. Membership data for the PSOE are sparse, but it is known it had 5,000 paid members in the Asturias in northern Spain in 1899 and seems to have had a national membership of about 9,000 in 1903. With limited industrialization, it failed to build mass support. Even allowing for official interference, the PSOE won only 25,400 votes in the elections of 1901 and even by 1914 there was only one socialist representative in the *Cortes* or parliament.

At the 1923 elections the PSOE increased in representation in the *Cortes* to seven, largely because of its opposition to Spain's war in Morocco, but was unable to make use of its gains because of a coup d'état by Primo de Rivera that began a period of dictatorship lasting until April 1931. The PSOE led a bloodless revolution against the dictatorship, which forced the abdication of the king, Alfonso XIII, in 1931. The elections of June 1931 increased the parliamentary representation of the PSOE to 117 out of 470 seats and enabled Niceto Alcalá Zamora (1877–1949) to become prime minister of Spain's first socialist-led government. The Zamora government brought a new constitution that contained the standard features of socialism at that time, namely an emphasis on **egalitarianism**, full adult **suffrage** at 23 years, and a critical attitude toward property and **wealth**. The government was also hostile to **religion** in the form of the Catholic Church, a policy that caused Zamora to resign. He was replaced by Manuel Azaña. The government faced serious challenges from many quarters. The conservatives did not accept its legitimacy. The military was not only conservative, but operated effectively outside of government control. Separatist movements were particularly strong in Catalonia (where a separate socialist party had been formed in 1923) and in the Basque region. In 1933 a more moderate government was elected, but tensions remained high. There was a revolt in Catalonia, and in the 1936 elections a **Popular Front** government was elected with 256 seats out of a total of 473. The **Spanish Civil War** began soon afterward. Defeated in **war**, the PSOE continued as a party in exile and was a full member of the **Socialist International** from 1951.

The dictator, Francisco Franco, died in 1975. Democracy was restored and the PSOE was legalized in February 1977; in that year it claimed 150,000 members. Under its leader **Felipe González**, the PSOE adopted more moderate policies, although it remained to the left end of the political spectrum; it also received financial assistance from the **German Social Democratic Party**. In 1982 the PSOE won government for the first time since 1939 under González. Along with the group known as the *renovators*, he gained control of the party from the senior party figure Alfonso Guerra and his followers (sometimes called "guerristas") and held power until the party's defeat in the elections of March 1996. Under his administration, the **welfare state** was increased, the role of government-owned enterprises in the economy was reduced, and Spain joined the North Atlantic Treaty Organization (NATO) despite long-standing opposition from within the PSOE. In the parliamentary elections of March 2004 the PSOE regained power, winning 164 of 350 seats with 42.6 percent of the vote. **José Luis Rodríguez Zapatero** became prime minister. In the elections to the European Parliament in June 2004 the PSOE obtained 24 of Spain's 54 seats, compared with 24 of 64 in 1999. The elected PSOE members worked in the **Party of European Socialists**, with which their party was affiliated.

SPENCE, WILLIAM GUTHRIE (1846–1926). One of Australia's leading labor leaders in the late nineteenth century, William Spence was born on one of the Orkney Islands of Scotland and emigrated with his family to Geelong, Victoria, in 1852. He had no formal **education** and worked as a butcher's boy, a miner, and a shepherd. He assisted with the recruiting drive that led to the formation of the Amalgamated Miners' Association in the gold-mining town of Bendigo in 1874. From the mid-1880s Spence was an early supporter of the need for organized labor to have political representation. He served as a Labor member in the New South Wales parliament from 1898 to 1901 and in the federal parliament from 1901 to 1917. In 1917 he was permitted to resign from the **Australian Labor Party** rather than be expelled for his support of conscription during World War I.

SPORTS. *See* SOCIALIST WORKERS' SPORTS INTERNATIONAL; INTERNATIONAL LABOUR SPORTS CONFEDERATION.

STATE SOCIALISM. *See* "SOCIALISM WITHOUT DOCTRINE."

STAUNING, THORVALD (1873–1942). Leader of the **Danish Social Democratic Party** (*Socialdemokraterne*—SD) Thorvald Stauning was born in Copenhagen. He became a cigar sorter and in 1886 became leader of the cigar employees' **trade union**, a position he held until he was elected to the lower house of the Danish parliament (*Folketing*) in 1908. In 1913 he was elected to the city council of Copenhagen. As leader of the SD, he joined the Social-Liberal-led ministry between 1916 and 1920, mainly as minister for labor. He served as prime minister from 1924 to 1926 and from 1929 to 1940. After the SD won a majority in the upper house of parliament (*Landsting*), Stauning was able to bring in a large number of progressive laws. He ceased to be prime minister after the Nazi takeover of Denmark in April 1940.

SUFFRAGE. Universal suffrage was the foremost demand of socialist/social-democratic parties by the 1890s. Significant advances were made during the nineteenth century to give the vote to men over 21 in North America, Australia, France, New Zealand, and the United Kingdom, but even these were often qualified by cumbersome registration procedures, unfair electoral practices, lack of payment for elected representatives, and the general exclusion of **women** from the franchise. Elsewhere, the suffrage was either nonexistent or operated under conditions that made it a farce. From the time of **Louis Blanc**, socialists who believed in the democratic process regarded the universal franchise as the essential political reform that would pave the way for the implementation of socialist policies. The **Erfurt Program** (1891) of the **German Social Democratic Party** made universal, equal, and direct suffrage for all men and women over 20 its first demand. It also wanted proportional representation, equality of electorates based on the population census, two-year parliaments, payments for elected representatives, and the elections being held on a legal day of rest.

The other European socialist/social-democratic parties also made suffrage and related electoral reform their first demand in their programs. In Austria and Eastern Europe these parties actively campaigned for universal suffrage in 1905. On 15 September 1905 the **Hungarian Social Democratic Party** held a demonstration in Budapest that attracted 100,000 people. On 31 October the **Austrian Social Democratic Party** conducted a demonstration of 50,000 people in Vienna for universal suffrage and electoral reform. On 28 November 1905 the party organized mass demonstrations in support of universal suffrage in Vienna (250,000), Bohemia (260,000), and Prague (100,000); in total about 1 million people took part in these demonstrations throughout the Austro-Hungarian empire with minimum violence, but it was not until 1907 that they achieved the reforms they demanded. Although suffrage in the United Kingdom was considerably widened in the nineteenth century, notably by the legislation of 1867 and 1884, registration procedures restricted it in practice. In February 1901 the Labour Representation Committee (the **British Labour Party** from 1906) supported adult franchise for both sexes. The Labour Party continued to support full adult suffrage for both sexes, but the issue of the vote for women was given a low priority by the party before 1913 because of the **middle-class** domination of the suffragette movement.

SWEDISH SOCIAL DEMOCRATIC WORKERS' PARTY [*SVERIGES SOCIALDEMOKRATISKA ARBETAREPARTI* (SAP)]. The SAP has long enjoyed a reputation for being the most successful and effective practitioner of democratic socialism in the world. It was formed in 1889 by skilled employees who had encountered socialist ideas in Germany, Denmark, and the United Kingdom. Its electoral progress was slow because universal male **suffrage** was only gradually introduced between 1907 and 1911; there was no SAP representative in the Swedish parliament until 1897. Furthermore, reforms did not apply to the upper chamber, which was dominated by wealthy urban businessmen and farmers until its reformation in 1917.

The membership of the SAP grew from 10,000 to 75,000 between 1895 and 1913 and to 143,000 by 1920. Between 1902 and 1911 the SAP's share of the national vote rose from 4 percent to 30 percent.

From 1917 to 1920 the SAP had its first taste of government when it ruled in coalition with the *Folk* (People's) Party, which had been formed in 1902 to press for universal male suffrage. But otherwise the members of the *Folk* Party had insufficient common ground to maintain their unity and the coalition broke up. The SAP continued as a minority government for six months. The **nationalization** policies of the SAP distinguished it from other major Swedish **political parties** and made it hard for it to form lasting coalitions in the 1920s. As a result there was a high turnover of governments, with the SAP forming governments between 1921 to 1923 and 1924 to 1926.

The election victory in 1932 marked a real watershed in modern Swedish politics, since this was the victory that enabled the SAP to lead Swedish governments until 1976, creating a model for the **welfare state**, and to regulate the economy without resort to direct nationalization. Thereafter, Sweden's high inflation rate and unfavorable balance of payments dented the SAP's electoral popularity. The SAP was a minority government between 1970 and 1976, 1982 and 1991, and from 1994 to date. After the assassination of **Sven Olaf Palme** in 1986, Ingvar Gösta Carlsson was prime minister until 1991 and from 1994 to 1995. Göran Persson became prime minister in March 1996. In the parliamentary elections of 1998 the SAP won 131 of the 349 seats with 36.4 percent of the vote. In the parliamentary elections of September 2002 the SAP took 144 seats with 39.8 percent of the vote. In the elections to the European Parliament in June 2004 it secured five of Sweden's 19 seats, one less than in 1999 when Sweden had 22 seats. The SAP members worked in the **Party of European Socialists**, with which their party was affiliated. *See also* HANSSON, PER ALBIN; ERLANDER, TAGE; WIGFORSS, ERNST.

SWISS SOCIAL DEMOCRATIC PARTY [*SOZIALDEMOKRATISCHE PARTEI DER SCHWEIZ* (SP)]. The SP began as the Swiss Socialist Party in 1888. By 1900 it had 9,000 members and attracted nearly a fifth of the national vote. During World War I the party turned increasingly left wing. In 1919 it withdrew from the **Second International** and the leadership applied to join the **Comintern**

while at the same time refusing to withdraw from parliamentary participation. The application to join the Comintern was rejected by the rank and file. Later the SP split and its left wing formed a **communist** party. The SP joined the **International Working Union of Socialist Parties** in 1921 and its replacement, the **Labor and Socialist International**, in 1923. In the 1920s and early 1930s the SP remained strongly antiwar, but the rise of Adolf Hitler in Germany and Engelbert Dollfuss in Austria forced it to adopt a policy that emphasized national defense. The SP was very concerned about **unemployment**; it wanted to use the defense surplus in the budget to reduce unemployment, but at a national referendum in 1935 this proposal—which was linked with a proposal to regulate the financial market and monopolies—received only 43 percent of the vote. In 1943 the SP increased its representation in parliament and became part of the governing coalition. In the same year it also adopted a policy known as "New Switzerland" that called for the expansion of the **welfare state**, economic planning, and the **nationalization** of privately owned monopolies in key parts of the economy; at the same time, the SP maintained its anticommunism.

During the 1960s the SP opposed **nuclear weapons** and supported graduated **taxation** and the use of popular initiatives for federal legislation; it claimed 55,000 members in 1975. It has been a leader in advancing the rights of **women** and has been a member of coalition governments since 1959. Coalition government has been a convention guided by an arrangement made in 1959 between the major parties. This arrangement, called the "magic formula," gives the SP two places in the executive Federal Council. In the national elections of October 1995, the SP obtained 21.8 percent of the vote (compared to 18.5 percent in 1991), making it the largest single Swiss political party. In October 1999 the SP won 51 seats in the 200-seat National Council with 22.56 percent of the vote. In October 2003 the SP achieved a slightly better result, taking 52 seats and 23.4 percent of the vote. In 2003 the SP also won eight seats in the 46-member upper house (Council of States). Although the magic formula was revised in January 2004 the party continued to participate in broad coalition governments, keeping its two places in the Federal Council. In December 2005 the holders of these places, Moritz Leuenberger and Micheline Calmy Rey, were elected by parliament to be president and vice president respectively of the Federal Council for 2006.

SYNDICALISM. Syndicalism was a set of practices and ideas developed by French organized labor in the 1890s and 1900s. It derived from the French *syndicat* meaning simply **trade union**. As an **ideology**, syndicalism (or revolutionary syndicalism) meant the aggressive use of unions to gain political and social change. The class **war** was central to syndicalist thought, which saw governments and **political parties**, including socialist parties, as instruments of **working-class** oppression. Syndicalist thought stressed direct action, particularly the general strike, as the means to gain its objectives. It owed as much, if not more, to work experience as to ideas. Syndicalism grew out of conditions peculiar to France, namely, its revolutionary tradition (1789, 1830, 1848, 1871), the self-reliant attitude of its working class, the relatively slow growth of industrialization, and the importance of small enterprises in the economy. The French Charter of Amiens (1906), which was adopted by the national organization of French labor, the *Confédération Générale du Travail*, called for higher wages and shorter hours to be won by taking over the **capitalist** class and the general strike.

In Italy, syndicalism began to emerge after 1902 as a reaction to reformism in the **Italian Socialist Party** and developed into an unstable combination of **Marxism** and populism. Some of the Italian syndicalists became fascists. For example, Edmondo Rossini (1884–1965), the head of the fascist trade union federation from 1922 to 1928, had been a revolutionary syndicalist labor organizer in Italy and New York before 1914. In Spain, syndicalism remained important until the late 1930s. In North America, the **Industrial Workers of the World** (IWW) represented an indigenous form of syndicalism but there was also a Syndicalist League of North America that was formed in Chicago and operated between 1912 and 1914; the league had about 2,000 members and unlike the IWW attempted to infiltrate established trade unions with syndicalist ideas. *See also* ANARCHISM; ANARCHO-SYNDICALISM; INTERNATIONAL OF REVOLUTIONARY SYNDICALISTS; MANN, TOM; PELLOUTIER, FERNAND LÉONCE EMILE; SOREL, GEORGES.

– T –

TANNER, VÄINÖ ALFRED (1885–1966). A Finnish socialist, **Väinö** Tanner was first elected to the parliament (*Diet*) in 1907 for the

Finnish Social Democratic Party (*Suomen Sosialidemokraattinen Puolue*—SDP). He served as minister for finance in 1917 and as prime minister of a minority government during 1926, during which time he was able to introduce old-age pensions and a **health** insurance scheme. He also became leader of the Finnish cooperative movement and played an important role in the **International Cooperative Alliance**. In 1937 he became minister for foreign affairs in a coalition government with the Agrarian Party and later served as minister for food supplies. He was strongly anticommunist and remained a force in Finnish politics in the 1940s and 1950s. He was leader of the SDP from 1957 to 1963.

TAWNEY, RICHARD HENRY (1880–1962). British historian and **Christian socialist** Richard Tawney was born in Calcutta, India, was educated at Oxford, and became active in the Workers' Educational Association. After military service, he became a professor at the London School of Economics in 1931, a post he held until 1949. A founder of modern economic history, he wrote *Religion and the Rise of Capitalism* (1926) and began a long-running debate about the role of the gentry in England between 1558 and 1640. His best-known socialist works were *The Acquisitive Society* (1921) and *Equality* (1931) in which he attacked both the British class system and the acquisitive behavior encouraged by **capitalism** as inherently corrupting. He advocated comprehensive welfare services and graduated **taxation** as ways of promoting greater social equality. *See also* EGALITARIANISM.

TAXATION. Graduated taxation was a standard feature of socialist policy from the 1840s. A heavy, graduated income tax was among the measures advocated by **Karl Marx** and **Friedrich Engels** in the *Communist Manifesto* (1848). By 1900 graduated taxation of incomes, profits, and **wealth** was a general item in the programs of European social-democratic/socialist parties. It was advocated as a replacement for consumption taxes, which bore heaviest on the **working class**. Ironically, it was high government expenditure caused by the arms race of the 1900s and its acceleration by World War I that brought about the introduction of the income tax in many Western countries (for example, in Australia in 1915). After World War II, social-democratic governments introduced high levels of taxation to pay for socialist objectives such as the **welfare state**. This led to tax revolts in Denmark (1973) and Sweden (1991).

TEMPERANCE. Temperance—the practice or advocacy of the temperate consumption of alcohol and tobacco or abstaining from them altogether—is a forgotten, but once notable feature of socialism before the 1930s. Temperance was not only a method of self-discipline for serious socialists, but also a way of denying income to brewers and publicans whom they saw as exploiters of the **working class**. British socialists **Keir Hardie** and **George Lansbury**, for instance, were total abstainers as was Arthur Henderson (1863–1935), who led the British Labour Party from 1908 to 1910 and from 1931 to 1932. An international body, the General Secretariat of Abstaining Socialists, was formed in 1910 and was replaced by the International Union of Socialist Teetotallers in 1921, but this body failed to survive into the 1930s. *See also* RELIGION.

TERRORISM. Most socialists oppose terrorism, which involves political violence used with the aim creating a climate of fear. This, terrorists hope, will lead to submission to their goals. Many socialists oppose the use of any violence and have argued for varying degrees of **pacifism**. Other socialists have argued that violence, but not terror, might be necessary in self-defense against aggression in a hostile world. **Karl Marx** and Marxists such as **V. I. Lenin** have argued that violence is often the only viable means of bringing social justice to society. Other Marxists such as **Karl Kautsky** have opposed violence. Some on the **anarchist** and **syndicalist** wings of socialism, such as **Michael Bakunin** and **Georges Sorel** respectively, have considered violence not only necessary, but also a creative force that would stimulate the masses to liberate themselves. Even among socialists who do defend the use of violence in some circumstances, most have not gone so far as to advocate terrorism, which aims to strike fear into large sections of society.

Most Marxists disagreed with terrorist campaigns, stressing that the emphasis should be on the organization of the **working class** for the class struggle. There are significant exceptions. **Leon Trotsky**, in *Terrorism and Communism* (1920), conceded that terror could not be defended logically in general, but argued that in a revolutionary war it was necessary to intimidate the reactionary class, which would otherwise be determined to struggle. Joseph Stalin (1879–1953) conducted state terrorism against the people of the Soviet Union, in the name of socialism, during his rule from 1922 to 1953.

During the 1970s and early 1980s a number of far-left groups in Europe became involved in terrorist activities. In Italy one particularly prominent group was the Red Brigades, which argued that the Italian Communist Party had abandoned revolutionary **Marxism** and **Leninism**. Formed in 1970 by Renato Curcio and Margherita Cagol, the Brigades were the most prominent of many far-left revolutionary groups that embarked on campaigns of terror in Europe. They famously kidnapped and murdered the Italian Christian Democratic leader and former prime minister Aldo Moro. Another prominent group was the Red Army Faction (Baader-Meinhof Gang) in West Germany. Four of the leaders of the Red Brigades renounced the armed struggle from their prison cells in 1984. Nevertheless, fear of far-left terror reemerged in 2002. After an economic advisor to Silvio Berlusconi's right-wing government was murdered, the Red Brigades for the Construction of a Combatant Communist Party claimed responsibility. In some Latin American countries such as Colombia and Peru, Marxist-inspired movements have taken up guerilla warfare and engaged in acts of terrorism.

THOMAS, NORMAN (1884–1968). Norman Thomas was the best-known American moderate socialist from the late 1920s to the late 1950s. Born in Marion, Ohio, he was educated at Princeton University and Union Theological Seminary and worked as a Presbyterian minister in New York City between 1912 and 1918. He resigned his position to devote himself full-time to the **Socialist Party of America** (SPA). A **pacifist**, Thomas supported conscientious objectors during World War I and protested the internment of Japanese Americans and mass bombing during World War II and later the Vietnam War. He advocated the introduction of a comprehensive social **welfare** system when it seemed a radical idea in American politics. He and his ideas became more widely known as a result of his unsuccessful attempts to be elected to public office, first in New York State in 1924 and then as the presidential candidate for the SPA between 1928 and 1948. In the 1932 presidential campaign he received 884,781 votes. He was also a great defender of civil liberties, such as the rights of employees to form **trade unions**, freedom of speech, and freedom of assembly.

TRADE UNIONS. Trade unions occupy a central place in the history of socialism. With **friendly societies** and **cooperatives**, they provided the essential foundation for socialism to become a mass movement in Western Europe. In their present form, that is, voluntary associations of employees that seek to maintain or improve the pay and conditions of employment of their members through collective bargaining, trade unions emerged in England by the eighteenth century, as a reflection of its commercial and industrial growth. Although intermittent as organizations, trade unions conducted a total of 383 labor disputes in Britain between 1717 and 1800 in more than 30 trades. The number of union members at the start of the nineteenth century in England is not known, but some indication of the extent of **working-class** organization is indicated by a petition to parliament opposing the repeal of the apprenticeship clauses in 1814. It was signed by 30,517 journeymen. The legal prohibition on unions was effectively lifted in 1824. Yet outside of Britain before 1835, trade unions seem to have existed only in France (where they were not legalized until 1884), the United States, Canada, and New South Wales, Australia.

Before 1880 unions were often ephemeral organizations whose membership fluctuated wildly according to the health of the economy. The core of their support came from skilled, relatively well-off employees. Although not political organizations as such, unions, with their demands for better pay and conditions, did play a political role not just through lobbying—where they were allowed to, notably in England—but less obviously through their implicit challenge to the distribution of **wealth** and power in society, a topic of central importance to socialist theorists from the 1840s. Between 1880 and 1913 the numerical strength of the unions grew from about 606,000 to 14.1 million worldwide, mainly in Western Europe. The United States was the outstanding exception to this growth. This growth reflected not just a surge of working-class mobilization generally, but also the beginnings of unionism among white-collar employees such as teachers and government employees.

Relations between trade unions and socialist/social-democratic parties were close. Indeed, in what is now Austria, the unions and the **Austrian Social Democratic Party** were not clearly differentiated until after 1909. The programs of the social-democratic/socialist parties in the 1890s show how close this relationship was in most of continental Europe. For instance, the **Erfurt Program** (1891) of the **German Social Democratic Party** included a separate section of demands for the protection of labor: an eight-hour working day, prohibition of employment for children under 14 years of age, prohibition of night work unless essential, an unbroken period of rest of at least 36 hours for all workers, prohibition of payment in kind, a system of factory inspectors, legal equality of **agricultural** workers and domestic servants with industrial workers, repeal of the laws governing masters and servants, confirmation of the right of association, and the assumption of workmen's insurance by the government with employees being given a share in its administration.

Similar kinds of demands were also included in the other programs of socialist/social-democratic parties of the time, although national experience differed widely. In France, the unions declared their independence from **political parties** in 1906. In the same year the German unions declared themselves equal partners with the German Social Democratic Party in the leadership of the working class. The histories of the trade unions and the social-democratic/socialist parties tended to parallel one another in most countries where they were legally permitted. Again, the United States is the exception to these developments because no social-democratic/socialist party based on trade unions ever became part of the political mainstream.

Like the social-democratic/socialist parties, the trade unions provided a focus for socialists and after 1919 a target for **communist** infiltration. Relations between trade unions and social-democratic parties have always varied greatly between countries. They have been particularly close in Sweden, the United Kingdom, Germany, Austria, Australia, and New Zealand—to the point of being regarded as natural allies—but far less close in most other countries. Where there is such a close relationship and the party is reformist rather than radical, this is sometimes described as "laborism." The distancing of trade unions from social-democratic/socialist parties (outside of northern Europe and Australia and New Zealand) arose from the weakness of trade unions (as in southern Europe where the parties sought out other allies), and the existence of significant **ideological** divisions among the trade unions that made it difficult for them to give their support as a single entity. In France and Italy, the major union federations have been dominated by communists since World War II, thus depriving socialist parties of an important source of potential political support. In some European countries such as Switzerland and Belgium trade unions are able to engage in corporatism with business and government. Even in countries where social-democratic parties and trade unions have a close relationship, there can still be disagreements about policies when social-democratic or socialist parties form governments, most notably over salaries and wages policy.

Since about 1980 trade union membership in many Western economies has declined substantially in response to decreases in manufacturing employment, increased part-time employment, the growth of employment in the service sector, and a failure by trade unions to actively recruit young employees. The weakened strength of trade unions has affected their political power within social-democratic and labor parties. This has been particularly evident in Britain where the number of trade union members affiliated with the **British Labour Party** fell from a peak of 6.5 million members in 1979 to 4.6 million members in 1992. This loss of strength enabled the party leader, **Tony Blair**, to be far more independent of trade union opinion in preparing policy than any previous Labour prime minister. In the whole of Western Europe union membership fell between 1980 and 2001 from 49.3 to 39.6 million, while in the United States in the same period membership fell from 23.5 to 19.3 million. Nevertheless, during that period membership of organized labor grew in Eastern Europe by 37 million, in Africa by 11 million, in Asia by almost 10 million, and in Latin America by 3 million. Overall, the worldwide membership of organized labor grew by 41 percent between 1980 and 2001.

Trade unionists still faced violence, oppression, and discrimination in many parts of the world. In 2005 an annual survey by the **International Confederation of Free Trade Unions** recorded that 145 people had been killed because of their trade union activities in 2004, 16 more than in the previous year. The survey also documented more than 700 violent attacks on trade unionists and almost 500 death threats in 2004. Governments and employees were, the report claimed, continuing to suppress workers' rights. Columbia, China, and Haiti were among the countries that were causing particular concern. Discrimination was also reported in industrialized countries including Australia and the United States. *See also* INTERNATIONAL FEDERATION OF TRADE UNIONS.

TRISTAN, FLORA (1803–44). French socialist, feminist, and author Flora Tristan (her full name was Flore Célestine Thérèsa Henriette Tristan-Moscoso) was born in Paris. Her father was a Peruvian Spaniard and her mother was French. Although her father was socially prominent, his unexpected death when she was young plunged the family into poverty. Because her parents had not completed the civil formalities needed to legalize their marriage, she had to suffer the stigma of illegitimacy. Her poverty denied her a formal education, but she demonstrated both literary and artistic talent. Humiliated by her illegitimacy, she compensated by claiming descent from the last Inca king, Montezuma. An unhappy marriage and various travels, including five years in service with an English family between 1825 and 1830, provided her with the material for an autobiography (1830) and a radical outlook on society. In 1840 she published *Promenades dans Londres* (Walks in London), which gave an account of English **working-class** living conditions and **Chartism**. She became interested in the emancipation of the working class and **women**. Inspired by the example of the clubs of French craftsmen (*compagnonnages*) and the failures to unite these clubs and other working-class societies, she proposed an international union for the working class in her book *L'Union ouvrière* (The Workers' Union) in 1843. Her idea was that all interested workers in all countries should contribute a small amount of money each year to build facilities in towns for education, **health**, and culture. She had no interest in **suffrage** for women, but ardently advocated women's right to **education** and employment on equal terms with men. She died prematurely of typhoid and was one of the grandmothers of Paul Gauguin.

TROTSKY, LEON (1879–1940). Born in Yanovka, Ukraine (then part of the Russian empire), as Lyov Davidovich Bronstein, Leon Trotsky was imprisoned twice in early adulthood for political activism. Escaping both times, he went into exile in Europe. He was a member of the Russian Social Democratic Labour Party and was active in the failed Russian Revolution of 1905. Although a **Marxist**, he was an advocate of workers' democracy, and thus disagreed with **V. I. Lenin** for many years regarding revolutionary strategy and Marxist theory. Trotsky put forward his theory of "permanent revolution," in which he argued that the series of revolutions predicted by Marx in the advanced **capitalist** countries could actually begin in backward Russia.

Like Lenin he believed that the **working class** should lead the bourgeois revolution that the conditions of undeveloped Russia would hold back. Trotsky argued that the working class should immediately begin the socialist revolution, and that revolutions in the developed capitalist countries needed to be simultaneously fostered by Marxists abroad. Otherwise, the Russian revolution would fail. When each accepted some of the other's ideas Trotsky eventually became, with Lenin, one of the two leading figures in the Bolshevik Revolution of 1917. Trotsky subsequently played important political and military roles in the new Soviet **communist** state.

Trotsky came to be the most prominent and influential critic of Joseph Stalin (1879–1953), who came to power in 1922, and the bureaucratization of the Soviet Union. Defeated in the power struggle with Stalin, Trotsky was exiled. He sought asylum unsuccessfully from many countries as he traveled the world. In 1936 he wrote his most famous anti-Stalinist work *The Revolution Betrayed*, which described the Soviet Union as a degenerated workers' state. He eventually settled in Mexico in 1937, and the following year founded the **Fourth International** in the belief that the **Comintern** was no longer a progressive revolutionary organization. He continued to air his critique of Stalinism and was murdered in Coyoacán, Mexico, by a Stalinist agent.

– U –

UNEMPLOYMENT. Unemployment had been a feature of European society well before the advent of the **Industrial Revolution**. In England the first legislation requiring the unemployed to be provided with work by local government was introduced as early as 1576. But it was during the nineteenth century that unemployment became a serious social problem, aggravated by population growth. Mass unemployment was seen by socialist critics from 1840 onward as one of the main reasons for the introduction of a new social system. The system of national workshops advocated by **Louis Blanc** was intended to alleviate unemployment. In the United Kingdom, unemployment was always a main policy concern of **Keir Hardie**. The large-scale and prolonged unemployment of the Depression in the 1930s made unemployment — expressed as a commitment to full employment — and social welfare top priorities for social-democratic governments after World War II.

After the economic boom following World War II, socialist parties in power in the advanced industrialized states faced the struggle against unemployment. This became a particularly pressing problem in many countries as the global slump began to bite in the late 1970s. In this climate social-democratic governments faced the prospect of eviction when unemployment increased under their tenure. In 1979 the **British Labour Party**, for example, was voted out of office partly in response to rising unemployment (which continued to rise still further under the subsequent Conservative government). Upon its election to government in 1981 the **French Socialist Party** (*Parti socialiste*—PS) sought to secure full employment but soon had to abort this policy. In part this was because of the balance of payments deficits and a foreign exchange crisis. Crucially, however, inflation was a major factor in the reversal of policy. The problem of inflation could not be solved, as the PS in government was reluctant to burden wage earners with the costs of reducing unemployment.

In the early 1990s the difficulties facing social-democratic governments became evident in Sweden, where in the previous decade the **Swedish Social Democratic Workers' Party** (*Sveriges Socialdemokratiska Arbetareparti*—SAP) achieved the highest employment figures per head of population among the advanced industrial countries and also a considerably **egalitarian** wage structure. In the period from 1990, with the SAP in office, to 1993, by which time the party had lost the general election of 1991, the situation changed, with recognized unemployment rising from 1.5 percent to 8.2 percent. The SAP had, in the 1980s, responded to rising inflation with monetary **policies** that led to higher saving, lower consumer demand, and a subsequent reduction in business investment. In 1990 the SAP government applied to join the European Community (EC) and thus attempted to combat inflation with a fixed exchange rate. This made it difficult to maintain coordinated wage restraint. The SAP's need to appease its traditional supporters meant that business leaders, who campaigned for a transition to a fully free-market economy, considered its response to the crisis insufficient. Under pressure from both sides the SAP lost the elections of 1991 to a right-wing coalition that governed until the SAP regained power in 1994.

In the 1990s right-wing governments in France did little to resolve the country's unemployment problem. In 1997 the PS was reelected at the head of a left-wing coalition with **Lionel Jospin** as prime minister, thus initiating a period of cohabitation with the right-wing president Jacques Chirac. Jospin launched a scheme to create 350,000 public-sector jobs in an effort to address the problem of rising **youth** unemployment. The PS also introduced a 35-hour working week, one goal of which was to create more jobs. Jospin's government created more than 2 million jobs. Nevertheless both youth and long-term unemployment remained high as Jospin insisted that jobs could only be created with economic growth. Moreover, his attempt to restrict redundancies by law when businesses began to lay off workers was nullified by the French Constitutional Council. The PS lost the support of its allies on the left and was unable to retain power at the general elections of 2002.

Unemployment remained a crucial issue for socialist governments. After increasing its share of the votes in the parliamentary elections of 2002 the minority SAP government in Sweden once again faced criticism for failing to reduce unemployment. In Germany the **German Social Democratic Party** (*Sozialdemokratische Partei Deutschlands*— SPD)-led minority government attempted to deal with rising unemployment by introducing substantial **welfare** cuts. The SPD subsequently lost power at the elections of September to October 2005. *See also* CAPITALISM.

UNION OF HAITIAN SOCIAL DEMOCRATS [*PATI FIZYON SOSYAL DEMOKRAT AYISYEN/PARTI FUSION DES SOCI- AUX-DEMOCRATES HAITIENS* (PFSDH)]. Formed in Haiti in 2005, the PFSDH was the result of a merger of the Revolutionary-Progressive Nationalist Party (*Parti Nationaliste Progressiviste Révolutionnaire*—PANPRA) and the Party of the National Congress of Democratic Movements (*Parti du Congrès National des Mouvements Démocratiques*—KONAKOM). The PANPRA was formed in Haiti in 1986, after the fall of the second generation of the brutal Duvalier (François, then Jean-Claude) dictatorships that had ruled Haiti for decades. In June 1989 the PANPRA was made a full member of the **Socialist International** (SI). Led by Serge Gilles, it became one of Haiti's leading **political parties** after the 1990 elections. In the 1990s Haitian politics was characterized by corruption, violence, and coups. The PANPRA participated in wide and unstable coalition governments that were dominated by the military, but pulled its representatives out of such governments in 1993 and 1995.

The KONAKOM was formed in 1987 and participated in unstable coalition governments during the turmoil of Haitian politics in the

1990s. In 1995 when other parties resigned, Jean-Claude Bajeux of the KONAKOM remained the sole opposition member in a government dominated by the party of outgoing President Jean-Bertrande Aristide. In 1996 the KONAKOM became a full member of the SI.

After the first round of parliamentary elections in May 2000 the KONAKOM and PANPRA, along with many other parties, complained of irregularities and boycotted the subsequent rounds in July and November. The Water Fall Family (*Famni Lavalas*) Party of Aristide, who won the presidency in 2000 after a constitutionally required gap after his presidency in the 1990s, dominated the parliamentary elections of 2000 that were condemned as corrupt by many domestic and international observers. After the elections of 2000 neither the PANPRA nor the KONAKOM held any seats in parliament. A wide range of **ideologically** diverse parties including the PANPRA and the KONAKOM, led by Victor Benoit, joined the Democratic Convergence opposition coalition. Aristide was overthrown by a coup in February 2004 and Haiti descended into chaos. The merger of the KONAKOM and PANPRA to form the PFSDH took place after encouragement and support from the SI at a meeting of the SI Committee for Latin America and the Caribbean in January 2005.

UNION OF LABOUR [*UNIA PRACY* (UP)]. The Polish UP was formed in June 1992. It comprised left-wing members of the Solidarity (*Solidarnoc*) **trade union** movement that had helped bring down **communism**, along with some members of the former communist Polish United Workers' Party (*Polska Zjednoczona Partia Robotnicza*). In the elections to the *Sejm* (parliament) in 1993, the UP gained 7.3 percent of the vote. Divisions within the UP meant that their expected participation in a coalition government with the **Democratic Left Alliance** (*Sojucz Lewicy Demokratycznej*—SLD) and Polish People's Party did not go ahead. In 1996 the UP gained full membership in the **Socialist International**.

In elections to the *Sejm* in 1997 the UP failed to gain the 5 percent required for representation. In elections to the *Sejm* in 2001 the UP campaigned in a list with the SLD, which had by then been transformed from an electoral coalition into a party. The SLD and UP formed a government after winning 216 of 460 seats with 41 percent of the vote. When, in 2004, poor economic performance and allegations of corruption led some SLD members to leave and form the Polish Social Democratic Party (*Socjaldemokracja Polska*—SdPL), Andrzej Celiński of the UP joined them. In elections to the *Sejm* in September 2005 and the presidency the following month the UP campaigned with the SdPL, rather than independently or with the SLD. The SdPL failed to obtain any seats. The SdPL's presidential candidate, Marek Borowski, won 10.33 percent of the vote.

UTOPIAN SOCIALISM. The term *utopian socialism* was used by **Karl Marx** and **Friedrich Engels** to describe their socialist predecessors; the *Communist Manifesto* (1848) refers to "critical-utopian socialism" to describe visionary schemes for separate societies practicing social equality as advocated by Étienne Cabet (1788–1856), **Robert Owen**, and **Charles Fourier**. The term *utopian* referred to *Utopia*, a Latin work published by Sir Thomas More in 1516 and first translated into English in 1551. Derived from Greek and meaning "Noplace," *Utopia* described an imaginary, ideal society located on an island off the Americas. The work was implicitly critical of the society of his day. More began a literary genre that has since been used by over 200 writers as a vehicle for the promotion of a range of social and political **ideologies**. **Karl Kautsky** published a study of More's *Utopia* in 1888. Three of the best-known utopian works that promoted socialism or influenced the development of socialism were **Edward Bellamy**'s *Looking Backward* (1887), **William Morris**'s *News from Nowhere* (1890), and **H. G. Wells**'s *A New Utopia* (1905).

Marx and Engels used utopian socialism as a contrast to their "scientific" socialism, and the term was later used in a derogatory sense against other socialists. Nevertheless, as the works of Bellamy, Morris, and Wells showed, the visionary idea of a future socialist society where poverty and **unemployment** would not exist was very strong from the 1880s to about 1914 and continued to be a feature of socialist writings into the 1930s. *See also* COMMUNES; LITERATURE.

– V –

VANDERVELDE, ÉMILE (1866–1938). Belgian socialist politician and theorist Émile Vandervelde was born in Ixelles, Belgium, and studied law and social science at the University of Brussels, from which he graduated with a doctorate. In 1886 he joined the Belgian

Workers' Party (*Belgische Werkliedenpartij*—PW), which later became the **Belgian Socialist Party**. In 1894 he was one of his party's 27 members elected to parliament. He was one of the founders of a program of university extension courses in 1892, the forerunner of the Center of Workers' Education set up by his party in 1911. He was a leader in the campaign to denounce appalling human rights abuses in the Congo perpetrated by King Leopold II. He visited the Congo and wrote an account of what he saw there. Unlike the bulk of his party, he realized that the only good option was to transfer control of the Congo to the Belgian parliament; this was in fact done in 1908.

Vandervelde was also a theorist. Unlike most of his German colleagues, he regarded socialism as an objective to be pursued not just by **political parties** but also by **trade unions**, the **cooperative movement**, and other bodies. He wrote *Le Collectivisme et l'évolution industrielle* (1900), which was translated into English as *Collectivism and Industrial Evolution* in 1907, and *Le Socialisme contre l'état* (Socialism against the State) in 1918.

Vandervelde was an active participant in international socialism and chairman of the International Bureau of the **Second International**. He was also a member of the executive of the **Labor and Socialist International** between 1923 and 1925.

As leader of the PW, he was invited to join the Belgian **war** cabinet in 1916, an appointment the party agreed to. He was minister for justice from 1918 to 1921 and was a minister in some capacity from 1925 until his death. He visited Russia in 1917 in support of the Allied war effort and denounced **Leninism** and the Bolshevik coup. Vandervelde was very much a **revisionist** socialist and was one of the few socialist leaders of his time to be concerned about the failure of socialism to gain supporters among **agricultural** workers. *See also* HUSYMANS, CAMILLE.

VIENNA INTERNATIONAL. *See* INTERNATIONAL WORKING UNION OF SOCIALIST PARTIES.

VIETNAM COMMUNIST PARTY [Đảng Cộng sản Việt Nam (ĐCVN)]. Formed in 1930 by Ho Chi Minh as the Indochinese Communist Party, the ĐCVN was dedicated to revolution. This led some socialists opposed to **communism** to join the Saigon chapter of the **French Socialist Party** in 1931. At the end of the Japanese occupation in August 1945 Ho seized power and formed the Democratic Republic of Vietnam. Vietnam had previously been under French **imperialism**. The French at first recognized the new republic but soon began an eight-year **war** against Ho. In 1954 the country was divided, with Ho's republic in the north and a pro-American regime in the South. The ĐCVN formed a people's democracy in the north—a communist state in which the ĐCVN controlled the National Assembly.

The noncommunist left secretly founded the Vietnamese Socialist Party in September 1952, which came to be legally recognized through support from the French Socialist Party and gained the status of a consultative member of the **Socialist International** between 1955 and 1969. Its leading figure was its secretary, Dr. Pham Van Ngoi. Representatives of the Vietnamese socialists were given observer status at the **Asian Socialist Conference** in 1953 and their party obtained full membership status in 1956, when it had about 1,000 members. The socialists wanted an independent Vietnam and universal **suffrage**. Repression by the government in the South as well as intense competition from the ĐCVN ensured that the Socialist Party did not survive beyond the 1960s.

After a land-reform program, based on Chinese communism in the 1950s, failed to produce the expected gains and led to repression of dissent, the ĐCVN organized **agriculture** into collectivized **cooperatives** and **nationalized** industry. In 1960 the ĐCVN resolved to step up its efforts to liberate South Vietnam. Alarmed at Soviet and Chinese support for the ĐCVN, the United States embarked on the war against North Vietnam—a war which escalated throughout the 1960s and destroyed much of Vietnam's infrastructure and industry. After huge losses on both sides the United States withdrew in 1973 and in 1975 the communists overran the South, leading to the unified Vietnamese communist state. Economic mismanagement and unexpected weather meant the failure of Vietnam's agricultural projects, leading to poverty and mass efforts to escape the country. The problems were worsened by war with China, which objected to Vietnam's intervention in Cambodia to remove the ultracommunist Khmer Rouge from power.

In the early 1990s the ĐCVN revamped the country's economy, introducing market reforms under the direction of the state. In the 1990s relations with China were normalized, good relations were established with noncommunist countries of the region, and businesses in the United States were encouraged to invest in Vietnam. Limited political reforms were also introduced, with collective ĐCVN leadership of Vietnam replaced by a cabinet system with a prime minister accountable to the Assembly. However, the Assembly remained under the domination of the ĐCVN, even though nonparty candidates were allowed to compete for seats. In the late 1990s economic growth declined for the first time since the reforms. Some political protest resulted. In 1998 to 1999 the ĐCVN determined that political stability would not be sacrificed for economic reform. Nevertheless, a stock exchange was set up in 2000 and foreign investment continued. In April 2001 Nong Duc Manh replaced Le Kha Phieu as secretary-general of the ĐCVN and announced that he intended to continue the modernization and industrialization of Vietnam.

– W –

WALZER, MICHAEL LABAN (1935–). Michael Walzer is a communitarian socialist and political philosopher. Born in New York City, he completed his PhD at Harvard University in 1961. He taught at Princeton University, then Harvard and then Princeton once again, where he is still based. In addition to education and writing political philosophy, he is editor of the socialist journal *Dissent*, thus conforming to his belief that social criticism is the business of every citizen. In his philosophy Walzer focuses on political culture and seeks to identify the institutions and political arrangements suitable for each existing society. He argues that no single conception of justice is applicable to every sphere of every society. Principles of justice must be derived from the way in which people understand the goods of their society. Things become valuable only within a web of social relations. Hence, justice is relative to social meanings, which are historical in character, but change over time.

This understanding of justice informs Walzer's book *Spheres of Justice* (1983), in which he argues that principles of justice are pluralistic. This means that different social goods should be distributed for different reasons. This is his idea of complex equality. He argues that a monopoly of goods within a particular sphere is not necessarily unjust. What is unjust is domination, which occurs when a monopoly in one type of good gives the holders power to command a wide range of other goods in other spheres. Walzer argues that the sphere of the market must be properly bounded. Also, the political sphere must be democratic to avoid dominance by money, social position, or other goods. He believes that the ideal of democracy is a key element of American history, traditions, and practices, and is the basis of much of the social criticism that he applauds. For him, the appropriate arrangements for American society involve a decentralized democratic socialism. A range of autonomous spheres would include companies and factories with workers' control, a strong **welfare state** run partly by local and amateur officials, protected **religion** and familial life, and a system of public honors unaffected by rank or class.

WAR. Except for purely defensive purposes, most socialists have been historically opposed to war and particularly to militarism. By the end of the nineteenth century socialists tended to regard war as the outcome of capitalist competition or the result of engineering by undemocratic forces within society to benefit **capitalism** and to divert the **working class** from uniting for social and economic reform. **Imperialism** was widely seen as a cause of war. The **Erfurt Program** (1891) of the **German Social Democratic Party** (*Sozialdemokratische Partei Deutschlands* — SPD) demanded that democratic processes decide questions of war and peace and that international disputes be resolved by arbitration. It also wanted Germany's standing army to be replaced by a militia based on military training for all. Similar sentiments were expressed in the other programs of the socialist/social-democratic parties of the period.

In Sweden the socialists helped avert a war when they threatened the government with mass demonstrations and strikes to allow Norway to secede peacefully in 1905. The buildup of international tensions in Western Europe and their outbreak into war was foreseen by the **Second International**, which attempted to use an appeal to the solidarity of the working class to prevent war.

Armies were suspect institutions among socialists because governments could use them to break strikes. In 1910 the French government of Aristide Briand (1862–1932), who had been a socialist until 1906, used the army to break a railroad strike. In 1911 the *Confédération du Travail* (French Confederation of Labor) introduced a policy of sending army conscripts a small payment from their **trade** unions to remind them of their links with, and obligation to, the working class. At the same time, it was generally recognized that armies were needed for defense. In 1910, **Jean Jaurès**, who led the **French Socialist Party**, advocated a nonprofessional citizens' army in his book *L'Armée nouvelle* (The New Army). Citizens would spend short periods of training and then return to their regular occupations. Such an army was designed only to defend against invasion.

In the 1930s **pacifist** sentiments were strong among socialists. But they were challenged by the menace of fascism and especially by the **Spanish Civil War**, which attracted many foreign socialists such as **George Orwell**, to fight on the republican side. During World War II European socialists and **communists** distinguished themselves in the resistance to the Nazis. For example, communists in Yugoslavia and Albania gained widespread support and took power after the war. In France, although initially prevented from doing so by the need to follow the line from Moscow, the French communists played a prominent role in the French resistance. German communists also played a role in World War II. Although most of the communist leaders were either executed or had fled to Moscow after Adolf Hitler imposed a ban on all parties other than the Nazis in 1933, a small network of Communist Party branches operated in secret during the war, spreading anti-Nazi propaganda. The German SPD had been banned in 1933 and most of its leaders were sent to concentration camps. Nevertheless Hans Vogel operated as president of the SPD from London during the war. He stressed that it would be the responsibility of the SPD after the war to educate all Germans to be good Europeans and good world citizens. He stressed that out of the chaos that Hitler would leave behind a new creative socialism could be built that would be committed to freedom. Recreated after the war, the SPD in opposition opposed rearmament.

In the United Kingdom the **British Labour Party** (Labour) played a prominent part in the war effort. Even before Winston Churchill took over from Neville Chamberlain as Conservative wartime prime minister in May 1940, Labour had issued *Labour's War Manifesto* demanding that there must be a sustained effort to defeat Hitler and to build a peace of justice that would remove the causes out of which war arises. All Labour members were called upon to resist the aggressor, but the manifesto stressed that Labour had no quarrel with the German people. The prominent Labour member Barbara Ayrton Gould argued that the alternative to defeating Hitler would be to suffer the "systematic terror" that had been reported to her in a letter from a German woman. **Harold Laski** argued that the struggle against Hitler must coincide with a struggle for socialism in order to ensure that it would be a victory for the common people of all lands. When Churchill took over as prime minister Labour cooperated in a wartime government. Labour politicians served in Churchill's cabinet.

In the Cold War that dominated international relations from 1945 to 1990 sharp divisions emerged in some Western European countries between communists and social democrats in the broader socialist movement. This was especially the case in France and Italy—countries with large, strong communist parties. Some of the more staunchly anticommunist social democrats opposed cooperation with the communists. **Giusseppe Saragat** in Italy, for example, left the **Italian Socialist Party** to form a new Italian Democratic Socialist Party (*Partito Socialista Democratico Italiano*). In the United Kingdom, where the Communist Party was small and weak, the divisions were within the Labour Party. Except for a short period in the early 1980s, the Labour leadership supported the Western alliance in the Cold War. **Ernest Bevin** was particularly anticommunist. There was always, however, a significant movement among the rank and file membership, sometimes gaining the support of senior figures such as Tony Benn, that wanted the United Kingdom to play no part in the Cold War and to abandon its **nuclear weapons**.

The Algerian war against the French colonial power, which lasted from 1954 to 1962, attracted opposition from the left, largely organized by and around the French communists. The war waged by the United States in Vietnam during the 1960s and early 1970s, following Washington's intervention against communism, attracted the hostility of the left. The **new left** in particular rallied against American involvement, with some support from trade unions and rather more from students. Many of the students were organized by the Students for a Democratic Society, and the protests became a broader antiwar movement that spread to campuses in other countries such as the United Kingdom and France in the mid to late 1960s.

In the United Kingdom the campaign against the Vietnam War was not supported by the Labour leader **Harold Wilson**, who provided diplomatic support to the Americans but nevertheless refused to send

British troops to fight in the conflict. By way of contrast, at the beginning of the twenty-first century the Labour leader **Tony Blair** was supportive of wars waged by the United States against the regimes in Afghanistan and Iraq in an effort to stamp out international **terrorism**. In each case Blair committed British troops to the conflict. The invasion and occupation of Iraq that began in 2003 were carried out in the belief that Iraqi dictator Saddam Hussein had acquired or built weapons of mass destruction. Saddam's *Baathist* regime was removed from power but the feared weapons were nowhere in evidence. The involvement in Afghanistan and Iraq caused great disruption among Labour Party members, many of whom resigned in protest. The Iraq War also created divisions between social-democratic leaders. **Gerhard Schröder** did not allow German involvement and the antiwar stance of **Jose Zapatero** in Spain brought his **Spanish Socialist Workers' Party** to power in March 2004 when voters rejected the incumbent government that had committed troops to the war. *See also* SOCIALIST FORCES FRONT; VIETNAM COMMUNIST PARTY.

WATSON, JOHN CHRISTIAN (1867–1941). John Watson was the first leader of the **Australian Labor Party** (ALP) to become head of the national government. He was born in Valparaiso, Chile, as his parents emigrated from Scotland to New Zealand, where he became a printer. He arrived in New South Wales, Australia, in 1886 and became president of the Sydney Trades and Labour Council (a **trade union** federation) in 1893 and the Australian Labour Federation, a trade union body that advocated the direct representation of labor in parliament. Watson joined the ALP and presided over the trade union conference in New South Wales in 1894. Labor candidates for parliament had to sign a pledge that bound them to follow the majority decisions of the parliamentary party (known as caucus). In 1894 he was also elected to the parliament of New South Wales. He entered federal politics in 1901 and was made leader of the parliamentary party. Because of the pledge, the Labor members were disciplined in their voting and therefore able to exert disproportionate influence on their disorganized opponents.

The ALP increased its representation in the federal parliament after the December 1903 election. Watson formed the first ALP government on 27 April 1903 with himself as prime minister and treas-

urer; he held office until 17 August 1904. During his brief administration, Watson endeavored, unsuccessfully, to bring in a labor arbitration law that would have included giving preference to employing
members of trade unions. He resigned as ALP leader in October 1907
due to ill health. He was succeeded by **Andrew Fisher**. In 1916 he,
like many other founding members of the ALP, supported conscription and was expelled from the party. Watson went on to have a business career and was one of the founders of the National Roads and
Motorists' Association in New South Wales.

WEALTH. The inequality of the distribution of wealth under **capitalism** was a concern of socialists from the 1840s. Their solution, foreshadowed as early as 1848 in **Karl Marx** and **Friedrich Engels**'s
Communist Manifesto, was a heavy graduated income **tax** and the
abolition of **inheritance**. Graduated income tax was a general objective in the programs of socialist parties by the 1890s. Ironically, a
number of nonsocialist governments introduced graduated income
taxes before 1914, although not to promote social equality, but rather
to pay for rising military expenditures. Wealth itself was harder to tax
than income because it was less easy to measure. Even so, Australia
(1915) and Canada (1919) both tried to measure the distribution of
wealth within their societies. Wealth distribution within capitalist society is a key objective of social-democratic parties. In 1910 the **Australian Labor Party**, which was then the federal government,
brought in a land tax. In 1982 the **French Socialist Party** in government introduced a wealth tax. *See also* MILL, JOHN STUART.

WEBB, MARTHA BEATRICE (1858–1943). Like her husband **Sidney Webb**, Beatrice Webb, *nee* Potter, was one of the prominent figures of British **Fabianism**. She was born in Gloucestershire, England, to prosperous parents, her father being a wealthy railway director. Although she enjoyed little formal education, she was self-
taught in a wide range of subjects during her childhood and **youth**.
As a young **woman** she engaged in charity work for the poor. She
then worked as a researcher for Charles Booth's study of poverty in
London. In 1892 she married Webb, thus beginning their intellectual
partnership that would continue for 50 years. Together they published
a range of works including studies of **trade unions**, industrial
democracy, local government, socialist constitutionalism, and, later,

a sympathetic study of Soviet **communism**. Together they founded the London School of Economics and Political Science (usually shortened to London School of Economics) and the *New Statesman* magazine. Her four-volume autobiographical diary, only the first volume of which was published before her death, is celebrated as a study of politics and society in her times.

WEBB, SIDNEY JAMES (1859–1947). Socialist author and intellectual Sidney Webb was born in London into a lower **middle-class** family. He left school at 16 and studied for legal qualifications part-time. He joined the **Fabian** Society in 1885. With **G. B. Shaw** and **H. G. Wells**, he was among its best-known members before 1912. Then a clerk with the Colonial Office, Webb devoted his legal training and remarkable memory to the cause of social justice though socialism. Socialism for Webb was an inevitable consequence of economic and social development. What he stressed was the importance of expert administration in the public interest. He had no interest in the dreams of **utopian socialism** and was opposed to **syndicalism**. Between 1905 and 1909 he served on the inquiry in the administration of the Poor Law. His unsuccessful minority report recommended that the social services provided by the boards of guardians (established in 1834) be given to the local government and that these services be expanded to include the unemployed. The extra cost would be paid for by more **taxation**, a proposal that foreshadowed the **welfare state**. Webb served on the London County Council between 1892 and 1910 and with **Beatrice Webb** formed an extraordinary intellectual partnership. Together they helped found the London School of Economics in 1895. Sidney Webb was an adviser to organized labor during World War I, and he greatly assisted the Miners' Federation of Great Britain before the Royal Commission on the Coal Mines in 1919. He drafted *Labour and the New Social Order* in 1918, which was the basis of **British Labour Party** (Labour) policies up to 1950. He served three terms as a Labour member of parliament in the 1920s, but left the House of Commons in 1929 to accept the title of Baron Passfield and to represent Labour in the House of Lords.

WELFARE STATE. The term *welfare state* was coined in the **Beveridge Report** in the United Kingdom in 1942. But its essential idea—the provision of comprehensive government benefits to the general population to cope with illness, **unemployment**, poverty, and old age—dated back to at least as early as the eighteenth century; for example, Thomas Paine suggested comprehensive welfare benefits to combat poverty in *The Rights of Man* (1791). In Germany Otto von Bismarck introduced a number of important welfare measures such as unemployment insurance that, together with the **Antisocialist Law**, were specifically designed to undercut popular support for socialism. Although the idea of the welfare state thus was not exclusively a socialist one, it was an idea that socialism championed from the 1860s.

By the 1890s the idea of the welfare state had become established in the programs of socialist/social-democratic parties. The **Erfurt Program** (1891) of the **German Social Democratic Party** (*Sozialdemokratische Partei Deutschlands*—SPD) demanded free medical and legal services and burial. The 1893 program of the Belgian Workers' Party (later **Belgian Socialist Party**) demanded that public charities be transformed into a general insurance system for all citizens to provide for unemployment, sickness, accident, old age, and benefits for widows and orphans.

Electoral wins by social-democratic parties in Sweden (1932), New Zealand (1935), and Denmark (1935) enabled their governments to lay the foundations for welfare states in these countries. In the United Kingdom (1945) and Australia (1946), convincing wins by their labor parties ensured that welfare states would be built there too. In other Western democracies the demand for welfare services was too great to be ignored by nonsocialist governments. Since the 1970s there has been increasing criticism of the cost of the welfare state because of the increased **taxation** it entails but also because of its alleged disincentive to actively seek employment. Nevertheless, in 2005 the SPD-led government in Germany alienated many of its supporters with measures to reduce welfare costs in an effort to revive the economy. The SPD was removed from power in the general elections that year. *See also* BEVERIDGE, WILLIAM HENRY; FRIENDLY SOCIETIES; SAVAGE, MICHAEL JOSEPH.

WELLS, HERBERT GEORGE (1866–1946). Born in Bromley, England, H. G. Wells is best remembered as the father of modern scientific fiction, rather than as a socialist. Nevertheless, he did play a significant role in popularizing socialist ideas, particularly among the lower **middle-class** English with some education, that is, people like himself. He was a member of the **Fabian** Society up to 1909, but fell out with **Sidney Webb**. Wells was too independent a figure and moved in too many **ideological** directions to be permanently identified with any single political philosophy. He popularized socialist ideas in *Anticipations* (1901), *Mankind in the Making* (1903), *A Modern Utopia* (1905), a Fabian tract called *The Misery of Boots* (1907), and most successfully in *New World for Old* (1908), the most influential work of its kind since **Robert Blatchford's** *Merrie England*. *See also* LITERATURE; UTOPIAN SOCIALISM.

WHITLAM, EDWARD GOUGH (1916–). Australian Labor Party (ALP) prime minister from December 1972 to November 1975, Edward Whitlam was born in Melbourne, Victoria, and graduated in arts and law from Sydney University. He entered federal politics in 1952 for a seat in southwestern Sydney. Narrowly elected deputy leader of the parliamentary party in 1960, he was elected leader in 1967 after the ALP's massive defeat in the 1966 elections. He set about reforming the ALP organization and advocated policies designed to attract support from the younger voters and the **middle class** in the outer suburbs of the large cities. Whitlam gained a remarkable swing of 7 percent to the ALP in the 1969 election and led it to victory at the elections of December 1972. However, Labor did not win a majority in the Senate, where the non-Labor parties were able to frustrate the government's programs of reform.

Building on a number of initiatives of the previous conservative government, Whitlam undertook a wide-ranging series of reforms in foreign relations and domestic policy. The government upgraded the **welfare state**, introduced universal **health** insurance, revised the divorce law, and devised programs to improve life in the cities, assist Aborigines, and improve the status of **women**.

The Whitlam government faced two great problems: the inflation and recession caused by the 1973 oil crisis and the hostility of the Liberal-Country coalition, which used its majority in the Senate to force the government to hold a new election in May 1974. Despite the reelection of Whitlam's government, the Senate refused to pass the budget (October 1975). Unexpectedly, the governor-general, a Whitlam appointee, intervened. He dismissed Whitlam and installed the leader of the opposition as prime minister of a caretaker government

(11 November 1975). At the election of 13 December 1975, Whitlam and the ALP were defeated. Whitlam remained as leader until 1977, when he resigned after a second electoral defeat in December. In May 1983 the new ALP government of **Bob Hawke** appointed Whitlam as Australia's ambassador to UNESCO.

WIGFORSS, ERNST (1881–1977). Swedish political theorist, politician, and author Ernst Wigforss played a central role in the creation of the **ideology** and **policies** of the **Swedish Social Democratic Workers' Party** (*Sveriges Socialdemokratiska Arbetareparti*—SAP). He was a member of the *Riksdag* (parliament) from 1919 to 1953, a member of the directorate of the SAP from 1920 to 1952, and a member of its executive committee from 1928 to 1952. In 1919 he largely drafted the Gothenburg Program, whose comprehensive **social security** schemes underpinned the policies and practices of the SAP after it won government in 1932. Although influenced by **guild socialism** and **syndicalism**, he recognized that the **working class** was getting better-off, not worse-off, and he argued for a gradual transition to socialism and for policies of ongoing social and economic reform to reduce the inequalities of **capitalism**. As minister for finance (1925–26, 1932–49), he was able to increase government spending to alleviate **unemployment**, a policy he deduced from socialist theories, thereby anticipating Keynes's anticyclical theory by four years.

WILDE, OSCAR FINGAL O'FLAHERTIE WILLS (1854–1900). Born in Dublin, Oscar Wilde studied at Trinity College, Dublin, and Magdalen College, Oxford. He is most famous for his plays including *The Importance of Being Earnest*, his novel *The Picture of Dorian Gray* and his short stories. He is well known for being imprisoned in 1895 for what were considered homosexual offenses. He also wrote an influential work called *The Soul of Man under Socialism*. With the abolition of private property and the diminishment of authority, socialism would allow individualism and artistic freedom to flourish. Widespread drudgery was no longer necessary given technological advancement. There was no need for the division of labor that led to the social injustice in which many endured lives of misery. Machines could now do the unpleasant work for humans. Wilde conceded that his ideas were utopian, but insisted that humanity should always strive to realize utopias.

WILSON, HAROLD (1916–95). Born in the northern English industrial town of Huddersfield, Wilson was **British Labour Party** prime minister from 1964 to 1970 and from 1974 to 1976. Raised in a nominally Anglican Nonconformist environment, he was educated at Oxford. He entered the **war** cabinet secretariat in 1940 working for **William Beveridge**, the planner of the United Kingdom's post-1945 **welfare state**. He was elected to parliament in the 1945 landslide election for the Labour Party. Originally on the left of the party, Wilson moved progressively to the center during the 1950s. He became party leader after the death of Hugh Gaitskell in 1963.

In October 1964 the Labour Party won a narrow victory in the national elections and Wilson began his first term as prime minister. His administration was characterized by a mixture of government economic planning that recognized the need for a strong private sector and the expansion of the welfare state. In his view socialism could be best achieved by policies that promoted greater efficiency, technological innovation, and equality. Nevertheless, Wilson supported the cultivation of merit. An astute politician, he used conciliation rather than confrontation to deal with governmental problems. Both his administrations faced serious economic problems, specifically a currency crisis in 1967 and high inflation in the mid-1970s. Wilson's achievements included the improvement of pensions and the establishment of the Open University program.

WOMEN. Improving the lot of women in society was a theme of socialism from its very beginnings in the early nineteenth century. It built on a campaign that was begun by liberal thinkers like Mary Wollstonecraft in *A Vindication of the Rights of Women* (1792) and by social theorists like the economist William Thompson (1775–1833), who argued the case for women's equality in his *Appeal of One Half of the Human Race, Women, against the Other Half, Men* in 1825.

Few women played prominent roles in socialism before the 1890s. One important exception was **Flora Tristan**, who advocated a proletarian international in her book *L'Union ouvrière* (The Workers' Union) in France in 1843. The socialist/social-democratic parties put the betterment of women on the political agenda as a general issue effectively for the first time. In 1883 **August Bebel** published *Die Frau und der Sozialismus* (Woman and Socialism), which championed women's emancipation and, through its large circulation, was important in making equal rights for women a priority in the political program of the socialist movement.

The **Erfurt Program** (1891) of the **German Social Democratic Party** (*Sozialdemokratische Partei Deutschlands*—SPD) demanded universal, equal, and direct **suffrage** for men and women alike and the abolition of all laws that disadvantaged women compared to men. The 1893 program of the Belgian Workers' Party (later **Belgian Socialist Party**) also called for the revision of divorce laws and the maintenance of the husband's liability to support his wife and children.

Socialist/social-democratic parties began to organize women from the 1900s. Legal difficulties in Germany prevented their being organized before 1908. *Die Gleichheit* (Equality), a journal begun in 1892 and edited by **Clara Zetlin**, had 125,000 subscribers in 1914. By then about 16 percent of the membership of the SPD was made up of women. From the 1980s women's working groups (*Arbeitsgemeinschaften*) operated within the SPD. The Dutch Social Democratic Party/Labor Party (later **Dutch Labor Party**) began actively recruiting women by special clubs from 1905, and these had a total of 1,500 members by 1914. The Bulgarian Social Democratic Party (later **Bulgarian Social Democrats**)—effectively a socialist movement that was by then divided into two parties—led the demand for women's equality and voting rights before 1914. The **Norwegian Labor Party** organized a women's federation in 1901 that claimed 2,000 members by 1914. Not every socialist/social-democratic party before 1914 welcomed women as members. The **Danish Social Democratic Party** (*Socialdemokraterne*—SD), although it resolved to organize women at its congress in 1908, effectively kept them out before 1914.

The **British Labour Party** established the Women's Labour League in 1906, which claimed 4,000 members by 1913, but at the time was otherwise rather conservative in its attitude toward women compared to the **Independent Labour Party**. The British Labour Party committed itself to a policy of full adult suffrage, that is, votes for both sexes for persons aged 21 or over, in 1904. In 1907 the party's conference resolved by 605,000 to 268,000 votes to oppose equal suffrage for women on the grounds that it would restrict the vote to women with sufficient property to qualify. In 1913 the party's conference agreed by a two to one majority to oppose any proposed suffrage legislation that omitted women.

An International Women's Congress was formed by the **Second International** in 1907, and the first international socialist women's conference was held in Copenhagen. An antiwar international conference of socialist women was held in Berne in 1915. The **International Socialist Women's Committee** was formed as part of the **Labor and Socialist International** (LSI) in Germany in 1923. In 1928 the member parties of the LSI claimed a total of 973,900 women members of which the largest number were in the United Kingdom (300,000), Austria (225,200), Germany (181,500), Belgium (80,000), Czechoslovakia (44,500), Sweden (26,000), and Hungary (22,000).

As a proportion of members, the highest level of women's membership among those parties based on individual affiliation in 1928 was in the **Austrian Social Democratic Party**—32.9 percent, a proportion that was maintained after World War II. The other social-democratic parties with high levels of women members in 1928 were Denmark (33 percent), the Netherlands (29 percent), Finland (27 percent), Czechoslovakia (24 percent), and Germany (21 percent). In July 1955 the **Socialist International Women** was formed in London as part of the **Socialist International**.

Although women are underrepresented in politics, several have played prominent roles for socialist parties in the highest offices of state. Benazir Bhutto of the **Pakistan People's Party** was twice elected prime minister of Pakistan, serving from 1988 to 1990 and 1993 to 1996, each time being removed from office by a president who alleged corruption. Edith Cresson of the **French Socialist Party** was prime minister of France in 1991 to 1992. **Helen Clarke** of the **New Zealand Labour Party** served as prime minister of her country for three successive terms following the elections of 1999, 2002, and 2005. In 2000 and 2006, Tarja Halonen of the **Finnish Social Democratic Party** was elected president of her country. Also in 2006, Michelle Bachelet of the **Socialist Party of Chile** was elected as Chile's first female president and Portia Simpson Miller of the **People's National Party** became the first woman to be prime minister of Jamaica.

Women who have led socialist parties but have not been elected to the senior offices of state include Takako Doi, who was head of the **Japan Socialist Party** from 1986 to 1991. She was also speaker of the Japanese House of Representatives from 1993 to 1996. Doi inspired many Japanese women to become involved in politics. In Canada Audrey McLaughlin led the social-democratic **New Democratic Party**

(NDP) from 1989 to 1995. Alexa McDonough was leader of the NDP from 1995 to 2003, having previously led the party in Nova Scotia from 1980 to 1994. In April 2005 the Danish SD elected Helle Thorning-Schmidt as party leader. Anna Lindh of the **Swedish Social Democratic Workers' Party** was widely expected to become party leader and prime minister of Sweden. However, while serving as Swedish minister for foreign affairs, she was murdered on a Stockholm street in September 2003. *See also* INTERNATIONAL WOMEN'S DAY; LUXEMBURG, ROSA; SOCIALIST FEMINISM; WEBB, MARTHA BEATRICE; YOUNG, IRIS MARION.

WOODCOCK, GEORGE (1912–95). An anarchist scholar and author, George Woodcock was born in Winnipeg, Canada. He was taken to the United Kingdom as a young child by his parents and he lived there until 1949. He came to **anarchism** though **pacifism** in the 1930s and was a conscientious objector during World War II. On his return to Canada, he developed the literary career he had begun in London. In 1959 he founded the journal *Canadian Literature*. Although not a university graduate, Woodcock made a substantial contribution to the scholarly study of socialism. He wrote biographies of **Peter Kropotkin** in 1950 (with Ivan Avakumović) and **Pierre-Joseph Proudhon** in 1956. In 1962 he published a detailed general history, *Anarchism: A History of Libertarian Ideas and Movements*, and edited an anthology of anarchist writings, *The Anarchist Reader*, which was published in 1972. In these works Woodcock demonstrated that anarchism was far from being the popular stereotype of mindless violence and destruction and that it was intimately connected with the quest for individual liberty in European thought and practice. In 1966 he wrote a study of **George Orwell**, *The Crystal Spirit*, for which he won the Governor-General's Literary Award. After an academic career teaching English at the Universities of Washington and British Columbia, he left **education** in 1963. Later he was elected a Fellow of the Royal Society of Canada.

WORKERS' PARTY [*PARTIDO DOS TRABALHADORES* (PT)]. The PT was formed in Brazil in 1978. This was an entirely new organization, the traditional left having been decimated under the military regime that ruled Brazil from 1964 to 1985. As a mass grassroots-based organization, the PT brought together **trade unionists**, a variety of **Marxist** currents, intellectuals, and church activists. Although unsuccessfully competing for the presidency throughout the 1990s after narrowly losing in 1989, the PT was more successful in local government. It held power for four years in Brazil's largest city, São Paulo, before divisions between radical and social-democratic wings led to defeat. The party was innovative in its administration of other cities, introducing popular means of public accountability, such as local citizens' assemblies. In Porto Alegre the PT administration introduced the Participatory Budget, which empowered poor community members by allowing them to take part in deliberations to formulate the annual investments of the city. Members of the poor communities discussed policy goals and agendas. The PT also gained considerable support among landless peasants.

In October 1998 the PT won 58 seats in the lower house of the legislature—the Chamber of Deputies—with 9.5 percent of the vote, and three seats in the Senate with 16.8 percent. The party leader **Luis Ignacio Lula da Silva** gained 31.7 percent of the vote for the presidency, losing out to Fernando Henrique Cardoso. The social-democratic elements of the party saw their policies, rather than those of the radical wing, become the dominant ones. In October 2002 Lula da Silva won the Brazilian presidency on the fourth attempt. The PT also increased its presence in both houses of the legislature that year, obtaining 91 seats (the largest share) in the lower house and 14 in the Senate. Hence, although the PT only held a minority in each of the two houses of the legislature (Congress) after the elections of 2002, with the social-democratic approach and policies Lula da Silva was able to govern with the support of several other parties, including the center-right Liberal Party.

Many on the left were disappointed when the PT became far less radical under Lula da Silva's presidency than they had expected. Governing in constraining economic circumstances, the PT pushed through **welfare** cuts that it had opposed in opposition and scaled down its Zero Hunger program. In 2004 several former PT members, led by Heloísa Helena, formed a new party: the Party of Socialism and Freedom (*Partido Socialismo e Liberdade*—P-Sol). As a Marxist party P-Sol began to attract the support of left-wingers including Trotskyists who had backed the PT. Other PT supporters stressed the need for patience, saying that the PT had to govern with caution in the difficult economic circumstances, that Zero Hunger had had some success, and that under the PT Brazil was promoting trade ties with other Latin American countries and using international trade meetings to press for increased access for poorer countries to Western markets. In the local elections of October 2004 the PT increased its share of seats and councils massively, including many in areas where it had hitherto been unsuccessful. Nevertheless it lost the key cities of São Paulo and Porto Alegre. In June and July 2005 allegations of corruption led to the resignation of several leading PT members.

WORKERS' PARTY OF KOREA (WPK) (*CHOSEN NODONG-TANG*). Formed in 1946 by Kim Il-Sung, the WPK took control of the northern part of Korea, which had been occupied by the Soviet Red Army since the end of World War II in 1945. Kim had been a major in the Soviet Army, along with which he had led his Korean partisans into Korea. He became chairman of the WPK. In 1948, when North Korea gained independence, he was declared premier. Since then North Korea has effectively been a one-party **communist** state, although a few powerless minor parties are allowed to exist.

In 1950, with Kim in total control of the WPK, North Korea invaded the South, thus starting the Korean **War** that sucked in the United States and People's Republic of China and which ended in stalemate three years later. After the death of the Soviet leader Joseph Stalin (1879–1953) that year, Kim moved away from the influence of the Soviet Union, promoting self-reliance (*juche*) for North Korea. Thereafter, Kim encouraged a personality cult that kept him and the WPK in power. In 1972 the WPK introduced a new communist constitution for North Korea and Kim officially became head of state. North Korea became one of the world's most secretive and totalitarian states. The personality cult, which attributed extraordinary powers to Kim, lasted beyond his death in 1994. He became eternal president after his death.

After a power struggle Kim's son Kim Jung Il became WPK chairman and effective absolute ruler of North Korea in 1996. In the second half of the 1990s millions of North Koreans died due partly to inadequate **policies** and resources for **agriculture** as North Korea concentrated its resources on strengthening its huge armed forces with medium-range missiles and other technology. By the early twenty-first century North Korea had also declared that it had developed its own **nuclear weapons**.

WORKING CLASS. The word *class* as a label for social divisions entered the main European languages during the last half of the eighteenth century. The use of the term *working class*, as applied to those who work in manual or industrial occupations for a wage, occurred by at least 1795 in England. The plural form, "working classes," was more commonly used before about 1870. As a plural term, it drew attention to the diversity of occupations and views among wage earners. **Robert Owen** used the expression "the poor and working classes" in 1813 to refer to what was later referred to as the working class.

As a singular term, *working class* was used by socialists not just to describe a social class but also to promote the idea of the unity of that class for its political, economic, and social improvement. The harsh working conditions and low wages of the working class made their improvement the driving imperative of socialist thought and policy. **Nationalization** of major industries was advocated as a way of ending the exploitation of their employees, not of improving the economic management or efficiency of those industries. The working class were commonly extolled in socialist propaganda—with varying degrees of accuracy—as heroic victims of **capitalist** oppression or as repositories of moral and national virtues. Many socialists have argued that the development of class consciousness is necessary for the working class to achieve social change.

The socialist emphasis on the working class was especially apt before the 1930s, when manual occupations dominated the employed labor forces of Western economies. In the United Kingdom, for instance, no less than 75 percent of the labor force worked in manual jobs in 1911, a proportion that had only fallen to 70 percent by 1931. From the 1930s the proportion of those in working-class jobs began to fall slowly, and it became more important for socialist/social-democratic parties to win over other groups in society if they were to win political power. Again using the example of Britain, the proportion of those in manual jobs in the employed labor force had fallen to 59 percent by 1961. New technology and the general maturation of Western economies favored white-collar employment and offered the chance for upward social mobility for many in the working class. At the same time, the effects of upward social mobility, which depended upon access to training and **education**, should not be exaggerated: individual members of the working class might rise on the social scale, but the working class as a whole could not. Consequently, class has continued to be an important factor in voting for socialist/social-democratic parties with those in manual jobs (the working class) still being proportionally far more likely to vote for these parties than other classes.

During the twentieth century, the working class contributed a declining proportion of the parliamentary representatives of socialist/social-democratic parties. For example, between 1910 and 1913 and 1958 and 1961 the proportion of federal parliamentarians belonging to the **Australian Labor Party** who were of working-class origin fell from 59 to 39 percent. Among **British Labour Party** parliamentarians, the proportion of those from working-class origins fell from 72 percent between 1918 and 1932 to 30 percent by 1964. Similar declines have also been found more generally among the **membership of socialist/social-democratic parties**. *See also* MIDDLE CLASS.

WORKINGMEN'S PARTY OF THE UNITED STATES (WPUS). The WPUS was the first nationwide socialist organization in the United States. It was founded in July 1876 from the merger of the Illinois Labor Party (which had been formed in 1874 and had in turn developed out of the Universal German Workingmen's Association founded by followers of **Ferdinand Lassalle** in Chicago in 1869), the Social Democratic Workmen's Party of North America (a **Marxist** party formed in New York in 1874), and groups that had been part of the **International Workingmen's Association**. One of its members was **Laurence Grönlund**. Another member was Samuel Gompers (1850–1924), who later became the leader of organized labor in the United States and a strong antisocialist. The WPUS claimed 7,000 members and drew most of its support from German Americans employed in skilled **working-class** jobs. The formation of the WPUS took place at the start of a period of widespread labor agitation and unrest, but the party played only a limited role in directing this discontent, which was largely unorganized. The WPUS split in October 1877 and gave rise to the **Socialist Labor Party of America**.

WORLD LABOR ZIONIST MOVEMENT (WLZM). The WLZM was originally organized in the German city of Danzig (now Gdansk in Poland) in 1932. It brought together **Zionist** groups in Europe and the United States. After 1945 it was based in Israel and was known as the World Union of Zionist Socialist Parties. It stands for the promotion of a Jewish secular state, complete social, economic, and political equality, social justice, and the peaceful settlement of the Arab-Israeli conflict. It has close links with the **Israel Labor Party** and has been an affiliated organization with the **Socialist International** since 1951. In 2002 the WLZM was active in 23 countries. *See also* INTERNATIONAL JEWISH LABOR BUND.

WORLD SOCIAL FORUM (WSF). Based in Brazil, where it first emerged, the WSF was conceived as neither a group nor an organization. As a contemporary progressive forum it is broadly left-wing and **anticapitalist**, concerned with issues and problems on which the socialist movement has traditionally campaigned. The Forum is styled as a meeting place for movements and nongovernmental organizations opposed to neoliberalism and all forms of **imperialism**. The Forum convenes annually, enabling participants opposed to **capitalist** domination of the world to share ideas, formulate proposals, and make plans for alternatives to neoliberalism. It meets at around the same time as the World Economic Forum (Davos Forum), which is an annual meeting of chief executives of the world's big capitalist corporations, along with some national political leaders.

The first three annual meetings of the WSF (2001, 2002, 2003) were held at Porto Alegre, Brazil. After the first meeting the organizing committee drew up a charter of principles that would guide the continued pursuit of the initiative. The charter is posted on the WSF website. The first principle declares that the Forum is a meeting place for groups and movements that oppose neoliberalism, capitalist world domination, and all forms of imperialism. Those groups and movements should be committed to building a worldwide society that aims to develop fruitful relationships among all people and between those people and the Earth. Proclaiming that "another world is possible," the charter also states that the Forum seeks alternatives to capitalist **globalization** dominated by large multinational corporations and their supporting governments, insists that the Forum is democratic and pluralist, upholds respect for human rights and opposes totalitarianism, and seeks to promote nonviolent resistance in the face of dehumanization and violence on the part of the state.

An indication of the growing significance of the Forum was the size of the second annual meeting; with between 65,000 to 85,000 attendees this was far larger than the first, which attracted approximately 12,000. In 2004 the Forum was held at Mumbai, India. In 2005 the fifth Forum was held once again at Porto Alegre. There are also linked regional Forums, such as the **European Social Forum** and **Americas Social Forum**, each of which shares the WSF's charter of principles.

– X –

XYZ GROUP. The XYZ Group consisted of left-wing British academic economists who operated during the 1930s. They were important in reshaping the policies of the **British Labour Party**.

– Y –

YOUNG, IRIS MARION (1949–). As a political philosopher Iris Marion Young presents the case for special rights to empower the exploited, dominated, and disadvantaged. Born in New York City, she completed her doctorate in 1974 at Pennsylvania State University. Formerly a professor at the University of Pittsburg, she is a professor of political science at the University of Chicago.

Young's socialism is in the **new left** tradition, which challenges the orthodox view that the relations between individuals and groups in contemporary liberal democracies allow formally recognized rights to be realized. She has contributed to **socialist feminism**, but her best-known book is *Justice and the Politics of Difference* (1990), which challenges liberal arguments that justice must be based entirely on impartial, universal rights. She argues that when such conceptions of justice prevail, the interpretations of justice held by the most powerful in society are dominant. To focus upon problems in the distribution of **wealth** is to neglect the even more fundamental exclusion from decision-making power over the economy. According to Young, the conception of citizenship that sees universality as inclusion is in tension with two other established conceptions of citizenship: universality as generality and universality as equal treatment. She argues that those other two conceptions should give way, whereupon special rights for oppressed groups would enable them to engage in participatory democracy on equal terms with others in society. Through special institutional channels representatives of the oppressed and disadvantaged groups could make the special rights effective. This would amount to what she calls "differentiated citizenship." In her book *Inclusion and Democracy* (2000) she once again examines the ideals of inclusion, the problems of exclusion, and the democratic processes required to overcome those problems.

YOUNG PEOPLE'S SOCIALIST LEAGUE (YPSL). The YPSL was an American **youth** organization that began on a national basis in 1915 under the auspices of the **Socialist Party of America** (SPA). Membership was open to those aged between 15 and 30 and the total number of members was claimed to be 10,000 by 1919. From 1920 the YPSL had a difficult history because of the decline of the SPA and the divisions in left-wing politics in the 1930s. In the early 1950s its leading figure was **Michael Harrington**. In the 1960s the YPSL faced strong competition from the Students for a Democratic Society (formed in 1962) and was made moribund when Harrington left in 1972. The YPSL was formally wound up in 1977.

YOUTH. No movement of any kind can survive it if neglects its youth. But it was not until the 1890s that socialism began to pay serious attention to recruiting young people. In the United Kingdom, the first socialist youth organization was the Clarion Scouts, established by **Robert Blatchford** in 1894. It claimed 120 clubs with 7,000 members by 1896. The members of the clubs traveled on bicycles to spread socialist ideas. The British journal *The Young Socialist* was first issued in 1901 and continued into the 1960s.

In northern Europe, organizations especially for youth were set up during the 1900s. The **Norwegian Labor Party** formed its first socialist youth organization in 1900 in Oslo and a national movement was formed in 1903. A socialist youth organization developed in Denmark between 1904 and 1907. But because of its affinities with **syndicalism**, it was shunned by the **Danish Social Democratic Party** (*Socialdemokraterne*—SD). The **German Social Democratic Party** did not begin to organize youth until after 1908 because of legal difficulties. Youth membership in the German party eventually came to be substantial, with young members coming to be known as

Jusos. The **Swedish Social Democratic Workers' Party** established a Young Socialist League by 1903; members of this league founded a breakaway party, the Swedish Young Socialist Party, in 1908. A Socialist Youth International was formed in Germany in 1907, but failed to survive the turmoil of World War I.

The International of Socialist Youth was formed in Hamburg in 1923 with the **Labor and Socialist International** (LSI). In 1928 parties affiliated with the LSI claimed youth organizations with a total membership of 260,000, of which the largest were in Germany (55,300), Sweden (41,200), Austria (31,000), Czechoslovakia (30,100), Belgium (24,600), Poland (16,200), the United Kingdom (12,000), and Denmark (11,300). After World War II, the **International Union of Socialist Youth** was formed in Paris in October 1946.

Social-democratic youth organizations have also served as nurseries for aspiring politicians. **Paul John Keating** began his political career in the Youth Council of the **Australian Labor Party**. Ingvar Gösta Carlsson, who was prime minister of Sweden from 1986 to 1991 and from 1994 to 1995, was president of the Swedish Social Democratic Youth League from 1961 to 1967. Karl August Fagerholm (1901–84), who was prime minister of Finland from 1948 to 1950, joined the youth organization of the **Finnish Social Democratic Party** in 1920 and became editor of the organization's newspaper in 1923. But the most successful example of a socialist youth organization was that of the SD in Denmark. No fewer than three prime ministers began their careers in its youth organization: **Hans Christian Hedtoft-Hansen**, **Hans Christian Hansen**, and **Jens Otto Krag**. *See also* EDUCATION; YOUNG PEOPLE'S SOCIALIST LEAGUE.

– Z –

ZAPATERO, JOSE LUIS RODRIGUEZ (1960–). Jose Luis Rodriguez Zapatero became Socialist prime minister of Spain in March 2004, as a result of an election held immediately after a terrorist bombing in Madrid, in which more than 200 people were killed. At the time of the bombing the **Spanish Socialist Workers' Party** (*Partido Socialista Obrero Español*—PSOE) was in opposition, campaigning under his leadership with the pledge to withdraw Spain's armed forces from the United States–led occupation of Iraq. He was born in Valladolid, in the Castile region of Spain, and in his youth studied law. He joined the PSOE as a teenager and was elected to the Spanish Parliament at the age of 26. He went on to become leader of his party in 2000. The PSOE was elected in 2004 without an absolute majority of seats but decided to govern by dialogue with other parties, rather than form a coalition. Zapatero immediately carried out his pledge to withdraw from Iraq and called for a new international alliance against **terrorism**.

ZETLIN, CLARA JOSEPHINE (1857–1933). A radical German socialist and schoolteacher, Clara Zetlin was born in Wiederau, Saxony, and was a member of the German delegation to the **Marxist** congress of the **Second International** in Paris in 1889. In 1892 she became editor of the **women**'s journal of the **German Social Democratic Party**, *Die Gleichheit* (Equality), a position she held until 1917. She opposed **revisionism** and supported the general strike as the prelude to social revolution. She was a leading campaigner of socialism for women and women's rights; she was one of the founders of the International Women's Socialist Congress, a secretariat of the Second International, in 1907. As secretary of the Second International's International Council of Socialist and Labor Organizations, she organized an international conference of socialist women from France, Germany, the United Kingdom, and other countries in March 1915 to protest World War I. In 1919 she joined the German **Communist** Party, and in 1923 she went to Moscow and persuaded **V. I. Lenin** that the left-wing uprisings were abortive and should not be supported.

ZIMMERWALD CONFERENCE. Initiated by Swiss and Italian socialists, this conference was held in secret in a peasant's house at Zimmerwald, Switzerland, in September 1915. It was attended by official delegates from Bulgaria, Italy, the Netherlands, Norway, Romania, Russia, Sweden, Switzerland, the **International Jewish Labor Bund**, and unofficial delegates from Germany. There were no British delegates because they were denied passports. **V. I. Lenin** attended for the Bolsheviks. The **Mensheviks** and Left Social Revolutionaries were also represented, making 42 delegates in all. The conference denounced World War I, blaming it on reactionary **capitalist** governments, and called for **working-class** unity to bring an end to the **war**, a peace without annexations or indemnities, and recognition of national rights of self-determination. The conference set up the International Socialist Commission, also known as the Zimmerwald Commission, made up of two Swiss, two Italians, and a Russian-born Italian resident, to work for an end to hostilities. *See also* KIENTHAL CONFERENCE.

ZIONISM. Zionism was effectively begun by Theodor Herzl (1860–1904) in 1897 to create a state for **Jews** in what was then Palestine. It took its name from Zion, the part of Jerusalem named in the Old Testament, and combined the European idea of **nationalism** with elements taken from socialism. The socialist aspects of Zionism were expressed in the **International Jewish Labor Bund** and the *Poalei Zion* (Workers of Zion), which was formed in the Jewish pale of settlement in the Russian empire in 1900. By 1928 *Poalei Zion* claimed a membership of 22,500, of whom 6,000 lived in the United States, 4,000 in Palestine, and 12,500 in Europe, and it was a member of the **Labor and Socialist International**. The growth of Jewish settlement in Palestine from the early 1900s was accompanied by the application of socialist principles, most notably in the idea of the *kibbutz* and the **cooperative movement**. *See also* WORLD LABOR ZIONIST MOVEMENT.

Glossary of Terms

This glossary provides a guide to terms and concepts that occur commonly in the extensive literature on socialism, although they are not always clearly defined. It does not pretend to be comprehensive. Terms within the definitions are in boldface type if they also appear as entries in the dictionary. There is an asterisk after each term that appears elsewhere as an entry in the glossary.

Arbeitsgemeinschaften A German term meaning "working groups" but referring specifically to groups within the **German Social Democratic Party** concerned with labor affairs and **women**. Originally set up in the 1980s, they became increasingly institutionalized in the early 1990s.

autogestion A term used by the French radical socialists in the early 1970s to refer to the desirability of employee participation in the decision-making process at the workplace, but also to encompass a broad vision of socialism that is based on the widest possible popular participation in decision making at all levels of society.

Bennite A follower of Tony Benn, a prominent left*-wing figure in the **British Labour Party** in the 1970s and 1980s.

branch stacking Term applied to the enrollment of groups of bogus members to branches of the **Australian Labor Party** (ALP) to influence voting for individuals or **policies**. The practice may involve members of a particular ethnic community and has occurred in branches in metropolitan New South Wales and Victoria since the late 1970s. Because the ALP is not a mass membership **political party**, it can be vulnerable to the practice.

bourgeoisie The term *bourgeoisie* originally referred to the freemen of a French town. It seems to have been used from the twelfth century but did not become widespread until after 1700, when it became a general term for the **middle class**. During the nineteenth century, it was applied to the middle classes of other countries. Associated with property ownership and the exercise of political, economic, and social power, the term was used pejoratively by socialists, particularly **Karl Marx**, who depicted the bourgeoisie as the natural enemies of the proletariat.* Ironically, many socialists came from the middle class, including Marx himself.

caucus A *caucus* means a meeting of the members of a parliamentary **political party**. The origins of the term are unclear. One explanation is that it was taken from a Latin (originally Greek) word for "drinking vessel" and therefore suggests conviviality. It was in use in the North American colonies by the mid-eighteenth century to refer to private political meetings; a Caucus Club existed in Boston by 1763. It was in use in its present sense in the British press by 1878 and in its Australian colonies by 1880. The term has been applied specifically to meetings of the parliamentary members of the **Australian Labor Party** since 1894 in New South Wales and in the federal parliament since 1911. It is also used in Canada.

center In political terms *center* is a moderate political position. The term originated in the first French National Assembly, after the revolution* of 1789. While opponents to change sat on the right* wing, and those who favored radical change sat on the left* wing of the chamber, moderates sat in the center.

centrism Also known as center-leftism, *centrism* is a French socialist term that referred to the composition of political alliances needed to form governments. A centrist alliance was one between a socialist party and **political parties** more to the center of the political spectrum, whereas a united leftist alliance (such as the French **Popular Front** in 1936–39) was one between only left*-wing parties, usually socialists and **communists**.

class consciousness A **Marxist** concept, class consciousness refers to the idea that the individuals in a class, particularly the **working class**, have a broad, collective view of themselves as belonging to one group that transcends divisions caused by different occupations, race, residence, or **religion**.

chattering classes Derisory term that came into vogue in the late 1980s to describe educated, articulate members of the **middle class** and upper class, often dependent for their living on government spending, who profess advanced political and social opinions. Often possessing extensive media contacts, they have been accused of exerting disproportionate influence on the policymaking processes of the **British Labour Party** and on the **Australian Labor Party** to the detriment of the **working class**. In Australia these groups have been called the new class.*

cohabitation The name given to those periods in recent French political history when the president and the prime minister represented different political parties and were therefore forced to "cohabit." There have been three such periods: from March 1986 to June 1988, from March 1993 to May 1995, and from June 1997 to 2002. In the first two periods the socialist president **François Mitterrand** shared power with the conservative coalitions led by Jacques Chirac and then by Edouard Balladur. Mitterrand was able to use his position to modify the policies of his conservative opponents. Between June 1997 and April 2002 the conservative president Jacques Chirac was forced to share power with the socialist prime minister **Lionel Robert Jospin**.

cooperation A key concern for socialists, cooperation is considered to be consistent with human nature, which is characterized by sociality.* Competition, socialists argue, should give way to cooperation, even though most socialists would not abolish competition entirely. Excessive competition is considered to be wasteful of resources and human energy, which can be expended on less divisive and more useful pursuits.

corporatism Before the 1920s corporatism was used as a synonym for **syndicalism**. During the 1920s **Benito Mussolini** organized "corporations" of occupations as means of economic, political, and social control. The term was revived in the 1970s to express loose cooperation between government, business, and **trade unions** to implement economic **policies** requiring their consent, notably over wages and technological change. It has also been called neocorporatism.

democracy Deriving from the ancient Greek term *demokratia*, which combined *demos* (people) and *kratia* (rule), democracy involves the exercise by the people of political power. This can be either direct participation in policy-making or the choice of those who make policy on behalf of the people. In the latter case the policy-makers must be responsive to an electorate that can replace them, either at regular intervals or within a given time limit. The more equal the participation and influence of persons, the more democratic is the state. Socialists believe that a state is democratic only to the degree that economic inequality and capitalist exploitation are reduced, thus allowing greater equality of political participation and influence.

Eisenachers Popular name given to the members of the Social Democratic Workers' Party (*Sozial Demokratische Arbeiterpartei*) formed at Eisenach in 1869. The party fused with the General Association of German Workers (Allgemeiner Deutscher Arbeiterverein) or Lassalleans to form the **German Social Democratic Party** in 1875.

embourgoisement A French term meaning "becoming **middle class**" and often used in a negative sense, *embourgoisement* refers to changes in the composition of **working-class** institutions or their political parties that see an increase in the proportion of members or supporters drawn from other social classes.

entrism Euphemism derived from the word entry referring to the infiltration of social-democratic parties by extreme left*-wing groups. The term has been applied to Trotskyite groups in the United Kingdom in relation to the **British Labour Party** in the 1970s and 1980s.

Eurocommunism A term coined in 1970 to describe attempts by the Communist Parties of France, Spain, and Italy to reconcile **communism** with liberal democracy* by emphasizing support for civil rights and recognizing the legitimacy of political opposition, that is, pluralism.*

Fraktion This is the name given to the parliamentary group formed by the two socialist parties in Germany after the elections in 1874. At their formal unification at Gotha in 1875 they became the **German Social Democratic Party**. The term was still being used at least up to 1918.

grouper This is a term originally applied to a member of the "industrial groups" formed by the **Australian Labor Party** (ALP) in 1947 to fight **communist** infiltration. After the ALP split in 1955, it was applied to members of the conservative, anticommunist breakaway members who formed the Democratic Labor Party.

guerristas With reference to the **Spanish Socialist Workers' Party**, guerristas were followers of Alfonso Guerra, who controlled the party machine during the 1980s. In March 1991 the guerristas were purged from the government of **Felipe González**.

H-J Vogel Circle This circle was a **middle-class** group of professionals and academics within the **German Social Democratic Party** that emerged in the late 1960s and became allied with the *Kanalarbeiten*.*

hegemony *Hegemony* is a term derived from a Greek word meaning "leader" or "ruler." It was given wider usage in socialist writings by the **Marxist** theorist **Antonio Gramsci** in the mid-1920s to describe the way in which the bourgeoisie,* as the dominant class, was able to organize the consent of the other social classes though political and economic **institutions**.

human rights Human rights are those rights that people have as human beings. Protection of human rights is essential if people are to enjoy a satisfactory life in their capacity as human beings. Human rights are moral rights, which are more fundamental than legal rights.

Juso This term, an abbreviation of *Jungsozialisten*, means young socialist and refers to members of the **German Social Democratic Party** who are under 35 years of age. The plural form is Jusos.

Kanalarbeiten This is a German term meaning literally "canal work," but referring to the generally conservative **trade union** members of the parliamentary **German Social Democratic Party** from the 1950s who carried out mechanical political functions.

laborism Laborism is a form of socialism characterized by a close relationship with organized labor and commitment to gradual political reforms by democratic means. Laborism is most commonly used to refer to the policies and practices of governments of labor parties, particularly those that respond to the immediate demands of labor as sectional groups without challenging the fundamental economic relationships of capitalist society. Its usage dates from about 1961 in English, but it was used by the Marxist **Antonio Gramsci** in 1921.

laborite A Laborite is a supporter or practitioner of laborism.*

labor theory of value This is an economic and moral concept which **Karl Marx** and others took from David Ricardo. It holds that the value of a commodity is largely dependent upon the amount of labor it took to produce it, that is, that labor is the true source of value, and by implication, **wealth**. The idea was used to justify the argument that labor should be paid more than simply a subsistence wage and also to criticize the wage system.

Lassalleans Followers of the General Association of German Workers (*Allgemeiner Deutscher Arbeiterverein*) founded by **Ferdinand Lassalle** on 23 May 1863. In 1875 it merged with the Eisenachers to form the **German Social Democratic Party**.

left The political use of the term *left* dates back to the first French National Assembly after the revolution* of 1789. The democratic and liberal members of the assembly sat to the left of the president's chair, the prerevolutionary nobility having traditionally sat to the king's right.* *Left* subsequently came to signify the position of those who favor wider and effective political participation, social reform, or revolution* over existing institutions, greater social and economic equality, and significant regulation or abolition of **capitalism**.

Leverkusen Circle The Leverkusen Circle was a left-wing parliamentary faction within the **German Social Democratic Party** that began as the Group of the Sixteenth Floor in 1972.

manualism Manualism refers to the idea that only manual workers—not the **middle class** or the intelligentsia—should represent manual workers in parliament or on other elected bodies. Manualism was recommended in the **Manifesto of the Sixty**.

maximalist A pre-1925 term applied to socialists, particularly in Italy and France, who desired the maximum, that is, the immediate attainment of socialism by violent revolution.*

minimalist In contrast to maximalist* socialists, minimalist socialists were those who favored the attainment of socialism by gradual, peaceful means.

municipal socialism This was a term used in Britain in the 1890s and into the early 1900s to describe the application of socialist ideas to local government administration. John Burns (1858–1943) was a leading exponent of municipal socialism in this period.

neoliberalism Based on "**liberalism**," which champions individual freedom, the term *neoliberalism* refers to the idea that **globalization** has brought about an international economy largely freed from what is considered as damaging interference and regulation by states. Opponents, including many socialists, argue that states in fact play an invaluable role for capital as guardians and administrators of vested interests.

Neue Mitte German for "New Middle" or "New Center," this term refers to the efforts of the leadership of the **German Social Democratic Party** to move the party's policies from the left* to the center* of the political spectrum in the late 1990s. It is the German equivalent of the Third Way.*

new class This is the Australian term for groups known as the chattering classes* in Britain.

Paulskirche movement This was a mass, extraparliamentary movement organized by the **German Social Democratic Party** and the **trade unions** in December 1954 to protest the proposed membership of West Germany in the North Atlantic Treaty Organization; the movement continued into 1955.

planning Socialists believe humans to be rational beings, who are able to plan their lives, rather than be helpless in face of their circumstances. Many nonsocialists since the Enlightenment have also stressed human rationality. Unlike them, socialists argue that sociality* requires that humans plan their lives collectively, rather than as atomistic individuals. Moreover, socialists stress that planning should have **egalitarian** motives and goals. For them planning is thus linked with social responsibility* and cooperation.*

pledge A pledge is a written undertaking by parliamentary members of the **Australian Labor Party** to adhere to the platform of the party and to follow the decisions of the caucus.* It was in use in New South Wales by 1894.

pluralism Pluralism refers to the acknowledgment and acceptance of political, functional, ethnic, or cultural differences within nations or organizations. The term was first used in this sense in the early twentieth century but has only become more common in political science since the mid-1960s.

political economy *Political economy* was the original term for what is now simply called "economics." Since the 1970s it has been revived to refer to a radical approach to economics that explores its political aspects.

proletariat/proletarian The term *proletariat* was originally used to refer to the poorest citizens of ancient Rome. Since they owned no property, they were deemed to contribute nothing to society other than their children (proles). With the rise of classical studies in Western Europe, the word was revived to refer to the poorest members of society. The term *proletarian* (a member of the proletariat) was used in England at least by 1658. By 1853 the term *proletariat* was used to describe the poorest class, usually in a hostile or demeaning way. In the *Communist Manifesto* (1848) **Karl Marx** used the terms *proletariat* and *proletarian* in a positive way to refer to the industrial **working class**.

rainbow alliance This is a term sometimes applied to political alliances between socialist or social-democratic parties and environmental or green **political parties**. It seems to have been derived from the term *rainbow coalition*, used to describe political groupings of minority races and other groups as used in the United States in 1982. Occasionally a rainbow coalition in government can emerge after elections.

renovatores *Renovatores* is the Spanish word for "renovators" but used in connection with the **Spanish Socialist Workers' Party** to mean those who wanted to end the domination of the party's machinery by the guerristas.*

revolution Revolution is a radical and long-term reconstruction in the political, social, and economic order, involving revolt from a section of the populace. The French Revolution of 1789 and the Russian Revolution in 1917 are classic examples. Revolutions often involve violence, but this is not necessarily the case if the existing order concedes defeat, as was the case in some eastern European countries in 1989.

right Like the terms *left** and *center*,* *right* originated in the first French National Assembly after the revolution* of 1789. Opponents of change gathered on the right of the Assembly. "Right-wing" typically implies conservative opposition to big government, which conceives of and implements change. However, right-wingers sometimes advocate change to reverse previous change. Moreover, "far-right" signifies fascism, which uses big government to reverse previous social change.

sarvodaya This is a Hindi term meaning "uplift of all" and used in socialist debates in India in the 1950s to describe expected outcomes from comprehensive economic and social reforms outlined in the Indian Socialist Party's platform of 4 July 1951.

social fascists A term of abuse used in the 1930s by **communist** parties in democratic countries to refer to noncommunist political parties on the left* of the political spectrum, that is, social-democratic parties.

sociality *Sociality* is a term referring to the quality of being social. It implies that human nature is social, involving interdependence between humans. Skills and abilities that are needed by humans are developed through **education** and cooperation* in society. Hence, those abilities are held in trust, to be used for the well being not only of the individual, but also for fellow human beings.

social justice In political terms justice is usually considered to require the equal treatment of equals. Socialists believe in human equality. When insisting on justice socialists are usually concerned with social justice, whereby the social order should be reconstructed with human needs taking priority.

social responsibility This is a requirement of socialism that rests on the concept of sociality.* Human beings ought to take an active interest in the wellbeing of their fellow humans. Selfishness is considered to be a trait associated with the perversion of human nature. Many socialists argue that selfishness has been intensified by **capitalism**.

social wage This is a view of wages that embraces not only the earnings of employment but also payments from the **social security** system and other benefits such as **health** insurance.

solidarity A term used to describe the common struggle by a group, whose members share political consciousness, against exploitation. As used by socialists, the group in question is often the **working class**.

Sozialdemokratische Wählerinitiative This is a post-1945 German term meaning "social-democratic voter initiative." It began as an electoral campaign group of intellectuals and leading figures from the arts. It has become a forum for the left*-wing intelligentsia within the **German Social Democratic Party**.

Third Way British term coined in the mid-1990s to describe the **ideology** and **policies** of the **British Labour Party** under **Tony Blair**. The objective of the term was to indicate that the traditional socialist outlook of the party had been updated and modified to meet changed social conditions and expectations. In practice, this has meant that the party has become more middle-of-the-road. It has provided the model for the German *neue Mitte*.*

unilateralism Used with reference to the **British Labour Party**'s policy adopted in 1960 of rejecting the use of **nuclear weapons** as the basis of a defense policy. The idea was that the United Kingdom would take this step on its own initiative without reference to other countries. The policy was repudiated in May 1989.

wobblies "Wobblies" was a popular name for members of the **Industrial Workers of the World**. The term also carries the suggestion that they could "wobble" or shake the economic and social order of **capitalism**.

Bibliography

INTRODUCTION

Since the words *socialist* and *socialism* were introduced into the political lexicon in the early nineteenth century, the literature surrounding the movement they represent has been immense and diverse, reflecting the many variants of the socialist tradition. Primary texts have been variously philosophical, polemical, ideological, critical, defensive, or, usually, some combination. Those texts, and the currents they represent within the movement, brought about the mosaic of traditions within socialism that has allowed thinkers, politicians, parties, and activists to be labeled, amongst other things, Marxist, utopian, anarchist, Christian socialist, or democratic socialist. Often a thinker or activist defies categorization. Should we, for example, describe Eduard Bernstein and Harold Laski as social democrats or Marxists? Was William Morris Marxist or Utopian? Where does one place G. D. H. Cole or Herbert Marcuse? For this reason, our lists of primary sources and anthologies of such sources are not partitioned into varieties of socialist thought. Likewise, our lists of works about those thinkers, and about socialist thought more generally, each include a variety of books and articles. Where the commentators or editors do specifically discuss a variant, we have placed them into appropriate sections.

Many books and articles on socialist politics in practice, rather than socialist political thought, focus on particular countries or on topics such as welfare or economics. We thus have sections on those countries and topics. We also list biographies, divided by country. Of course, this bibliography is representative rather than fully comprehensive. The section on Marxism, to take just one example, offers only a small selection from a vast range of works. The bibliography aims to help readers follow up on areas of interest. It is also worth noting that socialism is a living political philosophy and that the bibliography includes works—such as those on contemporary anticapitalism—which may not be historical as such, but raise interesting issues that may offer departure points for further research.

Our bibliography consists primarily of scholarly books and articles published in English. As a rule, we include more recent works, published since around 1970, than older ones. This is not to say that the older works are inferior or no longer worth reading. Indeed, in some instances, they may be superior to later works, but we aim to reflect the current scholarly view of the topic and guide the reader to other bibliographies for further research.

For general summaries of the politics of individual countries the annual *Statesman's Yearbook*, although too general to be listed here, is a valuable resource, as is the *Europa World Yearbook*. In addition, since the late 1980s the United States Department of Labor has published a series, based on information supplied by American embassies, on all the major countries called *Foreign Labor Trends*. These publications are updated periodically. Current information and research can be sought in journals, which are listed separately. Let us now focus on some of the sections in the bibliography, and identify some particularly useful titles.

BIBLIOGRAPHIES AND REFERENCE WORKS

Given the absence of bibliographical control over the whole subject of socialism, recourse must be made to a number of bibliographies. A good place to start for an annotated guide to the history of European socialism is in the guides to further reading included in Albert S. Lindemann's *A History of European Socialism*. The bibliographies in the first four volumes of G. D. H. Cole's *A History of Socialist Thought* provide a convenient guide to socialist writings up to the time of their publication in the 1950s. Cole died without having compiled the bibliography for the fifth volume. There is also a good bibliography, up to about 1960, in Harry W. Laidler, *History of Socialism: An Historical and Comparative Survey of Socialism, Communism, Co-operation, Utopianism, and Other Systems of Reform and Reconstruction*.

Two good single-volume bibliographies on socialism in English are: Donald D. Egbert and Stow Persons, eds., *Socialism and American Life*, and Lyman T. Sargent, ed., *British and American Utopian Literature, 1516–1985: An Annotated, Chronological Bibliography*. For the pre-1914 period, there is an excellent, up-to-date bibliography in Marcel van der Linden and Jürgen Rojahn, eds., *The Formation of Labour Movements, 1870–1914: An International Perspective*, Vol. II, 701–81. The latter is matchless for recent research on Eastern Europe in this period. For the post-1945 period, the most convenient bibliography is that in Donald Sassoon, *One Hundred Years of Socialism: The West European Left in the Twentieth Century*.

We list a number of reference works, dictionaries and sources of statistics. Readers will also find a list of journals that contain articles on socialism in section A.6. Some of the journals focus on socialism or the left; others are more general.

PRIMARY SOURCES

Section C lists an extensive range of works by writers in the socialist tradition. It includes works by socialists, edited anthologies of their work, and also literature, poetry, and music. We have made a point of giving some emphasis to the works of authors who popularized socialist ideas, many of whom now tend to be ignored in academic works.

Any reader who wishes to achieve an understanding of the socialist movement should seek to gain some acquaintance with the primary sources and not rely solely on the secondary works. Socialism is a subtle and complicated subject. Political ideas can undergo great violence in generalized works, and socialism is no exception. The only antidote to falling victim to these hazards is familiarity with the primary sources. Many of these works are difficult to find, but the anthologies are generally available and repay close study.

Scholars of socialism should certainly familiarize themselves with the work of Karl Marx. Only thus can one grasp the division within the socialist movement between those who adhere to some of Marx's ideas and those who are more critical. The best selection of Marx's works is David McLellan, ed., *Karl Marx: Selected Writings*, 2nd edition. To begin to explore the democratic socialist tradition, it is important to read Eduard Bernstein's *Preconditions of Socialism* (published in some editions as *Evolutionary Socialism*). First published in 1899, the best edition, which we list here, is in the Cambridge Texts in the History of Political Thought series (Cambridge University Press). Also, one of the few collections of documents that concentrate on democratic socialists is J. Alwin Shapiro, ed., *Movements of Social Dissent in Modern Europe*. The paths you take through the primary sources will then vary according to the interests you develop, perhaps after browsing the entries of this dictionary.

GENERAL SURVEYS OF SOCIALISM

A good, short, introductory text is Bernard Crick, *Socialism*, which has a British emphasis. Albert S. Lindemann, *A History of European Socialism*, is another good general survey of the history of European socialism for the pre-1939 period. It has the added advantage of annotated guides to further reading at the end of each chapter. The classic English-language global history of socialism is G. D. H. Cole, *A History of Socialist Thought*, which despite its age is the best comprehensive treatment of socialism. For the pre-1914 period readers should consult Marcel van der Linden and Jürgen Rojahn, eds., *The Formation of Labour Movements, 1870–1914: An International Perspective*. The research in this work for Eastern Europe is particularly good. Harry W. Laidler's *History of Socialism: An Historical and Comparative Survey of Socialism, Communism,*

Co-operation, Utopianism; and Other Systems of Reform and Reconstruction, was useful in its day, but should now only be used where there is no alternative. Donald Sassoon, *One Hundred Years of Socialism: The West European Left in the Twentieth Century*, contains a large-scale treatment of its subject. Despite its title, it is largely devoted to the post-1945 period, making a determined effort to place the development of socialism in its economic and social setting. Bhikhu Parekh's short introduction to his edited volume *The Concept of Socialism* is useful for its identification of some key principles of socialism. A good general survey of communism is the detailed study by Leslie Holmes, *Politics in the Communist World*, published in 1986, shortly before East European communism began to collapse.

SPECIFIC TOPICS

Many sections in this bibliography offer lists on specific topics (*see* structure of the bibliography below), such as socialist political thought, individual countries, and biographies. The section on socialist thought is divided into general studies and works that focus on particular thinkers such as Harold Laski, C. B. Macpherson, Herbert Marcuse, and many others.

For the social democratic parties of Western Europe, the treatment in William E. Paterson and Alastair H. Thomas, eds., *Social Democratic Parties in Western Europe*, is particularly good for the post-1945 period with lots of useful information hard to get elsewhere. Also see the same editors' *The Future of Social Democracy: Problems and Prospects of Social Democratic Parties in Western Europe*. As might be expected, the number of general books on socialist and social-democratic parties in non-English speaking countries written in English is limited. Specialists need to consult the research in the original language. We have omitted such works from this bibliography unless they are collections of source materials.

Some sections include useful dictionaries from the Scarecrow Press series to which the present work contributes. For an introduction to labor unions and labor matters generally, which occupy a central place in the history of socialism, see James C. Docherty, *Historical Dictionary of Organized Labor*, 2nd edition. Utopianism is covered by James M. Morris and Andrea L. Kross, *Historical Dictionary of Utopianism*, and the welfare state by Brent Greve, *Historical Dictionary of the Welfare State*, 2nd edition. These historical dictionaries include extensive bibliographies.

The interaction between art and the history of socialism is given large-scale treatment by Donald D. Egbert in *Social Radicalism and the Arts*. The use of culture to create a socialist way of life is well dealt with by Vernon L. Lidtke, *The Alternative Culture: Socialist Labor in Imperial Germany*. There is a general survey of war and socialism by S. F. Kisson, *War and the Marxists: Socialist Theory and Practice in Capitalist War*. This topic is also examined in J. M. Winter, *Socialism and the Challenge of War: Ideas and Politics in Britain, 1912–18*.

A rather general section comprises recent introductory works on ideologies. Each has at least one chapter on socialism. Andrew Heywood's *Political Ideologies* is particularly suitable for newcomers to the study of ideologies.

A section focusing on particular countries is divided by country. This will, hopefully, be useful for readers who wish to focus on socialist politics in one country or to embark on study in comparative politics. In the subsection on the United Kingdom a valuable annotated bibliography on the British Labour Party can be found in Kenneth O. Morgan, *Labour People: Leaders and Lieutenants, Hardie to Kinnock*, 2nd ed., 348–62. Also in that subsection, a useful study is Geoffrey Foote's *The Labour Party's Political Thought: A History*.

WEBSITES

The final section offers a selection of English language websites. A particularly useful site is that of the Socialist International, which includes links to the sites of most of the member parties. Also included are the websites of the contemporary social forums. Another useful site is the *Marxists.org Internet Archive*. This includes many Marxist writings, along with biographies, historical material, and an encyclopedia of Marxism.

COLLECTIONS AND INTERNET RESOURCES

Readers who wish to further their study of socialism can find an excellent collection of materials at The Working Class Movement Library (WCML) in Salford, England. Visitors need to book an appointment and much-needed donations are welcome. The WCML website is www.wcml.org.uk. Another resource is the International Institute of Social History, in Amsterdam, the Netherlands (www.iisg.nl). The World Wide Web has in recent years become a valuable resource. An excellent general politics website with links to a wide range of resources is *Richard Kimber's Political Science Resources*, www.psr.keele.ac.uk/.

STRUCTURE OF THE BIBLIOGRAPHY

The organization of this bibliography is as follows:

A. Research Guides

A.1 Bibliographies and finding aids: International
A.2 Bibliographies and finding aids: National
A.3 Dictionaries and reference works
A.4 Biographical dictionaries
A.5 Statistics

B. Journals and Magazines

C. Primary Sources

C.1 Individual primary sources
C.2 Anthologies
C.3 Novels, poetry, and music

D. General Survey Works on Socialism

E. Socialist Thought (Includes Biographies with Emphasis on Thought)

E.1 Works on specific thinkers
E.2 General works

F. Utopian Socialism

G. Marxism

H. Anarchism and Syndicalism

I. Social Democracy

J. Socialism and Religion

    J.1 Christian socialism
    J.2 Socialism and the Jews

K. Social Protest and Revolution

L. Contemporary Anticapitalism

M. Socialists and the Working Class

N. Socialism and Organized Labor

O. Socialism and Women

P. The Cooperative Movement and Other Voluntary Associations

Q. Socialism, Education, and the Arts

R. Socialism and the Welfare State

S. Socialism and the Economic Environment

T. Socialism and Liberalism

U. International Socialist Organizations

V. Socialism, Foreign Policy, and War

W. Ideologies

X. Autobiographies and Biographies of Politicians and Activists by Country

X.1 Australia
X.2 Austria
X.3 Belgium
X.4 France
X.5 Germany
X.6 India
X.7 Indonesia
X.8 Ireland
X.9 Japan
X.10 Mozambique
X.11 New Zealand
X.12 Portugal
X.13 Russia
X.14 United Kingdom
X.15 United States of America

Y. Studies of Specific Countries

Y.1 Argentina
Y.2 Australia
Y.3 Austria
Y.4 Belgium
Y.5 Brazil
Y.6 Canada
Y.7 Chile
Y.8 Czechoslovakia
Y.9 Denmark
Y.10 Egypt
Y.11 France
Y.12 Germany
Y.13 Greece
Y.14 India
Y.15 Indonesia
Y.16 Ireland
Y.17 Israel
Y.18 Italy
Y.19 Jamaica

Y.20 Japan
Y.21 Lithuania
Y.22 Mexico
Y.23 New Zealand
Y.24 Nicaragua
Y.25 Nigeria
Y.26 Peru
Y.27 Russia
Y.28 Spain
Y.29 Sweden
Y.30 Tanzania
Y.31 Tunisia
Y.32 Turkey
Y.33 United Kingdom
Y.34 United States of America
Y.35 Yugoslavia

Z. Websites

A. RESEARCH GUIDES

A.1 Bibliographies and finding aids: International

Dolléans, Edouard, and Michel Crozier, eds. *Mouvements Ouvriers et Socialistes: Chronologie et Bibliographie*. Paris: Editions Ouvrières, 1950–59. 5 vols.

Dowe, Dieter, ed. *Führer zu den Archiven, Bibliotheken und Forschungsein-richtungen zur Geschichte der europäischen Arbeiterbewegung.* Bonn: Verlag Neue Gesellschaft, 1984. [A guide to the holdings of labor movement materials in European archives and libraries.]

Haut, Georges, ed. *La Deuxième Internationale, 1889–1914: étude critique des sources, essai bibliographique*. Paris: Mouton, 1964.

International Labour Office. *International Labour Documentation*. Geneva: International Labour Office, 1965 to date.

———. *Labour Information: A Guide to Selected Sources*. Geneva: International Labour Office, 1991.

International Political Science Association. *International Political Science Abstracts*. Norwood, Mass.: SilverPlatter Information, 1951 to date. [Published every two months, this source provides abstracts of journal and yearbook articles.]

Jumba-Masagazi, A. H. K., ed. *African Socialism: A Bibliography and a Short Summary*. Nairobi, Kenya: East African Academy Research Information Centre, 1970.

Lee, A. H. *The Revolutionary Left in Europe: A Research Guide*. New York: New York Public Library, 1992.

Reference and Research Series. *The Left Index*. Santa Cruz, Calif.: Joan Hoardquista, 1984 to date. [A quarterly index to international left-wing periodicals.]

Rowbotham, Sheila, ed. *Women's Liberation and Revolution: A Bibliography*. 2nd ed. Bristol, England: Falling Wall Press, 1973.

Sargent, Lyman T., ed. *British and American Utopian Literature, 1516–1985: An Annotated, Chronological Bibliography*. New York: Garland, 1988. [Contains about 3,000 references.]

United Nations. *Poverty: A Bibliography*. Kuala Lumpur: Asian and Pacific Development Center Library, 1994.

Vanden, Harry E., ed. *Latin American Marxism: A Bibliography*. New York: Garland, 1991.

A.2 Bibliographies and finding aids: National

ABC-Clio Information Services. *Labor in America: A Historical Bibliography*. Santa Barbara, Calif.: ABC-Clio, 1985. [Annotated bibliography of journal articles.]

Archiv für Sozialgeschichte. *Bibliographie zur Geschichte der deutschen Arbeiterschaft und Arbeiterbewegung 1863 bis 1914: Berichtzeitraum 1945 bis 1975*. Bonn: Verlag Neue Gesellschaft, 1981.

Ashton, Owen, Robert Fyson, and Stephen Roberts, eds. *The Chartist Movement: A New Annotated Bibliography*. London: Mansell, 1995.

Blewett, Neal. *Cabinet Diary: A Political Record of the First Keating Government, 1991–1993*. Adelaide: Wakefield Press, 1999.

Brinkman, Maarten, ed. *Honderd jaar sociaal-democratie in boek en tijdschrift: Bibliografie van de geschiedenis van de SDAP en de PvdA, 1894–1994*. 3rd ed. Amsterdam: Stichting beheer IISG, 1994. [A greatly expanded bibliography containing 682 items on Dutch social democracy.]

Booker, Keith. *Film and the American Left: A Research Guide*. Westport, Conn.: Greenwood Press, 1999.

British Labour Party. *Labour History: Series One: British Labour Party Research Department Memoranda and Information Papers, 1941–1979*. Marlborough, England: Adam Matthew, 1998.

British Library of Political and Economic Science. *Labour Pamphlets Guide*. London: British Library of Political and Economic Science, 1997.

Burton, Alan, ed. *The British Co-operative Movement Film Catalogue*. Westport, Conn.: Greenwood Press, 1997.

Coleman, M. A., ed. *The New Zealand Labour Party, 1916–1966: A Bibliography*. Wellington: National Library of New Zealand, 1972.

Duffy, Susan, ed. *The Political Left in the American Theatre of the 1930's: A Bibliographical Sourcebook*. Lanham, Md.: Scarecrow Press, 1992.

Egbert, Donald D., and Stow Persons, eds. *Socialism and American Life*. Princeton, N.J.: Princeton University Press, 1952. 2 vols.

Gibbney, H. J., comp. *Labor in Print: A Guide to the People Who Created a Labor Press in Australia between 1850 and 1939*. Canberra: History Department, Research School of Social Sciences, Australian National University, 1975. [Lists 488 labor newspapers and publications.]

Goldwater, Walter, ed. *Radical Periodicals in America, 1890–1950*. New Haven, Conn.: Yale University Press, 1964.

Günther, Klaus, and Kurt Schmitz, eds. *SPD, KPD/DKP, DGB in den Westzonen und in der Bundesrepublik-Eine Bibliographie*. Bonn-Bad Godesberg: Verlag Neue Gesellschaft, 1976.

Ham, F. Gerald, ed. *Records of the Socialist Labor Party of America, 1877–1907: Guide to Microfilm Edition*. Alexandria, Va.: Chadwyck-Healey, 1970.

Harrison, J. F. C., and Dorothy Thompson, eds. *Bibliography of the Chartist Movement*. Hassocks, England: Harvester Press, 1978. [See also the updated supplement to this work by Owen Ashton, et al.]

Harrison, Royden, Gillian Woolven, and Robert Duncan, eds. *The Warwick Guide to British Labour Periodicals, 1790–1970: A Check List*. Atlantic Highlands, N.J.: Harvester Press, 1977. [Lists 4,125 periodicals.]

Harzig, Christiane, and Dirk Hoerder, eds. *The Immigrant Labor Press in North America, 1840s–1970s: An Annotated Bibliography*. New York: Greenwood Press, 1987.

Lamberet, Renée, ed. *Mouvements Ouvriers et Socialistes, Chronologie et Bibliographie: L'Espagne, 1750–1936*. Paris: Editions Ouvrières, 1953.

Ligthart Schenk A. H., ed. *Bibliografie van het christen—en religieus-socialisme in Nederland, 1900–1940*. Amsterdam: Bibliotheek-en documentatieschool, 1969.

Mayer, Henry, and L. Kirby, eds. *ARGAP: A Research Guide to Australian Politics and Cognate Subjects*. Melbourne: Cheshire, 1976. [A supplementary edition, *ARGAP 2*, was published by Longman Cheshire, Melbourne, in 1984.]

Miles, Dione, ed. *Something in Common: An IWW Bibliography*. Detroit, Mich.: Wayne State University Press, 1986.

Neufeld, Maurice F., Daniel J. Leab, and Dorothy Swanson, eds. *American Working Class History: A Representative Bibliography*. New York: R.R. Bowker Company, 1983. [A major work with about 7,200 entries including doctoral theses.]

Partisan Review. *Partisan Review: Cumulative Index, 1934–1999*. New York: AMS Press, 2000.

Rabin, Albert I., ed. *Kibbutz Studies: A Digest of Books and Articles on the Kibbutz by Social Scientists, Educators, and Others*. East Lansing: Michigan State University Press, 1971.

Research Publications, Ltd. *Archives of the British Labour Party, 1873–1973*. Reading, England: Research Publications, 1990.

Sbriccoli, Mario, ed. *Elementi per una bibliografia del Socialismo giuridico italiano*. Milan: Goiuffrè, 1976.

Sharma, Jaddish S., ed. *Indian Socialism: A Descriptive Bibliography*. Delhi: Vikas Publishing House, 1975.

Smethurst, John B., ed. *A Bibliography of Co-operative Societies' Histories*. Manchester: Co-operative Union, 1974. [A comprehensive bibliography.]

Smith, Harold, ed. *The British Labour Movement, 1945–1970: A Bibliography*. London: Mansell, 1981. [Contains 3,838 references.]

Steiner, Herbert, ed. *Bibliographie zur Geschichte der österreichischen Arbeiterbewegung*. Vienna: Europa Verlag, 1962. 3 vols. [Covers the period from 1867 to 1945.]

Uyehara, Cecil H., ed. *Leftwing Social Movements in Japan: An Annotated Bibliography*. Tokyo: Tuttle, 1959.

Wilcox, Laird, ed. *Guide to the American Left*. 21st ed. Olathe, Kans.: Editorial Research Service, 1999–2000. [First published in 1970.]

A.3 Dictionaries and reference works

Alexander, Robert J., ed. *Political Parties of the Americas*. Westport, Conn.: Greenwood Press, 1982. 2 vols. [Excludes the United States.]

Banks, Arthur S., William Overstreet, and Thomas Muller, eds. *Political Handbook of the World 2000–2002*. Washington D.C.: CQ Press, 2004. [Series began in 1975.]

Bottomore, Tom, ed. *A Dictionary of Marxist Thought*. 2nd ed. Oxford: Blackwell Publications, 1991. [First published in 1983, this comprehensive work has references at the end of entries.]

Buhle, Mari Jo, Paul Buhle, and Dan Georgakas, eds. *Encyclopedia of the American Left*. 2nd ed. New York: Oxford University Press, 1998. [Comprehensive and cross-referenced; it includes references after entries and an index.]

Day, Alan J., ed. *Political Parties of the World*. 4th ed. New York: Stockton, 1996. [The first two editions were edited with Henry W. Degenhardt in 1980 and 1984.]

Fukui, Haruhiro, ed. *Political Parties of Asia and the Pacific*. Westport, Conn.: Greenwood Press, 1985. 2 vols.

Jacobs, Francis, ed. *Western European Political Parties: A Comprehensive Guide*. Harlow, England: Longman, 1989.

Katz, Richard S., and Peter Mair, eds. *Party Organizations: A Data Handbook on Party Organizations in Western Democracies, 1960–1990.* London: Sage, 1992.

Kelly, Gary, and Edd Applegate, eds. *British Reform Writers, 1789–1832.* Detroit, Mich.: Gale Res., 1995.

Krieger, Joel. *The Oxford Companion to the Politics of the World.* 2nd ed. Oxford: Oxford University Press, 2001.

Leifer, Michael. *Dictionary of the Modern Politics of South-East Asia,* 3rd ed. London: Routledge, 2001. [First published in 1995.]

Lewis, D. S., and D. J. Sager, eds. *Political Parties of Asia and the Pacific: A Reference Guide.* Harlow, England: Longman, 1992.

McHale, Vincent E., and Sharon Skowronski, eds. *Political Parties of Europe.* Westport, Conn.: Greenwood Press, 1983. 2 vols. [As well as entries on individual parties, this work includes bibliographies for each country.]

McLean, Iain, and Alistair MacMillan. *The Concise Oxford Dictionary of Politics.* 2nd ed. Oxford: Oxford University Press, 2003.

Meyer, Thomas, et al., eds. *Lexikon des Sozialismus.* Cologne: Bund-Verlag, 1986.

Rappoport, Angelo S. *Dictionary of Socialism.* New York: Gordon Press, 1976. [First published in 1924.]

Ray, Donald I., ed. *Dictionary of the African Left: Parties, Movements and Groups.* Brookfield, Vt.: Gower, 1989.

Scruton, Roger. *A Dictionary of Political Thought.* London: Pan, 1983.

Snodgrass, Mary E., ed. *Encyclopedia of Utopian Literature.* Santa Barbara, Calif.: ABC-CLIO, 1995.

Stockwell, Foster, ed. *Encyclopedia of American Communes, 1663–1963.* Jefferson, N.C.: McFarland and Company, 1998.

Szajkowski, Bogdan, ed. *Political Parties of Eastern Europe, Russia and the Successor States.* Harlow, England: Longman, 1994.

Wilczynski, Joseph. *An Encyclopedic Dictionary of Marxism, Socialism and Communism.* London and Basingstoke: Macmillan, 1981.

A.4 Biographical dictionaries

Andreucci, Franco, and Detti Tommasco, eds. *Il movimento operaio italiano; Dizionario biografico, 1853–1943.* Rome: Riuniti, 1975–78. 5 vols.

Banks, O., ed. *The Biographical Dictionary of British Feminists.* New York: New York University Press, 1990. 2 vols.

Baylen, Joseph O., and Norbert J. Gossman, eds. *Biographical Dictionary of Modern British Radicals, 1770–1914.* Atlantic Highlands, N.J.: Humanities Press, 1979–1988. 4 vols.

Bédarida, François, et al., eds. *Dictionnaire Biographique du Mouvement Ouvrier International: Grand-Bretagne.* Paris: Les Editions Ouvrières, 1982, 1986. 2 vols.

Bellamy, Joyce, and John Saville, eds. *Dictionary of Labour Biography*. London: Macmillan, 1972–2000. Vol. 1–10. [British labor lives only.]

Gildart, Keith, David Howell, and Neville Kirk, eds. *Dictionary of Labour Biography*. London: Palgrave, 2003–2004. Vol. 11–12. [British labor lives only.]

Benewick, Robert, and Philip Green, eds. *The Routledge Dictionary of Twentieth-Century Political Thinkers*. 2nd ed. London: Routledge, 1998.

Bianco, L., and Y. Chevrier. *Dictionnaire Biographique du Mouvement Ouvrier International: La Chine*. Paris: Les Editions Ouvrières, 1985.

Bourdet, Y., et al., eds. *Dictionnaire Biographique du Mouvement Ouvrier International: L'Autriche*. Paris: Les Editions Ouvrières, 1988.

Droz, Jacques, ed. *Dictionnaire Biographique du Mouvement Ouvrier International: L'Allemagne*. Paris: Les Editions Ouvrières, 1990. [Covers the German labor movement up to the 1930s.]

Fink, Gary M., ed. *Biographical Dictionary of American Labor*. Rev. ed. Westport, Conn.: Greenwood Press, 1984. [Contains entries on about 750 individuals. First published in 1974.]

Greaves, Richard L., and Robert Zaller, eds. *Biographical Dictionary of British Radicals in the Seventeenth Century*. Brighton, England: Harvester Press, 1982, 1983, 1984. 3 vols.

Knox, William, ed. *Scottish Labour Leaders, 1918–39: A Biographical Dictionary*. Edinburgh: Mainstream Publishing, 1984.

Johnpoll, Bernard K., and Harvey Klehr, eds. *Biographical Dictionary of the American Left*. Westport, Conn.: Greenwood Press, 1986.

Lazitch, Branko, and Milorad M. Drachkovitch, eds. *Biographical Dictionary of the Comintern*. Stanford, Calif.: Hoover Institution Press, 1986. [First published in 1973.]

Maitron, Jean, ed. *Dictionnaire Biographique du Mouvement Ouvrier Français*. Paris: Les Editions Ouvrières, 1964–1993. 43 vols. [Covers the period 1789–1939.]

Meertens, van P. J., et al., eds. *Biografisch woordenboek van het socialisme en de arbeidersbeweging in Nederland*. 5 vols. Amsterdam: Sicting beheer IISG, 1986–92. [A biographical dictionary of Dutch socialists and labor leaders from 1840 to 1940.]

Nicholls, David, and Peter Marsh, eds. *A Biographical Dictionary of Modern European Radicals and Socialists. Volume 1: 1780–1815*. New York: St. Martin's Press, 1988.

Schröder, Wilhelm H., ed. *Sozialdemokratische Reichstagsabgeordnete und Reichstagskandidaten, 1898–1918*. Düsseldorf: Droste Verlag, 1986. [Contains biographies on about 700 German social-democratic candidates, both successful and unsuccessful, who stood for election to the *Reichstag*.]

———. *Sozialdemokratische Parlamentarier in den deutschen Reichs- und Landtagen, 1867–1933: Biographien, Chronik, Wahldokumentation: Ein*

Handbuch. Düsseldorf: Droste Verlag, 1995. [Contains details on 700 social-democratic parliamentarians.]

Shiota, S., ed. *Dictionnaire Biographique du Mouvement Ouvrier International: Japan*. Paris: Les Editions Ouvrières, 1982. 2 vols.

A.5 Statistics

Bairoch, Paul, et al., eds. *The Working Population and Its Structure*. Brussels: Free University of Brussels, 1968. [Contains census data on the industry structure of the labor force from the last half of the nineteenth century to the 1960s for every country.]

Crewe, Ivor, Neil Day, and Anthony Fox. *The British Electorate, 1963–1992: A Compendium of Data from the British Election Studies*. Rev. ed. Cambridge, England: Cambridge University Press, 1995.

Flora, Peter, Franz Kraus, and Winfried Pfenning. *State, Economy, and Society in Western Europe, 1815–1975: A Data Handbook*. Chicago: St. James Press, 1983, 1987. 2 vols.

Gorvin, Ian, ed. *Elections since 1945: A Worldwide Reference Compendium*. Harlow, England: Longman Group, 1989.

Harrison, A. *The Distribution of Wealth in Ten Countries. Royal Commission on the Distribution of Income and Wealth. Background Paper to Report No. 7*. London: Her Majesty's Stationery Office, 1979.

International Labor Office. *Year Book of Labour Statistics: Retrospective Edition on Population Censuses, 1945–1989*. Geneva: International Labour Office, 1990.

Katz, Richard S., and Peter Mair, eds. *Party Organizations: A Data Handbook on Party Organizations in Western Democracies, 1960–1990*. London: Sage, 1990.

Lacey, Michael, and Mary Fumer, eds. *The State and Social Investigation in Britain and the United States*. Cambridge, England: Cambridge University Press, 1993.

Mackie, Thomas T., and Richard Rose, eds. *The International Almanac of Electoral History*. 3rd ed. London: Macmillan, 1991. [First published in 1974.]

Mair, Peter, and Ingrid van Biezen. "Party Membership in Twenty European Democracies, 1980–2000." *Party Politics* 7, no. 1 (2001): 5–21.

B. JOURNALS AND MAGAZINES

Anarchist Studies (Cambridge, England), 1993 to date.
British Journal of Politics and International Relations (Oxford), 1999 to date.
Canadian Journal of Political Science (Ottawa, Ontario), 1967 to date.

Capital and Class (London), 1977 to date.
Comparative Studies in Society and History (London), 1958 to date.
Dissent (New York) 1954 to date.
Economy and Society (London), 1971 to date.
European Journal of Political Research (Dordrecht, Germany), 1972 to date.
European Journal of Political Theory (London), 2002 to date.
European Labour Forum (Nottingham, England), 1990 to date.
Government and Opposition (London), 1965 to date.
Historical Abstracts (New York), 1955 to date.
History of Political Economy (Durham, N.C.), 1990 to date.
History of Political Thought (Exeter, England), 1980 to date.
Imprint: A Journal of Analytical Socialism (Bristol, England), 1996 to date.
International Journal of Social Economics (Bradford, England), 1973 to date.
International Labor and Working Class History (Los Angeles), 1976 to date.
International Labour Review (Geneva), 1923 to date.
International Review of Social History (New York), 1956 to date.
International Socialism (London), 1960–78 (1st series), 1978 (2nd series) to date.
Journal of Contemporary History (London), 1966 to date.
Journal of Political Ideologies (Abingdon, England), 1996 to date.
Journal of Social History (Berkeley, Calif.), 1967 to date.
Labor History (New York), 1960 to date.
Labour/Le Travail (Halifax, Nova Scotia), 1976 to date.
Monthly Review (New York), 1965 to date.
New Left Review (London), 1960–99 (1st series), 2000 to date (2nd series).
New Statesman (London), 1913 to date.
Partisan Review (New York), 1934 to 2003.
Party Politics (London), 1995 to date.
Past and Present (Oxford), 1952 to date.
Politics and Society (Stoneham, Mass.), 1972 to date.
Political Quarterly (Oxford), 1930 to date.
Political Studies (Oxford), 1952 to date.
Political Theory (Newbury Park, Calif.), 1972 to date.
Politics (Oxford), 1980 to date.
Red Pepper (London), 1994 to date.
Review of International Studies (Cambridge, England), 1974 to date.
Review of Radical Political Economics (Cambridge, Mass.), 1993 to date.
Socialism and Democracy: The Bulletin of the Research Group on Socialism and Democracy (New York), 1982 to date.
Socialism Today (London), 1995 to date.
Socialist History (London), 1993 to date.
Socialist Register (London), 1964 to date.

Third World Quarterly (London), 1979 to date.
West European Politics (London), 1978 to date.

C. PRIMARY SOURCES

C.1 Individual primary sources

Bakunin, Mikhail Alexandrovich. *Statism and Anarchy*, ed. Marshall Shatz. Cambridge, England: Cambridge University Press, 1990.

Bebel, August. *Woman in the Past, Present, and Future*. London: Zwan Publications, 1988. [Originally published as *Woman and Socialism* in 1879, this title was used for the second edition in 1882.]

Bellamy, Edward. *Looking Backward*. Harmondsworth, England: Penguin, 1983. [First published in 1888.]

Benn, Tony. *A Future for Socialism: Agenda for the 21st Century*. London: Fount, 1991.

Berneri, Marie Louise. *Neither East nor West: Selected Writings, 1939–1948*. London: Freedom Press, 1988. [Anarchist author.]

Bernstein, Eduard. *Documente des Socialismus: Hefte für Geschichte, Urkunden und Bibliographie des Socialismus*. Frankfurt: Saur und Auvermann, 1968. 5 vols.

——. *The Preconditions of Socialism*, ed. and trans. Henry Tudor. Cambridge, England: Cambridge University Press, 1993. First published in 1899 as *Die Voraussetzungen des Socialismus und die Aufgaben der Socialdemokratie*. [This first full translation of Bernstein's classic statement of democratic socialism replaces the translation by Edith C. Harvey originally published in 1909 and reprinted by Schocken in 1961.]

Beveridge, (Sir) William. *Social Insurance and Allied Services*. New York: Macmillan, 1942. [Although Beveridge was a liberal, rather than a socialist, his ideas were hugely influential upon post-war British social democracy.]

Blair, Tony. *The Third Way: New Politics for the New Century*. London: Fabian Society, 1998.

Blatchford, Robert. *Merrie England*. London: Journeyman Press, 1976. [A facsimile of the first edition, first published in 1893.]

Blum, Léon. *L'Oeuvre de Léon Blum*. 3 vols. Paris: Albin Michel, 1955, 1972.

Chile, Vere G. *How Labour Governs: A Study of Workers' Representation in Australia*. Melbourne: Melbourne University Press, 1964. [First published in 1923.]

Cohen, G. A. *Self-Ownership, Freedom, and Equality*. Cambridge, England: Cambridge University Press, 1995.

——. *If You're an Egalitarian, How Come You're So Rich?* Cambridge, Mass.: Harvard University Press, 2000.

Cole, G. D. H. *The World of Labour*. 4th ed. London: Macmillan, 1928. [The first edition was published in 1913 and this fourth edition was first published in 1919 by G. Bell and sons, London.]

——. *The Next Ten Years in British Social and Economic Policy*. London, Macmillan: 1929.

——. *Socialism in Evolution*. Harmondsworth, England: Penguin, 1938.

——. *Self-Government in Industry*. London: J. G. Corina, 1972. [Facsimile of the original edition published in 1917 with two additional chapters and an appendix.]

——. *Guild Socialism Restated*. New Brunswick N.J.: Transaction Books, 1980. [Facsimile of the original edition published in 1920, with a new introduction by Richard Vernon.]

Crosland, C. A. R. *The Future of Socialism*. London: Jonathan Cape, 1956.

——. *Socialism Now and Other Essays*. London: Jonathan Cape, 1974.

Debs, Eugene V. *Gentle Rebel: Letters of Eugene V. Debs*, ed. J. Robert Constantine. Urbana, Ohio: University of Illinois Press, 1995.

De Man, Hendrik. *The Psychology of Socialism*. London: George Allen and Unwin, 1928.

Engels, Friedrich. *The Condition of the Working Class in England*. Oxford: Oxford University Press, 2004. [Written in 1842–44 and first published in English in 1892. This edition has an introduction by David McLellan.]

Ely, Richard T. *Socialism: An Examination of Its Nature, Its Strength, and Its Weakness, with Suggestions for Social Reform*. London: Swan Sonnenschein and Co., 1894.

Fromm, Erich. *The Working Class in Weimar Germany: A Psychological and Sociological Study*, ed. Wolfgang Bonss, trans. Barbara Weinberger. Leamington Spa, England: Berg, 1984. [A pioneering attitudinal study conducted in 1929 on 584 individuals.]

Godwin, William. *Enquiry Concerning Political Justice and Its Influence on Modern Morals and Happiness*, ed. Isaac Kramnick. Harmondsworth, England: Penguin, 1976. [First published in 1773, this is recognized as the first major work of what would be known as anarchist political philosophy.]

Gramsci, Antonio. *Pre-Prison Writings*, ed. Richard Bellamy, trans. Virginia Cox. Cambridge, England: Cambridge University Press, 1994.

——. *Selections from Prison Notebooks*, ed. and trans. Quentin Hoare and Geoffrey Nowell Smith London: Lawrence and Wishart, 1971.

Grönlund, Laurence. *The Cooperative Commonwealth*. Boston, Mass.: Lee and Shepard, 1884.

Hardie, Keir. *From Serfdom to Socialism*. Hassocks, England: Harvester Press, 1974. [First published in 1907.]

Hughes, William M. *The Case for Labor*. Sydney: Sydney University Press, 1970. [Facsimile edition with notes first published in 1910.]

Jay, Douglas. *The Socialist Case*. London: Faber, 1937. [A second edition was released in 1947.]

Jaurès, Jean. *Studies in Socialism*, trans. M. Minturn. London: Independent Labour Party, 1906.

Kautsky, Karl. *The Road to Power: Political Reflections on Growing into the Revolution*, ed. John H. Kautsky, trans. Raymond Mayer. Atlantic Highlands, N.J.: Humanities Press, 1996.

Laclau, Ernesto, and Chantal Mouffe. *Hegemony and Socialist Strategy: Towards a Radical Democratic Politics*. London: Verso, 1985.

Lange, Oskar, and Fred M. Taylor. *On the Economic Theory of Socialism*. New York: McGraw Hill, 1964. [First published in 1938.]

Lansbury, George. *My England*. London: Selwyn and Blount, 1934.

Laski, Harold J. *A Grammar of Politics*. 5th ed. London: Allen and Unwin, 1967. [First published in 1925, the 4th edition of 1938 included an important new introductory chapter, which is included in this edition.]

———. *Democracy in Crisis*. London: Allen and Unwin, 1933.

———. *The Rise of European Liberalism*. New Brunswick, N.J.: Transaction, 1997. [A facsimile of the original edition published in 1936 by Allen and Unwin: London.]

Le Bon, Gustav. *The Psychology of Socialism*. New Brunswick, N.J.: Transaction, 1982. [First published in 1899, this unsympathetic study viewed socialism as essentially a religion.]

MacKenzie, Norman, and Jeanne MacKenzie, eds. *The Diary of Beatrice Webb*. London: Virago in association with the London School of Economics and Political Science, 1982–85. 4 vols.

Macpherson, C. B. *Democratic Theory: Essays in Retrieval*. Oxford: Oxford University Press, 1973.

Mann, Tom. *Memoirs*. London: Labour Publishing, 1923.

Marcuse, Herbert. *Eros and Civilization*. London: Sphere, 1969. [Includes a new preface by Marcuse. First published by Beacon Press, 1955.]

———. *Soviet Marxism: A Critical Analysis*. Harmondsworth, England: Penguin, 1958.

———. *One Dimensional Man*. London: Routledge and Kegan Paul, 1986. [First published in 1964.]

———. *An Essay on Liberation*. Harmondsworth, England: Penguin, 1969.

Marx, Karl. *Capital. Volume 1*. Harmondsworth, England: Penguin, 1992. [First published, 1867; first English edition, 1886.]

———. *Capital. Volume 2*. Harmondsworth, England: Penguin, 1993. [First published, 1885, edited by Friedrich Engels; first English edition, 1893.]

———. *Capital. Volume 3*. Harmondsworth, England: Penguin, 1993. [First published, 1894, edited by Friedrich Engels; first English edition, 1909.]

Marx, Karl, and Friedrich Engels. *The Communist Manifesto*. Harmondsworth, England: Penguin, 2002. [First published in 1848.]

Métin, Albert. *Socialism without Doctrine*, trans. Russell Ward. Sydney: Alternative Publishing Co-operative Ltd., 1977. [First published as *Le Socialisme sans Doctrines* in 1901.]

Michels, Robert. *Political Parties: A Sociological Study of the Oligarchical Tendencies of Modern Democracy*, trans. Eden and Cedar Paul. New York: Free Press, 1962. [First published in English in 1915.]

Mill, John Stuart. *Principles of Political Economy*. London: Longman, People's edition, 1865. [The first edition was published in 1848. Although Mill was a liberal, his views in this book were influential upon the development of social democracy.]

Nursey-Bray, Paul, and Carol L. Bacchi, eds. *Left Directions: Is There a Third Way?* Perth: University of Western Australia Press, 2001.

Orwell, George. *The Road to Wigan Pier*. Harmondsworth, England: Penguin, 1962. [First published 1937 and reprinted many times thereafter.]

———. *The Lion and the Unicorn: Socialism and the English Genius*. Harmondsworth, England: Penguin, 1982. [First published in 1941, this edition has an introduction by Bernard Crick.]

Owen, Robert. *A New View of Society/Report to the County of Lanark*. Harmondsworth, England: Penguin, 1969. [First published in 1814.]

Panitch, Leo. *Renewing Socialism: Democracy, Strategy, and Imagination*. Boulder, Colo.: Westview Press, 2001.

Pimlott, Ben, ed. *The Political Diary of Hugh Dalton, 1918–40, 1945–60*. London: Cape in association with the London School of Economics and Political Science, 1986. 2 vols.

Proudhon, Pierre-Joseph. *What Is Property?* ed. and trans. Donald R. Kelly and Bonnie G. Smith. Cambridge, England: Cambridge University Press, 1994. [First published in 1840.]

Senghor, Léopold S. *On African Socialism*, trans. M. Cook. New York: Praeger, 1964.

Shaw, George B., ed. *Fabian Essays in Socialism*. London: Fabian Society and George Allen and Unwin, 1931. [First published in 1889, the 1931 edition includes a new preface by Shaw and Sidney Webb's introduction to the 1920 edition.]

Shaw, George B. *The Intelligent Woman's Guide to Socialism, Capitalism, Sovietism, and Fascism*. Harmondsworth, England: Penguin, 1996.

Sorel, Georges. *Reflections on Violence*, ed. Jeremy Jennings. Cambridge, England: Cambridge University Press, 1999.

Sombart, Werner. *Why Is There No Socialism in the United States?* trans. Patricia M. Hocking and C. T. Husbands. London: Macmillan Press, 1976. [First published in 1906.]

Tawney, R. H. *Equality*. London: George Allen and Unwin, 1931.

———. *Religion and the Rise of Capitalism*. Harmondsworth, England: Penguin, 1938. [First published in 1926.]

——. *The Acquisitive Society*. London: Fontana, 1961. [First published in 1921.]

Trotsky, Leon. *The Revolution Betrayed*. New York: Pathfinder, 1972. [Written in 1936.]

Walzer, Michael. *Spheres of Justice: A Defense of Pluralism and Equality*. New York: Basic Books, 1983.

Wilkinson, Ellen. *The Town That Was Murdered: The Life-Story of Jarrow*. London: Victor Gollancz, 1939.

Williams, Philip M., ed. *The Diary of Hugh Gaitskell, 1945–1956*. London: Cape, 1983.

Young, Iris Marion. *Justice and the Politics of Difference*. Princeton, N.J.: Princeton University Press, 1990.

——. *Inclusion and Democracy*. Oxford: Oxford University Press, 2000.

C.2 Anthologies

Ascher, Abraham, ed. *The Mensheviks in the Russian Revolution*. London: Thames and Hudson, 1976.

Attlee, C. R., et al. *Labour's Aims in War and Peace*. London: Lincolns-Prager, 1940. [A collection of early World War II statements by prominent Labour figures and the party's War Manifesto.]

Avrich, Paul, ed. *The Anarchists in the Russian Revolution*. London: Thames and Hudson, 1973.

——, ed. *Anarchist Voices: An Oral History of Anarchism in America*. Princeton, N.J.: Princeton University Press, 1995.

Aylmer, G. E., ed. *The Levellers in the English Revolution*. Ithaca, N.Y.: Cornell University Press, 1975.

Barker, Bernard, ed. *Ramsay MacDonald's Political Writings*. London: Allen Lane, 1972.

Bealy, Frank, ed. *The Social and Political Thought of the British Labour Party*. London: Weidenfeld and Nicolson, 1970.

Benn, Tony, ed. *Writings on the Wall: A Radical and Socialist Anthology, 1215–1984*. London: Faber and Faber, 1984.

Bernstein, Eduard. *Selected Writings of Eduard Bernstein, 1900–1921*, ed. and trans. Manfred Steger. Atlantic Highlands, N.J.: Humanities Press, 1996.

Brown, Gordon, and Tony Wright, eds. *Values, Visions, and Voices: An Anthology of Socialism*. Edinburgh: Mainstream, 1995.

Callinicos, Alex, ed. *Between Apartheid and Capitalism: Conversations with South African Socialists*. London: Bookmarks, 1992.

Christman, Henry M. *Essential Works of Lenin: "What is to be Done?" and Other Writings*. Mineola, N.Y.: Dover Publications, 1987.

Claeys, Gregory, ed. *Selected Works of Robert Owen*. London: William Pickering, 1993. 4 vols.

412 • BIBLIOGRAPHY

Coates, Ken, and Tony Topham, eds. *Workers' Control: A Book of Readings and Witnesses for Workers' Control*. London: Panther, 1970.

Cole, G. D. H., and A. W. Filson, eds. *British Working Class Movements: Select Documents, 1789–1875*. London: Macmillan, 1951. [A major collection of documents, reprinted in 1965 and again in 1967.]

Commons, John R., et al., eds. *A Documentary History of American Industrial Society*. New York: Russell and Russell, 1910–11. 10 vols.

Deutscher, Isaac, ed. *The Age of Permanent Revolution: A Trotsky Anthology*. New York: Dell, 1964.

Drew, Alison, ed. *South Africa's Radical Tradition: A Documentary History. Volume 1: 1907–1950*. Cape Town: UCT Press, 1996.

Ebbels, R. N., ed. *The Australian Labour Movement: Extracts from Contemporary Documents, 1850–1907*. Melbourne: Landsdowne Press, 1965. [First published in 1960.]

Edwards, Stewart, ed. *The Communards of Paris, 1871*. Ithaca, N.Y.: Cornell University Press, 1973.

Ensor, R. C. K., ed. and trans. *Modern Socialism as Set Forth by Socialists*. Rev. ed. London: Harper, 1910. [First published in 1903, this work remains a handy source for political programs.]

Fielding, Steven, ed. *The Labour Party: "Socialism" and Society since 1951*. Manchester: Manchester University Press, 1997. [Contains selections from almost 100 documents.]

Fried, Albert, and Ronald Sanders, eds. *Socialist Thought: A Documentary History*. Rev. ed. New York: Columbia University Press, 1993. [First published in 1964, this work is devoted to the writings of intellectuals.]

Fried, Albert, ed. *Socialism in America from the Shakers to the Third International: A Documentary History*. New York: Columbia University Press, 1992.

Goode, Patrick, ed. and trans. *Karl Kautsky: Selected Political Writings*. London: Macmillan Press, 1983.

Hampton, Christopher, ed. *A Radical Reader: The Struggle for Change in England*. Harmondsworth, England: Penguin, 1984.

Hanna, Sami A., and George Gardner, eds. *Arab Socialism: A Documentary Survey*. Salt Lake City, Utah: University of Utah Press, 1969.

Harris, Paul, and Stephen Levine, eds. *The New Zealand Politics Source Book*. Palmerston North, New Zealand: Dunmore Press, 1992. [Contains some source material for the New Zealand Labor Party.]

Harvester Press. *The Left in Britain*. Hassocks, England: Harvester Press, 1974 to date. [A series of primary sources on microfiche with bibliographical guides.]

Hirst, Paul Q., ed. *The Pluralist Theory of the State: Selected Writings of G.D.H. Cole, J.N. Figgis and H.J. Laski*. London: Routledge, 1989.

Hirst, Paul, ed. *The Collected Works of Harold Laski*. London: Routledge, 1997. 10 vols. [A useful, but far from comprehensive, collection of Laski's writings.]

Howe, Irving, ed. *A Handbook of Socialist Thought*. London: Victor Gollancz, 1972. [A comprehensive selection of Marxist and non-Marxist works.]

———. *Essential Works of Socialism*. New Haven, Conn.: Yale University Press, 1976.

Johar, K. L. *Struggles and Memoirs of the Socialists, 1947–1957*. New Delhi: Harman Publicity House, 1997.

Kameka, Eugene, ed. *The Portable Karl Marx*. New York: Viking Penguin Inc., 1983. [A particularly useful introductory compilation of Marx's voluminous writings that includes a detailed chronology of the life of Marx.]

Kelly, Alfred, ed. *The German Worker: Working-Class Autobiographies from the Age of Industrialization*. Berkeley: University of California Press, 1987.

Kornbluh, Joyce L., ed. *Rebel Voices: An IWW Anthology*. Chicago: Charles H. Kerr, 1988.

Kramer, Steven P., ed. *Socialism in Western Europe: The Experience of a Generation*. Boulder, Colo.: Westview Press, 1984. [Interviews with European socialists for the period from about 1930 onward.]

Laybourn, Keith. *The Labour Party, 1881–1951: A Reader in History*. Wolfboro, N.H.: Alan Sutton, 1988.

Leeson, R. A., ed. *Strike: A Live History, 1887–1971*. London: Allen and Unwin, 1973.

Litván, György, and János M. Bak, eds. *Socialism and Social Science: Selected Writings of Ervin Szabó*. London: Routledge and Kegan Paul, 1982. [This selected translation of the writings of the Hungarian social democrat Ervin Szabó covers the period from 1880 to 1918.]

Lorenz, E., ed. *Norsk socialisme i dokumenter*. Oslo: Pax, 1970.

McKinlay, Brian. *Australian Labor History in Documents. Volume 1: The Trade Union Movement; Volume 2: The Labor Party; Volume 3: The Radical Left*. Burwood, Victoria: Collins Dove, 1990. [A revised version of a work originally published in 1979.]

McLellan, David, ed. *Karl Marx: Selected Writings*. 2nd ed. Oxford: Oxford University Press, 2000.

Morris, William. *Political Writings—Contributions to Justice and Commonweal, 1883–1890*, ed. Nicholas Salmon. Bristol, England: Thoemmes, 1994.

Morton, A. L., ed. *Political Writings of William Morris*. New York: International Publishers, 1973.

Pelz, William A., ed. *Wilhelm Liebknecht and German Social Democracy: A Documentary History*, trans. Erich Hahn. Westport, Conn.: Greenwood Press, 1994.

Prasad, Bimla, ed. *Socialism, Sarvodaya, and Democracy: Selected Works of Jayaprakash Narayan*. Bombay: Asia Publishing House, 1964.

Price, Roger, ed. *1848 in France*. Ithaca, N.Y.: Cornell University Press, 1975.

Reisman, David, ed. *Democratic Socialism in Britain: Classic Texts in Economic and Political Thought, 1825–1952*. 10 vols. London: Pickering and Chatto, 1996. [A useful facsimile reprint of many works, some very difficult to obtain.]

Rose, Saul. *Socialism in Southern Asia*. London: Oxford University Press, 1959. [Contains many useful extracts from documents in the body of the text.]

Saint-Simon, Henri. *Selected Writings on Science, Industry, and Social Organisation*, ed. and trans. Keith Taylor. London: Croom Helm, 1975.

Schapiro, J. Salwin, ed. *Movements of Social Dissent in Modern Europe*. Princeton, N.J.: Van Nostrand, 1962. [Despite its title, this work is largely about democratic socialism; it contains a range of extracts, mainly from before 1920.]

Socialist Review Collectives, ed. *Unfinished Business: Twenty Years of Socialist Review*. London: Verso, 1991.

Tawney, R. H. *The Radical Tradition: Twelve Essays on Politics, Education and Literature*. Harmondsworth, England: Penguin, 1964.

Thompson, E. P., and Eileen Yeo, eds. *The Unknown Mayhew: Selections from the Morning Chronicle, 1849–50*. London: Merlin Press, 1971.

Tristan, Flora. *Flora Tristan: Utopian Feminist: Her Travel Diaries and Personal Crusade*, trans. Doris and Paul Beik. Bloomington: Indiana University Press, 1993. [A selection by the translators of Tristan's writings.]

Tudor, H., and J. M. Tudor, eds. and trans. *Marxism and Social Democracy: The Revisionist Debate, 1896–1898*. Cambridge, England: Cambridge University Press, 1988.

Waters, Mary-Alice. *Rosa Luxemburg Speaks*. New York: Pathfinder Press, 1970.

Weller, Patrick M., ed. *Caucus Minutes, 1901–1949: Minutes of the Meetings of the Federal Parliamentary Labor Party*. Melbourne: Melbourne University Press, 1975. 3 vols.

Weller, Patrick M., and Beverly Lloyd, eds. *Federal Executive Minutes, 1915–1955: Minutes of the Meetings of the Federal Executive of the Australian Labor Party*. Melbourne: Melbourne University Press, 1978.

Wilde, Oscar. *The Soul of Man and Prison Writings*, ed. Isobel Murray. Oxford: Oxford University Press, 1999. [Includes "The Soul of Man Under Socialism."]

Williams, Geraint L. *John Stuart Mill on Politics and Society*. Glasgow: Fontana, 1976. [This selection of Mill's writings includes his "Chapters on Socialism."]

Woodcock, George, ed. *The Anarchist Reader*. Glasgow: Fontana, 1977. [Includes a biographical supplement.]

Wright, Anthony, ed. *British Socialism: Socialist Thought from the 1880s to the 1960s*. London: Methuen, 1983.

Yassour, Avraham, ed. *A History of the Kibbutz: A Selection of Sources, 1905–1929*. Merhavia, Israel: University of Haifa, 1995.

C.3 Novels, poetry, and music

Bellamy, Edward. *Looking Backward: 2000–1887*. Boston, Mass.: Houghton Mifflin, 1926. [First published in 1888.]

——. *Equality*. New York: D. Appleton, 1897. [The sequel to *Looking Backward*.]

Bold, Alan, ed. *The Penguin Book of Socialist Verse*. Harmondsworth, England: Penguin, 1970.

Bush, Alan, and Randall, Swingler, eds. *The Left Song Book*. London: Victor Gollancz, 1938.

Carpenter, Edward. *Chants of Labor, with Music*. London: Sonnenheim and Co., 1892.

——. *Towards Democracy*. London: George Allen and Unwin, Complete edition, 1905. [The first edition published in 1883, more sections were gradually added and the complete edition was published in 1905.]

Claeys, Gregory, ed. *Utopias of the British Enlightenment*. Cambridge, England: Cambridge University Press, 1994.

Greenwood, Walter. *Love on the Dole*. London: Jonathan Cape, 1945. [First published in 1933, this edition includes a new note by the author on the text.]

London, Jack. *The Iron Heel*. London: Acro, 1966. [First published in 1907.]

More, Thomas. *Utopia*, trans. Paul Turner. Harmondsworth, England: Penguin, 1965.

Morris, William. *Dream of John Ball*. London: Reeves, 1889.

——. *Poems by the Way*. London: Reeves, 1891.

——. *News from Nowhere*, ed. Krishan Kumar. Cambridge, England: Cambridge University Press, 1995. [First published in 1890.]

Shelley, Percy Bysshe. *The Selected Poetry and Prose of Shelley*. Ware, England: Wordsworth, 2002. [Includes an introduction and notes by Bruce Woodcock.]

Sinclair, Upton. *The Jungle*. New York: Heritage Press, 1965. [First published in 1906.]

Tressell, Robert [Robert Noonan]. *The Ragged Trousered Philanthropists*. Oxford: Oxford University Press, 2005. [Written around 1910 and first published in full in London by Lawrence and Wishart in 1955.]

D. GENERAL SURVEY WORKS ON SOCIALISM

Anderson, Perry, and Patrick Camiller, eds. *Mapping the West European Left.* London: Verso, 1994.

Beaud, Michel. *Socialism in the Crucible of History*, trans. Thomas Dickman. Atlantic Highlands, N.J.: Humanities Press, 1993.

Beilharz, Peter. *Postmodern Socialism: Romanticism, City, and State.* Melbourne: Melbourne University Press, 1994.

Berki, R. N. *Socialism.* London: J.M. Dent and Sons, 1975.

Boggs, Carl. *The Socialist Tradition: From Crisis to Decline.* New York: Routledge, 1995.

Butler, Anthony. *Transformative Politics: The Future of Socialism in Western Europe.* Rev. ed. Basingstoke, England: Macmillan, 1997.

Busky, Donald F. *Democratic Socialism: A Global Survey.* Westport, Conn.: Praeger, 2000.

Cohen, Robert, and Harry Goulbourne, eds. *Democracy and Socialism in Africa.* Boulder, Colo.: Westview Press, 1991.

Crick, Bernard. "Socialist Literature in the 1950s." *The Political Quarterly* 31, no. 3 (1960): 361–73.

——. *Socialism.* Milton Keynes, England: Open University Press, 1987.

Derfler, Leslie. *Socialism since Marx: A Century of the European Left.* New York: St. Martin's Press, 1973.

Droz, Jacques, ed. *Histoire Générale du Socialisme.* Paris: Presses Universitaires de France, 1972–78. 4 vols.

Ellner, Steve, ed. *The Latin American Left: From the Fall of Allende to Perestroika.* Boulder, Colo.: Westview Press, 1993.

Geary, Dick, ed. *Labour and Socialist Movements in Europe before 1914.* Oxford: Berg, 1989. [Deals with the United Kingdom, France, Germany, Russia, Italy, and Spain.]

Goode, Stephen. *The Prophet and the Revolutionary: Arab Socialism in the Modern Middle East.* New York: Franklin Watts, 1975.

Gray, Alexander. *The Socialist Tradition: Moses to Lenin.* London: Longmans, Green and Co., 1946.

Holland, Stuart. *The Socialist Challenge.* London: Quartet Books, 1975.

Holmes, Leslie, *Politics in the Communist World.* Oxford: Clarendon Press, 1986.

Horn, Gerd-Rainer. *European Socialists' Response to Fascism: Ideology, Activism, and Contingency in the 1930s.* New York: Oxford University Press, 1996.

Hudson, Kate. *European Communism Since 1989: Towards a New European Left?* New York: Palgrave Macmillan, 2000.

Kilroy-Silk, Robert. *Socialism since Marx.* London: Allen Lane Penguin Books, 1972.

Laidler, Harry W. *History of Socialism: An Historical and Comparative Survey of Socialism, Communism, Co-operation, Utopianism; and Other Systems of Reform and Reconstruction.* London: Routledge and Kegan Paul, 1968. [First published as *Social-Economic Movements*, 1944.]

Lerner, Warren. *A History of Socialism and Communism in Modern Times: Theorists, Activists, and Humanists.* 2nd ed. Englewood Cliffs, N.J.: Prentice-Hall, 1993.

Lichtheim, George. *A Short History of Socialism.* London: Weidenfeld and Nicolson, 1970.

Lindemann, Albert S. *A History of European Socialism.* New Haven, Conn.: Yale University Press, 1983. [The best general survey of the period up to 1939 with annotated reading guides at the end of each chapter.]

Naarden, Bruno. *Socialist Europe and Revolutionary Russia: Perception and Prejudice, 1848–1923.* Cambridge, England: Cambridge University Press, 1992.

Newton, Douglas J. *British Labour, European Socialism and the Struggle for Peace, 1889–1914.* Oxford: Clarendon Press, 1985.

Parekh, Bhikhu, ed. *The Concept of Socialism.* London: Croom Helm, 1975. [Parekh's introduction is particularly useful.]

Sassoon, Donald. *One Hundred Years of Socialism: The West European Left in the Twentieth Century.* New York: I.B. Tauris Publishers, 1996. [The major survey of the post-1945 period.]

Sassoon, Donald, ed. *Looking Left: European Socialism after the Cold War.* London: I.B. Tauris in association with the Gramsci Foundation in Rome, 1997.

Tunçay, Mete, and Erik J. Zürcher, eds. *Socialism and Nationalism in the Ottoman Empire, 1876–1923.* London: British Academic Press, 1994.

van Holthoon, Frits, and Marcel van der Linden, eds. *Internationalism in the Labour Movement, 1830–1940.* Leiden, Netherlands: E. J. Brill, 1988. 2 vols.

White, Dan S. *Lost Comrades: Socialists of the Front Generation, 1918–1945.* Cambridge, Mass.: Harvard University Press, 1992. [Deals with Western Europe.]

Wilde, Lawrence. *Modern European Socialism.* Aldershot, England: Dartmouth Publishing Co., 1994.

Wright, Anthony. *Socialisms: Old and New.* 2nd ed. London: Routledge, 1996.

E. SOCIALIST THOUGHT (INCLUDES BIOGRAPHIES WITH EMPHASIS ON THOUGHT)

E.1 Works on specific thinkers

Carpenter, L. P. *G.D.H. Cole: An Intellectual Biography.* Cambridge, England: Cambridge University Press, 1973.

Carver, Terrell. "Engels's Feminism." *History of Political Thought* 6, no. 3 (1985): 479–89.

———. *The Postmodern Marx.* Manchester: Manchester University Press, 1998.

Davidson, Alistair. "Gramsci and Lenin 1917–1922." In *The Socialist Register 1974,* ed. Ralph Miliband and John Saville. London: Merlin Press, 1974.

Davis, Laurence. "Morris, Wilde, and Marx on the Social Preconditions of Individual Development." *Political Studies* 44, no. 4 (1996): 719–32.

Draper, Hal. "Marx on Democratic Forms of Government." In *The Socialist Register 1974,* ed. Ralph Miliband and John Saville. London: Merlin Press, 1974.

Fletcher, Don. "Iris Marion Young: The Politics of Difference, Justice and Democracy." In *Liberal Democracy and Its Critics: Perspectives in Contemporary Political Thought,* ed. April Carter and Geoffrey Stokes. Cambridge, England: Polity, 1998.

Geary, Dick. *Karl Kautsky.* Manchester: Manchester University Press, 1987.

Geoghegan, Vincent. *Reason and Eros: The Social Theory of Herbert Marcuse.* London: Pluto Press, 1981.

Greenleaf, W. H. "Laski and British Socialism." *History of Political Thought* 2, no. 3 (1981): 573–91.

Griffith, Gareth. *Socialism and Superior Brains: The Political Thought of Bernard Shaw.* London: Routledge, 1993.

Hoover, Kenneth R. "Ideologizing Institutions: Laski, Hayek, Keynes and the Creation of Contemporary Politics." *Journal of Political Ideologies* 4, no. 1 (1999): 87–115.

———. *Economics as Ideology: Keynes, Laski, Hayek, and the Creation of Contemporary Politics.* Lanham, Md.: Rowman and Littlefield, 2003.

Jennings, Jeremy. *Georges Sorel: The Character and Development of His Thought.* London: Macmillan, 1985.

Jones, Peter d'Alroy. *Henry George and British Socialism.* New York: Garland, 1991.

Kingwell, Mark. "Michael Walzer: Pluralism, Justice and Democracy." In *Liberal Democracy and Its Critics: Perspectives in Contemporary Political Thought,* ed. April Carter and Geoffrey Stokes. Cambridge, England: Polity, 1998.

Kramnick, Isaac, and Barry Sheerman. *Harold Laski: A Life on the Left.* London: Allen Lane, 1993.

Lamb, Peter. *Harold Laski: Problems of Democracy, the Sovereign State, and International Society.* New York: Palgrave Macmillan, 2004.

———. "G.D.H. Cole on the General Will: A Socialist Reflects on Rousseau." *European Journal of Political Theory* 4, no. 3 (2005): 283–300.

Lamb, Peter, and David Morrice. "Ideological Reconciliation in the Thought of Harold Laski and C. B. Macpherson." *Canadian Journal of Political Science* 35, no. 4 (2002): 795–810.

Le Bras-Chopard, Armelle. *De l'égalité dans la différence. Le socialisme de Pierre Leroux*. Paris: Presses de la Fondation Nationale de Sciences Politiques, 1986. [Pierre Leroux (1797–1871) invented the word "socialism."]

Lipow, Arthur. *Authoritarian Socialism in America: Edward Bellamy and the Nationalist Movement*. Berkeley: University of California Press, 1982.

McLellan, David. *The Thought of Karl Marx: An Introduction*. 3rd ed. London: Macmillan, 1995. [First published 1971.]

Miliband, Ralph. "Harold Laski: An Exemplary Public Intellectual." *New Left Review* 200 (1993): 175–81.

———. "Harold Laski's Socialism." In *The Socialist Register 1995*, ed. Leo Panitch. London: Merlin Press, 1995.

Morrice, David. "C.B. Macpherson's Critique of Liberal Democracy and Capitalism." *Political Studies* 42, no. 4 (1994): 646–61.

Mukherjee, Subrata. *A History of Socialist Thought from the Precursors to the Present*. Thousand Oaks, Calif.: Sage Publications, 2000.

Newman, Michael. *Harold Laski: A Political Biography*. Basingstoke, England: Macmillan, 1993.

———. "Harold Laski Today." *The Political Quarterly* 67, no. 3 (1996): 229–38.

Oishi, Takahisa. *The Unknown Marx: Reconstructing a Unified Perspective*. London: Pluto Press (in association with Takushoku University, Japan), 2001. [Foreword by Terrell Carver.]

Panitch, Leo. "Ralph Miliband, Socialist Intellectual, 1924–1994." In *The Socialist Register 1995*, ed. Leo Panitch. London: Merlin Press, 1995.

Pels, Dick. "Socialism Between Fact and Value: From Tony Blair to Hendrik de Man and Back." *Journal of Political Ideologies* 7, no. 3 (2002): 281–99.

Pemberton, Jo-Anne. "James and the Early Laski: The Ambiguous Legacy of Pragmatism." *History of Political Thought* 19, no. 2 (1998): 264–92.

Peretz, Martin. "Laski Redivivus." *Journal of Contemporary History* 1, no. 2 (1966): 87–101.

Showstack Sassoon, Anne. *Gramsci and Contemporary Politics*. London: Routledge, 2000.

Steenson, Gary P. *Karl Kautsky, 1854–1938: Marxism in the Classic Years*. Pittsburgh, Pa.: Pittsburgh University Press, 1979.

Steger, Manfred B. *The Quest for Evolutionary Socialism: Eduard Bernstein and Social Democracy*. Cambridge, England: Cambridge University Press, 1997.

Thomas, Paul. *Karl Marx and the Anarchists*. London: Routledge and Kegan Paul, 1980.

Townshend, Jules. *C.B. Macpherson and the Problem of Liberal Democracy*. Edinburgh: Edinburgh University Press, 2000.

Wright, Anthony. *R.H. Tawney*. Manchester: Manchester University Press, 1987.

Wright, A. W. *G.D.H. Cole and Socialist Democracy*. Oxford: Clarendon Press, 1979.

Yuan, Ji. *W.E.B. DuBois and His Socialist Thought*. Trenton, N.J.: Africa World Press, 1999.

E.2 General works

Barrow, Logie, and Bullock, Ian. *Democratic Ideas and the British Labour Movement, 1880–1914*. Cambridge, England: Cambridge University Press, 1996.

Beilharz, Peter. *Labour's Utopia: Bolshevism, Fabianism, Social Democracy*. London: Routledge, 1992.

Billington, James E. *Fire in the Minds of Men: Origins of the Revolutionary Faith*. New York: Basic Books, 1980.

Chauduri, Chitrita. *Rammounohar Lothia and the Indian Socialist Thought*. Calcutta, India: Minerva Associates, 1993.

Claeys, Gregory. *Machinery, Money and the Millennium: From Moral Economy to Socialism, 1815–1860*. Cambridge, England: Polity Press, 1987.

Cole, G. D. H. *A History of Socialist Thought*. New York: St. Martin's Press, 1953–60. 5 vols. [This classic work covers the period from the French Revolution to 1939.]

Crump, John. *The Origins of Socialist Thought in Japan*. New York: St. Martin's Press, 1983.

Cunningham, Frank. *Democratic Theory and Socialism*. Cambridge, England: Cambridge University Press, 1987.

Dorrien, Gary J. *The Democratic Socialist Vision*. Totawa, N.J.: Rowman and Littlefield, 1986. [Concerns the United States.]

Esposito, Anthony V. *The Ideology of the Socialist Party of America, 1901–1917*. New York: Garland Publishing Inc., 1997.

Foote, Geoffrey. *The Labour Party's Political Thought: A History*. 3rd ed. London: Croom Helm, 1997.

Hann, C. M., ed. *Socialism: Ideals, Ideologies, and Local Practice*. London: Routledge, 1993. [Anthropological perspective.]

Hill, Clive E. *Understanding the "Fabian Essays in Socialism" (1889)*. Lewiston, N.Y.: Edwin Mellen Press, 1996.

Jackson, Ben. "Equality of Nothing? Social Justice on the British Left, c. 1911–31." *Journal of Political Ideologies* 8, no. 1 (2003): 83–110.

Kloppenberg, James T. *Uncertain Victory: Social Democracy and Progressivism in European and American Thought, 1870–1920*. Oxford: Oxford University Press, 1986.

Lerner, Warren. *A History of Socialism in Modern Times: Theorists, Activists and Humanists*. Englewood Cliffs, N.J.: Prentice-Hall, 1982.

Leung, S. K. *Politics and Human Nature: Ideological Rooting of the Left*. London: Empiricus, 2000.

Levy, Carl, ed. *Socialism and the Intelligentsia, 1880–1914*. London: Routledge and Kegan Paul, 1987.

Macfarlane, Leslie J. *Socialism, Social Ownership, and Social Justice*. New York: St. Martin's Press, 1998.

Manton, Kevin. "The Fellowship of the New Life: English Ethical Socialism Reconsidered." *History of Political Thought* 24, no. 2 (2003): 282–304.

Martin, David E., and David Rubinstein, eds. *Ideology and the Labour Movement*. London: Croom Helm, 1979.

Pittenger, Mark. *American Socialists and Evolutionary Thought, 1870–1920*. Madison: University of Wisconsin Press, 1993.

Rubel, Maximilien, and John Crump, eds. *Non-Market Socialism in the Nineteenth and Twentieth Centuries*. London: Macmillan, 1987.

Ryle, Martin. *Ecology and Socialism*. London: Radius, 1988.

Schecter, Darrow. *Radical Theories: Paths beyond Marxism and Social Democracy*. Manchester: Manchester University Press, 1994.

Schwarzmantel, John. *Socialism and the Idea of the Nation*. London: Harvester Wheatsheaf, 1991.

Selucky, Radoslav. *Marxism, Socialism, and Freedom: Towards an Essential Democratic Theory of Labour-Managed Systems*. London: Macmillan, 1979.

Stears, Marc. "Guild Socialism and Ideological Diversity on the British Left, 1914–1926." *Journal of Political Ideologies* 3, no. 3 (1998): 289–307.

Thomas, John L. *Alternative America: Henry George, Edward Bellamy, Henry Demarest Lloyd, and the Adversary Tradition*. Cambridge, Mass.: Belknap Press, 1983.

Tingsten, Herbert. *The Swedish Social Democrats: Their Ideological Development*, trans. Greta Frankel and Patricia Howard-Rosen. Totawa, N.J.: Bedminister Press, 1973.

Werskey, Gary. *The Visible College*. London: Allen Lane, 1978. [A study of scientists and socialists in Britain in the 1930s.]

Wright, Anthony W. "Guild Socialism Revisited." *Journal of Contemporary History* 9 (1974): 165–80.

Wright, Anthony, ed. *Socialisms: Theories and Practices*. Oxford: Oxford University Press, 1986.

F. UTOPIAN SOCIALISM

Berry, Brian J. L. *America's Utopian Experiments: Communal Havens from Long-Wave Crises*. Hanover, N.H.: University of New England Press, 1992.

Brundage, W. Fitzhugh. *A Socialist Utopia in the New South: The Ruskin Colonies in Tennessee and Georgia, 1894–1901*. Urbana, Ohio: University of Illinois Press, 1996.

Guarneri, Carl J. *The Utopian Alternative: Fourierism in Nineteenth-Century America*. Ithaca, N.Y.: Cornell University Press, 1991.

Kumar, Krishna. *Utopianism*. Minneapolis: University of Minnesota Press, 1991. [An excellent introduction with an up-to-date bibliography.]

Levitas, Ruth. *The Concept of Utopia*. London: Philip Allan, 1990.

Loubère, L. A. *Utopian Socialism: Its History since 1800*. Cambridge, Mass.: Schenkman Publishing Co., 1974.

Manton, Kevin. "The British Nationalization of Labour Society and the Place of Edward Bellamy's *Looking Backward* in Late Nineteenth-Century Socialism and Radicalism." *History of Political Thought* 25, no. 2 (2004): 325–47.

Morris, James M., and Andrea L. Kross. *Historical Dictionary of Utopianism*. Lanham, Md.: Scarecrow Press, 2004.

Royle, Edward. *Robert Owen and the Commencement of the Millennium: A Study of the Harmony Community*. Manchester: Manchester University Press, 1998.

Taylor, Keith. *The Political Ideas of the Utopian Socialists*. London: Frank Cass, 1982.

G. MARXISM

Blackburn, Robin, ed. *Revolution and Class Struggle: A Reader in Marxist Politics*. Glasgow: Fontana, 1977.

Buhle, Paul. *Marxism in the US: Remapping the American Left*. London: Verso, 1987.

Callinicos, Alex. *Marxism and Philosophy*. Oxford: Oxford University Press, 1985.

Donald, Moira. *Marxism and Revolution: Karl Kautsky and the Russian Marxists, 1900–1924*. New Haven, Conn.: Yale University Press, 1993.

Fadndez, Julio. *Marxism and Democracy in Chile: From 1932 to the Fall of Allende*. New Haven, Conn.: Yale University Press, 1988.

Femia, Joseph V. *Marxism and Democracy*. Oxford: Oxford University Press, 1993.

Fernández-Morera, Daria. *American Academia and the Survival of Marxist Ideas*. Westport, Conn.: Praeger Publishers, 1996.

Gamble, Andrew, David Marsh, and Tony Tant. *Marxism and Social Science*. London: Routledge, 1999.

Judt, Tony. *Marxism and the French Left: Studies in Labour and Politics in France, 1830–1981*. Oxford: Clarendon Press, 1986.

Kolakowski, Leszek. *Main Currents of Marxism*, trans. P. S. Falla. Oxford: Clarendon Press, 1978. 3 vols. [A major work of intellectual history.]

Löwy, Michael, ed. *Marxism in Latin America from 1909 to the Present: An Anthology*. Atlantic Highlands, N.J.: Humanities Press, 1992.

Martin, Randy. *On Your Marx: Rethinking Socialism and the Left*. Minneapolis, Minn.: University of Minneapolis Press, 2001.

McLellan, David. *Marxism and Religion: A Descriptive Assessment of the Marxist Critique of Christianity*. London: Macmillan, 1987. [Contains an annotated bibliography.]

——. *Marxism after Marx: An Introduction*. 3rd ed. Basingstoke, England: Macmillan, 1998.

Rogers, Homer K. *Before the Revisionist Controversy: Kautsky, Bernstein, and the Meaning of Marxism*. New York: Garland Press, 1992.

Townshend, Jules. *The Politics of Marxism: The Critical Debates*. London: Leicester University Press, 1996.

H. ANARCHISM AND SYNDICALISM

Bookchin, Murray. *The Spanish Anarchists: The Heroic Years, 1868–1938*. New York: Free Life Editions, 1977.

Cahm, Caroline. *Kropotkin and the Rise of Revolutionary Anarchism, 1872–1886*. Cambridge, England: Cambridge University Press, 1989.

Carlson, Andrew R. *German Anarchism: The Early Movement*. Metuchen, N.J.: Scarecrow Press, 1972.

Crowder, George. *Classical Anarchism: The Political Thought of Godwin, Proudhon, Bakunin, and Kropotkin*. Oxford: Clarendon Press, 1991.

Dobofsky, Melvin. *We Shall Be All: A History of the Industrial Workers of the World*. 2nd ed. Urbana, Ohio: University of Illinois Press, 1988.

Jennings, Jeremy. *Syndicalism in France: A Study of Ideas*. London: Macmillan, 1990.

Joll, James. *The Anarchists*. 2nd ed. London: Methuen, 1979. [First published 1964.]

van der Linden, Marcel, and Wayne Thorpe, eds. *Revolutionary Syndicalism: An International Perspective*. Aldershot, England: Scolar Press, 1990.

Marshall, Peter. *Demanding the Impossible: A History of Anarchism*. London: HarperCollins, 1992.

Miller, David. *Anarchism*. London: J. M. Dent and Sons, 1984.

Quail, John. *The Slow Burning Fuse: The Lost History of the British Anarchists*. London: Paladin, 1978.

Vandervort, Bruce. *Victor Griffuelhes and French Syndicalism, 1895–1922*. Baton Rouge: Louisiana State University Press, 1996.

I. SOCIAL DEMOCRACY

Berman, Sheri. *The Social Democratic Movement: Ideas and Politics in the Making of Interwar Europe*. Cambridge, Mass.: Harvard University Press, 1998.

Bonoli, Guiliano, and Martin Powell, eds. *Social Democratic Party Policies in Contemporary Europe*. London: Routledge, 2004.

Brown, B. E., ed. *Eurocommunism and Eurosocialism*. New York: Cyrco Press, 1979.

Callaghan, John. *The Retreat of Social Democracy*. Manchester: Manchester University Press, 2000.

———. "Social Democracy and Globalisation: The Limits of Social Democracy in Historical Perspective." *British Journal of Politics and International Relations* 4, no. 3 (2002): 429–51.

Childs, David. *The Two Red Flags: European Social Democracy and Soviet Communism since 1945*. London: Routledge, 1999.

Daalder, Hans, and Peter Mair, eds. *Western European Party Systems: Continuity and Change*. London: Sage, 1983.

Dalton, Russell, and Manfred Kuechler, eds. *Challenging the Political Order: New Social and Political Movements in Western Democracies*. Cambridge, England: Polity Press, 1990.

Davis, Peter, ed. *Social Democracy in the Pacific: New Zealand Labour Perspective*. Auckland: Peter Davis in association with ROSS, 1983.

Dell, David S., and Eric Shaw, eds. *Conflict and Cohesion in Western European Social Democratic Parties*. London: Pinter Publishers, 1994.

Featherstone, Kevin. *Socialist Parties and European Integration: A Comparative History*. Manchester: Manchester University Press, 1988.

Fitzpatrick, Tony. *After the New Social Democracy: Social Welfare for the Twenty-first Century*. Manchester: Manchester University Press, 2003.

Gallagher, Tom, and Allan M. Williams, eds. *Southern European Socialism*. Manchester: Manchester University Press, 1989.

Gallie, Duncan. *Social Inequality and Class Radicalism in France and Britain*. Cambridge, England: Cambridge University Press, 1983.

Gamble, Andrew, and Tony Wright, ed. *The New Social Democracy*. Oxford: Blackwell Publishers, 1999.

Geyer, Robert. *The Uncertain Union: British and Norwegian Social Democrats in and Integrating Europe*. Aldershot, England: Avebury, 1997.

Giddens, Anthony. *The Third Way: The Renewal of Social Democracy*. Cambridge, England: Polity Press, 1998.

———. *The Third Way and Its Critics*. Cambridge, England: Polity Press, 2000.

Hamilton, Malcolm B. *Democratic Socialism in Britain and Sweden*. Basingstoke, England: Macmillan, 1988.

Hodge, Carl H. *The Trammels of Tradition: Social Democracy in Britain, France, and Germany.* Westport, Conn.: Greenwood Press, 1994.

Karvonen, Lauri, and Jan Sundberg, eds. *Social Democracy in Transition: Northern, Southern and Eastern Europe.* Brookfield, Vt.: Dartmouth Publishing, 1991.

Kitschelt, Herbert. *The Transformation of European Social Democracy.* New York: Cambridge University Press, 1994.

Korpi, Walter. *The Democratic Class Struggle.* London: Routledge and Kegan Paul, 1983.

Ladrech, Robert, and Philippe Marliere, eds. *Social Democratic Parties in the European Union: History, Organisation, Policies.* Basingstoke, England: Macmillan, 1999.

McLellan, David., ed. *Socialism and Democracy.* London: Macmillan, 1991.

Mitchell, Harvey, and Peter Stearns. *Workers and Protest: The European Labor Movement, the Working Class, and the Origins of Social Democracy, 1890–1914.* Itasca, Ill.: P.E. Peacock Publishers, 1974.

Moschonas, Gerassimos. *In the Name of Social Democracy: The Great Transformation, 1945 to the Present,* trans. Gregory Elliott. London: Verso, 2002.

Pagett, Stephen, and William E. Paterson. *A History of Social Democracy in Postwar Europe.* London: Longman, 1991.

Paterson, William E., and Alastair Thomas, eds. *Social Democratic Parties in Western Europe.* London: Croom Helm, 1977.

Paterson, William E., and Alastair Thomas. *The Future of Social Democracy: Problems and Prospects of Social Democratic Parties in Western Europe.* Oxford: Clarendon Press, 1986.

Paterson, William E., and Alastair Thomas, eds. *Social Democratic Parties in Western Europe.* London: Croom Helm, 1977. [An excellent source of data, much which is difficult to obtain.]

Pierson, Christopher. *Hard Choices: Social Democracy in the Twenty-First Century.* Oxford: Polity, 2001.

Pelinka, A. *Social Democratic Parties in Europe.* New York: Praeger, 1983.

Piven, Frances F., ed. *Labor Parties in Post Industrial Societies.* New York: Oxford University Press, 1992. [A study of Western Europe and North America.]

Pontusson, Jonas. *Swedish Social Democracy and British Labour: Essays on the Nature and Conditions of Social Democratic Hegemony.* Ithaca, N.Y.: Cornell University Press, 1988.

Przeworski, A., and J. Sprague. *Paper Stones: A History of Electoral Socialism.* Chicago: University of Chicago Press, 1986.

Vellinga, Menno, ed. *Social Democracy in Latin America: Prospects for Change.* Boulder, Colo.: Westview Press, 1993.

Waller, Michael, Bruno Coppieters, and Kris Deschouwer, eds. *Social Democracy in Post-Communist Europe.* Ilford, England: Frank Cass, 1994.

J. SOCIALISM AND RELIGION

J.1 Christian socialism

Bryant, Christopher. *Possible Dreams: A Personal History of British Christian Socialists*. London: Hodder and Stoughton, 1996.

Cort, John C. *Christian Socialism: An Informal History*. Maryknoll, New York: Orbis Books, 1988.

Dorn, Jacob H., ed. *Socialism and Christianity in Early 20th Century America*. Westport, Conn.: Greenwood Press, 1998.

Norman, Edward R. *The Victorian Christian Socialists*. Cambridge, England: Cambridge University Press, 1987.

Wilkinson, Alan. *Christian Socialism: Scott Holland to Tony Blair*. London: SCM, 1998.

J.2 Socialism and the Jews

Gorny, Joseph. *The British Labour Movement and Zionism, 1917–1948*. London: Frank Cass, 1983.

Mendelsohn, Ezra, ed. *Essential Papers on Jews and the Left*. New York: New York University Press, 1997.

Wistrich, Robert S. *Revolutionary Jews from Marx to Trotsky*. London: Harrap, 1976.

K. SOCIAL PROTEST AND REVOLUTION

Edwards, Stewart. *The Paris Commune*. London: Eyre and Spottiswoode, 1971.

Geary, Dick. *European Labour Protest, 1848–1939*. London: Methuen, 1981. [Good introduction.]

Haimson, L. H., and Tilly, C. (eds). *Strikes, Wars and Revolutions in an International Perspective*. Cambridge, England: Cambridge University Press, 1989. [Mainly concerned with the period up to 1920.]

Roseman, Mark, ed. *Generations in Conflict: Youth, Revolt and Generation Formation in Germany, 1770–1968*. Cambridge, England: Cambridge University Press, 1995.

Thompson, E. P. *The Making of the English Working Class*. Harmondsworth, England: Penguin, 1968. [First published in 1963.]

Thompson, Willie. *The Left in History: Revolution and Reform in Twentieth Century Politics*. London: Pluto Press, 1997.

Tilly, Charles, Louise Tilly, and Richard Tilly. *The Rebellious Century*. Cambridge, Mass.: Harvard University Press, 1975.

L. CONTEMPORARY ANTICAPITALISM

Bello, Walden. *Deglobalization: Ideas for a New World Economy*, updated edition. London: Zed Books, 2004. [First published in 2002.]

Callinicos. Alex. *An Anti-Capitalist Manifesto*. Cambridge, England: Polity, 2003.

George, Susan. *Another World is Possible if. . . .* Verso: London, 2004.

Kagarlitsky, Boris. *The Return of Radicalism: Reshaping the Left Institutions*, trans. Renfrey Clarke. London: Pluto, 2000.

Klein, Naomi. *No Logo*. London: Flamingo, 2000.

Mertes, Tom, ed. *A Movement of Movements: Is Another World Really Possible?* London: Verso, 2004.

Saul, John S. "Globalization, Imperialism, Development: False Binaries and Radical Resolutions." In The *Socialist Register 2004*, ed. Leo Panitch and Colin Leys. London: Merlin, 2004.

Teivainen, Teivo. "The World Social Forum and global democratization: learning from Porto Alegre." *Third World Quarterly* 23, no. 4 (2002): 621–32.

Tormey, Simon. *Anti-Capitalism: A Beginner's Guide*. Oxford: Oneworld, 2004.

M. SOCIALISTS AND THE WORKING CLASS

Bell, Lady Florence. *At the Works: A Study of a Manufacturing Town*. London: Virago Press, 1985. [First published by Edward Arnold, London, in 1907; this is a study of working-class life and tastes in Middlesborough, England.]

Cole, G. D. H. *A Short History of the British Working-Class Movement, 1789–1947*. London: Allen and Unwin, 1948.

Forester, T. *The Labour Party and the Working Class*. London: Heinemann, 1976. [An examination of the *embourgeoisement* of the Labour Party.]

Gorz, Andre. *Farewell to the Working Class: An Essay on Post-Industrial Socialism*, trans. Michael Sonenscher. London: Pluto Press, 1982.

Graham, Helen, and Paul Preston, eds. *The Popular Front in Europe*. Basingstoke, England: Macmillan, 1987.

Katznelson, Ira, and Aristide Zolberg, eds. *Working Class Formation: Nineteenth Century Patterns in Western Europe and the United States*. Princeton, N.J.: Princeton University Press, 1986.

Lovell, David. *Marx's Proletariat: The Making of a Myth*. London: Routledge, 1988.

Mayhew, Henry. *London Labour and the London Poor*. New York: Dover Publications, 1968. 4 vols. [Reproduction of the edition of 1861–62.]

Panitch, Leo. *Working-Class Politics in Crisis: Essays on Labour and the State*. London: Verso, 1986. [Concerned with the United Kingdom.]

Parkin, Frank. *Class Inequality and Political Order: Social Stratification in Capitalist and Communist Societies*. London: Paladin, 1972. [First published in 1971.]

Pierson, Stanley. *Marxist Intellectuals and the Working-Class Mentality in Germany, 1887–1912*. Cambridge, Mass.: Harvard University Press, 1993.

Seyd, Patrick, and Paul Whiteley. *Labour's Grass Roots: The Politics of Party Membership*. Oxford: Clarendon Press, 1992.

Scott, Andrew. *Fading Loyalties: The Australian Labor Party and the Working Class*. Sydney: Pluto Press, 1991. [Contains valuable data on the social composition of party members.]

Steenson, Gary P. *After Marx, before Lenin: Marxism and Socialist Working-Class Parties in Europe, 1884–1914*. Pittsburgh, Pa.: University of Pittsburgh Press, 1991. [Contains translations of socialist political platforms for Germany, Austria, and Italy.]

van der Linden, Marcel, and Jürgen Rojahn, eds. *The Formation of Labour Movements: An International Perspective, 1870–1914*. Leiden, Netherlands: E.J. Brill, 1990. 2 vols.

N. SOCIALISM AND ORGANIZED LABOR

Bridgford, Jeff. *The Politics of French Trade Unionism*. Leicester, England: Leicester University Press, 1991.

Docherty, James C. *Historical Dictionary of Organized Labor*. 2nd ed. Lanham, Md.: Scarecrow Press, 2004. [A general introduction from an international perspective.]

Fynes, Richard. *The Miners of Northumberland and Durham: A History of their Social and Political Progress*. Sunderland, England: Thos. Summerbell, 1963. [First published in 1873.]

Goodrich, Carter. *The Frontier of Control: A Study in British Workshop Politics*. London: Pluto Press, 1975. [Reprint of the original edition published in 1921 with notes.]

Kelly, John. *Trade Unions and Socialist Politics*. London: Verso, 1988.

Levy, Peter B. *The New Left and American Labor in the 1960s*. Urbana, Ohio: University of Illinois Press, 1994.

Marks, Gary. *Unions in Politics: Britain, Germany, and the United States in the Nineteenth and Early Twentieth Centuries*. Princeton, N.J.: Princeton University Press, 1989.

Minkin, Lewis. *The Contentious Alliance: Trade Unions and the Labour Party*. New York: Columbia University Press, 1992.

Nash, Michael. *Conflict and Accommodation: Coal Miners, Steel Workers, and Socialism, 1890–1920*. Westport, Conn.: Greenwood, 1982.

Webb, Sidney, and Beatrice Webb. *History of Trade Unionism*. Rev. ed. London: Longmans, Green, 1907. 2 vols. [First published in 1894.]

O. SOCIALISM AND WOMEN

Blaszak, Barbara J. *The Matriarchs of England's Cooperative Movement: A Study in Gender Politics and Female Leadership, 1883–1921*. Westport, Conn.: Greenwood Press, 2000.

Boxer, Marilyn, and Jean H. Quataert, eds. *Socialist Women: European Socialist Feminism in the Nineteenth and Early Twentieth Centuries*. New York: Elsevier, 1978.

Buhle, Mari Jo. *Women and Socialism, 1870–1920*. Urbana, Ohio: University of Illinois Press, 1981.

Deverall, Kate, et al., eds. *Party Girls: Labor Women Now*. Sydney: Pluto Press, 2000. [A study of women in the Australian Labor Party in the 1990s.]

Evans, Richard J. *Comrades and Sisters: Feminism, Socialism, and Pacifism in Europe, 1870–1945*. New York: St. Martin's Press, 1987.

Gaffin, J., and D. Thoms. *Caring and Sharing: The Centenary History of the Co-operative Women's Guild*. Manchester: Holyoake Books, 1983.

Graves, P. M. *Labour Women: Women in British Working-Class Politics, 1918–1939*. Cambridge, England: Cambridge University Press, 1994.

Grogan, Susan K. *French Socialism and Sexual Difference: Women and the New Society, 1803–44*. London: Macmillan, 1992.

Hannam, June, and Karen Hunt. *Socialist Women: Britain, 1880s–1920s*. London: Routledge, 2001.

Hilden, Patricia. *Women, Work and Politics: Belgium, 1830–1914*. Oxford: Clarendon Press, 1993.

Jaggar, Alison M. *Feminist Politics and Human Nature*. Lanham, Md.: Rowman and Littlefield, 1988. [An analysis of different types of feminist philosophy. Jaggar argues for socialist feminism.]

Miller, Sally M., ed. *Race, Ethnicity, and Gender in Early Twentieth-Century American Socialism*. New York: Garland, 1996.

Scott, Gillian. *Feminism and the Politics of Working Women: The Women's Co-operative Guild, 1880s to the Second World War*. London: UCL Press, 1998.

Slaughter, Jane, and Robert Kern. *European Women of the Left: Socialism and Feminism and the Problems Faced by Political Women 1890 to the Present*. Westport, Conn.: Greenwood Press, 1981.

Taylor, Barbara. *Eve and the New Jerusalem: Socialism and Feminism in the Nineteenth Century*. London: Virago, 1983.

P. THE COOPERATIVE MOVEMENT
AND OTHER VOLUNTARY ASSOCIATIONS

Birchall, Johnston. *Co-op: The People's Business*. Manchester: Manchester University Press, 1994.

Bolder, Patrick. *The Irish Co-operative Movement: Its History and Development*. Dublin: Institute of Public Administration, 1977.

Earle, John. *The Italian Cooperative Movement: A Portrait of the Lega Nazionale delle Cooperative e Mutue*. London: Allen and Unwin, 1986.

Furlough, Ellen. *Consumer Cooperation in France: The Politics of Consumption, 1834–1930*. Ithaca, N.Y.: Cornell University Press, 1991.

Furlough, Ellen, and Carl Strikwerda, eds. *Consumers against Capitalism: Consumer Cooperation in Europe, North America, and Japan, 1840–1990*. Lanham, Md.: Rowman and Littlefield, 1999.

Gosden, P. H. J. H. *Self-Help: Voluntary Associations in the 19th Century*. London: B.T. Batsford, 1973.

Gunn, Elisabeth, et al., eds. *Life and Times of the Lithgow Co-op: A Social and Industrial History*. Lithgow, New South Wales: Lithgow Co-operative Research Group, 2000.

Kasmir, Sharryn. *The Myth of Mondragón: Cooperatives, Politics, and Working Class Life in a Basque Town*. Albany: State University of New York Press, 1996.

Keillor, Steven J. *Cooperative Commonwealth: Co-ops in Rural Minnesota, 1859–1939*. St. Paul: Minnesota Historical Society Press, 2000.

Kinloch, James, and John Butt. *History of the Scottish CWS*. Manchester: Cooperative Wholesale Society, 1981.

Near, Henry, ed. *The Kibbutz Movement: A History. Volume 1: Origins and Growth, 1909–1939*. Oxford: Oxford University Press, 1992.

Richardson, William. *The CWS in War and Peace, 1938–1978*. Manchester: Cooperative Wholesale Society, 1977.

Russell, Raymond. *Utopia in Zion: The Israeli Experience with Worker Cooperatives*. Albany: State University of New York Press, 1995.

Shaffer, Jack. *Historical Dictionary of the Cooperative Movement*. Lanham, Md.: Scarecrow Press, 1999.

Walker, Thomas J. E. *Pluralistic Fraternity: The History of the International Workers' Order*. New York: Garland, 1991. [Deals with a friendly society.]

Watkins, W. P. *The International Co-operative Alliance, 1895–1970*. London: International Co-operative Alliance, 1970.

Q. SOCIALISM, EDUCATION, AND THE ARTS

Boyer, John W. *Culture and Crisis in Vienna*. Chicago: University of Chicago Press, 1995.

Davis, Tracey C. *George Bernard Shaw and the Socialist Theater*. Westport, Conn.: Greenwood Press, 1994.

Egbert, Donald D. *Social Radicalism and the Arts: A Cultural History from the French Revolution to 1968*. New York: Alfred Knopf, 1970. [A large-scale study of the subject.]

Kinna, Ruth. *William Morris and the Art of Socialism*. Cardiff: University of Wales Press, 2000.

Klaus, Gustav H. *The Rise of Socialist Fiction, 1880–1914*. New York: St. Martin's Press, 1987.

Reuss, Richard A., and JoAnne C. Reuss. *American Folk Music and Left Wing Politics, 1927–1957*. Lanham, Md.: Scarecrow Press, 2000.

Schulz, Hans-Joachim. *German Socialist Literature, 1860–1914: Predicaments of Criticism*. Columbia, S.C.: Camden House, 1993.

Teitelbaum, Kenneth. *Schooling for "Good Rebels": Socialist Education for Children in the United States, 1900–1920*. Philadelphia: Temple University Press, 1993.

Waters, Chris. *British Socialism and the Politics of Popular Culture, 1884–1914*. Stanford University, Calif.: Stanford University Press, 1990.

Watt, David, and Alan Filewod. *Worker's Playtime: Theatre and the Labour Movement in Australia, Canada, and the United Kingdom*. Melbourne: Cambridge University Press, 2000.

R. SOCIALISM AND THE WELFARE STATE

Ashford, D. E. *The Emergence of the Welfare States*. Oxford: Basil Blackwell, 1986.

Baldwin, Peter. *The Politics of Solidarity: Class Bases of the European Welfare State, 1875–1975*. Cambridge, England: Cambridge University Press, 1990.

Esping-Anderson, Gösta. *The Three Worlds of Welfare Capitalism*. Princeton, N.J.: Princeton University Press, 1990.

Flora, Peter, and Arnold J. Heidenheimer, eds. *The Development of Welfare States in Europe and America*. New Brunswick, N.J.: Transaction Books, 1981.

Greve, Bent. *Historical Dictionary of the Welfare State*. 2nd ed. Lanham, Md.: Scarecrow Press, 2006.

Korpi, W. *The Working Class in Welfare Capitalism*. London: Routledge and Kegan Paul, 1978.

Little, Adrian. *Post-Industrial Socialism: Towards a New Politics of Welfare*. London: Routledge, 1998.

Mishra, Ramesh. *The Welfare State in Crisis: Social Thought and Social Change*. Brighton, England: Wheatsheaf Books, 1984.

Pierson, Christopher. *Beyond the Welfare State: The New Political Economy of Welfare*. 2nd ed. Cambridge, England: Polity, 1998.
Webster, Charles. *The National Health Service: A Political History*. Oxford: Oxford University Press, 1998.

S. SOCIALISM AND THE ECONOMIC ENVIRONMENT

Archer, Robin. *Economic Democracy: The Politics of Feasible Socialism*. Oxford: Oxford University Press, 1995.
Artis, Michael, and David Cobham, eds. *Labour's Economic Policies, 1974–1979*. Manchester: Manchester University Press, 1991.
Beckerman, Wilfred, ed. *The Labour Government's Economic Record, 1964–1970*. London: Duckworth, 1972.
Berger, Suzanne D., ed. *Organizing Interests in Western Europe: Pluralism, Corporatism and the Transformation of Politics*. Cambridge, England: Cambridge University Press, 1981.
Cipolla, Carl M., ed. *The Fontana Economic History of Europe*. Glasgow: Collins/Fontana Books, 1972–76.
Esping-Andersen, G. *Politics against Markets: The Social Democratic Road to Power*. Princeton, N.J.: Princeton University Press, 1985.
Glyn, Andrew. "Social Democracy and Full Employment." *New Left Review* 211 (1995): 33–55.
Hicks, Alexander. *Social Democracy and Welfare Capitalism: A Century of Income Security Politics*. Ithaca, N.Y.: Cornell University Press, 2000.
Horvat, Branko. *The Political Economy of Socialism*. New York: M.E. Sharpe, 1982.
Howard, Michael C., and J. E. King. *A History of Marxian Economics. Volume 1, 1883–1929*. Princeton, N.J.: Princeton University Press, 1989.
Hutchinson, Frances. *The Political Economy of Social Credit and Guild Socialism*. London: Routledge, 1997.
Itoh, Makoto. *Political Economy for Socialism*. New York: St. Martin's Press, 1995.
Lash, Scott, and John Urry. *The End of Organised Capitalism*. Cambridge, England: Cambridge University Press, 1987.
Le Grand, Julian, and Saul Estin, eds. *Market Socialism*. Oxford: Clarendon Press, 1989.
Machin, Howard, and Vincent Wright, eds. *Economic Policy and Policy-Making under the Mitterrand Presidency, 1981–1984*. London: Frances Pinter, 1985.
Maddison, Anfus. *Dynamic Force in Capitalist Development*. Oxford: Oxford University Press, 1991.

Middleton, Roger. *Government versus the Market: The Growth of the Public Sector, Economic Management, and British Economic Performance, c. 1890–1979*. Cheltenham, England: Elgar Press, 1996.

Miller, David. *Market, State and Community: Theoretical Foundations of Market Socialism*. Oxford: Clarendon Press, 1990.

Millward, Robert, and John Singleton. *The Political Economy of Nationalisation in Britain, 1920–1950*. Cambridge, England: Cambridge University Press, 1995.

Nove, Alec. *The Economics of Feasible Socialism Revisited*. London: Harper-Collins, 1991. [The word "Revisited" was not in the title of the first edition of 1983.]

Offe, Claus. *Disorganised Capitalism*. Cambridge, England: Cambridge University Press, 1985.

Ollman, Bertell, ed. *Market Socialism: The Debate Among Socialists*. New York: Routledge, 1998.

Pierson, Christopher. *Socialism after Communism: The New Market Socialism*. University Park: Pennsylvania State University, 1995.

Pollard, Sidney. *Peaceful Conquest: The Industrialization of Europe, 1760–1970*. Oxford: Oxford University Press, 1981.

Przworski, A. *Capitalism and Social Democracy*. Cambridge, England: Cambridge University Press, 1985.

Radice, Giles, and Lisanne Radice. *Socialists and the Recession: The Search for Solidarity*. Basingstoke, England: Macmillan, 1986.

Schott, Kerry. *Policy, Power, and Order: The Persistence of Economic Problems in Capitalist Societies*. New Haven, Conn.: Yale University Press, 1984.

Schmitter, P., ed. *Experimenting with Scale*. Cambridge, England: Cambridge University Press, 1990.

Senghaas, Dieter. *The European Experience: A Historical Critique of Development Theory*. Dover, N.J.: Berg Publishers, 1985.

Stauber, Leland G. *A New Program for Democratic Socialism: Lessons from the Market-Planning Experience of Austria*. Carbondale, Ill.: Four Willows Press, 1987.

Stearns, Peter N., ed. *The Industrial Revolution in World History*. Boulder, Colo.: Westview Press, 1993.

Teeple, Gary. *Globalization and the Decline of Social Reform*. Atlantic Highlands, N.J.: Humanities Press, 1995.

Tomlinson, Jim. *Democratic Socialism and Economic Policy: The Attlee Years, 1945–1951*. Cambridge, England: Cambridge University Press, 1997.

Williamson, P. *Corporatism in Perspective*. London: Sage, 1989.

Yunker, James A. *Socialism Revised and Modernized: The Case for Pragmatic Market Socialism*. New York: Praeger, 1992.

T. SOCIALISM AND LIBERALISM

Bellamy, Richard. *Liberalism and Modern Society: An Historical Argument.* Cambridge, England: Polity Press, 1992.

Blaazer, David. *The Popular Front and the Progressive Tradition: Socialists, Liberals, and the Quest for Unity, 1884–1939.* Cambridge, England: Cambridge University Press, 1992.

Clarke, P. F. *Liberals and Social Democrats in Historical Perspective.* Cambridge, England: Cambridge University Press, 1978.

Kirchner, Emil J., ed. *Liberal Parties in Western Europe.* Cambridge, England: Cambridge University Press, 1988.

Laybourn, Keith, and Jack Reynolds. *Liberalism and the Rise of Labour, 1890–1918.* New York: St Martin's Press, 1984.

Luebbert, Gregory M. *Liberalism, Fascism, and Social Democracy.* New York: Oxford University Press, 1991.

Marquand, David. *The Progressive Dilemma.* London: Heinemann, 1991.

Osborne, Peter, ed. *Socialism and the Limits of Liberalism.* London: Verso, 1991.

Ramsay, Maureen. *What's Wrong With Liberalism? A Radical Critique of Liberal Political Philosophy.* London: Leicester University Press, 1997.

U. INTERNATIONAL SOCIALIST ORGANIZATIONS

Archer, Julian P. W. *The First International in France, 1864–1872: Its Origins, Theories, and Impact.* Lanham, Md.: University Press of America, 1997.

Braunthal, Julius. *History of the International. Volume 1, 1864–1914; Volume 2, 1914–1943,* trans. Henry Collins and Kenneth Mitchell. London: Nelson, 1966. [Originally published in German in 1961 and 1963.]

Braunthal, Julius. *History of the International. Volume 3: 1943–1968,* trans. Henry Collins and Kenneth Mitchell. London: Gollancz, 1980. [Originally published in German in 1971.]

Butler, William E., ed. *A Sourcebook on Socialist International Organizations.* Dordrecht, Germany: Kluwer Academic Publishing, 1980.

Collette, Christine. *The International Faith: Labour's Attitude to European Socialism, 1918–39.* Aldershot, England: Ashgate, 1998.

Devin, Guillaume. *L'Internationale Socialiste: Histoire et sociologie du socialisme international (1945–1990).* Paris: Presses de la Fondation Nationale des Sciences Politiques, 1993.

Forman, Michael. *Nationalism and the International Labor Movement: The Idea of the Nation in Socialist and Anarchist Theory.* University Park: Pennsylvania State University Press, 1998.

Hallas, Duncan. *The Comintern*. London: Bookmarks, 1985.

Haupt, Georges. *Socialism and the Great War: The Collapse of the Second International*. Oxford: Clarendon Press, 1972.

———. *Aspects of International Socialism, 1871–1914*. Cambridge, England: Cambridge University Press, 1986.

Joll, James. *The Second International, 1889–1914*. 2nd ed. New York: Harper and Row, 1965.

Socialist International. *The Socialist International: A Short History*. London: Socialist International, 1969.

Wrynn, J. E. *The Socialist International and the Politics of European Reconstruction, 1919–1930*. Amsterdam: University of Amsterdam, 1976.

V. SOCIALISM, FOREIGN POLICY, AND WAR

Bullock, Alan. *Ernest Bevin: Foreign Secretary*. London: Heinemann, 1983.

Featherstone, Kevin. *Socialist Parties and European Integration: A Comparative History*. Manchester: Manchester University Press, 1988.

George, Bruce. *The British Labour Party and Defense*. New York: Praeger, 1991.

Griffiths, Richard T. *Socialist Parties and the Question of Europe in the 1950s*. Leiden, Netherlands: E. J. Brill, 1993.

Gupta, Partha S. *Imperialism and the British Labour Movement, 1914–1964*. London: Macmillan, 1975.

Jenkins, Mark. *Bevanism—Labour's High Tide: The Cold War and the Democratic Mass Movement*. Nottingham, England: Spokesman, 1979.

Kirby, David. *War, Peace, and Revolution: International Socialism at the Crossroads, 1914–1918*. Aldershot, England: Gower, 1986. [Pays special attention to Scandinavia.]

Kisson, S. F. *War and the Marxists: Socialist Theory and Practice in Capitalist War*. London: Andre Deutsch, 1988, 1989. 2 vols.

Little, Richard, and Mark Wickham-Jones, eds. *New Labour's Foreign Policy: A New Moral Crusade?* Manchester: Manchester University Press, 2000.

Naylor, John F. *Labour's International Policy: The Labour Party in the 1930s*. London: Weidenfeld and Nicolson, 1969.

Newman, Michael. *Socialism and European Unity: The Dilemma of the Left in Britain and France*. London: Junction Books, 1983.

Newton, Douglas J. *British Labour, European Socialism, and the Struggle for Peace, 1889–1914*. Oxford: Clarendon Press, 1985.

Robins, Lynton J. *The Reluctant Party: Labour and the European Economic Community, 1951–1975*. Ormskirk, England: G. W. and A. Hesketh, 1979.

Scott, Leonard V. *Conscription and the Attlee Governments: The Politics and Policy of National Service, 1945–1951*. Oxford: Clarendon Press, 1993.

Vickers, Rhiannon. *The Labour Party and the World. Volume 1: The Evolution of Labour's Foreign Policy, 1900–51.* Manchester: Manchester University Press, 2004.

Winter, J. M. *Socialism and the Challenge of War: Ideas and Politics in Britain, 1912–18.* London and Boston: Routledge and Kegan Paul, 1974.

W. IDEOLOGIES

Ball, Terence, and Richard Dagger, *Political Ideologies and the Democratic Ideal.* 5th ed. New York: Longman, 2004.

Eatwell, Roger, and Anthony Wright, eds. *Contemporary Political Ideologies.* 2nd ed. London: Pinter, 1999.

Eccleshall, Robert, Alan Finlayson, Vincent Geoghegan, Michael Kenny, Moya Lloyd, Iain MacKenzie, and Rick Wilford. *Political Ideologies: An Introduction.* 3rd ed. London and New York: Routledge, 2003.

Freeden, Michael. *Ideologies and Political Theory: A Conceptual Approach.* Oxford: Oxford University Press, 1996.

Heywood, Andrew. *Political Ideologies: An Introduction.* 3rd ed. Basingstoke, England: Palgrave, 2003.

Vincent, Andrew. *Modern Political Ideologies.* 2nd ed. Oxford: Blackwell, 2001.

X. AUTOBIOGRAPHIES AND BIOGRAPHIES OF POLITICIANS AND ACTIVISTS BY COUNTRY

X.1 Australia

Carew, Edna. *Paul Keating: Prime Minister.* Sydney: Allen and Unwin, 1992.

Day, David. *John Curtin: A Life.* London: HarperCollins, 1999.

——. *Ben Chifley.* London: HarperCollins, 2001.

Fitzhardinge, L. F. *William Morris Hughes: A Political Biography.* Sydney: Angus and Robertson, 1964, 1979. 2 vols.

Guy, Bill. *A Life on the Left: A Biography of Clyde Cameron.* Adelaide: Wakefield Press, 1999.

Holt, Stephen. *A Veritable Dynamo: Lloyd Ross and Australian Labour, 1901–1987.* St. Lucia: Queensland University Press, 1996.

Murphy, D. J. *Hayden: A Political Biography.* Sydney: Angus and Robertson, 1980.

Nairn, Bede. *The "Big Fella": Jack Lang and the Australian Labor Party, 1891–1949.* Melbourne: Melbourne University Press, 1986.

Rickard, John. *H.B. Higgins: The Rebel as Judge.* Sydney: Allen and Unwin, 1985.

Robertson, John. *J.H. Scullin: A Political Biography.* Perth: University of Western Australia Press, 1974.

Ross, Lloyd. *John Curtin: A Biography.* Melbourne: Sun Books, 1983. [First published in 1977.]

Spaull, Andrew. *John Dedman: A Most Unexpected Labor Man.* Melbourne: Hyland Press, 1998.

Uren, Tom. *Straight Left.* Sydney: Random House, 1994. [Autobiography of a prominent left-wing Australian Labor Party politician.]

X.2 Austria

Smaldone, William. *Rudolf Hilferding: The Tragedy of a Social Democrat.* Dekalb: Northern Illinois University Press, 1998.

X.3 Belgium

Polaksy, Janet L. *The Democratic Socialism of Émile Vandervelde: Between Reform and Revolution.* Oxford: Berg Publishers, 1995.

X.4 France

Beecher, Jonathan. *Charles Fourier: The Visionary and His World.* Berkeley: University of California Press, 1986.

Cole, Alistair. *François Mitterrand: A Study in Political Leadership.* 2nd ed. London: Routledge, 1997.

Cross, Marie, and Tim Gray. *The Feminism of Flora Tristan.* Oxford: Berg Publishers, 1992.

Derfler, Leslie. *Alexandre Millerand: The Socialist Years.* The Hague, Netherlands: Mouton and Co., 1977.

———. *Paul Lafargue and the Flowering of French Socialism, 1882–1911.* Cambridge, Mass.: Harvard University Press, 1998.

Lefebvre, Denis. *Guy Mollet: Le mal aimé.* Paris: Plon, 1992.

Singer, Daniel. *Is Socialism Doomed? The Meaning of Mitterrand.* New York: Oxford University Press, 1988.

Vincent, K. Steven. *Between Marxism and Anarchism: Benoît Malon and French Reformist Socialism.* Berkeley: University of California Press, 1992.

X.5 Germany

Brandt, Willy. *My Life in Politics,* trans. Anthea Bell. New York: Penguin Books, 1993.

Edinger, L. *Kurt Schumacher: A Study in Personality and Political Behavior*. Stanford, Calif.: Stanford University Press, 1965.

X.6 India

Benundhar, Pradham. *The Socialist Thought of Jawaharlal Nehru*. Bombay: South Asia Books, 1974.

X.7 Indonesia

Rose, Mavis. *Indonesia Free: A Political Biography of Mohammed Hatta*. Ithaca, N.Y.: Cornell University, 1987. [Hatta (1902–80), the first president of Indonesia, had close contacts with Dutch left-wing socialists in the 1920s and early 1930s.]

X.8 Ireland

Anderson, W. K. *James Connolly and the Irish Left*. Dublin: Irish Academic Press and the National Center for Australian Studies, 1994.

X.9 Japan

Kublin, Hyman. *Asian Revolutionary: The Life of Sen Katayama*. Princeton, N.J.: Princeton University Press, 1964.

X.10 Mozambique

Christie, Iain. *Samora Michel: A Biography*. London, Panaf, 1989.

X.11 New Zealand

Gustafson, Barry. *From the Cradle to the Grave: A Biography of Michael Joseph Savage*. Auckland: Reed Methuen, 1986.
Hayward, Margaret. *Diary of the Kirk Years*. Wellington: Reid, 1981.
Sinclair, Keith. *William Pember Reeves: New Zealand Fabian*. Oxford: Oxford University Press, 1965.
Wright, Vernon. *David Lange: Prime Minister*. Wellington: Unwin Paperbacks with Port Nicholson Press, 1984.

X.12 Portugal

Janitschek, Hans. *Mario Soares: Portrait of a Hero*. London: Weidenfeld and Nicolson, 1985.

X.13 Russia

Service, Robert. *Lenin: A Biography*. Basingstoke, England: Macmillan, 2000. [A recent life based on the Lenin archives.]

Volkogonov, Dmitri. *Lenin: Life and Legacy*, trans. Harold Shukman. London: HarperCollins, 1994. [An important biography that uses previously unavailable Soviet archival sources.]

X.14 United Kingdom

Bullock, Alan. *The Life and Times of Ernest Bevin*. London: Heinemann, 1960, 1967, 1983. 3 vols.

Burridge, Trevor. *Clement Attlee: A Political Biography*. London: Jonathan Cape, 1985.

Callaghan, James. *Time and Chance*. London: Collins, 1987. [Autobiography.]

Campbell, John. *Nye Bevan and the Mirage of British Socialism*. London: Weidenfeld and Nicolson, 1987.

Coombes, B. L. *These Poor Hands: The Autobiography of a Miner Working in South Wales*. London: Victor Gollancz, 1939.

Crick, Bernard. *George Orwell: A Life*. London: Secker and Warburg, 1981.

Fraser, W. Hamish. *Alexander Campbell and the Search for Socialism*. Manchester: Holyoake Books, 1996. [Life of an Owenite, cooperative leader, and founder of the Glasgow Trades Council.]

Gideon, Godfrey. *Labour's Visionary: Lord Hirshfield*. London: Cohen Books, 1998.

Gormley, Joe. *Battered Cherub: The Autobiography of Joe Gormley*. London: Hamilton, 1982.

Harris, Kenneth. *Attlee*. London: Weidenfeld and Nicolson, 1982.

Healey, Denis. *The Time of My Life*. London: Michael Joseph, 1989.

Holroyd, Michael. *Bernard Shaw*. London: Chatto and Windus, 1988–92. 5 vols.

Jenkins, Robert. *Tony Benn: A Political Biography*. London: Writers and Readers, 1980.

Jones, Mervyn. *Michael Foot*. London: Victor Gollancz, 1994.

MacCarthy, Fiona. *William Morris: A Life for Our Time*. London: Faber and Faber, 1995.

Marquand, David. *Ramsay MacDonald*. London: Jonathan Cape, 1977.

Morgan, Kenneth O. *Labour People: Leaders and Lieutenants, Hardie to Kinnock*. 2nd ed. Oxford: Oxford University Press, 1992. [First published 1987; contains a good annotated bibliography.]

———. *Callaghan: A Life*. Oxford: Oxford University Press, 1997.

Mortimer, Jim W. *A Life on the Left*. Lews, England: The Book Guild, 1998.

Myers, Jeffrey. *Orwell: Wintry Conscience of a Generation*. New York: W.W. Norton, 2000.

Newsinger, John. *Orwell's Politics*. Basingstoke, England: Macmillan, 1999.

Pankhurst, Richard. *William Thompson (1775–1833): Pioneer Socialist*. London: Pluto, 1991.

Pimlott, Ben. *Harold Wilson*. London: HarperCollins, 1992. [See also the biography of Wilson by Philip Ziegler.]

———. *Hugh Dalton*. London: Cape, 1985.

Reid, Fred. *Keir Hardie: The Making of a Socialist*. London: Croom Helm, 1978.

Seymour-Jones, Carole. *Beatrice Webb: Woman of Conflict*. London: Pandora Press, 1993. [First published in 1992 by Allison and Busby, London.]

Romano, Mary A. *Beatrice Webb (1858–1943): The Socialist With A Sociological Imagination*. Lewiston, N.Y.: Mellen Press, 1998.

Smith, Dai. *Aneurin Bevan and the World of South Wales*. Cardiff: University of South Wales Press, 1993.

Tsuzuki, Chushichi. *Tom Mann, 1856–1941: The Challenge of Labour*. Oxford: Clarendon Press, 1991.

Vernon, Betty D. *Ellen Wilkinson*. London: Croom Helm, 1982.

Williams, P. M. *Hugh Gaitskell: A Political Biography*. London: Cape, 1979.

Ziegler, Philip. *Wilson: The Authorised Life of Lord Wilson of Rievaulx*. London: Weidenfeld and Nicolson, 1993. [A biography of Harold Wilson that makes extensive use of his personal papers. See also the unauthorized biography of Wilson by Ben Pimlott.]

X.15 United States of America

Barrett, James R. *William Z. Foster and the Tragedy of American Radicalism*. Urbana: University of Illinois Press, 1999.

Gorman, Robert A. *Michael Harrington: Speaking American*. New York: Routledge, 1995.

Miller, Sally M. *Victor Berger and the Promise of Constructive Socialism, 1910–1920*. Westport, Conn.: Greenwood Press, 1973.

Ovenden, Kevin. *Malcolm X: Socialism and Black Nationalism*. London: Bookmarks, 1992.

Pratt, Norma F. *Morris Hillquit: A Political History of American Jewish Socialist*. Westport, Conn.: Greenwood Press, 1979.

Reed, Adolph L. Jr. *W.E.B. Du Bois and American Political Thought: Fabianism and the Color Line*. New York: Oxford University Press, 1997.

Salvatore, Nick. *Eugene V. Debs: Citizen and Socialist*. Urbana, University of Illinois Press, 1982.

Scott, Ivan. *Upton Sinclair: The Forgotten Socialist*. Lewiston, N.Y.: Mellen Press, 1997.

Seretan, L. Glen. *Daniel DeLeon: The Odyssey of an American Marxist*. Cambridge, Mass: Harvard University Press, 1979.

Swanberg, W. A. *Norman Thomas: The Last Idealist*. New York: Scribners, 1976.

Y. STUDIES OF SPECIFIC COUNTRIES

Y.1 Argentina

Munck, Ronaldo. *Argentina: From Anarchism to Peronism: Workers, Unions and Politics, 1855–1985*. Atlantic Highlands, N.J.: Zed Books, 1987.

Y.2 Australia

Bergmann, V. *In Our Time: Socialism and the Rise of Labor, 1885–1905*. Sydney: Allen and Unwin, 1985.

Bongiorno, Frank. *The People's Party: Victorian Labor and the Radical Tradition, 1875–1914*. Melbourne: Melbourne University Press, 1996.

Coghlan, Timothy A. *Labour and Industry in Australia from the First Settlement in 1788 to the Establishment of the Commonwealth in 1901*. Melbourne: Macmillan, 1969. 4 vols. [First published in 1918; volumes 3 and 4 are still important for the rise of the labor movement and the Australian Labor Party.]

Farrell, Frank. *International Socialism and Australian Labour: The Left in Australia, 1919–1939*. Sydney: Hale and Iremonger, 1981.

Hagan, James, and Ken Turner. *A History of the Labor Party in New South Wales 1891–1991*. Melbourne: Longman Cheshire, 1991.

Lavelle, Ashley. "Social Democrats and Neo-Liberalism: A Case Study of the Australian Labor Party." *Political Studies* 53, no. 4 (2005): 753–71.

MacIntyre, Stuart, and John Faulkner, eds. *True Believers: The Story of the Federal Parliamentary Labor Party*. Sydney: Allen and Unwin, 2001.

Markey, Ray. *The Making of the Labor Party in New South Wales, 1880–1910*. Sydney: Sydney University Press, 1988.

McMullin, Ross. *The Light on the Hill: The Australian Labor Party, 1891–1991*. Melbourne: Oxford University Press, 1991.

Moss, Jim. *Sound of Trumpets: History of the Labour Movement in South Australia*. Adelaide: Wakefield Press, 1985.

Murphy, D. J., ed. *Labor in Politics: The State Labor Parties in Australia, 1880–1920*. St. Lucia: University of Queensland Press, 1975.

Murphy, D. J., et al., eds. *Labor in Power: The Labor Party and Governments in Queensland, 1915–1957*. St. Lucia: Queensland University Press, 1980.

Murray, Robert. *The Split: Australian Labor in the Fifties*. Melbourne: Cheshire, 1970. [Reprinted by Hale and Iremonger, Sydney, in 1984.]

Pierson, Chris, and Francis G. Castles. "Australian Antecedents of the Third Way." *Political Studies* 50, no. 4 (2002): 683–702.

Reeves, Pember. *State Experiments in Australia and New Zealand*. Melbourne: Macmillan, 1969. 2 vols. [First published in 1902.]

Scates, Bruce. *A New Australia: Citizenship, Radicalism and the First Republic*. Melbourne: Cambridge University Press, 1997. [A study of the late nineteenth and twentieth centuries.]

Singleton, Gwynnoth. *The Accord and the Australian Labour Movement*. Melbourne: Melbourne University Press, 1990.

Whitlam, Gough. *The Whitlam Government, 1972–1975*. Melbourne: Viking, 1985. [A detailed examination of the policies of the most reformist national government in Australian history since 1950 by its leader.]

Y.3 Austria

Jeffry, Charlie. *Social Democracy in the Austrian Provinces, 1918–34: Beyond Red Vienna*. Madison, N.J.: Fairleigh Dickinson University Press, 1995.

Knapp, Vincent J. *Austrian Social Democracy, 1889–1914*. Washington, D.C.: University Press of America, 1980.

Sully, Melanie A. *Continuity and Change in Austrian Socialism: The Eternal Quest for the Third Way*. New York: Columbia University Press, 1982.

Y.4 Belgium

Fitzmaurice, J. *The Politics of Belgium: Crisis and Compromise in a Plural Society*. 2nd ed. London: Hurst and Co., 1988. [First published in 1983.]

Y.5 Brazil

Abers, Rebecca Neaera. *Inventing Local Democracy: Grassroots Politics in Brazil*. London: Eurospan, 2000.

Keck, M. E. *The Workers' Party and Democratization in Brazil*. New Haven, Conn.: Yale University Press, 1992. [Mainly concerned with the 1980s.]

Y.6 Canada

McCormack, A. Ross. *Reformers, Rebels, and Revolutionaries in the Western Canadian Radical Movement, 1899–1919*. Toronto: University of Toronto Press, 1977.

Whitehorn, Alan. *Canadian Socialism: Essays on the CCF-NDP*. Toronto: Oxford University Press, 1992.

Y.7 Chile

Hite, Katherine. *When the Romance Ended: Leaders of the Chilean Left, 1968–1998*. New York: Columbia University Press, 1999.

Miliband, Ralph. "The Coup in Chile." In *The Socialist Register 1973*, ed. Ralph Miliband and John Saville. London: Merlin Press, 1973.
Roberts, Kenneth M. *Deepening Democracy: The Modern Left and Social Movements in Chile and Peru*. Stanford, Calif.: Stanford University Press, 1998.

Y.8 Czechoslovakia

Wigfield, Nancy M. *Minority Politics in a Multicultural State: The German Social Democrats in Czechoslovakia, 1918–1938*. New York: Columbia University Press, 1989.

Y.9 Denmark

Logue, John. *Socialism and Abundance: Radical Socialism in the Danish Welfare State*. Minneapolis: University of Minnesota Press, 1982.
Thomas, Alastair H. *Parliamentary Parties in Denmark, 1945–1972*. Occasional Paper no. 13. Glasgow: University of Strathclyde Survey Research Centre, 1972.

Y.10 Egypt

Ginat, R. *Egypt's Incomplete Revolution: Lutfi Al-Khuli and Nasser's Socialism in the 1960s*. London: Cass and Co., 1997.

Y.11 France

Amdur, Kathryn E. *Syndicalist Legacy: Trade Unions and Politics in Two French Cities in the Era of World War I*. Urbana: University of Illinois Press, 1986. [The cities examined are Saint-Etienne and Limoges.]
Beecher, Jonathan. *Victor Considerant and the Rise and Fall of French Romantic Socialism*. Berkeley: University of California Press, 2001.
Bell, David S., and Byron Criddle. *The French Socialist Party: The Emergence of Party Government*. 2nd ed. Oxford: Oxford University Press, 1988. [First published in 1984.]
Blaazer, David. *The Popular Front and the Progressive Tradition: Socialists, Liberals, and the Quest for Unity, 1884–1939*. Cambridge, England: Cambridge University Press, 1992.
Cole, Alistair. *French Political Parties in Transition*. Aldershot, England: Dartmouth, 1990.
———. "Studying Political Leadership: The Case of François Mitterrand." *Political Studies* 42, no. 3 (1994): 453–68.

Corcoran, Paul E. *Before Marx: Socialism and Communism in France, 1830–1848.* New York: St. Martin's Press, 1983.

Christopherson, Thomas R. *The French Socialists in Power, 1981–1986.* Cranbury, N.J.: University of Delaware Press, 1991.

Friend, Julius W. *The Long Presidency: France in the Mitterrand Years, 1881–1995.* Boulder, Colo.: Westview Press, 1998.

Graham, B. D. *Choice and Democratic Order: The French Socialist Party, 1937–1950.* Cambridge, England: Cambridge University Press, 1994.

Hanley, David. *Keeping Left? Ceres and the French Socialist Party: A Contribution to the Study of Factionalism in Political Parties.* Manchester: Manchester University Press, 1986.

Jackson, Julian. *The Popular Front in France: Defending Democracy, 1934–38.* Cambridge, England: Cambridge University Press, 1988.

Marian, Michel. "France 1997–2002: Right-Wing President, Left-Wing Government." *The Political Quarterly* 73, no. 3 (2002): 258–65.

Steinhouse, Adam. *Workers' Participation in Post-Liberation France.* Lanham Md.: Lexington, 2001.

Stuart, Robert C. *Marxism at Work: Ideology, Class, and French Socialism during the Third Republic.* Cambridge, England: Cambridge University Press, 1992.

Williams, Stuart, ed. *Socialism in France: From Jaurès to Mitterrand.* New York: St. Martin's Press, 1983.

Wilson, F. L. *The French Democratic Left, 1963–69: Towards a Modern Party System.* Stanford, Calif.: Stanford University Press, 1971.

Y.12 Germany

Barclay, David E., and Eric D. Weitz, eds. *Between Reform and Revolution: German Socialism and Communism from 1840 to 1990.* New York and Oxford: Berghahn Books, 1998.

Braunthal, Gerard. *The German Social Democrats since 1969: A Party in Power and Opposition.* 2nd ed. Boulder, Colo.: Westview Press, 1994. [First published 1983.]

Dettke, Dieter, ed. *The Challenge of Globalization for Germany's Social Democracy: A Policy Agenda for the 21st Century.* Oxford: Berghahn, 1998.

Guttsman, W. L. *The German Social Democratic Party, 1875–1933: From Ghetto to Government.* London: George Allen and Unwin, 1981.

Hough, Dan. *The Fall and Rise of the PDS in Eastern Germany.* Birmingham: University of Birmingham Press, 2001.

Hough, Daniel, and Jonathan Grix. "The PDS and the SDP's Dilemma of Governance in the Eastern German *Länder*." *Politics* 21, no. 3 (2001): 158–67.

Lidtke, Vernon L. *The Alternative Culture: Socialist Labor in Imperial Germany.* New York: Oxford University Press, 1985.

Martkovits, Andrei S., and Philip S. Gorski. *The German Left: Red, Green, and Beyond*. Cambridge, England: Polity Press, 1993.

Narsch, Donna. *German Social Democracy and the Rise of Nazism*. Durham: University of North Carolina Press, 1993.

Steenson, Gary P. *"Not One Man! Not One Penny!" German Social Democracy, 1865–1914*. Pittsburgh, Pa.: University of Pittsburgh Press, 1981.

Y.13 Greece

Featherstone, K. *Political Change in Greece: Before and After the Colonels*. London: Croom Helm, 1987.

Kassimeris, G. "The 2004 Greek Election: PASOK's Monopoly Ends." *West European Politics* 27, no. 5 (2004): 943–53.

Spourdalakis, M. *The Rise of the Greek Socialist Party*. London: Routledge, 1988.

Tzannatos, Zapiris. *Socialism in Greece: The First Four Years*. Aldershot, England: Gower, 1986.

Y.14 India

Chopra, Pran N. *A Century of the Indian National Congress, 1885–1985*. Delhi: Agam Prakashan, 1986.

Jawaid, Sohail. *Socialism in India*. London: Sangam, 1987.

Mehnotra, Nanak C. *The Socialist Movement in India*. London: Sangam, 1995.

Y.15 Indonesia

Mintz, J. S. *Mohammed, Marx and Marhaen: The Roots of Indonesian Socialism*. New York: Praeger, 1965.

Y.16 Ireland

Lane, Fintan. *The Origins of Modern Irish Socialism, 1881–1896*. Cork, Ireland: Cork University Press, 1997.

Y.17 Israel

Cohen, Mitchell. *Zion and State: Nation, Class, and the Shaping of Modern Israel*. New York: Columbia University Press, 1992.

Y.18 Italy

Barkan, Joanne. *Visions of Emancipation: The Italian Workers' Movement since 1945*. New York: Praeger, 1984.

De Grand, Alexander. *The Italian Left in the Twentieth Century: A History of the Socialist and Communist Parties*. Bloomington: Indiana University Press, 1989. [Contains a useful bibliographical essay.]
Fouskas, Vassilis. *Italy, Europe and the Left*. Aldershot: Ashgate, 1999.
Miller, James E. *From Elite to Mass Politics: Italian Socialism in the Giolittian Era, 1900–1914*. Kent State University, Ohio: Kent State University Press, 1990.
Scala, Spencer M. Di, ed. *Italian Socialism: Between Politics and History*. Amherst: University of Massachusetts Press, 1996.

Y.19 Jamaica

Keith, Nelson W. *The Social Origins of Democratic Socialism in Jamaica*. Philadelphia: Temple University Press, 1992.
Stephens, Evelyn H. *Democratic Socialism in Jamaica: The Political Movement and Social Transformation in Dependent Capitalism*. Basingstoke, England: Macmillan, 1986.

Y.20 Japan

Baerwald, Hans H. *Party Politics in Japan*. Boston, Mass.: Allen and Unwin, 1986.
Kume, Ikuo. *Disparaged Success: Labor Politics in Postwar Japan*. Ithaca, N.Y.: Cornell University Press, 1998.
Large, Stephen S. *Organized Workers and Socialist Politics in Interwar Japan*. New York: Cambridge University Press, 1981.
Plotkin, Ira L. *Anarchism in Japan: A Study of the Great Treason Affair, 1910–1911*. Lewiston, N.Y.: Mellen, 1990.

Y.21 Lithuania

Sabaliunas, Leonas. *Lithuanian Social Democracy in Perspective, 1893–1914*. Durham, N.C.: Duke University Press, 1990.

Y.22 Mexico

Bruhn, Kathleen. *Taking on Goliath: The Emergence of a New Left Party and the Struggle for Democracy in Mexico*. University Park: Pennsylvania State Press, 1997.

Y.23 New Zealand

Bassett, Michael. *The Third Labour Government: A Personal History*. Palmerston North, New Zealand: Dunmore Press, 1976.

Boston, Jonathan, Stephen Church, Stephen Levine, Elizabeth McLeay, and Nigel S. Roberts, eds. *Left Turn: The New Zealand Election of 1999*. Wellington, Victoria University Press, 2000.

Clark, Margaret, ed. *The Labour Party after 75 Years*. Wellington, New Zealand: Department of Politics, Victoria University of Wellington, 1992.

Gustafson, Barry. *Labour's Path to Political Independence: The Origins and Establishment of the New Zealand Labour Party, 1900–19*. Auckland: Auckland University Press, 1980.

Holland, Martin, and Jonathan Boston, eds. *The Fourth Labour Government: Politics and Policy in New Zealand*. 2nd ed. Auckland: Oxford University Press, 1990.

Wilson, Margaret A. *Labour in Government, 1984–1987*. Wellington: Allen and Unwin/Port Nicholson Press, 1989.

Y.24 Nicaragua

Black, George. *Triumph of the People: The Sandinista Revolution in Nicaragua*. London: Zed Press, 1981.

Melrose, Diana. *Nicaragua: The Threat of a Good Example?* Oxford: Oxfam, 1985.

Prevost, Gary. "The Nicaraguan Revolution—Six Years after the Sandinista Electoral Defeat." *Third World Quarterly* 17, no. 2 (1996): 307–27.

Y.25 Nigeria

Madunagu, Eddie. *Problems of Socialism: The Nigerian Challenge*. London: Zed Books, 1982.

Y.26 Peru

Schönwälder, Gerd. *Linking Civil Society and the State: Urban Popular Movements, the Left, and Local Government in Peru, 1980–1992*. University Park: Pennsylvania State University Press, 2002.

Y.27 Russia

Bonnell, Victoria E. *Roots of Rebellion: Workers' Politics and Organizations in St. Petersburg and Moscow, 1900–1914*. Berkeley: University of California Press, 1983.

Liebich, André. *From the Other Shore: Russian Social Democracy after 1921*. Cambridge, Mass.: Harvard University Press, 1997.

Malie, Martin. *The Soviet Tragedy: A History of Socialism in Russia, 1917–1991*. New York: The Free Press, 1994.

Y.28 Spain

Fisherman, Robert M. *Working-Class Organization and the Return to Democracy in Spain*. Ithaca, N.Y.: Cornell University Press, 1991.

Gillespie, R. *The Spanish Socialist Party: A History of Factionalism*. Oxford: Clarendon Press, 1989.

Graham, Helen. *Socialism and War: The Spanish Socialist Party in Power and Crisis, 1936–1939*. Cambridge, England: Cambridge University Press, 1991.

Heywood, Paul. *Marxism and the Failure of Organized Socialism in Spain, 1879–1936*. Cambridge, England: Cambridge University Press, 1990.

Peirata, José. *Anarchists in the Spanish Revolution*. London: Freedom Press, 1990.

Share, D. *Dilemmas of Social Democracy; The Spanish Socialist Workers' Party in the 1980s*. Westport, Conn.: Greenwood Press, 1989.

Y.29 Sweden

Misgeld, Klaus, Karl Molin, and Klas Amark, eds. *Creating Social Democracy: A Century of the Social Democratic Labor Party in Sweden*. University Park: Pennsylvania State University Press, 1993.

Rothstein, Bo. *The Social Democratic State: The Swedish Model and the Bureaucratic Problem of Social Reforms*. Pittsburgh, Pa.: Pittsburgh University Press, 1996.

Tilton, T. A. *The Political Theory of Swedish Social Democracy: Through the Welfare State to Socialism*. Oxford: Clarendon Press, 1990.

Y.30 Tanzania

McHenry, Dean E. *Limited Choices: The Political Struggle for Socialism in Tanzania*. Boulder, Colo.: Lynne Rienner, 1994.

Resnick, Idrian N. *The Long Tradition: Building Socialism in Tanzania*. New York: Monthly Review Press, 1981.

Y.31 Tunisia

Sadiki, Larbi. "The Search for Citizenship in Bin Ali's Tunisia: Democracy versus Unity." *Political Studies* 50, no. 3 (2002): 497–513.

Y.32 Turkey

Lipovsky, Igor P. *The Socialist Movement in Turkey, 1960–1980*. New York: Brill, 1992.

Y.33 United Kingdom

Barnsby, George J. *Socialism in Birmingham and the Black Country, 1850–1939*. Wolverhampton, England: Integrated Publishing Services, 1998.

Bevir, Mark. "New Labour: A Study in Ideology." *British Journal of Politics and International Relations* 2, no. 3 (2000): 277–301.

Brown, K. D., ed. *The First Labour Party, 1906–1914*. London: Croom Helm, 1985. [Excellent issues-based approach.]

Callaghan, John, Steven Fielding, and Steve Ludlam, eds. *Interpreting the Labour Party: Approaches to Labour Politics and History*. Manchester: Manchester University Press, 2003.

Calven, Jim. *The Centre is Mine: Tony Blair, New Labour, and the Future of Electoral Politics*. Sydney: Pluto Press, 2000. [Considers the implications of New Labour for other countries.]

Charlton, John. *The Chartists: The First National Workers' Movement*. London: Pluto Press, 1997.

Claeys, Gregory. *Citizens and Saints: Politics and Anti-Politics in Early British Socialism*. Cambridge, England: Cambridge University Press, 1989.

Coates, David. "Capitalist Models and Social Democracy: The Case of New Labour." *British Journal of Politics and International Relations* 3, no. 3 (2001): 284–307.

Coates, David, and Peter Lawler. *New Labour in Power*. Manchester: Manchester University Press, 2000.

Coates, Ken. "Socialists and the Labour Party." In *The Socialist Register 1973*, ed. Ralph Miliband and John Saville. London: Merlin Press, 1973.

Cook, Chris, and Taylor, Ian. *The Labour Party: An Introduction to its History, Structure and Politics*. London: Longman, 1980.

Crewe, Ivor, and Anthony King. *SDP: The Birth, Life and Death of the Social Democratic Party*. Oxford: Oxford University Press, 1995.

Donachie, Ian, Christopher Harvie, and Ian S. Wood, eds. *Forward: Labour Politics in Scotland, 1888–1988*. Edinburgh: Polygon, 1989.

Elliott, Gregory. *Labourism and the English Genius: The Strange Death of Labour England?* London: Verso, 1993.

Fielding, Steven. *The Labour Governments 1964–70: Labour and Cultural Change*. Manchester: Manchester University Press, 2003.

Foote, Geoffrey. *The Labour Party's Political Thought: A History*. 3rd ed. London: Croom Helm, 1997.

Gould, Philip. *The Unfinished Revolution: How the Modernisers Saved the Labour Party*. Polmont, England: Little Brown, 1998.

Holmes, Martin. *The Labour Government, 1974–1979*. London: Macmillan, 1985.

Howell, David. *British Social Democracy: A Study in Development and Decay*. 2nd ed. London: Croom Helm, 1980. [First published 1976.]

——. *British Workers and the Independent Labour Party, 1888–1906.* Manchester: Manchester University Press, 1983.

——. *A Lost Left: Three Studies in Socialism and Nationalism.* Manchester: Manchester University Press, 1986.

——. *MacDonald's Party: Labour Identities and Crisis 1922–1931.* Oxford: Oxford University Press, 2002.

Jefferys, Kevin. *The Labour Party since 1945.* New York: St. Martin's Press, 1993.

Jefferys, Kevin, ed. *Labour Forces: From Ernest Bevin to Gordon Brown.* London: I.B. Tauris, 2002.

Jones, Barry, and Michael Keating. *Labour and the British State.* Oxford: Clarendon Press, 1985.

Kavanagh, D., ed. *The Politics of the Labour Party.* London: Allen and Unwin, 1982.

Leonard, Dick, ed. *Crosland and New Labour.* Basingstoke, England: Macmillan and the Fabian Society, 1999.

Levitas, Ruth. *The Inclusive Society? Social Exclusion and New Labour.* Basingstoke, England: Macmillan, 1998.

McKibbin, Ross. "The Economic Policy of the Second Labour Government 1929–31." *Past and Present* 68, August (1975): 95–123.

McAllister, Laura. *Plaid Cymru: The Emergence of a Political Party.* Bridgend, Wales: Seren, 2001.

McKinlay, Alan, and R. J. Morris, eds. *The ILP on Clydeside, 1893–1932: From Foundation to Disintegration.* Manchester: Manchester University Press, 1991.

Morgan, Kenneth O. *Labour in Power, 1945–1951.* Oxford: Oxford University Press, 1984.

Pelling, Henry. *A Short History of the Labour Party.* 8th ed. London: Macmillan, 1985. [First published 1961, this remains a reliable introduction to the subject.]

Pierson, Stanley. *British Socialists: The Journey from Fantasy to Politics.* Cambridge: Mass.: Harvard University Press, 1979.

Pimlott, Ben. *Labour and the Left in the 1930s.* Cambridge, England: Cambridge University Press, 1977.

Powell, David. *What's Left? Labour Britain and the Socialist Tradition.* London: Peter Owen Ltd., 1998.

Seyd, Patrick. *The Rise and Fall of the Labour Left.* London: Macmillan, 1987.

Shaw, Eric. *The Labour Party since 1979: Crisis and Transformation.* London and New York: Routledge, 1994.

Smith, Martin, and Joanna Spear. *The Changing Labour Party.* London: Routledge, 1992.

Tanner, Duncan. *Political Change and the Labour Party, 1900–1918.* Cambridge, England: Cambridge University Press, 1990.

Tanner, Duncan, Pat Thanne, and Nick Tiratsoo, eds. *Labour's First Century*. Cambridge, England: Cambridge University Press, 2000.

Thompson, Noel. *Left in the Wilderness: The Political Economy of British Democratic Socialism since 1979*. Chesham: Acumen, 2002.

Thorpe, Andrew. *A History of the British Labour Party*. Basingstoke, England: Macmillan, 1997. [A survey of the period up to 1992.]

Warde, A. *Consensus and Beyond: The Development of Labour Party Strategy since the Second World War*. Manchester: Manchester University Press, 1982.

Wickham-Jones, Mark. "New Labour in the Global Economy: Partisan Politics and the Social Democratic Model." *British Journal of Politics and International Relations* 2, no. 1 (2000): 1–25.

White, Stuart, ed. *New Labour: The Progressive Future*. Basingstoke, England: Palgrave, 2001.

Wright, Tony, and Matt Carter. *The People's Party: The History of the Labour Party*. London: Thames and Hudson, 1997. [A profusely illustrated general history with a chronology and short bibliography.]

Y.34 United States of America

Buhle, Paul, and Dan Georgakas, eds. *The Immigrant Left in the United States*. New York: State University Press of New York, 1996.

Commons, John R., et al. *History of Labor in the United States*. New York: Macmillan, 1918–1935. 4 vols.

Crichlow, Donald T., ed. *Socialism in the Heartland: The Midwestern Experience, 1900–1925*. Notre Dame, Ind.: University of Notre Dame Press, 1986.

Diggins, John P. *The Rise and Fall of the American Left*. New York: W.W. Norton, 1992.

Fitrakis, Robert J. *The Idea of Democratic Socialism in America and the Decline of the Socialist Party*. New York: Garland Press, 1993.

Foner, Philip. *American Socialism and Black Americans*. Westport, Conn.: Greenwood Press, 1977.

Girard, Frank, and Ben Perry. *The Socialist Labor Party: A Short History*. Philadelphia: Livra Books, 1991.

Gosse, Van. *Where the Boys Are: Cuba, Cold War America, and the Making of the New Left*. London: Verso, 1993.

Horowitz, Ruth L. *Political Ideologies of Organized Labor*. New Brunswick, N.J.: Transaction Books, 1978.

Iton, Richard. *Solidarity Blues: Race, Culture, and the American Left*. Chapel Hill: University of North Carolina Press, 2000.

Judd, Richard W. *Socialist Cities: Municipal Politics and the Grass Roots of American Socialism*. Albany: State University of New York, 1989.

Laslett, John H. M., ed. *Failure of a Dream: Essays in the History of American Socialism.* Garden City, N.Y.: Anchor Press, 1974.

Laslett, John. *Labor and the Left: A Study of Socialist and Radical Influences in the American Labor Movement, 1881–1924.* New York: Basic Books, 1970.

Lipset, Seymour Martin, and Gary Marks. *It Didn't Happen Here: Why Socialism Failed in the United States.* London: Norton, 2000.

Hillquit, Morris, *History of Socialism in the United States.* 5th ed. New York: Russell and Russell, 1965. [First published in 1903.]

Shor, Francis R. *Utopianism and Radicalism in a Reforming America, 1888–1918.* Westport, Conn.: Greenwood Press, 1997.

Weinstein, James. *The Decline of Socialism in America, 1912–1925.* New Brunswick, N.J.: Rutgers University Press, 1984. [First published in 1967.]

Wohlforth, Tim. *The Prophet's Children: Travels on the American Left.* Atlantic Highlands, N.J.: Humanities Press, 1994.

Y.35 Yugoslavia

Lydall, Harold. *Yugoslav Socialism: Theory and Practice.* Oxford: Clarendon Press, 1984.

Z. WEBSITES

Americas Social Forum, www.forosocialamericas.org/index.phtml.en [accessed 6 January 2006].

Commission for Socialist Education in the European Union, www.helsingfors-demare.com/CSEEU [accessed 6 January 2006].

European Forum for Democracy and Solidarity, www.europeanforum.net/index.php [accessed 6 January 2006].

European Social Forum, www.fse-esf.org/rubrique.php3?id_rubrique=17 [accessed 6 January 2006].

International Committee of the Fourth International, *World Socialist Web Site,* www.wsws.org/index.shtml [accessed 6 January 2006].

International Confederation of Free Trade Unions, www.icftu.org [accessed 6 January 2006].

International Cooperative Alliance, www.ica.coop [accessed 6 January 2006].

International Social Democratic Union for Education, www.isdue.net [accessed 6 January 2006].

International Union of Socialist Youth, www.iusy.org [accessed 6 January 2006].

Marxists.org Internet Archive, www.marxists.org/index.htm [accessed 6 January 2006].

Party of European Socialists, www.eurosocialists.org [accessed 6 January 2006].

Party of the European Left, www.european-left.org [accessed 6 January 2006].

Socialist International, www.socialistinternational.org [accessed 6 January 2006].

World Social Forum, www.forumsocialmundial.org.br/index.php?cd_language=2&id_menu= [accessed 6 January 2006].

About the Authors

Peter Lamb was born in Stoke on Trent, England, in 1960. He is a graduate of Staffordshire Polytechnic (B.A. Hons), Keele University (M.Sc.), and the University of Manchester (M.A. Econ, Ph.D.). Presently a research fellow at Keele University, he has taught politics at Keele University, Staffordshire University, the University of Manchester, Manchester Metropolitan University, the University of Liverpool, and the Open University. His publications include *Harold Laski: Problems of Democracy, the Sovereign State and International Society* (2004). He has also published articles on the socialist thought of Laski in *History of Political Thought* (1997), *Politics* (1999, 2002), *Journal of Political Ideologies* (1999), and *Review of International Studies* (1999); on Laski and C. B. Macpherson (with coauthor David Morrice) in *Canadian Journal of Political Science* (2002); and on G. D. H. Cole in *European Journal of Political Thought* (2005). He contributed the entry on G. D. H. Cole to the *Dictionary of Twentieth Century British Philosophers*, edited by Stuart Brown (2005), and entries on Cole, Laski, democracy, equality, and foundations of state to the multivolume *Encyclopedia of British Philosophy*, edited by A. C. Grayling, Andrew Pyle, and Naomi Goulder (2006).

James C. Docherty was born in Gosford, New South Wales, Australia, in 1949. He is a graduate of the University of Newcastle, New South Wales (B.A. with First Class Honors and the University Medal in History, 1972) and the Australian National University (M.A. 1974 and Ph.D., 1978). He worked as a research assistant with the Australian Dictionary of Biography at the Australian National University in 1974. Between 1978 and 2004, he worked for the Australian federal public service in various departments including the Australian Bureau of Statistics, the Department of Employment and Industrial Relations, and, lastly, in the citizenship program of the Department of Immigration and Multicultural and Indigenous Affairs. He was also an honorary research associate with the National Centre for Australian Studies at Monash University from 1990 to 1996.

His publications include *Selected Social Statistics of New South Wales, 1861–1976* (1982), *Newcastle: The Making of an Australian City* (1983), and "English Settlement in Newcastle and the Hunter Valley" in *The Australian People: An Encyclopedia of the Nation, Its People and Their Origins* (1988). He was an editorial consultant to *Australians: Historical Statistics* (1987), contributed the entries on Australian history, politics, labor relations, and institutions to *The Cambridge Encyclopedia* (1990), and was an editor and contributor to *Workplace Bargaining in the International Context* (1993). He is the author of *Historical Dictionary of Australia* (2nd ed., 1999), *Historical Dictionary of Organized Labor* (2nd ed., 2004), and the first edition of *Historical Dictionary of Socialism* (1997).